T0180413

Lecture Notes in Computer Science 13494

More information about this series at https://link.springer.com/bookseries/558

Khoa Nguyen · Guomin Yang · Fuchun Guo ·
Willy Susilo (Eds.)

Information Security and Privacy

27th Australasian Conference, ACISP 2022
Wollongong, NSW, Australia, November 28–30, 2022
Proceedings

Springer

Editors
Khoa Nguyen (ID)
University of Wollongong
Wollongong, NSW, Australia

Guomin Yang (ID)
University of Wollongong
Wollongong, NSW, Australia

Fuchun Guo (ID)
University of Wollongong
Wollongong, NSW, Australia

Willy Susilo (ID)
University of Wollongong
Wollongong, NSW, Australia

ISSN 0302-9743 ISSN 1611-3349 (electronic)
Lecture Notes in Computer Science
ISBN 978-3-031-22300-6 ISBN 978-3-031-22301-3 (eBook)
https://doi.org/10.1007/978-3-031-22301-3

This Springer imprint is published by the registered company Springer Nature Switzerland AG
The registered company address is: Gewerbestrasse 11, 6330 Cham, Switzerland

Preface

The 27th Australasian Conference on Information Security and Privacy (ACISP 2022) was held during November 28–30, 2022, in Wollongong, Australia. The conference had a hybrid format, with some presentations made in person, and some delivered virtually. The conference was hosted by the Institute of Cybersecurity and Cryptology (IC2) at the University of Wollongong.

The Program Committee consisted of 79 members from all over the world. In response to the call for papers, 62 papers were submitted to the conference. The papers were reviewed in a double-blind manner. Each paper was carefully evaluated by three to five reviewers, and then discussed among the Program Committee. Finally, 25 papers were selected for presentation at the conference. The selection process was assisted by 67 external reviewers. This volume contains the revised versions of the 25 papers that were selected, together with the abstracts of three keynote talks. The final revised versions of papers were not reviewed again and the authors are responsible for their contents.

The program of ACISP 2022 featured three excellent keynote talks. Huaxiong Wang delivered a Jennifer Seberry Lecture on "Combinatorial Cryptography", Jing Chen spoke on "Technical Challenges in Blockchains", and Yuval Yarom gave a talk entitled "Just About Time."

Based on the reviews and votes by Program Committee members, the following two papers were given the Best Paper Awards:

- "Key Structures: Improved Related-Key Boomerang Attack against the Full AES-256", by Jian Guo, Ling Song, and Haoyang Wang; and
- "CCOM: Cost-Efficient and Collusion-Resistant Oracle Mechanism for Smart Contracts", by Xiaofei Wu, Hao Wang, Chunpeng Ge, Lu Zhou, Qiong Huang, Lanju Kong, Lizhen Cui, and Zhe Liu.

Many people contributed to the success of ACISP 2022. We would like to thank the authors for submitting their research results to the conference and the keynote speakers for delivering their excellent talks. We are very grateful to the Program Committee members and external reviewers for contributing their knowledge and expertise, and for the tremendous amount of work that was done with reading papers and contributing to the discussions. We thank the local organizers for their great efforts in planning and executing this event. We are very grateful to the Publication Chairs, Yudi Zhang and Xueqiao Liu, for their valuable helps in the preparation of the proceedings and the conference website administration.

We would like to give special thanks to the Abelian Foundation for their generous sponsorship for ACISP 2022.

Last but not least, we would like to thank the LNCS editorial team at Springer for handling the publication of this volume.

November 2022   Khoa Nguyen
                                                        Guomin Yang
                                                        Fuchun Guo
                                                        Willy Susilo

Organization

General Chairs

Willy Susilo   University of Wollongong, Australia
Fuchun Guo   University of Wollongong, Australia

Program Chairs

Guomin Yang   University of Wollongong, Australia
Khoa Nguyen   University of Wollongong, Australia

Publication Chairs

Yudi Zhang   University of Wollongong, Australia
Xueqiao Liu   University of Wollongong, Australia

Program Committee

Masayuki Abe   NTT, Japan
Cristina Alcaraz   University of Malaga, Spain
Man Ho Au   The University of Hong Kong, Hong Kong
Shi Bai   Florida Atlantic University, USA
Zhenzhen Bao   Nanyang Technological University, Singapore
Carsten Baum   Aarhus University, Denmark
Rishiraj Bhattacharyya   NISER, India
Anupam Chattopadhyay   Nanyang Technological University, Singapore
Jinjun Chen   Swinburne University of Technology, Australia
Liqun Chen   University of Surrey, UK
Rongmao Chen   National University of Defense Technology, China
Xiaofeng Chen   Xidian University, China
Chitchanok Chuengsatiansup   The University of Adelaide, Australia
Mauro Conti   University of Padua, Italy
Hui Cui   Murdoch University, Australia
Xuhua Ding   Singapore Management University, Singapore
Josep Domingo-Ferrer   Universitat Rovira i Virgili, Spain
Rafael Dowsley   Monash University, Australia
Keita Emura   National Institute of Information and Communications Technology, Japan

Pierangela Samarati	Università degli Studi di Milano, Italy
Leonie Simpson	Queensland University of Technology, Australia
Daniel Slamanig	Austrian Institute of Technology, Austria
Bing Sun	National University of Defense Technology, China
Atsushi Takayasu	The University of Tokyo, Japan
Benjamin Hong Meng Tan	Institute for Infocomm Research, A*STAR, Singapore
Qiang Tang	The University of Sydney, Australia
Viet Cuong Trinh	Hong Duc University, Vietnam
Vijay Varadharajan	University of Newcastle, Australia
Damien Vergnaud	Sorbonne Université, France
Ding Wang	Peking University, China
Huaxiong Wang	Nanyang Technological University, Singapore
Yanhong Xu	Shanghai Jiao Tong University, China
Guomin Yang	University of Wollongong, Australia
Yuval Yarom	The University of Adelaide, Australia
Xun Yi	RMIT University, Australia
Zuoxia Yu	The University of Hong Kong, Hong Kong
Tsz Hon Yuen	The University of Hong Kong, Hong Kong
Mingwu Zhang	Hubei University of Technology, China
Cong Zhang	University of Maryland, USA
Liangfeng Zhang	Shanghai Tech University, China
Kehuan Zhang	The Chinese University of Hong Kong, Hong Kong

External Reviewers

Sanidhay Arora
Anubhab Baksi
Enkeleda Bardhi
Cyril Bouvier
Alessandro Brighente
Andrea Caforio
Kwan Yin Chan
Jinrong Chen
Xin Chen
Xinjian Chen
Cristòfol Daudén-Esmel
Zhili Dong
Rami Haffar
Sara Jafarbeiki
Corentin Jeudy

Huang Jianye
Floyd Johnson
Huang Junhao
Kallol Krishna Karmakar
Pengzhen Ke
Mustafa Khairallah
Andrea Lesavourey
Hongbo Li
Nan Li
Xinyu Li
Yongqiang Li
Ziyi Li
Chao Lin
Jiahao Liu
Jing Liu

Qinju Liu
Xueqiao Liu
Xingye Lu
Junwei Luo
Qian Mei
Arash Mirzaei
Tran Ngo
Shimin Pan
Simeone Pizzi
Maxime Plancon
Sebastian Ramacher
Simon Rastikian
Arnab Roy
Rahul Saha
Abiola Salau
Hwajeong Seo
Jun Shen
Danping Shi

Hanh Tang
Guohua Tian
Uday Tupakula
Hao Wang
Ruida Wang
Yi Wang
Yunling Wang
Yuzhu Wang
Zhe Xia
Qiaoer Xu
Haiyang Xue
Hailun Yan
Yingfei Yan
Xin Yin
Jiaming Yuan
Jipeng Zhang
Yudi Zhang
Yanwei Zhou

Keynote Talks

Combinatorial Cryptography

Huaxiong Wang

School of Physical and Mathematical Sciences, Nanyang Technological University,
Singapore
hxwang@ntu.edu.sg

Abstract. Combinatorics has been playing an active role in cryptography, from the designs of cryptographic constructions, security proofs to cryptanalysis. Combinatorial cryptography refers to a sub-field of cryptography where combinatorics and cryptography are interacted significantly. In this talk, I will present several concrete examples to illustrate how combinatorial objects and techniques are applied to the constructions of cryptographic schemes such as in secret sharing, threshold cryptography and secure multiparty computation.

Part of this research was funded by Singapore Ministry of Education under Research Grant MOE2019-T2-2-083.

Technical Challenges in Blockchains

Jing Chen

Algorand

Abstract. In the past decade blockchain technology has attracted tremendous attention from both academia and industry. It is the technology of choice to realize decentralized ledgers that are transparent, autonomous, and tamperproof. It reduces the dependence on intermediaries and introduces a new trust structure in transaction systems, so that entities from all over the world can transact directly.

The development of blockchains has been enabled by and has in turn triggered research in many fields such as distributed computation, cryptography, and programming languages, just to name a few. In this talk I'll discuss several important technical challenges and research topics brought up by blockchains.

Just About Time

Yuval Yarom

School of Computer Science, University of Adelaide, Australia

Abstract. When multiple programs execute on the same computer, they share the use of the microarchitectural resources. Because program execution affects the state of the microarchitecture and the state of the architecture affects program execution time, measuring execution time can reveal information on the state of the microarchitecture, and with it on prior execution of other programs. Thus, such micoroarchitectural timing attacks leak information by measuring variations in program execution time.

As these attacks often measure minute variations, at the order of few nanoseconds, multiple proposed defences aim at depriving attackers of high-resolution clocks. In response, counter-proposals that show how to overcome these defences have been published. In this talk we look at the ensuing armed-race and explore techniques for limiting timer resolution and for carrying out attacks with restricted timers. We will take a close look at the impact of low-resolution clocks on microarchitectural attacks, explore techniques for amplifying signals by over six orders of magnitude, and demonstrate how attackers can perform high-frequency, high-resolution attacks without using high-resolution clocks.

Contents

Public-Key Cryptography

Post-quantum Cryptography

Cryptographic Protocols

Blockchain

Symmetric-Key Cryptography

Key Structures: Improved Related-Key Boomerang Attack Against the Full AES-256

Jian Guo[1], Ling Song[2], and Haoyang Wang[3](✉)

[1] Nanyang Technological University, Singapore, Singapore
guojian@ntu.edu.sg
[2] Jinan University, Guangzhou, China
songling.qs@gmail.com
[3] Shanghai Jiao Tong University, Shanghai, China
haoyang.wang@sjtu.edu.cn

Abstract. This paper introduces structure to key, in the related-key attack settings. While the idea of structure has been long used in key-recovery attacks against block ciphers to enjoy the birthday effect, the same had not been applied to key materials due to the fact that key structure results in uncontrolled differences in key and hence affects the validity or probabilities of the differential trails. We apply this simple idea to improve the related-key boomerang attack against AES-256 by Biryukov and Khovratovich in 2009. Surprisingly, it turns out to be effective, *i.e.*, both data and time complexities are reduced by a factor of about 2^8, to 2^{92} and 2^{91} respectively, at the cost of the amount of required keys increased from 4 to 2^{19}. There exist some tradeoffs between the data/time complexity and the number of keys. To the best of our knowledge, this is the first essential improvement of the attack against the full AES-256 since 2009. It will be interesting to see if the structure technique can be applied to other AES-like block ciphers, and to tweaks rather than keys of tweakable block ciphers so the amount of required keys of the attack will not be affected.

Keywords: AES · Differential · Boomerang · Key structure · Related key

1 Introduction

The Birth of AES. After the *Data Encryption Standard* (DES) was attacked by differential cryptanalysis due to Biham and Shamir [7,8] and later by linear cryptanalysis due to Matsui [29,30], the U.S. National Institute of Standards and Technology (NIST) initiated the public AES competition (1997–2000), out of which Rijndael [16] designed by Daemen and Rijmen won the competition and became officially the *Advanced Encryption Standard* in 2001. There are three variants, *i.e.*, AES-k with $k \in \{128, 192, 256\}$ denoting the key sizes in bits. AES became *de facto* the most popular and important block cipher in the world now

© The Author(s), under exclusive license to Springer Nature Switzerland AG 2022
K. Nguyen et al. (Eds.): ACISP 2022, LNCS 13494, pp. 3–23, 2022.
https://doi.org/10.1007/978-3-031-22301-3_1

for data protection, widely adopted by both industry and government agencies. The computation power nowadays is still far from breaking AES by bruteforce, even against the smallest variant AES-128, and due to the existence of AES-256, it will remain sound even under attack by the future quantum computers. Hence, a much longer lifespan is expected if no security flaw is discovered.

The Security. Since the design of Rijndael, AES has attracted tremendous efforts from the research community in security analysis. One of the most important security features of AES is its *proven* resistance against differential and linear cryptanalysis, which were applied to its predecessor—DES. It achieved this by the so-called *wide trail strategy* [15], *e.g.*, the minimum number of active S-boxes (those with non-zero differences) in 4 consecutive AES rounds for any differential characteristic in the single-key setting is 25. It has been analyzed by many cryptanalysis techniques[1], just to name a few here. Biryukov, Khovratovich, and Nikolić gave the first key-recovery attack against AES-256 by differentials [11] in 2009, the complexity of which was later improved in [10] by using related-key boomerang attack. In [28], Lu *et al.* gave 7-round attacks against AES-128 and AES-192, and 8-round against AES-256 by using impossible differentials. Leveraging integral cryptanalysis, Ferguson *et al.* [20] gave a practical attack against 6-round AES and then the first attack against 7-round AES. In terms of complexities of the key-recovery attacks in the single-key setting, the best attacks up to date are due to the Demirci-Selçuk meet-in-the-middle attack [17–19]. The meet-in-the-middle attack, which was previously known to be powerful for finding preimages of hash functions, led to attacks against 7-round AES in some hashing modes [31]. Many more attacks were found under other attack settings *e.g.*, single-key, related-key, hashing modes, for various security aspects, *e.g.*, key-recovery, collision/preimage finding in hashing modes, distinguisher, etc. Up to date, the most successful key-recovery[2] attack against AES-128/192/256 is for 7, 9, and 9 out of 10, 12, and 14 rounds respectively in the single-key setting, due to Derbez *et al.* [18] and an improvement by Li *et al.* [27].

The Boomerang Attack. To the best of our knowledge, the best attack against AES, in terms of number of attacked rounds, is due to Biryukov *et al.* [10,11] which dates back to 2009, where the key of the full version of AES-256 and AES-192 can be recovered under the related (sub-)key setting. While the bound given by the wide trail strategy could not be overcome in the differential attack under the single-key setting, differential characteristics with much higher probability exist in the related-key settings, where the differences from round keys and the data path can be cancelled out. Also, the boomerang attack is able to utilize two high-probability differential characteristics for small number of rounds. The attack succeeds due to these two properties.

---

[1] Only a few papers are cited here as examples since there are simply too many results.
[2] Besides those optimized brute-force style attacks, such as [12].

Our Contributions. Biryukov et al.'s works remain as the best publicly known key-recovery attack against the full version of AES-256, and there exists no essential improvement since 2009. In this paper, we try to improve their attack, in terms of data and time complexities, under the same related-subkey boomerang attack framework. The core idea comes from the observation that, while *structure* has been used in plaintext to enjoy the birthday effect and improve cryptanalysis, the same could potentially be applied to key material as well, even though this has not been tried yet. It is necessary to note that similar expressions to "key structure" already existed in some papers before, such as [6]. Their purpose is to generate some required subkey differences from key structure, due to non-linear key schedule of their targeted ciphers. However, our aim in this paper is to make further improvement by enjoying birthday effect of a key structure. There are many technical difficulties to overcome in the key structure boomerang attack framework, before the idea can eventually work out.

- Firstly, when *structure* rather than a fixed or chosen difference is introduced in the key material, one has to ensure that the uncontrollable difference in the key will not affect the validity of the two differential characteristics in the data path of the boomerang attack.
- Secondly, when *structure* is applied to the key, one has to ensure that the two differentials are neutral to each other in two halves of the key schedule, i.e., the differential characteristics in the key schedule in one half will not affect the other half regardless of the actual key difference chosen from the structure.
- Thirdly, one has to ensure that the key difference will not affect the probability of the differential characteristics. Note that Biryukov *et al.* chose the high probability difference transition of the S-box (those with 2^{-6}, rather than the 2^{-7} ones for the AES S-box) in order to increase the overall probability of the differential characteristics. In our case of structure, we only utilize those 2^{-6} difference pairs to achieve the same optimization. Although this only happens once in every 2^8 difference pairs (so we lose most of the pairs), we gain back by enforcing the high probability 2^{-6} transition once, and re-use it multiple times in the differential characteristics.

The final result, presented in Sect. 4, turns out to improve both the time and data complexities of Biyukov *et al.* attack by a factor of about 2^8, at the expense of the number of required keys being increased from 4 to 2^{19}. A detailed comparison is provided in Table 1.

Organization. The rest of the paper is organized as follows. Section 2 gives the necessary preliminaries for understanding the attack, and Sect. 3 explains the ideas behind key structures. The details of the improved attack are given in Sect. 4. Finally, Sect. 5 concludes the paper.

Table 1. Comparison with previous key-recovery attacks on full AES-256

Attack	Time	Data	Memory	# keys	Reference
Related-Key Differential	2^{131}	2^{131}	2^{65}	2^{35}	[11]
Related-Key Boomerang	$2^{99.5}$	$2^{99.5}$	2^{77}	4	[10]
Key-Structure Boomerang	$2^{92.5+s}$	2^{92+s}	2^{89-s}	2^{17-s}	Ours
	2^{92+s}	2^{91+s}	2^{89-s}	2^{19-s}	

Note: $0 \leq s \leq 7.5$

2 Preliminaries

2.1 Description of AES

The Advanced Encryption Standard (AES) [16] is an iterated block cipher which encrypts 128-bit plaintext with secret key of sizes 128, 192, and 256 bits. Its internal state can be represented as a 4×4 matrix whose elements are byte value (8 bits) in a finite field of $GF(2^8)$. The round function consists of four basic transformations in the following order:

- SubBytes (SB) is a nonlinear substitution that applies the same S-box to each byte of the internal state.
- ShiftRows (SR) is a cyclic rotation of the i-th row by i bytes to the left, for $i = 0, 1, 2, 3$.
- MixColumns (MC) is a multiplication of each column with a Maximum Distance Separable (MDS) matrix over $GF(2^8)$.
- AddRoundKey (AK) is an exclusive-or with the round key.

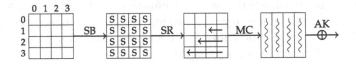

Fig. 1. AES round function

At the very beginning of the encryption, an additional whitening key addition is performed, and the last round does not contain MixColumns. AES-128, AES-192, and AES-256 share the same round function with different number of rounds: 10, 12, and 14, respectively.

The key schedule of AES transforms the master key into subkeys which are used in each of the rounds. Here, we describe the key schedule of AES-256. The 256-bit master key is divided into 8 32-bit words ($W[0], W[1], ..., W[7]$), then

$W[i]$ for $i \geqslant 8$ is computed as

$$W[i] = \begin{cases} W[i-8] \oplus \text{SB}(\text{RotByte}(W[i-1])) \oplus Rcon[i/8] & i \equiv 0 \bmod 8, \\ W[i-8] \oplus \text{SB}(W[i-1]) & i \equiv 4 \bmod 8, \\ W[i-8] \oplus W[i-1] & \text{otherwise} \end{cases}$$

The i-th *subkey* is of size 256-bit denoted by K^i, K^0 is the master key. RotByte is a cyclic shift by one byte to the left, and $Rcon$ is the round constant. The key schedule of AES-128 and AES-192 is slightly different due to the different key sizes, since this paper does not focus on these two variants, we refer to [16] for details.

Property of the AES S-box. The details of the S-box and the Difference Distribution Table (DDT) could be found in [16]. For any input difference $\Delta_{in} \neq 0$, there exists exactly one Δ_{out} such that $\text{DDT}(\Delta_{in}, \Delta_{out}) = 4$ (this results in the highest probability 2^{-6} for the AES S-box transition), 126 values of Δ_{out} such that $\text{DDT}(\Delta_{in}, \Delta_{out}) = 2$ (*i.e.*, probability 2^{-7}), and the rest 129 values of Δ_{out} with $\text{DDT}(\Delta_{in}, \Delta_{out}) = 0$. Those $(\Delta_{in}, \Delta_{out})$'s with $\text{DDT}(\Delta_{in}, \Delta_{out}) \neq 0$ are called *compatible*, and others are *incompatible*. These statistics will be used in our attack later.

2.2 Boomerang Attack

The boomerang attack was introduced in [33]. It regards the target cipher as a composition of two sub-ciphers E_0 and E_1. The first sub-cipher is supposed to have a differential $\alpha \to \beta$, and the second one to have a differential $\gamma \to \delta$, with probabilities p and q, respectively. The basic boomerang attack requires an adaptive chosen plaintext/ciphertext scenario, and plaintext pairs result in a right quartet with probability $p^2 q^2$. It works with four plaintext/ciphertext pairs $(P_1, C_1), (P_2, C_2), (P_3, C_3), (P_4, C_4)$, and the basic attack procedure is as follows. The attacker queries the encryption oracle with the input P_1 and $P_2 = P_1 \oplus \alpha$ to obtain C_1 and C_2, and calculate $C_3 = C_1 \oplus \delta$ and $C_4 = C_2 \oplus \delta$, which are sent to the decryption oracle to obtain P_3 and P_4. Later, Kelsey *et al.* [24] developed the amplified boomerang which is pure chosen-plaintext attack and a right quartet is obtained with probability $p^2 q^2 2^{-n}$. Further, it was pointed out in [4,5,33] that any value of β and γ is allowed as long as $\beta \neq \gamma$. As a result, the probability of the right quartet is increased to $2^{-n} \hat{p}^2 \hat{q}^2$, where $\hat{p} = \sqrt{\Sigma_i \Pr^2(\alpha \to \beta_i)}$ and $\hat{q} = \sqrt{\Sigma_j \Pr^2(\gamma_j \to \delta)}$. This improved attack framework is named the *rectangle attack*.

Related-Key Boomerang Attack. Boomerang and rectangle attacks under related-key setting were formulated in [6,25,26]. Let ΔK and ∇K be the key differences for E_0 and E_1, respectively. The attacker needs to access four related-key oracles with $K_1 \in \mathbb{K}$, where $\mathbb{K}$ is the key space, $K_2 = K_1 \oplus \Delta K$, $K_3 = K_1 \oplus \nabla K$ and $K_4 = K_1 \oplus \Delta K \oplus \nabla K$. In the related-key boomerang attack, paired plaintexts P_1, P_2 such that $P_1 \oplus P_2 = \alpha$ are queried to K_1 encryption oracle and K_2 encryption oracle, and the attacker receives ciphertexts C_1 and C_2. Then C_3 and C_4 are calculated by $C_3 = C_1 \oplus \delta$ and $C_4 = C_2 \oplus \delta$, and then queried to K_3 decryption oracle and K_4 decryption oracle. The resulting plaintext difference $P_3 \oplus P_4$ equals to α with probability $p^2 q^2$. Related-key rectangle attacks can be similarly formulated.

Boomerang Switch and Boomerang Connectivity Table. The boomerang switch was used to gain free rounds in the middle of the cipher in the attacks against the full AES-192 and AES-256 [10]. The idea was to optimize the transition between the differential characteristics of E_0 and E_1 in order to minimize the overall complexity of the distinguisher. In [10], three types of switch were introduced which are the *Feistel switch*, the *ladder switch* and the *S-box switch*. These switches were further generalized in the *boomerang connectivity table* (BCT) [14].

In this paper, we utilize the ladder switch to optimize our attack. The idea of the ladder switch is to realize that a cipher can be decomposed into smaller parallel transformations instead of rounds by default. The principle can be explained in the framework of BCT, see Fig. 2 with the case when $\Delta \neq 0$ and $\nabla = 0$. For any values of x_1 and x_2, with difference Δ, their outputs after S-box application are y_1 and y_2, respectively. Since the boomerang shift happens when $\nabla = 0$, we have $y_3 = y_1 \oplus \nabla = y_1$ and $y_4 = y_2 \oplus \nabla = y_2$. Thus, after the inversed S-box is applied, the paired values (x_3, x_4) is equal to (x_1, x_2) with probability 1, *i.e.*, the returned pair will always have difference Δ. The same also holds when $\Delta = 0$ and $\nabla \neq 0$.

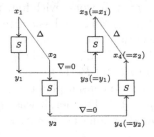

Fig. 2. The ladder switch on a single S-box

2.3   Notations

The byte at i-th row, j-th column of an internal state a is denoted by $a_{i,j}$, as illustrated in Fig. 1, where i and j start from 0. We refer to the byte of plaintext by $p_{i,j}$, the byte of the r-th subkey by $k_{i,j}^r$, and the byte of the r-th internal state after SubBytes by $x_{i,j}^r$. For the differential characteristics of boomerang distinguisher, we denote the difference used in E_0 by Δ and the difference in E_1 by ∇.

3   Key Structures

In differential cryptanalysis as [8], the attacker tries to find a distinguisher of a cipher so that he can distinguish the cipher from a random permutation. Then, key recovery attacks can be mounted based on the distinguisher directly, or with additional rounds added before and/or after the distinguisher. In this paper, we focus on the latter one.

We assume that there is a distinguisher which consists of a differential $\alpha \rightarrow \beta$ with probability p covering the last r_1 rounds of the target cipher. In order to launch a full-round attack (r rounds), ($r - r_1$) rounds should be prepended to the distinguisher. The aim of the attacker is to obtain enough ciphertext pairs with difference β by querying the encryption oracle with pre-chosen plaintexts. We define V to be the space spanned by all the plaintext differences that may lead to the difference α after the first ($r - r_1$) rounds, and let $m = log_2|V|$.

Structure from Plaintext. The first step of the attack is to generate pairs of plaintexts whose output differences after the first ($r - r_1$) rounds are the expected input difference α of the differential. The way to improve the efficiency of this step is to build a structure of plaintexts which consists of $P \oplus v_i$, where P is chosen randomly and $v_i \in V$. The XOR difference between any two elements of the structure belongs to V. In this way, at most 2^{2m-1} unordered plaintext pairs (P_i, P_j) (the order of i, j does not matter) can be composed from a single structure, while the data and time complexity to prepare this structure is only 2^m. We refer to the ratio between the number of pairs generated and the size of structure as *gain* (this is also called birthday effect in other places), quantitatively it is $2^{(2m-1)-m} = 2^{m-1}$ here. If more plaintext pairs are needed for the attack, another new structure can be constructed in the same way by selecting another random value of P. However, this would not increase the overall gain. As can be seen, the gain only depends on the structure size. Thus, if the structure size could be increased, the attack complexity would be reduced accordingly.

Structure from Key. In the related-key setting [3], the attacker is allowed to choose a desired relation between keys. The most common form is: for an unknown key K_1, the attacker uses a XOR difference D to produce another key $K_2 = K_1 \oplus D$. Then, the subkey additions in round functions can be used to cancel some differences in the differential attack in order to obtain better differential characteristics. Compared with the single-key setting, the related-key setting provides additional freedom in choosing the key difference D. In our case, this fact enlightens us that a key structure utilizing the key difference could be used to improve the attack.

For a related-key differential characteristic with key difference D, we can build a key structure from the original secret key K_1, and let $\{K_1 \oplus v_i \mid v_i \in V_D\}$ be the set of keys inside the structure, where V_D is the space consisting of the differences that have the same truncated difference as that of D. Similarly, we define $m_k = log_2|V_D|$. Together with a plaintext structure, at most a total of $2^{2(m+m_k)-1}$ unordered pairs of $((P_i, K_i), (P_j, K_j))$ can be obtained, while only 2^{m+m_k} data/queries are used. Thus, the gain increases to $2^{2(m+m_k)-1-(m+m_k)} = 2^{m+m_k-1}$, compared to the use of plaintext structure alone.

The Use of Key Structure. Key structure should be applied together with plaintext structure to provide additional advantage. However, compared to plaintext structure, key structure has more constraints in its application. Due to the fact that each plaintext in the plaintext structure will be encrypted with each key in the key structure during an attack, the difference between the pairs of keys will not be fixed, thus the subkey differences in the whole rounds are difficult to control and are unlikely to match the exact differential characteristic $\alpha \rightarrow \beta$.

Hence, in order to have as many valid key pairs as possible, the key schedule is better to be linear or the proportion of the non-linear part is small, and the key difference should not have strong impact on the truncated differential characteristic, which means that the truncated differential characteristic should be able to be instantiated with many differences. Otherwise, if the differential characteristic is valid with only a small proportion of key pairs, smaller than 2^{-m_k}, the use of key structure will only weaken the attack. On the other hand, the distinguisher obtained with key structure might not be as good as the original one without key structure, because the probability of the differential characteristic will vary according to key difference since the propagation of non-linear part in the internal state will be different. All in all, in order to make good use of key structure, the extra data and time consumption of it should be lower than the gain it offers.

Last but not least, it is necessary to mention that at most one key structure can be constructed in an attack as the key structure is created from the original secret key which is fixed.

4   Improved Boomerang Attack on AES-256

In this section, we apply key structure to the related-key boomerang attack on AES-256, which is based on the attack in [10]. We will first give an overview of the boomerang distinguisher, then describe the construction of the key structure, and finally explain the details of the attack.

The differential characteristics used in our boomerang attack are depicted in Fig. 3. The differential characteristic of E_1 is fixed, while the differential characteristic of E_0 has a lot of candidates. In Fig. 3, different colors refer to different values. The differentials for all the active S-boxes of the differential characteristic of E_1 are set to be (0x01, 0x1f), which holds with probability 2^{-6}. For the differential characteristic of E_0, the red and blue hashed cells are not fixed but always pass the S-box differential with the maximal probability 2^{-6}, and the green cells are unknown. The switching position of the boomerang distinguisher is pointed by the green ovals.

The differences in the key schedule are given in Table 2. Since the differential characteristic of E_0 is not fixed, we use the variables R, B and G_i to represent its truncated pattern, $i = 1, 2, 3, 4$. Given the value of R, B is then derived from the table DDT with the requirement that $\text{DDT}(R, B) = 4$, lastly the value of G_i is uniquely determined by B through the MixColumns transformation:

$$\begin{pmatrix} 0 \\ B \\ 0 \\ 0 \end{pmatrix} \xrightarrow{\text{MixColumns}} \begin{pmatrix} G_1 \\ G_2 \\ G_3 \\ G_4 \end{pmatrix}.$$

Table 2. Key schedule difference for the boomerang attack on AES-256. The values are given in hexadecimal notation.

														ΔK^i													
0	?	00	00	00	G_1	G_1	G_1	G_1	1	00	00	00	00	G_1	00	G_1	00	2	00	00	00	00	G_1	G_1	00	00
	?	R	R	R	?	G_2	G_2	G_2		00	R	00	R	G_2	00	G_2	00		00	R	R	00	G_2	G_2	00	00
	?	00	00	00	G_3	G_3	G_3	G_3		00	00	00	00	G_3	00	G_3	00		00	00	00	00	G_3	G_3	00	00
	?	00	00	00	G_4	G_4	G_4	G_4		00	00	00	00	G_4	00	G_4	00		00	00	00	00	G_4	G_4	00	00
3	00	00	00	00	G_1	00	00	00	4	00	00	00	00	G_1	G_1	G_1	G_1									
	00	R	00	00	G_2	00	00	00		00	R	R	R	?	?	?	?									
	00	00	00	00	G_3	00	00	00		00	00	00	00	G_3	G_3	G_3	G_3									
	00	00	00	00	G_4	00	00	00		00	00	00	00	G_4	G_4	G_4	G_4									

														∇K^i													
0	?	?	?	?	?	00	?	00	1	?	01	?	00	?	?	00	00	2	?	?	00	00	?	00	00	00
	X	X	X	X	1f	00	1f	00		X	00	X	00	1f	1f	00	00		X	X	00	00	1f	00	00	00
	?	?	?	?	1f	00	1f	00		?	00	?	00	1f	1f	00	00		?	?	00	00	1f	00	00	00
	?	?	?	?	21	00	21	00		?	00	?	00	21	21	00	00		?	?	00	00	21	00	00	00
3	?	01	01	01	3e	3e	3e	3e	4	01	00	01	00	3e	00	3e	00	5	01	01	00	00	3e	3e	00	00
	X	00	00	1f	1f	1f	1f	1f		00	00	00	00	1f	00	1f	00		00	00	00	00	1f	1f	00	00
	?	00	00	00	1f	1f	1f	1f		00	00	00	00	1f	00	1f	00		00	00	00	00	1f	1f	00	00
	?	00	00	00	21	21	21	21		00	00	00	00	21	00	21	00		00	00	00	00	21	21	00	00
6	01	00	00	00	3e	00	00	00	7	01	01	01	01	?	?	?	?									
	00	00	00	00	1f	00	00	00		00	00	00	00	1f	1f	1f	1f									
	00	00	00	00	1f	00	00	00		00	00	00	00	1f	1f	1f	1f									
	00	00	00	00	21	00	00	00		00	00	00	00	21	21	21	21									

4.1 Construction of the Key Structure

The key relation used in our attack is a complex form that allows the attacker to choose a desired XOR difference of a subkey at any round. This setting is also defined as the related-subkey setting in [9].

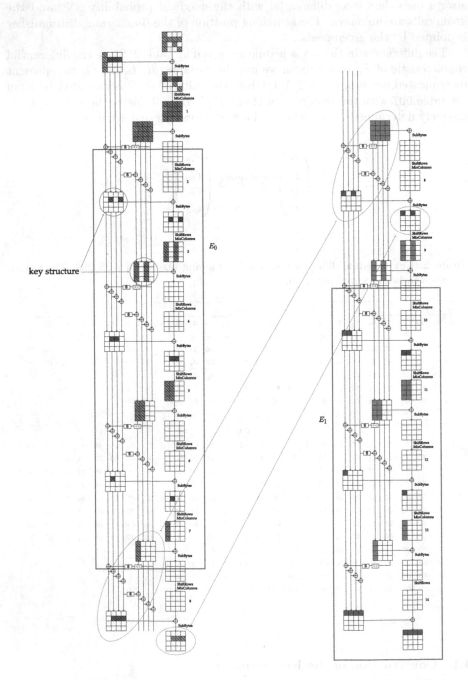

Fig. 3. The differential characteristics of the boomerang attack against AES-256

Now, we describe how to construct the key structure, denoted by S_k. The key structure is generated from the second subkey K^1. One can observe in Fig. 3 that the difference of the second 256-bit subkey has 10 active bytes, but the difference cannot be chosen randomly. The differential characteristic of E_0, as well as the one of E_1, is constructed following the idea of local collision [13], that is, once a subkey difference is added to the internal state, the next subkey difference will try to cancel it in the next round. Therefore, in order to generate such a differential characteristic for E_0, the two active bytes in the first half of ΔK^1 must take the same difference value, thus it can choose 2^8 values at most. Besides, for the second half of ΔK^1, the differences of the two active columns are also required to be the same value, because the two active columns are supposed to cancel the two active columns in the internal state according to the differential characteristic of E_0, and each active column in the internal state is computed from a single active byte through MixColumns and the two active bytes are equal. Furthermore, this relation also implies that the two active columns of ΔK^1 can only choose 2^8 values at most. To sum up, there are 2^{16} valid values for ΔK^1, each of which is denoted by ΔK_i^1, $1 \leq i \leq 2^{16}$.

For a secret key K_0, the key structure S_k is generated by adding the non-zero difference ΔK_i^1 to the second subkey of K_0, from which a new secret key K_i can be uniquely determined, see Fig. 4(a). Finally, the key structure consists of 2^{16} keys, from which 2^{31} unordered key pairs can be composed.

Note that the keys in the key structure are used in the encryption side of the boomerang attack. For the key K_i' used in the decryption side, they are computed by adding the fixed difference ∇K to the jointed state of the second half of K_i^3 and the first half of K_i^4, then the full K_i' can be uniquely determined by the obtained eight consecutive columns, see Fig. 4(b). By doing so, the differential characteristic of E_1 will be fixed. The actual value of ∇K can be found in Table 2, it will make sure that the differential characteristic of E_1 is the optimal one $i.e.$, all S-box transitions happen with probability 2^{-6}.

Given a pair of keys (K_A, K_B) chosen from the key structure S_k, together with the corresponding key pair (K_A', K_B') used in the decryption side, the four keys form a key quartet. For a key quartet, the differences in the key schedule for both the differential characteristics of E_0 and E_1 can be found in Table 2. In particular, for the differential characteristic of E_1 (where the key pair (K_A, K_A') or (K_B, K_B') is applied), some byte in ∇K^i for $i = 1, 2, 3$ can even be determined due to the slow diffusion of the key schedule. These values will play an important role in the following key recovery attack. Last but not least, we note that only one key structure is used in our attack.

4.2 Boomerang Distinguisher

Let us compute the probability of the boomerang distinguisher covering rounds 2–14. For the differential characteristic of E_0 which covers rounds 2–8, there are 5 active S-boxes and the differentials $(\Delta_{in}, \Delta_{out})$ for all of them are the same. Because of the use of key structure, the values for both Δ_{in} and Δ_{out} are not fixed, but they are directly related to the subkey differences, which are

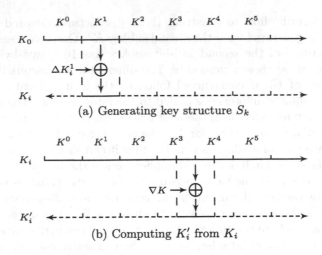

(a) Generating key structure S_k

(b) Computing K_i' from K_i

Fig. 4. Key generation

determined by the key pair used in the differential characteristic. Among the total of 2^{31} key pairs that can be composed from the key structure, $(2^7 - 2)/2^8$ of it will make the differential $(\Delta_{in}, \Delta_{out})$ happen with probability 2^{-7}, while a proportion of $1/2^8$ will lead the probability to 2^{-6}. Accordingly, the 5 active S-boxes in rounds 2–8 are passed with probability $2^{-7 \times 5} = 2^{-35}$ for the first case and $2^{-6 \times 5} = 2^{-30}$ for the second case.

The boomerang is switched in round 9. Although the differential characteristic of E_0 is not fixed, its truncated pattern is uniquely determined. Accordingly, we can ensure that there is no overlapped active S-box in round 9 between the differential characteristics of E_0 and E_1. Thus, according to the BCT, the two differential characteristics are compatible for the boomerang attack and the switching probability is 1. Besides, it was reported recently that the boomerang switch can actually happen in multiple rounds in [32,34], so we have also verified the switching effect in rounds 8–10, and it matches our evaluation.

For the differential characteristic of E_1, there are 3 active S-boxes in rounds 10–14. Note that only one differential characteristic is used for E_1 and the differentials for all the active S-boxes are optimal with probability 2^{-6}, thus the probability of the differential characteristic of E_1 of rounds 10–14 is $2^{-6 \times 3} = 2^{-18}$.

Finally, the probability of the boomerang distinguisher is either $2^{2 \times (-35-18)} = 2^{-106}$ or $2^{2 \times (-30-18)} = 2^{-96}$, depending on the key pair from the key structure.

4.3   A Detailed Description of the Attack

One round is added at the beginning of the boomerang distinguisher to launch the full-round attack. The plaintext difference pattern, as show in Fig. 3, is deduced from both the first subkey difference and the internal state difference in the second round. The attack procedure is described in Algorithm 1.

Algorithm 1: Related-key boomerang attack on AES-256 using key structure

---

Prepare a plaintext structure consisting of 2^{72} plaintexts, which traverses all

values of the 9 gray cells in , and takes arbitrary constants in the others.

Create a hash table H of size 2^{88}.

> **for** *each of the 2^{16} keys K in the key structure S_K* **do**
> > **for** *each of the 2^{72} plaintexts P in the plaintext structure* **do**
> > > Encrypt P under key K, denote the ciphertext as C.
> > >
> > > Compute $C' = C \oplus \Delta C$.
> > >
> > > Decrypt C' with K', K' being computed from the corresponding K, and denote the new plaintext by P'.
> > >
> > > Insert the plaintext pair (P, P') into the hash table H, indexed by the 7 bytes of P' where constants of the plaintext structure fall and 2 bytes of $P \oplus P'$ at positions $(2,0)$ and $(3,0)$.
> >
> > **end**
>
> **end**

For each key pair, we can compose 2^{144} plaintext pairs from 1 plaintext structure, out of which $2^{144-72} = 2^{72}$ will pass through the first round with the desired input difference of the boomerang distinguisher. In total, 2^{103} pairs pass the first round for all the 2^{31} key pairs. The probability of the boomerang distinguisher is 2^{-106} for a proportion of $(2^7 - 2)/2^8$ key pairs, thus around $2^{103} \cdot (2^7 - 2)/2^8 \cdot 2^{-106} \approx 2^{-4}$ right quartets are expected. On the other hand, $2^{103} \cdot 1/2^8 \cdot 2^{-96} = 2^{-1}$ right quartets are expected when the probability of the boomerang distinguisher is 2^{-96} for $1/2^8$ of key pairs. Compared to the first case, the boomerang distinguisher in the second case is much better, so we will only adopt the second one in our attack. Therefore, in order to obtain 4 right quartets, 2^3 plaintext structures are required. We need to repeat Algorithm 1 2^3 times with different plaintext structures and the same key structure.

In the following, we will explain how to gradually filter out wrong quartets and recover key bits. Let us compute the number of quartet candidates after Algorithm 1. Firstly, there is a 56-bit filter at the output of the boomerang. Then, observe in Table 2 that $\nabla k_{i,7}^0 = 0$ for $i > 1$, so $\Delta k_{i,0}^0$ should be equal for both pairs (K_A, K_B) and (K'_A, K'_B) in a key quartet, which implies that $\Delta p_{i,0}$ should be equal for both plaintext pairs (P_1, P_2) and (P'_1, P'_2) for the right quartet as well, because $\Delta k_{i,0}^0$ is equal to $\Delta p_{i,0}$ according to the differential characteristic of E_0. This is a 16-bit filter. So there are on average $2^{72+16-56-16} = 2^{16}$ collisions for each index of the hash table H, from which 2^{31} quartets can be composed. In total, $2^{31+72} = 2^{103}$ quartet candidates are left for all the 2^{72} indices of the hash table, and thus 2^{106} quartet candidates for all the 2^3 plaintext structures. These candidates are further filtered by the following steps. The key bytes that can be recovered are listed in Fig. 5.

7						5
3	4	2	2	4D		7
D	4					5
D		4				5

Fig. 5. The AES-256 key state with key information obtained at each step. Digits stand for the sub-steps in step II, "D" means difference.

Step I. Note that the key pairs of a right quartet must meet the requirement that the active S-boxes in the differential characteristic of E_0 are passed with probability 2^{-6}. The requirement is satisfied with probability 2^{-8}, thus $2^{106-8} = 2^{98}$ quartet candidates are eligible. Now we explain how to obtain the 2^{98} quartet candidates. The differential of the active S-boxes can be deduced by the difference in the key schedule. For example, $\Delta k_{1,1}^1$ is the input difference of the S-box at the position $(1,1)$ in the third round, and $\Delta k_{2,4}^1$ is the corresponding output difference due to the ShiftRows and MixColumns. Thus, we can simply check whether the differential $(\Delta k_{1,1}^1, \Delta k_{2,4}^1)$ is optimal for the AES S-box. Once it is confirmed, the differentials of the 5 active S-boxes will also be determined. Note that the differential characteristics of E_0 used in both sides of the boomerang are the same, thus we only need to check the encryption side, the details are given in Algorithm 2.

Algorithm 2: Filtration in Step I

---

for *each index of the hash table H* **do**

    Insert the 2^{16} collisions into a new hash table H' indexed by the difference of $k_{1,1}^1$ between the current key and the original key K_0.

    for *each index i of H'* **do**

        Insert the $2^{16-8} = 2^8$ collisions (on average) into a new hash table H_i'' indexed by the difference of $k_{2,4}^1$ between the current key and the original key K_0.

    end

    for *index i of H' from 0 to $2^8 - 2$* **do**

        for *index j of H' from i+1 to $2^8 - 1$* **do**

            Compute $\Delta k_{1,1}^1 = i \oplus j$, and find the value of $\Delta k_{2,4}^1$ such that DDT$(\Delta k_{1,1}^1, \Delta k_{2,4}^1) = 4$.

            for *each index s of H_i''* **do**

                Compute $t = s \oplus \Delta k_{2,4}^1$. Check whether t is in H_j''. If yes, the pairs of H_i'' and H_j'' compose quartet candidates.

            end

        end

    end

end

Step II. There are $2^{31-8} = 2^{23}$ key quartets remaining after Step I, and each has on average $2^{98-23} = 2^{75}$ quartet candidates. In the following steps, we will proceed with each key quartet independently, and use K_A, K_B, K'_A and K'_B to denote the four keys.

1) There is a 2-bit filter at $\Delta p_{1,2}$ and $\Delta p_{1,3}$ due to the S-box compatibility, thus 4-bit at both sides of the boomerang in total. Besides, there is also a 2-bit filter at $\Delta p_{2,0}$ and $\Delta p_{3,0}$ due the S-box compatibility in the key schedule. Thus, the number of quartets is reduced to $2^{75-6} = 2^{69}$.

2) Each quartet proposes 2^2 candidates of $k^0_{1,2}$ and $k^0_{1,3}$ for K_A and K'_A each, thus there are in total 2^4 candidates. As can be seen from Table 2, the four "X" of ∇K^0 are equal and take only 2^7 values. Hence, the differences $\Delta k^0_{1,2}$ and $\Delta k^0_{1,3}$ between K_A and K'_A have to be equal to X, which is a 16-bit filter for the key candidates. Thus, $2^{69+4+7-16} = 2^{64}$ quartet candidates are left, and the values of $k^0_{1,2}$ and $k^0_{1,3}$ are suggested.

3) Observe that the value of $\Delta k^0_{1,0}$ is determined by $k^0_{2,7}$ and $\nabla k^0_{2,7} = 0$ from Table 2, the values of $\Delta k^0_{1,0}$ should be the same for both the key pairs (K_A, K_B) and (K'_A, K'_B). Since $\Delta k^0_{2,7}$ is known, $\Delta k^0_{1,0}$ can take 2^7 values. For each guess of $\Delta k^0_{1,0}$, it has to be compatible with $\Delta p_{1,0}$ and $\Delta x^0_{1,0}$ through the S-box, which is a 2-bit filter for both sides of the boomerang. After that, each quartet proposes two candidates of $k^0_{1,0}$ for K_A and K'_A, respectively. Moreover, there is an 8-bit filter because the difference $\nabla k^0_{1,0}$ between K_A and K'_A should be equal to X. In the end, the number of quartet candidates is reduced to $2^{64+7-2+2-8} = 2^{63}$, and the value of $k^0_{1,0}$ is suggested.

4) Notice that $\nabla k^1_{1,3} = 0$, a reasoning similar to the one above can be applied to $\Delta k^0_{1,4}$, which can take 2^7 values. For each guess of $\Delta k^0_{1,4}$, the values of $\Delta x^0_{0,0}, \Delta x^0_{1,1}, \Delta x^0_{2,2}, \Delta x^0_{3,3}$ can be uniquely computed by inverting the MixColumns transformation. There is a 1-bit filter on $\Delta x^0_{1,1}, \Delta x^0_{2,2}, \Delta x^0_{3,3}$ each due to the S-box compatibility, then 6-bit filter in total on both sides of the boomerang. Each quartet proposes two candidates of $k^0_{1,1}, k^0_{2,2}, k^0_{3,3}$ for K_A and K'_A, respectively. However, the difference $\nabla k^0_{1,1}$ between K_A and K'_A is restricted to X, which results in an 8-bit filter. To summarize, the number of quartets is reduced to $2^{63+7-6+6-8} = 2^{62}$ and the values of $k^0_{1,1}, k^0_{2,2}, k^0_{3,3}$ as well as $\Delta k^0_{1,4}$ are suggested.

5) Since $\Delta k^0_{1,0}$, $\Delta k^0_{2,0}$ and $\Delta k^0_{3,0}$ are known, it will provide 2 guesses for each of $k^0_{2,7}$, $k^0_{3,7}$ and $k^0_{0,7}$. However, these guesses for K_A and K'_A are the same because the differences $\nabla k^0_{2,7}$, $\nabla k^0_{3,7}$ and $\nabla k^0_{0,7}$ between K_A and K'_A are all 0. Thus, in this step, the number of key candidates is increased to $2^{62+3} = 2^{65}$, and the values of $k^0_{2,7}$, $k^0_{3,7}$ and $k^0_{0,7}$ are suggested.

6) Note that the key bytes $k^0_{2,7}$, $k^0_{1,0}$, $k^0_{1,1}$, $k^0_{1,2}$, $k^0_{1,3}$ and the difference $\Delta k^0_{1,4}$ have been derived in the above steps. On the other hand, we notice that $\Delta k^0_{1,4}$ can be computed from $k^0_{2,7}$, $k^0_{1,0}$, $k^0_{1,1}$, $k^0_{1,2}$ and $k^0_{1,3}$ according to the key schedule. This constraint can provide an 8-bit filter, and thus the number of key proposals is reduced to 2^{57}.

7) Make a guess of $k_{1,7}^0$ of K_A, which has 2^8 choices, then $k_{1,7}^0$ will be known for all the four keys and $\Delta k_{0,0}^0$ can be computed. After that, for each side of the boomerang there is a 1-bit filter on $\Delta k_{0,0}^0$ due to the S-box compatibility, then each quartet will propose 2 candidates of $k_{0,0}^0$ for K_A and K_A', respectively. Thus $2^{57+8-2+2} = 2^{65}$ key proposals are obtained.

In the end, 2^{65} key candidates are proposed and 11 key bytes for each of K_A, K_B, K_A' and K_B' are suggested. However, many bytes are strongly related according to Table 2. Among them, at least $k_{0,0}^0$, $k_{1,1}^0$, $k_{2,2}^0$ and $k_{3,3}^0$ of K_A and K_A' are independent, so we can recover 15 bytes with 2^{65} proposals for each key quartet, and thus 2^{88} proposals for all the 2^{23} key quartets. Additionally, differences of 3 bytes are recovered: $\Delta k_{1,4}^0$, $\Delta k_{2,0}^0$, $\Delta k_{3,0}^0$, where $\Delta k_{2,0}^0$ and $\Delta k_{3,0}^0$ can be directly obtained from plaintext difference, but they can not be used to derive the corresponding key bytes.

Recover the Key. Recall that 4 right quartets are expected for the attack, which are supposed to be distinguishable from other wrong quartets. However, the 4 right quartets are very likely to be combined with different key pairs due to the key structure, thus the correct key bytes proposed by them will belong to different keys, which is hard to be distinguished. So we have to deduce all the proposed key bytes to the original keys K_0 and K_0'. Looking at Table 2, we can see that most bytes of the first subkey difference between K_0 and all the other keys are known, except $\Delta k_{1,4}^0$ and $\Delta k_{i,0}^0$ where $0 \le i \le 3$. Hence, for those key bytes whose differences are known, all the proposals can be deduced to K_0. The same reasoning applies to K_0'. As for the two unknown differences $\Delta k_{0,0}^0$ and $\Delta k_{1,0}^0$, since the value of $k_{1,7}^0$ was derived and the difference of $\Delta k_{1,7}^0$ is known, the difference $\Delta k_{0,0}^0$ can be easily computed through the key schedule. Same trick holds for $\Delta k_{1,0}^0$, it can be computed from $k_{2,7}^0$ and $\Delta k_{2,7}^0$. Then, we can deduce the proposals of the two bytes to K_0 and K_0'.

In the end, all the proposed key bytes can be deduced to K_0 and K_0'. We have 2^{88} proposals for 120 key bits, and the correct proposal is supposed to appear 4 times. The probability that a wrong key is suggested 4 times is $\binom{2^{88}}{4} \cdot (2^{-120})^4 \cdot (1 - 2^{-120})^{2^{88}-4} \approx 2^{-138.5}$, thus the expect number of such a key is $2^{120-138.5} = 2^{-18.5}$, while the 4 right quartets would always vote for the correct one. Therefore, no wrong key will survive and the correct 120 key bits will be recovered. With the knowledge of the recovered key bits, the remaining part of the key can be found with many approaches, which will not dominate the cost of the whole attack.

Complexity. In our attack, a total of 2^{92} plaintexts and ciphertexts are generated, thus the data complexity is 2^{92}. In Algorithm 1, there are 2^{88} encryption oracle calls, 2^{88} XOR operations, and 2^{88} decryption oracle calls. As the plaintexts are added into the hash table, each plaintext requires one memory access, thus 2^{88} memory accesses in total. Thus, for the 2^3 plaintext structures, the total time complexity of Algorithm 1 is 2^{92} encryption/decryption oracle calls and 2^{91} memory accesses.

In Algorithm 2, the plaintext pairs (P, P') in H are added into many new hash tables, which requires $2^{72} \times (2^{16} + 2^{16}) = 2^{89}$ memory accesses. The lookups in DDT require $2^{72+15} = 2^{87}$ memory accesses. The lookups in the hash table H_i'' require $2^{72+23} = 2^{95}$ memory accesses, which dominates the algorithm. In sum, for the entire 2^3 plaintext structures, Step I requires $2^{95+3} = 2^{98}$ memory accesses.

For Step II 1), it requires 1 memory access for each quartet to check whether these bytes are compatible. Therefore, the time complexity of this step is 2^{98} memory accesses.

After Step II 1), the number of remaining quartets is 2^{92}, and the number is continuously decreasing in the following steps, thus the following computation will not dominate the cost of the whole attack.

Following the idea from [5,9,20], where memory access can be converted to equivalent amount of encryption/decryption oracle calls, one AES-256 encryption/decryption is equivalent to roughly 2^8 memory accesses by counting the number of S-box lookups. Therefore, the 2^{98} memory accesses to the hash table H_i'' in Step I can be converted to 2^{90} encryptions/decryptions, and the same can be done for the 2^{98} memory accesses in Step II 1). Finally, we conclude that the whole attack requires 2^{92} plaintexts and ciphertexts, the time complexity being equivalent to $2^{92.5}$ encryptions (2^{92} encryptions/decryptions and 2^{99} memory accesses $\approx 2^{91}$ encryptions), and the memory complexity is 2^{89}.

Further Improvement. In the attack, the key structure is only added in K_A and K_B in E_0, the same idea could be extended to the K_A' and K_B' in E_1. However, this attempt could not work. For a right quartet, the differentials of E_0 in both sides of the boomerang should be the same, which determines that the differential characteristic in the key schedule of (K_A', K_B') must be the same as that of (K_A, K_B). In order to meet this condition, the switch in the key schedule should be the same for a quartet, i.e., the differences ∇K added to K_A and K_B at the middle of the fourth and fifth subkey should be the same. Even if we use a structure of ∇K, we still need to find right quartets for each value of ∇K separately. Thus, this method does not provide additional improvement to the attack.

Although the potential key structure is a failure, it can also be used to improve the attack slightly. As discussed above, the functionality of the key structure is equivalent to plaintext structure: using a different ∇K leads to a different set of (P_1', P_2'). In our attack, 2^3 plaintext structures are required to produce 4 right quartets. Instead of choosing 2^3 plaintext structures, we could also choose $2^3 \nabla K$ (There are $2^8 - 1$ values of ∇K to produce the optimal differential characteristic of E_1). In this way, 2^{88} encryptions and $2^{88+3} = 2^{91}$ decryptions are needed, thus the number of decryptions dominates the complexity. The time and data complexity is reduced to 2^{92} and 2^{91}, respectively. The number of keys will increase to $2^{16+3} = 2^{19}$.

More Tradeoffs. One key structure consists of 2^{16}, and hence the total number of keys required in this attack is 2^{17} (2^{16} for the encryption and decryption oracles each). There is a tradeoff between the number of keys required, and the time and data complexities, by reducing the size of the key structure, *i.e.*, with a 2^{16-s} key structures, the resulted complexities of the attack will be: Time 2^{92+s}, Data 2^{91+s}, and # Keys 2^{17-s}, for $0 \leq s \leq 16$. Further to note, when $s \geq 7.5$ the time complexity becomes higher than that in [10], and our attack offers no more advantage, so the tradeoff makes sense only for $0 \leq s \leq 7.5$.

5   Conclusion

In this paper, we brought the idea of structures to key materials, and successfully applied it to the related-key boomerang attack against AES-256. This improved the best known attack against AES-256 by reducing the data/time complexities by a factor of about 2^8, at the cost of more required keys. While the general principle is simple, its deployment contains many details and it is important to ensure that the introduction of key structure will not invalidate or significantly reduce the probability of the differential characteristics. More tradeoffs are provided between time/data complexity and the number of required keys.

Other Potential Applications. We note that our structure technique was applied to key material, and hence increases the number of required keys for the attack to succeed. However, this may be avoided when the attack is applied to AES-based tweakable block ciphers so that the structure is applied to tweak, rather than keys. There are two such cases: TAES [1] and the TBCs following TWEAKEY framework [22]. TAES is basically AES-256 with the concatenation of a 128-bit secret key and a 128-bit tweak as the 256-bit key input. The TWEAKEY framework treats the key and tweak in the same way and names the combined input "tweakey". Following it, there are several dedicated AES-like proposals such as the Deoxys-BC in the Deoxys AE design [23], SKINNY [2], and Kiasu [21]. Users will have the choice to decide which are the bits to be used as key or tweak material. The potential application of our technique is that, when the structure is applied to the tweak of either TAES or AES-based TWEAKEY designs, the increased requirement applies to the tweak only, and that of keys remains un-affected.

Inapplicability to AES-192 [10] **and Differential Attack** [11]. The boomerang attack was applied to AES-192 as well in [10], so the idea of key structure naturally applies. However, looking into the details, the key bytes recovered in the AES-192 attack falls in two different locations, in both the pre- and post-whitening keys. Note that in our improved attack on AES-256, we are able to deduce the count of key suggestions of all keys to the original key K_0 and K_0', however this becomes impossible for both pre- and post-whitening keys simultaneously in case of AES-192. The direct application of the idea of key structure to the differential attack in [11] seems difficult, as the probability of the differentials will drop significantly, which overrules the potential gain key structures might brings. It will be interesting to see if these technical difficulties could be overcome and find more applications of key structures.

Acknowledgements. This research is partially supported by the Nanyang Technological University in Singapore under Grant 04INS000397C230, Singapores Ministry of Education under Grants RG91/20 and MOE2019-T2-1-060, the National Natural Science Foundation of China (Grants 62022036, 62132008, 62172410, 61732021), and the National Key Research and Development Program of China (Grant 2018YFA0704704).

References

1. Bao, Z., Guo, J., Iwata, T., Minematsu, K.: ZOCB and ZOTR: Tweakable Blockcipher modes for authenticated encryption with full absorption. IACR Trans. Symmetric Cryptol. **2019**(2), 1–54 (2019)
2. Beierle, C., et al.: The SKINNY family of block ciphers and its low-latency variant MANTIS. In: Robshaw, M., Katz, J. (eds.) CRYPTO 2016. LNCS, vol. 9815, pp. 123–153. Springer, Heidelberg (2016). https://doi.org/10.1007/978-3-662-53008-5_5
3. Biham, E.: New types of cryptanalytic attacks using related keys. J. Cryptol. **7**(4), 229–246 (1994)
4. Biham, E., Dunkelman, O., Keller, N.: The rectangle attack — rectangling the serpent. In: Pfitzmann, B. (ed.) EUROCRYPT 2001. LNCS, vol. 2045, pp. 340–357. Springer, Heidelberg (2001). https://doi.org/10.1007/3-540-44987-6_21
5. Biham, E., Dunkelman, O., Keller, N.: New results on boomerang and rectangle attacks. In: Daemen, J., Rijmen, V. (eds.) FSE 2002. LNCS, vol. 2365, pp. 1–16. Springer, Heidelberg (2002). https://doi.org/10.1007/3-540-45661-9_1
6. Biham, E., Dunkelman, O., Keller, N.: Related-key boomerang and rectangle attacks. In: Cramer, R. (ed.) EUROCRYPT 2005. LNCS, vol. 3494, pp. 507–525. Springer, Heidelberg (2005). https://doi.org/10.1007/11426639_30
7. Biham, E., Shamir, A.: Differential cryptanalysis of DES-like cryptosystems. In: Menezes, A.J., Vanstone, S.A. (eds.) CRYPTO 1990. LNCS, vol. 537, pp. 2–21. Springer, Heidelberg (1991). https://doi.org/10.1007/3-540-38424-3_1
8. Biham, E., Shamir, A.: Differential cryptanalysis of the full 16-round DES. In: Brickell, E.F. (ed.) CRYPTO 1992. LNCS, vol. 740, pp. 487–496. Springer, Heidelberg (1993). https://doi.org/10.1007/3-540-48071-4_34
9. Biryukov, A., Dunkelman, O., Keller, N., Khovratovich, D., Shamir, A.: Key recovery attacks of practical complexity on AES-256 variants with up to 10 rounds. In: Gilbert, H. (ed.) EUROCRYPT 2010. LNCS, vol. 6110, pp. 299–319. Springer, Heidelberg (2010). https://doi.org/10.1007/978-3-642-13190-5_15
10. Biryukov, A., Khovratovich, D.: Related-key cryptanalysis of the full AES-192 and AES-256. In: Matsui, M. (ed.) ASIACRYPT 2009. LNCS, vol. 5912, pp. 1–18. Springer, Heidelberg (2009). https://doi.org/10.1007/978-3-642-10366-7_1
11. Biryukov, A., Khovratovich, D., Nikolić, I.: Distinguisher and related-key attack on the full AES-256. In: Halevi, S. (ed.) CRYPTO 2009. LNCS, vol. 5677, pp. 231–249. Springer, Heidelberg (2009). https://doi.org/10.1007/978-3-642-03356-8_14
12. Bogdanov, A., Khovratovich, D., Rechberger, C.: Biclique cryptanalysis of the full AES. In: Lee, D.H., Wang, X. (eds.) ASIACRYPT 2011. LNCS, vol. 7073, pp. 344–371. Springer, Heidelberg (2011). https://doi.org/10.1007/978-3-642-25385-0_19

13. Chabaud, F., Joux, A.: Differential collisions in SHA-0. In: Krawczyk, H. (ed.) CRYPTO 1998. LNCS, vol. 1462, pp. 56–71. Springer, Heidelberg (1998). https://doi.org/10.1007/BFb0055720

14. Cid, C., Huang, T., Peyrin, T., Sasaki, Yu., Song, L.: Boomerang connectivity table: a new cryptanalysis tool. In: Nielsen, J.B., Rijmen, V. (eds.) EUROCRYPT 2018. LNCS, vol. 10821, pp. 683–714. Springer, Cham (2018). https://doi.org/10.1007/978-3-319-78375-8_22

15. Daemen, J.: Cipher and Hash function design strategies based on linear and differential cryptanalysis. Ph.D. thesis, Doctoral Dissertation, March 1995, KU Leuven (1995)

16. Daemen, J., Rijmen, V.: The Design of Rijndael: AES - The Advanced Encryption Standard. Information Security and Cryptography. Springer, Heidelberg (2002). https://doi.org/10.1007/978-3-662-04722-4

17. Demirci, H., Selçuk, A.A.: A meet-in-the-middle attack on 8-round AES. In: Nyberg, K. (ed.) FSE 2008. LNCS, vol. 5086, pp. 116–126. Springer, Heidelberg (2008). https://doi.org/10.1007/978-3-540-71039-4_7

18. Derbez, P., Fouque, P.-A., Jean, J.: Improved key recovery attacks on reduced-round , in the single-key setting. In: Johansson, T., Nguyen, P.Q. (eds.) EUROCRYPT 2013. LNCS, vol. 7881, pp. 371–387. Springer, Heidelberg (2013). https://doi.org/10.1007/978-3-642-38348-9_23

19. Dunkelman, O., Keller, N., Shamir, A.: Improved single-key attacks on 8-round AES-192 and AES-256. In: Abe, M. (ed.) ASIACRYPT 2010. LNCS, vol. 6477, pp. 158–176. Springer, Heidelberg (2010). https://doi.org/10.1007/978-3-642-17373-8_10

20. Ferguson, N., et al.: Improved cryptanalysis of Rijndael. In: Goos, G., Hartmanis, J., van Leeuwen, J., Schneier, B. (eds.) FSE 2000. LNCS, vol. 1978, pp. 213–230. Springer, Heidelberg (2001). https://doi.org/10.1007/3-540-44706-7_15

21. Jean, J., Nikolić, I., Peyrin, T.: KIASU v1. Additional first-round candidates of CAESAR compeition (2014)

22. Jean, J., Nikolić, I., Peyrin, T.: Tweaks and keys for block ciphers: the TWEAKEY framework. In: Sarkar, P., Iwata, T. (eds.) ASIACRYPT 2014. LNCS, vol. 8874, pp. 274–288. Springer, Heidelberg (2014). https://doi.org/10.1007/978-3-662-45608-8_15

23. Jean, J., Nikolić, I., Peyrin, T., Seurin, Y.: Deoxys-II. Finalist of CAESAR compeition (2014)

24. Kelsey, J., Kohno, T., Schneier, B.: Amplified boomerang attacks against reduced-round MARS and serpent. In: Goos, G., Hartmanis, J., van Leeuwen, J., Schneier, B. (eds.) FSE 2000. LNCS, vol. 1978, pp. 75–93. Springer, Heidelberg (2001). https://doi.org/10.1007/3-540-44706-7_6

25. Kim, J., Hong, S., Preneel, B., Biham, E., Dunkelman, O., Keller, N.: Related-key boomerang and rectangle attacks: theory and experimental analysis. IEEE Trans. Inf. Theory 58(7), 4948–4966 (2012)

26. Kim, J., Kim, G., Hong, S., Lee, S., Hong, D.: The related-key rectangle attack – application to SHACAL-1. In: Wang, H., Pieprzyk, J., Varadharajan, V. (eds.) ACISP 2004. LNCS, vol. 3108, pp. 123–136. Springer, Heidelberg (2004). https://doi.org/10.1007/978-3-540-27800-9_11

27. Li, L., Jia, K., Wang, X.: Improved single-key attacks on 9-Round AES-192/256. In: Cid, C., Rechberger, C. (eds.) FSE 2014. LNCS, vol. 8540, pp. 127–146. Springer, Heidelberg (2015). https://doi.org/10.1007/978-3-662-46706-0_7

28. Lu, J., Dunkelman, O., Keller, N., Kim, J.: New impossible differential attacks on AES. In: Chowdhury, D.R., Rijmen, V., Das, A. (eds.) INDOCRYPT 2008. LNCS, vol. 5365, pp. 279–293. Springer, Heidelberg (2008). https://doi.org/10.1007/978-3-540-89754-5_22
29. Matsui, M.: Linear cryptanalysis method for DES cipher. In: Helleseth, T. (ed.) EUROCRYPT 1993. LNCS, vol. 765, pp. 386–397. Springer, Heidelberg (1994). https://doi.org/10.1007/3-540-48285-7_33
30. Matsui, M.: The first experimental cryptanalysis of the data encryption standard. In: Desmedt, Y.G. (ed.) CRYPTO 1994. LNCS, vol. 839, pp. 1–11. Springer, Heidelberg (1994). https://doi.org/10.1007/3-540-48658-5_1
31. Sasaki, Yu.: Meet-in-the-middle preimage attacks on AES hashing modes and an application to whirlpool. In: Joux, A. (ed.) FSE 2011. LNCS, vol. 6733, pp. 378–396. Springer, Heidelberg (2011). https://doi.org/10.1007/978-3-642-21702-9_22
32. Song, L., Qin, X., Hu, L.: Boomerang connectivity table revisited. Application to SKINNY and AES. IACR Trans. Symmetric Cryptol. **2019**(1), 118–141 (2019)
33. Wagner, D.: The boomerang attack. In: Knudsen, L. (ed.) FSE 1999. LNCS, vol. 1636, pp. 156–170. Springer, Heidelberg (1999). https://doi.org/10.1007/3-540-48519-8_12
34. Wang, H., Peyrin, T.: Boomerang switch in multiple rounds. Application to AES variants and deoxys. IACR Trans. Symmetric Cryptol. **2019**(1), 142–169 (2019)

Truncated Differential Properties of the Diagonal Set of Inputs for 5-Round AES

Lorenzo Grassi[1,2(✉)] and Christian Rechberger[2]

[1] Digital Security Group, Radboud University, Nijmegen, The Netherlands
l.grassi@science.ru.nl
[2] IAIK, Graz University of Technology, Graz, Austria
christian.rechberger@iaik.tugraz.at

Abstract. In the last couple of years, a new wave of results appeared, proposing and exploiting new properties of round-reduced AES. In this paper we survey and combine some of these results (namely, the multiple-of-n property and the mixture differential cryptanalysis) in a systematic way in order to answer more general questions regarding the probability distribution of encrypted diagonal sets. This allows to analyze this special set of inputs, and report on new properties regarding the probability distribution of the number of different pairs of corresponding ciphertexts are equal in certain anti-diagonal(s) after 5 rounds.

An immediate corollary of the multiple-of-8 property is that the variance of such a distribution can be shown to be higher than for a random permutation. Surprisingly, also the mean of the distribution is significantly different from random, something which cannot be explained by the multiple-of-8 property. We propose a theoretical explanation of this, by assuming an APN-like assumption on the S-Box which closely resembles the AES-Sbox. By combining the multiple-of-8 property, the mixture differential approach, and the results just mentioned about the mean and the variance, we are finally able to formulate the probability distribution of the diagonal set after 5-round AES as a sum of independent binomial distributions.

Keywords: AES · Truncated-differential cryptanalysis · Distinguisher

1 Introduction

AES (Advanced Encryption Standard) [9] is probably the most used and studied block cipher. Since the development of cryptanalysis of AES and AES-like constructions in the late 1990s, the set of input which differ only in one diagonal has special importance. Indeed, it appears in several attacks and distinguishers, including various (truncated) differential [16,17], integral [8], and impossible differential attacks [4], among others. In particular, given a diagonal set of plaintexts and the corresponding ciphertexts after 4 rounds, it is well known that the XOR-sum of the ciphertexts is equal to zero [8], or that each pair of ciphertexts cannot be equal in any of the four anti-diagonals, as shown by Biham and Keller in [5].

© The Author(s), under exclusive license to Springer Nature Switzerland AG 2022
K. Nguyen et al. (Eds.): ACISP 2022, LNCS 13494, pp. 24–45, 2022.
https://doi.org/10.1007/978-3-031-22301-3_2

Table 1. *Expected properties of a diagonal set after 5-round encryption.* Given a set of 2^{32} chosen plaintexts all equal in three diagonals (that is, a diagonal set), we consider the *distribution* of the number of different pairs of ciphertexts that are equal in one anti-diagonal (equivalently, that lie in a particular subspace $\mathcal{ID}_I$ for $I \subseteq \{0, 1, 2, 3\}$ fixed with $|I| = 3$). *Expected values for mean and variance* of these distributions are given in this table for 5-round AES and for a random permutation. Practical results on AES are close and are discussed in Sect. 7.2.

	Random permutation	5-round AES
Mean* (Theorem 4)	$2\,147\,483\,647.5 \approx 2^{31}$	$2\,147\,484\,685.6 \approx 2^{31} + 2^{10}$
Variance (Theorem 4)	$2\,147\,483\,647 \approx 2^{31}$	$76\,842\,293\,834.905 \approx 2^{36.161}$
Multiple-of-8 [14]		✓

$\cdot^\star \equiv$ assuming an "APN-like" S-Box (for the 5-round AES case).

While a lot is known about the encryption of a *diagonal set of plaintexts* – that is, a set of plaintexts with one (or more) active diagonal(s) – for up to 4-round AES, an analysis for 5 or more rounds AES is still missing. At Eurocrypt 2017, a new property which is *independent* of the secret key has been found for 5-round AES [14]. By appropriate choices of a number of input pairs, it is possible to make sure that the number of times that the difference of the resulting output pairs lie in a particular subspace $\mathcal{ID}$ is always a multiple of 8. Such a distinguisher has then been exploited in, e.g., [2,11] for setting up new competitive distinguishers and key-recovery attacks on round-reduced AES.

At the same time, some open questions arise from the result provided in [14]: *does this property influence the average number of output pairs that lie in such a particular subspace (i.e., the mean)? Are other parameters (including the variance and the skewness) affected by the multiple-of-8 property?*

In this paper, given a diagonal set of plaintexts, we consider the probability distribution of the corresponding number of pairs of ciphertexts that are equal in one fixed anti-diagonal after 5-round AES (without the final MixColumns operation) – equivalently, that belong to the same coset of a particular subspace $\mathcal{ID}$ – denoted in the following as the "(average) number of collisions".

1.1 Contributions

As the main contribution, we perform for the first time a differential analysis of such distribution after 5-round AES, and find significant deviations from random, supported by practical implementations and verification. For a theoretical explanation we have to resort to an APN-like assumption on the S-Box, which closely resembles the AES-Sbox. A numerical summary is given in Table 1. All the results presented in this paper are independent of the secret-key.

Mean of 5-Round AES. Firstly, by an appropriate choice of 2^{32} plaintexts in a diagonal space $\mathcal{D}$, we prove for the first time that *the average number of times that the resulting output pairs are equal in one fixed anti-diagonal* (equivalently, the average number of times that the difference of the resulting output pairs lie in a particular subspace $\mathcal{ID}$) *is (a little) bigger for 5-round AES than for a random permutation, independently of the secret key.* A complete proof of this result – under an "APN-like" assumption on the S-Box which closely resembles the AES S-Box – can be found in Sect. 6.

Variance of 5-Round AES. Secondly, *we theoretically compute the variance of the probability distribution just defined, and we show that it is higher (by a factor of approximately 36) for 5-round AES than for a random permutation.* As we are going to show, this result is mainly due to the "multiple-of-8" result [14] proposed at Eurocrypt 2017. For this reason, with respect to the mean value, the variance is independent of the details of the S-Box.

Practical Verification and Influence of the S-Box Details on the Mean. We practically verified the mean on small-scale 5-round AES (namely, AES defined over $\mathbb{F}_{2^4}^{4 \times 4}$ as proposed in [7]), and the variance both for small-scale and real 5-round AES. As discussed in Sect. 7, practical results are close to the theoretical ones in both cases. Before going on, we mention that the theoretical and the practical results regarding the mean (almost) match if the S-Box satisfies an "APN-like" assumption on the S-Box which closely resembles the AES S-Box, namely, if the solutions of the equality S-Box$(\cdot \oplus \Delta_I) \oplus$ S-Box$(\cdot) = \Delta_O$ are uniformly distributed for each non-zero input/output differences $\Delta_I, \Delta_O \neq 0$. In the case in which this assumption – also used in other related works as [1,3] – is not satisfied, then a gap between the theoretical and the practical results can occur, as showed and discussed in details in the extended version of this paper – see [13, App. C].

Probability Distribution of 5-Round AES. By combining the multiple-of-8 property presented in [14], the mixture differential cryptanalysis [11,12] and the results just mentioned about the mean and the variance, in Sect. 3 we show the following: given a diagonal space of 2^{32} plaintexts with one active diagonal, the probability distribution of the number of different pairs of ciphertexts which are equal in one fixed anti-diagonal after 5-round AES (without the final MixColumns operation) with respect to (1st) all possible secret keys and (2nd) all possible initial diagonal spaces is well described *by a sum of independent binomial distributions* $\mathfrak{B}(n, p)$, that is

$$2^3 \times \mathfrak{B}(n_3, p_3) + 2^{10} \times \mathfrak{B}(n_{10}, p_{10}) + 2^{17} \times \mathfrak{B}(n_{17}, p_{17})$$

where the values of n_3, n_{10}, n_{17} and p_3, p_{10}, p_{17} are provided in the following.

1.2   Follow-Up Works: Truncated Differentials for 5-/6-Round AES

Before going on, we recall the other results concerning truncated differentials for 5- or 6-round AES present in the literature.

In [1], Bao, Guo and List presented "extended expectation cryptanalysis" (or "extended truncated differential") on round-reduced AES. By making use of expectation-based distinguishers, they are able to show how to extend the well-known 3-round integral distinguisher to truncated differential secret-key distinguishers over 4, 5 and even 6 rounds. The technique exploited to derive such a result is based on results by Patarin [20], who observed that the expected (average) number of collisions differs slightly for a sum of permutations from the ideal. At the same time, authors showed that *their results (namely, the expectation distinguishers over 4-, 5- and 6-round AES proposed in the main part of* [1]) *can be derived exploiting the same technique/strategy that we are going to propose in this paper* in Sect. 6, as showed in details in [1, App. C].

Later on, in [3] Bardeh and Rønjom developed another technique in order to set an equivalent truncated differential distinguishers for up to 6-round AES. Such technique – called the "exchange equivalence attack" – resembles the yoyo technique [21] and the mixture differential cryptanalaysis [11], and it allows to give a precise estimation of the average number of pairs of ciphertexts that are equal in fixed anti-diagonal(s), given a particular set of chosen plaintexts. The corresponding secret-key distinguisher on 6-round AES has complexity of about $2^{88.2}$ computations and chosen texts.

Remark. Before going on, we remark that *all these results are valid only under the "APN" assumption of the S-Box* previously mentioned. Namely, both our and the theoretical results proposed in [1,3] regarding the average number of collisions after 5 or more rounds of AES hold only in the case in which the solutions of the equality S-Box$(\cdot \oplus \Delta_I) \oplus$ S-Box$(\cdot) = \Delta_O$ are uniformly distributed for each non-zero input/output differences $\Delta_I, \Delta_O \neq 0$, an assumption that is (almost) satisfied by the AES S-Box. More details about this are provided in the following.

2   Preliminary

2.1   Advanced Encryption Standard (AES)

AES [9] is a *Substitution-Permutation network* based on the "Wide Trail Design" strategy [10], that supports key size of 128, 192 and 256 bits. The 128-bit plaintext initializes the internal state as a 4×4 matrix of bytes as values in the finite field $\mathbb{F}_{2^8}$. Depending on the version of AES, N_r rounds are applied to the state: $N_r = 10$ for AES-128, $N_r = 12$ for AES-192 and $N_r = 14$ for AES-256. An AES round applies four operations to the state matrix:

- *SubBytes* (S-Box) - applying the same 8-bit to 8-bit invertible S-Box 16 times in parallel on each byte of the state (provides non-linearity in the cipher);
- *ShiftRows* (*SR*) - cyclic shift of each row to the left;
- *MixColumns* (*MC*) - multiplication of each column by a constant 4×4 invertible matrix (*MC* and *SR* provide diffusion in the cipher);
- *AddRoundKey* (*ARK*) - XORing the state with a 128-bit subkey k.

One round of AES can be described as $R(x) = k \oplus MC \circ SR \circ$ S-Box(x). In the first round an additional AddRoundKey operation (using a whitening key) is applied, and in the last round the MixColumns operation is omitted.

Notation Used in the Paper. Let x denote a plaintext, a ciphertext, an intermediate state or a key. Then, $x_{i,j}$ with $i,j \in \{0, \dots, 3\}$ denotes the byte in the row i and in the column j. We denote by R one round of AES (and R_f if the MixColumns operation is omitted), while we denote r rounds of AES by R^r (where we use the notation R_f^r in the case in which the last MixColumns operation is omitted). We also define the diagonal and the anti-diagonal of a text as follows. The i-th *diagonal* of a 4×4 matrix A is defined as the elements that lie on row r and column c such that $r - c \equiv_4 i$. The i-th *anti-diagonal* of a 4×4 matrix A is defined as the elements that lie on row r and column c such that $r + c \equiv_4 i$.

2.2   Properties of an S-Box

Given a bijective S-Box function on $\mathbb{F}_{2^n}$, let $\Delta_I, \Delta_O \in \mathbb{F}_{2^n}$. Let N_{Δ_I, Δ_O} denotes the number of solutions of the equation

$$\text{S-Box}(x \oplus \Delta_I) \oplus \text{S-Box}(x) = \Delta_O \tag{1}$$

for each $\Delta_I \neq 0$ and $\Delta_O \neq 0$. Obviously, (i) x is a solution if and only if $x \oplus \Delta_I$ is a solution, and (ii) if $\Delta_O = 0$, then any $x \in \mathbb{F}_{2^n}$ is a solution if and only if $\Delta_I = 0$ (the S-Box is bijective).

Let's analyze the probability distribution related to N_{Δ_I, Δ_O}.

Mean Value. *Independently of the details of the S-Box*, the *mean value* (or the average value) of N_{Δ_I, Δ_O} is equal to $\mathbb{E}[N_{\Delta_I, \Delta_O}] = \frac{2^n}{2^n - 1}$. Indeed, observe that for each x and for each $\Delta_I \neq 0$ there exists $\Delta_O \neq 0$ (since S-Box is bijective) that satisfies Eq. (1). Thus, the average number of solutions is $\frac{2^n \cdot (2^n - 1)}{(2^n - 1)^2} = \frac{2^n}{(2^n - 1)}$ independently of the details of the (bijective) S-Box.

Variance. The *variance* $\text{Var}(N_{\Delta_I, \Delta_O})$ *depends on the details of the S-Box*. For the AES S-Box case, for each $\Delta_I \neq 0$ there are 128 values of $\Delta_O \neq 0$ for which Eq. (1) has no solution, 126 values of $\Delta_O \neq 0$ for which Eq. (1) has 2 solutions ($\hat{x}$ is a solution if and only if $\hat{x} \oplus \Delta_I$ is a solution) and finally 1 value of $\Delta_O \neq 0$ for which Eq. (1) has 4 solutions. The variance for the AES S-Box is so equal to $\text{Var}_{AES}(N_{\Delta_I, \Delta_O}) = 2^2 \cdot \frac{126}{255} + 4^2 \cdot \frac{1}{255} - \left(\frac{256}{255}\right)^2 = \frac{67\,064}{65\,025}$.

Maximum Differential Probability. The *Maximum Differential Probability* $\text{DP}_{\max}$ of an S-Box is defined as

$$\text{DP}_{\max} = 2^{-n} \cdot \max_{\Delta_I \neq 0, \Delta_O} N_{\Delta_I, \Delta_O}. \tag{2}$$

Since $\max_{\Delta_I \neq 0, \Delta_O} N_{\Delta_I, \Delta_O} \geq 2$, $\text{DP}_{\max}$ is always bigger than or equal to 2^{-n+1}. Permutations with $\text{DP}_{\max} = 2^{-n+1}$ are called Almost Perfect Nonlinear (APN).

"Homogeneous" S-Box. Finally, given $\Delta_I \neq 0$ (respectively, $\Delta_O \neq 0$), consider the probability distribution of N_{Δ_I, Δ_O} with respect to $\Delta_O \neq 0$ (respectively, $\Delta_I \neq 0$): we say that the S-Box is (differential) *"homogeneous"* if such distribution is independent of Δ_I (respectively, Δ_O). As a concrete example, the AES S-Box is differential "homogeneous", since for each $\Delta_I \neq 0$ (fixed),

$\Pr(N_{\Delta_I, \Delta_O} = 2) = \frac{126}{255}$ and $\Pr(N_{\Delta_I, \Delta_O} = 4) = \frac{1}{255}$. Other examples of S-Boxes that are/are not differential "homogeneous" are given in the extended version of this paper – see [13, App. C].

3 Probability Distribution for 5-Round AES

In this section, we first recall some results already published in the literature about round-reduced AES. Then, given a diagonal space of 2^{32} plaintexts with one active diagonal, we present the probability distribution of the number of different pairs of ciphertexts which are equal in one fixed anti-diagonal after 5-round AES (without the final MixColumns operation).

3.1 Truncated Differentials for 2-Round AES

Here we recall the truncated differential for 2-round AES using the subspace trail notation introduced in [15]. In the following, we only work with vectors and vector spaces over $\mathbb{F}_{2^n}^{4 \times 4}$, and we denote by $\{e_{0,0}, \dots, e_{3,3}\}$ the unit vectors of $\mathbb{F}_{2^n}^{4 \times 4}$ (e.g., $e_{i,j}$ has a single 1 in row i and column j).

Definition 1. *For each $i \in \{0, 1, 2, 3\}$:*

- *The column spaces $\mathcal{C}_i$ are defined as $\mathcal{C}_i = \langle e_{0,i}, e_{1,i}, e_{2,i}, e_{3,i} \rangle$.*
- *The diagonal spaces $\mathcal{D}_i$ are defined as $\mathcal{D}_i = SR^{-1}(\mathcal{C}_i)$. Similarly, the inverse-diagonal spaces $\mathcal{ID}_i$ are defined as $\mathcal{ID}_i = SR(\mathcal{C}_i)$.*
- *The i-th mixed spaces $\mathcal{M}_i$ are defined as $\mathcal{M}_i = MC(\mathcal{ID}_i)$.*

Definition 2. *For each $I \subseteq \{0, 1, 2, 3\}$, let $\mathcal{C}_I$, $\mathcal{D}_I$, $\mathcal{ID}_I$ and $\mathcal{M}_I$ be defined as*

$$\mathcal{C}_I = \bigoplus_{i \in I} \mathcal{C}_i, \qquad \mathcal{D}_I = \bigoplus_{i \in I} \mathcal{D}_i, \qquad \mathcal{ID}_I = \bigoplus_{i \in I} \mathcal{ID}_i, \qquad \mathcal{M}_I = \bigoplus_{i \in I} \mathcal{M}_i.$$

Definition 3. *Let $t \in \mathbb{F}_{2^n}^{4 \times 4}$ be a text in a coset of a space $\mathcal{X} \subseteq \mathbb{F}_{2^n}^{4 \times 4}$ such that $\mathcal{X} = \langle x_0, x_1, \dots, x_{d-1} \rangle$ where $\dim(\mathcal{X}) = d$, namely $t \in \mathcal{X} \oplus \gamma$. Given γ, $(t_0, t_1, \dots, t_{d-1}) \in \mathbb{F}_{2^n}^d$ are the generating variables of t if the following holds:*

$$t \equiv (t_0, t_1, \dots, t_{d-1}) \qquad \text{if and only if} \qquad t = \gamma \oplus \bigoplus_{j=0}^{d-1} t_j \cdot x_j.$$

As shown in detail in [15], for any coset $\mathcal{D}_I \oplus \alpha$ there exists $\beta \in \mathbb{F}_{2^8}^{4 \times 4}$ such that $R(\mathcal{D}_I \oplus \alpha) = \mathcal{C}_I \oplus \beta$. In a similar way, for any coset $\mathcal{C}_I \oplus \beta$ there exists $\gamma \in \mathbb{F}_{2^8}^{4 \times 4}$ such that $R(\mathcal{C}_I \oplus \beta) = \mathcal{M}_I \oplus \gamma$.

Theorem 1. ([15]). *For each $I \subseteq \{0, 1, 2, 3\}$ and for each $\alpha \in \mathbb{F}_{2^8}^{4 \times 4}$, there exists $\beta \in \mathbb{F}_{2^8}^{4 \times 4}$ such that $R^2(\mathcal{D}_I \oplus \alpha) = \mathcal{M}_I \oplus \beta$. Equivalently:*

$$Prob(R^2(x) \oplus R^2(y) \in \mathcal{M}_I \mid x \oplus y \in \mathcal{D}_I) = 1. \tag{3}$$

3.2 Multiple-of-8 Property and Mixture Differential Cryptanalysis

As already recalled in the introduction, the first known property independent of the secret-key for 5-round AES – called "multiple-of-8" property [14] – has been presented at Eurocrypt 2017.

Theorem 2. ([14]). *Let $\{p^i\}_{i \in \{0,1,\ldots,2^{32 \cdot d}-1\}}$ be $2^{32 \cdot d}$ plaintexts with $1 \leq d \leq 3$ active diagonals, or equivalently in the same coset of a diagonal subspace $\mathcal{D}_I$ for a certain $I \subseteq \{0,1,2,3\}$ with $|I| = d$. Consider the corresponding ciphertexts after 5 rounds (without the final MixColumns operation), that is, (p^i, c^i) for $i \in \{0,\ldots,2^{32 \cdot |I|}-1\}$ where $c^i = R_f^5(p^i)$. The number of different pairs[1] of ciphertexts (c^i, c^j) that are equal in $1 \leq a \leq 3$ anti-diagonals (i.e., that belong to the same coset of a subspace $\mathcal{ID}_J$ for a certain $J \subseteq \{0,1,2,3\}$ with $|J| = 4 - a$) is always a multiple of 8, independently of the secret key, of the details of the S-Box and of the MixColumns matrix.*

We refer to [6,11,14] for details. Such a result is strictly related to the mixture differential cryptanalysis [11] proposed at FSE/ToSC'19.

Theorem 3. ([11]). *Let t^1, t^2 be two texts in $\mathcal{C}_i \oplus \gamma$ for a certain $i \in \{0,1,2,3\}$, namely two plaintexts that differ in the i-th column only. Let $t^1 \equiv (x_0^1, x_1^1, x_2^1, x_3^1)$ and $t^2 \equiv (x_0^2, x_1^2, x_2^2, x_3^2)$ be their generating variables. Let $s^1, s^2 \in \mathcal{C}_i \oplus \gamma$ be defined as following:*

- *if $x_i^1 \neq x_i^2$ for a certain $i \in \{0,1,2,3\}$: the i-th generating variable s_i^1 of s^1 is either x_i^1 or x_i^2, and the i-th generating variable of s^2 is $\{x_i^1, x_i^2\} \setminus s_i^1$;*
- *if $x_i^1 = x_i^2$ for a certain $i \in \{0,1,2,3\}$: the i-th generating variable s_i^1 of s^1 is equal to the i-th generating variable of s^2 (no condition on the value).*

The following holds:

1. *$R^2(t^1) \oplus R^2(t^2) = R^2(s^1) \oplus R^2(s^2)$;*
2. *for each $J \subseteq \{0,1,2,3\}$:*

$$R^4(t^1) \oplus R^4(t^2) \in \mathcal{M}_J \quad \text{if and only if} \quad R^4(s^1) \oplus R^4(s^2) \in \mathcal{M}_J.$$

3.3 Main Result: Probability Distribution for 5-Round AES

Given a set of $2^{32 \cdot d}$ plaintexts with $1 \leq d \leq 3$ active diagonal(s), consider the probability distribution of the number of pairs of ciphertexts which are equal in $1 \leq a \leq 3$ fixed anti-diagonal(s) (without the final MixColumns operation):

- what can we say about the mean, the variance and the skewness of this distribution?
- does the multiple-of-8 property influence the average number of output pairs that lie in a particular subspace (i.e., the mean)? Are other parameters (as the variance and the skewness) affected by the multiple-of-8 property?

---

[1] Two pairs (s, t) and (t, s) are considered to be equivalent (i.e., they count per 1).

Here we answer these questions.

Theorem 4. *Given an AES-like cipher that works with texts in $\mathbb{F}_{2^8}^{4\times4}$, assume that (1st) the MixColumns matrix is an MDS matrix and that (2nd) the solutions of the equation S-Box$(x \oplus \Delta_I) \oplus$ S-Box$(x) = \Delta_O$ are uniformly distributed for each non-zero input/output difference $\Delta_I \neq 0$ and $\Delta_O \neq 0$.*

Given 2^{32} plaintexts $\{p^i\}_{i\in\{0,1,\ldots,2^{32}-1\}}$ with one active diagonal (i.e., in a coset of a diagonal subspace $\mathcal{D}_i$ for $i \in \{0,1,2,3\}$), consider the number of different pairs of ciphertexts (c^h, c^j) for $h \neq j$ that belong into the same coset of $\mathcal{ID}_J$ for any fixed $J \subseteq \{0,1,2,3\}$ with $|J| = 3$. The corresponding probability distribution – denoted in the following by $\mathfrak{D}_{5\text{-}AES}$ – with respect to

- *all possible initial coset of the diagonal space $\mathcal{D}_i$, and*
- *all possible secret keys*

is given by

$$\mathfrak{D}_{5\text{-}AES} = 2^3 \times \mathfrak{B}(n_3, p_3) + 2^{10} \times \mathfrak{B}(n_{10}, p_{10}) + 2^{17} \times \mathfrak{B}(n_{17}, p_{17}), \qquad (4)$$

where $\mathfrak{B}_i \sim \mathfrak{B}(n_i, p_i)$ for $i \in \{3,10,17\}$ are binomial distributions, and where n_i and p_i for $i \in \{3,10,17\}$ are equal to

$$n_3 = 2^{28} \cdot (2^8 - 1)^4, \qquad\qquad p_3 = 2^{-32} + 2^{-53.983};$$
$$n_{10} = 2^{23} \cdot (2^8 - 1)^3, \qquad\qquad p_{10} = 2^{-32} - 2^{-45.989};$$
$$n_{17} = 3 \cdot 2^{15} \cdot (2^8 - 1)^2, \qquad\qquad p_{17} = 2^{-32} + 2^{-37.986}.$$

Such distribution has mean value $\mu = 2\,147\,484\,685.6$, and standard deviation $\sigma = 277\,204.426$.

In order to prove Theorem 4, we first derive the values n_i for $i = 3, 10, 17$ and prove the result given in Eq. (4). In the next sections, we formally compute the probabilities p_i for $i \in \{3, 10, 17\}$, the value of the mean and the variance.

4   Initial Considerations

About the S-Box: "Uniform Distribution of the Solutions of S-Box$(\cdot \oplus \Delta_I) \oplus$ S-Box$(\cdot) = \Delta_O$". Before going further, we discuss the assumptions of Theorem 4, focusing on the one related to the properties/details of the S-Box. The fact that "the solutions of Eq. (1) are uniformly distributed for each $\Delta_I \neq 0$ and $\Delta_O \neq 0$" basically corresponds to an S-Box that satisfies the following properties:

1. it is "homogeneous" (defined in Sect. 2.2);
2. its variance $\text{Var}(N_{\Delta_I, \Delta_O})$ is as "lower" as possible.[2]

---

[2] Note that even if the variance $\text{Var}(N_{\Delta_I, \Delta_O})$ is related to $\text{DP}_{\max}$, S-Boxes with equal $\text{DP}_{\max}$ can have very different variance. Moreover, the variance of an S-Box S_1 can be bigger than the corresponding variance of an S-Box S_2 even if $\text{DP}_{\max}$ of S_1 is lower than $\text{DP}_{\max}$ of S_2.

This is close to being true if the S-Box is APN, or if the S-Box is "close" to be APN. Although much is known for (bijective) APN permutations in odd dimension, it is known that there is no APN permutation of dimension 4 [18], there is at least one APN permutation, up to equivalence, of dimension 6 (that is, the Dillon's permutation), while the question of finding an APN bijective (n,n)-function for even $n \geq 8$ is still open. As a result, in the case of dimensions equal to a power of 2 (e.g., $\mathbb{F}_{2^4}$ or $\mathbb{F}_{2^8}$), *the only (known) S-Box that (approximately) matches the assumptions of the Theorem in dimensions 4 or 8 is the one generated by the multiplicative-inverse permutation*[3], as for example the AES S-Box, which is not APN but differentially 4-uniform [19] (e.g., note that the variance of the AES S-Box is $67\,064/65\,025$ vs $64\,004/65\,025$ of an APN S-Box). As we are going to show, our practical results on small-scale AES (for which the S-Box has the same property as the full-size AES one) are very close to the one predicted by the previous Theorem.

We remark that even if the assumptions on the S-Box of Theorem 4 are restrictive, they match criteria used to design an S-Box which is strong against differential and linear cryptanalysis. As a result, many ciphers in the literature are built using S-Boxes which (are close to) satisfy the assumptions of Theorem 4.

Influence of the S-Box. If the S-Box does not satisfy the required properties related to the assumption of the Theorem, then the average number of collisions can be different from the one previously given. To be more concrete, in the extended version of this paper [13, App. C], we provide several practical examples of the dependency of the average number of collisions for small-scale AES-like ciphers with respect to the properties of the S-Box. We also mention that, in the case in which the assumption about the S-Box is not fulfilled, it turned out (by practical tests) that also the details of the MixColumns matrix can influence the average number of collisions.

Probability Distribution of a Random Permutation. Here we briefly compare the probability distribution for 5-round AES and the one of a random permutation. This fact can be used to set up new truncated differential distinguishers for 5-round AES, as we are going to show concretely in the extended version of this paper [13, Sect. 8].

Proposition 1. *Consider 2^{32} plaintexts $\{p^i\}_{i\in\{0,1,\dots,2^{32}-1\}}$ with one active diagonal (equivalently, a coset of a diagonal space $\mathcal{D}_i$ for $i \in \{0,1,2,3\}$), and the corresponding (cipher)texts generated by a random permutation Π, that is $c^i = \Pi(p^i)$. The probability distribution of the number of different pairs of ciphertexts (c^h, c^j) that belong to the same coset of $\mathcal{ID}_J$ for any fixed $J \subseteq \{0,1,2,3\}$ with $|J|=3$ is given by a binomial distribution $\mathfrak{B}(n,p)$, where $n = \binom{2^{32}}{2} = 2^{31} \cdot (2^{32}-1)$ and $p = \frac{2^{96}-1}{2^{128}-1} \approx 2^{-32}$. The average number of*

---

[3] Variance, homogeneous differential property and $\mathrm{DP}_{\max}$ of an S-Box $\mathcal{S}$ remain unchanged if affine transformations are applied in the domain or co-domain of $\mathcal{S}$.

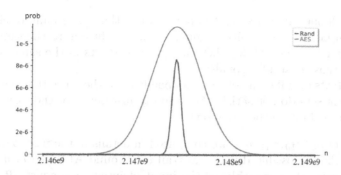

Fig. 1. Comparison between the theoretical probability distribution of the number of collisions between 5-round AES (*approximated* – only here – by a normal distribution) and a random permutation. *Remark:* since the AES probability distribution – *in red* – satisfies the multiple-of-8 property, then the probability in the case in which the number of collision n is not a multiple of 8 is equal to zero, namely $Prob(n \neq 8 \cdot n') = 0$. (Color figure online)

collisions of such distribution is equal to $2^{31} - 0.5 = 2\,147\,483\,647.5$, while its variance is equal to $2\,147\,483\,647 \simeq 2^{31}$.

It follows that:

– independently of the secret key, the average number of pairs of ciphertexts which are equal in one fixed anti-diagonal is (a little) bigger for 5-round AES than for a random permutation (approximately $1\,038.1$ more collisions);
– independently of the secret key, the variance of the probability distribution of the number of collisions is much bigger for 5-round AES than for a random permutation (approximately of a factor 36).

To highlight this difference, Fig. 1 proposes a comparison between the probability distribution of the number of collisions for the AES case (approximated here for simplicity by a normal distribution) in red and of the random case in blue.

5   Proof of Theorem 4: Sum of Binomial Distributions

Consider a set of 2^{32} plaintexts with one active diagonal and the corresponding ciphertexts after 5-round AES (without the final MixColumns operation). As shown by the multiple-of-8 property [14] and by the mixture differential crypt-analysis [11], *the corresponding pairs of ciphertexts of such set of plaintexts are not independent/unrelated.* In particular, these pairs of texts can be divided in $n_3 + n_{10} + n_{17} + n_{24}$ sets defined as in [11] (recalled in Theorem 3) such that

1. for each $i \in \{3, 10, 17, 24\}$, exactly n_i sets have cardinality 2^i;
2. each one of these sets contains pairs of texts for which i out of the four generating variables are equal (and $4 - i$ are different) after 1-round encryption;

3. given each one of such sets, it is not possible that some pairs of ciphertexts are equal in $1 \le a \le 3$ anti-diagonals (i.e., that belong to the same coset of $\mathcal{ID}_J$) after 5-round, while other pairs of ciphertexts in the same set are not equal in those a anti-diagonals;
4. pairs of texts of different sets are independent (in the sense that pairs of texts of different sets do not satisfy the property just given for the case of pairs of texts that belong to the same set).

The values of $n_3, n_{10}, n_{17}, n_{24}$ are computed in details in the next paragraph.

Due to the impossible differential trail on 4-round AES [5,15], if three out of the four generating variables of the input plaintexts are equal *after 1-round encryption*, then the corresponding ciphertexts cannot be equal in any anti-diagonal. In other words, the probability p_{24} is equal to zero. For this reason, we will only focus on n_3, n_{10}, n_{17} in the following.

About the Values of n_3, n_{10}, n_{17}. Given a set of 2^{32} chosen texts with one active column[4], the number of pairs of texts with $0 \le v \le 3$ equal generating variables (and $4 - v$ different generating variables) *after one round* is given by

$$\binom{4}{v} \cdot 2^{31} \cdot (2^8 - 1)^{4-v}. \tag{5}$$

Indeed, note that if v variables are equal for the two texts of the given pair, then these variables can take $(2^8)^v$ different values. For each one of the remaining $4 - v$ variables, the variables must be different for the two texts. Thus, these $4 - v$ variables can take exactly $\left[2^8 \cdot (2^8 - 1)\right]^{4-v}/2$ different values. The result follows from the fact that there are $\binom{4}{v}$ different combinations of v variables.

Due to Eq. (5), the number n_v of the sets of pairs of texts with "no equal generating variables" (namely, $v = 0$), the set of pairs of texts with "one equal and three different generating variable(s)" (namely, $v = 1$) and finally the set of pairs of texts with "two equal and two different generating variable" (namely, $v = 2$) are given by:

$$\forall v \in \{0, 1, 2\}: \qquad n_{7 \cdot v + 3} = \binom{4}{v} \cdot \frac{2^{31} \cdot (2^8 - 1)^{4-v}}{2^{7 \cdot v + 3}}. \tag{6}$$

About Binomial Distributions $B_i \sim \mathfrak{B}(n_i, p_i)$ for $i \in \{3, 10, 17\}$. Due to the previous facts, it follows that the probability of the event "$n = 8 \cdot n'$ pairs of ciphertexts equal in one fixed anti-diagonal" for $n' \in \mathbb{N}$ – equivalently, "$n = 8 \cdot n'$ collisions" in a coset of $\mathcal{ID}_J$ for $J \subseteq \{0, 1, 2, 3\}$ with $|J| = 3$ – corresponds to the sum of the probabilities to have "$2^3 \cdot k_3$ collisions in the first set *and* $2^{10} \cdot k_{10}$ collisions in the second set *and* $2^{17} \cdot k_{17}$ collisions in the third set" *for each* k_3, k_{10}, k_{17} such that $2^3 \cdot k_3 + 2^{10} \cdot k_{10} + 2^{17} \cdot k_{17} = n$.

---

[4] One active diagonal is mapped to one active column after 1-round AES encryption.

Each one of these (independent) events is well characterized by a *binomial distribution*. By definition, a binomial distribution with parameters n and p is the discrete probability distribution of the number of successes in a sequence of n independent yes/no experiments, each of which yields success with probability p. In our case, given n pairs of texts, each one of them satisfies or not the above property/requirement with the same probability p.

Probability Distribution. Due to all these initial considerations (based on the multiple-of-8 property and on the mixture differential cryptanalysis), it follows that the distribution 5-AES of the number of collisions for the AES case is well described by

$$\mathfrak{D}_{5\text{-AES}} = 2^3 \times \mathfrak{B}_3 + 2^{10} \times \mathfrak{B}_{10} + 2^{17} \times \mathfrak{B}_{17},$$

where $\mathfrak{B}_i \sim \mathfrak{B}(n_i, p_i)$ for $i = 3, 10, 17$ are independent binomial distributions. In the following, we formally compute the values of n_i and of p_i.

Mean Value and Variance. Due to the results just presented, it follows that the mean value μ of 5-AES is given by

$$\begin{aligned} \mu &= \mathbb{E}[\mathfrak{D}_{5\text{-AES}}] = \mathbb{E}[2^3 \times \mathfrak{B}_3 + 2^{10} \times \mathfrak{B}_{10} + 2^{17} \times \mathfrak{B}_{17}] \\ &= 2^3 \cdot \mathbb{E}[\mathfrak{B}_3] + 2^{10} \cdot \mathbb{E}[\mathfrak{B}_{10}] + 2^{17} \cdot \mathbb{E}[\mathfrak{B}_{17}] \\ &= 2^3 \cdot n_3 \cdot p_3 + 2^{10} \cdot n_{10} \cdot p_{10} + 2^{17} \cdot n_{17} \cdot p_{17}, \end{aligned}$$

where $\mathbb{E}[a \cdot X + b \cdot Y + c] = a \cdot \mathbb{E}[X] + b \cdot \mathbb{E}[Y] + c$ for each $a, b, c \in \mathbb{R}$ and for each random variable X and Y. Similarly, the variance σ^2 is given by

$$\begin{aligned} \sigma^2 &= \mathsf{Var}(\mathfrak{D}_{5\text{-AES}}) = \mathsf{Var}(2^3 \times \mathfrak{B}_3 + 2^{10} \times \mathfrak{B}_{10} + 2^{17} \times \mathfrak{B}_{17}) \\ &= 2^6 \cdot \mathsf{Var}(\mathfrak{B}_3) + 2^{20} \cdot \mathsf{Var}(\mathfrak{B}_{10}) + 2^{34} \cdot \mathsf{Var}(\mathfrak{B}_{17}) \\ &= 2^6 \cdot n_3 \cdot p_3 \cdot (1 - p_3) + 2^{10} \cdot n_{10} \cdot p_{10} \cdot (1 - p_{10}) + 2^{17} \cdot n_{17} \cdot p_{17} \cdot (1 - p_{17}), \end{aligned}$$

where $\mathsf{Var}(a \cdot X + b \cdot Y + c) = a^2 \cdot \mathsf{Var}(X) + b^2 \cdot \mathsf{Var}(Y)$ for each $a, b, c \in \mathbb{R}$ *under the assumption that X and Y are independent random variables* (remember that $\mathfrak{B}_3, \mathfrak{B}_{10}, \mathfrak{B}_{17}$ are independent).

6 Proof of Theorem 4: About the Probabilities p_3, p_{10}, p_{17}

6.1 Reduction to the Middle Round

In order to compute the probabilities p_3, p_{10} and p_{17} given before for 5 rounds AES, the idea is to work on an equivalent result on a single round. Due to the 2-round truncated differential with prob. 1 recalled in Sect. 3.1, we have that

$$\mathcal{D}_i \oplus \delta \xrightarrow[\text{prob. 1}]{R^2(\cdot)} \mathcal{M}_i \oplus \omega \xrightarrow{R(\cdot)} \mathcal{D}_J \oplus \delta' \xrightarrow[\text{prob. 1}]{R_f^2(\cdot)} \mathcal{ID}_J \oplus \omega'. \tag{7}$$

For this reason, it is sufficient to focus on the middle round $\mathcal{M}_i \oplus \omega \xrightarrow{R(\cdot)} \mathcal{D}_J \oplus \delta'$ in order to compute the desired result.

Sketch and Organization of the Proof. W.l.o.g., we limit ourselves to consider plaintexts in the same coset of $\mathcal{M}_0$ and to count the number of texts which are equal in the first diagonal after one round (the other cases are analogous). By definition of $\mathcal{M}_0$, if $p^1, p^2 \in \mathcal{M}_0 \oplus \omega$, then there exist $x^i, y^i, z^i, w^i \in \mathbb{F}_{2^8}$ for $i \in \{1, 2\}$ such that:

$$p^i = \omega \oplus \begin{bmatrix} 2 \cdot x^i & y^i & z^i & 3 \cdot w^i \\ x^i & y^i & 3 \cdot z^i & 2 \cdot w^i \\ x^i & 3 \cdot y^i & 2 \cdot z^i & w^i \\ 3 \cdot x^i & 2 \cdot y^i & z^i & w^i \end{bmatrix},$$

where $2 \equiv 0 \times 02$ and $3 \equiv 0 \times 03$. In the following, we say that p^1 is "generated" by the generating variables (x^1, y^1, z^1, w^1) and that p^2 is "generated" by the generating variables (x^2, y^2, z^2, w^2). As before, we use the notation $p^i \equiv (x^i, y^i, z^i, w^i)$. The proof is organized as follows:

1. first of all, we limit ourselves to consider a subset of 2^{16} texts with only 2 active bytes. Since this case is much simpler to analyze than the generic one, it allows us to highlight the crucial points of the proof;
2. we then present the complete proof for the case of 2^{32} texts in the same coset of $\mathcal{M}_0$. Roughly speaking, this case is split in various sub-cases: each one of them is studied/analyzed independently of the others using the same strategy proposed for the simplest case of 2^{16} texts. The final result is obtained by simply combining the results of each one of these sub-cases.

We emphasize that the following computations are *not* influenced by neither the value of the secret key nor the value of the initial coset of the diagonal subspace $\mathcal{D}_i$. That is, the following results are the average with respect to these two values.

6.2   A "Simpler" Case: 2^{16} Texts with Two Equal Generating Variables

As a first case, we consider 2^{16} texts for which two generating variables are equal, e.g., $z^1 = z^2$ and $w^1 = w^2$. Given two texts p^1 generated by $(x^1, y^1, 0, 0)$ and p^2 generated by $(x^2, y^2, 0, 0)$, they are equal in the first diagonal after one round if and only if the following four equations are satisfied

$$(R(p^1) \oplus R(p^2))_{0,0} = 2 \cdot (\text{S-Box}(2 \cdot x^1 \oplus a_{0,0}) \oplus \text{S-Box}(2 \cdot x^2 \oplus a_{0,0}))$$
$$\oplus 3 \cdot (\text{S-Box}(y^1 \oplus a_{1,1}) \oplus \text{S-Box}(y^2 \oplus a_{1,1})) = 0,$$

$$(R(p^1) \oplus R(p^2))_{1,1} = \text{S-Box}(3 \cdot x^1 \oplus a_{3,0}) \oplus \text{S-Box}(3 \cdot x^2 \oplus a_{3,0})$$
$$\oplus \text{S-Box}(y^1 \oplus a_{0,1}) \oplus \text{S-Box}(y^2 \oplus a_{0,1}) = 0,$$

$$(R(p^1) \oplus R(p^2))_{2,2} = 2 \cdot (\text{S-Box}(x^1 \oplus a_{2,0}) \oplus \text{S-Box}(x^2 \oplus a_{2,0}))$$
$$\oplus 3 \cdot (\text{S-Box}(2 \cdot y^1 \oplus a_{3,1}) \oplus \text{S-Box}(2 \cdot y^2 \oplus a_{3,1})) = 0,$$

$$(R(p^1) \oplus R(p^2))_{3,3} = \text{S-Box}(x^1 \oplus a_{1,0}) \oplus \text{S-Box}(x^2 \oplus a_{1,0})$$
$$\oplus \text{S-Box}(3 \cdot y^1 \oplus a_{2,1}) \oplus \text{S-Box}(3 \cdot y^2 \oplus a_{2,1}) = 0,$$

where $a_{.,.} \in \mathbb{F}_{2^8}$ depends on the initial key and on the constant $w \in \mathbb{F}_{2^8}^{4 \times 4}$ that defines the coset. Equivalently, four equations of the form

$$A \cdot \left(\text{S-Box}(B \cdot x^1 \oplus a) \oplus \text{S-Box}(B \cdot x^2 \oplus a)\right)$$
$$\oplus C \cdot \left(\text{S-Box}(D \cdot y^1 \oplus c) \oplus \text{S-Box}(D \cdot y^2 \oplus c)\right) = 0 \tag{8}$$

must be satisfied, where $A, B, C, D \in \mathbb{F}_{2^8}$ depend on the MixColumns matrix, while $a, c \in \mathbb{F}_{2^8}$ depend on the secret key and on the initial constant w.

Number of Solutions of Each Equation. Consider one of these four equations. By simple observation, Eq. (8) is satisfied if and only if the following system of equations is satisfied

$$\text{S-Box}(\hat{x} \oplus \Delta_I) \oplus \text{S-Box}(\hat{x}) = \Delta_O$$
$$\text{S-Box}(\hat{y} \oplus \Delta_I') \oplus \text{S-Box}(\hat{y}) = \Delta_O'$$
$$\Delta_O' = C^{-1} \cdot A \cdot \Delta_O \tag{9}$$

for each value of Δ_O, where $\hat{x} = B \cdot x^1 \oplus a$, $\Delta_I = B \cdot (x^1 \oplus x^2)$, $\hat{y} = D \cdot y^1 \oplus c$ and $\Delta_I' = D \cdot (y^1 \oplus y^2)$. We emphasize that we exclude null solutions.

What is the number of different (not null) solutions $\{(x^1, y^1), (x^2, y^2)\}$ of Eq. (8)? Given $\Delta_O \neq 0$, each one of the first two equations of (9) admits 256 different solutions $(\hat{x}, \Delta_I)$ (respectively, $(\hat{y}, \Delta_I')$), since for each value of $\hat{x} \in \mathbb{F}_{2^8}$, there exists $\Delta_I \neq 0$ that satisfies the first equation (similar for $\hat{y}$ and Δ_I'). It follows that the number of different solutions $\{(x^1, y^1), (x^2, y^2)\}$ of Eq. (8) considering all the 255 possible values of Δ_O is exactly equal to

$$\frac{1}{2} \cdot 255 \cdot (256)^2 = 255 \cdot 2^{15},$$

Independent of the Details of the S-Box. The factor $1/2$ is due to the fact that we consider only different solutions, that is, two solutions of the form $(p^1 \equiv (x^1, y^1), p^2 \equiv (x^2, y^2))$ and $(p^2 \equiv (x^1, y^1), p^1 \equiv (x^2, y^2))$ are equivalent. In other words, a solution $\{(x^1, y^1), (x^2, y^2)\}$ is valid if $x^2 \neq x^1$ and $y^1 < y^2$.

Probability of Common Solutions. Knowing the number of solutions of Eq. (8), what is the number of common (different) solutions $\{(x^1, y^1), (x^2, y^2)\}$ of four equations of the form (8)? We have just seen that each equation of the form (8) has exactly $255 \cdot 2^{15}$ different (not null) solutions $\{(x^1, y^1), (x^2, y^2)\}$. Assuming the APN-like assumption on the S-Box and the fact that the MixColumns is defined by an MDS matrix, the probability that two equations admit the same solution (i.e., that $\{(x^1, y^1), (x^2, y^2)\}$ – solution of one equation – is equal to $\{(\hat{x}^1, \hat{y}^1), (\hat{x}^2, \hat{y}^2)\}$ – solution of another equation) is

$$(256 \cdot 255)^{-1} \cdot (255 \cdot 128)^{-1} = 255^{-2} \cdot 2^{-15}. \tag{10}$$

To explain this probability, the first term $(256 \cdot 255)^{-1}$ is due to the fact that $x^1 = \hat{x}^1$ with probability 256^{-1}, while $x^2 = \hat{x}^2$ with probability 255^{-1}, since by assumption x^2 (respectively, $\hat{x}^2$) cannot be equal to x^1 (respectively, $\hat{x}^1$). The second term $(128 \cdot 255)^{-1}$ is due to the assumption on the second variable, that is $y^1 < y^2$. To explain it, note that the possible number of pairs (y^1, y^2) with $y^1 < y^2$ is $\sum_{i=0}^{255} i = \frac{255 \cdot (255+1)}{2} = 255 \cdot 128.$[5] It follows that y^1 and y^2 are equal to $\hat{y}^1$ and $\hat{y}^2$ with probability $(128 \cdot 255)^{-1}$.

Total Number of (Different) Common Solutions. In conclusion, the average number of common (different) solutions $\{(x^1, y^1), (x^2, y^2)\}$ of 4 equations of the form (8) is given by

$$(255 \cdot 2^{15})^4 \cdot (255^{-2} \cdot 2^{-15})^3 = \frac{2^{15}}{255^2} \simeq 0.503929258 \simeq 2^{-1} + 2^{-7.992}.$$

For comparison, in the case in which the ciphertexts are generated by a random permutation, the average number of pairs of ciphertexts that satisfy the previous property is approximately given by

$$\binom{2^{16}}{2} \cdot (2^{-8})^4 = \frac{2^{16}-1}{2^{17}} \simeq 0.499992371 \simeq 2^{-1} - 2^{-17}.$$

Remark: About the MDS Assumption. We highlight that the *probability (10) strongly depends on the assumptions that*

- the solutions of Eq. (1) – hence, the numbers N_{Δ_I, Δ_O} – are uniformly distributed for each $\Delta_I \neq 0$ and $\Delta_O \neq 0$;
- there is *"no (obvious/non-trivial) relation"* between the solutions of the studied system of four equations of the form (8). This means that the four Eqs. (8) must be independent/unrelated, in the sense that the solution of one equation is *not* a solution of another one with probability different than the one given in (10).

Focusing here on this second requirement, a relation among solutions of different equations *can* arise if some relations hold between the coefficients A, B, C, D of different equations of the form (8). Since these are the coefficients of the MixColumns matrix and since such matrix is MDS, no non-trivial linear relation among the rows/columns of any submatrix exists.

6.3   Generic Case: 2^{32} Texts

As next step, we adapt the strategy just presented in order to analyze the case of 2^{32} texts in the same coset of $\mathcal{M}_0$. Two texts p^1, p^2 are equal in one diagonal

---

[5] E.g., if $y^1 = $ 0x0 then y^2 can take 255 different values (all values except 0), if $y^1 = $ 0x1 then y^2 can take 254 different values (all values except 0x0, 0x1) and so on. Given $y^1 = d$ with $0 \le d \le 255$, then y^2 can take $255 - d$ different values.

after one round if and only if four equations of the form

$$
\begin{aligned}
&A \cdot \left(\text{S-Box}(B \cdot x^1 \oplus b) \oplus \text{S-Box}(B \cdot x^2 \oplus b)\right) \\
&\oplus C \cdot \left(\text{S-Box}(D \cdot y^1 \oplus d) \oplus \text{S-Box}(D \cdot y^2 \oplus d)\right) \\
&\oplus E \cdot \left(\text{S-Box}(F \cdot z^1 \oplus f) \oplus \text{S-Box}(F \cdot z^2 \oplus f)\right) \\
&\oplus G \cdot \left(\text{S-Box}(H \cdot w^1 \oplus h) \oplus \text{S-Box}(H \cdot w^2 \oplus h)\right) = 0
\end{aligned}
\tag{11}
$$

are satisfied, where $A, B, C, D, E, F, G, H \in \mathbb{F}_{2^8}$ depend only on the MixColumns matrix, while $b, d, f, h \in \mathbb{F}_{2^8}$ depend on the secret key and on the constant ω that defined the initial coset, as before. Each one of these equations is equivalent to a system of equations like (9), that is:

$$
\text{S-Box}(\hat{x} \oplus \Delta_I) \oplus \text{S-Box}(\hat{x}) = \Delta_O \qquad \text{S-Box}(\hat{y} \oplus \Delta_I') \oplus \text{S-Box}(\hat{y}) = \Delta_O'
$$
$$
\text{S-Box}(\hat{z} \oplus \Delta_I'') \oplus \text{S-Box}(\hat{z}) = \Delta_O'' \qquad \text{S-Box}(\hat{w} \oplus \Delta_I''') \oplus \text{S-Box}(\hat{w}) = \Delta_O'''
$$

together with one of the following conditions

1. $\Delta_O''' = \Delta_O'' = 0$ and $\Delta_O' = C^{-1} \cdot A \cdot \Delta_O \neq 0$, or analogous (six possibilities in total);
2. $\Delta_O''' = 0$ and $\Delta_O, \Delta_O', \Delta_O'' \neq 0$ and $\Delta_O'' = E^{-1} \cdot (A \cdot \Delta_O \oplus C \cdot \Delta_O')$, or analogous (four possibilities in total);
3. $\Delta_O, \Delta_O', \Delta_O'', \Delta_O''' \neq 0$ and $\Delta_O''' = G^{-1} \cdot (A \cdot \Delta_O \oplus C \cdot \Delta_O' \oplus E \cdot \Delta_O'')$.

First Case. Since the first case ($\Delta_O''' = \Delta_O'' = 0$) is analogous to the case in which two generating variables are equal, we can limit ourselves to re-use the previous computation. In the case $\Delta_O''' = \Delta_O'' = 0$ and $\Delta_O' = C^{-1} \cdot A \cdot \Delta_O \neq 0$, the only possible solutions of the third and fourth equations are of the form $(\hat{z}, \Delta_I'' = 0)$ and $(\hat{w}, \Delta_I''' = 0)$ for each possible value of $\hat{z}, \hat{w} \in \mathbb{F}_{2^8}$. Using the same computation as before, the average number of common solutions for this case is

$$
\binom{4}{2} \cdot 256^2 \cdot \frac{2^{15}}{255^2} = \frac{2^{32}}{21\,675} \simeq 198\,153.047 .
\tag{12}
$$

About Probability p_{17}. By definition of probability, the probability p_{17} – given in Theorem 4 – that pairs of texts with two equal (and two different) generating variables are equal in one diagonal after one round is given by:

$$
p_{17} = \frac{1}{2^{17} \times n_{17}} \cdot \frac{2^{32}}{21\,675} = 2^{-32} + 2^{-37.98588} ,
\tag{13}
$$

where $2^{17} \times n_{17}$ is the *total* number of pairs of texts with two equal (and two different) generating variables.

Second Case. Consider now the case $\Delta_O''' = 0$ and $\Delta_O, \Delta_O', \Delta_O'' \neq 0$ (i.e., $\Delta_I, \Delta_I', \Delta_I'' \neq 0$). First of all, note that $\Delta_O \neq 0$ can take 255 different values, while $\Delta_O' \neq 0$ can take only 254 different values (since it must be different from 0 and from $C^{-1} \cdot A \cdot \Delta_O$).

Using the same argumentation given before, for each Eq. (11) the number of different solutions $\{(x^1, y^1, z^1, w^1), (x^2, y^2, z^2, w^2)\}$ – with $z^1 < z^2$ and where $w^1 = w^2$ – is given by $\binom{4}{1} \cdot 256 \cdot (\frac{1}{2} \cdot 255 \cdot 254 \cdot (256)^3) = 2^{10} \cdot (32\,385 \cdot 2^{24})$, where the initial factor $\binom{4}{1} \cdot 256$ is due to the condition $w^1 = w^2$ and on the fact that there are four analogous cases (namely, $x^1 = x^2$ or $y^1 = y^2$ or $z^1 = z^2$). Similar to before, the probability that two equations of the form (11) – where $w^1 = w^2$ – have a common solution is given by $(256 \cdot 255)^{-2} \cdot (128 \cdot 255)^{-1} = 2^{-23} \cdot 255^{-3}$ *under* (1st) the assumption of uniform distribution of the solutions n_{Δ_I, Δ_O} of Eq. (1) and (2nd) the assumption that there is "no (obvious/non-trivial) relation" between the solutions of the studied system of four equations of the form (11). It follows that the average number of common solutions for the four equations of the form (11) is

$$\binom{4}{1} \cdot 256 \cdot (32\,385 \cdot 2^{24})^4 \cdot (2^{-23} \cdot 255^{-3})^3 = \frac{127^4 \cdot 2^{37}}{255^5} \simeq 33\,160\,710.047 \,. \quad (14)$$

About Probability p_{10}. As before, the probability p_{10} – given in Theorem 4 – that pairs of texts with one equal (and three different) generating variable(s) are equal in one diagonal after one round is given by:

$$p_{10} = \frac{1}{2^{10} \times n_{10}} \cdot \frac{127^4 \cdot 2^{37}}{255^5} = 2^{-32} - 2^{-45.98874} \,. \quad (15)$$

Third Case. We finally consider the case $\Delta_O, \Delta_O', \Delta_O'', \Delta_O''' \neq 0$. By simple computation, the number of different values that satisfy $\Delta_O''' = G^{-1} \cdot (A \cdot \Delta_O \oplus C \cdot \Delta_O' \oplus E \cdot \Delta_O'')$. is given by $255^3 - (255 \cdot 254) = 16\,516\,605$. Indeed, the total number of $\Delta_O, \Delta_O', \Delta_O'' \neq 0$ is 255^3, while $255 \cdot 254$ is the total number of values $\Delta_O, \Delta_O', \Delta_O'' \neq 0$ for which Δ_O''' is equal to zero (which is not possible since $\Delta_O''' \neq 0$ by assumption). In more detail, *firstly* observe that for each value of Δ_O there is a value of Δ_O' that satisfies $A \cdot \Delta_O = C \cdot \Delta_O'$. For this pair of values $(\Delta_O, \Delta_O' = C^{-1} \cdot A \cdot \Delta_O)$, the previous equation $\Delta_O''' = G^{-1} \cdot E \cdot \Delta_O''$ is always different from zero, since $\Delta_O'' \neq 0$. *Secondly*, for each one of the $255 \cdot 254$ values of the pair $(\Delta_O, \Delta_O' \neq C^{-1} \cdot A \cdot \Delta_O)$, there is only one value of Δ_O'' such that the previous equation is equal to zero.

Hence, the total number of different solutions $\{(x^1, y^1, z^1, w^1), (x^2, y^2, z^2, w^2)\}$ with $w^1 < w^2$ of each equation corresponding to (11) is $\frac{1}{2} \cdot 16\,516\,605 \cdot (256)^4 = 16\,516\,605 \cdot 2^{31}$. Since the probability that two solutions $\{(x^1, y^1, z^1, w^1), (x^2, y^2, z^2, w^2)\}$ and $\{(\hat{x}^1, \hat{y}^1, \hat{z}^1, \hat{w}^1), (\hat{x}^2, \hat{y}^2, \hat{z}^2, \hat{w}^2)\}$ are equal is $(255 \cdot 256)^{-3} \cdot (255 \cdot 128)^{-1} = 255^{-4} \cdot 2^{-31}$ *under* (1st) the assumption of uniform distribution of the solutions of Eq. (1) and (2nd) the assumption that there is "no (obvious/non-trivial) relation" between the solutions of the studied system of four equations of the form (11), the average number of common solutions (with no equal generating variables) is

$$\left(16\,516\,605 \cdot 2^{31}\right)^4 \cdot (255^{-4} \cdot 2^{-31})^3 = \frac{64\,771^4 \cdot 2^{31}}{255^8} \simeq 2\,114\,125\,822.5 \,. \tag{16}$$

About Probability p_3. As before, the probability p_3 given in Theorem 4 that pairs of texts with no equal generating variable are equal in one diagonal after one round is given by:

$$p_3 = \frac{1}{2^3 \times n_3} \cdot \frac{64\,771^4 \cdot 2^{31}}{255^8} = 2^{-32} + 2^{-53.98306} \,. \tag{17}$$

Total Number of (Different) Common Solutions. Based on the results just proposed, given plaintexts in the same coset of $\mathcal{M}_0$, the number of different pairs of ciphertexts that are equal in one fixed diagonal after 1-round (equivalently, the number of collisions in $\mathcal{D}_J$ for $|J| = 3$) is

$$2\,114\,125\,822.5 + 33\,160\,710.047 + 198\,153.047 \simeq 2\,147\,484\,685.594 \simeq 2^{31} + 2^{10.02} \,.$$

Since the total number of pairs of texts is $2^{31} \cdot (2^{32} - 1)$, the probability for the AES case that a couple of ciphertexts (c^1, c^2) satisfies $c^1 \oplus c^2 \in \mathcal{D}_J$ for $|J| = 3$ fixed is equal to

$$p_{AES} \simeq \frac{2\,147\,484\,685.594}{2^{31} \cdot (2^{32} - 1)} \simeq 2^{-32} + 2^{-52.9803}$$

versus $\approx 2^{-32} - 2^{-128}$ for the case of a random permutation.

7 Practical Results for 5-Round AES

We have practically verified the mean and the variance for 5-round AES given above (in Theorem 4) using a C/C++ implementation[6]. In particular, we have verified the mean value on a small-scale AES as proposed in [7], and the variance value both on full-size and on the small-scale AES.

7.1 Probability Distribution of 5-Round AES over $(\mathbb{F}_{2^n})^{4\times4}$

Firstly, we generalize Theorem 4 for the case of 5-round AES defined over $\mathbb{F}_{2^n}^{4\times4}$.

Proposition 2. *Consider an AES-like cipher that works with texts in $\mathbb{F}_{2^n}^{4\times4}$, such that (1st) the MixColumns matrix is an MDS matrix and such that (2nd) the solutions of Eq. (1) are uniformly distributed for each input/output difference $\Delta_I \neq 0$ and $\Delta_O \neq 0$. Given 2^{4n} plaintexts $\{p^i\}_{i\in\{0,1,\ldots,2^{4n}-1\}}$ with one active diagonal (equivalently, in a coset of a diagonal space $\mathcal{D}_i$ for $i \in \{0,1,2,3\}$), consider the corresponding ciphertexts after 5 rounds without the final MixColumns operation, that is, $c^i = R_f^5(p^i)$. Independently of*

---

[6] The source codes of the distinguishers/attacks can be found at https://github.com/Krypto-iaik/TruncatedDiff5roundAES.

- *the initial coset of $\mathcal{D}_i$, and*
- *the value of the secret key,*

the average number of different pairs of ciphertexts (c^h, c^j) for $h \neq j$ that belong to the same coset of $\mathcal{ID}_J$ for any fixed $J \subseteq \{0, 1, 2, 3\}$ with $|J| = 3$ is equal to

$$\frac{2^{4n-1} \cdot (2^{2n} - 3 \cdot 2^n + 3)^4}{(2^n - 1)^8} + \frac{(2^{n-1} - 1)^4 \cdot 2^{4n+5}}{(2^n - 1)^5} + 3 \cdot \frac{2^{4n}}{(2^n - 1)^2}, \tag{18}$$

and the variance of such distribution is given by

$$\frac{2^{4n+2} \cdot (2^{2n} - 3 \cdot 2^n + 3)^4}{(2^n - 1)^8} + \frac{(2^{n-1} - 1)^4 \cdot 2^{5n+7}}{(2^n - 1)^5} + \frac{3 \cdot 2^{6n+1}}{(2^n - 1)^2}. \tag{19}$$

The proof is analogous to the one just given for $\mathbb{F}_{2^8}^{4 \times 4}$.

7.2   Practical Results for 5-Round AES over $\mathbb{F}_{2^n}^{4 \times 4}$ for $n \in \{4, 8\}$

Practical Results: Variance of 5-round AES over $\mathbb{F}_{2^8}^{4 \times 4}$. Our practical results regarding the variance σ^2 for full-size AES *over 320 different initial cosets and keys* are

$$\sigma_T^2 = 76\,842\,293\,834.905 \simeq 2^{36.161} \quad versus \quad \sigma_P^2 = 73\,288\,132\,411.36 \simeq 2^{36.093},$$

where the subscript $\cdot_T$ denotes the theoretical value and the subscript $\cdot_P$ the practical one.

Practical Results for 5-round AES over $\mathbb{F}_{2^4}^{4 \times 4}$. Our practical results for small-scale AES regarding the mean μ *over 125 000 $\simeq 2^{17}$ different initial cosets and keys* are

$$\mu_{AES}^T = 32\,847.124 \qquad versus \qquad \mu_{AES}^P = 32\,848.57;$$
$$\mu_{rand}^T = 32\,767.5 \qquad versus \qquad \mu_{rand}^P = 32\,768.2.$$

Our practical results for small-scale AES regarding the standard deviation σ *over 100 different initial cosets and keys* are

$$\sigma_{AES}^T = 1036.58 \qquad versus \qquad \sigma_{AES}^P = 1027.93;$$
$$\sigma_{rand}^T = 181.02 \qquad versus \qquad \sigma_{rand}^P = 182.42.$$

The Probability Distribution for 5-Round AES Is *not* Symmetric. Figure 2 highlights the difference between the *practical* probability distribution of the number of collisions for small-scale AES and for a random permutation.

By Fig. 2, it turns out that small-scale 5-round AES distribution has a positive skew, while the skew of the random distribution is approximately equal to zero. The skewness is the parameter that measures the asymmetry of the

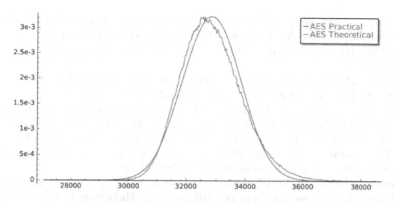

Fig. 2. Comparison between the probability distribution of the number of collisions between *theoretical* small-scale 5-round AES (approximated by a normal distribution) and the *practical* one. *Remark:* since the AES probability distribution satisfies the multiple-of-8 property, then the probability in the case in which the number of collisions n is not a multiple of 8 is equal to zero.

probability distribution of a real-valued random variable about its mean. We practically derived the values of the skewness γ both for full-size AES and for small-scale one using 2^9 initial cosets, and we got the following results:

$$\gamma^{AES} \simeq 0.43786 \qquad and \qquad \gamma^{AES}_{\text{small-scale}} \simeq 0.4687 \,,$$

where the skew of a random permutation is close to zero. We leave the open problem to theoretically compute the skew for small/real-size AES (and to set up a corresponding distinguisher if possible) as a future work.

Acknowledgements. This work was accomplished when L. Grassi was at IAIK, Graz University of Technology, Austria. Authors thank also anonymous reviewers for their valuable comments and suggestions. L. Grassi is currently supported by the European Research Council under the ERC advanced grant agreement under grant ERC-2017-ADG Nr. 788980 ESCADA.

References

1. Bao, Z., Guo, J., List, E.: Extended truncated-differential distinguishers on round-reduced AES. IACR Trans. Symmetric Cryptol. **2020**(3), 197–261 (2020)
2. Bar-On, A., Dunkelman, O., Keller, N., Ronen, E., Shamir, A.: Improved key recovery attacks on reduced-round AES with practical data and memory complexities. In: Shacham, H., Boldyreva, A. (eds.) CRYPTO 2018. LNCS, vol. 10992, pp. 185–212. Springer, Cham (2018). https://doi.org/10.1007/978-3-319-96881-0_7
3. Bardeh, N.G., Rønjom, S.: The exchange attack: *how to distinguish six rounds of AES with* $2^{88.2}$ *chosen plaintexts.* In: Galbraith, S.D., Moriai, S. (eds.) ASIACRYPT 2019. LNCS, vol. 11923, pp. 347–370. Springer, Cham (2019). https://doi.org/10.1007/978-3-030-34618-8_12

4. Biham, E., Biryukov, A., Shamir, A.: Cryptanalysis of skipjack reduced to 31 rounds using impossible differentials. In: Stern, J. (ed.) EUROCRYPT 1999. LNCS, vol. 1592, pp. 12–23. Springer, Heidelberg (1999). https://doi.org/10.1007/3-540-48910-X_2

5. Biham, E., Keller, N.: Cryptanalysis of reduced variants of Rijndael (2001). Unpublished. http://csrc.nist.gov/archive/aes/round2/conf3/papers/35-ebiham.pdf

6. Boura, C., Canteaut, A., Coggia, D.: A general proof framework for recent AES distinguishers. IACR Trans. Symmetric Cryptol. **2019**(1), 170–191 (2019)

7. Cid, C., Murphy, S., Robshaw, M.J.B.: Small scale variants of the AES. In: Gilbert, H., Handschuh, H. (eds.) FSE 2005. LNCS, vol. 3557, pp. 145–162. Springer, Heidelberg (2005). https://doi.org/10.1007/11502760_10

8. Daemen, J., Knudsen, L., Rijmen, V.: The block cipher square. In: Biham, E. (ed.) FSE 1997. LNCS, vol. 1267, pp. 149–165. Springer, Heidelberg (1997). https://doi.org/10.1007/BFb0052343

9. Daemen, J., Rijmen, V.: The Design of Rijndael: AES - The Advanced Encryption Standard, Ser. Information Security and Cryptography. Springer, Heidelberg (2002). https://doi.org/10.1007/978-3-662-04722-4

10. Daemen, J., Rijmen, V.: Security of a wide trail design. In: Menezes, A., Sarkar, P. (eds.) INDOCRYPT 2002. LNCS, vol. 2551, pp. 1–11. Springer, Heidelberg (2002). https://doi.org/10.1007/3-540-36231-2_1

11. Grassi, L.: Mixture differential cryptanalysis: a new approach to distinguishers and attacks on round-reduced AES. IACR Trans. Symmetric Cryptol. **2018**(2), 133–160 (2018)

12. Grassi, L.: Probabilistic mixture differential cryptanalysis on round-reduced AES. In: Paterson, K.G., Stebila, D. (eds.) SAC 2019. LNCS, vol. 11959, pp. 53–84. Springer, Cham (2020). https://doi.org/10.1007/978-3-030-38471-5_3

13. Grassi, L., Rechberger, C.: Truncated Differential Properties of the Diagonal Set of Inputs for 5-round AES (Extended Version), Cryptology ePrint Archive, Report 2018/182 (2018). https://ia.cr/2018/182

14. Grassi, L., Rechberger, C., Rønjom, S.: A new structural-differential property of 5-round AES. In: Coron, J.-S., Nielsen, J.B. (eds.) EUROCRYPT 2017. LNCS, vol. 10211, pp. 289–317. Springer, Cham (2017). https://doi.org/10.1007/978-3-319-56614-6_10

15. Grassi, L., Rechberger, C., Rønjom, S.: Subspace trail cryptanalysis and its applications to AES. IACR Trans. Symmetric Cryptol. **2016**(2), 192–225 (2017)

16. Knudsen, L.R.: Truncated and higher order differentials. In: Preneel, B. (ed.) FSE 1994. LNCS, vol. 1008, pp. 196–211. Springer, Heidelberg (1995). https://doi.org/10.1007/3-540-60590-8_16

17. Lai, X.: Higher order derivatives and differential cryptanalysis. In: Blahut, R.E., Costello, D.J., Maurer, U., Mittelholzer, T. (eds.) Communications and Cryptography. The Springer International Series in Engineering and Computer Science, vol. 276, pp. 227–233. Springer, Boston (1994). https://doi.org/10.1007/978-1-4615-2694-0_23

18. Leander, G., Poschmann, A.: On the classification of 4 bit S-boxes. In: Carlet, C., Sunar, B. (eds.) WAIFI 2007. LNCS, vol. 4547, pp. 159–176. Springer, Heidelberg (2007). https://doi.org/10.1007/978-3-540-73074-3_13

19. Nyberg, K.: Perfect nonlinear S-boxes. In: Davies, D.W. (ed.) EUROCRYPT 1991. LNCS, vol. 547, pp. 378–386. Springer, Heidelberg (1991). https://doi.org/10.1007/3-540-46416-6_32

20. Patarin, J.: Generic attacks for the Xor of k random permutations. In: Jacobson, M., Locasto, M., Mohassel, P., Safavi-Naini, R. (eds.) ACNS 2013. LNCS, vol. 7954, pp. 154–169. Springer, Heidelberg (2013). https://doi.org/10.1007/978-3-642-38980-1_10

21. Rønjom, S., Bardeh, N.G., Helleseth, T.: Yoyo tricks with AES. In: Takagi, T., Peyrin, T. (eds.) ASIACRYPT 2017. LNCS, vol. 10624, pp. 217–243. Springer, Cham (2017). https://doi.org/10.1007/978-3-319-70694-8_8

PNB-Focused Differential Cryptanalysis of ChaCha Stream Cipher

Shotaro Miyashita[1], Ryoma Ito[2(✉)], and Atsuko Miyaji[1,3]

[1] Osaka University, Suita, Japan
miyashita@cy2sec.comm.eng.osaka-u.ac.jp, miyaji@comm.eng.osaka-u.ac.jp
[2] National Institute of Information and Communications Technology,
Koganei, Japan
itorym@nict.go.jp
[3] Japan Advanced Institute of Science and Technology, Nomi, Japan

Abstract. This study focuses on differential cryptanalysis of the ChaCha stream cipher. In the conventional approach, an adversary first searches for an input/output differential pair with the highest differential bias and then analyzes the *probabilistic neutral bits* (PNB) based on the obtained input/output differential pair. However, although the time and data complexities for the attack can be estimated by the differential bias and PNB obtained by this approach, the combination of the differential bias and PNB is not always optimal. In addition, the existing studies have not performed a comprehensive analysis of the PNB; thus, they have not provided an upper bound on the number of rounds required for a differential attack that uses a single-bit truncated differential to be successful. To address these limitations, we propose a *PNB-focused differential attack* on reduced-round ChaCha by first comprehensively analyzing the PNB for all possible single-bit truncated output differences and then searching for the input/output differential pair with the highest differential bias based on the obtained PNB. The best existing attack on ChaCha, proposed by Beierle et al. at CRYPTO 2020, works on up to 7 rounds, whereas the most extended attack we observed works on up to 7.25 rounds using the proposed PNB-focused approach. The time complexity, data complexity, and success probability of the proposed attack are $2^{255.62}$, $2^{48.36}$, and 0.5, respectively. Although the proposed attack is less efficient than a brute force attack, it is the first dedicated attack on the target and provides both a baseline and useful components (*i.e.*, differential bias and PNB) for improved attacks.

Keywords: Stream cipher · ChaCha · Differential cryptanalysis · PNB

1 Introduction

ChaCha [4] is a stream cipher designed by Bernstein in January 2008. It was motivated by the ECRYPT Stream Cipher Project (eSTREAM)[1] finalist, Salsa [5],

---

[1] http://www.ecrypt.eu.org/stream.

K. Nguyen et al. (Eds.): ACISP 2022, LNCS 13494, pp. 46–66, 2022.
https://doi.org/10.1007/978-3-031-22301-3_3

which was proposed by the same designer in April 2005. After the release of Salsa and ChaCha, several studies performed the security evaluations of both ciphers [1,3,6–16,18]. One of the most relevant of these evaluations is the differential attack based on the concept of *probabilistic neutral bits* (PNB), proposed by Aumasson et al. at FSE 2008 [1]. The PNB concept is to divide secret key bits into two sets – a set of *significant key bits* and a set of *non-significant key bits* – and to use a *neutral measure* as an evaluation indicator to distinguish them. The fewer the elements in the set of significant key bits, the lower the time complexity required for an adversary to recover the unknown secret key; thus, it is crucial to analyze the PNB concept for the differential attacks on Salsa and ChaCha.

Aumasson et al. [1] first searched for the input/output differential pair with the highest differential bias; then, based on this pair, they divided the secret key bits into two sets using the PNB concept; finally, they performed a differential attack on the 7-round version of ChaCha, ChaCha20/7, with time and data complexities of 2^{248} and 2^{27}, respectively. Several researchers later reported improvements to this attack [3,6–9,16,18]. To the best of our knowledge, the best key recovery attack on ChaCha works on up to seven rounds with time and data complexities of $2^{230.86}$ and $2^{48.80}$, respectively, proposed by Beierle et al. at CRYPTO 2020 [3].

The existing studies [1,3,6–9,16,18] have focused on searching for the input/output differential pair with the highest differential bias; however, no study focusing on PNB analysis has been conducted thus far. For this reason, the combination of differential biases and PNB obtained from the existing attacks may not always be optimal. The theoretical time and data complexities for the attacks can be estimated from the combination of differential biases and PNB. In addition, the differential biases and PNB can be analyzed independently; therefore, focusing on the PNB analysis may help provide an upper bound on the number of rounds required for a differential attack that uses a single-bit truncated differential to be successful. The above suggests that PNB-focused analysis has the potential to improve the existing attacks.

Our Contributions. In this study, we propose a *PNB-focused differential attack*. The proposed attack targets reduced-round ChaCha by first analyzing the PNB for all possible single-bit truncated output differences ($\mathcal{OD}$s) and then searching for the input difference ($\mathcal{ID}$) bit position with the highest differential bias in the obtained $\mathcal{OD}$ bit position. The primary aims of the proposed attack are to identify the best combination of the differential bias and PNB through PNB-focused analysis and to provide an upper bound on the number of rounds required for a differential attack that uses a single-bit truncated differential to be successful. Our contributions can be summarized as follows.

Comprehensive Analysis of PNB. By focusing on PNB analysis, we first clarify the distribution of the number of non-significant key bits in each round. Furthermore, we demonstrate that the number of non-significant key bits varies significantly depending on the $\mathcal{OD}$ bit position. In particular, all 0-th single-bits (*i.e.*, all the least significant bits) of each word in all intermediate rounds of reduced-round ChaCha are $\mathcal{OD}$ bit positions with a large number of non-significant key bits.

Upper Bound on the Number of Rounds for the Attacks. Based on the comprehensive analysis of the PNB, we examine the values of the average neutral measure for each round of the inverse round function. Consequently, we determine that the PNB-focused differential attack on reduced-round ChaCha should work on up to 7.25 rounds. In addition, our investigation suggests that the number of intermediate rounds must be at least 3.5 to improve the existing attacks [1,3,6–9,16,18].

Best Combinations of Differential Bias and PNB. Let $\Delta_i^{(r)}[j]$ be a single-bit difference for the j-th bit of the i-th word in the r-round internal state. By analyzing the differential biases at the obtained $\mathcal{OD}$ bit positions (*i.e.*, all 0-th single-bit positions of each word in 3.5 intermediate rounds), we report the $\mathcal{ID}$-$\mathcal{OD}$ pairs with a high differential bias to use in the attack, such as $(\Delta_{15}^{(0)}[6], \Delta_0^{(3.5)}[0])$, $(\Delta_{12}^{(0)}[6], \Delta_1^{(3.5)}[0])$, $(\Delta_{13}^{(0)}[6], \Delta_2^{(3.5)}[0])$, and $(\Delta_{14}^{(0)}[6], \Delta_3^{(3.5)}[0])$. Our investigation suggests that at least one of these $\mathcal{ID}$-$\mathcal{OD}$ pairs should yield the best combination of the differential bias and PNB.

Differential Attacks on Reduced-Round ChaCha. Based on the combinations of the differential bias and PNB, we present a differential attack on ChaCha20/7 with a time complexity of $2^{231.63}$, data complexity of $2^{49.58}$, and success probability of 0.5 using the $\mathcal{ID}$-$\mathcal{OD}$ pair of $(\Delta_{14}^{(0)}[6], \Delta_3^{(3.5)}[0])$. Furthermore, by using the $\mathcal{ID}$-$\mathcal{OD}$ pair of $(\Delta_{15}^{(0)}[6], \Delta_0^{(3.5)}[0])$, we present a differential attack on ChaCha20/7.25 with a time complexity of $2^{255.62}$, data complexity of $2^{48.36}$, and success probability of 0.5.

Table 1 summarizes our proposed attack as well as existing attacks on reduced-round ChaCha[2]. As illustrated in this table, our attack does not offer an improvement over the best existing attack on ChaCha20/7. However, we demonstrate that the PNB-focused differential attack on reduced-round ChaCha should work on up to 7.25 rounds. There have been no studies focusing on attacks on ChaCha20/7.25 thus far. It is crucial to thoroughly analyze the security evaluations of symmetric-key ciphers while gradually increasing the nonlinear operations, such as S-boxes and modular additions. In other words, it is important to thoroughly analyze the security of reduced-round ChaCha for each 0.25 round since the round function in ChaCha adds four wordwise modular additions every 0.25 round.

In conventional attacks on ChaCha, if the time complexity for the attack is beyond that of an exhaustive search for the unknown secret key, cryptanalysts

---

[2] According to [8], Coutinho and Neto stated that their initial results presented at EUROCRYPT 2021 [9] were erroneous. That is, a differential attack on ChaCha20/7 with time and data complexities of $2^{228.51}$ and $2^{80.51}$, respectively, is infeasible. Furthermore, Coutinho and Neto presented a differential attack on ChaCha20/7 with time and data complexities of 2^{224} and 2^{224}, respectively [8]. This was similar to the best attacks on ChaCha20/7; however, verification is beyond the scope of this study because this was a distinguishing attack, not a key recovery attack.

Table 1. Summary of the proposed and existing key recovery attacks.

Target	Time	Data	Reference
ChaCha20/6	2^{139}	2^{30}	[1]
	2^{136}	2^{28}	[18]
	$2^{127.5}$	$2^{27.5}$	[6]
	$2^{102.2}$	2^{56}	[7]
	$2^{77.4}$	2^{58}	[3]
ChaCha20/7	2^{248}	2^{27}	[1]
	$2^{246.5}$	2^{27}	[18]
	$2^{242.59}$	$2^{69.58}$	[8]
	$2^{238.9}$	2^{96}	[16]
	$2^{237.7}$	2^{96}	[6]
	$2^{231.9}$	2^{50}	[7]
	$\mathbf{2^{231.63}}$	$\mathbf{2^{49.58}}$	**This work**
	$2^{230.86}$	$2^{48.8}$	[3]
ChaCha20/7.25	$\mathbf{2^{255.62}}$	$\mathbf{2^{48.36}}$	**This work**

utilize an approach that reduces the number of target rounds for the attack or selects an $\mathcal{ID}$-$\mathcal{OD}$ pair with a higher differential bias. In our approach, we focus on the fact that the PNB concept has a strong influence on the theoretical time complexity. We demonstrate the relevance of the comprehensive analysis of PNB for ChaCha for the first time and conclude that it is crucial to analyze not only differential biases but also PNB.

Organization. The rest of this paper is organized as follows. In Sect. 2, we briefly describe the ChaCha specification. In Sect. 3, we review generic techniques for the existing attack based on the PNB concept. In Sect. 4, we present and discuss the experimental results of the comprehensive analysis of PNB. In Sect. 5, we examine the differential bias at the $\mathcal{OD}$ bit position obtained in Sect. 4 and perform a differential attack on ChaCha20/7, ChaCha20/7.25, and ChaCha20/7.5. Finally, we summarize related works in Sect. 6 and conclude this study in Sect. 7.

2 Specification of ChaCha

ChaCha [4] performs the following three steps to generate a keystream block of 16 words, where the size of each word is 32 bits:

Step 1. The initial state matrix $X^{(0)}$ of order 4×4 is initialized from a 256-bit secret key $k = (k_0, k_1, \ldots, k_7)$, a 96-bit nonce $v = (v_0, v_1, v_2)$, a 32-bit block counter t_0, and four 32-bit constants $c = (c_0, c_1, c_2, c_3)$, such as

$c_0 = $ 0x61707865, $c_1 = $ 0x3320646e, $c_2 = $ 0x79622d32, and $c_3 = $ 0x6b206574. After initialization, the following initial state matrix is obtained:

$$X^{(0)} = \begin{pmatrix} x_0^{(0)} & x_1^{(0)} & x_2^{(0)} & x_3^{(0)} \\ x_4^{(0)} & x_5^{(0)} & x_6^{(0)} & x_7^{(0)} \\ x_8^{(0)} & x_9^{(0)} & x_{10}^{(0)} & x_{11}^{(0)} \\ x_{12}^{(0)} & x_{13}^{(0)} & x_{14}^{(0)} & x_{15}^{(0)} \end{pmatrix} = \begin{pmatrix} c_0 & c_1 & c_2 & c_3 \\ k_0 & k_1 & k_2 & k_3 \\ k_4 & k_5 & k_6 & k_7 \\ t_0 & v_0 & v_1 & v_2 \end{pmatrix}.$$

Step 2. The round function of ChaCha comprises four simultaneous computations of the **quarterround** function. According to the procedure, a vector $(x_a^{(r)}, x_b^{(r)}, x_c^{(r)}, x_d^{(r)})$ in the internal state matrix $X^{(r)}$ is updated by sequentially computing the following:

$$\begin{cases} x_{a'}^{(r)} = x_a^{(r)} + x_b^{(r)}; & x_{d'}^{(r)} = x_d^{(r)} \oplus x_{a'}^{(r)}; & x_{d'}^{(r)} = x_{d'}^{(r)} \lll 16; \\ x_{c'}^{(r)} = x_c^{(r)} + x_{d''}^{(r)}; & x_{b'}^{(r)} = x_b^{(r)} \oplus x_{c'}^{(r)}; & x_{b''}^{(r)} = x_{b'}^{(r)} \lll 12; \\ x_a^{(r+1)} = x_{a'}^{(r)} + x_{b''}^{(r)}; & x_{d'''}^{(r)} = x_{d''}^{(r)} \oplus x_a^{(r+1)}; & x_d^{(r+1)} = x_{d'''}^{(r)} \lll 8; \\ x_c^{(r+1)} = x_{c'}^{(r)} + x_d^{(r+1)}; & x_{b'''}^{(r)} = x_{b''}^{(r)} \oplus x_c^{(r+1)}; & x_b^{(r+1)} = x_{b'''}^{(r)} \lll 7; \end{cases}$$

where the symbols "$+$", "$\oplus$", and "$\lll$" represent wordwise modular addition, bitwise XOR, and bitwise left rotation, respectively. For odd-numbered rounds, which are called **columnrounds**, the quarterround function is applied to the following four column vectors: $(x_0^{(r)}, x_4^{(r)}, x_8^{(r)}, x_{12}^{(r)})$, $(x_1^{(r)}, x_5^{(r)}, x_9^{(r)}, x_{13}^{(r)})$, $(x_2^{(r)}, x_6^{(r)}, x_{10}^{(r)}, x_{14}^{(r)})$, and $(x_3^{(r)}, x_7^{(r)}, x_{11}^{(r)}, x_{15}^{(r)})$. For even-numbered rounds, which are called **diagonalrounds**, the quarterround function is applied to the following four diagonal vectors: $(x_0^{(r)}, x_5^{(r)}, x_{10}^{(r)}, x_{15}^{(r)})$, $(x_1^{(r)}, x_6^{(r)}, x_{11}^{(r)}, x_{12}^{(r)})$, $(x_2^{(r)}, x_7^{(r)}, x_8^{(r)}, x_{13}^{(r)})$, and $(x_3^{(r)}, x_4^{(r)}, x_9^{(r)}, x_{14}^{(r)})$.

Step 3. A 512-bit keystream block is computed as $Z = X^{(0)} + X^{(R)}$, where R is the final round. The original version of ChaCha has $R = 20$ rounds, and the reduced-round version of ChaCha is denoted as ChaCha20/R.

The round function of ChaCha is reversible. In other words, an input vector $(x_a^{(r+1)}, x_b^{(r+1)}, x_c^{(r+1)}, x_d^{(r+1)})$ in the internal state matrix $X^{(r+1)}$ is backdated by sequentially computing the following:

$$\begin{cases} x_{b'''}^{(r)} = x_b^{(r+1)} \lll 25; & x_{b''}^{(r)} = x_{b'''}^{(r)} \oplus x_c^{(r+1)}; & x_{c'}^{(r)} = x_c^{(r+1)} - x_d^{(r+1)}; \\ x_{d'''}^{(r)} = x_d^{(r+1)} \lll 24; & x_{d''}^{(r)} = x_{d'''}^{(r)} \oplus x_a^{(r+1)}; & x_{a'}^{(r)} = x_a^{(r+1)} - x_{b''}^{(r)}; \\ x_{b'}^{(r)} = x_{b''}^{(r)} \lll 20; & x_b^{(r)} = x_{b'}^{(r)} \oplus x_{c'}^{(r)}; & x_c^{(r)} = x_{c'}^{(r)} - x_{d''}^{(r)}; \\ x_{d'}^{(r)} = x_{d''}^{(r)} \lll 16; & x_d^{(r)} = x_{d'}^{(r)} \oplus x_{a'}^{(r)}; & x_a^{(r)} = x_{a'}^{(r)} - x_b^{(r)}; \end{cases}$$

where the symbol "$-$" represents wordwise modular subtraction.

For a more accurate analysis of the round function, we further divide it into four rounds: 0.25, 0.5, 0.75, and 1 round. For example, the 0.25 round signifies that all **quarterround** functions in the round function have 0.25 round.

The 0.25-round quarterround function comprises one wordwise modular addition, one bitwise XOR, and one bitwise left rotation; thus, the ChaCha round function adds four wordwise modular additions every 0.25 round.

3 Differential Cryptanalysis of ChaCha

In this section, we review generic techniques for a differential attack based on the PNB concept, proposed by Aumasson et al. at FSE 2008 [1]. This attack comprises precomputation and online phases. In the precomputation phase, we examine single-bit differential biases and PNB and perform a probabilistic backward computation (PBC). Subsequently, we execute the online phase to recover the unknown key.

3.1 Precomputation Phase

Single-Bit Differential Biases. Let $x_i^{(r)}[j]$ be the j-th bit of the i-th word in the r-round internal state matrix $X^{(r)}$ for $0 \leq i \leq 15$ and $0 \leq j \leq 31$, and let $x_i'^{(r)}[j]$ be an associated bit with the difference $\Delta_i^{(r)}[j] = x_i^{(r)}[j] \oplus x_i'^{(r)}[j]$. Based on the difference $\Delta_i^{(0)}[j] = 1$ to the initial state matrix $X^{(0)}$, which is called the *input difference* or $\mathcal{ID}$, we obtain the corresponding initial state matrix $X'^{(0)}$. Then, we execute the round function of ChaCha using these initial state matrices $X^{(0)}$ and $X'^{(0)}$ as inputs and obtain $\Delta_p^{(r)}[q] = x_p^{(r)}[q] \oplus x_p'^{(r)}[q]$ from the r-round output internal state matrices $X^{(r)}$ and $X'^{(r)}$, which is called the *output difference* or $\mathcal{OD}$. For a fixed key and all possible choices of nonces and block counters, the single-bit differential probability is defined as

$$\Pr\left(\Delta_p^{(r)}[q] = 1 \mid \Delta_i^{(0)}[j] = 1\right) = \frac{1}{2}(1 + \epsilon_d), \tag{1}$$

where ϵ_d denotes the $\mathcal{OD}$ bias. Note that we use the specified 1-bit $\mathcal{ID}$ and then obtain the truncated 1-bit $\mathcal{OD}$.

To estimate the number of samples to distinguish two distributions of random bit strings, we use the following theorem provided by Baignères et al. at ASIACRYPT 2004 [2].

Theorem 1 ([2, Theorem 6]). *Let $Z_1, \ldots, Z_n$ be independent and identically distributed random variables over the set $\mathcal{Z}$ of distribution D, D_0 and D_1 be two distributions of same support which are close to each other, and n be the number of samples of the best distinguisher between $\mathsf{D} = \mathsf{D}_0$ or $\mathsf{D} = \mathsf{D}_1$. Let d be a real number such that*

$$n = \frac{d}{\sum_{z \in \mathcal{Z}} \frac{\epsilon_z^2}{p_z}}, \tag{2}$$

where p_z and $p_z + \epsilon_z$ are probabilities of a random variable z following D_0 and D_1, respectively. Then, the overall probability of error is $P_e \approx \Phi(-\sqrt{d}/2)$, where $\Phi(\cdot)$ is the distribution function of the standard normal distribution.

Let D_0 and D_1 be the uniform distribution and a distribution of the truncated $\mathcal{OD}$ bit strings obtained from the internal state of ChaCha, respectively. In this case, the target event occurs in D_0 and D_1 with probabilities of $\frac{1}{2}$ and $\frac{1}{2} \cdot (1 + \epsilon_d)$, respectively (*i.e.*, $p_0 = p_1 = \frac{1}{2}$ and $|\epsilon_0| = |\epsilon_1| = \frac{\epsilon_d}{2}$). Based on this, the number of samples of the best distinguisher between $D = D_0$ and $D = D_1$ can be estimated as $\frac{4}{\epsilon_d^2}$ with an overall probability of error of $P_e \approx \Phi(-\sqrt{4}/2) = \Phi(-1)$.

PNB. The PNB divides secret key bits into sets of m-bit significant and n-bit non-significant key bits. To differentiate between the sets, Aumasson et al. [1] focused on the degree of influence of each secret key bit on the $\mathcal{OD}$. The degree of influence is called the *neutral measure* and is defined as follows:

Definition 1 ([1, Definition 1]). *The neutral measure of the key bit position κ with respect to the $\mathcal{OD}$ is defined as γ_κ, where $\frac{1}{2}(1 + \gamma_\kappa)$ is the probability that complementing the key bit κ does not change the $\mathcal{OD}$.*

For example, we have the following singular cases of neutral measure:

- $\gamma_i = 1$: $\mathcal{OD}$ does not depend on the i-th key bit (*i.e.*, it is non-significant).
- $\gamma_i = 0$: $\mathcal{OD}$ is statistically independent of the i-th key bit (*i.e.*, it is significant).
- $\gamma_i = -1$: $\mathcal{OD}$ linearly depends on the i-th key bit.

By performing the following steps, we compute the neutral measure and divide the secret key bits into two sets – a set of m-bit significant key bits and a set of n-bit non-significant key bits:

Step 1. Compute the R-round internal state matrix pair $(X^{(R)}, X'^{(R)})$ corresponding to the input pair $(X^{(0)}, X'^{(0)})$ with $\Delta_i^{(0)}[j] = 1$, and derive the keystream blocks $Z = X^{(0)} + X^{(R)}$ and $Z' = X'^{(0)} + X'^{(R)}$, respectively.

Step 2. Prepare a new input pair $(\overline{X}^{(0)}, \overline{X'}^{(0)})$ with the key bit position κ_i of the original input pair $(X^{(0)}, X'^{(0)})$ flipped by one bit.

Step 3. Compute the r-round internal state matrix pair $(Y^{(r)}, Y'^{(r)})$ for $r < R$ with $Z - \overline{X}^{(0)}$ and $Z' - \overline{X'}^{(0)}$ as inputs to the inverse round function of ChaCha.

Step 4. Compute $\Gamma_p^{(r)}[q] = y_p^{(r)}[q] \oplus y_p'^{(r)}[q]$ for the fixed $\mathcal{OD}$ bit, where $y_p^{(r)}[q]$ and $y_p'^{(r)}[q]$ denote the q-th bit of the p-th word of $Y^{(r)}$ and $Y'^{(r)}$, respectively.

Step 5. Repeat Steps 1–4 using different initial state matrices with the same $\Delta_i^{(0)}[j] = 1$, and compute the neutral measure as $\Pr(\Delta_p^{(r)}[q] = \Gamma_p^{(r)}[q] \mid \Delta_i^{(0)}[j] = 1) = \frac{1}{2}(1 + \gamma_i)$, where $\Delta_p^{(r)}[q]$ is the $\mathcal{OD}$ obtained when searching for single-bit differential biases.

Step 6. Set a threshold γ and place all key bits with $\gamma_\kappa < \gamma$ into the set of m-bit significant key bits and those with $\gamma_\kappa \geq \gamma$ into the set of n-bit non-significant key bits.

PBC. As explained at the beginning of this subsection, we obtain r-round single-bit differential biases from the initial state matrices with the selected $\mathcal{ID}$, indicating that these biases can be obtained by performing forward computation in the target cipher. Moreover, we can obtain the r-round single-bit differential biases for ChaCha20/R from the obtained keystream by performing the following backward computation, which is called *PBC*:

Step 1. Compute the R-round internal state matrix pair $(X^{(R)}, X'^{(R)})$ corresponding to the input pair $(X^{(0)}, X'^{(0)})$ with $\Delta_i^{(0)}[j] = 1$, and derive the keystream blocks $Z = X^{(0)} + X^{(R)}$ and $Z' = X'^{(0)} + X'^{(R)}$, respectively.

Step 2. Prepare a new input pair $(\hat{X}^{(0)}, \hat{X}'^{(0)})$ with only non-significant key bits reset to a fixed value (*e.g.*, all zeros) from the original input pair $(X^{(0)}, X'^{(0)})$.

Step 3. Compute the r-round internal state matrix pair $(\hat{Y}^{(r)}, \hat{Y}'^{(r)})$ for $r < R$ with $Z - \hat{X}^{(0)}$ and $Z' - \hat{X}'^{(0)}$ as inputs to the inverse round function of ChaCha.

Step 4. Compute $\hat{\Gamma}_p^{(r)}[q] = \hat{y}_p^{(r)}[q] \oplus \hat{y}_p'^{(r)}[q]$ for the fixed $\mathcal{OD}$ bit, where $\hat{y}_p^{(r)}[q]$ and $\hat{y}_p'^{(r)}[q]$ are the q-th bit of the p-th word of $\hat{Y}^{(r)}$ and $\hat{Y}'^{(r)}$, respectively.

Step 5. Repeat Steps 1–4 using different initial state matrices with the same $\Delta_i^{(0)}[j] = 1$. Compute the r-round bias ϵ_a as $\Pr(\Delta_p^{(r)}[q] = \hat{\Gamma}_p^{(r)}[q] \mid \Delta_i^{(0)}[j] = 1) = \frac{1}{2}(1+\epsilon_a)$, where $\Delta_p^{(r)}[q]$ is the $\mathcal{OD}$ obtained when searching for single-bit differential biases.

The bias of $\hat{\Gamma}_p^{(r)}[q]$ is denoted by ϵ, that is, $\Pr(\hat{\Gamma}_p^{(r)}[q] = 1 \mid \Delta_i^{(0)}[j] = 1) = \frac{1}{2}(1 + \epsilon)$. According to [1], the bias ϵ is approximated as $\epsilon_d \cdot \epsilon_a$ and is used to compute the overall complexity of the attack on the R-round target cipher.

3.2   Online Phase

After the precomputation phase, we perform the following steps to recover an unknown key:

Step 1. For an unknown key, collect N keystream block pairs where each pair is generated by a random input pair satisfying the relevant $\mathcal{ID}$.

Step 2. For each choice of the subkey (*i.e.*, m-bit significant key bits), the following steps should be performed:

  Step 2–1. Derive the r-round single-bit differential biases from the obtained N keystream block pairs by performing backward computation.

  Step 2–2. If the optimal distinguisher legitimates the subkeys candidate as (possibly) correct, perform an additional exhaustive search over the n-bit non-significant key bits to confirm the correctness of the filtered subkey and identify the n-bit non-significant key bits.

  Step 2–3. Stop if the correct key is reported and output the recovered key.

Complexity Estimation. Given N keystream block pairs and a false alarm probability of $P_{fa} = 2^{-\alpha}$, the time complexity of the attack is

$$2^m(N + 2^n P_{fa}) = 2^m N + 2^{256-\alpha}, \text{ where } N \approx \left(\frac{\sqrt{\alpha \log 4} + 3\sqrt{1 - \epsilon^2}}{\epsilon}\right)^2,$$

for a probability of non-detection $P_{nd} = 1.3 \times 10^{-3}$. In practice, α and thus N are selected to minimize the time complexity of the attack. Based on an existing study [1], we use the median bias ϵ in our attack; therefore, we note that our attack has a success probability of approximately 0.5.

4 Analysis of PNB

4.1 Search for PNB with High Neutral Measures

Typically, differential attacks on Salsa and ChaCha first determine the $\mathcal{ID}$-$\mathcal{OD}$ pair with a higher differential bias and then explore neutral measures of the target $\mathcal{OD}$ bit position. The existing studies [1,3,6–9,16,18] analyzed the differential bias and optimized the combination of the differential bias and PNB, as this combination can be used to determine the time and data complexities for the attack. Optimizing this combination by focusing on PNB analysis may help improve differential attacks on Salsa and ChaCha.

In this section, we perform a comprehensive analysis of the PNB and examine the conditions that produce a large number of non-significant key bits because the size of the PNB directly influences the theoretical time complexity of an attack, as described in Sect. 3.2. No study focusing on analyzing PNB has been conducted. If the conditions that produce a large number of non-significant key bits can be clarified, it can be claimed that existing attacks require improvement.

We perform the following procedure to search for conditions that produce a large number of non-significant key bits:

Step 1. Generate a known key $k = (k_0, \ldots, k_7)$ uniformly at random.

Step 2. Select the $\mathcal{ID}$ bit position $\Delta_i^{(0)}[j]$, nonce, and block counter uniformly at random. Then, generate the initial state matrix $X^{(0)}$ and the corresponding initial matrix $X'^{(0)} = X^{(0)} \oplus \Delta_i^{(0)}[j]$.

Step 3. From the input pair $(X^{(0)}, X'^{(0)})$, compute the r-round internal state matrix pair $(X^{(r)}, X'^{(r)})$ and R-round internal state matrix pair $(X^{(R)}, X'^{(R)})$, where R is the target round for the attack on ChaCha20/R.

Step 4. From the r-round internal state matrix pair $(X^{(r)}, X'^{(r)})$, compute the $\mathcal{OD}$ for each bit, such as $\Delta_p^{(r)}[q] = X_p^{(r)}[q] \oplus X_p'^{(r)}[q]$ for all possible choices of p and q.

Step 5. From the R-round internal state matrix pair $(X^{(R)}, X'^{(R)})$, obtain keystream blocks $Z = X^{(0)} + X^{(R)}$ and $Z' = X'^{(0)} + X'^{(R)}$.

Step 6. Complement a particular key bit position κ ($\kappa \in \{0, \ldots, 255\}$) to yield states $\overline{X}^{(0)}$ and $\overline{X'}^{(0)}$. Then, compute the r-round internal state matrix pair

$(Y^{(r)}, Y'^{(r)})$ with $Z - \overline{X}^{(0)}$ and $Z' - \overline{X'}^{(0)}$ as inputs to the inverse round function of ChaCha, and derive $\Gamma_p^{(r)}[q] = Y_p^{(r)}[q] \oplus Y'^{(r)}_p[q]$ for all possible choices of p and q.

Step 7. Increase the counter for each p, q, and κ only if $\Delta_p^{(r)}[q] = \Gamma_p^{(r)}[q]$.

Step 8. Repeat Steps 2–7 for the required number of samples.

After completing multiple trials with the above steps, we compute the neutral measures γ_κ for each key bit position and then count the number of non-significant key bits for each $\mathcal{OD}$ bit position with a specified threshold value γ. We note that the number of trials represents the number of different keys used in our experiments, while the number of samples represents the number of different initial state matrices generated from a fixed $\mathcal{ID}$ bit in each trial.

4.2 Experimental Results

This subsection presents our experimental results based on the search procedure described in Sect. 4.1. The following is our experimental environment: five Linux machines with 40-core Intel Xeon CPU E5-2660 v3 (2.60 GHz), 128.0 GB of main memory, a gcc 7.2.0 compiler, and the C programming language. We use the Mersenne Twister[3], which is a pseudorandom number generator proposed by Matsumoto and Nishimura [17], to generate the secret keys and samples used in all our experiments, and thus did not reuse secret keys and samples in any of the experiments.

To search for the conditions that produce a large number of non-significant key bits, we conduct experiments with 2^8 trials using 2^{21} samples for each of the possible 2^7 $\mathcal{ID}$s (*i.e.*, 2^{28} total samples). Based on Theorem 1, let D_0 and D_1 be the uniform distribution and a distribution of $\Delta_p^{(r)}[q] = \Gamma_p^{(r)}[q]$ obtained from the r-round internal state matrices of ChaCha20/R, respectively. The target event occurs in D_0 and D_1 with probabilities of $\frac{1}{2}$ and $\frac{1}{2} \cdot (1 + \gamma_\kappa)$, respectively; thus, the number of samples of the best distinguisher between $\mathsf{D} = \mathsf{D}_0$ and $\mathsf{D} = \mathsf{D}_1$ can be estimated as $\frac{4}{\gamma_\kappa^2}$. Our results are reliable when the derived neutral measures γ_κ are greater than 2^{-13} (≈ 0.000122), as 2^{28} samples are used.

ChaCha20/7. Figure 1 presents the number of non-significant key bits for each $\mathcal{OD}$ bit position in ChaCha20/7. In this figure, the vertical axis represents the number of non-significant key bits at each $\mathcal{OD}$ bit position, the horizontal axis represents the $\mathcal{OD}$ bit position, and the auxiliary lines on the vertical axis separate the $\mathcal{OD}$ word positions (*i.e.*, the word positions are $0, 1, \ldots, 15$ in order from left to right). The blue (top), orange (center), and green (bottom) lines represent the number of non-significant key bits when the number of intermediate rounds r is 3, 3.5, and 4, respectively.

---

[3] The source code is available at https://github.com/omitakahiro/omitakahiro.github.io/blob/master/random/code/MT.h.

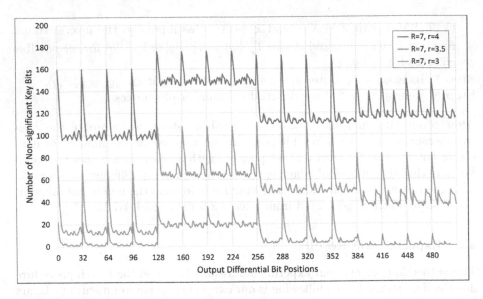

Fig. 1. Number of non-significant key bits for each $\mathcal{OD}$ bit position when the number of intermediate rounds r is 3, 3.5, and 4 in ChaCha20/7. We use $\gamma = 0.35$ as the threshold value. (Color figure online)

Figure 1 indicates that the number of non-significant key bits tends to be larger at all 0-th $\mathcal{OD}$ bit positions (*i.e.*, all least significant $\mathcal{OD}$ bit positions) of each word regardless of the number of intermediate rounds. Therefore, optimizing the combination of the differential bias and PNB by focusing on all 0-th $\mathcal{OD}$ bit positions may improve the differential attack on ChaCha20/7. Referring to the existing studies [1,16,18], the 0-th $\mathcal{OD}$ bit positions with a high average neutral measure were selected in the third round (*i.e.*, $\Delta_{11}^{(3)}[0]$); thus, it is difficult to improve the differential attack on ChaCha20/7 even for 3 intermediate rounds r. This is because the smaller the number of the intermediate rounds r, the smaller the number of non-significant key bits. Therefore, to improve the differential attack on ChaCha20/7, we should focus on more than 3 intermediate rounds.

The PNB analysis in this subsection cannot be directly compared with that in existing studies (*e.g.*, [3,6,11]) because a multi-bit differential or differential-linear technique was employed in the existing studies, whereas we focus solely on the single-bit differential technique. From a computational complexity perspective, we have searched for the number of non-significant key bits for only a single-bit $\mathcal{OD}$ bit position. Similarly, we should search for the number of non-significant key bits for multi-bit $\mathcal{OD}$ bit positions, which is left for future work.

ChaCha20/7.25, ChaCha20/7.5, and ChaCha20/7.75. Figure 2 presents the number of non-significant key bits for each 3.5-round $\mathcal{OD}$ bit position when the number of target rounds R is 7, 7.25, 7.5, and 7.75. In this figure, the vertical and horizontal axes and the auxiliary lines on the vertical axis are the same as in Fig. 1. The blue (top), orange (second from the top), green (second from the bottom), and yellow (bottom) lines represent the number of non-significant key

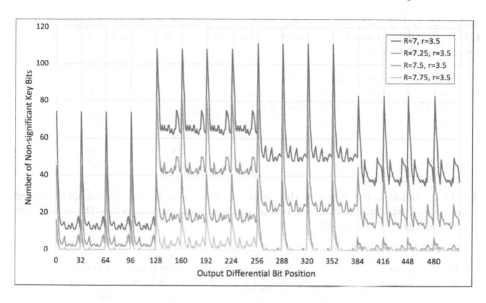

Fig. 2. Number of non-significant key bits for each $\mathcal{OD}$ bit position when the number of intermediate rounds r is 3.5 and number of target rounds R is 7, 7.25, 7.5, and 7.75. We use $\gamma = 0.35$ as the threshold value. (Color figure online)

bits when the number of intermediate rounds r is 3.5 and number of target rounds R is 7, 7.25, 7.5, and 7.75, respectively.

Similar to the experimental results for ChaCha20/7, the number of non-significant key bits tends to be larger at all 0-th $\mathcal{OD}$ bit positions of each word regardless of the number of target rounds. Therefore, optimizing the combination of the differential bias and PNB by focusing on all 0-th $\mathcal{OD}$ bit positions may be effective for performing a differential attack on ChaCha20/7.25, ChaCha20/7.5, and ChaCha20/7.75.

4.3   Discussion

Relationship Between PNB and Inverse Round Function. We discuss the relationship between the PNB (or the number of non-significant key bits) and inverse round function of ChaCha. To this end, we investigate the relationship between the input word position to the inverse quarterround function and the cumulative number of wordwise modular subtractions. This is because wordwise modular addition/subtraction plays a crucial role in ensuring the security of ARX ciphers. In our investigation, the cumulative number of wordwise modular subtractions is counted as follows:

Wordwise modular subtraction. The cumulative number of wordwise modular subtractions is counted only when wordwise modular subtraction is executed. Moreover, we calculate the sum of the cumulative number of wordwise modular subtractions in two input words to wordwise modular subtraction. For example, when the wordwise modular subtraction, $A' = A - B$, is executed and the cumulative number of wordwise modular subtractions in the

Table 2. Relationship between the input word position to the inverse quarterround function and the cumulative number of modular subtractions when the number of target rounds R is 7 or 7.5.

Input Word position	Cumulative number of modular subtractions for $R - r$ rounds.				
	3 rounds ($r = 4$ or 4.5)	3.25 rounds ($r = 3.75$ or 4.25)	3.5 rounds ($r = 3.5$ or 4)	3.75 rounds ($r = 3.25$ or 3.75)	4 rounds ($r = 3$ or 3.5)
A	70	70	156	156	349
B	37	85	85	192	192
C	48	107	107	236	236
D	58	128	128	128	284

Table 3. Relationship between the input word position to the inverse quarterround function and the cumulative number of modular subtractions when the number of target rounds R is 7.25 or 7.75.

Input Word position	Cumulative number of modular subtractions for $R - r$ rounds.				
	3 rounds ($r = 4.25$ or 4.75)	3.25 rounds ($r = 4$ or 4.5)	3.5 rounds ($r = 3.75$ or 4.25)	3.75 rounds ($r = 3.5$ or 4)	4 rounds ($r = 3.25$ or 3.75)
A	48	107	107	236	236
B	58	58	128	128	284
C	70	70	156	156	349
D	37	85	85	192	192

two input words A and B are 70 and 85, respectively, 156 is the cumulative number of wordwise modular subtractions in the output word A'.

Bitwise XOR. We calculate only the sum of the cumulative number of wordwise modular subtractions in two input words to bitwise XOR. For example, when the bitwise XOR operation, $B' = B \oplus C$, is executed and the cumulative number of wordwise modular subtractions in the two input words B and C are 37 and 48, respectively, 85 is the cumulative number of wordwise modular subtractions in the output word B'.

Bitwise left rotation. The cumulative number of wordwise modular subtractions did not change after the execution of bitwise left rotation.

Tables 2 and 3 present the results of examining the cumulative number of wordwise modular subtractions. In Table 2, the number of target rounds R is 7 or 7.5, whereas in Table 3, the number of target rounds R is 7.25 or 7.75. In these tables, the input word position column contains the word positions, such as a vector (A, B, C, D), input to the inverse quarterround function. Note that each input word position always transitions to the same input word position in the next round (refer to Sect. 2 for more details).

Tables 2 and 3 indicate that the cumulative number of wordwise modular subtractions differ depending on the input word position relative to the inverse round function and the number of intermediate rounds r. In particular, the cumulative number of wordwise modular subtractions is smaller in the order of the input word positions B, C, D, and A when the number of intermediate rounds r is 3, 3.5, 4, and 4.5. In contrast, the cumulative number of wordwise modular subtractions is smaller in the order of the input word positions D, A,

Table 4. Maximum, minimum, average, and median values of the average neutral measures $\hat{\gamma}_\kappa$ for each target round R when $r = 3.5$, where p and q are the word and bit positions of the $\mathcal{OD}$, respectively (*i.e.*, $\Delta_p^{(r)}[q]$).

R	Maximum			Minimum			Average	Median
	$\hat{\gamma}_\kappa$	p	q	$\hat{\gamma}_\kappa$	p	q		
7	0.382	11	0	0.050	2	13	0.169	0.174
7.25	0.282	6	0	0.018	3	13	0.097	0.087
7.5	0.151	4	0	0.004	0	13	0.034	0.016
7.75	0.075	9	0	0.001	0	13	0.011	0.005

B, and C when the number of intermediate rounds r is 3.25, 3.75, 4.25, and 4.75. We now compare the experimental results presented in Fig. 2 with the results when $r = 3.5$, as illustrated in Tables 2 and 3. Note that the range of input word positions A, B, C, and D corresponds to the $\mathcal{OD}$ bit positions 0 to 127, 128 to 255, 256 to 383, and 384 to 511, respectively. From Fig. 2, the number of non-significant key bits is larger in the order of the input word positions B, C, D, and A when the number of intermediate rounds r is 3.5 (all 0-th bit positions are exceptions); thus, the smaller the cumulative number of wordwise modular subtractions, the larger the number of non-significant key bits. The 0-th bit position is uninfluenced by the carry-in wordwise modular subtraction (*i.e.*, it is uninfluenced by the $\mathcal{ID}/\mathcal{OD}$). This has been suggested to be a special case.

In summary, the number of non-significant key bits depends on the input word position relative to the inverse round function and is affected by the cumulative number of wordwise modular subtractions. Specifically, the conditions that produce the number of non-significant key bits depend on the $\mathcal{OD}$ bit position, particularly all 0-th $\mathcal{OD}$ bit positions.

Upper Bound on the Number of Rounds for the Attacks. We discuss the upper bound on the number of rounds required for a PNB-focused differential attack that uses a single-bit truncated differential to be successful. To this end, we investigate the value of the average neutral measures $\hat{\gamma}_\kappa$ for each round of the inverse round function. Table 4 presents the maximum, minimum, average, and median values of the average neutral measures $\hat{\gamma}_\kappa$ for each target round R when the number of intermediate rounds r is 3.5[4]. These findings can be obtained by a detailed analysis of the experimental results described in Sect. 4.2. The R column in Table 4 lists the number of target rounds for our attack, and the number of rounds of the inverse round function can be calculated as $R - r$.

Our experimental results are reliable when the derived average neutral measures $\hat{\gamma}_\kappa$ are greater than 2^{-13} (≈ 0.000122), as 2^{28} samples are used. As illus-

---

[4] The latest study presented by Coutinho and Neto at EUROCRYPT 2021 [9] used $\Delta_5^{(3.5)}[0]$ $(= \Delta_5^{(4)}[7] \oplus \Delta_{10}^{(4)}[0])$ as the $\mathcal{OD}$ to perform a differential attack on ChaCha20/7. Accordingly, we focused solely on $r = 3.5$.

trated in Table 4, all values of $\hat{\gamma}_\kappa$ are reliable when the number of target rounds R is 7, 7.25, 7.5, and 7.75; thus, the upper bound on the number of rounds required for a PNB-focused differential attack that uses a single-bit truncated differential to be successful is at most 7.75 rounds. However, given that the threshold γ used in the existing attacks, such as [3,6,9], was $\gamma = 0.27$ or 0.35, it is practically difficult to perform a differential attack when the number of target rounds R is 7.5 or 7.75 because $\hat{\gamma}_\kappa$ is too small; thus, our results suggest that a PNB-focused differential attack on reduced-round ChaCha should work on up to 7.25 rounds. To verify this claim, we perform a PNB-focused differential attack on reduced-round ChaCha with target rounds of 7, 7.25, and 7.5.

5   PNB-Focused Differential Attack

In this section, we describe a PNB-focused differential attack on reduced-round ChaCha. First, based on the PNB analysis described in Sect. 4, we determine the target $\mathcal{OD}$ bit position for the proposed attack. Next, we analyze the differential biases at the target $\mathcal{OD}$ bit positions and then obtain the $\mathcal{ID}$ bit position with the best differential bias at the target $\mathcal{OD}$ bit positions. Finally, we estimate the time and data complexities for our attack using the combination of the differential bias and PNB.

5.1   Analysis of Single-Bit Differential Biases

In Sect. 4, we comprehensively analyze the PNB for all possible single-bit truncated $\mathcal{OD}$s. Accordingly, by analyzing the $\mathcal{ID}$ bit position with the highest differential bias at the target $\mathcal{OD}$ bit position, we can determine the $\mathcal{ID}$-$\mathcal{OD}$ pair to use for our attack.

To identify the $\mathcal{ID}$ bit position with the highest differential bias $|\epsilon_d|$ at the target $\mathcal{OD}$ bit positions, we conduct experiments with 2^6 trials using 2^{28} samples for a fixed $\mathcal{ID}$; thus, the results are reliable when the derived differential biases $|\epsilon_d|$ are greater than 2^{-13} (≈ 0.000122), as 2^{28} samples are used. In our experiments, the target $\mathcal{OD}$s are $\Delta_0^{(3.5)}[0]$, $\Delta_1^{(3.5)}[0]$, $\Delta_2^{(3.5)}[0]$, $\Delta_3^{(3.5)}[0]$, $\Delta_{12}^{(3.5)}[0]$, $\Delta_{13}^{(3.5)}[0]$, $\Delta_{14}^{(3.5)}[0]$, and $\Delta_{15}^{(3.5)}[0]$. Consequently, our results are reliable at $\Delta_0^{(3.5)}[0]$, $\Delta_1^{(3.5)}[0]$, $\Delta_2^{(3.5)}[0]$, and $\Delta_3^{(3.5)}[0]$ because these absolute biases are at least 0.000430, but not at $\Delta_{12}^{(3.5)}[0]$, $\Delta_{13}^{(3.5)}[0]$, $\Delta_{14}^{(3.5)}[0]$, and $\Delta_{15}^{(3.5)}[0]$ because these absolute biases are at most 0.000028. Moreover, these results lead to unreliable at other 0-th $\mathcal{OD}$ bit positions, such as $\Delta_4^{(3.5)}[0]$, $\Delta_5^{(3.5)}[0]$, $\Delta_6^{(3.5)}[0]$, $\Delta_7^{(3.5)}[0]$, $\Delta_8^{(3.5)}[0]$, $\Delta_9^{(3.5)}[0]$, $\Delta_{10}^{(3.5)}[0]$, and $\Delta_{11}^{(3.5)}[0]$, because the results are affected by the unreliable results at $\Delta_{12}^{(3.5)}[0]$, $\Delta_{13}^{(3.5)}[0]$, $\Delta_{14}^{(3.5)}[0]$, and $\Delta_{15}^{(3.5)}[0]$ according to the computations of the quarterround function (see Sect. 2 for details). Consequently, we determine the following $\mathcal{ID}$-$\mathcal{OD}$ pairs to use for our attack: $(\Delta_{15}^{(0)}[6], \Delta_0^{(3.5)}[0])$, $(\Delta_{12}^{(0)}[6], \Delta_1^{(3.5)}[0])$, $(\Delta_{13}^{(0)}[6], \Delta_2^{(3.5)}[0])$, and $(\Delta_{14}^{(0)}[6], \Delta_3^{(3.5)}[0])$.

To obtain more precise single-bit differential biases for the derived $\mathcal{ID}$-$\mathcal{OD}$ pairs, we conduct additional experiments with 2^8 trials using 2^{34} samples for a

Table 5. Best single-bit differential biases $|\epsilon_d|$ at the 0-th $\mathcal{OD}$ bit positions of each word for 3.5 rounds of ChaCha. Experiments are conducted with 2^8 trials using 2^{34} samples for a fixed $\mathcal{ID}$; thus, the results are reliable when the derived differential biases $|\epsilon_d|$ are greater than 2^{-16} (≈ 0.000015), as 2^{34} samples are used.

$\mathcal{ID}$	$\mathcal{OD}$	$|\epsilon_d|$
$\Delta_{15}^{(0)}[6]$	$\Delta_{0}^{(3.5)}[0]$	0.000469
$\Delta_{12}^{(0)}[6]$	$\Delta_{1}^{(3.5)}[0]$	0.000478
$\Delta_{13}^{(0)}[6]$	$\Delta_{2}^{(3.5)}[0]$	0.000504
$\Delta_{14}^{(0)}[6]$	$\Delta_{3}^{(3.5)}[0]$	0.000478

fixed $\mathcal{ID}$; thus, the results are reliable when the derived differential biases $|\epsilon_d|$ are greater than 2^{-16} (≈ 0.000015), as 2^{34} samples are used. Table 5 lists the additional experimental results of the best differential biases $|\epsilon_d|$ at the target $\mathcal{OD}$ bit positions: $\Delta_{0}^{(3.5)}[0]$, $\Delta_{1}^{(3.5)}[0]$, $\Delta_{2}^{(3.5)}[0]$, and $\Delta_{3}^{(3.5)}[0]$. As displayed in this table, we can obtain reliable results at the target positions; then, we use the listed biases $|\epsilon_d|$ to estimate the time and data complexities for our attack.

5.2 Complexity Estimation

To estimate the time and data complexities for the PNB-focused differential attack on the target rounds of ChaCha (*i.e.*, 7, 7.25, and 7.5 rounds), the remaining steps should be performed as follows (see Sect. 3 for details):

Step 1. Recalculate the neutral measures corresponding to the derived $\mathcal{ID}$-$\mathcal{OD}$ pairs and divide the secret key bits into two sets – a set of m-bit significant and a set of n-bit non-significant key bits.

Step 2. By performing PBC, obtain the biases $|\epsilon_a|$ for each threshold γ from the obtained keystream and approximate the overall bias $\epsilon \approx \epsilon_d \cdot \epsilon_a$ for the attack on the target rounds of ChaCha.

Step 3. Perform the online phase and estimate the time and data complexities to recover the unknown key, as described in Sect. 3.2.

To perform the above-mentioned steps, we conduct experiments with 2^8 trials using 2^{30} samples for the fixed $\mathcal{ID}$; thus, the results are reliable when the derived biases $|\epsilon_a|$ are greater than 2^{-14} (≈ 0.000061), as 2^{30} samples are used.

ChaCha20/7. Table 6 presents the best parameters for each target $\mathcal{ID}$-$\mathcal{OD}$ pair to estimate the time and data complexities for our attack on ChaCha20/7. The threshold γ is set from 0.10 to 0.95 at intervals of 0.05 (*i.e.*, total 18 patterns), n represents the number of non-significant key bits, $|\epsilon_d|$ is derived from Table 5, $|\epsilon_a|$ is obtained by performing PBC for each threshold γ, and α is selected to minimize the time complexity of our attack.

Consequently, we can perform our attack on ChaCha20/7 with time and data complexities of $2^{231.63}$ and $2^{49.58}$, respectively, using the best parameters, where

Table 6. Best parameters for the proposed attack on ChaCha20/7.

$\mathcal{ID}$	$\mathcal{OD}$	γ	n	$|\epsilon_d|$	$|\epsilon_a|$	α	Time	Data
$\Delta_{15}^{(0)}[6]$	$\Delta_0^{(3.5)}[0]$	0.35	74	0.000469	0.000662	29	$2^{231.74}$	$2^{49.68}$
$\Delta_{12}^{(0)}[6]$	$\Delta_1^{(3.5)}[0]$	0.35	74	0.000478	0.000556	29	$2^{232.17}$	$2^{50.13}$
$\Delta_{13}^{(0)}[6]$	$\Delta_2^{(3.5)}[0]$	0.35	74	0.000504	0.000615	29	$2^{231.74}$	$2^{49.69}$
$\Delta_{14}^{(0)}[6]$	$\Delta_3^{(3.5)}[0]$	0.35	74	0.000478	0.000674	29	$2^{231.63}$	$2^{49.58}$

Table 7. Best parameters for the proposed attack on ChaCha20/7.25.

$\mathcal{ID}$	$\mathcal{OD}$	γ	n	$|\epsilon_d|$	$|\epsilon_a|$	α	Time	Data
$\Delta_{15}^{(0)}[6]$	$\Delta_0^{(3.5)}[0]$	0.30	49	0.000469	0.000564	3	$2^{255.62}$	$2^{48.36}$
$\Delta_{12}^{(0)}[6]$	$\Delta_1^{(3.5)}[0]$	0.35	45	0.000478	0.002200	3	$2^{255.64}$	$2^{44.38}$
$\Delta_{13}^{(0)}[6]$	$\Delta_2^{(3.5)}[0]$	0.35	45	0.000504	0.001783	2	$2^{256.02}$	$2^{44.61}$
$\Delta_{14}^{(0)}[6]$	$\Delta_3^{(3.5)}[0]$	0.35	45	0.000478	0.002186	3	$2^{255.65}$	$2^{44.40}$

the $\mathcal{ID}$-$\mathcal{OD}$ pair is $(\Delta_{14}^{(0)}[6], \Delta_3^{(3.5)}[0])$, γ is 0.35, n is 74, α is 29, and the list of PNB is {6, 7, 8, 9, 10, 11, 12, 13, 14, 19, 27, 28, 29, 30, 31, 34, 35, 36, 37, 46, 71, 79, 80, 83, 98, 99, 100, 101, 102, 103, 104, 105, 106, 109, 110, 111, 112, 113, 114, 115, 116, 117, 118, 119, 122, 123, 127, 128, 129, 130, 148, 149, 150, 159, 187, 188, 189, 190, 191, 200, 223, 224, 225, 231, 232, 239, 240, 243, 244, 251, 252, 253, 254, 255}.

ChaCha20/7.25 and ChaCha20/7.5. Similar to the complexity estimation for ChaCha20/7, we present the best parameters for each target $\mathcal{ID}$-$\mathcal{OD}$ pair to estimate the time and data complexities for our attack on ChaCha20/7.25 and ChaCha20/7.5 in Tables 7 and 8, respectively.

As illustrated in Table 7, our attack on ChaCha20/7.25 can be performed with time and data complexities of $2^{255.62}$ and $2^{48.36}$, respectively, using the best parameters, where the $\mathcal{ID}$-$\mathcal{OD}$ pair is $(\Delta_{15}^{(0)}[6], \Delta_0^{(3.5)}[0])$, γ is 0.30, n is 49, α is 3, and the list of PNB is {2, 3, 10, 13, 14, 19, 20, 26, 27, 31, 40, 44, 45, 46, 51, 59, 60, 61, 62, 63, 128, 129, 130, 135, 136, 143, 144, 147, 148, 155, 156, 157, 158, 159, 160, 161, 162, 180, 181, 182, 191, 219, 220, 221, 222, 223, 224, 232, 255}. ChaCha provides a 256-bit security level against key recovery attacks. Given that the success probability is approximately 0.5, our attack on ChaCha20/7.25 is slightly less efficient than a brute force attack; however, it is the first dedicated attack on the target to be reported. It provides both a baseline and useful components (*i.e.*, differential bias and PNB) for improved attacks.

In addition, as displayed in Table 8, our attack on ChaCha20/7.5 can be performed with time and data complexities of $2^{273.49}$ and $2^{37.49}$, respectively, using the best parameters, where the $\mathcal{ID}$-$\mathcal{OD}$ pair is $(\Delta_{15}^{(0)}[6], \Delta_0^{(3.5)}[0])$, γ is 0.30, n is 20, α is 1, and the list of PNB is {6, 7, 14, 22, 25, 31, 39, 40, 41, 42, 56, 57, 58, 63, 191, 219, 220, 221, 222, 223}. Thus, our attack on ChaCha20/7.5 is inefficient because this is beyond the security level of ChaCha.

Table 8. Best parameters for the proposed attack on ChaCha20/7.5.

$\mathcal{ID}$	$\mathcal{OD}$	γ	n	$|\epsilon_d|$	$|\epsilon_a|$	α	Time	Data
$\Delta_{15}^{(0)}[6]$	$\Delta_0^{(3.5)}[0]$	0.30	20	0.000469	0.020269	1	$2^{273.49}$	$2^{37.49}$
$\Delta_{12}^{(0)}[6]$	$\Delta_1^{(3.5)}[0]$	0.30	20	0.000478	0.014840	1	$2^{274.33}$	$2^{38.33}$
$\Delta_{13}^{(0)}[6]$	$\Delta_2^{(3.5)}[0]$	0.30	20	0.000504	0.017594	1	$2^{273.69}$	$2^{37.69}$
$\Delta_{14}^{(0)}[6]$	$\Delta_3^{(3.5)}[0]$	0.30	20	0.000478	0.018693	1	$2^{273.67}$	$2^{37.67}$

6 Related Works

Aumasson et al. [1] proposed a framework for a differential attack based on the PNB concept and applied it to reduced-round Salsa, ChaCha, and Rumba. They first obtained an $\mathcal{ID}$-$\mathcal{OD}$ pair, $(\Delta_{13}^{(0)}[13], \Delta_{11}^{(3)}[0])$, with a high differential bias using a single-bit differential technique. Then, they determined the PNB at the target $\mathcal{OD}$ bit position and estimated the time and data complexities for their attack on ChaCha20/7. Their attack can be performed with time and data complexities of 2^{248} and 2^{27}, respectively.

Shi et al. [18] proposed new techniques, called the column chaining distinguisher (CCD) and probabilistic neutral vector (PNV) concept, to improve Aumasson et al.'s attack. They used the same $\mathcal{ID}$-$\mathcal{OD}$ pair, $(\Delta_{13}^{(0)}[13], \Delta_{11}^{(3)}[0])$, obtained by Aumasson et al., constructed a 4-step CCD, determined the PNV at the target $\mathcal{OD}$ bit position, and estimated the time and data complexities as well as the success probability for their attack on ChaCha20/7. Their attack can be performed with time and data complexities of $2^{246.5}$ and 2^{27}, respectively, and a success probability of approximately 0.43.

Maitra [16] further improved Aumasson et al.'s attack by using the chosen-IV technique. Maitra used the same $\mathcal{ID}$-$\mathcal{OD}$ pair, $(\Delta_{13}^{(0)}[13], \Delta_{11}^{(3)}[0])$, obtained by Aumasson et al. and explored how to appropriately select IVs corresponding to the secret keys, given the target $\mathcal{ID}$, $\Delta_{13}^{(0)}[13]$. This attack can be performed on ChaCha20/7 with the time and data complexities of $2^{238.94}$ and $2^{23.89}$, respectively.

Choudhuri and Maitra [6] used a differential-linear technique to extend the existing 3-round single-bit differential, $(\Delta_{13}^{(0)}[13], \Delta_{11}^{(3)}[0])$, to 4-, 4.5-, and 5-round multi-bit differentials, such that the 4.5-round $\mathcal{OD}$ is $\Delta_0^{(4.5)}[0] \oplus \Delta_0^{(4.5)}[8] \oplus \Delta_1^{(4.5)}[0] \oplus \Delta_5^{(4.5)}[12] \oplus \Delta_{11}^{(4.5)}[0] \oplus \Delta_9^{(4.5)}[0] \oplus \Delta_{15}^{(4.5)}[0] \oplus \Delta_{12}^{(4.5)}[16] \oplus \Delta_{12}^{(4.5)}[24]$. Using such multi-bit differentials, their attack on ChaCha20/7 can be performed with time and data complexities of $2^{237.65}$ and $2^{31.6}$, respectively.

Beierle et al. [3] presented a generic framework for differential-linear attacks with a special focus on ARX ciphers. Then, they applied this framework to

ChaCha20/7 and improved the best existing attacks. To perform a differential-linear attack on ChaCha20/7, the target cipher is divided into a differential part covering 1 round, a middle part covering 2.5 rounds, a linear part covering 2.5 rounds, and a key guessing part covering 1 round. As a result, their attack can be performed on ChaCha20/7 with time and data complexities of $2^{230.86}$ and $2^{48.83}$, respectively.

As summarized above, the best existing attack on reduced-round ChaCha works on up to 7 rounds with time and data complexities of $2^{230.86}$ and $2^{48.83}$, respectively. Our attack has the time and data complexities of $2^{231.63}$ and $2^{49.58}$, respectively; thus, it is not an improvement over the best existing attack on ChaCha20/7. However, our analysis suggests that a PNB-focused differential attack on reduced-round ChaCha should work on up to 7.25 rounds. No study focusing on attacks on ChaCha20/7.25 has been conducted until now. Although the proposed attack on ChaCha20/7.25 is less efficient than a brute force attack, it is the first dedicated attack on the target. It provides both a baseline and useful components (*i.e.*, differential bias and PNB) for improved attacks.

7   Conclusion

In this study, we have proposed a new approach for differential cryptanalysis against the ChaCha stream cipher. Our approach focuses on analyzing PNB rather than searching for differential biases; therefore, we refer to the proposed approach as a *PNB-focused differential attack*. The proposed approach allows us to perform the most effective differential attack on the 7.25-round ChaCha (*i.e.*, ChaCha20/7.25) with a time complexity of $2^{255.62}$, a data complexity of $2^{48.36}$, and a success probability of 0.5. Although this attack is less efficient than a brute force attack, it is the first dedicated attack on the target. It provides both a baseline and useful components (*i.e.*, differential bias and PNB) for improved attacks.

Our work can be extended in the following directions in the future. First, in this study, we have focused solely on the truncated single-bit differential technique. However, it may be possible to improve the proposed attack by employing multi-bit differential or differential-linear techniques, especially in the framework proposed by Beierle et al. [3]. In addition, our analysis have not fully considered both the differential bias and PNB to obtain the best combination because these characteristics can be analyzed independently. The next step is thus to consider these characteristics together to obtain stricter evaluation results. Finally, the PNB-focused differential attack can be used to improve existing differential attacks on the Salsa stream cipher.

Acknowledgment. We would like to thank the reviewers for their valuable feedback that helped improve the quality of our paper. This work is partially supported by JSPS KAKENHI Grant Number JP21H03443, and Innovation Platform for Society 5.0 at MEXT.

References

1. Aumasson, J.-P., Fischer, S., Khazaei, S., Meier, W., Rechberger, C.: New features of Latin dances: analysis of Salsa, ChaCha, and Rumba. In: Nyberg, K. (ed.) FSE 2008. LNCS, vol. 5086, pp. 470–488. Springer, Heidelberg (2008). https://doi.org/10.1007/978-3-540-71039-4_30

2. Baignères, T., Junod, P., Vaudenay, S.: How far can we go beyond linear cryptanalysis? In: Lee, P.J. (ed.) ASIACRYPT 2004. LNCS, vol. 3329, pp. 432–450. Springer, Heidelberg (2004). https://doi.org/10.1007/978-3-540-30539-2_31

3. Beierle, C., Leander, G., Todo, Y.: Improved differential-linear attacks with applications to ARX ciphers. In: Micciancio, D., Ristenpart, T. (eds.) CRYPTO 2020. LNCS, vol. 12172, pp. 329–358. Springer, Cham (2020). https://doi.org/10.1007/978-3-030-56877-1_12

4. Bernstein, D.J.: ChaCha, a variant of Salsa20. In: Workshop Record of SASC, vol. 8 (2008)

5. Bernstein, D.J.: The Salsa20 family of stream ciphers. In: Robshaw, M., Billet, O. (eds.) New Stream Cipher Designs. LNCS, vol. 4986, pp. 84–97. Springer, Heidelberg (2008). https://doi.org/10.1007/978-3-540-68351-3_8

6. Arka Rai Choudhuri and Subhamoy Maitra: Significantly improved multi-bit differentials for reduced round Salsa and ChaCha. IACR Trans. Symmetric Cryptol. 2016(2), 261–287 (2016)

7. Coutinho, M., Souza Neto, T.C.: New multi-bit differentials to improve attacks against ChaCha. IACR Cryptology ePrint Archive, p. 350 (2020)

8. Coutinho, M., Souza Neto, T.C.: Improved linear approximations to ARX ciphers and attacks against ChaCha. IACR Cryptology ePrint Archive, p. 224 (2021)

9. Coutinho, M., Souza Neto, T.C.: Improved linear approximations to ARX ciphers and attacks against ChaCha. In: Canteaut, A., Standaert, F.-X. (eds.) EUROCRYPT 2021. LNCS, vol. 12696, pp. 711–740. Springer, Cham (2021). https://doi.org/10.1007/978-3-030-77870-5_25

10. Deepthi, K.K.C., Singh, K.: Cryptanalysis of Salsa and ChaCha: revisited. In: Hu, J., Khalil, I., Tari, Z., Wen, S. (eds.) MONAMI 2017. LNICST, vol. 235, pp. 324–338. Springer, Cham (2018). https://doi.org/10.1007/978-3-319-90775-8_26

11. Dey, S., Sarkar, S.: Improved analysis for reduced round Salsa and Chacha. Discret. Appl. Math. 227, 58–69 (2017)

12. Dey, S., Sarkar, S.: Proving the biases of Salsa and ChaCha in differential attack. Des. Codes Crypt. 88(9), 1827–1856 (2020). https://doi.org/10.1007/s10623-020-00736-9

13. Dey, S., Sarkar, S.: A theoretical investigation on the distinguishers of Salsa and ChaCha. Discret. Appl. Math. 302, 147–162 (2021)

14. Ishiguro, T., Kiyomoto, S., Miyake, Y.: Latin dances revisited: new analytic results of Salsa20 and ChaCha. In: Qing, S., Susilo, W., Wang, G., Liu, D. (eds.) ICICS 2011. LNCS, vol. 7043, pp. 255–266. Springer, Heidelberg (2011). https://doi.org/10.1007/978-3-642-25243-3_21

15. Ito, R.: Rotational cryptanalysis of salsa core function. In: Susilo, W., Deng, R.H., Guo, F., Li, Y., Intan, R. (eds.) ISC 2020. LNCS, vol. 12472, pp. 129–145. Springer, Cham (2020). https://doi.org/10.1007/978-3-030-62974-8_8

16. Maitra, S.: Chosen IV cryptanalysis on reduced round ChaCha and Salsa. Discret. Appl. Math. 208, 88–97 (2016)

17. Matsumoto, M., Nishimura, T.: Mersenne twister: a 623-dimensionally equidistributed uniform pseudo-random number generator. ACM Trans. Model. Comput. Simul. **8**(1), 3–30 (1998)
18. Shi, Z., Zhang, B., Feng, D., Wu, W.: Improved key recovery attacks on reduced-round Salsa20 and ChaCha. In: Kwon, T., Lee, M.-K., Kwon, D. (eds.) ICISC 2012. LNCS, vol. 7839, pp. 337–351. Springer, Heidelberg (2013). https://doi.org/10.1007/978-3-642-37682-5_24

Improved Differential Attack on Round-Reduced LEA

Yuhan Zhang[1,2], Wenling Wu[1,2(✉)], and Lei Zhang[1,2]

[1] Trusted Computing and Information Assurance Laboratory, Institute of Software
Chinese Academy of Science, Beijing 100190, China
{yuhan2019,wenling}@iscas.ac.cn
[2] University of Chinese Academy of Sciences, Beijing 100049, China

Abstract. LEA is both the national standard of the Republic of Korea and an ISO/IEC standard. In this paper, we focus on differential attack on LEA with the automatic analysis technique and improve the previous searching strategy in ARX ciphers. For new strategy, we no longer just pay attention to the internal difference with only one active bit. By studying the differential property of modular addition, we choose the proper difference in the middle round. We construct a 13-round differential characteristic whose probability is better than the best previous one with a factor of about 2. Furthermore, We take the differential effect into consideration and obtain a 13-round differential whose probability is better than the best previous one with a factor of about 4. Moreover, we mount key-recovery on 14-round LEA-128, 14-round LEA-192 and 15-round LEA-256. Utilizing the property for key schedule, we obtain the lower time complexity than that evaluated by Dinur's method.

Keywords: Differential cryptanalysis · Key-recovery attack · Automatic search · MILP · ARX · LEA

1 Introduction

In symmetric cryptography, ARX ciphers with excellent performance in software are a large class of symmetric-key primitives consisting of three operations: modular addition, bit rotations and XOR. For example: the block ciphers SPECK [3], LEA [15], HIGHT [16], SPARX [12], TEA [24], the stream ciphers Salsa20 [7], ChaCha [6], and the SHA-3 finalists Skein [11] and Blake [1]. Some other examples are: message authentication code algorithm Chaskey [19], ARX-box Alzette [4] and authenticated encryption with associated data SPARKLE [5], which is one of the 10 finalists to move forward to the final round of the selection process in NIST Lightweight Cryptography Standardization process(LWC).

Differential cryptanalysis introduced by Biham and Shamir in [8] is an important method in evaluating security of symmetric-key cryptographic algorithms. As for S-boxes based ciphers, there exist many automatic search algorithms such as the work in [23]. The security against differential is evaluated by the number of active S-boxes. However, modular addition, the non-linear operation in ARX ciphers, is very different from the S-boxes. It is difficult to evaluate the security for ARX ciphers against differential in a similar way. To fill this gap, a variety of methods have been proposed and they can be divided into the following three classes.

The first category of the automatic methods for differential cryptanalysis is based on Matsui's branch and bound algorithm. In [9,10], Biryukov et al. proposed an automatic differential cryptanalysis method using partial difference distribution tables. Many best differential characteristics for ARX ciphers, such as SPECK, are found with their method. However, with the round increasing, it is infeasible to find the best characteristics in a reasonable time. Another important branch of the automatic searching algorithms is the methods using mixed integer linear programming(MILP). In [14], Fu et al., proposed a MILP-based method to search for the best differential characteristics for SPECK. However, when the number of rounds or the block size is large, the optimal characteristics cannot be found. In [2], Bagherzadeh et al. extend Fu's method. They show how to construct the MILP model of modular addition with one constant and search for the long-round characteristics by connecting two short-round differential characteristics. The search method based on the boolean satisfiability problem(SAT) [22] also plays an crucial role in automatic searching algorithm. In [20], Mouha et al. proposed a framework to search for the best differential characteristics for Salsa20. They use some logical equations in Conjunctive Normal Form(CNF) to describe the differential propagations through round function of ARX ciphers and add the logical equation system to SAT solver STP to find the best differential characteristics for ARX ciphers. In [21], Song et al. extend the Mouha's algorithm by connecting two short-round characteristics to construct a long-round differential characteristic. In the first place, they choose an internal difference with one active bit, then search forward and backward. Consequently, they obtained the improved results for LEA and SPECK. However, the way of choosing internal difference is limited, which may miss the better differential characteristics.

Our Contributions. In this paper, we pay attention to the automatic differential cryptanalysis of LEA with respect to XOR-difference. Our searching method is based on Fu's framework using MILP. We improved the Song's and Bagherzadeh's work by proposing a new method to choose the proper internal difference based on the differential property for modular addition. The new searching strategy helps us find the better differential characteristics for LEA. For round-reduced LEA, we find a new 13-round differential characteristic whose probability is twice as large as the best previous results. We take the differential effect into consideration and obtain a more powerful 13-round differential than the previous best one. What's more, we improve the key-recovery attack. We extract the property in key schedule. Using the relations between round keys, we mount the key-recovery on 14-round LEA-128, 14-round LEA-192 and 15-round LEA-256. We obtain the lower complexity than that evaluated by Dinur's method [13].

Outline. The rest of this paper is organized as follows. In Sect. 2, we review Fu's MILP model of ARX ciphers. In Sect. 3, we show the details of our improved searching strategy. The application to round-reduced LEA are detailed in Sect. 4. Finally, we conclude our work in Sect. 5.

2 Fu's MILP Model for Differential Characteristics of ARX Ciphers

In this section, we first present Fu et al.'s algorithm, we can refer to [14] for detailed work. We first give some definitions and theorems.

Definition 1. Let α, β and γ be fixed n-bit XOR differences. The XOR-differential probability (DP) of addition modular 2^n (xdp^+) is the probability with which α and β propagate to γ through the ADD operation, computed over all pairs of n-bit inputs (x, y) :

$$xdp^+(\alpha, \beta \to \gamma) = 2^{-2n} \cdot \# \{(x, y) : ((x \oplus \alpha) \boxplus (y \oplus \beta)) \oplus (x \boxplus y) = \gamma\} \quad (1)$$

Theorem 1 ([18]). The differential $(\alpha, \beta \to \gamma)$ is possible iff $(\alpha[0] \oplus \beta[0] \oplus \gamma[0]) = 0$ and $\alpha[i-1] = \beta[i-1] = \gamma[i-1] = \alpha[i] \oplus \beta[i] \oplus \gamma[i]$ for $\alpha[i-1] = \beta[i-1] = \gamma[i-1], i \in [1, n-1]$.

Theorem 2 ([18]). Assume that $(\alpha, \beta \to \gamma)$ is a possible differential characteristic, then the differential probability $xdp^+ = 2^{-\sum_{i=0}^{n-2} \neg eq(\alpha[i], \beta[i], \gamma[i])}$, where

$$eq(\alpha[i], \beta[i], \gamma[i]) = \begin{cases} 1, \alpha[i] = \beta[i] = \gamma[i] \\ 0, others \end{cases} \quad (2)$$

Note, the 0-th bit is the least significant bit and the $\neg$ means logical negation.

Next, we describe the constraints for XOR and modular addition operation and objective function in Fu's MILP model.

Constraints of XOR Operation. Assume that a, b and c are two input differences and output difference for XOR operation, respectively. Then we can use the following inequalities to describe the differential propagation for XOR operation

$$\begin{cases} a + b + c \geq 2d \\ d \geq a \\ d \geq b \\ d \geq c \\ a + b + c \leq 2 \end{cases} \quad (3)$$

where d is a dummy bit variable, the value of d is 0 if $a = 0, b = 0$ and $c = 0$, 1 otherwise.

Constraints of Modular Addition Operation. According to Theorem 1 and Theorem 2, all 65 possible vectors $(\alpha[i], \beta[i], \gamma[i], \alpha[i+1], \beta[i+1], \gamma[i+1], \neg eq(\alpha[i], \beta[i], \gamma[i]))$ for modular addition can be obtained. With the **inequality_generator()** function in the **sage.geometry** and the greedy algorithm in [23], the following inequalities can describe the differential propagation for modular addition

$$\begin{cases}
\beta[i] - \gamma[i] + (\neg eq(\alpha[i], \beta[i], \gamma[i])) \geq 0 \\
\alpha[i] - \beta[i] + (\neg eq(\alpha[i], \beta[i], \gamma[i])) \geq 0 \\
-\alpha[i] + \gamma[i] + (\neg eq(\alpha[i], \beta[i], \gamma[i])) \geq 0 \\
-\alpha[i] - \beta[i] - \gamma[i] - (\neg eq(\alpha[i], \beta[i], \gamma[i])) \geq -3 \\
\alpha[i] + \beta[i] + \gamma[i] - (\neg eq(\alpha[i], \beta[i], \gamma[i])) \geq 0 \\
-\beta[i] + \alpha[i+1] + \beta[i+1] + \gamma[i+1] + (\neg eq(\alpha[i], \beta[i], \gamma[i])) \geq 0 \\
\beta[i] + \alpha[i+1] - \beta[i+1] + \gamma[i+1] + (\neg eq(\alpha[i], \beta[i], \gamma[i])) \geq 0 \\
\beta[i] - \alpha[i+1] + \beta[i+1] + \gamma[i+1] + (\neg eq(\alpha[i], \beta[i], \gamma[i])) \geq 0 \\
\alpha[i] + \alpha[i+1] + \beta[i+1] - \gamma[i+1] + (\neg eq(\alpha[i], \beta[i], \gamma[i])) \geq 0 \\
\gamma[i] - \alpha[i+1] - \beta[i+1] - \gamma[i+1] + (\neg eq(\alpha[i], \beta[i], \gamma[i])) \geq -2 \\
-\beta[i] + \alpha[i+1] - \beta[i+1] - \gamma[i+1] + (\neg eq(\alpha[i], \beta[i], \gamma[i])) \geq -2 \\
-\beta[i] - \alpha[i+1] + \beta[i+1] - \gamma[i+1] + (\neg eq(\alpha[i], \beta[i], \gamma[i])) \geq -2 \\
-\beta[i] - \alpha[i+1] - \beta[i+1] + \gamma[i+1] + (\neg eq(\alpha[i], \beta[i], \gamma[i])) \geq -2
\end{cases} \qquad (4)$$

Besides, we can easily get the inequalities corresponding $\alpha[0] \oplus \beta[0] = \gamma[0]$ by constraints of XOR operation.

Objective Function of Differential Model. Based on the computation of xdp^+, the objective function is to minimize $\sum_{i=0}^{n-2} \neg eq(\alpha[i], \beta[i], \gamma[i])$.

3   Automatic Search for Characteristics and Differentials for Round-Reduced LEA

In this section, we propose an improved strategy for searching for long-round differential characteristics for ARX cipher. In the previous searching methods for ARX ciphers, authors prefer to choose the input difference in the middle round with one active bit to find the high probability differential characteristics. In this section, we extend the previous work and propose an improved searching strategy to long-round characteristics. We first study the differential property for modular addition i.e. which input difference may lead to the high differential probability. Then, we choose the input difference in the middle round based on the above property to search for long-round differential characteristics with high probability.

3.1   Differential Property for Modular Addition

Lipmaa and Moriai prove that the differential probability through modular addition can be computed by

$$xdp^+ = 2^{-\sum_{i=0}^{n-2} \neg eq(\alpha[i], \beta[i], \gamma[i])} \qquad (5)$$

when the differential $(\alpha, \beta \rightarrow \gamma)$ is possible. According to the definition of $\neg eq(x, y, z)$,

$$eq(x, y, z) = (\neg x \oplus y)(\neg x \oplus z) \tag{6}$$

we can easily get that the value of $eq(x, y, z)$ is 1 if and only if $x = y = z$. In order to obtain the high differential probability through modular addition, we hope that the value of $\sum_{i=0}^{n-2} \neg eq(\alpha[i], \beta[i], \gamma[i])$ is small. To achieve this goal, the number of bits that satisfy $eq(\alpha[i], \beta[i], \gamma[i]) = 1$ should be as many as possible, i.e. the number of bits which satisfy $\alpha[i] = \beta[i] = \gamma[i]$ should be covered large scale.

Besides, considering the diffusion, the input difference with few active bits may be easier to lead to high differential probability, so if we want to find the good differential for modular addition, the number of active bits in input difference should be as fewer as possible. The above phenomenon can be summarized as the following two observations,

Observation 1. To get high differential probability in modular addition, the number of bits in α, β having the same value should be as many as possible.

Observation 2. To get high differential probability in modular addition, the number of non-active bits in α, β should be as many as possible.

Based on the above observations, we try various input differences and compute its best differential probability P through modular addition. As a consequence, we obtain the three classes of input difference which will lead to high probability and less active bits in the output difference. Assuming that $x = (x_{n-1}, ..., x_1, x_0), y = (y_{n-1}, ..., y_1, y_0)$ are input differences for modular addition, #Ac represents the number of active bits in input difference and the ID is the input difference set corresponding to the certain class. The three classes are summarized in Table 1. According to the input difference in Table 1, we desire to decide the input difference which may lead to better differential characteristics in the middle round.

Table 1. The classes for input difference for nodular addition with high probability

Class	#Ac	Input difference set
$P = 1$	1	$ID = \{(x, y) \mid x_{n-1} = 1, y_{n-1} = 0, x_i = y_i = 0, i = 0, 1, ..., n-2\}$
	2	$ID = \{(x, y) \mid x_{n-1} = 1, y_{n-1} = 1, x_i = y_i = 0, i = 0, 1, ..., n-2\}$
$P = \frac{1}{2}$	1	$ID = \{(x, y) \mid x_i = 1, y_i = 0, x_j = y_j = 0, i = 0, 1, ..., n-2, j \neq i\}$
	2	$ID = \{(x, y) \mid x_i = 1, y_i = 1, x_j = y_j = 0, i = 0, 1, ..., n-2, j \neq i\}$
		$ID = \{(x, y) \mid x_i = 1, x_{i-k} = 1, x_j = 0, j \neq i, i-k, y = 0, i = n-1, k-1\}$
		$ID = \{(x, y) \mid x_i = 1, y_{i-k} = 1, x_j = 0, j \neq i, y_l = 0, l \neq i-k, i = n-1, k-1\}$
$P = \frac{1}{4}$	2	$ID = \{(x, y) \mid x_i = 1, x_{i-k} = 1, x_j = 0, j \neq i, i-k, y = 0, i \neq n-1, k-1\}$
		$ID = \{(x, y) \mid x_i = 1, y_{i-k} = 1, x_j = 0, j \neq i, y_l = 0, l \neq i-k, i \neq n-1, k-1\}$

3.2   Improved Searching Strategy for Long-Round Differential Characteristics

With the number of rounds increasing, the solving time for MILP model increases sharply. As a result, it is infeasible to find the best long-round differential characteristics. Inspired by the phenomenon that many optimal characteristics have a special input difference which has few active bits in the middle round, we search for the long-round differential characteristics by Algorithm 1, where S is the set of internal difference corresponding to the input difference for modular addition in Table 1, and $E = E_2 \circ E_1$. Our searching process is based on the Markov cipher assumption [17]. The details are as follow.

Firstly, we choose one value of internal difference $diff$ in S.

Secondly, we build MILP model M_1 and add linear inequalities with respect to XOR-difference for every modular addition, XOR and rotation of r_1-round E_1 as constraints into M_1 . Then we add constraints to fix the value of output difference for r_1-round E_1 to $diff$ to M_1. The constraints corresponding to output difference can help us connect two short-round characteristics perfectly. Besides, we set the objective function according to Theorem 2. Next, we solve M_1 and obtain the best differential characteristic and the corresponding probability p_1 under the above constraints.

Thirdly, MILP model M_2 is built to search r_2-round best differential characteristic and probability p_2 for E_2 under the constraints: the value of input difference is fixed to $diff$.

Finally, r-round differential characteristic can be obtained by connecting r_1-round characteristic with r_2-round characteristic, and the probability p can be computed by $p_1 \cdot p_2$.

We traverse the value of internal difference $diff$ in S to get the max probability p corresponding r-round differential characteristic for E. Generally, we choose $r_1 = r_2 = r/2$ when r is even and we choose $|r_1 - r_2| = 1$ when r is odd.

We use Algorithm 1 to SPECK to search for the long-round characteristics. The results show that more powerful differential characteristics can be found effectively, i.e. if we choose the proper internal difference and search for the short-round differential characteristic forward and backward, we will obtain the good long-round differential characteristics for SPECK family. The experiment results are summarized in Table 2. The results illustrate that it is possible to find good long-round differential characteristics for ARX ciphers in a feasible time with the improved searching strategy. Note the probability in the Table 2 are all the best differential probability for SPECK.

Algorithm 1. Searching good long-round differential characteristics

---

Input: number of rounds r for E, number of rounds r_1 for E_1 , number of rounds r_2 for E_2

Output: differential characteristic DC, differential probability p

1: $p = 0$

2: $DC \leftarrow \emptyset$

3: **for** $diff$ in S:

4:    /*search backward r_1-round characteristic*/

5:    Construct the MILP model M_1 for r_1-round E_1

6:    Add constraints fixed the r_1-round output difference equal to $diff$

7:    Solving M_1 and get the best r_1-round differential probability p_1

8:    /*search forward r_2-round characteristic*/

9:    Construct the MILP model M_2 for r_2-round E_2

10:   Add constraints fixed the input difference equal to $diff$

11:   Solving M_2 and get the best r_2-round differential probability p_2

12:   **if** $p_1 \cdot p_2 > p$:

13:      $p = p_1 \cdot p_2$

14:      $DC \leftarrow r_1 - round\ characteristic || r_2 - round\ characteristics$

15:   **end if**

16:**end for**

17:**return** p, DC

Table 2. The experiment results for SPECK .

Variant	Rounds	Internal difference	r_1, r_2, p_1, p_2	Probability
SPECK32	9	$x_{15} = y_8 = 1$	$r_1 = 4, r_2 = 5, p_1 = 2^{-13}, p_2 = 2^{-17}$	2^{-30}
SPECK48	10	$x_{23} = y_{16} = 1$	$r_1 = 4, r_2 = 6, p_1 = 2^{-15}, p_2 = 2^{-25}$	2^{-40}
SPECK128	9	$x_{63} = y_{56} = 1$	$r_1 = 5, r_2 = 5, p_1 = 2^{-27}, p_2 = 2^{-2}$	2^{-49}

4 Application to Round-Reduced LEA

In this section, we apply the improved searching strategy in Sect. 3 to round-reduced LEA. We would like to find the longer characteristics with higher probability. Note that all of the characteristics are searched with MILP solver Gurobi on a personal computer(Intel(R) Core(TM) i7-6700 CPU @ 3.40 GHz 3.41 GHz,16 GB RAM).

4.1 Description of LEA

LEA is an ARX block cipher designed by Hong et al. [15]. The block size of LEA is 128 bits, the key size has three visions, i.e. 128bits, 192bits and 256 bits. We denote the algorithms by LEA-128, LEA-192 and LEA-256 respectively according to key size.

The encryption rounds r is 24, 28 and 32 for LEA-128, LEA-192 and LEA-256 respectively. Assume that the input of the i-th round is (x^i, y^i, w^i, z^i), output is $(x^{i+1}, y^{i+1}, w^{i+1}, z^{i+1})$, and the round key is $rk^i = (rk_0^i, rk_1^i, rk_2^i, rk_3^i, rk_4^i, rk_5^i)$, $x^i, y^i, w^i, z^i, rk_0^i, rk_1^i, rk_2^i, rk_3^i, rk_4^i, rk_5^i \in F_2^{32}$. The round function for round $i, 0 \le i < r$ is defined as follows:

$$x^{i+1} \leftarrow ((x^i \oplus rk_0^i) \boxplus (y^i \oplus rk_1^i)) \lll 9,$$
$$y^{i+1} \leftarrow ((y^i \oplus rk_2^i) \boxplus (w^i \oplus rk_3^i)) \ggg 5,$$
$$w^{i+1} \leftarrow ((w^i \oplus rk_4^i) \boxplus (z^i \oplus rk_5^i)) \ggg 3,$$
$$z^{i+1} \leftarrow x^i.$$

We take LEA-256 as an example to illustrate the key schedule. Let $k = (k_0, k_1, ..., k_7)$ be a 256-bit key. We set $t_i = k_i, 0 \le i < 8$. Round key $rk^i = (rk_0^i, rk_1^i, rk_2^i, rk_3^i, rk_4^i, rk_5^i), 0 \le i < 32$ are computed by the following relations:

$$t_{6i\,mod\,8} \leftarrow (t_{6i\,mod\,8} \boxplus \delta_{i\,mod\,8} \lll i) \lll 1$$
$$t_{6i+1\,mod\,8} \leftarrow (t_{6i+1\,mod\,8} \boxplus \delta_{i\,mod\,8} \lll i+1) \lll 3$$
$$t_{6i+2\,mod\,8} \leftarrow (t_{6i+2\,mod\,8} \boxplus \delta_{i\,mod\,8} \lll i+2) \lll 6$$
$$t_{6i+3\,mod\,8} \leftarrow (t_{6i+3\,mod\,8} \boxplus \delta_{i\,mod\,8} \lll i+3) \lll 11$$
$$t_{6i+4\,mod\,8} \leftarrow (t_{6i+4\,mod\,8} \boxplus \delta_{i\,mod\,8} \lll i+4) \lll 13$$
$$t_{6i+5\,mod\,8} \leftarrow (t_{6i+5\,mod\,8} \boxplus \delta_{i\,mod\,8} \lll i+5) \lll 17$$
$$rk^i = (t_{6i\,mod\,8}, t_{6i+1\,mod\,8}, t_{6i+2\,mod\,8}, t_{6i+3\,mod\,8}, t_{6i+4\,mod\,8}, t_{6i+5\,mod\,8})$$

where $\delta_i, 0 \le i < 8$ are the constant for generating round keys, which are defined as follows.

$$\delta_0 = 0xc3efe9db, \delta_1 = 0x44626b02,$$
$$\delta_2 = 0x79e27c8a, \delta_3 = 0x78df30ec,$$
$$\delta_4 = 0x715ea49e, \delta_5 = 0xc785da0a,$$
$$\delta_6 = 0xe04ef22a, \delta_7 = 0xe5c40957.$$

The relations between round keys play an important role in reducing complexity in key-recovery process. Figure 1 provides a schematic view on the round function of LEA.

4.2   Characteristics and Differentials of Round-Reduced LEA

Characteristics of Round-Reduced LEA. According to the Algorithm 1 in Sect. 3, we search for the 13-round differential characteristics. In the searching process, we first generate the internal difference set S according to the high probability differential through modular addition in Table 1. Then we divide 13-round LEA denoted by E into 6-round E_1 and 7-round E_2. Traversing the internal difference in S, we found a better 13-round differential characteristic

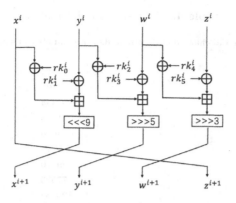

Fig. 1. Round function of LEA

Table 3. The new 13-round differential characteristic for LEA

Rounds	Δx	Δy	Δw	Δz	$\sum log_2 p$
0	0x00000900	0x80000900	0x80402900	0x80402100	
1	0x00000100	0x00020100	0x00000100	0x00000900	
2	0x04000000	0x00001000	0x00000100	0x00000100	
3	0x00600008	0x000001f8	0x00000000	0x04000000	
4	0x40040001	0x40000001	0x00800000	0x00600008	
5	0x08000000	0x0ffc0000	0x00040001	0x40040001	
6	**0x08000000**	**0x08000000**	**0x08000000**	**0x08000000**	−83
7	0x00000000	0x00000000	0x00000000	0x08000000	
8	0x00000000	0x00000000	0x01000000	0x00000000	
9	0x00000000	0x00080000	0x00400000	0x00000000	
10	0x10000000	0x0001e000	0x00040000	0x00000000	
11	0x00800020	0x00000200	0x00008000	0x10000000	
12	0x00044001	0x00000410	0x02001000	0x00100020	
13	0x08882400	0x801000a0	0x00500204	0x00044001	−126

than the best previous results with the following internal difference:

$$\Delta x_m = 0x08000000$$

$$\Delta y_m = 0x08000000$$

$$\Delta w_m = 0x08000000$$

$$\Delta z_m = 0x08000000$$

where $(\Delta x_m, \Delta y_m, \Delta w_m, \Delta z_m)$ is the internal difference, i.e. it represents the output difference for 6-round E_1 and the input difference for 7-round E_2. With this internal difference, we can get the following 13-round differential characteristic with probability of 2^{-126}, which is connected by 6-round characteristic with probability of 2^{-83} and 7-round characteristic with probability of 2^{-43}. The details of this characteristic are shown in Table 3.

Table 4. The results for differential

Differenctial characteristic probability	the number of solutions
2^{-126}	8
2^{-127}	16
2^{-128}	108
2^{-129}	354
2^{-130}	1186
2^{-131}	3660
2^{-132}	10713
2^{-133}	29270
2^{-134}	77503
2^{-135}	196884
2^{-136}	481462
2^{-137}	1146163
2^{-138}	2649128
2^{-139}	5967464
2^{-140}	13142204
2^{-141}	28328269
Differential probability	$2^{-113.59}$

Differentials of Round-Reduced LEA. Besides, we analyse the differential probability for 13-round LEA. Based on the above 13-round differential characteristic connecting by 6-round characteristic with 7-round characteristic with the internal difference $(0x08000000, 0x08000000, 0x08000000, 0x08000000)$, We fix the input difference, internal difference and output difference to search for all 13-round differential characteristics satisfied the above constraints. The differential probability can be obtained by the following step,

Step 1: Adding the constraints to fix the input difference and output difference equal to the input difference for 13-round differential characteristic, i.e. $(0x00000900, 0x80000900, 0x80402900, 0x80402100)$ and internal difference , i.e. $(0x08000000, 0x08000000, 0x08000000, 0x08000000)$ respectively to the 6-round MILP model M_1. Then, adding constraints to limit the differential probability which is equal to 2^{-83-N} and searching all the solutions satisfying above constraints by Gurobi and recording the number of solutions.

Step 2: Adding constraints to fix input difference and output difference to 7-round MILP model M_2 similarly to step1. Then, adding constraints to limit the differential probability which is equal to 2^{-43-N}, searching and recording the number of solutions. In our searching process, we take the value of N from 0 to 15.

Step 3: Connecting two short-round characteristics to obtain the 13-round characteristics and recording the number of 13-round characteristics satisfying the certain probability. The details of our searching results are shown in Table 4.

Comparison. Table 5 compares the differential of round-reduced LEA we found with the previous results. We find a 13-round differential with the probability $2^{-113.59}$ higher than the previous best result.

Table 5. Comparison of our differential of LEA with previous best one

#Rounds	characteristic probability	differential probability	Reference
13	2^{-127}	$2^{-115.86}$	[2]
13	2^{-126}	$2^{-113.59}$	**This paper**

4.3 Differential Attacks on Round-Reduced LEA

According to the round function and the output difference for new 13-round differential, we can easily obtain the representation of the output difference of 14-round and 15-round for LEA, and the details are shown in Fig. 2, where the $0x$ represents hexadecimal, $0b$ is binary and $*$ represent the value of this bit can take value 0 or 1, $(\Delta x^i, \Delta y^i, \Delta w^i, \Delta z^i)$ is the input difference of the i-th round.

14-Round Key-Recovery for LEA-128 and LEA-192. For convenience, we first refine relations between $(x^{13}, y^{13}, w^{13}, z^{13})$ and $(x^{14}, y^{14}, w^{14}, z^{14})$ from round function. Then, we mount the key-recovery on 14-round LEA-128 and 14-round LEA-192.

Relations in Round Function. From the round function of LEA, we can easily gain the following relations.

$$\mathcal{L}_1 : x^{13} = z^{14}$$
$$\mathcal{L}_2 : y^{13} \oplus rk_1^{13} = (x^{14} \ggg 9 \boxminus (x^{13} \oplus rk_0^{13}))$$
$$\mathcal{L}_3 : w^{13} \oplus rk_3^{13} = (y^{14} \lll 5 \boxminus (y^{13} \oplus rk_1^{13} \oplus (rk_1^{13} \oplus rk_2^{13})))$$
$$\mathcal{L}_4 : z^{13} \oplus rk_5^{13} = (w^{14} \lll 3 \boxminus (w^{13} \oplus rk_3^{13} \oplus (rk_3^{13} \oplus rk_4^{13})))$$

Key-Recovery. The key-recovery is divided into collection phase and key-guessing phase. The details of 14-round key-recovery are as follows,

Collection Phase:

1. Choose 2^N pairs (P_i, P_i') such that their difference is $P_i \oplus P_i' = (\Delta x^0, \Delta y^0, \Delta w^0, \Delta z^0)$.

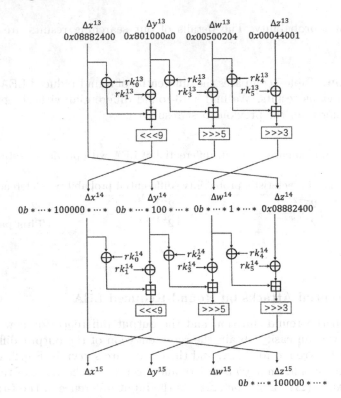

Fig. 2. Two rounds of LEA

2. Encrypt 2^N pairs (P_i, P_i') to ciphertext pairs (C_i, C_i') with a 14-round LEA encryption oracle, where $C_i = E_k(P_i), C_i' = E_k(P_i')$. Derive the output difference and check whether the difference meets the representation of $(\Delta x^{14}, \Delta y^{14}, \Delta w^{14}, \Delta z^{14})$, i.e. $\Delta x^{14} = 0b * \ldots * 100000 * \ldots *$, $\Delta y^{14} = 0b * \ldots * 100 * \ldots *$, $\Delta w^{14} = 0b * \ldots * 1 * \ldots *$ and $\Delta z^{14} = 0x08882400$. If it is not satisfied the above difference form, we discard the corresponding pairs and store the remaining pairs in a list C_0. Through this step, the number of remaining pairs is 2^{N-42}.

Key-Guessing Phase:

In the following, we focus on recovering the key bits: $(rk_0^{13})_{5-31}$, $(rk_1^{13} \oplus rk_2^{13})_{2-31}$, $rk_3^{13} \oplus rk_4^{13}$.

Initialize a list of $2^{89} counters$.
  1. Guess the 27 bits $(rk_0^{13})_{5-31}$,
     – Partially decrypt (C_i, C_i') in list C_0 to the state of y_{13} keyed by rk_1^{13} by $\mathcal{L}_1$ and $\mathcal{L}_2$, and derive the value of Δy^{13}. If $\Delta y^{13} = 0x801000a0$ is not hold, the corresponding pairs should be discarded. Then, store

the remaining pairs in a list C_1 and the number of remaining pairs is $2^{N-42-26} = 2^{N-68}$.

2. Guess the value of 30 bits $(rk_1^{13} \oplus rk_2^{13})_{2-31}$,
   - Partially decrypt (C_i, C_i') in list C_1 to the state of w_{13} keyed by rk_3^{13} by $\mathcal{L}_3$, and derive the value of Δw^{13}. If $\Delta w^{13} = 0x00500204$ is not hold, the corresponding pairs should be discarded. Then, store the remaining pairs in a list C_2 and the number of remaining pairs is $2^{N-68-29} = 2^{N-97}$.

3. Guess the value of the 32 bits $rk_3^{13} \oplus rk_4^{13}$,
   - Partially decrypt (C_i, C_i') in list C_2 to the state of z_{13} keyed by rk_5^{13} by $\mathcal{L}_4$, and derive the value of Δz^{13}. If $\Delta z^{13} = 0x00044001$ is hold, then increment the counter for the current key candidate. Otherwise, the corresponding pairs should be discarded.

The differential probability for 13-round LEA is $2^{-113.59}$. We hope that the key as potentially correct has a counter of at least two, so we take the value of N as 114.59.

Complexity. When the value of N is 114.59, our attack require $2^{114.59}$ chosen plaintext pairs. So the data complexity is $2^{114.59}$. The time complexity can be computed as follows. In the collection phase, 2^N 14-round LEA encryptions are needed, then in the key-guessing phase $2^{N-42} \cdot 2^{27} \cdot \frac{1}{14}$ 14-round LEA encryptions, $2^{N-68} \cdot 2^{57} \cdot \frac{1}{14}$ 14-round LEA encryptions and $2^{N-97} \cdot 2^{89} \cdot \frac{1}{14}$ 14-round LEA encryptions are needed in step 1, 2 and 3 respectively. When $N = 114.59$, the total time complexity is about $2^{114.59}$ 14-round LEA encryptions. In the key-guessing phase, 2^{89} counters are needed, so the memory complexity is 2^{89}.

15-Round Key-Recovery for LEA-256. In key-recovery for 15-round LEA-256, some properties in key schedule help us saving 32-bit key guessing. In the following, we first extract the relations between round keys and summarize the relations between $(x^{13}, y^{13}, w^{13}, z^{13})$, $(x^{14}, y^{14}, w^{14}, z^{14})$ and $(x^{15}, y^{15}, w^{15}, z^{15})$. Then, we introduce the details for key-recovery.

Property in Key Schedule. We study the property in key schedule for LEA and obtain the relations between round key rk^{13} and round key rk^{14}. We can easily obtain the following relations from the key schedule of LEA-256, when $i = 13$,

$$t_6 \leftarrow (t_7 \boxplus \delta_5 \lll 13) \lll 1$$
$$t_7 \leftarrow (t_6 \boxplus \delta_5 \lll 14) \lll 3$$
$$t_0 \leftarrow (t_0 \boxplus \delta_5 \lll 15) \lll 6$$
$$t_1 \leftarrow (t_1 \boxplus \delta_5 \lll 16) \lll 11$$
$$t_2 \leftarrow (t_2 \boxplus \delta_5 \lll 17) \lll 13$$
$$t_3 \leftarrow (t_3 \boxplus \delta_5 \lll 18) \lll 17$$
$$rk^{13} = (t_6, t_7, t_0, t_1, t_2, t_3)$$

when $i = 14$,

$$t_4 \leftarrow (t_4 \boxplus \delta_6 \lll 14) \lll 1$$
$$t_5 \leftarrow (t_5 \boxplus \delta_6 \lll 15) \lll 3$$
$$t_6 \leftarrow (t_6 \boxplus \delta_6 \lll 16) \lll 6$$
$$t_7 \leftarrow (t_7 \boxplus \delta_6 \lll 17) \lll 11$$
$$t_0 \leftarrow (t_0 \boxplus \delta_6 \lll 18) \lll 13$$
$$t_1 \leftarrow (t_1 \boxplus \delta_6 \lll 19) \lll 17$$
$$rk^{14} = (t_4, t_5, t_6, t_7, t_0, t_1)$$

We obtain that $rk_2^{14}, rk_3^{14}, rk_4^{14}, rk_5^{14}$ can be computed by $rk_0^{13}, rk_1^{13}, rk_2^{13}, rk_3^{13}$.

From the round function, we get the following relations,

$\mathcal{L}_5 : x^{14} = z^{15}$

$\mathcal{L}_6 : y^{14} \oplus rk_1^{14} = (x^{15} \ggg 9 \boxminus (x^{14} \oplus rk_0^{14}))$

$\mathcal{L}_7 : w^{14} \oplus rk_3^{14} = (y^{15} \lll 5 \boxminus (y^{14} \oplus rk_1^{14} \oplus (rk_1^{14} \oplus rk_2^{14})))$

$\mathcal{L}_8 : z^{14} \oplus rk_5^{14} = (w^{15} \lll 3 \boxminus (w^{14} \oplus rk_3^{14} \oplus (rk_3^{14} \oplus rk_4^{14})))$

$\mathcal{L}_9 : x^{13} = z^{14}$

$\mathcal{L}_{10} : y^{13} \oplus rk_1^{13} = (x^{14} \ggg 9 \boxminus (z^{14} \oplus rk_5^{14} \oplus (rk_5^{14} \oplus rk_0^{13})))$

$\mathcal{L}_{11} : w^{13} \oplus rk_3^{13} = (((y^{14} \oplus rk_1^{14}) \oplus rk_1^{14}) \lll 5 \boxminus (y^{13} \oplus rk_1^{13} \oplus (rk_1^{13} \oplus rk_2^{13})))$

$\mathcal{L}_{12} : z^{13} \oplus rk_5^{13} = (((w^{14} \oplus rk_3^{14}) \oplus rk_3^{14}) \lll 3 \boxminus (w^{13} \oplus rk_3^{13} \oplus (rk_3^{13} \oplus rk_4^{13})))$

Key-Recovery. The details of 15-round key-recovery for LEA-256 are as follows. We use $\Delta_{i_0,i_1,...,i_p}$ to represent the difference whose active bits are in i_0-th, i_1-th,...,i_p-th bit.

Collection Phase:

1. Choose 2^N pairs (P_i, P_i') such that their difference is $P_i \oplus P_i' = (\Delta x^0, \Delta y^0, \Delta w^0, \Delta z^0)$.
2. Encrypt 2^N pairs (P_i, P_i') to ciphertext pairs (C_i, C_i') with a 15 round LEA encryption oracle, where $C_i = E_k(P_i), C_i' = E_k(P_i')$. Derive the output difference and check whether the difference meets the representation of $(\Delta x^{15}, \Delta y^{15}, \Delta w^{15}, \Delta z^{15})$, i.e. $\Delta z^{15} = 0b * ... * 100000 * ...*$. If it is not satisfied the above difference form, we discard the corresponding pairs. Then store the remaining pairs in a list D_0. Through this step, the number of remaining pairs is 2^{N-6}.

Key-Guessing Phase:

In the following, we focus on recovering the key bits: rk_0^{14}, $rk_1^{14} \oplus rk_2^{14}$, rk_1^{14}, $rk_3^{14} \oplus rk_4^{14}$, $(rk_5^{14} \oplus rk_0^{13})_{5-31}$, $(rk_1^{13} \oplus rk_2^{13})_{2-31}$, $rk_3^{13} \oplus rk_4^{13}$.

Initialize a list of $2^{217} counters$.

1. Guess the value of the 32 bits rk_0^{14},

   Partially decrypt (D_i, D_i') in list D_0 to the state of y_{14} keyed by rk_1^{14} by $\mathcal{L}_5$ and $\mathcal{L}_6$, and derive the value of Δy^{14}. If $\Delta y^{14} = \Delta_{26,27,28}$ is not hold, the corresponding pairs should be discarded. Then, store the remaining pairs in a list D_1 and the number of remaining pairs is $2^{N-6-3} = 2^{N-9}$.

2. Guess the value of the 32 bits $rk_1^{14} \oplus rk_2^{14}$,

   Partially decrypt (D_i, D_i') in list D_1 to the state of w_{14} keyed by rk_3^{14} by $\mathcal{L}_7$, and derive the value of Δw^{14}. If $\Delta w^{14} = \Delta_{28}$ is not hold, the corresponding pairs should be discarded. Then, store the remaining pairs in a list D_2 and the number of remaining pairs is $2^{N-9-1} = 2^{N-10}$.

3. Guess the value of the 32 bits $rk_3^{14} \oplus rk_4^{14}$,

   Partially decrypt (D_i, D_i') in list D_2 to the state of z_{14} keyed by rk_5^{14} by $\mathcal{L}_8$, and derive the value of Δz^{14}. If $\Delta z^{14} = 0x08882400$ is not hold, the corresponding pairs should be discarded. Then, store the remaining pairs in a list D_3 and the number of remaining pairs is $2^{N-10-32} = 2^{N-42}$.

4. Guess the value of the 27 bits $(rk_5^{14} \oplus rk_0^{13})_{5-31}$,

   Partially decrypt (D_i, D_i') in list D_3 to the state of y_{13} keyed by rk_1^{13} by $\mathcal{L}_{10}$, and derive the value of Δy^{13}. If $\Delta y^{13} = 0x801000a0$ is not hold, the corresponding pairs should be discarded. Then, store the remaining pairs in a list D_4 and the number of remaining pairs is $2^{N-42-26} = 2^{N-68}$.

5. Guess the value of the 30 bits $(rk_1^{13} \oplus rk_2^{13})_{2-31}$ and 32 bits rk_1^{14},

   Partially decrypt (D_i, D_i') in list D_4 to the state of w_{13} keyed by rk_3^{13} by $\mathcal{L}_{11}$, and derive the value of Δw^{13}. If $\Delta w^{13} = 0x00500204$ is not hold, the corresponding pairs should be discarded. Then, store the remaining pairs in a list D_5 and the number of remaining pairs is $2^{N-68-29} = 2^{N-97}$.

6. Guess the value of the 32 bits $rk_3^{13} \oplus rk_4^{13}$,

   Partially decrypt (D_i, D_i') in list D_5 to the state of z_{13} keyed by rk_5^{13} by $\mathcal{L}_{12}$, and derive the value of Δz^{13}. If $\Delta z^{13} = 0x00044001$ is hold, then increment the counter for the current key candidate. Otherwise, the corresponding pairs should be discarded.

In the above procedure, the following should be noted: when the value of $z^{13} \oplus rk_5^{13}$ are guessed, the value of key rk_3^{14} is needed. Next, we explain why the guess of rk_3^{14} is omitted. Using the property extracted from key schedule, we can see that rk_3^{14} can be deduced by the value of rk_1^{13} and rk_4^{14} can be computed by rk_2^{13}. Before the value of z^{13} are guessed, we have obtained the value of $rk_1^{13} \oplus rk_2^{13}$ and $rk_3^{14} \oplus rk_4^{14}$.

$$rk_3^{14} = (rk_1^{13} \boxplus \delta_6 \lll 17) \lll 11$$
$$rk_4^{14} = (rk_2^{13} \boxplus \delta_6 \lll 18) \lll 13$$
$$keyguess_1 = rk_3^{14} \oplus rk_4^{14}$$
$$keyguess_2 = rk_1^{13} \oplus rk_2^{13}$$
$$\delta_6 = 0xe04ef22a$$

where $keyguess_1, keyguess_2$ are the value that have been guessed. So we have obtained four equations with four variables. As a result, the value of rk_3^{14} can be easily determined, which allows saving the guessing of a 32-bit key world directly.

The differential probability for 13-round LEA is $2^{-113.59}$. We hope that the key as potentially correct has a counter of at least two, so we take the value of N as 114.59.

Complexity . When the value of N is 114.59, our attack require $2^{114.59}$ chosen plaintext pairs. So the data complexity is $2^{114.59}$. The time complexity can be computed as follows. In the collection phase, 2^N 15-round LEA encryption are needed, then in the key-guessing phase $2^{N-6} \cdot 2^{32} \cdot \frac{1}{15}$ 15-round LEA encryptions, $2^{N-9} \cdot 2^{64} \cdot \frac{1}{15}$ 15-round LEA encryptions , $2^{N-10} \cdot 2^{96} \cdot \frac{1}{15}$ 15-round LEA encryptions, $2^{N-42} \cdot 2^{123} \cdot \frac{2}{15}$ 15-round LEA encryptions, $2^{N-68} \cdot 2^{185} \cdot \frac{2}{15}$ 15-round LEA encryptions, $2^{N-97} \cdot 2^{217} \cdot \frac{2}{15}$ 15-round LEA encryptions, are needed in step 1, 2, 3, 4, 5 and 6 respectively. When $N = 114.59$, the total time complexity is about $2^{231.69}$ 15-round LEA encryptions. In the key-guessing phase, 2^{217} counters are needed, so the memory complexity is 2^{217}.

The time, data and memory complexity of key-recovery for 14-round LEA-128, 14-round LEA-192 and 15-round LEA-256 are shown in Table 6.

Table 6. Comparison of our attack complexity of LEA with the previous one

Variant	#Rounds	Time complexity	Data complexity	Memory complexity	Reference
LEA-128	14	$2^{124.79}$	$2^{124.79}$	2^{22}	[21]
LEA-128	14	$2^{114.59}$	$2^{114.59}$	2^{89}	This paper
LEA-192	14	$2^{124.79}$	$2^{124.79}$	2^{22}	[21]
LEA-192	14	$2^{114.59}$	$2^{114.59}$	2^{89}	This paper
LEA-256	15	$2^{252.79}$	$2^{124.79}$	2^{22}	[21]
LEA-256	15	$2^{231.69}$	$2^{114.59}$	2^{217}	This paper

5 Conclusion

In this paper, we apply Fu's MILP framework to search for differential characteristics of ARX ciphers. We extend the Song's long-round differential characteristics searching strategy. Compared to selecting the input difference of the middle round with only one active bit in previous work, we carefully choose the internal difference depending on the differential property for modular addition. Using our improved searching strategy, we find a better 13-round differential characteristic for LEA with probability of 2^{-126}. Furthermore, we obtain a more powerful 13-round differential with probability $2^{-113.59}$. Moreover, using the relations derived by the key schedule of LEA, we mount key-recovery on 14-round LEA-128, 14-round LEA-192 and 15-round LEA-256.

Acknowledgement. The authors would like to thank Dr. Rishiraj Bhattacharyya and the anonymous reviewers for their detailed and very helpful comments and suggestions to improve this article. This work is supported by the National Natural Science Foundation of China (No. 62072445).

References

1. Andreeva, E., Mennink, B., Preneel, B., Škrobot, M.: Security analysis and comparison of the SHA-3 finalists BLAKE, Grøstl, JH, Keccak, and Skein. In: Mitrokotsa, A., Vaudenay, S. (eds.) AFRICACRYPT 2012. LNCS, vol. 7374, pp. 287–305. Springer, Heidelberg (2012). https://doi.org/10.1007/978-3-642-31410-0_18
2. Bagherzadeh, E., Ahmadian, Z.: Milp-based automatic differential search for LEA and HIGHT block ciphers. IET Inf. Secur. **14**(5), 595–603 (2020)
3. Beaulieu, R., Shors, D., Smith, J., Clark, S.T., Weeks, B., Wingers, L.: The SIMON and SPECK familiies of lightweight block ciphers. Technical report, Cryptology ePrint Archive, Report 2013/404, (2013)
4. Beierle, C., et al.: Alzette: a 64-Bit ARX-box. In: Micciancio, D., Ristenpart, T. (eds.) CRYPTO 2020. LNCS, vol. 12172, pp. 419–448. Springer, Cham (2020). https://doi.org/10.1007/978-3-030-56877-1_15
5. Beierle, C., et al.: Lightweight AEAD and hashing using the sparkle permutation family. IACR Trans. Symmetric Cryptol. **2020**(S1), 208–261 (2020)
6. Bernstein, D.J.: The salsa20 family of stream ciphers. In: Robshaw, M., Billet, O. (eds.) New Stream Cipher Designs. LNCS, vol. 4986, pp. 84–97. Springer, Heidelberg (2008). https://doi.org/10.1007/978-3-540-68351-3_8
7. Bernstein, D.J.: The salsa20 family of stream ciphers. In: Robshaw, M., Billet, O. (eds.) New Stream Cipher Designs. LNCS, vol. 4986, pp. 84–97. Springer, Heidelberg (2008). https://doi.org/10.1007/978-3-540-68351-3_8
8. Biham, E., Shamir, A.: Differential cryptanalysis of des-like cryptosystems. J. Cryptol. **4**(1), 3–72 (1991)
9. Biryukov, A., Velichkov, V.: Automatic search for differential trails in ARX ciphers. In: Benaloh, J. (ed.) CT-RSA 2014. LNCS, vol. 8366, pp. 227–250. Springer, Cham (2014). https://doi.org/10.1007/978-3-319-04852-9_12
10. Biryukov, A., Velichkov, V., Le Corre, Y.: Automatic search for the best trails in ARX: application to block cipher SPECK. In: Peyrin, T. (ed.) FSE 2016. LNCS, vol. 9783, pp. 289–310. Springer, Heidelberg (2016). https://doi.org/10.1007/978-3-662-52993-5_15
11. Aumasson, J.-P., Çalık, Ç., Meier, W., Özen, O., Phan, R.C.-W., Varıcı, K.: Improved cryptanalysis of skein. In: Matsui, M. (ed.) ASIACRYPT 2009. LNCS, vol. 5912, pp. 542–559. Springer, Heidelberg (2009). https://doi.org/10.1007/978-3-642-10366-7_32

12. Dinu, D., Perrin, L., Udovenko, A., Velichkov, V., Großschädl, J., Biryukov, A.: Design strategies for ARX with provable bounds: SPARX and LAX. In: Cheon, J.H., Takagi, T. (eds.) ASIACRYPT 2016. LNCS, vol. 10031, pp. 484–513. Springer, Heidelberg (2016). https://doi.org/10.1007/978-3-662-53887-6_18

13. Dinur, I.: Improved differential cryptanalysis of round-reduced speck. In: Joux, A., Youssef, A. (eds.) SAC 2014. LNCS, vol. 8781, pp. 147–164. Springer, Cham (2014). https://doi.org/10.1007/978-3-319-13051-4_9

14. Fu, K., Wang, M., Guo, Y., Sun, S., Hu, L.: MILP-based automatic search algorithms for differential and linear trails for speck. In: Peyrin, T. (ed.) FSE 2016. LNCS, vol. 9783, pp. 268–288. Springer, Heidelberg (2016). https://doi.org/10.1007/978-3-662-52993-5_14

15. Hong, D., Lee, J.-K., Kim, D.-C., Kwon, D., Ryu, K.H., Lee, D.-G.: LEA: a 128-bit block cipher for fast encryption on common processors. In: Kim, Y., Lee, H., Perrig, A. (eds.) WISA 2013. LNCS, vol. 8267, pp. 3–27. Springer, Cham (2014). https://doi.org/10.1007/978-3-319-05149-9_1

16. Hong, D., et al.: HIGHT: a new block cipher suitable for low-resource device. In: Goubin, L., Matsui, M. (eds.) CHES 2006. LNCS, vol. 4249, pp. 46–59. Springer, Heidelberg (2006). https://doi.org/10.1007/11894063_4

17. Lai, X., Massey, J.L., Murphy, S.: Markov ciphers and differential cryptanalysis. In: Davies, D.W. (ed.) EUROCRYPT 1991. LNCS, vol. 547, pp. 17–38. Springer, Heidelberg (1991). https://doi.org/10.1007/3-540-46416-6_2

18. Lipmaa, H., Moriai, S.: Efficient algorithms for computing differential properties of addition. In: Matsui, M. (ed.) FSE 2001. LNCS, vol. 2355, pp. 336–350. Springer, Heidelberg (2002). https://doi.org/10.1007/3-540-45473-X_28

19. Mouha, N., Mennink, B., Herrewege, A.V., Watanabe, D., Preneel, B., Verbauwhede, I.: Chaskey: an efficient MAC algorithm for 32-bit microcontrollers. In: IACR Cryptology. ePrint Arch., pp. 386 (2014)

20. Nicky Mouha and Bart Preneel. Towards finding optimal differential characteristics for ARX. Technical report, Cryptology ePrint Archive, Report 2013/328 (2013)

21. Song, L., Huang, Z., Yang, Q.: Automatic differential analysis of ARX block ciphers with application to SPECK and LEA. In: Liu, J.K., Steinfeld, R. (eds.) ACISP 2016. LNCS, vol. 9723, pp. 379–394. Springer, Cham (2016). https://doi.org/10.1007/978-3-319-40367-0_24

22. Soos, M., Nohl, K., Castelluccia, C.: Extending SAT solvers to cryptographic problems. In: Kullmann, O. (ed.) SAT 2009. LNCS, vol. 5584, pp. 244–257. Springer, Heidelberg (2009). https://doi.org/10.1007/978-3-642-02777-2_24

23. Sun, S., Hu, L., Wang, P., Qiao, K., Ma, X., Song, L.: Automatic security evaluation and (related-key) differential characteristic search: application to SIMON, PRESENT, LBlock, DES(L) and other bit-oriented block ciphers. In: Sarkar, P., Iwata, T. (eds.) ASIACRYPT 2014. LNCS, vol. 8873, pp. 158–178. Springer, Heidelberg (2014). https://doi.org/10.1007/978-3-662-45611-8_9

24. Kaps, J.-P.: Chai-tea, cryptographic hardware implementations of xTEA. In: Chowdhury, D.R., Rijmen, V., Das, A. (eds.) INDOCRYPT 2008. LNCS, vol. 5365, pp. 363–375. Springer, Heidelberg (2008). https://doi.org/10.1007/978-3-540-89754-5_28

Implementing Grover Oracle for Lightweight Block Ciphers Under Depth Constraints

Subodh Bijwe[1], Amit Kumar Chauhan[2(✉)], and Somitra Kumar Sanadhya[2]

[1] Independent Researcher, Mumbai, India
[2] Indian Institute of Technology Jodhpur, Jodhpur, India
akcindia.macs@gmail.com, somitra@iitj.ac.in

Abstract. Grover's search algorithm allows a quantum attack against block ciphers by searching for an n-bit secret key in time $O(2^{n/2})$. In the PQC standardization process, NIST defined the security categories by imposing the upper bound on the depth of the quantum circuit of the Grover oracle. In this work, we study quantum key search attacks on lightweight block ciphers under depth constraints. We design optimized quantum circuits for GIFT, SKINNY, and SATURNIN and enumerate the quantum resources to implement the Grover oracle in terms of the number of qubits, Clifford+T gates, and circuit depth. We also give the concrete cost of Grover oracle for these ciphers in both the gate-count and depth-times-width cost models. We then present the cost estimates of Grover-based key search attacks on these ciphers under NIST's depth constraints. We also release Q# implementations of the full Grover oracle for all the variants of GIFT, SKINNY, and SATURNIN to automatically reproduce our quantum resource estimates.

Keywords: Quantum cryptanalysis · Grover's algorithm · Lightweight block ciphers · GIFT · SKINNY · SATURNIN · Q#

1 Introduction

The seminal work by Shor [25] shows that a sufficiently large quantum computer would solve the problems of integer factorization and discrete logarithm in a polynomial time. Consequently, the hugely deployed asymmetric cryptosystems such as RSA, ECDSA, and ECDH would become insecure. In contrast, symmetric cryptosystems like block ciphers and hash functions are widely considered post-quantum secure. Grover's algorithm [10] provides a quadratic speedup to exhaustive key search attacks against an ideal block cipher. The conventional wisdom suggests that doubling the key size of the block cipher will make it post-quantum secure. However, this only gives a rough idea of the security penalties that quantum computers impose on symmetric cryptographic primitives, mainly because the cost of evaluating Grover's oracle is often ignored. It is thus essential to know the actual cost of quantum algorithms for the specific parameters that provide concrete security measurements.

© The Author(s), under exclusive license to Springer Nature Switzerland AG 2022
K. Nguyen et al. (Eds.): ACISP 2022, LNCS 13494, pp. 85–105, 2022.
https://doi.org/10.1007/978-3-031-22301-3_5

In its call for proposals to PQC standardization process [22], NIST proposes security categories based on the concrete cost of quantum resources(quantum gates, and circuit depth and width) for exhaustive key search on the block cipher AES and collision search for the hash function SHA-3. Since the total gate count of Grover's algorithm increases with parallelization, NIST imposes a restriction on the maximum depth of a quantum circuit, called MAXDEPTH (ranges from 2^{40} to 2^{96}). For a meaningful definition of the security categories, NIST derives gate cost estimates from the gate-level descriptions of the Grover oracle for key search on AES by Grassl et al. [9]. They gave Grover's key search cost estimates on AES by minimizing the circuit width, i.e., the number of qubits needed. Almazrooie et al. [1] improved the quantum circuit of AES-128 by reducing the total number of Toffoli gates. Langenberg et al. [20] proposed an optimized quantum circuit of AES S-box based on the work by Boyar and Peralta [6] that further reduces the total number of Toffoli gates. Zou et al. [29] further reduced the number of qubits needed to design the quantum circuit of AES by introducing an optimized implementation of the inverse S-box operation.

Recently, block ciphers other than AES have also been considered. Schlieper [23] presents the in-place implementation of Gimli cipher by conducting XOR operations after performing ANDs and ORs. Anand et al. [3] studied SIMON intending to verify the implementation via quantum simulations. Jang et al. [13] estimated quantum resources required for running Grover on SPECK. Jang et al. [12] evaluated quantum resources for Korean block ciphers, including HIGHT, LEA, and CHAM. Anand et al. [2] studied the quantum search attacks on the feedback shift register based ciphers like Grain, TinyJambu, LIZARD. Jang et al. [14] studied the block cipher PRESENT and GIFT by applying Grover's algorithm to its quantum circuit. However, they provided the cost of Grover-based key search attacks without considering the depth restriction.

In a nutshell, most previous works focus on reducing the number of T gates and qubits in their quantum circuit implementation. In a different direction of work, Kim et al. [19] discussed time-space trade-offs of quantum resources needed for key search on block ciphers and applied their methods on AES as an example. Recently, Jaques et al. [15] studied the quantum key-search attacks on AES under NIST's MAXDEPTH constraint [22] at the cost of a few qubits. Finally, they proposed a circuit that minimizes the (a) gate-count and (b) depth-times-width cost metrics under the MAXDEPTH constraint. As a working example, they implemented the full Grover's oracle for key search on AES and LowMC in Q# quantum programming language developed by Microsoft [26].

1.1 Our Contributions

In this paper, we present quantum implementations of the full Grover oracle for key search on lightweight block ciphers such as GIFT, SKINNY, and SATURNIN in Q#. We first design quantum circuits for each of the operations in the block ciphers, primarily focusing on the S-box and the invertible linear map (permutation). We use an in-place PLU decomposition method for implementing invertible linear maps. We then derive the cost estimates for the full ciphers regarding the number of qubits, Clifford+T gates, and overall circuit depth, including T-depth.

Our quantum circuit implementations do not aim for the lowest possible number of qubits. Instead, following the work [15], we focus on minimizing the gate-count and depth-times-width cost metrics for the quantum circuit under depth constraints. The gate-count metric is relevant for security categories defined by NIST in the PQC competition. When the quantum error correction is deployed, the depth-times-width cost metric is a more realistic measure of quantum resources. Zalka [28] showed that Grover's algorithm does not parallelize well. Therefore, minimizing depth rather than width is crucial to make the most out of the available depth.

We then present our results for quantum key search attacks against all the variants of GIFT, SKINNY, and SATURNIN ciphers under NIST's MAXDEPTH constraints. The source code of Q# implementations of Grover oracles for all the variants of GIFT, SKINNY, and SATURNIN will be publicly available[1] under a free license. It allows independent verification of our results, further investigation of different trade-offs and cost models, and re-costing as the Q# compiler improves further.

1.2 Organization of the Paper

In Sect. 2, we review basic facts concerning quantum computation and cost metrics for the quantum circuit. In Sect. 3, we examine how the Grover search works with parallelization improving upon the generic Grover-based attacks. Sections 4, 5 and 6 describe the quantum circuits for block ciphers GIFT, SKINNY and SATURNIN, and Sect. 7 provides the resource estimates for their full encryption circuits. In Sect. 8, we estimate the resources needed for quantum key search attack against GIFT, SKINNY, and SATURNIN in both the gate count and depth-time-width cost models. Section 9 concludes this work.

2 Preliminaries

Throughout this paper, we assume that readers have basic knowledge about quantum computation (see textbooks such as [21] for an introduction).

2.1 Fault-Tolerant Gate Set

We adopt the computation model presented in [16]. The quantum circuits operating on qubits are composed of Clifford+T gates, which form a commonly used universal fault-tolerant set of gates by several families of quantum error-correcting codes. The primitive gates consist of single-qubit Clifford (denoted as 1qClifford) gates, controlled-NOT (CNOT) gates, T gates, and measurements. We make the standard assumption of full parallelism, meaning that a quantum

---

[1] https://github.com/amitcrypto/LWC-Q.

circuit can apply any number of gates simultaneously as long as these gates act on disjoint sets of qubits [11].

All quantum circuits for GIFT, SKINNY, and SATURNIN described in this paper are designed and tested in the Q# programming language [26]. Q# allows to describe circuits in terms of single-qubit gates (the Pauli gates X, Y, Z, the Hadamard gate H, the phase gate S, the T gate, general rotation gates), and controlled gates. Furthermore, it makes classical control logic around quantum operations transparent so that loops and conditional statements based on measurement output can be easily expressed. The Q# compiler allows us to compute circuit depth automatically by moving gates around through a circuit if the qubits it acts on were previously idle. Further, Q# enables the circuit to allocate auxiliary qubits as needed, which adds new qubits initialized to $|0\rangle$. If an auxiliary qubit is returned to state $|0\rangle$ after it has been operated on, the circuit can release it. Such a qubit is no longer entangled with the state used for computation, and the circuit can now maintain or measure it.

The asymptotic cost of Grover's algorithm for searching an n-bit secret key is $O(2^{n/2})$. However, it is not easy to translate the asymptotic cost to an exact number for any practical design. This is further complicated due to the different costs of quantum gates used in implementing Grover's oracle. In particular, most of the previous works [1,9,20] assumed that T gates constitute the main cost. However, Fowler [8] argued that T gates are exceptionally expensive for a surface code. It is quite possible that T gates might be cheaper for some other error-correcting code families.

In implementing the S-box, we often use Toffoli gates to realize the functionality of the classical AND gate. The Toffoli gate can be implemented using Selinger's approach [24] which requires 7 T gates, 16 CNOT gates, 2 single-qubit Clifford gates, and 4 ancillae with an overall depth of 7. For implementation of quantum AND gate in terms of Clifford+T gates, we use a combination of Selinger's [24] and Jones' [18] circuits. Quantum circuit of AND gate uses 4 T gates and 11 Clifford gates in T-depth 1 and total depth 8 [15].

2.2   Cost Metrics for Quantum Circuit

For meaningful cost analysis, we assume an adversary has fixed constraints on their total available resources and a specific cost metric they wish to minimize. In this work, we use two cost metrics that are considered by Jaques and Schanck [16]. The first cost metric is called G-cost which counts the total number of gates. It assumes non-volatile (passive) quantum memory. Therefore it models quantum circuits that incur some cost with every gate, but where no cost is incurred in time units during which a qubit is not operated on.

The second cost metric is the product of circuit depth and width, called DW-cost. This is a more realistic model when quantum error correction is necessary. It assumes a volatile (active) memory, which incurs some cost to correct errors on every qubit in each time step, i.e., each layer of the total circuit depth. In this cost model, a released auxiliary qubit would not require error correction, and the cost to correct it could be omitted.

For both cost metrics, we can choose to count only T gates towards gate count and depth, or count all gates equally.

3   Finding Key for Block Cipher with Grover's Algorithm

Given plaintext-ciphertext pairs created by encrypting a small number of messages with a block cipher under a common key, Grover's search algorithm [10] can be used to find such key.

3.1   Key Search Problem for Block Cipher

Let $E : \{0,1\}^k \times \{0,1\}^n \to \{0,1\}^n$ be a block cipher with block size n and a key size k for a key $K \in \{0,1\}^k$. Given r plaintext-ciphertext pairs $\{(P_i, C_i)\}_{i=1}^r$ with $C_i = E(K, P_i)$, our goal is to apply Grover's algorithm to find the unknown key K. The Boolean function f for the Grover oracle takes a key K as input, and is defined as

$$f_r(K) = \begin{cases} 1, & \text{if } E(K, P_i) = C_i \text{ for all } 1 \leq i \leq r \\ 0, & \text{otherwise.} \end{cases} \tag{1}$$

so that we can evaluate f upon elements of the domain $\{0,1\}^k$ until we find the unique element (the user's key) for which we are searching. However, other possible keys could exist than K that encrypt the known plaintexts to the same ciphertexts. Such keys are called *spurious keys*. If there are $M-1$ such spurious keys, then the M-solution version of Grover's algorithm has the same probability of measuring such spurious keys as of measuring the correct key K.

The probability that K is the unique key consistent with r plaintext-ciphertext pairs can be approximated as $e^{-2^{k-rn}}$. Thus, we can choose r such that rn is slightly larger than k, i.e., $rn = k + 10$ gives the probability 0.999. In a block cipher where $k = b \cdot n$ is a multiple of n, taking $r = b + 1$ will give the unique key K with probability at least $1 - 2^{-n}$, which is negligibly close to 1 for typical block sizes. If $rn < k$, then K is almost certainly not unique. Even $rn = k - 3$ gives less than a 1% chance of a unique key. Hence, r must be at least $\lceil \frac{k}{n} \rceil$ (see Sect. 2.2 of [15]).

3.2   Grover's Algorithm

We briefly recall the interface that we need to provide for realizing a key search, namely Grover's algorithm [10]. Given a search space of 2^k elements, say $\{x : x \in \{0,1\}^k\}$ and a Boolean function or predicate $f : \{0,1\}^n \to \{0,1\}$, the Grover's algorithm requires about $O(\sqrt{2^k})$ evaluations of the quantum oracle $\mathcal{U}_f$ that outputs $\sum_x a_x \ket{x} \ket{y \oplus f(x)}$ upon input of $\sum_x a_x \ket{x} \ket{y}$. First, we construct a uniform superposition of states

$$\ket{\psi} = \frac{1}{\sqrt{2^k}} \sum_{x \in \{0,1\}^k} \ket{x},$$

by applying the Hadamard transformation $H^{\otimes k}$ to $|0\rangle^{\otimes k}$. We prepare the joint state $|\psi\rangle \otimes |\phi\rangle$ with $|\psi\rangle$ and $|\phi\rangle = (|0\rangle - |1\rangle)/\sqrt{2}$. We define the Grover operator G as

$$G = (2|\psi\rangle\langle\psi| - I)U_f,$$

where $(2|\psi\rangle\langle\psi| - I)$ can be viewed as an inversion about the mean amplitude. We then iteratively apply the Grover operator $(2|\psi\rangle\langle\psi| - I)\mathcal{U}_f$ to $|\psi\rangle$ such that the amplitudes of those values x with $f(x) = 1$ are amplified. Each iteration can be viewed as a rotation of the state vector in the plane spanned by two orthogonal vectors; the superposition of all indices corresponding to solutions and non-solutions, respectively. The operator G rotates the vector by a constant angle towards the superposition of solution indices. Let $1 \leq M \leq N$ be the number of solutions and let $0 < \theta \leq \pi/2$ such that $\sin^2(\theta) = M/N$.

When measuring the first qubits after $j > 0$ iterations of G, the success probability $p(j)$ for obtaining one of the solutions is $p(j) = \sin^2((2j + 1)\theta)$, which is close to 1 for $j \approx \frac{\pi}{4\theta}$. Hence, after $\left\lceil \frac{\pi}{4}\sqrt{\frac{N}{M}} \right\rceil$ iterations, measurement yields a solution with overwhelming probability of at least $1 - \frac{N}{M}$. The exact complexity of the Grover search can be estimated by implementing the oracle circuit efficiently. It is thus essential to have a precise estimate of the quantum resources needed to implement the oracle.

3.3 Cost Metrics for Grover's Algorithm with Parallelization

Suppose a single Grover oracle call G costs G_G gates, has depth G_D, and uses G_W qubits. Let $S = 2^s$ be the number of parallel machines that are used with inner parallelization method by dividing the search space into S disjoint subsets. In order to achieve a certain success probability p, the required number of iterations j can be deduced from $p \leq \sin^2((2j+1)\theta)$ which yields $j = \frac{1}{2} \cdot \lceil(\arcsin(\sqrt{p})/\theta - 1)\rceil \approx \frac{1}{2} \cdot \arcsin(\sqrt{p}) \cdot \sqrt{N/S}$.

Let $c_p := \frac{1}{2} \cdot \arcsin(\sqrt{p})$, then the total depth of a j-fold Grover iteration is

$$D = j \cdot \mathsf{G}_D \approx c_p \cdot \sqrt{N/S} \cdot \mathsf{G}_D = c_p \cdot 2^{\frac{k-s}{2}} \cdot \mathsf{G}_D \text{ cycles.} \tag{2}$$

Note that for $p \approx 1$, we have $c_p \approx c_1 = \pi/4$. Each machines uses $j \cdot \mathsf{G}_G \approx c_p \cdot \sqrt{N/S} \cdot \mathsf{G}_G = c_p \cdot 2^{\frac{k-s}{2}} \cdot \mathsf{G}_G$ gates, i.e., the total G-cost over all S machines is

$$G = S \cdot j \cdot \mathsf{G}_G \approx c_p \cdot \sqrt{N \cdot S} \cdot \mathsf{G}_G = c_p \cdot 2^{\frac{k+s}{2}} \cdot \mathsf{G}_G \text{ gates.} \tag{3}$$

Finally, the total width is $W = S \cdot \mathsf{G}_W = 2^s \cdot \mathsf{G}_W$ qubits, which leads to a DW-cost

$$DW \approx c_p \cdot \sqrt{N.S} \cdot \mathsf{G}_D\mathsf{G}_W = c_p \cdot 2^{\frac{k+s}{2}} \cdot \mathsf{G}_D\mathsf{G}_W \text{ qubit-cycles.} \tag{4}$$

The cost expressions given in (3) and (4) show that minimizing the number $S = 2^s$ of parallel machines reduces both G-cost and DW-cost. Hence, under fixed limits on depth, width, and the number of gates, the adversary's best course of action is to use the entire depth budget and parallelize as little as possible. Under this premise, the depth limit fully determines the optimal attack strategy for a given Grover oracle. For more details, Sect. 3.4 in [15] may be referred.

3.4 Cost Metrics for Grover's Algorithm with Parallelization Under a Depth Limit

Let D_{max} be a fixed depth limit of the circuit. Given the depth G_D of the oracle, we need to run $j_{max} = \lfloor D_{max}/\mathsf{G}_D \rfloor$ Grover iterations of the oracle G in order to find a solution. For a target success probability $p = \sin^2((2j_{max}+1)\sqrt{S/N})$, we obtain the number S of parallel instances as

$$S = \left\lceil \frac{N \cdot \arcsin^2(\sqrt{p})}{(2 \cdot \lfloor D_{max}/\mathsf{G}_D \rfloor + 1)^2} \right\rceil \approx c_p^2 \cdot 2^k \cdot \frac{\mathsf{G}_D^2}{D_{max}^2}. \tag{5}$$

Using this in equation (3) gives the total gate count of

$$G = c_p^2 \cdot 2^k \cdot \frac{\mathsf{G}_D \mathsf{G}_G}{D_{max}} \text{ gates.} \tag{6}$$

Equation (6) suggests that for reducing the cost G, we should aim to minimize the product $\mathsf{G}_D\mathsf{G}_G$. Similarly, the total DW cost under the depth limit is

$$DW = c_p^2 \cdot 2^k \cdot \frac{\mathsf{G}_D^2 \mathsf{G}_W}{D_{max}} \text{ qubit-cycles.} \tag{7}$$

In equation (7), the higher power on G_D suggests that minimizing depth should be prioritized over minimizing G_W. Therefore, we focus on reducing $\mathsf{G}_D^2\mathsf{G}_W$ cost of the oracle circuit to minimize total DW (see Sect. 3.4 in [15]).

4 Quantum Circuit of GIFT

GIFT [4] is a family of lightweight block ciphers with SPN structure. It consists of two ciphers, namely GIFT-64/128 and GIFT-128/128, where GIFT-n/k operates on n-bit plaintexts and k-bit secret key. The smaller version has 28 rounds while the larger version uses 40 rounds.

Next, we describe GIFT cipher's round function and key scheduling with the required number of quantum resources for their circuit implementation.

4.1 Round Function

Each round of GIFT-64/128 and GIFT-128/128 consists of there major subroutines in the following order: SubCells, PermBits and AddRoundKey, which are described as follows.

- **SubCells:** The S-box is applied to each nibble of the cipher state X. The GIFT S-box is given in Table 1.
  The quantum circuit implementation of GIFT S-box requires 4 Toffoli gates, 2 CNOT gates, and 6 Pauli-X gates. We ignore the SWAP gate as it can be implemented freely via reshuffling of wires. The quantum circuit for 4-bit S-box is shown in Fig. 1.

Table 1. Specifications of the 4-bit S-box of GIFT.

x	0	1	2	3	4	5	6	7	8	9	10	11	12	13	14	15
GS(x)	1	10	4	12	6	15	3	9	2	13	11	7	5	0	8	14

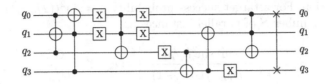

Fig. 1. In-place implementation of 4-bit S-box of GIFT.

- **PermBits:** The bit permutation P_{64} (resp. P_{128}) used in GIFT-64/128 (resp. GIFT-128/128) map bit position i of the cipher state to bit position $P(i)$. The quantum circuit implementation of PermBits operation requires no quantum gates, since it is just a permutation of qubits which can be done by shifting the wires.
- **AddRoundKey:** This step consists of adding the round key and round constants. An $n/2$-bit round key RK is extracted from the key state. It is further partitioned into 2 s-bit words $RK = U\|V = u_{31}\ldots u_0\|v_{31}\ldots v_0$, where $s = 16$ (resp. 32) for GIFT-64/128 (resp. GIFT-128/128).
  For GIFT-64/128, U and V are XOR'ed to b_{4i+1} and b_{4i} of cipher state.

$$b_{4i+1} \leftarrow b_{4i+1} \oplus u_i, b_{4i} \leftarrow b_{4i} \oplus v_i, \forall i \in \{0,\ldots,15\}.$$

For GIFT-128/128, U and V are XOR'ed to b_{4i+2} and b_{4i+1} of cipher state.

$$b_{4i+2} \leftarrow b_{4i+2} \oplus u_i, b_{4i+1} \leftarrow b_{4i+1} \oplus v_i, \forall i \in \{0,\ldots,31\}.$$

Furthermore, a single bit "1" and a 6-bit round constant $C = c_5\ldots c_0$ are XOR'ed into the cipher state at bit position 127, 23, 19, 15, 11, 7 and 3. The quantum circuit implementation of AddRoundKey operation requires 32 CNOT gates for one round of GIFT-64/128 and 64 CNOT gates for one round of GIFT-128/128.

4.2   Key Schedule and Round Constants

The key schedule and round constants are the same for both versions of GIFT, the only difference is the round key extraction. A round key is first extracted from the key state before updating it. The key state is then updated as follows:

$$k_7\|k_6\|\ldots\|k_0 \leftarrow (k_1 \ggg 2)\|(k_0 \ggg 12)\|k_7\|\ldots\|k_2,$$

where $\ggg i$ is an i bits right rotation within a 16-bit word.

The round constants $(c_5, c_4, c_3, c_2, c_1, c_0)$ for GIFT are updated as follows:

$$(c_5, c_4, c_3, c_2, c_1, c_0) \leftarrow (c_4, c_3, c_2, c_1, c_0, c_5 \oplus c_4 \oplus 1).$$

The quantum circuit implementation of updating the key state requires no quantum gates since it is just a permutation of wires. We pre-compute the round constants, and hence adding them to appropriate qubits in each round requires only a few Pauli-X gates. The number of Pauli-X gates depends on the number of 1's in the binary representation of round constants.

5   Quantum Circuit of SKINNY

SKINNY [5] is a family of lightweight tweakable block ciphers which follows the TWEAKEY framework by Jean et al. [17]. The term 'tweakey' refers to an input that can be both tweak and/or key material. SKINNY consists of 64-bit and 128-bit block versions with three different tweakey sizes. For a block size n, the tweakey size is defined as $t = n$, $t = 2n$ or $t = 3n$. The number of rounds for SKINNY depends upon the size of the block and tweakey. SKINNY-64/64, SKINNY-64/128, and SKINNY-64/192 consist of 32, 36, and 40 rounds, respectively. SKINNY-128/128, SKINNY-128/256, and SKINNY-128/384 consist of 40, 48, and 56 rounds, respectively.

The internal state of SKINNY can be viewed as a 4×4 square array of cells, where each cell is a nibble (when $n = 64$) or a byte (when $n = 128$). The tweakey size t to block size n ratio is denoted by z.

Next, we describe the round function of SKINNY with the required number of quantum resources for their circuit implementation.

5.1   Round Function

One encryption round of SKINNY is composed of five operations in the following order: SubCells, AddConstants, AddRoundTweakey, ShiftRows and Mix-Columns. These operations are described as follows.

- **SubCells:** An s-bit S-box is applied to every cell of the cipher internal state. For $s = 4$, the SKINNY-64 cipher uses an S-box S_4, while for $s = 8$, the SKINNY-128 cipher uses an S-box S_8. The Sbox is applied to every cell of the internal state X.

  The S-box S_4: A 4-bit S-box S_4 can be described with four NOR and four XOR operations. If $x_0, \ldots, x_3$ represent the eight input bits then the S-box applies the following transformation on the 4-bit state:

  $$(x_3, x_2, x_1, x_0) \rightarrow (x_3, x_2, x_1, x_0 \oplus (\overline{x_3 \vee x_2})),$$

  followed by a left shift bit rotation. This process is repeated four times, except for the last iteration where the bit rotation is omitted.

The S-box S_8: A 8-bit S-box S_8 is applied to every cell of the internal state X. If $x_0, \ldots, x_7$ represent the eight input bits then the Sbox applies the following transformation on the 8-bit state:

$$(x_7, x_6, x_5, x_4, x_3, x_2, x_1, x_0) \rightarrow (x_7, x_6, x_5, x_4 \oplus (\overline{x_7 \vee x_6}), x_3, x_2, x_1, x_0 \oplus (\overline{x_3 \vee x_2})),$$

followed by the bit permutation:

$$(x_7, x_6, x_5, x_4, x_3, x_2, x_1, x_0) \rightarrow (x_2, x_1, x_7, x_6, x_4, x_3, x_3, x_5),$$

repeating this process 4 times, except the last iteration where there is just a bit swap between x_1 and x_2.

The quantum circuit for 4-bit S-box and 8-bit S-box are shown in Figs. 2 and 3, respectively. The quantum circuit implementation of 4-bit S-box operation requires 4 Toffoli gates and 10 Pauli-X gates. The quantum circuit implementation of 8-bit S-box operation requires 8 Toffoli gates and 22 Pauli-X gates. We ignore the count of SWAP gates as these can be implemented freely via simple reshuffling of wires.

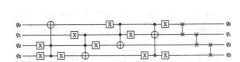

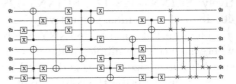

Fig. 2. In-place implementation of S_4.   **Fig. 3.** In-place implementation of S_8.

- **AddConstants:** A 6-bit affine LFSR, whose state is denoted as $(rc_5, rc_4, rc_3, rc_2, rc_1, rc_0)$, is used to generate round constants. Its update function is defined as

$$(rc_5, rc_4, rc_3, rc_2, rc_1, rc_0) \rightarrow (rc_4, rc_3, rc_2, rc_1, rc_0, rc_4 \oplus rc_4 \oplus 1).$$

The six bits are initialized to zero, and updated before use in a given round. The round constants are combined with the state, respecting array positioning, using bitwise exclusive-or. We precompute all the round constants, and hence adding constants to appropriate qubits in each round requires only Pauli-X gates. The number of Pauli-X gates depends on the the number of 1's in the binary representation of round constants.

- **AddRoundTweakey:** The first and second rows of all tweakey arrays $TK1, TK2$ and $TK3$ are extracted and bitwise exclusive-xored to the cipher internal state X. More formally, for $i = \{0, 1\}$ and $j = \{0, 1, 2, 3\}$, we have:
  - $X_{i,j} = X_{i,j} \oplus TK1_{i,j}$ when $z = 1$,
  - $X_{i,j} = X_{i,j} \oplus TK1_{i,j} \oplus TK2_{i,j}$ when $z = 2$,
  - $X_{i,j} = X_{i,j} \oplus TK1_{i,j} \oplus TK2_{i,j} \oplus TK3_{i,j}$ when $z = 3$.

Tweakey array TK_1 is updated according to a fixed permutation, while TK_2 and TK_3 are individually updated with an LFSR.

Observe that the AddRoundTweakey operation uses only XOR operations to update the state. Hence, its quantum circuit implementation requires CNOT gates only.

– **ShiftRows:** The rows of the cipher state array are rotated to the right. The second, third, and fourth cell rows are rotated by 1, 2, and 3 positions to the right, respectively. This operation is similar to AES.

   The quantum circuit implementation of ShiftRows operation is free since it is just a permutation of qubits.

– **MixColumns:** Each column of the cipher internal state array is multiplied by the following binary matrix:

$$M = \begin{pmatrix} 1 & 0 & 1 & 1 \\ 1 & 0 & 0 & 0 \\ 0 & 1 & 1 & 0 \\ 1 & 0 & 1 & 0 \end{pmatrix}.$$

The PLU decomposition of matrix M implemented in SageMath [27] gives

$$\begin{pmatrix} 1 & 0 & 1 & 1 \\ 1 & 0 & 0 & 0 \\ 0 & 1 & 1 & 0 \\ 1 & 0 & 1 & 0 \end{pmatrix} = \begin{pmatrix} 1 & 0 & 0 & 0 \\ 0 & 0 & 1 & 0 \\ 0 & 1 & 0 & 0 \\ 0 & 0 & 0 & 1 \end{pmatrix} \cdot \begin{pmatrix} 1 & 0 & 0 & 0 \\ 0 & 1 & 0 & 0 \\ 1 & 0 & 1 & 0 \\ 1 & 0 & 0 & 1 \end{pmatrix} \cdot \begin{pmatrix} 1 & 0 & 1 & 1 \\ 0 & 1 & 1 & 0 \\ 0 & 0 & 1 & 1 \\ 0 & 0 & 0 & 1 \end{pmatrix}.$$

The permutation P does not require any quantum gates in its implementation, as it can be realized by appropriately rewiring. The lower- and upper-triangular components L and U of the decomposition can be implemented using CNOT gates only. The quantum circuit implementation of binary matrix M requires $4 \times 6 = 24$ CNOT gates, and $8 \times 6 = 48$ CNOT gates for SKINNY-64 and SKINNY-128, respectively. As for the full MixColumns operation, we need to apply M four times on each column. Therefore, we need $(4 \times 24) = 96$ and $(4 \times 48) = 192$ CNOT gates for the MixColumns operation of SKINNY-64 and SKINNY-128, respectively.

6 Quantum Circuit of SATURNIN

SATURNIN [7] is an SPN-based 256-bit block cipher with an even number of rounds. It uses a 256-bit internal state X and a 256-bit key state K, and both are represented as a $4 \times 4 \times 4$ cube of nibbles.

Next, we describe the round function and key scheduling of SATURNIN with the required number of quantum resources for their circuit implementation.

6.1 Round Function

Each round consists of five transformations in the following order: S-box layer, Nibble permutation, Linear layer, Inverse of nibble permutation, and AddRound-Key. These operations are described as follows.

Table 2. Specifications of 4-bit S-boxes of SATURNIN-256.

x	0	1	2	3	4	5	6	7	8	9	10	11	12	13	14	15
$\sigma_0(x)$	0	6	14	1	15	4	7	13	9	8	12	5	2	10	3	11
$\sigma_1(x)$	0	9	13	2	15	1	11	7	6	4	5	3	8	12	10	14

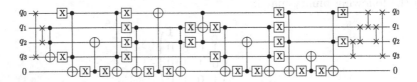

Fig. 4. In-place implementation of σ_0.

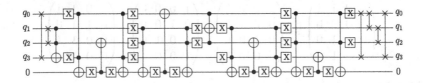

Fig. 5. In-place implementation of σ_1.

- **Sbox layer:** An Sbox layer applies a 4-bit S-box σ_0 to all nibbles with an even index, and a 4-bit S-box σ_1 to all nibbles with an odd index. These two S-boxes are defined in Table 2, and their quantum circuit implementations are shown in Figs. 4 and 5.

  The quantum circuit implementation of SATURNIN S-boxes requires 10 Toffoli gates, 4 CNOT gates, and 24 Pauli-X gates. Additionally, we need 4 qubits and 1 ancilla to implement the S-boxes. We ignore the count of SWAP gates as these can be implemented freely via simple reshuffling of the wires.

- **Nibble permutation:** A nibble permutation SR_r depends on the round number r. For all even rounds, SR_r is an identity function. For odd rounds with index r where $r \bmod 4 = 1$, $SR_r = SR_{\text{slice}}$ maps (x, y, z) to $(x + y \bmod 4, y, z)$. For odd rounds with index r where $r \bmod 4 = 3$, $SR_r = SR_{\text{sheet}}$ maps (x, y, z) to $(x, y, z + y \bmod 4)$.

  No quantum gate is required to implement the nibble permutation since it is just a reshuffling of the wires in the implementation.

- **Linear layer:** A linear layer MC is composed of 16 copies of a linear operation M over $(\mathbb{F}_2^4)^4$ which is applied in parallel to each column of the internal state. The transformation M is defined as

$$M : \begin{pmatrix} a \\ b \\ c \\ d \end{pmatrix} \mapsto \begin{pmatrix} \alpha^2(a) \oplus \alpha^2(b) \oplus \alpha(b) \oplus c \oplus d \\ a \oplus \alpha(b) \oplus b \oplus \alpha^2(c) \oplus c \oplus \alpha^2(d) \oplus \alpha(d) \oplus d \\ a \oplus b \oplus \alpha^2(c) \oplus \alpha^2(d) \oplus \alpha(d) \\ \alpha^2(a) \oplus a \oplus \alpha^2(b) \oplus \alpha(b) \oplus b \oplus c \oplus \alpha(d) \oplus d \end{pmatrix}$$

where a is the nibble with the lowest index, and α transforms the four bits (x_0, x_1, x_2, x_3) of each nibble by the following multiplication

$$\alpha : \begin{pmatrix} x_0 \\ x_1 \\ x_2 \\ x_3 \end{pmatrix} \mapsto \begin{pmatrix} 0 & 1 & 0 & 0 \\ 0 & 0 & 1 & 0 \\ 0 & 0 & 0 & 1 \\ 1 & 1 & 0 & 0 \end{pmatrix} \begin{pmatrix} x_0 \\ x_1 \\ x_2 \\ x_3 \end{pmatrix}.$$

The PLU decomposition of the above binary matrix gives

$$\begin{pmatrix} 0 & 1 & 0 & 0 \\ 0 & 0 & 1 & 0 \\ 0 & 0 & 0 & 1 \\ 1 & 1 & 0 & 0 \end{pmatrix} = \begin{pmatrix} 0 & 1 & 0 & 0 \\ 0 & 0 & 1 & 0 \\ 0 & 0 & 0 & 1 \\ 1 & 0 & 0 & 0 \end{pmatrix} \cdot \begin{pmatrix} 1 & 0 & 0 & 0 \\ 0 & 1 & 0 & 0 \\ 0 & 0 & 1 & 0 \\ 0 & 0 & 0 & 1 \end{pmatrix} \cdot \begin{pmatrix} 1 & 1 & 0 & 0 \\ 0 & 1 & 0 & 0 \\ 0 & 0 & 1 & 0 \\ 0 & 0 & 0 & 1 \end{pmatrix}.$$

One CNOT gate is required to implement the transformation α, and two CNOT gates are required to implement the transformation α^2. Overall, only $(8 \times 4 + 2 \times 1 + 2 \times 2) = 38$ CNOT gates are required to implement one transformation M. As the linear layer needs 16 parallel copies of M, we need a total of $(16 \times 38) = 608$ CNOT gates to implement MC.
- **Inverse of nibble permutation:** Apply SR_r^{-1}.
  The quantum circuit implementation of the inverse of nibble permutation is free, i.e., no quantum gates are required.
- **AddRoundKey:** The sub-key addition is performed at odd rounds only.
  The quantum circuit implementation of key addition requires 256 CNOT gates for every two consecutive rounds (one super-round) of SATURNIN-256.

6.2   Key Schedule and Round Constants

The subkey is composed of XOR of a round constant and either the master key, or a rotated version of the master key.

- **Round constant:** The round constants RC_0 and RC_1 are updated by clocking two independent LFSRs in Galois mode 16 times.
  We precompute the round constants on a classical computer, and hence the quantum circuit implementation of adding round constants to the current states requires 16 Pauli-X gates.

- **Round key:** If the round index r is such that $r \mod 4 = 3$, the master key is XOR'ed to the internal state; otherwise a rotated version of the key is added instead. The nibble with index i receives the key nibble with index $(i + 20)$ mod 64 for $0 \leq i \leq 63$.

  The quantum circuit implementation of subkey generation requires CNOT gates for XOR operations or no quantum gates for rotations of key bits.

7 Quantum Resource Estimates for Implementing the Circuits of GIFT, SKINNY, and SATURNIN

In this section, we give concrete cost estimates for the quantum circuits of GIFT, SKINNY, and SATURNIN based on their Q# implementation. The total cost estimates of full GIFT-64/128, GIFT-128/128, SKINNY-64/64, SKINNY-64/128, SKINNY-64/192, SKINNY-128/128, SKINNY-128/256, SKINNY-128/384, and SATURNIN-256 encryption circuits are given in Table 3.

We stress that the numbers given in Table 3 include the cost estimates for two encryption calls as used in Grover oracle since we need to reverse all the operations executed on the wires (refer to Fig. 6).

Table 3. Cost of the full encryption circuits of GIFT, SKINNY, and SATURNIN.

Operation	#Quantum gates				Depth		#Qubits
	CNOT	1qClifford	T	M	T-depth	full depth	(full width)
GIFT-64/128	61056	12768	25088	0	224	1851	260
GIFT-128/128	174336	36160	71680	0	320	2643	388
SKINNY-64/64	73792	18720	28672	0	256	2537	196
SKINNY-64/128	85888	21054	32256	0	288	2851	260
SKINNY-64/192	98624	23396	35840	0	320	3176	324
SKINNY-128/128	184448	48996	71680	0	320	3243	388
SKINNY-128/256	228224	58772	86016	0	384	3891	516
SKINNY-128/384	254720	63666	93184	0	416	4215	644
SATURNIN-256	455168	112960	179200	0	400	3763	773

8 Grover Oracles and Key Search Resource Estimates

This section describes the Q# implementations of full Grover oracles for lightweight block ciphers: GIFT, SKINNY, and SATURNIN. Based on the cost estimates obtained automatically from these Q# Grover oracles, we provide quantum resource estimates for full key search attacks via Grover's algorithm. We emphasize evaluating algorithms with respect to a total depth limit, for which we consider NIST's values for MAXDEPTH from [22]. This means that we must parallelize. We use inner parallelization method via splitting up the search space as considered by Kim et al. [19].

8.1   Grover Oracle

As discussed in Sect. 3, we must determine the parameter r, the number of known plaintext-ciphertext pairs that are required for a successful key recovery attack. The main idea of the key-search algorithm is as follows. For a message-ciphertext pair (m, c), the Grover oracle first encrypts m under different keys and checks if the ciphertext obtained matches with c. If this match fails then this particular key is wrong. On the other hand, when the match succeeds, it does not guarantee that the key is correct. This could be due to spurious keys. To eliminate spurious keys and get the right candidate, we require a few (i.e., r many) plaintext-ciphertext pairs. When $r > 1$, the Grover oracle will encrypt all the r plaintexts under the candidate keys and will match with the corresponding ciphertexts. The construction of Grover oracle is shown in Fig. 6 for $r = 2$.

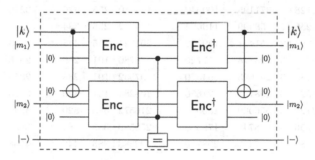

Fig. 6. Grover oracle construction for block cipher using two message-ciphertext pairs. Enc represents the Encryption operator. The operator ($=$) compares the output of Enc with given ciphertexts and flips the target qubit if they are equal.

Cost of Grover Oracle for GIFT. Table 4 shows the resources needed for our implementations of the full GIFT Grover oracles for $r \in \{1, 2\}$.

Table 4. Cost estimates for the GIFT Grover oracle operator for r plaintext-ciphertext pairs. All operations are performed in-place.

Operation	r	#CNOT	#1qClifford	#T	#M	T-depth	full depth	width
GIFT-64/128	1	61567	13288	25340	63	224	1850	2049
GIFT-128/128	1	175365	37204	72188	127	320	2642	5505
GIFT-64/128	2	123387	26560	50684	127	224	1851	4097
GIFT-128/128	2	350951	74328	144380	255	320	2644	11009

Cost of Grover Oracle for SKINNY. The resources for our implementations of the full SKINNY Grover oracles for $r \in \{1, 2, 3\}$ are shown in Table 5.

Cost of Grover Oracle for SATURNIN. Table 6 shows the resources needed for our implementation of the full SATURNIN Grover oracle for $r \in \{1, 2\}$.

Table 5. Cost estimates for the SKINNY Grover oracle operator for r plaintext-ciphertext pairs. All operations are performed in-place.

Operation	r	#CNOT	#1qClifford	#T	#M	T-depth	full depth	width
SKINNY-64/64	1	74289	19212	28924	63	256	2536	2241
SKINNY-64/128	1	86381	21538	32508	63	288	2850	2561
SKINNY-64/192	1	99113	23872	36092	63	320	3176	2881
SKINNY-128/128	1	185487	50060	72188	127	320	3242	5505
SKINNY-128/256	1	229245	59800	86524	127	384	3890	6657
SKINNY-128/384	1	275311	69560	100860	127	448	4538	7809
SKINNY-64/64	2	148731	38464	57852	127	256	2536	4481
SKINNY-64/128	2	173027	43084	65020	127	288	2850	5121
SKINNY-64/192	2	198657	47828	72188	127	320	3176	5761
SKINNY-128/128	2	371195	100040	144380	255	320	3242	11009
SKINNY-128/256	2	458999	119584	173052	255	384	3890	13313
SKINNY-128/384	2	551421	139172	201724	255	448	4538	15617
SKINNY-64/64	3	223175	57720	86780	191	256	2536	6721
SKINNY-64/128	3	259693	64670	97532	191	288	2850	7681
SKINNY-64/192	3	298137	71656	108284	191	320	3176	8641
SKINNY-128/128	3	556909	150032	216572	383	320	3242	16503
SKINNY-128/256	3	688749	179360	259580	383	384	3890	19969
SKINNY-128/384	3	827499	208720	302588	383	448	4538	23425

Table 6. Cost estimates for the SATURNIN Grover oracle operator for r plaintext-ciphertext pairs. All operations are performed in-place.

Operation	r	#CNOT	#1qClifford	#T	#M	T-depth	full depth	width
SATURNIN-256	1	457197	114980	180220	255	400	3762	5889
SATURNIN-256	2	914655	229960	360444	511	400	3764	11777

8.2 Cost Estimates for Lightweight Block Cipher Key Search

Based on the cost estimates for the GIFT, SKINNY, and SATURNIN Grover oracles given in Sect. 8.1, this section provides cost estimates for quantum key search attacks on lightweight block ciphers. Firstly, we provide cost estimates without any depth limit and parallelization requirements. Table 7 shows cost estimates for a full run of Grover's algorithm when using $\lfloor \frac{\pi}{4} 2^{k/2} \rfloor$ iterations of the GIFT Grover operator without parallelization. We only consider the costs imposed by the unitary operator U_f and ignore the cost of the operator $2 |\psi\rangle \langle\psi| - I$. The G-cost is the total number of gates which is the sum of the first four columns in the table. These columns correspond to the numbers of single-qubit Clifford and CNOT gates, T gates, and measurements M. The DW-cost is the product of full circuit depth and width, corresponding to columns 6 and 7 in the table.

Tables 8 and 9 show cost estimates for SKINNY and SATURNIN, respectively in the same setting as GIFT.

Table 7. Cost estimates for Grover's algorithm with $\left\lfloor \frac{\pi}{4} 2^{k/2} \right\rfloor$ GIFT oracle iterations for attacks with high success probability p_s, without depth restrictions.

Scheme	r	#CNOT	#1qClifford	#T	#M	T-depth	full depth	width	G-cost	DW-cost	p_s
GIFT-64/128	1	$1.47 \cdot 2^{79}$	$1.27 \cdot 2^{77}$	$1.21 \cdot 2^{78}$	$1.54 \cdot 2^{69}$	$1.37 \cdot 2^{71}$	$1.41 \cdot 2^{74}$	2049	$1.19 \cdot 2^{80}$	$1.41 \cdot 2^{85}$	$1/e$
GIFT-64/128	2	$1.47 \cdot 2^{80}$	$1.27 \cdot 2^{78}$	$1.21 \cdot 2^{79}$	$1.55 \cdot 2^{70}$	$1.37 \cdot 2^{71}$	$1.41 \cdot 2^{74}$	4097	$1.19 \cdot 2^{81}$	$1.41 \cdot 2^{86}$	1
GIFT-128/128	1	$1.05 \cdot 2^{81}$	$1.78 \cdot 2^{78}$	$1.73 \cdot 2^{79}$	$1.55 \cdot 2^{70}$	$1.96 \cdot 2^{71}$	$1.01 \cdot 2^{75}$	5505	$1.70 \cdot 2^{81}$	$1.35 \cdot 2^{88}$	$1/e$
GIFT-128/128	2	$1.05 \cdot 2^{82}$	$1.78 \cdot 2^{79}$	$1.73 \cdot 2^{80}$	$1.56 \cdot 2^{71}$	$1.96 \cdot 2^{71}$	$1.01 \cdot 2^{75}$	11009	$1.70 \cdot 2^{82}$	$1.35 \cdot 2^{88}$	1

Table 8. Cost estimates for Grover's algorithm with $\left\lfloor \frac{\pi}{4} 2^{k/2} \right\rfloor$ SKINNY oracle iterations for attacks with high success probability p_s, without depth restrictions.

Scheme	r	#CNOT	#1qClifford	#T	#M	T-depth	full depth	width	G-cost	DW-cost	p_s
SKINNY-64/64	1	$1.78 \cdot 2^{47}$	$1.84 \cdot 2^{45}$	$1.38 \cdot 2^{46}$	$1.54 \cdot 2^{37}$	$1.57 \cdot 2^{39}$	$1.94 \cdot 2^{42}$	2241	$1.46 \cdot 2^{48}$	$1.06 \cdot 2^{54}$	$1/e$
SKINNY-64/64	2	$1.78 \cdot 2^{48}$	$1.84 \cdot 2^{46}$	$1.38 \cdot 2^{47}$	$1.55 \cdot 2^{38}$	$1.57 \cdot 2^{39}$	$1.94 \cdot 2^{42}$	4481	$1.46 \cdot 2^{49}$	$1.06 \cdot 2^{55}$	1
SKINNY-64/128	2	$1.03 \cdot 2^{81}$	$1.03 \cdot 2^{79}$	$1.55 \cdot 2^{79}$	$1.55 \cdot 2^{70}$	$1.76 \cdot 2^{71}$	$1.09 \cdot 2^{75}$	5121	$1.67 \cdot 2^{81}$	$1.36 \cdot 2^{87}$	$1/e$
SKINNY-64/128	3	$1.55 \cdot 2^{81}$	$1.55 \cdot 2^{79}$	$1.16 \cdot 2^{80}$	$1.17 \cdot 2^{71}$	$1.76 \cdot 2^{71}$	$1.09 \cdot 2^{75}$	7681	$1.25 \cdot 2^{82}$	$1.02 \cdot 2^{88}$	1
SKINNY-64/192	2	$1.19 \cdot 2^{113}$	$1.14 \cdot 2^{111}$	$1.73 \cdot 2^{111}$	$1.55 \cdot 2^{102}$	$1.96 \cdot 2^{103}$	$1.21 \cdot 2^{107}$	5761	$1.90 \cdot 2^{113}$	$1.70 \cdot 2^{119}$	$1/e$
SKINNY-64/192	3	$1.78 \cdot 2^{113}$	$1.71 \cdot 2^{111}$	$1.29 \cdot 2^{112}$	$1.17 \cdot 2^{103}$	$1.96 \cdot 2^{103}$	$1.21 \cdot 2^{107}$	8641	$1.42 \cdot 2^{113}$	$1.27 \cdot 2^{120}$	1
SKINNY-128/128	1	$1.11 \cdot 2^{81}$	$1.19 \cdot 2^{79}$	$1.73 \cdot 2^{79}$	$1.55 \cdot 2^{70}$	$1.96 \cdot 2^{71}$	$1.24 \cdot 2^{75}$	5505	$1.84 \cdot 2^{81}$	$1.66 \cdot 2^{87}$	$1/e$
SKINNY-128/128	2	$1.11 \cdot 2^{82}$	$1.19 \cdot 2^{80}$	$1.73 \cdot 2^{80}$	$1.56 \cdot 2^{71}$	$1.96 \cdot 2^{71}$	$1.24 \cdot 2^{75}$	11009	$1.84 \cdot 2^{81}$	$1.66 \cdot 2^{88}$	1
SKINNY-128/256	2	$1.37 \cdot 2^{146}$	$1.43 \cdot 2^{144}$	$1.03 \cdot 2^{145}$	$1.56 \cdot 2^{135}$	$1.17 \cdot 2^{136}$	$1.49 \cdot 2^{139}$	13313	$1.12 \cdot 2^{147}$	$1.21 \cdot 2^{153}$	$1/e$
SKINNY-128/256	3	$1.03 \cdot 2^{147}$	$1.07 \cdot 2^{145}$	$1.55 \cdot 2^{145}$	$1.17 \cdot 2^{136}$	$1.17 \cdot 2^{136}$	$1.49 \cdot 2^{139}$	19969	$1.68 \cdot 2^{147}$	$1.81 \cdot 2^{153}$	1
SKINNY-128/384	2	$1.65 \cdot 2^{210}$	$1.66 \cdot 2^{208}$	$1.20 \cdot 2^{209}$	$1.56 \cdot 2^{199}$	$1.37 \cdot 2^{200}$	$1.74 \cdot 2^{203}$	15617	$1.33 \cdot 2^{211}$	$1.65 \cdot 2^{217}$	$1/e$
SKINNY-128/384	3	$1.23 \cdot 2^{211}$	$1.25 \cdot 2^{209}$	$1.81 \cdot 2^{209}$	$1.17 \cdot 2^{200}$	$1.37 \cdot 2^{200}$	$1.74 \cdot 2^{203}$	23425	$1.99 \cdot 2^{211}$	$1.23 \cdot 2^{218}$	1

Table 9. Cost estimates for Grover's algorithm with $\left\lfloor \frac{\pi}{4} 2^{k/2} \right\rfloor$ SATURNIN oracle iterations for attacks with high success probability p_s, without depth restrictions.

Scheme	r	#CNOT	#1qClifford	#T	#M	T-depth	full depth	width	G-cost	DW-cost	p_s
SATURNIN-256	1	$1.37 \cdot 2^{146}$	$1.38 \cdot 2^{144}$	$1.08 \cdot 2^{145}$	$1.56 \cdot 2^{135}$	$1.22 \cdot 2^{136}$	$1.44 \cdot 2^{139}$	5889	$1.13 \cdot 2^{147}$	$1.03 \cdot 2^{152}$	$1/e$
SATURNIN-256	2	$1.37 \cdot 2^{147}$	$1.38 \cdot 2^{145}$	$1.08 \cdot 2^{146}$	$1.56 \cdot 2^{136}$	$1.22 \cdot 2^{136}$	$1.44 \cdot 2^{139}$	11777	$1.13 \cdot 2^{148}$	$1.03 \cdot 2^{153}$	1

8.3 Cost Estimates for Grover Search Under MAXDEPTH Limit

Tables 10, 11, 12 and 13 show the cost estimates for running Grover's algorithm against GIFT, SKINNY and SATURNIN under a given depth limit, respectively. Imposing a depth restriction forces the parallelization of Grover's algorithm.

In Tables 10, 11, 12 and 13, MD is the MAXDEPTH, r is the number of plaintext-ciphertext pairs used in the Grover oracle, S is the number of subsets in which the key-space is divided, SKP is the probability that spurious keys are present in the subset holding the target key, W is the qubit width of the full circuit, D is the full depth. After the execution of the Grover oracle is completed, each of S measured candidate keys is classically checked against a sufficient number of plaintext-ciphertext pairs.

Table 10. Circuit sizes for parallel Grover key search against GIFT-64 and GIFT-128 under a depth limit MAXDEPTH with *inner* parallelization.

scheme	MD	r	S	$\log_2(\text{SKP})$	D	W	G-cost	DW-cost
GIFT-64/128	2^{40}	1	$1.01 \cdot 2^{69}$	-69.01	$1.00 \cdot 2^{40}$	$1.01 \cdot 2^{80}$	$1.70 \cdot 2^{114}$	$1.01 \cdot 2^{120}$
GIFT-128/128	2^{40}	1	$1.03 \cdot 2^{70}$	-70.04	$1.00 \cdot 2^{40}$	$1.38 \cdot 2^{82}$	$1.73 \cdot 2^{116}$	$1.38 \cdot 2^{122}$
GIFT-64/128	2^{64}	1	$1.01 \cdot 2^{21}$	-21.01	$1.00 \cdot 2^{64}$	$1.01 \cdot 2^{32}$	$1.70 \cdot 2^{90}$	$1.01 \cdot 2^{96}$
GIFT-128/128	2^{64}	1	$1.03 \cdot 2^{22}$	-22.04	$1.00 \cdot 2^{64}$	$1.38 \cdot 2^{34}$	$1.73 \cdot 2^{92}$	$1.38 \cdot 2^{98}$
GIFT-64/128	2^{96}	2	$1.00 \cdot 2^{0}$	-128.00	$1.42 \cdot 2^{74}$	$1.00 \cdot 2^{12}$	$1.20 \cdot 2^{81}$	$1.42 \cdot 2^{86}$
GIFT-128/128	2^{96}	2	$1.00 \cdot 2^{0}$	-128.00	$1.01 \cdot 2^{75}$	$1.34 \cdot 2^{13}$	$1.71 \cdot 2^{82}$	$1.36 \cdot 2^{88}$

Table 11. Circuit sizes for parallel Grover key search against SKINNY-64 under a depth limit MAXDEPTH with *inner* parallelization.

scheme	MD	r	S	$\log_2(\text{SKP})$	D	W	G-cost	DW-cost
SKINNY-64/64	2^{40}	1	$1.91 \cdot 2^{5}$	-69.93	$1.00 \cdot 2^{40}$	$1.04 \cdot 2^{17}$	$1.43 \cdot 2^{51}$	$1.03 \cdot 2^{57}$
SKINNY-64/128	2^{40}	1	$1.19 \cdot 2^{70}$	-70.26	$1.00 \cdot 2^{40}$	$1.49 \cdot 2^{81}$	$1.84 \cdot 2^{115}$	$1.49 \cdot 2^{121}$
SKINNY-64/192	2^{40}	1	$1.48 \cdot 2^{134}$	-70.57	$1.00 \cdot 2^{40}$	$1.04 \cdot 2^{146}$	$1.16 \cdot 2^{180}$	$1.04 \cdot 2^{186}$
SKINNY-64/64	2^{64}	1	$1.00 \cdot 2^{0}$	-64.00	$1.95 \cdot 2^{42}$	$1.09 \cdot 2^{11}$	$1.47 \cdot 2^{48}$	$1.06 \cdot 2^{54}$
SKINNY-64/128	2^{64}	1	$1.19 \cdot 2^{22}$	-22.26	$1.00 \cdot 2^{64}$	$1.49 \cdot 2^{33}$	$1.84 \cdot 2^{91}$	$1.49 \cdot 2^{97}$
SKINNY-64/192	2^{64}	1	$1.48 \cdot 2^{86}$	-22.57	$1.00 \cdot 2^{64}$	$1.04 \cdot 2^{98}$	$1.16 \cdot 2^{156}$	$1.04 \cdot 2^{162}$
SKINNY-64/64	2^{96}	1	$1.00 \cdot 2^{0}$	-64.00	$1.95 \cdot 2^{42}$	$1.09 \cdot 2^{11}$	$1.47 \cdot 2^{48}$	$1.06 \cdot 2^{54}$
SKINNY-64/128	2^{96}	2	$1.00 \cdot 2^{0}$	-128.00	$1.09 \cdot 2^{75}$	$1.25 \cdot 2^{12}$	$1.69 \cdot 2^{81}$	$1.37 \cdot 2^{87}$
SKINNY-64/192	2^{96}	2	$1.48 \cdot 2^{22}$	-86.57	$1.00 \cdot 2^{96}$	$1.04 \cdot 2^{35}$	$1.16 \cdot 2^{125}$	$1.04 \cdot 2^{131}$

Table 12. Circuit sizes for parallel Grover key search against SKINNY-128 under a depth limit MAXDEPTH with *inner* parallelization.

scheme	MD	r	S	$\log_2(\text{SKP})$	D	W	G-cost	DW-cost
SKINNY-128/128	2^{40}	1	$1.55 \cdot 2^{70}$	-70.63	$1.00 \cdot 2^{40}$	$1.04 \cdot 2^{83}$	$1.15 \cdot 2^{117}$	$1.04 \cdot 2^{123}$
SKINNY-128/256	2^{40}	1	$1.11 \cdot 2^{199}$	-71.15	$1.00 \cdot 2^{40}$	$1.81 \cdot 2^{211}$	$1.68 \cdot 2^{245}$	$1.81 \cdot 2^{251}$
SKINNY-128/384	2^{40}	1	$1.51 \cdot 2^{327}$	-71.60	$1.00 \cdot 2^{40}$	$1.44 \cdot 2^{340}$	$1.16 \cdot 2^{374}$	$1.44 \cdot 2^{380}$
SKINNY-128/128	2^{64}	1	$1.55 \cdot 2^{22}$	-22.63	$1.00 \cdot 2^{64}$	$1.04 \cdot 2^{35}$	$1.15 \cdot 2^{93}$	$1.04 \cdot 2^{99}$
SKINNY-128/256	2^{64}	1	$1.11 \cdot 2^{151}$	-23.15	$1.00 \cdot 2^{64}$	$1.81 \cdot 2^{163}$	$1.68 \cdot 2^{221}$	$1.81 \cdot 2^{227}$
SKINNY-128/384	2^{64}	1	$1.51 \cdot 2^{279}$	-23.60	$1.00 \cdot 2^{64}$	$1.44 \cdot 2^{292}$	$1.16 \cdot 2^{350}$	$1.44 \cdot 2^{356}$
SKINNY-128/128	2^{96}	2	$1.00 \cdot 2^{0}$	-128.00	$1.24 \cdot 2^{75}$	$1.34 \cdot 2^{13}$	$1.85 \cdot 2^{82}$	$1.67 \cdot 2^{88}$
SKINNY-128/256	2^{96}	2	$1.11 \cdot 2^{87}$	-87.15	$1.00 \cdot 2^{96}$	$1.81 \cdot 2^{100}$	$1.68 \cdot 2^{190}$	$1.81 \cdot 2^{196}$
SKINNY-128/384	2^{96}	2	$1.51 \cdot 2^{215}$	-87.60	$1.00 \cdot 2^{96}$	$1.44 \cdot 2^{229}$	$1.16 \cdot 2^{319}$	$1.44 \cdot 2^{325}$

Table 13. Circuit sizes for parallel Grover key search against SATURNIN-256 under a depth limit MAXDEPTH with *inner* parallelization.

Scheme	MD	r	S	$\log_2$ (SKP)	D	W	G-cost	DW-cost
SATURNIN-256	2^{40}	1	$1.04 \cdot 2^{199}$	-199.06	$1.00 \cdot 2^{40}$	$1.50 \cdot 2^{211}$	$1.63 \cdot 2^{246}$	$1.50 \cdot 2^{251}$
SATURNIN-256	2^{64}	1	$1.04 \cdot 2^{151}$	-151.06	$1.00 \cdot 2^{64}$	$1.50 \cdot 2^{163}$	$1.63 \cdot 2^{222}$	$1.50 \cdot 2^{227}$
SATURNIN-256	2^{96}	1	$1.04 \cdot 2^{87}$	-87.06	$1.00 \cdot 2^{96}$	$1.50 \cdot 2^{99}$	$1.63 \cdot 2^{190}$	$1.50 \cdot 2^{195}$

9 Conclusion

We explored the resource estimates for Grover key search on lightweight block ciphers such as GIFT, SKINNY, and SATURNIN under MAXDEPTH limitations as proposed by NIST's PQC standardization process. First, we implemented the Grover oracle for GIFT, SKINNY, and SATURNIN in Q# quantum programming language. We then presented concrete costs of quantum circuits for these ciphers. We also provided concrete cost estimations for all variants of these ciphers while parallelizing Grover's algorithm under NIST's MAXDEPTH limit. As a future work, it would be interesting to implement other ciphers in Q# for estimating resources against Grover-based attacks.

Acknowledgment. We would like to thank the anonymous reviewers of ACISP 2022 for their insightful comments and suggestions, which has significantly improved the presentation and technical quality of this work. The second author would also like to thank MATRICS grant 2019/1514 by the Science and Engineering Research Board (SERB), Dept. of Science and Technology, Govt. of India for supporting the research carried out in this work.

References

1. Almazrooie, M., Samsudin, A., Abdullah, R., Mutter, K.N.: Quantum reversible circuit of AES-128. Quantum Inf. Process. **17**(5), 112 (2018)
2. Anand, R., Maitra, A., Maitra, S., Mukherjee, C.S., Mukhopadhyay, S.: Quantum resource estimation for fsr based symmetric ciphers and related grover's attacks. In: Adhikari, A., Küsters, R., Preneel, B. (eds.) INDOCRYPT 2021. LNCS, vol. 13143, pp. 179–198. Springer, Cham (2021). https://doi.org/10.1007/978-3-030-92518-5_9
3. Anand, R., Maitra, A., Mukhopadhyay, S.: Grover on SIMON. Quantum Inf. Process. **19**(9), 340 (2020)
4. Banik, S., Pandey, S.K., Peyrin, T., Sasaki, Yu., Sim, S.M., Todo, Y.: GIFT: a small present. In: Fischer, W., Homma, N. (eds.) CHES 2017. LNCS, vol. 10529, pp. 321–345. Springer, Cham (2017). https://doi.org/10.1007/978-3-319-66787-4_16
5. Beierle, C., et al.: The SKINNY family of block ciphers and its low-latency variant MANTIS. In: Robshaw, M., Katz, J. (eds.) CRYPTO 2016. LNCS, vol. 9815, pp. 123–153. Springer, Heidelberg (2016). https://doi.org/10.1007/978-3-662-53008-5_5

6. Boyar, J., Peralta, R.: A small depth-16 circuit for the aes s-box. In: Gritzalis, D., Furnell, S., Theoharidou, M. (eds.) SEC 2012. IAICT, vol. 376, pp. 287–298. Springer, Heidelberg (2012). https://doi.org/10.1007/978-3-642-30436-1_24

7. Canteaut, A., et al.: Saturnin: a suite of lightweight symmetric algorithms for post-quantum security. IACR Trans. Symmetric Cryptol. **2020**(S1), 160–207 (2020)

8. Fowler, A.G., Mariantoni, M., Martinis, J.M., Cleland, A.N.: Surface codes: towards practical large-scale quantum computation. Phys. Rev. A **86**, 032324 (2012)

9. Grassl, M., Langenberg, B., Roetteler, M., Steinwandt, R.: Applying grover's algorithm to aes: quantum resource estimates. In: Takagi, T. (ed.) PQCrypto 2016. LNCS, vol. 9606, pp. 29–43. Springer, Cham (2016). https://doi.org/10.1007/978-3-319-29360-8_3

10. Grover, L.K.: A fast quantum mechanical algorithm for database search. In: Proceedings of the Twenty-Eighth Annual ACM Symposium on the Theory of Computing, pp. 212–219. ACM, Pennsylvania, USA (1996)

11. Grover, L.K., Rudolph, T.: How significant are the known collision and element distinctness quantum algorithms? Quantum Inf. Comput. **4**(3), 201–206 (2004)

12. Jang, K., Choi, S., Kwon, H., Kim, H., Park, J., Seo, H.: Grover on korean block ciphers. Appl. Sci. **10**, 1–25 (2020)

13. Jang, K., Choi, S., Kwon, H., Seo, H.: Grover on SPECK: quantum resource estimates. IACR Cryptol. ePrint Arch, p. 640 (2020)

14. Jang, K., Song, G., Kim, H., Kwon, H., Kim, H., Seo, H.: Efficient implementation of PRESENT and GIFT on quantum computers. Appl. Sci. **11**(11), 4776 (2021)

15. Jaques, S., Naehrig, M., Roetteler, M., Virdia, F.: Implementing Grover oracles for quantum key search on AES and LowMC. In: Canteaut, A., Ishai, Y. (eds.) EUROCRYPT 2020. LNCS, vol. 12106, pp. 280–310. Springer, Cham (2020). https://doi.org/10.1007/978-3-030-45724-2_10

16. Jaques, S., Schanck, J.M.: Quantum cryptanalysis in the ram model: claw-finding attacks on SIKE. In: Boldyreva, A., Micciancio, D. (eds.) CRYPTO 2019. LNCS, vol. 11692, pp. 32–61. Springer, Cham (2019). https://doi.org/10.1007/978-3-030-26948-7_2

17. Jean, J., Nikolić, I., Peyrin, T.: Tweaks and keys for block ciphers: the TWEAKEY framework. In: Sarkar, P., Iwata, T. (eds.) ASIACRYPT 2014. LNCS, vol. 8874, pp. 274–288. Springer, Heidelberg (2014). https://doi.org/10.1007/978-3-662-45608-8_15

18. Jones, C.: Low-overhead constructions for the fault-tolerant toffoli gate. Phys. Rev. A **87**, 022328 (2013)

19. Kim, P., Han, D., Jeong, K.C.: Time-space complexity of quantum search algorithms in symmetric cryptanalysis: applying to AES and SHA-2. Quantum Inf. Process. **17**(12), 339 (2018)

20. Langenberg, B., Pham, H., Steinwandt, R.: Reducing the cost of implementing the advanced encryption standard as a quantum circuit. IEEE Trans. Quantum Eng. **1**, 1–12 (2020)

21. Nielsen, M.A., Chuang, I.L.: Quantum Computation and Quantum Information: 10th anniversary edition. Cambridge University Press (2010)

22. NIST: Submission requirements and evaluation criteria for the post-quantum cryptography standardization process (2016). https://csrc.nist.gov/CSRC/media/Projects/Post-Quantum-Cryptography/documents/call-for-proposals-final-dec-2016.pdf/

23. Schlieper, L.: In-place implementation of quantum-gimli (2020). https://arxiv.org/abs/2007.06319

24. Selinger, P.: Quantum circuits of t-depth one. Phys. Rev. A **87**, 042302 (2013)
25. Shor, P.W.: Polynomial time algorithms for discrete logarithms and factoring on a quantum computer. In: Adleman, L.M., Huang, M.-D. (eds.) ANTS 1994. LNCS, vol. 877, pp. 289–289. Springer, Heidelberg (1994). https://doi.org/10.1007/3-540-58691-1_68
26. Svore, K.M., et al.: Q#: Enabling scalable quantum computing and development with a high-level DSL. In: Proceedings of the Real World Domain Languages Workshop, pp. 7:1–7:10. ACM, Austria (2018)
27. William Stein et al.: Sagemath, the sage mathematics software system version 8.1 (2017). https://www.sagemath.org
28. Zalka, C.: Grover's quantum searching algorithm is optimal. Phys. Rev. A **60**(4), 2746–2751 (1999)
29. Zou, J., Wei, Z., Sun, S., Liu, X., Wu, W.: Quantum circuit implementations of AES with fewer qubits. In: Moriai, S., Wang, H. (eds.) ASIACRYPT 2020. LNCS, vol. 12492, pp. 697–726. Springer, Cham (2020). https://doi.org/10.1007/978-3-030-64834-3_24

Improved Division Property for Ciphers with Complex Linear Layers

Yongxia Mao[1,2], Wenling Wu[1,2(✉)], Bolin Wang[1,2], and Li Zhang[1,2]

[1] Trusted Computing and Information Assurance Laboratory, Institute of Software
Chinese Academy of Sciences, Beijing 100190, China
{yongxia2018,wenling,bolin2018,zhangli2021}@iscas.ac.cn
[2] University of Chinese Academy of Sciences, Beijing 100049, China

Abstract. The division property proposed by Todo at EUROCRYPT 2015 as a generalized integral property has been applied to many symmetric ciphers. Automatic search methods of the division property assisted by modeling technique, such as Mixed Integer Linear Programming (MILP) and Boolean Satisfiability Problem (SAT), have become the most popular approach to searching integral distinguishers. The accuracy of the model in searching algorithms has an effect on the search results of integral distinguishers. For the block cipher, constructing an accurate and efficient model of the division property propagation on complex linear layers remains hard. This paper observes that the non-independent propagations of the bit-based division property (BDP) on complex linear layers can generate redundant division trails, which will affect the accuracy of the model if it is not taken into account in modeling. Based on this, we propose a method that can build a more accurate model by handling matrices containing non-independent propagations in the linear layer. To verify the effectiveness of our method, we apply the method to two block ciphers uBlock-128 and MIBS. For uBlock-128, our results improve the previous 8-round integral distinguisher by more balanced bits. For MIBS, a 9-round integral distinguisher is given for the first time, which is 4 rounds longer than the previous best.

Keywords: Division property · Linear layer · Block cipher · MILP · Cryptanalysis

1 Introduction

Integral cryptanalysis was originally proposed by Knudsen et al. [1] at FSE 2002, also known as Square attack [2], and is a powerful cryptanalysis method. Todo [3] further generalized integral cryptanalysis as division property at EUROCRYPT 2015. At ASIACRYPT 2016, Xiang et al. [4] introduced the MILP technique into bit-based division property for the first time, which improved the block size of the block cipher that can be automatically searched. Since then, the automatic modeling tool of integral cryptanalysis has been widely used in evaluating the security of symmetric encryptions, and a series of remarkable results have been

K. Nguyen et al. (Eds.): ACISP 2022, LNCS 13494, pp. 106–124, 2022.
https://doi.org/10.1007/978-3-031-22301-3_6

obtained [5–10]. Recently, Hebborn et al. [11] demonstrated the upper bound on the round number of integral distinguishers on several block ciphers such as PRESENT and SKINNY-64, using the automatic modeling method of BDP at ASIACRYPT 2021.

The automatic search method with modeling technique mainly including MILP and SAT for division property can be summarized as follows. At first, the basic component model of block cipher needs to be established by following the propagation rules of division property. Next, the r-round model is built and the initial division property is given. At last, the entire model is solved with the help of solving tools, such as Gurobi and SAT/SMT solvers. In the process, the number of conditional constraints determines the time that it takes to solve and the round number of the integral distinguisher that can be obtained. For the linear component, it only needs to exchange the position of variables to build constraints when the linear layer is simple, such as PRESENT, GIFT, etc. When the linear layer is complex, such as AES, uBlock, MIBS, etc., it needs to follow the propagation rules of COPY/XOR operations to build the constraints, which often leads to redundancy and errors.

For the problem of how to model the complex linear layer, there are mainly S method [12], ZR method [13] and HW method [14]. The S method is a general method for modeling the division property propagation of complex linear layers. However, the disadvantage is that it does not consider the cancellation between terms, so it can easily introduce invalid division trails resulting in a quicker loss of the balanced property than the cipher itself would. Both the ZR method and HW method can create very accurate models, but their applications have certain limitations. For example, the ZR method needs to construct a one-to-one correspondence between the division trails of the invertible matrix M and the invertible sub-matrices, so it is not suitable for the non-binary linear layer and non-invertible matrices. The HW method can only be modeled by SAT and cannot be applied to the MILP model. As far as the current modeling methods of the division property for S-boxes, the accuracy of the SAT solving model is weaker than that of the MILP model. Hence, the HW method is not suitable for block ciphers with S-boxes.

Our Contribution. In this paper, we analyze why errors arise in the solving model of division property propagations for the complex linear layer. In other words, the *non-independent division property propagation* of variables in the linear layer will produce redundant division trails, which reduces the accuracy of the model, and ultimately affects the judgment of integral distinguishers. Then, we propose a strategy to effectively remove redundant division trails for the *non-independent division property propagation*: replacing the original representation of the linear layer with an equivalent one which only includes the *independent division property propagation*. According to this strategy, an algorithm (Algorithm 2) is proposed to construct the MILP model of BDP propagation for the complex linear layer. Finally, we apply our method to two block ciphers uBlock-128 and MIBS. For uBlock-128, we find an 8-round integral distinguisher where all the 128 bits are balanced. For MIBS, we find a 9-round integral distinguisher with 32 balanced bits which is better than the best known result. We list all our new BDP results obtained in Table 1.

Organization. The rest of this paper is organized as follows. Section 2 introduces some notations of this paper and revisits the definition related to division property. Section 3 presents our observations and the new method of this paper. Section 4 mainly presents improved integral distinguishers on uBlock-128 and MIBS by using our new method. Section 5 is the conclusion and outlook for future work.

Table 1. Number of rounds of the best known integral distinuisher vs. our results on the block cipher uBlock-128 and MIBS.

Cipher	# Rounds	log_2 (Data)	# Balanced bits	Reference
uBlock	7	124	128	[16]
	8	124	64	[17]
	8	124	96	Sect. 4.1
	8	127	128	Sect. 4.1
MIBS	5	8	8	[21]
	5	12	32	Sect. 4.2
	6	32	32	Sect. 4.2
	7	52	32	Sect. 4.2
	8	61	32	Sect. 4.2
	8	63	64	Sect. 4.2
	9	63	32	Sect. 4.2

2   Notations and Division Property

In this section, we are going to show some notations, and recall the fundamental definitions and modeling techniques of division property.

For a block cipher, we use the following notation to represent the integral property of a nibble in the plaintext and ciphertext.

- $\mathcal{C}$: Each bit of the nibble at the plaintext is fixed to constant.
- $\mathcal{A}$: All bits of the nibble at the plaintext are active.
- $\mathcal{B}$: Each bit of the nibble at the ciphertext is balanced.
- $\mathcal{U}$: A nibble at the ciphertext with unknown status.

For the integral property of a single bit in integral distinguishers, we use c, a, b, and u denote a constant bit, an active bit, a balanced bit and an unknown bit, respectively. For a matrix $M \in \mathbb{F}_2^{m \times n}$, we use the notation $M[i][j]$ to represent the element of M located at the i-th row and j-th column, $l_i = M[i]$ to represent the i-th row, and $M[*][j]$ to represent the j-th column. A bold letter represents a vector, e.g., $\boldsymbol{u} \in \mathbb{F}_2^m$. Let $\boldsymbol{k}$ and $\boldsymbol{k'}$ be two vectors in $\mathbb{F}_2^m$, we define $\boldsymbol{k} \succcurlyeq \boldsymbol{k'}$ if $k_i \geq k'_i$ for all i.

Bit Product Function [3]: Let $\pi_u : \mathbb{F}_2^n \to \mathbb{F}_2$ be a function for any $u \in \mathbb{F}_2^n$. Let $x \in \mathbb{F}_2^n$ be an input of π_u, then $\pi_u(x)$ is defined as

$$\pi_u(x) = \prod_{i=0}^{n-1} x_i^{u_i},$$

where $x_i^0 = 1$ and $x_i^1 = x_i$.

Definition 1 (Bit-based Division Property [15]**).** *Let $\mathbb{X}$ be a multiset whose elements take a value of $\mathbb{F}_2^m$, and $k \in \mathbb{F}_2^m$. When the multiset $\mathbb{X}$ has the division property $D_{\mathbb{K}}^{1,m}$, it fulfils the following conditions:*

$$\bigoplus_{x \in \mathbb{X}} \pi_u(x) = \begin{cases} unknown, & \text{if there are } k \in \mathbb{K} \text{ s.t. } u \succcurlyeq k, \\ 0, & otherwise. \end{cases}$$

Definition 2 (Division Trail [4]**).** *Let f be the round function of an iterated block cipher. Assume the input multiset set to the block cipher has initial division property $D_{\mathbb{K}_0}^{1,n}$, and denote the division property after i rounds through f by $D_{\mathbb{K}_i}^{1,n}$. Then we have the following chain of division property propagations:*

$$\{k\} \equiv \mathbb{K}_0 \xrightarrow{f} \mathbb{K}_1 \xrightarrow{f} \cdots \xrightarrow{f} \mathbb{K}_r.$$

For any vector $k_{i+1}^* \in \mathbb{K}_{i+1}$, there must exist a vector $k_i^* \in \mathbb{K}_i$ such that k_i^* can propagate to k_{i+1}^*. Furthermore, for $(k_0, k_1, \ldots, k_r) \in (\mathbb{K}_0 \times \mathbb{K}_1 \times \mathbb{K}_2 \times \cdots \times \mathbb{K}_r)$, if for all $i \in \{0, 1, \cdots, r-1\}$, k_i can propagate to k_{i+1}, we call $(k_0 \to k_1 \to \ldots \to k_r)$ a r-round division trail.

MILP Modeling Rule for COPY [12]. If $a \xrightarrow{COPY} (b_0, b_1, \cdots, b_{m-1})$ is a division trail of COPY function, it is sufficient to describe the propagation using the following inequalities

$$\begin{cases} a - b_0 - b_1 - \cdots - b_{m-1} = 0, \\ a, b_0, b_1, \cdots, b_{m-1} \text{ are binaries.} \end{cases}$$

MILP Modeling Rule for XOR [12]. If $(a_0, a_1, \cdots, a_{m-1}) \xrightarrow{XOR} b$ is a division trail of XOR function, it is sufficient to describe the propagation using the following inequalities

$$\begin{cases} a_0 + a_1 + \cdots + a_{m-1} - b = 0, \\ a_0, a_1, \cdots, a_{m-1}, b \text{ are binaries.} \end{cases}$$

The Judgment Condition of Division Property. If there exists a division trail that satisfies $k_0 \xrightarrow{E_k} k_r = e_j$, where e_j is a unit vector, $j \in \{0, \cdots, n-1\}$, then the j-th bit of ciphertext is unknown. If there is no division trail $k_0 \xrightarrow{E_k} k_r = e_j$, then the j-th bit of ciphertext is balanced.

3   A Method to Reduce Redundant Division Trails for Complex Linear Layers

With the help of the MILP modeling rules, the linear inequalities of the division property propagation for the linear layer can be established. We can easily observe the following rules: for the same linear layer, the more COPY/XOR operations in MILP model are used, the lower accuracy achieved in characterizing division property propagations. For example, obviously, if the linear layer is a simple bit permutation, the model of the linear layer will not produce error and redundancy, because we only need to exchange the position of variables without adding extra constraints to model for describing the division property propagation on linear layer. For complex linear layers, the situation becomes different.

Assuming that $L : (x_0, x_1, x_2, x_3, x_4, x_5) \to (y_0, y_1, y_2, y_3, y_4, y_5)$ is a linear transformation corresponding to a complex linear layer, and the equivalent linear transformation matrix is M which always is a full rank matrix. In this paper, "complex" also means that there are at least two rows in M that have the element 1 on at least two of the same columns, i.e., there exist i, j s.t. $\sum_k M[i][k] \cdot M[j][k] \geq 2$. If we establish constaints based on the original matrix M, then at least two independent constraints about COPY on the input variables need to be added to the MILP model. In fact, the two COPY constraints are not independent since they occur simultaneously in the constraints about XOR for two different output variables. At this point, an error occurs. Similarly, when $\sum_k M[i][k] \cdot M[j][k] = 4$, we need to add 4 independent constraints on COPY from M. Suppose $M[1] = (0, 1, 1, 1, 1, 1)$ and $M[2] = (1, 1, 0, 1, 1, 1)$. If we set $t_1 = x_1 + x_3$ and $t_2 = x_4 + x_5$ using the method in [18], then only two independent constraints on COPY and two independent constraints on XOR need to be added. However, the two COPY constraints are still not independent in fact because they appear in the XOR constraints of both y_1 and y_2. Errors in the MILP model eventually lead to redundant division trails through L.

Generally speaking, when several output bits contain multiple common input variables during propagations, the model established on some of the bits based on the MILP modeling rule for COPY cannot accurately describe the correlation between them. In other words, some non-independent bits are incorrectly propagated as independent bits if we build the MILP model of linear layers directly from the original matrix. As a result, the division property of multiple outputs is 1 at the same time in places where it should not be. Thus, there will be some redundant division trails. To this end, we give the following definition and observation.

Definition 3. *Let $F : \mathbb{F}_2^n \to \mathbb{F}_2^m$ be a linear transformation , defined as $F(x) = y$, and M be the equivalent linear transformation matrix satisfying $M \cdot x = y$. The division property of x and y is denoted as $a = (a_0, a_1, ..., a_{n-1})$ and $b = (b_0, b_1, ..., b_{m-1})$, respectively. That is, $a \xrightarrow{F} b$ is a division trail through F. We call $a_{i_1}, a_{i_2}, ..., a_{i_s} \xrightarrow{F} b_{j_1}, b_{j_2}, ..., b_{j_t}$ is a non-independent division prop-*

erty propagation through F, if $M[j_*][i_*] = 1$ for all $i_* \in \{i_1, i_2, ..., i_s\}$, $j_* \in \{j_1, j_2, ..., j_t\}$, $n \geq s \geq 2$, $m \geq t \geq 2$, i.e., $\sum_{k=0}^{n-1} M[j_1][k] \cdot M[j_2][k] \cdot ... \cdot M[j_t][k] \geq 2$, where $\{i_1, i_2, ..., i_s\}$ and $\{j_1, j_2, ..., j_t\}$ are two index sets. Otherwise, it is called an independent division property propagation.

Observation. When modeling the non-independent division property propagations, redundant division trails will be generated if we use the MILP model of independent propagations to characterize that of non-independent propagations. If all the common variables that lead to non-independent division property propagations in the linear function F are all replaced at once by variables $T_1, \cdots, T_N$ newly introduced, the propagation through F that are described in new expressions containing variables $T_1, \cdots, T_N$ will be transformed into independent division property propagations. In this way, the redundant division trails can be effectively reduced.

Example 1. Assume that the linear transformation $P : \mathbb{F}_2^8 \to \mathbb{F}_2^8$ has following expressions:

$$z_0 = y_0 + y_1 + y_3 + y_4 + y_6 + y_7,$$
$$z_1 = y_1 + y_2 + y_3 + y_4 + y_5 + y_6,$$
$$z_2 = y_0 + y_1 + y_2 + y_4 + y_5 + y_7,$$
$$z_3 = y_1 + y_2 + y_3 + y_6 + y_7,$$
$$z_4 = y_0 + y_2 + y_3 + y_4 + y_7,$$
$$z_5 = y_0 + y_1 + y_3 + y_4 + y_5,$$
$$z_6 = y_0 + y_1 + y_2 + y_5 + y_6,$$
$$z_7 = y_0 + y_2 + y_3 + y_5 + y_6 + y_7,$$

where $(y_0, y_1, y_2, y_3, y_4, y_5, y_6, y_7)$ and $(z_0, z_1, z_2, z_3, z_4, z_5, z_6, z_7)$ are the inputs and outputs, respectively. Let the corresponding division property be $(a_0, a_1, a_2, a_3, a_4, a_5, a_6, a_7)$ and $(b_0, b_1, b_2, b_3, b_4, b_5, b_6, b_7)$, respectively.

We take b_1 and b_3 as examples, and focus on division trails with the form of $(a_0, a_1, a_2, a_3, a_4, a_5, a_6, a_7) \to (*, b_1, *, b_3, *, *, *, *)$. Let the input division property be $(0, 1, 1, 1, 0, 0, 1, 0)$, so we only consider the output division property with form $(0, *, 0, *, 0, 0, 0, 0)$. According to traditional models,

$$b_1 = a_1 + a_2 + a_3 + a_4 + a_5 + a_6,$$
$$b_3 = a_1 + a_2 + a_3 + a_6 + a_7.$$

a_1, a_2, a_3, a_6 need to establish constraints separately by using the MILP modeling rule for COPY, so the output division property is $(0, 1, 0, 1, 0, 0, 0, 0)$, $(0, 1, 0, 0, 0, 0, 0, 0)$, and $(0, 0, 0, 1, 0, 0, 0, 0)$. For b_1, when i (≤ 4) variables of a_1, a_2, a_3, a_6 take 1, the output division property $(0, 1, 0, 1, 0, 0, 0, 0)$ will be obtained. However, since $(0, 1, 0, 1, 0, 0, 0, 0) \succcurlyeq (0, 1, 0, 0, 0, 0, 0, 0)$, $(0, 1, 0, 1, 0, 0, 0, 0)$ is redundant.

We noticed that $(*, a_1, a_2, a_3, *, *, a_6, *) \to (*, b_1, *, b_3, *, *, *, *)$ is the non-independent division property propagation, and a_1, a_2, a_3, a_6 are the common variables of b_1, b_3. If we denote $t = a_1 + a_2 + a_3 + a_6$, then $b_1 = t + a_4 + a_5$ and $b_3 = t + a_7$ are new expressions. At this point, we only need to do COPY operation once on t. For b_1, when any i variables of a_1, a_2, a_3, a_6 take 1, $i < 4$, that is, the t contained in b_1 takes 1, the other t contained in b_3 must take constant 0 after COPY operation, hence the output division property must be $(0, 1, 0, 0, 0, 0, 0, 0)$. After variable substitution, the output division property of the form $(0, *, 0, *, 0, 0, 0, 0)$ contains only $(0, 1, 0, 0, 0, 0, 0, 0)$, $(0, 0, 0, 1, 0, 0, 0, 0)$. Similarly, redundant vectors like the above can be removed by updating the linear layer expression using a series of variable substitutions.

Before building the constraints of the MILP model of the linear layer, we first pair the rows of the implementation matrix that is a linear transformation matrix so that we can extract the common variables for each pair. It is not difficult to find that for the entire reduction process, the more common variable that can be extracted, the better the effect of removing redundant trails and the more accurate the model. Following the reduction idea, We present Algorithm 1 for screening and pairing the rows of the linear transformation matrix.

Algorithm 2 is used to build the MILP model of the BDP propagation for the linear layer. Let the initial matrix of the linear layer be M, the matrix corresponding to the new variable that are introduced by replacing the common variable be B. A new matrix P with size $n \times (n + n/2)$ is generated in Algorithm 2 which is equivalent to M, and the last $n/2$ columns of P correspond to new binary variable $T_1, \cdots, T_N$. Additionally, we point out that Algorithm 2 can also make models using SAT method based on Algorithm 1, and they are equivalent.

Algorithm 1. Row pairing algorithm for a linear transformation matrix

---

Input: An implementation matrix M of the linear layer
Output: A row partition of M
1: $count = 0_{n \times n}$ //a $n \times n$ all-zero matrix
2: **for** $i \in \{0, n\}, j \in \{0, n\}$ **do**
3:     **if** $i < j$ **then**
4:         $count[i][j] = \sum\limits_{k=0}^{n-1} l_i^k \wedge l_j^k$
5:     **else**
6:         $count[i][j] = 0$
7:     **end if**
8: **end for**
9: **while** True **do**
10:     $Global\_max = max(count)$
11:     **if** $Global\_max = 0$ **then**
12:         break
13:     **end if**
14:     **if** $row\_max = Global\_max$ **then** //the row row_max is located
15:         $Row = (row\_max = Global\_max)[0]$
16:     **end if**
17:     **for** $j \in J = \{j | count[Row][j] = row\_max\}$ **do**
18:         **if** $max(count[j]) < row\_max$ **then**//the column row_max is located

19:          $Col = j$; break
20:      **end if**
21:    **end for**
22:    **if** $len(Col) = 0$ **then**
23:        $Col = J[0]$
24:    **end if**
25:    $result \leftarrow (Row, Col)$
26:    $count[Row] = 0, count[Col] = 0, count[*][Row] = 0, count[*][Col] = 0$
27: **end while**
28: **return** $result$

Algorithm 2. Construct the MILP model of linear layer BDP propagation

---

Input: An Implementation matrix M of the linear layer
Output: The MILP model $\mathcal{M}$ of BDP propagation
 1: Build an empty MILP model $\mathcal{M}$
 2: $\mathcal{M}.var \leftarrow a_i, b_i, u_i$ $//a_i, b_i$ denote the input and output BDP of linear layer, u_i denotes a new binary variable introduced by COPY
 3: $B = [\,]$ $//$a $n \times \frac{n}{2}$ all-zero matrix
 4: **for** (i, j) in $result$ **do**
 5:    $B[i][N] = 1, B[j][N] = 1$
 6:    $l = \left(l_i^0 \wedge l_j^0, l_i^1 \wedge l_j^1, \ldots, l_i^n \wedge l_j^n\right)$
 7:    $M[i] = M[i] + l, M[j] = M[j] + l$
 8:    $Constr \leftarrow T_N = \sum\limits_{k=0}^{n-1} x_k \cdot \left(l_i^k \wedge l_j^k\right)$
 9:    $Constr \leftarrow y_i = T_N + \sum\limits_{k=0}^{n-1} x_k \cdot \left(l_i^k \oplus l^k\right), y_j = T_N + \sum\limits_{k=0}^{n-1} x_k \cdot \left(l_j^k \oplus l^k\right)$
10:    $\mathcal{M}.con \leftarrow T_N = \sum\limits_{k=0}^{n-1} a_k \cdot \left(l_i^k \wedge l_j^k\right)$
11: **end for**
12: $P = [M, B]$
13: **for** $j \in (0, n + n/2), i \in (0, n)$ **do**
14:    $\mathcal{M}.con \leftarrow a_j = \sum\limits_{k=0}^{n-1} u_k \cdot P[i][j]$
15: **end for**
16: **for** $i \in (0, n), j \in (0, n + n/2)$ **do**
17:    $\mathcal{M}.con \leftarrow b_i = \sum\limits_{k=0}^{n-1} u_k \cdot P[i][j]$
18: **end for**
19: **return** $\mathcal{M}$

Traditional models usually added the corresponding constraints based on the initial expression of the linear layer and combined with the BDP model of COPY/XOR operations. If there exist non-independent division property propagations in it, then redundant vectors must be produced, for example the method of [12]. Hong et al. [18] proposed a method using the optimal implementation of the linear layer to reduce the number of COPY/XOR constraints, and finally obtained the same integral distinguisher as the best at the time. [18] is an example of reducing errors caused by non-independent division property propagations, and it also supports our observation in this section, but the method of [18] is effective for the cipher like Midori-64, Skinny-64 and LED (because the non-independent propagation in the linear layer of these ciphers contains at most 3 common variables, our model contains i common variables, $i \geq 2$). In other words, for the cipher with complex linear layers, such as uBlock and MIBS ($i \geq 3$), only a part of the redundancy can be reduced using method in [18].

4   Applications

In this section, for two block ciphers uBlock-128 and MIBS, we first briefly introduce their encryption structures, then apply our new method to them, and finally show the complete process of constructing MILP models for them.

4.1   Application to uBlock-128

uBlock-128. uBlock is a block cipher family proposed by Wu et al. [16]. It adopts a SP network and supports 128-bit and 256-bit block lengths. Moreover, uBlock-128 supports 128-bit and 256-bit key lengths, and the number of encryption rounds are 16 and 24, respectively. Let the round function of uBlock-128 be $f = P \circ X \circ S$, where S represents the S layer, X represents the cyclic shift and XOR operation in the middle, and P represents the last nibble-based permutation. The round function is shown in Fig. 1, where s represents a 4-bit nonlinear S-box, and $\lll 4$ represents that a block rotates 4 bits to the left in units of 32. PL_{128} and PR_{128} represent two 8-byte vector permutations respectively, where $PL_{128} = \{1, 3, 4, 6, 0, 2, 7, 5\}$ and $PR_{128} = \{2, 7, 5, 0, 1, 6, 4, 3\}$.

uBlock is the winner in the National Cryptographic Algorithm Design Competition held by the Chinese Association for Cryptologic Research in 2019 because of its adaptability to software and hardware platforms, simple and effective hardware implementations, and strong security. For the integral cryptanalysis, based on Todo et al.'s conclusion on the division property of the (l, d, m)-SPN in [3], the uBlock designers presented a 7-round integral distinguisher [16]. Besides, the current optimal integral distinguisher is the 8-round distinguisher found by Tian et al. [17] by using the optimized representation of S-box in division property propagation.

Searching the Integral Distinguisher of uBlock-128. Let the input of the X layer be $x = (x_3, x_2, x_1, x_0)$ and the output be $y = (y_3, y_2, y_1, y_0)$. Then the linear matrix corresponding to the transformation X can be expressed as the juxtaposition of two nibble-based matrices $M_{16 \times 16}$, denoted as

$$M_{16 \times 16} = \begin{bmatrix} A_{8 \times 16} \\ B_{8 \times 16} \end{bmatrix}.$$

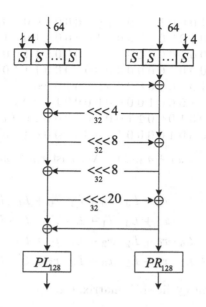

Fig. 1. Round function of uBlock-128.

$$A = \begin{bmatrix} 0\,0\,1\,1\,1\,0\,1\,1\,1\,1\,0\,1\,0\,1\,1\,1 \\ 1\,0\,0\,1\,1\,1\,0\,1\,1\,1\,1\,0\,1\,0\,1\,1 \\ 1\,1\,0\,0\,1\,1\,1\,0\,1\,1\,1\,1\,0\,1\,0\,1 \\ 0\,1\,1\,0\,0\,1\,1\,1\,1\,1\,1\,1\,1\,0\,1\,0 \\ 1\,0\,1\,1\,0\,0\,1\,1\,0\,1\,1\,1\,1\,1\,0\,1 \\ 1\,1\,0\,1\,1\,0\,0\,1\,1\,0\,1\,1\,1\,1\,1\,0 \\ 1\,1\,1\,0\,1\,1\,0\,0\,0\,1\,0\,1\,1\,1\,1\,1 \\ 0\,1\,1\,1\,0\,1\,1\,0\,1\,0\,1\,0\,1\,1\,1\,1 \end{bmatrix} \quad B = \begin{bmatrix} 1\,1\,0\,1\,0\,1\,1\,1\,1\,0\,1\,1\,0\,0\,1\,1 \\ 1\,1\,1\,0\,1\,0\,1\,1\,1\,1\,0\,1\,1\,0\,0\,1 \\ 1\,1\,1\,1\,0\,1\,0\,1\,1\,1\,1\,0\,1\,1\,0\,0 \\ 1\,1\,1\,1\,1\,0\,1\,0\,0\,1\,1\,1\,0\,1\,1\,0 \\ 0\,1\,1\,1\,1\,1\,0\,1\,0\,0\,1\,1\,1\,0\,1\,1 \\ 1\,0\,1\,1\,1\,1\,1\,0\,1\,0\,0\,1\,1\,1\,0\,1 \\ 0\,1\,0\,1\,1\,1\,1\,1\,1\,0\,0\,1\,1\,1\,0 \\ 1\,0\,1\,0\,1\,1\,1\,1\,0\,1\,1\,0\,0\,1\,1\,1 \end{bmatrix}$$

In other words, the input x is transformed by the matrix $A_{8\times16}$ and then output y_2 and y_3, and x is also transformed by the matrix $B_{8\times16}$ and then output y_0 and y_1. It can be observed from the initial matrix A and B that any two of the rows contain multiple common columns with a constant 1. Thus the division property propagation of $(x_0, *, x_2, *) \to y_0, y_2$ and $(*, x_1, *, x_3) \to y_1, y_3$ are both non-independent. After operating on the linear transformation matrix A and B by using Algorithm 1 and Algorithm 2, we get the new matrix representation corresponding to the X transformation under the basis $(x_3, x_2, x_1, x_0, T_1, T_0)$. That is

$$A' = \begin{bmatrix} 0\,0\,1\,0\,1\,0\,0\,0\,1\,1\,0\,0\,0\,1\,0\,0\,0\,0\,0\,1\,0\,0\,1\,1 \\ 0\,0\,0\,1\,0\,1\,0\,0\,0\,1\,1\,0\,0\,0\,1\,0\,1\,0\,0\,0\,1\,0\,0\,1 \\ 0\,0\,0\,0\,1\,0\,1\,0\,0\,0\,1\,1\,0\,0\,0\,1\,1\,1\,0\,0\,0\,1\,0\,0 \\ 0\,0\,0\,0\,0\,1\,0\,1\,1\,0\,0\,1\,1\,0\,0\,0\,0\,1\,1\,0\,0\,0\,1\,0 \\ 1\,0\,0\,0\,0\,0\,1\,0\,0\,1\,0\,0\,1\,1\,0\,0\,0\,0\,1\,1\,0\,0\,0\,1 \\ 0\,1\,0\,0\,0\,0\,0\,1\,0\,0\,1\,0\,0\,1\,1\,0\,1\,0\,0\,1\,1\,0\,0\,0 \\ 1\,0\,1\,0\,0\,0\,0\,0\,0\,1\,0\,0\,1\,1\,0\,1\,0\,0\,1\,1\,0\,0 \\ 0\,1\,0\,1\,0\,0\,0\,0\,1\,0\,0\,0\,1\,0\,0\,1\,0\,0\,1\,0\,0\,1\,1\,0 \end{bmatrix}$$

$$B' = \begin{bmatrix} 0\,1\,0\,0\,0\,1\,0\,0\,0\,0\,1\,0\,0\,0\,0\,0\,1\,0\,0\,1\,0\,0\,1\,1 \\ 0\,0\,1\,0\,0\,0\,1\,0\,0\,0\,0\,1\,0\,0\,0\,0\,1\,1\,0\,0\,1\,0\,0\,1 \\ 0\,0\,0\,1\,0\,0\,0\,1\,0\,0\,0\,0\,1\,0\,0\,0\,1\,1\,1\,0\,0\,1\,0\,0 \\ 1\,0\,0\,0\,1\,0\,0\,0\,0\,0\,0\,0\,0\,1\,0\,0\,0\,1\,1\,1\,0\,0\,1\,0 \\ 0\,1\,0\,0\,0\,1\,0\,0\,0\,0\,0\,0\,0\,0\,1\,0\,0\,0\,1\,1\,1\,0\,0\,1 \\ 0\,0\,1\,0\,0\,0\,1\,0\,0\,0\,0\,0\,0\,0\,0\,1\,1\,0\,0\,1\,1\,1\,0\,0 \\ 0\,0\,0\,1\,0\,0\,0\,1\,1\,0\,0\,0\,0\,0\,0\,0\,0\,1\,0\,0\,1\,1\,1\,0 \\ 1\,0\,0\,0\,1\,0\,0\,0\,0\,1\,0\,0\,0\,0\,0\,0\,0\,0\,1\,0\,0\,1\,1\,1 \end{bmatrix}$$

where $T_0 = x_0 + x_2$, $T_1 = x_1 + x_3$. The X transformation can be expressed as follows

$$y_0 = L_2 \cdot x_0 + L_1 \cdot x_2 + L_5 \cdot x_2 + L_0 \cdot T_0 + L_3 \cdot T_0 + L_6 \cdot T_0 + L_7 \cdot T_0$$

$$y_1 = L_2 \cdot x_1 + L_1 \cdot x_3 + L_5 \cdot x_3 + L_0 \cdot T_1 + L_3 \cdot T_1 + L_6 \cdot T_1 + L_7 \cdot T_1$$

$$y_2 = L_0 \cdot x_0 + L_1 \cdot x_0 + L_5 \cdot x_0 + L_2 \cdot x_2 + L_4 \cdot x_2 + L_3 \cdot T_0 + L_6 \cdot T_0 + L_7 \cdot T_0$$

$$y_3 = L_0 \cdot x_1 + L_1 \cdot x_1 + L_5 \cdot x_1 + L_2 \cdot x_3 + L_4 \cdot x_3 + L_3 \cdot T_1 + L_6 \cdot T_1 + L_7 \cdot T_1$$

where L_i is a 32×32 left cyclic shift matrix, e.g.

$$L_2 = \begin{bmatrix} 0\,0\,1\,0\,0\,\ldots\,0\,0\,0\,0 \\ 0\,0\,0\,1\,0\,\ldots\,0\,0\,0\,0 \\ 0\,0\,0\,0\,1\,\ldots\,0\,0\,0\,0 \\ \vdots\,\vdots\,\vdots\,\vdots\,\vdots\,\quad\vdots\,\quad\vdots\,\vdots \\ 0\,1\,0\,0\,0\,\ldots\,0\,0\,0\,0 \end{bmatrix}.$$

It is easy to observe that any two rows of A' and B' have at most one common column with 1 in the first n columns. Therefore, the representation of X is transformed into the new form which not contains non-independent division property propagations.

Let the input division property of X be $(a_3, a_2, a_1, a_0, U_1, U_0) \in (\mathbb{F}_2^{32})^6$ and the output division property be $(b_3, b_2, b_1, b_0) \in (\mathbb{F}_2^{32})^4$. We can easily obtain the linear inequality constraints in terms of new expressions. Firstly, the following constraints corresponding to the substitution variables need to be added to the MILP model $\mathcal{M}$:

$$\begin{cases} U_0 = a_0 + a_2, \\ U_1 = a_1 + a_3, \\ U_1, U_0 \text{ are binaries.} \end{cases}$$

Then, according to the linear matrices A' and B' with independent division property propagations, we can easily write the corresponding constraints. For example, for y_0, y_2, the first column of A' and B' corresponds to x_2^7, then we have the COPY constraint

$$\begin{cases} a_2^7 = A_0^7 + A_1^7 + \cdots + A_5^7, \\ A_0^7, \cdots, A_5^7 \text{ are binaries.} \end{cases}$$

The last column of A' and B' corresponds to T_0^7, then we have the COPY constraint

$$\begin{cases} U_0^7 = u_0^0 + u_1^0 + \cdots + u_6^0, \\ u_0^0, \cdots, u_6^0 \text{ are binaries.} \end{cases}$$

The first row of B' corresponds to y_0^7, then we have the XOR constraint

$$\begin{cases} b_0^7 = A_0^6 + A_0^2 + \cdots + t_1^0 + t_0^0, \\ b_0^7 \text{ is binary.} \end{cases}$$

For the nonlinear layer of uBlock-128, we need to use the SAGE tool to convert division trails of the S-box into some linear inequalities, and then reduce them through the Greedy Algorithm (refer to [4] for more details). Algorithm 3 describes the whole process of building a MILP model for the BDP of uBlock-128. Based on Algorithm 3, for uBlock-128, we verified the 7-round integral distinguisher in the design document and 6-, 7-, 8-round integral distinguishers in [17], and obtained better results shown in the following.

8-Round Integral Distinguishers. When the least significant 4 bits of the input are constant and other positions are active, the output after 8 rounds has 96 balanced bits; when the most significant 4 bits of the input are constant and other positions are active, the output after 8 rounds has 96 balanced bits; when the least significant 1 bits of the input are constant and other positions are active, the output after 8 rounds are all balanced.

$$\begin{bmatrix} C & A & A & A & A & A & A & A \\ A & A & A & A & A & A & A & A \\ A & A & A & A & A & A & A & A \\ A & A & A & A & A & A & A & A \end{bmatrix} \xrightarrow{8R} \begin{bmatrix} bubb & bubb & bubb & bubb & bubb & bubb & bubb & bubb \\ bubb & bubb & bubb & bubb & bubb & bubb & bubb & bubb \\ bubb & bubb & bubb & bubb & bubb & bubb & bubb & bubb \\ bubb & bubb & bubb & bubb & bubb & bubb & bubb & bubb \end{bmatrix}$$

$$\begin{bmatrix} A & A & A & A & A & A & A & A \\ A & A & A & A & A & A & A & A \\ A & A & A & A & A & A & A & A \\ A & A & A & A & A & A & A & C \end{bmatrix} \xrightarrow{8R} \begin{bmatrix} bubb & bubb & bubb & bubb & bubb & bubb & bubb & bubb \\ bubb & bubb & bubb & bubb & bubb & bubb & bubb & bubb \\ bubb & bubb & bubb & bubb & bubb & bubb & bubb & bubb \\ bubb & bubb & bubb & bubb & bubb & bubb & bubb & bubb \end{bmatrix}$$

$$\begin{bmatrix} A & A & A & A & A & A & A & A \\ A & A & A & A & A & A & A & A \\ A & A & A & A & A & A & A & A \\ A & A & A & A & A & A & A & \text{aaac} \end{bmatrix} \xrightarrow{8R} \begin{bmatrix} B & B & B & B & B & B & B & B \\ B & B & B & B & B & B & B & B \\ B & B & B & B & B & B & B & B \\ B & B & B & B & B & B & B & B \end{bmatrix}$$

Algorithm 3 A MILP model for BDP propagation of uBlock-128

Input: S-box, the linear layer
Output: A MILP model $\mathcal{M}$ for BDP propagation of uBlock-128.
 1: Build an empty MILP model $\mathcal{M}$.
 2: $\mathcal{M}.var \leftarrow a_i, b_i, U_i, u_i, A_i$ //a_i, b_i denote the input and output BDP of linear layer, the rest are newly introduced binary variables
 3: //Generating Constrained Inequalities for S-boxes
 4: Call Algorithm 2 in [4] to calculate the division trail of S-box: $V = \{a_i \rightarrow b_i\}$
 5: Use $inequality\_generator()$ in SAGE to generate inequalities of V : $\mathcal{L}(a_i, b_i)$
 6: Reduce $\mathcal{L}(a_i, b_i)$ to $\mathcal{L}'(a_i, b_i)$ by using the Greedy Algorithm
 7: $\mathcal{M}.con \leftarrow \mathcal{L}'(a_i, b_i)$
 8: //Generating Constraned Inequalities for Linear Layers
 9: Write the implementation matrix M of linear layer
10: Call Algorithm 2 to generate constraints: $\mathcal{L}''(b_i, a_i, U_i, u_i, A_i)$
11: $\mathcal{M}.con \leftarrow \mathcal{L}''(b_i, a_i, U_i, u_i, A_i)$
12: **for** i in range$(0, n)$ **do**
13:     $\mathcal{M}.con \leftarrow \mathcal{L}'(a_i, b_i)$
14:     $\mathcal{M}.con \leftarrow \mathcal{L}''(b_i, a_i, U_i, u_i, A_i)$
15:     $\mathcal{M}.con \leftarrow \mathcal{L}'''(PL_{128}(b_i, a_{i+1}), PR_{128}(b_i, a_{i+1}))$
16: **end for**
17: Return $\mathcal{M}$

4.2   Application to MIBS

MIBS. MIBS is a lightweight block cipher proposed by Izadi M et al. at CANS 2009 [19]. Its overall encryption structure uses the Feistel network, and the round function adopts the SP network. The cipher has a 64-bit block length and supports 64-bit and 80-bit two key lengths. The number of iterative rounds is 32. All iterative operations in MIBS are based on nibble. The round function includes a XOR subkey, a S-box layer and a linear layer M denoted as $M = L \circ XOR \circ P$, where L represents the left and right permutations, XOR represents XOR with the input of the right half, P represents the linear transformation in the middle. The round function of MIBS is shown in Fig. 2.

MIBS has good resistance to differential cryptanalysis, linear cryptanalysis and integral cryptanalysis. The current best cryptanalytic result for MIBS is the 18-round linear cryptanalysis on MIBS-80 with the time complexity $2^{76.13}$, but the success probability is only 72.14% [20]. The existing integral attacks on it are mainly obtained by the derivation of the structure, and the known optimal integral distinguisher is a 5-round one proposed by Li et al. [21].

Searching the Integral Distinguisher of MIBS. Let the input of transformation P be $x = (x_7, x_6, x_5, x_4, x_3, x_2, x_1, x_0)$ and the output be $y = (y_7, y_6, y_5, y_4, y_3, y_2, y_1, y_0)$. The division property propagation is expressed as $(a_7, a_6, a_5,$

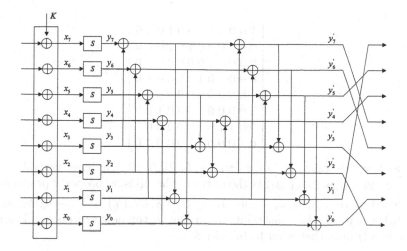

Fig. 2. Round function of MIBS.

$a_4, a_3, a_2, a_1, a_0) \xrightarrow{P} (b_7, b_6, b_5, b_4, b_3, b_2, b_1, b_0)$. The transformation matrix of P is expressed as follows:

$$M = \begin{bmatrix} 1 & 1 & 1 & 0 & 1 & 1 & 0 & 1 \\ 0 & 1 & 1 & 0 & 0 & 1 & 1 & 1 \\ 0 & 0 & 1 & 1 & 1 & 0 & 1 & 1 \\ 1 & 0 & 0 & 1 & 1 & 1 & 0 & 1 \\ 1 & 1 & 0 & 0 & 1 & 1 & 1 & 0 \\ 1 & 0 & 1 & 1 & 0 & 1 & 1 & 1 \\ 0 & 1 & 1 & 1 & 1 & 1 & 1 & 0 \\ 1 & 1 & 0 & 1 & 1 & 0 & 1 & 1 \end{bmatrix}.$$

To convert the non-independent division property propagations involved in transformation P into independent propagations, the following new variables are introduced in using Algorithm 2.

$$\begin{cases} T_0 = x_0 + x_3 + x_4 + x_7, \\ T_1 = x_1 + x_2 + x_3 + x_6, \\ T_2 = x_0 + x_1 + x_4 + x_5, \\ T_3 = x_0 + x_2 + x_5 + x_6. \end{cases}$$

Transform the matrix into

$$M' = \begin{bmatrix} 1 & 0 & 0 & 0 & 1 & 0 & 0 & 0 & 1 & 0 & 0 & 0 \\ 0 & 0 & 0 & 0 & 0 & 0 & 1 & 0 & 1 & 0 & 0 & 0 \\ 0 & 0 & 0 & 0 & 1 & 0 & 0 & 0 & 0 & 1 & 0 & 0 \\ 0 & 0 & 0 & 0 & 0 & 1 & 0 & 0 & 0 & 0 & 1 & 0 \\ 1 & 0 & 0 & 0 & 0 & 0 & 0 & 0 & 0 & 0 & 0 & 1 \\ 1 & 0 & 0 & 0 & 1 & 0 & 0 & 0 & 1 & 0 & 0 \\ 0 & 0 & 1 & 1 & 0 & 0 & 0 & 0 & 0 & 0 & 0 & 1 \\ 0 & 1 & 0 & 0 & 0 & 0 & 1 & 0 & 0 & 0 & 1 & 0 \end{bmatrix}.$$

Take $x = (x_7, x_6, x_5, x_4, x_3, x_2, x_1, x_0, T_3, T_2, T_1, T_0)$ as new variables, and $y = (y_7, y_6, y_5, y_4, y_3, y_2, y_1, y_0)$ is the output. The division property propagation is expressed as $(a_7, a_6, a_5, a_4, a_3, a_2, a_1, a_0, U_3, U_2, U_1, U_0) \xrightarrow{P} (b_7, b_6, b_5, b_4, b_3, b_2, b_1, b_0)$. Create model constraints according to the new expression. The new variable constraints that need to be added are

$$\begin{cases} U_0 = a_0 + a_3 + a_4 + a_7, \\ U_1 = a_1 + a_2 + a_3 + a_6, \\ U_2 = a_0 + a_1 + a_4 + a_5, \\ U_3 = a_0 + a_2 + a_5 + a_6, \\ U_3, \cdots, U_0 \text{ are binaries.} \end{cases}$$

Using Algorithm 4, we can find an integral distinguisher up to 9 rounds with 63 active bits and 32 balanced bits. For the 8-round MIBS, the output of ciphertext are all balanced if plaintexts are chosen as 63 active bits and one constant bit. The following shows a list of integral distinguishers found by Algorithm 4. In particular, the 6-, 7-, 8- and 9-round integral distinguisher of MIBS all have longer rounds than the currently known ones.

$$\begin{bmatrix} \mathcal{C},\mathcal{C},\mathcal{C},\mathcal{C},\mathcal{C},\mathcal{C},\mathcal{C},\mathcal{C}, \\ \mathcal{C},\mathcal{C},\mathcal{C},\mathcal{C},\mathcal{C},\mathcal{A},\mathcal{A},\mathcal{A} \end{bmatrix} \xrightarrow{5R} \begin{bmatrix} \mathcal{B},\mathcal{B},\mathcal{B},\mathcal{B},\mathcal{B},\mathcal{B},\mathcal{B},\mathcal{B}, \\ \mathcal{U},\mathcal{U},\mathcal{U},\mathcal{U},\mathcal{U},\mathcal{U},\mathcal{U},\mathcal{U} \end{bmatrix}$$

$$\begin{bmatrix} \mathcal{C},\mathcal{C},\mathcal{C},\mathcal{C},\mathcal{C},\mathcal{C},\mathcal{C},\mathcal{C}, \\ \mathcal{A},\mathcal{A},\mathcal{A},\mathcal{A},\mathcal{A},\mathcal{A},\mathcal{A},\mathcal{A} \end{bmatrix} \xrightarrow{6R} \begin{bmatrix} \mathcal{B},\mathcal{B},\mathcal{B},\mathcal{B},\mathcal{B},\mathcal{B},\mathcal{B},\mathcal{B}, \\ \mathcal{U},\mathcal{U},\mathcal{U},\mathcal{U},\mathcal{U},\mathcal{U},\mathcal{U},\mathcal{U} \end{bmatrix}$$

$$\begin{bmatrix} \mathcal{C},\mathcal{C},\mathcal{C},\mathcal{A},\mathcal{A},\mathcal{A},\mathcal{A},\mathcal{A}, \\ \mathcal{A},\mathcal{A},\mathcal{A},\mathcal{A},\mathcal{A},\mathcal{A},\mathcal{A},\mathcal{A} \end{bmatrix} \xrightarrow{7R} \begin{bmatrix} \mathcal{B},\mathcal{B},\mathcal{B},\mathcal{B},\mathcal{B},\mathcal{B},\mathcal{B},\mathcal{B}, \\ \mathcal{U},\mathcal{U},\mathcal{U},\mathcal{U},\mathcal{U},\mathcal{U},\mathcal{U},\mathcal{U} \end{bmatrix}$$

$$\begin{bmatrix} ccca,\mathcal{A},\mathcal{A},\mathcal{A},\mathcal{A},\mathcal{A},\mathcal{A},\mathcal{A}, \\ \mathcal{A},\mathcal{A},\mathcal{A},\mathcal{A},\mathcal{A},\mathcal{A},\mathcal{A},\mathcal{A} \end{bmatrix} \xrightarrow{8R} \begin{bmatrix} \mathcal{B},\mathcal{B},\mathcal{B},\mathcal{B},\mathcal{B},\mathcal{B},\mathcal{B},\mathcal{B}, \\ \mathcal{U},\mathcal{U},\mathcal{U},\mathcal{U},\mathcal{U},\mathcal{U},\mathcal{U},\mathcal{U} \end{bmatrix}$$

$$\begin{bmatrix} caaa,\mathcal{A},\mathcal{A},\mathcal{A},\mathcal{A},\mathcal{A},\mathcal{A},\mathcal{A}, \\ \mathcal{A},\mathcal{A},\mathcal{A},\mathcal{A},\mathcal{A},\mathcal{A},\mathcal{A},\mathcal{A} \end{bmatrix} \xrightarrow{8R} \begin{bmatrix} \mathcal{B},\mathcal{B},\mathcal{B},\mathcal{B},\mathcal{B},\mathcal{B},\mathcal{B},\mathcal{B}, \\ \mathcal{B},\mathcal{B},\mathcal{B},\mathcal{B},\mathcal{B},\mathcal{B},\mathcal{B},\mathcal{B} \end{bmatrix}$$

$$\begin{bmatrix} caaa,\mathcal{A},\mathcal{A},\mathcal{A},\mathcal{A},\mathcal{A},\mathcal{A},\mathcal{A}, \\ \mathcal{A},\mathcal{A},\mathcal{A},\mathcal{A},\mathcal{A},\mathcal{A},\mathcal{A},\mathcal{A} \end{bmatrix} \xrightarrow{9R} \begin{bmatrix} \mathcal{B},\mathcal{B},\mathcal{B},\mathcal{B},\mathcal{B},\mathcal{B},\mathcal{B},\mathcal{B}, \\ \mathcal{U},\mathcal{U},\mathcal{U},\mathcal{U},\mathcal{U},\mathcal{U},\mathcal{U},\mathcal{U} \end{bmatrix}$$

Algorithm 4. A MILP model for BDP propagation of MIBS

Input: S-box, the linear layer
Output: A MILP model $\mathcal{M}$ for BDP propagation of MIBS
 1: Build an empty MILP model $\mathcal{M}$.
 2: $\mathcal{M}.var \leftarrow a_i, d_i, b_i, c_i, U_i, u_i, A_i$ //a_i, b_i denote the input and output BDP of
    linear layer, the rest are newly introduced binary variables
 3: //COPY Operation in the Left of Feistel Structure
 4: $\mathcal{M}.con \leftarrow \mathcal{L}\,(a_i = d_i + a_{i+1})$
 5: // Generating Constrained Inequalities for S-boxes
 6: Use Algorithm 2 [4] to calculate the division trail of S-box: $V = \{d_i \rightarrow b_i\}$
 7: Use $inequality\_generator()$ in SAGE to generate inequalities of V : $\mathcal{L}\,(d_i, b_i)$
 8: Reduce $\mathcal{L}\,(d_i, b_i)$ to $\mathcal{L}'\,(d_i, b_i)$ by using the Greedy Algorithm
 9: $\mathcal{M}.con \leftarrow \mathcal{L}'\,(d_i, b_i)$
10: //Generating Constraned Inequalities for transformation P
11: Write the implementation matrix M of P
12: Call Algorithm 2 to generate constraints: $\mathcal{L}''\,(b_i, c_i, U_i, u_i, A_i)$
13: $\mathcal{M}.con \leftarrow \mathcal{L}''\,(b_i, c_i, U_i, u_i, A_i)$
14: // XOR Operation in the Right of Feistel Network
15: $\mathcal{M}.con \leftarrow \mathcal{L}'''\,(a_i + c_i = a_{i+1})$
16: **for** i in range$(0, n)$ **do**
17:     $\mathcal{M}.con \leftarrow \mathcal{L}\,(a_i = d_i + a_{i+1})$
18:     $\mathcal{M}.con \leftarrow \mathcal{L}'\,(d_i, b_i)$
19:     $\mathcal{M}.con \leftarrow \mathcal{L}''\,(b_i, c_i, U_i, u_i, A_i)$
20:     $\mathcal{M}.con \leftarrow \mathcal{L}'''\,(a_i + c_i = a_{i+1})$
21: **end for**
22: Return $\mathcal{M}$

---

5   Conclusion

In this paper, we proposed a method to improve the accuracy of modeling the BDP propagation of complex linear layers using MILP model, which can also make models using SAT, and showed the effectiveness of this approach by applying it to two block ciphers uBlock-128 and MIBS. For uBlock-128, we found an integral distinguisher with the same round number as the longest known one, but our results has more balance bits. For MIBS, our method can attack more rounds than previous generic integral attacks. However, we cannot guarantee that the number of active bits is a tight lower bound for the 6-, 7- and 8-round integral distinguisher of MIBS due to the problem of solving time. Therefore, continuing to optimize the entire MILP model and improve the solving efficiency, and applying to other block ciphers with the complex linear layer are issues of our further investigations.

Acknowledgement. The authors would like to thank Prof. Guomin Yang and the anonymous reviewers for their detailed and very helpful comments and suggestions to improve this article. This work is supported by the National Natural Science Foundation of China (No. 62072445).

A   Linear Inequalities for S-Boxes in uBlock-128

The following inequalities are the 12 inequalities used to describe uBlock S-box in MILP model of BDP, and $(a_3, a_2, a_1, a_0) \rightarrow (b_3, b_2, b_1, b_0)$ denotes a division trail of S-box.

$$
\begin{cases}
a_3 + a_2 + a_1 + a_0 - b_3 - b_2 - b_1 - b_0 \geq 0 \\
-3a_3 - a_2 - 2a_1 - 4a_0 + 3b_3 + b_2 + 2b_1 - b_0 \geq -5 \\
2a_3 - a_0 - 2b_3 - b_2 - b_1 + b_0 \geq -2 \\
-4a_3 - 3a_2 - 2a_1 - 2a_0 - b_3 + 3b_2 + b_1 + 2b_0 \geq -6 \\
-a_1 + 2a_0 - b_3 - b_2 + b_1 - 2b_0 \geq -2 \\
-a_3 - a_2 - 2a_0 + b_3 + 2b_2 + 3b_1 + 2b_0 \geq 0 \\
a_3 + a_0 + b_3 - 2b_2 - 2b_1 - b_0 \geq -2 \\
a_1 + 2a_0 - b_3 - b_2 - b_1 - b_0 \geq -1 \\
a_3 - b_1 - b_0 \geq -1 \\
-a_3 - a_1 + b_3 + 2b_2 + b_1 + b_0 \geq 0 \\
a_1 - b_3 - b_1 \geq -1 \\
a_2 - b_2 - b_1 \geq -1
\end{cases}
$$

B   Linear Inequalities for S-Boxes in MIBS

The following inequalities are the 12 inequalities used to describe MIBS S-box in MILP model of BDP, and $(d_3, d_2, d_1, d_0) \rightarrow (b_3, b_2, b_1, b_0)$ denotes a division trail of S-box.

$$
\begin{cases}
d_3 + d_2 + 4d_1 + d_0 - 2b_3 - 2b_2 - 2b_1 - 2b_0 \geq -1 \\
3d_2 - b_3 - b_2 - b_1 - b_0 \geq -1 \\
-d_3 - 2d_2 - 2d_1 - d_0 - b_3 - 2b_2 + 4b_1 - b_0 \geq -6 \\
-d_3 - 2d_2 - 2d_1 - d_0 + 5b_3 + 4b_2 + 5b_1 + 5b_0 \geq 0 \\
-d_3 - d_2 - d_1 - b_3 + 3b_2 - 2b_1 - b_0 \geq -4 \\
-d_3 - d_0 - 2b_3 - b_2 - b_1 + 3b_0 \geq -3 \\
d_3 + b_3 - b_2 - b_1 - b_0 \geq -1 \\
-d_3 - d_2 - d_0 + b_3 + 2b_2 + 2b_1 + b_0 \geq -1 \\
-d_1 - b_3 - b_2 + 2b_1 - b_0 \geq -2
\end{cases}
$$

References

1. Knudsen, L., Wagner, D.: Integral cryptanalysis. In: Daemen, J., Rijmen, V. (eds.) FSE 2002. LNCS, vol. 2365, pp. 112–127. Springer, Heidelberg (2002). https://doi.org/10.1007/3-540-45661-9_9

2. Daemen, J., Knudsen, L., Rijmen, V.: The block cipher Square. In: Biham, E. (ed.) FSE 1997. LNCS, vol. 1267, pp. 149–165. Springer, Heidelberg (1997). https://doi.org/10.1007/BFb0052343

3. Todo, Y.: Structural evaluation by generalized integral property. In: Oswald, E., Fischlin, M. (eds.) EUROCRYPT 2015. LNCS, vol. 9056, pp. 287–314. Springer, Heidelberg (2015). https://doi.org/10.1007/978-3-662-46800-5_12

4. Xiang, Z., Zhang, W., Bao, Z., Lin, D.: Applying MILP method to searching integral distinguishers based on division property for 6 lightweight block ciphers. In: Cheon, J.H., Takagi, T. (eds.) ASIACRYPT 2016. LNCS, vol. 10031, pp. 648–678. Springer, Heidelberg (2016). https://doi.org/10.1007/978-3-662-53887-6_24

5. Wang, Q., Hao, Y., Todo, Y., Li, C., Isobe, T., Meier, W.: Improved division property based cube attacks exploiting algebraic properties of superpoly. In: Shacham, H., Boldyreva, A. (eds.) CRYPTO 2018. LNCS, vol. 10991, pp. 275–305. Springer, Cham (2018). https://doi.org/10.1007/978-3-319-96884-1_10

6. Liu, M., Yang, J., Wang, W., Lin, D.: Correlation cube attacks: from weak-key distinguisher to key recovery. In: Nielsen, J.B., Rijmen, V. (eds.) EUROCRYPT 2018. LNCS, vol. 10821, pp. 715–744. Springer, Cham (2018). https://doi.org/10.1007/978-3-319-78375-8_23

7. Wang, S., Hu, B., Guan, J., Zhang, K., Shi, T.: MILP-aided method of searching division property using three subsets and applications. In: Galbraith, S.D., Moriai, S. (eds.) ASIACRYPT 2019. LNCS, vol. 11923, pp. 398–427. Springer, Cham (2019). https://doi.org/10.1007/978-3-030-34618-8_14

8. Hao, Y., Leander, G., Meier, W., Todo, Y., Wang, Q.: Modeling for three-subset division property without unknown subset. In: Canteaut, A., Ishai, Y. (eds.) EUROCRYPT 2020. LNCS, vol. 12105, pp. 466–495. Springer, Cham (2020). https://doi.org/10.1007/978-3-030-45721-1_17

9. Hebborn, P., Lambin, B., Leander, G., Todo, Y.: Lower bounds on the degree of block ciphers. In: Moriai, S., Wang, H. (eds.) ASIACRYPT 2020. LNCS, vol. 12491, pp. 537–566. Springer, Cham (2020). https://doi.org/10.1007/978-3-030-64837-4_18

10. Hu, K., Sun, S., Wang, M., Wang, Q.: An algebraic formulation of the division property: revisiting degree evaluations, cube attacks, and key-independent sums. In: Moriai, S., Wang, H. (eds.) ASIACRYPT 2020. LNCS, vol. 12491, pp. 446–476. Springer, Cham (2020). https://doi.org/10.1007/978-3-030-64837-4_15

11. Hebborn, P., Lambin, B., Leander, G., Todo, Y.: Strong and tight security guarantees against integral distinguishers. In: Tibouchi, M., Wang, H. (eds.) ASIACRYPT 2021. LNCS, vol. 13090, pp. 362–391. Springer, Cham (2021). https://doi.org/10.1007/978-3-030-92062-3_13

12. Sun, L., Wang, W., Wang, M.Q.: MILP-aided bit-based division property for primitives with non-bit-permutation linear layers. IET Inf. Secur. **14**, 12–20 (2020)

13. Zhang, W.Y., Rijmen, V.: Division cryptanalysis of block ciphers with a binary diffusion layer. IET Inf. Secur. **13**, 87–95 (2019)

14. Hu, K., Wang, Q.J., Wang, M.Q.: Finding bit-based division property for ciphers with complex linear layers. IACR Trans. Symmetric Cryptol. **2020**, 396–424 (2020)

15. Todo, Y., Morii, M.: Bit-based division property and application to SIMON family. In: Peyrin, T. (ed.) FSE 2016. LNCS, vol. 9783, pp. 357–377. Springer, Heidelberg (2016). https://doi.org/10.1007/978-3-662-52993-5_18

16. Wu, W.L., Zhang, L., Zheng, Y.F., Li, L.C.: The block cipher uBlock. J. Cryptol. Res. **6**(6), 690–703 (2019). (in Chinese)

17. Tian, W., Hu, B.: Integral cryptanalysis on two block ciphers Pyjamask and uBlock. IET Inf. Secur. **14**, 572–579 (2020)

18. Hong, C., Zhang, S., Chen, S., Lin, D., Xiang, Z.: More accurate division property propagations based on optimized implementations of linear layers. In: Yu, Yu., Yung, M. (eds.) Inscrypt 2021. LNCS, vol. 13007, pp. 212–232. Springer, Cham (2021). https://doi.org/10.1007/978-3-030-88323-2_11

19. Izadi, M., Sadeghiyan, B., Sadeghian, S.S., Khanooki, H.A.: MIBS: a new lightweight block cipher. In: Garay, J.A., Miyaji, A., Otsuka, A. (eds.) CANS 2009. LNCS, vol. 5888, pp. 334–348. Springer, Heidelberg (2009). https://doi.org/10.1007/978-3-642-10433-6_22

20. Bay, A., Nakahara, J., Vaudenay, S.: Cryptanalysis of reduced-round MIBS block cipher. In: Heng, S.-H., Wright, R.N., Goi, B.-M. (eds.) CANS 2010. LNCS, vol. 6467, pp. 1–19. Springer, Heidelberg (2010). https://doi.org/10.1007/978-3-642-17619-7_1

21. Li, Y.J., Sun, Q., Ou, H.W., et al.: Improved integral attacks on MIBS-64 block cipher. J. Cryptol. Res. **8**(4), 669–679 (2021). (in Chinese)

Fast Skinny-128 SIMD Implementations for Sequential Modes of Operation

Alexandre Adomnicai[1]([✉]), Kazuhiko Minematsu[2,3]([✉]), and Maki Shigeri[4]([✉])

[1] CryptoNext Security, Paris, France
`alex.adomnicai@gmail.com`
[2] NEC, Kawasaki, Japan
`k-minematsu@nec.com`
[3] Yokohama National University, Yokohama, Japan
[4] NEC Solution Innovators, Hokuriku, Japan
`m-shigeri_pb@nec.com`

Abstract. This paper reports new software implementation results for the Skinny-128 tweakable block ciphers on various SIMD architectures. More precisely, we introduce a decomposition of the 8-bit S-box into four 4-bit S-boxes in order to take advantage of vector permute instructions, leading to significant performance improvements over previous constant-time implementations. Since our approach is of particular interest when Skinny-128 is used in sequential modes of operation, we also report how it benefits to the Romulus authenticated encryption scheme, a finalist of the NIST LWC standardization process.

Keywords: Skinny · Romulus · NIST LWC · SIMD

1 Introduction

The Internet of Things (IoT) does not come without its challenges, and security concerns remain a major barrier to its adoption. One of the technical considerations is the efficiency/security trade-off of cryptographic implementations on IoT devices. The restrictions in terms of power and memory introduce challenges that do not exist when using cryptography in more conventional IT platforms. Moreover, environments in which IoT devices are deployed make these devices vulnerable to unforeseen physical threats where attackers may tamper with them directly. It implies that cryptographic implementations must show some resilience against physical attacks to avoid key recoveries that might lead to a compromised network, as already demonstrated in practice [27]. Therefore, numerous symmetric-key ciphers have been proposed by taking all these aspects into consideration at the design level. They are categorized as lightweight cryptography, aiming at providing better hardware and/or software implementation properties on embedded devices. In this context, the National Institute of Standards and Technology (NIST) initiated a process that started in 2018, with the goal of selecting the future Authenticated Encryption with Associated Data (AEAD) standard(s) for constrained envi-

© The Author(s), under exclusive license to Springer Nature Switzerland AG 2022
K. Nguyen et al. (Eds.): ACISP 2022, LNCS 13494, pp. 125–144, 2022.
https://doi.org/10.1007/978-3-031-22301-3_7

ronments [23]. AEAD algorithms ensure confidentiality, integrity, and authenticity of data in a single primitive. Romulus [19] is one of the ten proposals currently competing for standardization in the final round. It is based on Skinny [7], a tweakable block cipher standardized in ISO/IEC 18033-7. If Skinny shows outstanding results when implemented in hardware, the picture is more mixed when it comes to software. Although recent works have been undertaken to optimize its performance on 32-bit microcontrollers, for example by Adomnicai and Peyrin [2], it is not clear what is the best implementation strategy on more advanced architectures. Although the main goal of lightweight cryptography is to provide optimized encryption and authentication solutions for resource-constrained devices (e.g. low-cost microcontrollers), it will be inevitably deployed on more sophisticated platforms for interoperability purposes. For instance, many IoT networks adopt a star topology where numerous low-end devices communicate with a single server that has to decrypt received data. Mobile devices (e.g. smartphones, tablets) are also commonly used for network monitoring purposes, requiring to handle secure communications with many nodes simultaneously. Therefore, software performance of lightweight cryptography does matter on mid-range to high-end microprocessors as well. Most of these platforms are now equipped with single instruction multiple data (SIMD) units whose goal is to vectorize calculations by performing the same operation on multiple data operands concurrently. On Intel processors, SIMD units have been available since the advent of the MMX instruction set architecture extension, initially designed to speed up the performance of multimedia applications. Similarly, ARM introduced SIMD extensions with the NEON technology being implemented on all ARM Cortex-A series processors. To date, the best software Skinny-128 implementation results reported on SIMD architectures are obtained by processing many 128-bit blocks in parallel (e.g. 64 using AVX2 [7]) thanks to bitslicing. While relying on implementations that operate on a large amount of data at once is not necessarily relevant in the context of IoT, where payloads are usually a few dozen of bytes only, it is even less of interest for sequential (i.e. non-parallelizable) modes of operation as in Romulus.

Our Contributions. In this paper, we optimize the performance of Skinny-128 for sequential modes of operation on SIMD platforms, with a focus on ARM processors with NEON technology. First, we briefly review various publicly available software implementations of Skinny-128 and highlight that the 8-bit S-box component is the most-time consuming part of the encryption process. To address this issue, we propose an optimization trick which consists in decomposing the S-box into smaller ones so that we can take advantage of SIMD-specific vector permute instructions to reach competitive performance without introducing secret-dependent timing variations. While it has already been shown that lightweight ciphers with 4-bit S-boxes can highly benefit from such instructions [5,8], it is less trivial for designs with larger (e.g. 8-bit) S-boxes. Still, a similar implementation trick has been first proposed by Hamburg for AES on Intel processors [18]. Our work shows that this is also quite effective for Skinny-128 by introducing a novel decomposition of its 8-bit S-box into 4 tables. As a result, we observe a speedup by a factor that ranges from 1.5 to 3.5 depending on the computing platform, compared to the fixsliced implementation strategy [2], which is currently the fastest option for Skinny-128 when used in non-parallelizable operating modes. We also port our implementations on Intel platforms, improving the performance by a factor of 4. These results straightforwardly apply to Romulus as shown by our benchmarks. Finally, our software implementations are released into the public domain at https://github.com/aadomn/skinny.

2   Skinny in Software

2.1   The Skinny-128 Tweakable Block Ciphers

A tweakable block cipher is family of permutations where both key and tweak are used to select a permutation. Skinny follows the tweakey framework [21] which treats the tweak and the key in the same way in a structure called *tweakey*. It is up to the user what part of this tweakey will be key material and/or tweak material. The internal state of Skinny-128 as well as the tweakey states consist of a 4×4 square arrays of bytes. The number of tweakey states ranges from one to three (namely $TK1$, $TK2$ and $TK3$), and is directly linked to the quantity of tweakey material which is either 128, 256, or 384 bits. The corresponding versions are denoted by Skinny-128-128, Skinny-128-256, and Skinny-128-384, and are composed of 40, 48, and 56 encryption rounds, respectively. One encryption round is itself composed of five operations in the following order: SubCells, AddConstants, AddRoundTweakey, ShiftRows and MixColumns as illustrated in Fig. 1.

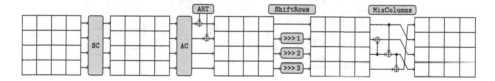

Fig. 1. The Skinny round function (from [20])

SubCells refers to the non-linear layer and consists in applying an 8-bit S-box, depicted in Fig. 2, to each byte individually.

AddConstants consists in combining three round constants c_0, c_1, c_2 with the three topmost bytes in the first state column using bitwise exclusive-OR (XOR). The round constants are defined as below:

$$c_0 = 0 \parallel 0 \parallel 0 \parallel 0 \parallel rc_3 \parallel rc_2 \parallel rc_1 \parallel rc_0$$
$$c_1 = 0 \parallel 0 \parallel 0 \parallel 0 \parallel 0 \parallel 0 \parallel rc_5 \parallel rc_4$$
$$c_2 = 0 \parallel 0 \parallel 0 \parallel 0 \parallel 0 \parallel 0 \parallel 1 \parallel 1$$

where rc_i are defined by the following 6-bit LFSR

$$(rc_5 \parallel rc_4 \parallel rc_3 \parallel rc_2 \parallel rc_1 \parallel rc_0) \rightarrow (rc_4 \parallel rc_3 \parallel rc_2 \parallel rc_1 \parallel rc_0 \parallel rc_5 \oplus rc_4 \oplus 1).$$

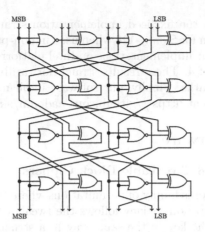

Fig. 2. The Skinny-128 S-box (from [20])

`AddRoundTweakey` extracts the two topmost rows of each tweakey array and adds them to the internal state using bitwise XOR. Then all tweakey arrays are updated by applying a byte permutation to the state and an 8-bit LFSR to each byte, as illustrated in Fig. 3. Finally, `ShiftRows` and `MixColumns` refer to the linear layer, ensuring diffusion within the state.

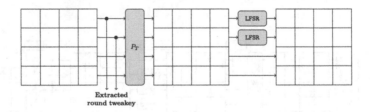

Extracted
round tweakey

Fig. 3. Tweakey state update (from [20])

2.2   Publicly Available Software Implementations

The original publication of Skinny reports efficient bitsliced implementations[1] with Skinny-128-128 running at 3.78 and 3.43 cycles per byte (cpb) on Haswell and Skylake architectures respectively, by taking advantage of Intel AVX2 instructions. However, it requires to process 64 blocks in parallel which makes it quite inefficient for sequential modes of operation since it would basically decrease computation speed by a factor of 64.

Regarding 32-bit implementations, as for the AES T-tables, it is possible to combine multiple steps of the round function into table lookups. This has

---

[1] https://github.com/kste/skinny_avx.

been investigated in [14] in order to optimize ForkAE [3], which is based on the Skinny round function, but there are no implementation results reported for Skinny itself. For platforms where cache-based attacks are a concern, one should favor constant-time implementations to avoid timing side-channels that could leak information about the secret key. An application of the fixslicing technique to Skinny-128 was recently proposed in this regard [2]. Fixslicing is a specific instance of bitslicing where at least one slice remains fixed (potentially leading to an alternative representation for a few rounds), with the aim of optimizing the diffusion layer. It was originally proposed by Adomnicai, Najm and Peyrin [1] with an application to GIFT-COFB, a NIST LWC finalist based on the GIFT block cipher [6] and the COFB mode of operation [13]. According to [2], fixsliced Skinny-128-128 runs around 191 cpb on ARMv7-M when processing a single block at a time (with precomputed round tweakeys). Note that there is also a constant-time implementation from Weatherley which stores the internal state in a byte-wise fashion but implements the S-box in a bitsliced manner by means of bitmasks and bitwise operations [31]. While it is around 2.5 times slower than the fixsliced version on ARMv7-M when processing a single block at time [2], it requires half RAM to store the round tweakeys. Still, the improvement factor should be significantly reduced on 64-bit platforms since the byte-wise representation can benefit from larger registers to apply the S-box on only two 64-bit words instead of four 32-bit words.

There has also been work on Skinny-128 optimizations using the ARM NEON extension, with the objective to enhance the performance of the ForkAE lightweight encryption scheme [14]. The implementation strategy is the same as [31]: the authors use a single 128-bit NEON register to store the entire internal state and rely on a bitsliced approach for the S-box, requiring 63 instructions in total[2]. Because no implementation results are reported for Skinny-128 itself, it is not clear how it performs compared to the fixsliced[3] and byte-wise[4] implementations. To clarify this point, we performed a simple benchmark on the following three ARM CPUs implementing the NEON extension: the Cortex-A7, Cortex-A53 and Cortex-A72 processors briefly described hereafter. We used the SUPERCOP benchmarking suite [9] using gcc 8.3.0. The results are reported in Table 1.

ARM Cortex-A7. The Cortex-A7 is an in-order pipeline CPU core with moderate performance but an extremely small die size and very low power consumption. It was initially introduced for entry-level smartphones and now progressively finds its place in system-on-chips dedicated to the IoT [22]. It is based on the 32-bit ARMv7-A architecture which has 16 32-bit general-purpose ARM registers R_0-R_{15} and 32 64-bit NEON registers D_0-D_{31}. These NEON registers can

---

[2] https://github.com/ArneDeprez1/ForkAE-SW/blob/master/Neon_SIMD/sbox_neon.S.

[3] https://github.com/aadomn/skinny/tree/master/crypto_tbc/skinny128/1_block/opt32.

[4] https://github.com/rweather/skinny-c.

also be manipulated as 16 128-bit registers Q_0-Q_{15} where each Q_i maps to the pair (D_{2i}, D_{2i+1}). For our benchmarks, we use the Raspberry Pi 2 Model B featuring the 900 MHz quad-core Cortex-A7 Broadcom BCM2836 chipset running Raspbian 10 (buster).

ARM Cortex-A53. The Cortex-A53 is one of the first two processors implementing the ARMv8-A architecture and is typically found in entry-level smartphone and other embedded devices. ARMv8-A introduces a new 64-bit instruction set known as A64 which operates in the 64-bit execution state called AArch64. It also provides a 32-bit execution state called AArch32 to ensure backward compatibility with ARMv7-A. While AArch32 has the same number of registers as ARMv7-A, AArch64, by comparison, has 31 64-bit ARM registers X_0-X_{30} and 32 128-bit NEON registers V_0-V_{31}. For our benchmarks, we use the Raspberry Pi 3 Model B featuring the 1.2 GHz quad-core Cortex-A53 Broadcom BCM2837 chipset running Debian 10 (buster).

ARM Cortex-A72. Finally, the Cortex-A72 is based on the ARMv8-A architecture and is designed for the mobile market. It is considered as a high performant core which is often combined with lower performance processors such as the Cortex-A53 to achieve better tradeoffs between energy and performance. For our benchmarks, we use the Raspberry Pi 4 Model B featuring the 1.5 GHz quad-core Cortex-A72 Broadcom BCM2711 chipset running Debian 10 (buster).

Table 1. Performance comparison between three Skinny-128 implementations. Best results are bolded.

Algorithm	Implementation	Speed (clock cycles)		
		A7	A53	A72
	Fixsliced [2]	**5 492**	**2 814**	**2 655**
Skinny-128-384 block encryption	Byte-wise [31]	10 328	3 055	2 993
	ARMv7-A NEON [14]	10 563	-	-
	Fixsliced [2]	**3 901**	3 210	2 082
Skinny-128-384 tweakey schedule	Byte-wise [31]	7 855	**2 294**	**1 568**
	ARMv7-A NEON [14]	4 127	-	-

As expected, fixslicing appears as the most efficient implementation strategy for the encryption round function. While the byte-wise approach shows better performance for the tweakey schedule on 64-bit platforms, we decide to take the fixsliced implementation as a reference in terms of performance since many operation modes leave some tweakey states unchanged across calls to Skinny-128. Another observation that stems from our benchmark is that the use of NEON on the Cortex-A7 outperforms the non-vectorized byte-wise implementation for the tweakey schedule only, resulting in similar performance for the encryption round function. This is likely due to the fact that, on the Cortex-A7, while most NEON instructions have a throughput of either 1 and 2 instructions per clock cycle when operating on doubleword and quadword registers, respectively, latencies are typically 4 cycles or more [28]. Therefore, directly using the result of the previous instruction will cause a stall. While the ARMv7-A NEON S-box implementation tries to mitigate such additional costs by carefully scheduling instructions, its sequential aspect makes it impossible to completely avoid it. The performance bottleneck of the encryption round function is clearly the 8-bit S-box, which is responsible for about 60% of the clock cycles in the fixsliced setting, versus 80% in the byte-wise setting. Therefore, optimizing this operation would significantly enhance the overall Skinny-128 performance.

3   Optimizing the S-Box Layer

3.1   NEON Vector Permute Instructions

NEON instruction set features a vector permute instruction named tbl which performs a table lookup at byte level. As originally introduced in ARMv7-A, it operates on doubleword registers providing a 64-bit output at a time. The table can be specified from 1 to 4 double-word registers, allowing up to 32 bytes. While the tbl instruction insert zeroes for out-of-bounds indices, its sister instruction tbx leaves the destination unchanged instead. In ARMv8-A, these instructions are operating on 128-bit wide registers allowing to specify a table of up to 64 bytes. Therefore, a single instruction is enough to compute an S-box up to either 5-bit or 6-bit on ARMv7-A and ARMv8-A, respectively. It is also possible to go further by combining several tbl/tbx calls. For instance, on ARMv8-A, given an 8-bit S-box one can split it into four 6-bit S-boxes: the first one covering bytes from 0 to 63, the second one covering bytes from 64 to 127, etc. First, a tbl instruction with the first 6-bit S-box is performed. If a byte is out-of-bounds the result is set to 0, or the final S-box output otherwise. Then, 64 is subtracted to each byte before applying the second 6-bit S-box using the tbx instruction (so that non-zero bytes calculated in the previous instruction are not affected). The same reasoning applies for the two remaining 6-bit S-boxes as detailed in Listing 1.1. This technique was actually applied to the AES S-box in order to boost its performance for ARMv8-A processors that do not include the optional Cryptography Extension [11,15]. Although the same trick applies to ARMv7-A as well, the limited number of registers coupled with the fact that permute instructions operate on 64-bit doublewords makes it inefficient for an 8-bit S-box, as it would occupy all the 32 NEON registers available. It would be still possible to store it in memory and perform loads during the calculation, but it would have a significant impact on performance. Another drawback of this technique is its inefficiency in some processors. It has been observed that tbl/tbx performance can greatly vary from one platform to another [4]. For instance, in AArch64 mode, a `tbl` instruction with 4 input registers has a latency of 15 cycles on the A72 compared to only 5 on the A53, as summarized in Table 2. Those latency issues can be mitigated by executing several instances in parallel. However, because the internal state fits in a single 128-bit register, it is only of interest for parallelizable modes of operation. Another potential solution would be to use a clever decomposition of the S-box rather than simply splitting it into several parts.

```
1  tbl v1.16b, {v16.16b - v19.16b}, v0.16b // S-box for bytes in [0,63]
2  sub v0.16b, v0.16b, v15.16b             // Subtracts 64 to each byte
3  tbx v1.16b, {v20.16b - v23.16b}, v0.16b // S-box for bytes in [64,127]
4  sub v0.16b, v0.16b, v15.16b             // Subtracts 64 to each byte
5  tbx v1.16b, {v24.16b - v27.16b}, v0.16b // S-box for bytes in [128,191]
6  sub v0.16b, v0.16b, v15.16b             // Subtracts 64 to each byte
7  tbx v1.16b, {v28.16b - v31.16b}, v0.16b // S-box for bytes in [192,255]
```

Listing 1.1. ARMv8-A NEON implementation of an 8-bit S-box stored in v16–v31. The input register is v0 and while the output register is v1. v15 is supposed to contain 0x40...40.

Table 2. Effective execution latency and throughput for Neon vector permute instructions.

Execution Mode	Instructions	Throughput (ops/cycle)			Latency (cycles)		
		A7	A53	A72	A7	A53	A72
Aarch32	vtbl/vtbx from 1/2 sources (64-bit wide)	1	1	2	4	2	3
	vtbl/vtbx from 3/4 sources (64-bit wide)	1/2	1/2	1	5	3	6
Aarch64	tbl/tbx from n sources (64-bit wide)	-	$1/n$	$2/n$	-	$n+1$	$3n$
	tbl/tbx from n sources (128-bit wide)	-	$1/n$	$1/(2n-1)$	-	$n+1$	$3n+3$

3.2 S-Box Decomposition

The decomposition of an S-box into smaller ones is a well-known technique to achieve compact hardware implementations. Building large S-boxes from smaller ones is actually a design strategy that has been used in many ciphers (e.g. Whirlpool [30], CLEFIA [29], Streebog and Kuznyechik [25]). This is also useful for side-channel countermeasures such as threshold implementations, where having a decomposition into functions with lower algebraic degrees allows to reach a secure implementation with fewer shares. Note that improvements for first-order threshold implementations of Skinny-128 have been recently proposed thanks to novel S-box decompositions [12]. Such decompositions are also of interest in software, as it allows to build S-boxes that combine strong cryptanalytic properties and efficient bitsliced implementations (see e.g. Scream [17], Robin and Fantomas [16]). More closely related to our case study, a decomposition of the AES S-box has been proposed to achieve a constant-time implementation on Intel SIMD architectures [18]. It consists in representing $\mathbb{F}_{2^8}$ as a degree-2 field extension of $\mathbb{F}_{2^4}$ which allows computation of the AES S-box using small look-up tables that fit in `pshufb` instructions.

In the case of Skinny-128, we aim at finding an S-box decomposition that minimizes the number of inner S-boxes as well as their input size. Limiting the number of inner S-boxes will reduce the number of vector permute instructions while limiting their input size will reduce the number of input registers for these instructions (which has an impact on latency). Note that their output size can be anything between 1 and 8 bits since vector permute instructions operate at byte level. Another criterion to take into account is the way the input bits are positioned within bytes. Indeed for vector permute instructions, we want to be able to extract these input bits easily in order to store them in a contiguous manner. The ideal instruction to do so would be an SIMD equivalent of Intel `pext` which, for each byte, would apply a bitmask and pack the selected bits (either contiguous or non-contiguous) into contiguous low-order bit positions, as illustrated in Fig. 4.

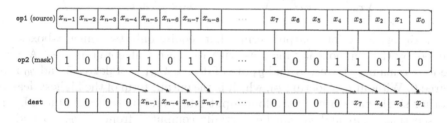

Fig. 4. Byte-wise SIMD parallel bit extract instruction. Each cell refers to a bit.

Unfortunately, there is no such instruction on ARM and replicating it in pure software is non-trivial as it would require many bit manipulations. To avoid such additional costs, we considered decompositions such that input bits of the inner S-boxes are always stored contiguously so that they can be extracted using a single bitmask or bitshift. We naturally started our investigations by looking at what can be done when applying a 4-bit S-box to each nibble individually. As highlighted in Fig. 5, it appears that a single output term, namely y_6, exclusively depends on the most significant nibble while two output terms, namely y_5 and y_3, exclusively depend on the less significant nibble. It implies that additional inner S-boxes are necessary to compute the remaining five terms, with their inputs consisting of output terms from both previous 4-bit S-boxes. Because those S-box outputs will be stored in two distinct registers, we will inevitably spend some cycles to end up with output terms from both S-boxes in the same register. To mix up these output bits, we suggest taking advantage of the fact that the output size of inner S-boxes is up to 8 bits. Therefore, without additional cost, we can do some bit rearrangement with the next inner S-boxes in mind before merging both outputs in the same register using a bitwise XOR. This way we can simply extract the input bits using a single bitmask or bitshift as done previously. Note that a clever merge of both outputs using a bitwise XOR also allows computing some logic gates for free. This is typically the case for the XOR required to compute the output term $y_2 = \neg(x_2 \vee x_1) \oplus x_6$, which means that after the merge, we now have four (instead of three) output terms among eight: y_2, y_3, y_5, y_6 as highlighted in Fig. 5. As a result, we are not simply interested in pure table decompositions, but rather in decompositions with potential additional bitwise operations. In order to investigate what would be the best strategy for the remaining four terms, we give a more formal definition of the 8-bit S-box in Eq. (1).

$$
S \colon \{0,1\}^8 \to \{0,1\}^8
$$

$$
\begin{pmatrix} x_7 \\ x_6 \\ x_5 \\ x_4 \\ x_3 \\ x_2 \\ x_1 \\ x_0 \end{pmatrix} \mapsto \begin{pmatrix} y_7 \\ y_6 \\ y_5 \\ y_4 \\ y_3 \\ y_2 \\ y_1 \\ y_0 \end{pmatrix} = \begin{pmatrix} (x_7 \vee x_6 \oplus x_4) \wedge (x_3 \vee x_2 \oplus x_0) \oplus x_5 \\ \neg(x_7 \vee x_6) \oplus x_4 \\ \neg(x_3 \vee x_2) \oplus x_0 \\ \neg((\neg(y_6 \vee y_5) \oplus x_5) \vee y_6) \oplus x_3 \\ \neg(y_5 \vee x_3) \oplus x_1 \\ \neg(x_2 \vee x_1) \oplus x_6 \\ \neg(y_7 \vee y_2) \oplus x_7 \\ \neg(y_1 \vee y_3) \oplus x_2 \end{pmatrix} \quad (1)
$$

In all logic, the four output terms that require only two inner S-boxes are defined by the component functions with the lowest algebraic degree. Among the four remaining terms, y_7 and y_4 are of degree 4, y_1 is of degree 5 and y_0 is of degree 6. Without considering y_0, which is the output term of the highest degree, another single inner S-box with four input bits would be sufficient. Indeed, one can see that y_7, y_4 and y_1 can be partially computed from y_6, y_5, y_2 and x_5 which are all available after the first layer of inner S-boxes (including the merge step). Note that we would actually need x_7 and x_3 as well for additional bitwise XORs, but we assume that they can be included in the computation for free with a clever merge as detailed above. However, y_0 makes things more complicated as it requires to consider two additional terms: x_7 and y_3. Therefore, we could theoretically get the remaining four output terms with a single 6-bit S-box call, but this option is only worth consideration for the ARMv8-A architecture since ARMv7-A vtbl and Intel SSSE3 pshufb instructions do not support such sizes. Instead, we suggest to slightly decompose the last output term as detailed in Eq. (2) so that each operand of the bitwise XOR can be computed separately and then merged together. It still requires to consider y_3 as additional input, resulting in a 5-bit S-box.

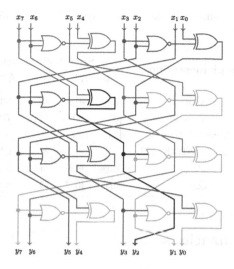

Fig. 5. The Skinny-128 S-box. Two inner S-boxes with 4-bit input (respectively highlighted in red and blue) are sufficient to get four output terms (including XOR when merging outputs, highlighted in black). (Color figure online)

$$y_0 = \neg(y_1 \lor y_3) \oplus x_2$$
$$= \neg((\neg(y_7 \lor y_2) \oplus x_7) \lor y_3) \oplus x_2$$
$$= (y_7 \lor y_2 \oplus x_7) \land \neg y_3 \oplus x_2$$
$$= \big[(y_7 \lor y_2) \land \neg y_3\big] \oplus \big[x_7 \land \neg y_3 \oplus x_2\big]$$

$$(2)$$

In order to achieve a version with 4-bit inner S-boxes only, one can use an additional bitwise AND operation at the cost of latency cycles. Both approaches, namely D_{4444} and D_{4454}, are formally defined in Appendixes A and B, respectively. Note that those decompositions are not the only possible ones, and other similar solutions surely exist. Still, given the restriction on the contiguous storage of the input bits, we believe that it is not possible to reach less than four inner S-box calls when limiting the number of input bits to 4 or 5. As shown in Table 3, our decompositions make the S-box layer faster on all processors, except on the A72 where they reach the same performance as the fixsliced version. According to the performance, it seems that one should favor D_{4454} over D_{4444}. However, the fact that the 5-bit inner S-box S_2 requires an additional 128-bit register is troublesome on the ARMv7-A architecture. We suggest to keep this register free on ARMv7-A as it allows to avoid stack usage during the entire Skinny-128 encryption as detailed in Sect. 4.2.

Table 3. Performance comparison of various software implementations of the Skinny-128 S-box.

Implementation	Ref	Speed (clock cycles)		
		A7	A53	A72
Fixsliced	[2]	40	32	33
Byte-wise	[31]	169	62	70
ARMv7-A NEON	[14]	163	-	-
ARMv8-A `tbl/tbx` split	[11]	-	26	64
D_{4444}	Ours	34	14	33
D_{4454}	Ours	30	13	33

4   Other Optimizations

4.1   Linear Layer

The linear layer consists of the `ShiftRows` followed by the `MixColumns`. The main complication with our representation, i.e. the 128-bit internal state stored row-wise in a 128-bit register, is that XORs within the `MixColumns` are performed row-wise. In order to avoid additional bitmasks and bitshifts to add the corresponding rows together, our implementations take again advantage of vector permute instructions by expressing the `MixColumns` as the XOR of three operands as detailed in Eq. (3).

$$\texttt{MixColumns} \begin{pmatrix} r_0 \\ r_1 \\ r_2 \\ r_3 \end{pmatrix} = \begin{pmatrix} r_0 \oplus r_2 \oplus r_3 \\ r_0 \\ r_1 \oplus r_2 \\ r_0 \oplus r_2 \end{pmatrix} = \begin{pmatrix} r_3 \\ r_0 \\ r_1 \\ r_2 \end{pmatrix} \oplus \begin{pmatrix} r_2 \\ 0 \\ r_2 \\ r_0 \end{pmatrix} \oplus \begin{pmatrix} r_0 \\ 0 \\ 0 \\ 0 \end{pmatrix} \quad (3)$$

Since the operands are just different rows reordering of the internal state, they can be easily computed using a table lookup instruction. We also include the `ShiftRows` calculation within those instructions as it comes at no cost. Note that because the third operand only consists of the first row, whose bytes are not shifted by the `ShiftRows`, we simply perform a bitwise AND instead of a table lookup instruction. Therefore, the entire linear layer can be computed using 2 128-bit wide vector permute instructions, 1 bitwise AND, and 2 XORs. This translates to 6 and 5 instructions on ARMv7-A and ARMv8-A architectures, respectively.

4.2 Tweakey Schedule

When it comes to the tweakey expansion, two options are left to the implementer: precalculation versus on-the-fly computation. It usually refers to a time-memory trade-off as on-the-fly computations allow to reduce memory usage at the cost of additional operations, and vice-versa. In our case, we decided to consider both approaches depending on the target platform. For instance, as highlighted in Table 3, our implementations suffer from many stall cycles on the A7 and A72 processors due to the latency of vector permute instructions on those platforms. Therefore, we suggest to take advantage of these stall cycles in order to compute the round tweakeys on-the-fly, in the background. We naturally implement the byte permutation using vector permute instructions while using bitwise operations for the LFSRs. On the ARMv8-A architecture, we compute double updates at once as illustrated in Fig. 6 so that we can divide by a factor of two the number of instructions. Thanks to the large number of registers available in the NEON SIMD unit, we can fit all the working variables in the NEON bank register without additional usage of the stack, even for Skinny-128-384 which requires three 128-bit tweakey states. This is what motivates us to use the D_{4444} decomposition on ARMv7-A since it requires two fewer 64-bit registers than D_{4454} (which would imply additional loads/stores on the stack).

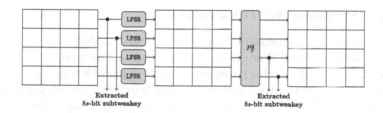

Fig. 6. Tweakey state double update

5   Implementation Results

5.1 ARM NEON

Table 4 reports benchmark results on the selected ARM NEON processors for Skinny-128-384+ and Romulus using the SUPERCOP benchmarking suite [9]. Skinny-128-384+ is a round-reduced version of Skinny-128-384 (decreased from 56 to 40) used in Romulus in order to enhance the performance while preserving a high security margin[5]. The latest specification of Romulus includes a nonce-based AE (Romulus-N), a nonce-misuse-resistant AE [26] (Romulus-M),

---

[5] https://groups.google.com/a/list.nist.gov/g/lwc-forum/c/5_mqi9irD0U.

a leakage-resilient AE (Romulus-T) based on TEDT [10], and a hash function (Romulus-H) based on MDPH [24]. We implemented and benchmarked all these members in order to compare our work with the fixsliced approach, which defines the most efficient software implementation available on this platform as highlighted in Sect. 2. For the sake of completeness, we considered both alternatives with precalculated and on-the-fly calculated round tweakeys. On top of running faster, a clear advantage of our NEON implementations over previous work is the RAM usage, which is smaller by a factor of 4 when computing the tweakey schedule on the fly. As expected, taking advantage of stall cycles on the A7 and A72 to compute the tweakey schedule in the background allows to reach the best performance on those platforms. Still, precomputing the round tweakeys is the most efficient approach on the A53. This is not only because there are fewer cycles latency for vector permute instructions on this platform: in each variant of Romulus, the tweakey is only differing from a byte or so across many calls to Skinny-128-384+ (see the Romulus specification for more details [19]). Therefore, it is possible to run some precalculations since the tweakeys $TK2$ and $TK3$ remain fixed. In the end, the improvement factor of our NEON implementations over fixslicing differs significantly depending on the processor. For Skinny-128-384+ (including the tweakey schedule) and Romulus, it is roughly 1.5, 2, and 3.5 on the A72, A7, and A53, respectively.

5.2 Intel Streaming SIMD Extensions

We also ported our implementations on Intel using Supplemental Streaming SIMD Extensions 3 (SSSE3) intrinsics. To do so, we naturally opted for the D_{4444} decomposition since the vector permute instruction pshufb operates on 16-byte vectors only. In order to save 1 instruction per S-box call, we simply reordered the output bits of S_0 and S_1 so that we can extract y_3 using a single bitmask instead of a shift (there is no _mm_srli_epi8 so we would need _mm_srli_epi16 followed by _mm_and_si128 to discard the bits from adjacent bytes). Because there are no high latency issues related to pshufb and because the amount of RAM usage is relatively small for such platforms, we only considered the variant with precalculation of the round tweakeys in order to reach the best performance. As reported in Table 5, the improvement in terms of performance ranges between 4 and 5 on Whiskey Lake and Comet Lake microarchitectures. Note that the advanced vector extension AVX2 should not lead to significant enhancements since its vpshufb instruction operates within 128-bit lanes. The only

Table 4. Benchmark on ARM Cortex-A processors. Results are given when processing 4096 bytes for Romulus (2048-byte additional data and 2048-byte message) and a single block (i.e. 16 bytes) for Skinny-128-384+. The function 'encryption only' takes as input the round tweakeys fully precomputed while 'encryption + tweakey schedule' simply requires the 48-byte tweakey.

Algorithm	Implementation	Speed (cycles/byte)			RAM
		A7	A53	A72	(bytes)
Skinny-128-384+					
encryption only	Fixsliced [2]	254	129	123	-
	Ours	**127**	**57**	**111**	-
encryption + tweakey schedule	Fixsliced [2]	431	321	201	736
	Ours (precalculate)	177	**84**	148	368
	Ours (on-the-fly)	**143**	85	**112**	**16**
Romulus					
Romulus-N nonce-based AEAD	Fixsliced [2]	239	165	137	1 088
	Ours (precalculate)	112	**48**	94	544
	Ours (on-the-fly)	**110**	64	**85**	**240**
Romulus-M nonce misuse-resistant AEAD	Fixsliced [2]	337	245	199	1 136
	Ours (precalculate)	153	**69**	130	640
	Ours (on-the-fly)	**144**	83	**113**	**272**
Romulus-T leakage-resilient AEAD	Fixsliced [2]	705	551	387	1 136
	Ours (precalculate)	321	**145**	273	640
	Ours (on-the-fly)	**289**	158	**226**	**272**
Romulus-H hash function	Fixsliced [2]	318	227	187	1 104
	Ours (precalculate)	161	**71**	138	544
	Ours (on-the-fly)	**150**	85	**116**	**224**

advantage is to either (1) process two blocks in parallel (which is only of interest for Romulus-H that rely on the MDPH mode) or (2) to use a sparse representation by storing bytes within 16-bit words in order to use a single _mm_srli_epi16 instruction when extracting topmost nibbles for the S-box decomposition. Still, the vpshufb instruction in AVX512 allows to handle permutations across entire 512-bit registers, making possible to implement the D_{4454} decomposition on Intel as well.

Table 5. Benchmark on Intel processors. Results are given when processing 4096 bytes for Romulus (2048-byte additional data and 2048-byte message) and a single block (i.e. 16 bytes) for Skinny-128-384+. The function 'encryption only' takes as input the round tweakeys fully precomputed while 'encryption + tweakey schedule' simply requires the 48-byte tweakey. Benchmarks were run by carefully disabling the TurboBoost technology.

Algorithm	Implementation	Speed (cycles/byte)	
		i5-8365U (Whiskey Lake)	i7-10510U (Comet Lake)
Skinny-128-384+			
encryption only	Fixsliced [2]	150	165
	Ours	**44**	**47**
encryption + tweakey schedule	Fixsliced [2]	282	305
	Ours	**58**	**62**
Romulus			
Romulus-N nonce-based AEAD	Fixsliced [2]	161	175
	Ours	**37**	**40**
Romulus-M nonce misuse-resistant AEAD	Fixsliced [2]	234	252
	Ours	**51**	**55**
Romulus-T leakage-resilient AEAD	Fixsliced [2]	453	491
	Ours	**109**	**118**
Romulus-H hash function	Fixsliced [2]	220	238
	Ours	**54**	**58**

6   Conclusion and Future Work

We introduced SIMD implementations of Skinny-128 whose performance outperform previous work by up to a factor of 4 on various platforms. The main optimization consists in decomposing the 8-bit S-box in smaller S-boxes with 4/5-bit inputs in order to take advantage of vector permute instructions. It is very likely that other S-boxes in the literature may benefit from a similar implementation technique, and developing a generic tool that would list the relevant decompositions regarding vector permute instructions could be useful for other designs. More generally, we believe that the design of large S-boxes with efficient decompositions could provide attractive trade-offs between security and performance on SIMD platforms. Our work also highlights that performance can greatly vary from a microarchitecture to another, due to possible design discrepancies regarding vector permute instructions. Finally, we did not discuss the integration of countermeasures against power side-channel attacks but studying the relevance of lookup table masking schemes combined with vector permute instructions might be an interesting direction for future research.

Acknowledgements. We are grateful to Thomas Peyrin as well as the anonymous reviewers for their comments that improved the quality of this article.

Appendix

This appendix formally defines the S-box decompositions D_{4444} and D_{4454} introduced in Sect. 3.

A D_{4444} Decomposition

$$S_0 \begin{pmatrix} x_7 \\ x_6 \\ x_5 \\ x_4 \end{pmatrix} = \begin{pmatrix} 0 \\ 0 \\ 0 \\ x_7 \\ x_5 \\ \neg(x_7 \vee x_6) \oplus x_4 \\ 0 \\ x_6 \end{pmatrix} \qquad S_1 \begin{pmatrix} x_3 \\ x_2 \\ x_1 \\ x_0 \end{pmatrix} = \begin{pmatrix} \neg((\neg(x_3 \vee x_2) \oplus x_0) \vee x_3) \oplus x_1 \\ x_3 \\ x_2 \\ 0 \\ 0 \\ 0 \\ \neg(x_3 \vee x_2) \oplus x_0 \\ \neg(x_2 \vee x_1) \end{pmatrix}$$

$$S_2 \begin{pmatrix} x_7 \\ x_6 \\ x_5 \\ x_4 \end{pmatrix} = \begin{pmatrix} 0 \\ 0 \\ 0 \\ x_6 \\ x_7 \\ 0 \\ x_4 \\ (x_7 \vee \neg x_4) \oplus x_5 \end{pmatrix} \qquad S_3 \begin{pmatrix} x_3 \\ x_2 \\ x_1 \\ x_0 \end{pmatrix} = \begin{pmatrix} \neg(x_2 \vee x_1) \oplus x_3 \\ x_2 \\ x_1 \\ \neg((\neg(x_2 \vee x_1) \oplus x_3) \vee x_2) \\ 0 \\ x_0 \\ \neg((\neg(x_2 \vee x_1) \oplus x_3) \vee x_0) \\ \neg((\neg(x_2 \vee x_1) \oplus x_3) \vee x_0) \end{pmatrix}$$

$$S_0 \begin{pmatrix} x_7 \\ x_6 \\ x_5 \\ x_4 \end{pmatrix} \oplus S_1 \begin{pmatrix} x_3 \\ x_2 \\ x_1 \\ x_0 \end{pmatrix} = \begin{pmatrix} y_3 \\ x_3 \\ x_2 \\ x_7 \\ x_5 \\ y_6 \\ y_5 \\ y_2 \end{pmatrix} \qquad S_2 \begin{pmatrix} y_3 \\ x_3 \\ x_2 \\ x_7 \end{pmatrix} \oplus S_3 \begin{pmatrix} x_5 \\ y_6 \\ y_5 \\ y_2 \end{pmatrix} \vee \begin{pmatrix} 0 \\ 0 \\ 0 \\ 0 \\ 0 \\ 0 \\ 0 \\ y_3 \end{pmatrix} = \begin{pmatrix} y_7 \\ y_6 \\ y_5 \\ y_4 \\ y_3 \\ y_2 \\ y_1 \\ y_0 \end{pmatrix}$$

B D_{4454} Decomposition

$$S_0 \begin{pmatrix} x_7 \\ x_6 \\ x_5 \\ x_4 \end{pmatrix} = \begin{pmatrix} x_5 \\ \neg(x_7 \lor x_6) \oplus x_4 \\ 0 \\ x_6 \\ 0 \\ 0 \\ 0 \\ x_7 \end{pmatrix} \qquad S_1 \begin{pmatrix} x_3 \\ x_2 \\ x_1 \\ x_0 \end{pmatrix} = \begin{pmatrix} 0 \\ 0 \\ \neg(x_3 \lor x_2) \oplus x_0 \\ \neg(x_2 \lor x_1) \\ \neg((\neg(x_3 \lor x_2) \oplus x_0) \lor x_3) \oplus x_1 \\ x_3 \\ x_2 \\ 0 \end{pmatrix}$$

$$S_2 \begin{pmatrix} x_7 \\ x_6 \\ x_5 \\ x_4 \\ x_3 \end{pmatrix} = \begin{pmatrix} \neg(x_6 \lor x_5) \oplus x_7 \\ x_6 \\ x_5 \\ \neg((\neg(x_6 \lor x_5) \oplus x_7) \lor x_6) \\ 0 \\ x_4 \\ \neg((\neg(x_6 \lor x_5) \oplus x_7) \lor x_4) \\ \neg((\neg(x_6 \lor x_5) \oplus x_7) \lor x_4) \lor x_3) \end{pmatrix} \qquad S_3 \begin{pmatrix} x_3 \\ x_2 \\ x_1 \\ x_0 \end{pmatrix} = \begin{pmatrix} 0 \\ 0 \\ 0 \\ x_2 \\ x_3 \\ 0 \\ x_0 \\ (x_3 \lor \neg x_0) \oplus x_1 \end{pmatrix}$$

$$S_0 \begin{pmatrix} x_7 \\ x_6 \\ x_5 \\ x_4 \end{pmatrix} \oplus S_1 \begin{pmatrix} x_3 \\ x_2 \\ x_1 \\ x_0 \end{pmatrix} = \begin{pmatrix} x_5 \\ y_6 \\ y_5 \\ y_2 \\ y_3 \\ x_3 \\ x_2 \\ x_7 \end{pmatrix} \qquad S_2 \begin{pmatrix} x_5 \\ y_6 \\ y_5 \\ y_2 \\ y_3 \end{pmatrix} \oplus S_3 \begin{pmatrix} y_3 \\ x_3 \\ x_2 \\ x_7 \end{pmatrix} = \begin{pmatrix} y_7 \\ y_6 \\ y_5 \\ y_4 \\ y_3 \\ y_2 \\ y_1 \\ y_0 \end{pmatrix}$$

References

1. Adomnicai, A., Najm, Z., Peyrin, T.: Fixslicing: a new GIFT representation fast constant-time implementations of GIFT and GIFT-COFB on ARM cortex-m. IACR Trans. Cryptogr. Hardw. Embed. Syst. **2020**(3), 402–427 (2020)
2. Adomnicai, A., Peyrin, T.: Fixslicing AES-like ciphers: new bitsliced AES speed records on ARM-Cortex M and RISC-V. IACR Trans. Cryptogr. Hardw. Embed. Syst. **2021**(1), 402–425 (2020). https://tches.iacr.org/index.php/TCHES/article/view/8739
3. Andreeva, E., Lallemand, V., Purnal, A., Reyhanitabar, R., Roy, A., Vizár, D.: ForkAE v.1. Submission to the NIST Lightweight Cryptography Project (2019)
4. Aufranc, J.L.: How ARM Nerfed NEON Permute Instructions in ARMv8 (2017). https://www.cnx-software.com/2017/08/07/how-arm-nerfed-neon-permute-instructions-in-armv8. Accessed 25 Nov 2021
5. Banik, S., et al.: WARP: revisiting GFN for lightweight 128-bit block cipher. In: Dunkelman, O., Jacobson, Jr., M.J., O'Flynn, C. (eds.) SAC 2020. LNCS, vol. 12804, pp. 535–564. Springer, Cham (2021). https://doi.org/10.1007/978-3-030-81652-0_21

6. Banik, S., Pandey, S.K., Peyrin, T., Sasaki, Yu., Sim, S.M., Todo, Y.: GIFT: a small present - towards reaching the limit of lightweight encryption. In: Fischer, W., Homma, N. (eds.) CHES 2017. LNCS, vol. 10529, pp. 321–345. Springer, Cham (2017). https://doi.org/10.1007/978-3-319-66787-4_16

7. Beierle, C., et al.: The SKINNY family of block ciphers and its low-latency variant MANTIS. In: Robshaw, M., Katz, J. (eds.) CRYPTO 2016. LNCS, vol. 9815, pp. 123–153. Springer, Heidelberg (2016). https://doi.org/10.1007/978-3-662-53008-5_5

8. Benadjila, R., Guo, J., Lomné, V., Peyrin, T.: Implementing lightweight block ciphers on x86 architectures. In: Lange, T., Lauter, K., Lisoněk, P. (eds.) SAC 2013. LNCS, vol. 8282, pp. 324–351. Springer, Heidelberg (2014). https://doi.org/10.1007/978-3-662-43414-7_17

9. Bernstein, D.J., Lange, T.: eBACS: ECRYPT Benchmarking of Cryptographic Systems. https://bench.cr.yp.to. Accessed 25 Feb 2022

10. Berti, F., Guo, C., Pereira, O., Peters, T., Standaert, F.: TEDT, a leakage-resist AEAD mode for high physical security applications. IACR Trans. Cryptogr. Hardw. Embed. Syst. 2020(1), 256–320 (2020)

11. Biesheuvel, A.: Accelerated AES for the Arm64 Linux kernel (2017). https://www.linaro.org/blog/accelerated-aes-for-the-arm64-linux-kernel/. Accessed 25 Oct 2021

12. Caforio, A., Collins, D., Glamocanin, O., Banik, S.: Improving First-Order Threshold Implementations of SKINNY. Cryptology ePrint Archive, Report 2021/1425 (2021). https://ia.cr/2021/1425

13. Chakraborti, A., Iwata, T., Minematsu, K., Nandi, M.: Blockcipher-based authenticated encryption: how small can we go? In: Fischer, W., Homma, N. (eds.) CHES 2017. LNCS, vol. 10529, pp. 277–298. Springer, Cham (2017). https://doi.org/10.1007/978-3-319-66787-4_14

14. Deprez, A., Andreeva, E., Mera, J.M.B., Karmakar, A., Purnal, A.: Optimized software implementations for the lightweight encryption scheme ForkAE. In: Liardet, P.-Y., Mentens, N. (eds.) CARDIS 2020. LNCS, vol. 12609, pp. 68–83. Springer, Cham (2021). https://doi.org/10.1007/978-3-030-68487-7_5

15. Fujii, H., Rodrigues, F.C., López, J.: Fast AES implementation using ARMv8 ASIMD without cryptography extension. In: Seo, J.H. (ed.) ICISC 2019. LNCS, vol. 11975, pp. 84–101. Springer, Cham (2020). https://doi.org/10.1007/978-3-030-40921-0_5

16. Grosso, V., Leurent, G., Standaert, F.-X., Varıcı, K.: LS-designs: bitslice encryption for efficient masked software implementations. In: Cid, C., Rechberger, C. (eds.) FSE 2014. LNCS, vol. 8540, pp. 18–37. Springer, Heidelberg (2015). https://doi.org/10.1007/978-3-662-46706-0_2. https://hal.inria.fr/hal-01093491/document

17. Grosso, V., Varici, A.K., Gaspar, L.: Scream - side-channel resistant authenticated encryption with masking (2015). https://competitions.cr.yp.to/round2/screamv3.pdf

18. Hamburg, M.: Accelerating AES with vector permute instructions. In: Clavier, C., Gaj, K. (eds.) CHES 2009. LNCS, vol. 5747, pp. 18–32. Springer, Heidelberg (2009). https://doi.org/10.1007/978-3-642-04138-9_2

19. Iwata, T., Khairallah, M., Minematsu, K., Peyrin, T.: Duel of the titans: the romulus and remus families of lightweight AEAD algorithms. IACR Trans. Symmetric Cryptol. 2020(1), 43–120 (2020). https://tosc.iacr.org/index.php/ToSC/article/view/8560

20. Jean, J.: TikZ for Cryptographers (2016). https://www.iacr.org/authors/tikz/

21. Jean, J., Nikolic, I., Peyrin, T.: Tweaks and keys for block ciphers: the TWEAKEY framework. In: ASIACRYPT (2014)
22. Mauro, A.D., Fatemi, H., de Gyvez, J.P., Benini, L.: Idleness-aware dynamic power mode selection on the i.MX 7ULP IoT edge processor. J. Low Power Electron. Appl. **10**(2), 19 (2020), https://www.mdpi.com/2079-9268/10/2/19
23. McKay, K., Bassham, L., Turan, M.S., Mouha, N.: Report on Lightweight Cryptography (2017). https://tsapps.nist.gov/publication/get_pdf.cfm?pub_id=922743
24. Naito, Y.: Optimally indifferentiable double-block-length hashing without post-processing and with support for longer key than single block. In: Schwabe, P., Thériault, N. (eds.) LATINCRYPT 2019. LNCS, vol. 11774, pp. 65–85. Springer, Cham (2019). https://doi.org/10.1007/978-3-030-30530-7_4
25. Perrin, L.: Partitions in the S-Box of Streebog and Kuznyechik. IACR Trans. Symmetric Cryptol. **2019**(1), 302–329 (2019). https://tosc.iacr.org/index.php/ToSC/article/view/7405
26. Rogaway, P., Shrimpton, T.: A provable-security treatment of the key-wrap problem. In: Vaudenay, S. (ed.) EUROCRYPT 2006. LNCS, vol. 4004, pp. 373–390. Springer, Heidelberg (2006). https://doi.org/10.1007/11761679_23
27. Ronen, E., Shamir, A., Weingarten, A.O., O'Flynn, C.: IoT goes nuclear: creating a ZigBee chain reaction. In: 2017 IEEE Symposium on Security and Privacy (SP), pp. 195–212 (2017)
28. Rullgard, M.: Cortex-A7 instruction cycle timings (2014). https://hardwarebug.org/2014/05/15/cortex-a7-instruction-cycle-timings. Accessed 25 Oct 2021
29. Shirai, T., Shibutani, K., Akishita, T., Moriai, S., Iwata, T.: The 128-bit blockcipher CLEFIA (extended abstract). In: Biryukov, A. (ed.) FSE 2007. LNCS, vol. 4593, pp. 181–195. Springer, Heidelberg (2007). https://doi.org/10.1007/978-3-540-74619-5_12
30. S.L.M, P., Rijmen, V.: The Whirlpool Hashing Function (2003)
31. Weatherley, R.: SKINNY tweakable block cipher (2017). https://github.com/rweather/skinny-c

Public-Key Cryptanalysis

Handle the Traces: Revisiting the Attack on ECDSA with EHNP

Jinzheng Cao[1] , Yanbin Pan[2], Qingfeng Cheng[1(✉)] , and Xinghua Li[3]

[1] Strategic Support Force Information Engineering University,
Zhengzhou 450001, China
`qingfengc2008@sina.com`
[2] Key Laboratory of Mathematics Mechanization, Academy of Mathematics
and Systems Science, Chinese Academy of Sciences, Beijing 100190, China
[3] Xidian University, Xi'an 710071, China

Abstract. The Elliptic Curves Digital Signature Algorithm (ECDSA) is a standard public key signature protocol. It has become essential to the security of blockchain, digital currency, and many more Internet applications. Currently, it is still one of the most popular algorithms used for digital signing and SSL/TLS transport. Among the possible attacks on ECDSA, side-channel attack poses a serious threat against hardware and software implementations. In particular, Extended Hidden Number Problem can be used when ECDSA leaks side-channel information about the double-and-add chains. The problem is then converted to the shortest vector problem and solved with lattice algorithms. In this paper, we analyze the Extended Hidden Number Problem and present an improved EHNP lattice attack on ECDSA implementations that adopt leaky scalar multiplication. Our attack requires information of double-and-add chains or traces extracted from side-channel results. In addition to methods such as elimination and merging that have been introduced, we make further improvements according to the specific structure of the lattice basis. In fact, the specific property of EHNP allows us to find a sublattice that contains the target vector. We simulate the attack to the **secp256k1**, and the result shows that three signatures are enough to lead to a success rate greater than 0.8. When 4 or 5 traces are known, the success rate is close to 1. The new algorithm significantly improves the performance of attacks using EHNP methods.

Keywords: ECDSA · Side-channel attack · Lattice · Extended hidden number problem

1 Introduction

The Elliptic Curves Digital Signature Algorithm (ECDSA) algorithm is essential to many practical cryptographic protocols, such as TLS and SSH, and is a necessary part of the security of IoT communication, blockchain, and crypto currencies. However, to protect privacy and unforgeability, the signatures should

K. Nguyen et al. (Eds.): ACISP 2022, LNCS 13494, pp. 147–167, 2022.
https://doi.org/10.1007/978-3-031-22301-3_8

be carefully generated. The security of ECDSA is based on the computational intractability of the elliptic curve discrete logarithm problem (ECDLP). The signature requires a point P on a certain elliptic curve to be multiplied by a scalar nonce k. To accelerate the time-consuming procedure of scalar multiplication, the windowed Non-Adjacent Form (wNAF) is introduced as the representation of the nonce k. This method involves fewer executions of scalar multiplication compared with binary representation, thus improving the efficiency [12]. The wNAF representation is implemented in Bitcoin, Cryptlib, Apple's Common-Crypto, and more than one branch of OpenSSL. This multiplication method, however, makes the signature vulnerable to side-channel attacks.

Initiated by Kocher et al. [16], the side-channel attack has recently become a useful approach to analyzing possible vulnerabilities of implementations of ECDSA. Side-channel attacks have been mounted against numerous schemes [6,17] and pose a serious threat to the security of Internet protocols and mobile devices. Among the vulnerable protocols, ECDSA is one of the essential signature schemes [14]. Currently, constant-time and constant-memory implementations can avoid some side-channel attacks, but wNAF is still relevant, especially in some old versions of libraries that are not updated in time. Genkin et al. were able to extract traces from Android and iOS devices via physical side-channels [11]. A recent survey [15] shows that wNAF is still implemented in SunEC, Intel PP Crypto, Crypto++ libraries. Different types of side information determine what method should be chosen to recover the secret. If the most significant bits of nonce are known, recovering the key can be reduced to the Hidden Number Problem (HNP) [4] using the method proposed by Nguyen and Shparlinski [19]. Dall et al. [7] considered errors in the traces and showed that the HNP attack is still possible with erroneous information. The attack has been mounted in the wild on systems such as Bitcoin by Breitner et al. [5]. With biased nonces, the attackers are able to compute hundreds of Bitcoin private keys.

An alternative side-channel detection, FLUSH+RELOAD [25,26], was proposed by Yarom and Falkner as a cache side-channel attack that enables the attacker to observe the scalar multiplication process of ECDSA. The attack extracts the sequence of double-and-add (referred to as DA chain or trace) in the execution of scalar multiplication. Van de Pol et al. [21] derived an effective way of extracting information from 13 traces, but still used the HNP to recover the key. This method omitted much of the side information. To make the full use of the traces, new tools are required. Such a lattice-based attack on ECDSA was proposed by Fan, Wang, and Cheng [10]. Their attack relies on the positions of non-zero coefficients in the wNAF or other presentations. Based on the information, an instance of the Extended Hidden Number Problem (EHNP) can be constructed. The authors solved the EHNP instances by lattice reduction algorithm and successfully recovered the key with four traces. This attack was optimized by De Micheli et al. [8], who introduced preselecting of data to make sure traces of smaller weight are taken as input to construct a lattice basis. With optimized parameters, they improved the probability of success of key recovery and reduced the time cost. The authors successfully recovered a key from three traces but with very low probability.

Our Contributions: In this paper, we try to analyze the factors that affect the success probability of the EHNP attack on ECDSA. The result of our work is an improved algorithm for recovering the key from the EHNP lattice. We also experimentally demonstrate the performance of our algorithms in the context of ECDSA signatures with wNAF information about nonces. Our work improves on previous research in multiple ways.

- **Analysis:** In order to estimate the success condition, we analyze the structure of the EHNP lattice and propose a new observation of the target vector. For example, a new estimation on the norm of the target vector is given, based on probabilities and the average case of the problem. Further, we illustrate that the target vector can be found in a sublattice of smaller dimension, which cancels the effect of parameters such as δ and reduces the dimension of the lattice.
- **Algorithm:** Based on the observations, we propose a strategy to efficiently recover the target vector. For example, we restrict the target vector in a sublattice. Also, it is possible to improve the chance of success by modifying and selecting the traces used to construct the instance and control the size of the lattice. An extended attack algorithm is proposed based on our analysis.

We carry out experiments to test the efficiency of our attack compared with previous algorithms. With up to 5 traces, our attack can reach a success rate close to 1, significantly higher than previous attacks. With 3 traces, the algorithm allows us to achieve a success probability > 0.5. This is a remarkable improvement compared with [8] that only achieved a lower probability (0.002).

2 Preliminaries

2.1 ECDSA

Let E be an elliptic curve on finite field $\mathbb{F}_p$, where p is prime. G is a known point on E of a large prime order q. H is a hash function. The secret key is an integer $0 < \alpha < q$. The public key is the point $Q = \alpha G$. The main steps to sign a message m are as follows:

1) Choose nonce $0 < k < q$ randomly.
2) Compute $(x, y) = kG$, let $r \equiv x \bmod q$; go back to step 1) if $r = 0$.
3) Compute $s = k^{-1}(H(m) + r \cdot \alpha) \bmod q$; if $s = 0$, then go to step (1).

The pair (r, s) is an ECDSA signature of message m. Given k and public information (s, r, m), the secret key can be recovered by computing

$$\alpha = r^{-1}(s \cdot k - H(m)) \bmod q. \tag{1}$$

2.2 ECDSA Scalar Multiplication and Side-Channel Attack

Definition 1 (windowed Non-Adjacent Form). *Consider a window size w, the windowed Non-Adjacent Form (wNAF) of a scalar k is a sequence of digits $\{m_i\}$, where $m_i \in \{0, \pm 1, \pm 3, \ldots, \pm(2^w - 1)\}$. When we denote the non-zero digits among $\{m_i\}$ as $\{k_i\}_{i=1}^l$, k can be rewritten as*

$$k = \sum_{j=1}^{l} k_j 2^{\lambda_j},$$

where $|k_i| \leq 2^w - 1$, l is the number of non-zero digits k_j, and λ_j the position of the digit k_j in the wNAF representation. Every non-zero digit must be followed by at least w zeros. In this way, the scalar k is converted to the wNAF, represented by a sequence of digits.

Algorithm 1: kG using wNAF

Input: wNAF representation for k, $m_0, m_1, \ldots, m_v$, precomputed points
      $\pm G, \pm 3G, \ldots, \pm(2^w - 1)G$, window size w
Output: kG
$Q = G$;
for $i = v, v - 1, \ldots, 0$ **do**
    $Q = 2Q$;
    if $m_i \neq 0$ **then**
        $Q = Q + m_i G$;
    end
end

Algorithm 1 shows the scalar multiplication kG using wNAF. According to the structure of multiplication, if an attacker is able to detect whether the **if-then** block is executed in the **for** loop, then he can determine whether m_i is zero. The double-and-add chain or trace can be presented as a sequence of "A" and "D", where "A" represents an add operation in the **if-then** block, and "D" a double operation. We refer to the Hamming weight or number of non-zero digits of the trace as length. From side-channel information, we can only decide if a digit is zero or not, yet the exact values of the non-zero digits are not revealed.

2.3 EHNP

The Extended Hidden Number Problem (EHNP) was initially introduced to study DSA signatures [13]. We will use the problem to attack ECDSA.

Definition 2 (Extended Hidden Number Problem). *Let N be a prime, given u congruences*

$$\beta_i x + \sum_{j=1}^{l_i} a_{i,j} k_{i,j} \equiv c_i \bmod N, 1 \leq i \leq u,$$

where $k_{i,j}$ and x are unknown. $0 \leq k_{i,j} \leq 2^{\epsilon_{i,j}}$. $\beta_i, a_{i,j}, c_i, l_i$ and known. The EHNP is to find the hidden number x that satisfies the conditions above.

The EHNP can be reduced to an approximate SVP instance with suitable parameters.

2.4   Lattice

We will provide basic concepts about lattices, necessary assumptions, and hard problems. More details about lattice can be seen in [20].

Definition 3 (Lattice). *Let* $\mathbf{b}_1, \mathbf{b}_2, \ldots, \mathbf{b}_d \in \mathbb{R}^d$ *be linearly independent vectors. We define the lattice basis as* $B = [\mathbf{b}_1, \mathbf{b}_2, \ldots, \mathbf{b}_d]$. *The lattice generated by* B *is* $\mathcal{L}(B) = \{\sum_{i=1}^{d} x_i \mathbf{b}_i : x_i \in \mathbb{Z}\}$.

We refer to $\mathcal{L}$ as the full lattice compared with the sublattice generated by the submatrix of full basis B.

For a given basis B, π_i are the projections orthogonal to the span of $\mathbf{b}_1, \mathbf{b}_2, \ldots,$ $\mathbf{b}_i$ and the Gram-Schmidt orthogonalization of B is $B^* = [\mathbf{b}_1^*, \mathbf{b}_2^*, \ldots, \mathbf{b}_d^*]$, where $\mathbf{b}_i^* = \pi_i(\mathbf{b}_i)$. The determinant of $\mathcal{L}$ denotes the volume of the fundamental area, $\det \mathcal{L} = \det B = \|\mathbf{b}_1^*\| \|\mathbf{b}_2^*\| \ldots \|\mathbf{b}_d^*\|$.

Definition 4 (Shortest Vector Problem). *Given a basis B of a lattice $\mathcal{L}$, find a non-zero lattice vector $v \in \mathcal{L}$ of minimal length* $\lambda_1(\mathcal{L}) = \min_{0 \neq \mathbf{w} \in L} \|\mathbf{w}\|$.

There are a variety of algorithms to solve the SVP, such as enumeration, sieve and lattice reduction (LLL or BKZ).

Gaussian Heuristic: To describe the quality of the lattice, we use the Gaussian heuristic [18] to estimate the norm of the shortest vector in the lattice. Let $K \subset \mathbb{R}^d$ be a measurable body, then $|K \cap \mathcal{L}| \approx \mathrm{vol}(K)/\det(\mathcal{L})$. When applying the heuristic to a d-dimension ball of volume $\det(\mathcal{L})$ we get

$$\lambda_1(\mathcal{L}) = \frac{\Gamma\left(\frac{d}{2} + 1\right)^{\frac{1}{d}} \det(\mathcal{L})^{\frac{1}{d}}}{\sqrt{\pi}} \approx \sqrt{\frac{d}{2\pi e}} \det(\mathcal{L})^{1/d}.$$

We denote the heuristic length by $gh(\mathcal{L})$ or $\mathrm{GH}(\mathcal{L})$ in short. In a random lattice $\mathcal{L}$, we assume the shortest vector will have norm $\mathrm{GH}(\mathcal{L})$.

3   Framework of EHNP Attack

In this section, we introduce the main point of the EHNP attack against ECDSA initiated by [10]. With the information obtained from FLUSH+RELOAD, one can set up an EHNP instance to recover the secret key. We produce many ECDSA signatures (r, s), each one with a different nonce k. We assume that the trace of every nonce is known to the attacker, but the values of the non-zero coefficients are unknown. Our goal is to recover α with the traces.

3.1 Preparation

In the attack, we assume the entire chain is known after FLUSH+ RELOAD or other attacks. Suppose that there are l different 'A's, whose positions are shown as $\lambda_i (1 \leq i \leq l)$, then k is rewritten as $k = \sum_{i=1}^{l} k_i 2^{\lambda_i}$, where $k_i \in \{\pm 1, \pm 3, \ldots, \pm(2^w - 1)\}$. Obviously the i-th non-zero digit k_i is odd, so we rewrite it as $k_i = 1 + 2 \cdot k_i'$, where $k_i' \in [-2^{w-1}, 2^{w-1} - 1]$. Let $d_i = k_i' + 2^{w-1} \in [0, 2^w - 1]$, so k can be rewritten as

$$k = \sum_{i=1}^{l} k_i 2^{\lambda_i} = \sum_{i=1}^{l} (1 + 2 \cdot k_i') \cdot 2^{\lambda_i} = \overline{k} + \sum_{i=1}^{l} d_i 2^{\lambda_i + 1}, \tag{2}$$

where $\overline{k} = \sum_{i=1}^{l} 2^{\lambda_i} - \sum_{i=1}^{l} 2^{\lambda_i + w}$. On average, every trace of a 257-bit nonce $k + q$ has $(\lfloor \log_2 q \rfloor + 1)/(w + 2) - 1 = 50.4$ non-zero digits [10].

3.2 Formulating EHNP

According to the ECDSA algorithm, we have $\alpha r - sk + H(m) \equiv 0 \bmod q$. With information about k and (2), we know that there is a $t \in \mathbb{Z}$ such that

$$\alpha r - \sum_{j=1}^{l} (2^{\lambda_i + 1} \cdot s) d_j - (s\overline{k} - H(m)) + tq = 0, \tag{3}$$

where $0 < \alpha < q, 0 \leq d_j \leq 2^w - 1$ and t are unknown.

With u signatures (r_i, s_i) of message $m_i (1 \leq i \leq u)$ using one secret key α, we can build following equations:

$$\begin{cases} \alpha r_1 - \displaystyle\sum_{j=1}^{l_1} (2^{\lambda_{1,j}+1} \cdot s_1) d_{1,j} - (s_1 \overline{k_1} - H(m_1)) + t_1 q = 0, \\ \qquad\qquad\qquad \cdots \\ \alpha r_u - \displaystyle\sum_{j=1}^{l_u} (2^{\lambda_{u,j}+1} \cdot s_u) d_{u,j} - (s_u \overline{k_u} - H(m_u)) + t_u q = 0, \end{cases} \tag{4}$$

where l_i denotes the number of non-zero digits of nonce k_i, $\lambda_{i,j}$ is the position of the j-th non-zero digit $k_{i,j}$. The definition of $\overline{k_i}$ and $d_{i,j}$ are discussed as above. The value of $\alpha, d_{i,j}$ and h_i are unknown. To reduce the complexity of solving the EHNP instance, eliminating and merging are introduced.

Merging: The technique of merging minimizes the number of unknown bits in a trace, reducing the number of non-zero digits of each nonce [8]. The main operation is to merge consecutive non-zero digits into one. After merging, the distance of two adjacent non-zero digits is $\lambda_{i+1} - \lambda_i \geq w + 1 (1 \leq i \leq l - 1)$. From literature, we have the following conclusion ([10], Theorem 1):

Theorem 1. *For $h \geq 1$, suppose $h+1$ consecutive digits $d_i, \ldots, d_{i+h}$ are merged as a new digit d_i'. Then we have $0 \leq d_i' \leq 2^{\mu_i} - 1$, where $\mu_i = \lambda_{i+h} - \lambda_i + w$ is the window size of d_i'.*

This result gives the upper bound of the unknown d'. In addition, $\lambda_{i+h} - \lambda_i + w = w + \sum_{j=1}^{h}(\lambda_{i+j} - \lambda_{i+j-1}) \geq h(w + 1) + w$. The equality holds if and only if $\lambda_{i+j} - \lambda_{i+j-1} = w + 1, 1 \leq j \leq h$. In this case, we can minimize the number of unknown bits. We adopt the merging technique from [10], in which the consecutive non-zero digits whose distance is $w + 1$ are merged. This strategy ensures that we can reduce about half the number of non-zero digits while keeping the number of unknown bits as small as possible.

$$
M = \begin{bmatrix}
q & & & & & & & & & & \\
 & \ddots & & & & & & & & & \\
 & & q & & & & & & & & \\
\tau_{1,2} & \cdots & \tau_{1,u} & \delta/2^{\mu_{1,1}} & & & & & & & \\
\vdots & & \vdots & & \ddots & & & & & & \\
\tau_{l_1,2} & & \tau_{l_1,u} & & & \delta/2^{\mu_{1,l_1}} & & & & & \\
\sigma_{2,1} & & & & & & \delta/2^{\mu_{2,1}} & & & & \\
\vdots & & & & & & & \ddots & & & \\
\sigma_{2,l_2} & & & & & & & & \delta/2^{\mu_{2,l_2}} & & \\
 & \ddots & & & & & & & & \ddots & \\
 & & \sigma_{u,1} & & & & & & & & \delta/2^{\mu_{u,1}} \\
 & & \vdots & & & & & & & & \\
 & & \sigma_{u,l_u} & & & & & & & & \\
\gamma_2 & \cdots & \gamma_u & \delta/2 & \cdots & \delta/2 & \delta/2 & \cdots & \delta/2 & \cdots & \delta/2 & \cdots & \delta/2 & \delta/2
\end{bmatrix}
$$

$$
= \begin{bmatrix} qI_{u-1} & \mathbf{0} \\ A & \delta B \end{bmatrix}
$$

$$(5)$$

Eliminating α: One straightforward improvement is to eliminate α from the equations, thus reducing the dimension by 1 [10]. We denote the i-th equation in (4) as E_i. To eliminate α, we compute $r_1 E_i - r_i E_1$ for $1 < i \leq u$. As a result, we have the following equations:

$$
\sum_{j=1}^{l_1} \underbrace{(2^{\lambda_{1,j}+1} s_1 r_i)}_{\tau_{j,i}} d_{1,j} + \sum_{j=1}^{l_i} \underbrace{(-2^{\lambda_{i,j}+1} s_i r_1)}_{\sigma_{i,j}} d_{i,j} - \underbrace{[r_1(s_i \overline{k}_i - H(m_i)) - r_i(s_1 \overline{k}_1 - H(m_1))]}_{\gamma_i} + t_i q = 0,
$$

where $0 \leq d_{1,j}, d_{i,j} \leq 2^{\mu_{i,j}} - 1$ and t_i are unknown.

3.3   Lattice Basis

With the information extracted from traces, we can construct a lattice $\mathcal{L}$ spanned by the basis M to solve the EHNP instance. The basis matrix is shown in (5). In fact, let $T = \sum_{i=1}^{u} l_i$, then M is a $(T+u) \times (T+u)$ matrix. The row vectors in M form a basis of a lattice $\mathcal{L}(M)$ of dimension $d = T + u$, and there exists a vector

$$\mathbf{z} = [t_2, \dots, t_u, d_{1,1}, \dots, d_{1,l_1}, \dots, d_{u,1}, \dots, d_{u,l_u}, -1] \cdot M$$

$$= (0, \dots, 0, \frac{d_{1,1}}{2^{\mu_{1,1}}}\delta - \frac{\delta}{2}, \dots, \frac{d_{1,l_1}}{2^{\mu_{1,l_1}}}\delta - \frac{\delta}{2}, \dots, \frac{d_{u,1}}{2^{\mu_{u,1}}}\delta$$

$$- \frac{\delta}{2}, \dots, \frac{d_{u,l_u}}{2^{\mu_{u,l_u}}}\delta - \frac{\delta}{2}, -\frac{\delta}{2}) \in \mathcal{L}.$$

The determinant of $\mathcal{L}$ is $vol(\mathcal{L}) = q^{u-1}\delta^{T+1}/2^{U+1}, U = \sum_{i=1}^{u}\sum_{j=1}^{l_u}\mu_{i,j}$. The vector $\mathbf{z}$ has norm $\|\mathbf{z}\| \leq \frac{\delta}{2}\sqrt{T+1}$. When a small δ is chosen, $\mathbf{x}$ will be short enough to be found by lattice reduction algorithms. In this work, the choice of δ follows the instructions of [10] and [8]. After finding the vector, k and α can be recovered by (4).

4   New Analysis of ECDSA-EHNP

Section 3 introduces the general idea of EHNP attack of ECDSA with wNAF information. However, previous works leave several problems unsolved. For example, the relatively loose upper bound for $\|\mathbf{z}\|$, the lack of analysis of the EHNP-lattice basis, and most importantly, whether the target vector is short enough to be found by LLL or BKZ. In this section, we try to shed light on the structure of the basis and provide possible strategies to improve the attack.

4.1   New Estimation for $\|\mathbf{z}\|$

Estimating the norm of target vector $\mathbf{z}$ helps the attacker evaluate the success condition and optimize the parameters. Generally, a shorter vector is easier to find with SVP algorithms. Prior work used an upper bound for $\|\mathbf{z}\|$ as the estimated norm [8,10]. In many practical cases, however, the target vector is shorter. When instances are randomly sampled, we can use the expected norm of a uniformly oriented vector instead of the loose upper bound for the target. The length of the target vector $\mathbf{z}$ can be estimated with the expected value of its norm [3].

$$\mathbb{E}(\|\mathbf{z}\|^2) = \mathbb{E}\left[\sum_{1 \leq i \leq u,\ 1 \leq j \leq l_u} \left(\frac{d_{i,j}}{2^{\mu_{i,j}}}\delta - \frac{\delta}{2}\right)^2 + \left(\frac{\delta}{2}\right)^2\right]$$

$$= \delta^2 \cdot T \cdot \mathbb{E}\left[\left(\frac{d_{i,j}}{2^{\mu_{i,j}}} - \frac{1}{2}\right)^2\right] + \frac{\delta^2}{4}.$$

Assuming $d_{i,j}$ is distributed uniformly in $[0, 2^{\mu_{i,j}} - 1]$, we have

$$\mathbb{E}\left[\left(d_{i,j} - 2^{\mu_{i,j}-1}\right)^2\right] = \frac{1}{2^{\mu_{i,j}}} \sum_{k=0}^{2^{\mu_{i,j}}-1} \left(k - 2^{\mu_{i,j}-1}\right)^2 = \frac{2^{2\mu_{i,j}}}{12} + \frac{1}{6},$$

$$\mathbb{E}\left[\left(\frac{d_{i,j}}{2^{\mu_{i,j}}} - \frac{1}{2}\right)^2\right] = \frac{1}{2^{2\mu_{i,j}}}\mathbb{E}\left[\left(d_{i,j} - 2^{\mu_{i,j}-1}\right)^2\right] = \frac{1}{12} + \frac{1}{6 \cdot 2^{2\mu_{i,j}}},$$

and

$$\mathbb{E}(\|\mathbf{z}\|^2) = \mathbb{E}\left[\sum_{1\leq i\leq u,\ 1\leq j\leq l_u} \left(\frac{d_{i,j}}{2^{\mu_{i,j}}}\delta - \frac{\delta}{2}\right)^2 + \left(\frac{\delta}{2}\right)^2\right]$$

$$\approx \delta^2 \left(\frac{T}{12} + \frac{1}{4}\right).$$

In fact, we have $\mu_{i,j} \geq 3$ after merging, so

$$\mathbb{E}(\|\mathbf{z}\|^2) \leq \delta^2 \left(\frac{T}{12} + \frac{1}{4} + \frac{T}{6 \cdot 2^6}\right)$$

$$= \delta^2 \left(\frac{3T}{32} + \frac{1}{4}\right) < \frac{\delta^2}{8}(T+1) \quad \text{(when } T > 16\text{)}.$$

The new expected norm is shorter than the upper bound $\|\mathbf{z}\| \leq \delta\sqrt{T+1}/2$. Therefore, some problems previously seen as difficult can possibly be solved. Taking a larger block size for BKZ or calling SVP solvers can help find the short vector $\mathbf{z}$.

4.2   Sublattice Analysis

Previous attacks tend to use Gaussian heuristic to estimate parameters such as δ. However, the lattice basis M contains special structures, which allow extended analysis of the EHNP instance generated from ECDSA. We divide M into blocks as shown in (5), where $A \in \mathbb{Z}^{(T+1)\times(u-1)}, B \in \mathbb{Z}^{(T+1)\times(T+1)}$. The analysis of sublattices allows us to find more specific structures. The target vector $\mathbf{z}$ can be rewritten as $\mathbf{z} = [\mathbf{t}, \mathbf{d}] \cdot M = [\mathbf{0}_{u-1}, \mathbf{b}]$, where $\mathbf{t} \in \mathbb{Z}^{u-1}, \mathbf{d} \in \mathbb{Z}^{T+1}, \mathbf{b} \in \mathbb{Z}^{T+1}$. From the equation, we have

$$\begin{aligned} \mathbf{0}_{u-1} &= \mathbf{t} \cdot qI_{u-1} + \mathbf{d} \cdot A, \\ \mathbf{b} &= \mathbf{d} \cdot B. \end{aligned} \tag{6}$$

Therefore, the target vector can be described with additional conditions, which lead to a smaller space. Here we introduce the definition of sublattice, which contains the target $\mathbf{b}$.

Definition 5. *For a $(T+u) \times (T+u)$-EHNP basis $M = \begin{bmatrix} qI_{u-1} & \mathbf{0} \\ A & \delta B \end{bmatrix}$ as defined in 5, the sublattice of M is $\mathcal{L}' = \mathcal{L}_{\mathsf{sub}}(M) = \{\mathbf{d} \cdot \delta B \in \mathcal{L}(\delta B) : \mathbf{d} \cdot A = \mathbf{0}_{u-1}$ (mod q)$\}$.*

The target vector $\mathbf{b}$ is a short vector in the sublattice $\mathcal{L}' = \{\mathbf{d} \cdot \delta B \in \mathcal{L}(\delta B) : \mathbf{d} \cdot A = \mathbf{0}_{u-1}$ (mod q)$\}$. An interesting finding is that $\mathbf{z}$ must have consecutively $u - 1$ zeros at the left end. Therefore, vectors with non-zero elements at the left will not contribute to the target.

Theorem 2. *At least $u - 1$ vectors in the basis of $\mathcal{L}$ are independent to the target vector $\mathbf{z} = [\mathbf{0}_{u-1}, \mathbf{b}]$.*

Proof. To solve the equation $\mathbf{d} \cdot A = \mathbf{0}_{u-1}$ (mod q) is equivalent to solving

$$\mathbf{t} \cdot qI_{u-1} + \mathbf{d} \cdot A = \mathbf{0}_{u-1},$$

where t and d are integer vectors. So vector $[\mathbf{t}, \mathbf{d}]$ is in the left kernel of block $\begin{bmatrix} qI_{u-1} \\ A \end{bmatrix} \in \mathbb{Z}^{(T+u) \times (u-1)}$. The kernel of the block has rank $T + 1$. Therefore, there exist $u - 1$ independent vectors $\mathbf{b}'$ such that $\mathbf{d}' \cdot A \neq \mathbf{0}_{u-1}$ (mod q).

In fact, we can compute the shape of the $u-1$ irrelevant vectors. Recall that q is a prime number, so $\gcd(q, \tau_{i,j}) = \gcd(q, \sigma_{i',j'}) = 1$. Thus, after some linear combination, there is a vector with a 1 element in the first $u - 1$ positions.

$$\mathbf{c}_i = [\underbrace{0, \ldots, 1, 0, \ldots,}_{u-1} \underbrace{\mathbf{c}'_i}_{T+1}].$$

Take $\mathbf{c}_1$ (corresponding to the first column of M) as an example. There exist integers $m, g_1, \ldots, g_{l_1}, h_1, \ldots, h_{l_2}$ such that $mq + \sum_{i=1}^{l_1} g_i\tau_{i,2} + \sum_{i=1}^{l_2} h_i\sigma_{2,i} = \gcd(q, \tau_{1,2}, \ldots, \sigma_{2,1}, \ldots)$. It is obvious that $\gcd(q, \tau_{1,2}, \ldots, \sigma_{2,1}, \ldots) = 1$ (for q is prime). Therefore, there is a lattice vector

$$\mathbf{c}_1 = [m, 0, \ldots, 0, g_1, \ldots, g_{l_1}, h_1, \ldots, h_{l_2}, 0, \ldots] \cdot M$$
$$= [1, 0, \ldots, 0, \frac{\delta g_1}{2^{\mu_{1,1}}}, \ldots, \frac{\delta g_{l_1}}{2^{\mu_{1,l_1}}}, \frac{\delta h_1}{2^{\mu_{2,1}}}, \ldots, \frac{\delta h_{l_2}}{2^{\mu_{2,l_2}}}, 0, \ldots].$$

This vector is independent to target vector, which has the form $(0, \ldots, 0, *, *, \ldots)$. Our aim is to construct the basis of sublattice $\mathcal{L}'$ that doesn't contain $\mathbf{c}_i$. The target in the sublattice is $\mathbf{b}$. Further, we show that the different δ parameters proposed in [13] actually lead to isomorphic sublattices.

Theorem 3. *For two basis $M_{\delta_1}, M_{\delta_2}$ generated by the same EHNP instance and two δ values δ_1, δ_2, they contain sublattices $\mathcal{L}_{\mathsf{sub}}(M_{\delta_1})$ and $\mathcal{L}_{\mathsf{sub}}(M_{\delta_2})$ which are isomorphic.*

Proof. We first give the basis of $\mathcal{L}_{\mathbf{sub}}(M_{\delta_1})$ and $\mathcal{L}_{\mathbf{sub}}(M_{\delta_2})$. From the definition of M, M_{δ_1} and M_{δ_2} share the same left block $\begin{bmatrix} qI_{u-1} \\ A \end{bmatrix}$. As a q-ary matrix, the block has the Hermite Normal Form I_{u-1}. Therefore, there is a unimodular matrix R such that $R \begin{bmatrix} qI_{u-1} \\ A \end{bmatrix} = \begin{bmatrix} I_{u-1} \\ 0 \end{bmatrix}$. Similarly, $RM = \begin{bmatrix} I_{u-1} & C' \\ 0 & \delta B' \end{bmatrix}$, and $\delta b_1, \ldots, \delta b_{T+1}$ are the basis vectors of sublattice $\mathcal{L}_{\mathbf{sub}}(M_\delta)$, where $b_1, \ldots, b_{T+1}$ are the rows of B'.

Define a homomorphic map

$$\phi : \mathcal{L}_{\mathbf{sub}}(M_{\delta_1}) \rightarrow \mathcal{L}_{\mathbf{sub}}(M_{\delta_2})$$

$$[\delta_1 a_1, \delta_1 a_2, \ldots, \delta_1 a_{T+1}] \rightarrow [\delta_2 a_1, \delta_2 a_2, \ldots, \delta_2 a_{T+1}].$$

For every basis $\delta_1 b_i \in \mathcal{L}_{\mathbf{sub}}(M_{\delta_1})$, $\phi(\delta_1 b_i) = \delta_2 b_i$ is a corresponding basis vector in $\mathcal{L}_{\mathbf{sub}}(M_{\delta_1})$. Therefore, ϕ is an isomorphic map.

By extracting the sublattice, we reduce the dimension of the basis from $T + u$ to $T + 1$. What's more, putting the target vector in the sublattice eliminates the influence of δ on solving EHNP. In the previous method, the attacker uses δ to empirically balance the size of sublattice $\mathcal{L}'$ and the full basis, expecting the target vector appears in the reduced basis. However, Theorem 3 constructs a sublattice basis, which will generate the target vector. In the following sections, we just assume $\delta = 1$ and cancel its effect.

4.3   Evaluating the Instance

In the previous subsection, we show that the target vector can be found in a sublattice $\mathcal{L}'$. In this part, we discuss the factors that affect the quality of the sub-basis, and the shortness of the target vector.

We first compute $\det(\mathcal{L}')$. Theorem 3 introduces unimodular R such that $RM = \begin{bmatrix} I_{u-1} & C' \\ 0 & B' \end{bmatrix}$. Therefore, we have $|M| = |RM| = |I_{u-1}||B'|$.

$\det(\mathcal{L}') = |B'| = |M| = q^{u-1} 2^{-U-1}$, where $U = \sum_{i=1}^{u} \sum_{j=1}^{l_u} \mu_{i,j}$. We usually use the merging technique to shorten the traces, or reduce the number of non-zero coefficients. As a side effect, this operation will increase U. The merging algorithm only merges two digits when their distance is $w + 1$. Suppose $k_0, k_1, \ldots, k_m$ are consecutive non-zero digits to be merged of position $\lambda_0, \lambda_1, \ldots, \lambda_m$, where $\lambda_{i+1} - \lambda_i = 4, i = 0, 1, \ldots, m$. The original $\mu_0, \mu_1, \ldots, \mu_m$ are all 3 (the window size w). After m merging operations, the m digits are merged into new digit with $\mu'_0 = 3 + \lambda_m - \lambda_0 = 3 + 4m = \sum_{i=-0}^{m} \mu_i + m$.

Before merging, $U = 3T$, where T is the total length of u. After x mergings, $T' = T - x, U' = U + x$. In fact, if we assume the traces have the average length l, then $T = lu$. Recall that in Subsect. 4.1, we estimate that $\mathbb{E}(\|\mathbf{z}\|) < \frac{\sqrt{T+1}}{\sqrt{8}}$. On the other hand, the Gaussian Heuristic of $\mathcal{L}'$ can be computed as

$$\mathrm{GH} = \sqrt{\frac{T'+1}{2\pi e}} q^{\frac{u-1}{T'+1}} 2^{-\frac{U'+1}{T'+1}}.$$

To find the secret key, we expect that the target vector is significantly shorter than the Gaussian heuristic. In other words, $GH/\mathbb{E}(\|\mathbf{z}\|)$ should be as large as possible. Based on our analysis, $GH/\mathbb{E}(\|\mathbf{z}\|) = \Omega(q^{\frac{u-1}{T'+1}} 2^{-\frac{U'+1}{T'+1}})$. We define $f = \log_2(q^{\frac{u-1}{T'+1}} 2^{-\frac{U'+1}{T'+1}}) = \frac{u-1}{T-x+1} \log_2 q - \frac{U+x+1}{T-x+1} \log_2 2$.

For easier analysis, we can approximate $\log_2 q$ as 256 and replace T, U with $lu, 3lu$. Thus, we use the **scoring function**

$$f = \frac{u-1}{lu-x+1}256 + \frac{3lu+x+1}{lu-x+1} \tag{7}$$

to evaluate the ECDSA-EHNP instance and estimate the chance of recovering the target vector.

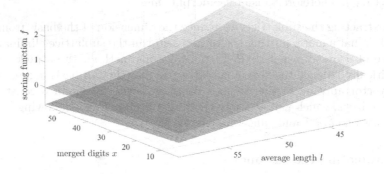

Fig. 1. $f(x, l)$ for different u

To describe the shape and tendency of f, we compute its partial derivatives.

$$\begin{aligned}
\frac{\partial f}{\partial x} &= \frac{256u - 256}{(lu-x+1)^2} - \frac{x+3lu+1}{(lu-x+1)^2} - \frac{1}{lu-x+1}, \\
\frac{\partial f}{\partial l} &= \frac{u(x+3lu+1)}{(lu-x+1)^2} - \frac{3u}{lu-x+1} - \frac{u(256u-256)}{(lu-x+1)^2}.
\end{aligned} \tag{8}$$

With u fixed, f only has a singular point $(x, l) = (64u - 63.5, 64 - 64.5/u)$ but no extreme point in $S = \{0 \le x \le 3u, l > 0\}$. In fact, for $u \ge 2$, $\frac{\partial f}{\partial l} < 0$, which makes f continuously drop with l increasing. As shown in Fig. 1, larger u also has a significant improvement on f. To ensure a short target vector, traces with smaller l and larger x should be used to construct an EHNP instance.

4.4   Short Vectors

We have constructed a sublattice $\mathcal{L}'$ where $\mathbf{b}$ is the desired target vector. However, $\mathbf{b}$ may not be the shortest vector in $\mathcal{L}(B)$. For example, the rows of submatrix A are not linearly independent, which leads to a set of non-unique solutions to the equation $\mathbf{x} \cdot A = \mathbf{0}_{u-1} \pmod q$. Consider in B's row vectors corresponding to $\lambda_{i,j}$ and $\lambda_{i,j+1}$, or in other words, the $(u - 1 + \sum_{k=1}^{i-1} l_k + j)$-th row $v_{i,j}$ and $(u + \sum_{k=1}^{i-1} l_k + j)$-th row $v_{i,j+1}$ of M, $0 \le j \le l_i - 1$. To compare the two rows, one can take $\sigma_{i,j}$ and $\sigma_{i,j+1}$ as an example. Here we assume the traces have been merged and T, U are properly updated. By definition of σ we have

$$\sigma_{i,j+1} = -2^{\lambda_{i,j+1}+1} \cdot s_i r_1 = 2^{\lambda_{i,j+1}-\lambda_{i,j}} \cdot \sigma_{i,j},$$

so we can get a short vector by $v_{i,j+1}$ minus $2^{\lambda_{i,j+1}-\lambda_{i,j}}$ times $\mathbf{v}_{i,j}$:

$$\mathbf{v} = (0, \ldots, 0, - \cdot 2^{\lambda_{i,j+1}-\lambda_{i,j}-\mu_{i,j}}, \cdot 2^{-\mu_{i,j+1}}, 0, \ldots, 0). \tag{9}$$

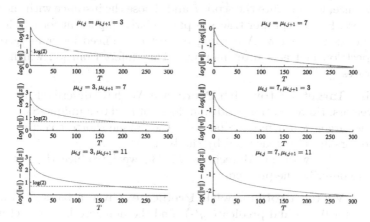

Fig. 2. $\log \|\mathbf{v}\| - \log \|\mathbf{z}\|$ in different conditions

After merging, in $3/4$ of the cases, the distance between two consecutive non-zero digits is larger than $2w$. We expect $\mathbf{v}$ to be relatively long compared with $vol(\mathcal{L})^{1/(T+u)}$, which requires T/u to be large. This (again) means longer traces (traces with more non-zero digits) are required.

Measuring Vectors: Knowing $\mu_{i,j}$ and $\mu_{i,j+1}$ allows more accurate discussion on the length of $\mathbf{v}$ and $\mathbf{z}$. In fact, the value of $\mu_{i,j}$ has a significant effect on the length of v, then we have

$$\log \|\mathbf{v}\| - \log \|\mathbf{z}\| \approx \frac{1}{2} \log(2^{4w} \cdot 2^{-2\mu_{i,j}} + 2^{-2\mu_{i,j+1}})$$

$$- \frac{1}{2} \log(T/12 + 1/4).$$

Figure 2 shows the estimated $\log \|\mathbf{v}\| - \log \|\mathbf{z}\|$. When $\mu_{i,j} = 3$, $\|\mathbf{z}\|$ is shorter than $0.5\|\mathbf{v}\|$ when $T < 200$. After merging, we get $\mu_{i,j} = 3$ in more than half of the cases. Therefore, we expect $T < 200$ will make $\mathbf{z}$ shorter than half of the $\mathbf{v}$ vectors, enough to be found by SVP solvers. In particular, the average Hamming weight (number of 'A's) of a trace falls between 25 and 30, so expect to use fewer than 10 traces to recover the key.

5   Algorithms

This subsection summarizes our method of attacking ECDSA and provides our algorithms for recovering the private key. We begin with the basic procedures of our attack.

5.1   Strategy

Choice of Traces: According to [10], at least 3 traces are required to recover a 256-bit secret key. To improve the probability of recovering the secret with 3 traces, we preselect the traces to construct a better basis. For every possible EHNP instance, we compute the score f and choose the instance with the highest possible score. Finding proper traces is particularly important for $u = 3$, for the average success rate is low. According to Sect. 4, we need fewer merged digits, so we expect longer traces after merging. This differs from [8], which asks for shorter traces.

Describing Target Vector with Predicate: We have described the existence of short vectors. However, this condition does not lead to a unique-SVP instance. In fact, the target vector may be far from the unique shortest vector, for many shorter vectors are also generated by the basis.

Similar to the work of Albrecht et al. [3], we introduce the α-SVP with predicate to describe the problem.

α-Shortest Vector Problem with Predicate: Given a basis B of a lattice $\mathcal{L}$, a parameter $0 < \alpha$ and predicate $g(\cdot)$, find the non-zero lattice vector $\mathbf{v} \in \mathcal{L}$ satisfying $\mathrm{GH}(\mathcal{L}) > \alpha \cdot \|\mathbf{v}\|$ and $g(\mathbf{v}) = 1$.

For an EHNP instance generated from traces, the $\{\mu_{i,j}\}$ and basis matrix M are known. Therefore, we can define a predicate to find vector $\mathbf{z}$ as in Algorithm 2.

Algorithm 2: Predicate $g(\cdot)$

Input: Vector $\mathbf{v} = [v_1, v_2, \dots, v_d]$
Output: $g(\mathbf{z})$
if $v_1, \dots, v_{u-1} \neq 0$ **then**
| return *FALSE*;
end
Compute $\mathbf{u} = \mathbf{v} \cdot M^{-1} = [t_2, \dots, t_u, d_{1,1}, \dots, d_{1,l_1}, \dots, d_{u,1}, \dots, d_{u,l_u}, n]$;
if $n \neq -1$ **then**
| return *FALSE*;
end
Solve equation $\alpha r_i - \sum_{j=1}^{l}(2^{\lambda_{i,j}+1} \cdot s_i)d_{i,j} - (s_i \overline{k_i} - H(m_i)) + t_i q = 0$, get α';
if $Q == \alpha' \cdot G$ **then**
| return *TRUE*;
end
else
| return *FALSE*;
end

5.2   The Attack

In addition to BKZ, our main algorithm adopts sieving as the SVP solver. The BKZ reduction is still included in the procedure at the preprocess stage. To accelerate the process, we may use the BKZ 2.0 implementation. According to previous work, we make use of the set of relatively short vectors or "database" that a sieve call outputs on a projected block [2]. In fact, after a sieve call terminates, it will output a database L that contains all vectors shorter than $\sqrt{4/3}vol(\mathcal{L})$. After the sieve call, we run a predicate check to find the target vector.

Algorithm 3: Sieving attack

Input: Lattice basis M, dimension d, block size β_{max}, predicate $g(\cdot)$
Output: Vector $\mathbf{z} = (\mathbf{0}, v)$ such that $g(\mathbf{z}) = 1$
Extract sublattice basis M' from M with LLL;
Set β to be the number of quasi-reduced rows in M';
while $\beta < \beta_{max}$ **do**
   | BKZ tour on M' with block size β;
   | Increase β;
   | **if** *row vector* $\mathbf{v}$ *in* M' *satisfies* $g(\mathbf{v}) = 1$ **then**
   | | **return** $(\mathbf{0}, \mathbf{v})$
   | **end**
end
Run sieving algorithm on projected sublattice of M', denote output list by L';
Lift the vectors in L', get list of vectors L;
for $\mathbf{v} \in L$ **do**
   | **if** $g(\mathbf{0}, \mathbf{v}) = 1$ **then**
   | | **return** $(\mathbf{0}, \mathbf{v})$
   | **end**
end

Implementation: Several detailed modifications are made to the algorithm. First, according to the work of Albrecht [1], parameters such as size of database and saturation ratio need to be modified to find the required vector. Second, we preprocess the basis with BKZ-$(d - 30)$ before sieving. The effect of sieving is significantly affected by the quality of the input basis. Therefore, BKZ reduction is necessary before sieve is called. We use a progressive algorithm to gradually update the basis.

Using Subsieve: Currently, the most efficient sieve variants benefit from the "dimensions for free technique". This technique makes use of all vectors that a sieve call can output. In fact, **Subsieve** solves SVP in dimension d with a sieve in dimension $d' = d - \Theta(d/\log d)$. Assuming the projected lattice $\mathcal{L}_{d-d'}$ contains a short vector $\|\pi_{d-d'}(v)\| \leq \sqrt{4/3}vol(\mathcal{L}_{d-d'})$, it can be obtained by a sieve call. The entire vector $\mathbf{v}$ can be found by Babai's Nearest Plane Algorithm.

Lucas proposed $d' = d - \frac{d \log(4/3)}{\log(d/(2\pi e))}$ for random lattice [9]. In practice, our target vector may be longer than the Gaussian heuristic, so we can empirically choose the dimensions for free.

6   Simulation Analysis

We test our attack on the elliptic curve **secp256k1** and show our new results of attacking with at least 3 traces. We used the personal computer on an Intel Core i7-10750H CPU running at 2.60 GHz in six threads. Recall that Fan et al. used an Intel Core i7-3770 CPU running at 3.40 GHz while De Micheli et al. used the cluster Grid'5000 on a single core of an Intel Xeon Gold 6130. The implementation of BKZ and Sieve functions are based on FPLLL [22,23] and G6K [24].

6.1   Attacking with 3 Traces

Our algorithm is able to attack ECDSA with 3 traces. Fan et al. conjectured that 3 independent traces are enough to recover the secret key, but did not mount a successful attack with 3 traces. In 2019, De Micheli et al. were able to reach a success probability of 0.002. Based on the discussion in Subsect. 4.2, the traces should not have too few non-zero digits. In the attack, we adopt the preselecting technique. We compare the success rate and time cost of attacking different traces in Table 1. The T is the sum of weight of the traces. The dimension of the EHNP-lattice is $T + u = T + 3$. Time is in CPU-seconds. Using 3 traces, we achieved a success probability up to 0.85, significantly superior to [8].

Table 1. Key recovery with 3 traces

T	Probability	Time	
		BKZ stage	Sieve stage
$T > 110$	0.59	3 min	19.7 min
$105 < T \leq 110$	0.85	2.3 min	18.3 min
$95 < T \leq 105$	0.36	1.5 min	15.3 min

Table 2. New record of attacking ECDSA

u	Our attack		De Micheli's attack		Fan's attack		van de Pol's attack	
	Probability	Time	Probability	Time	Probability	Time	Probability	Time
3	0.85[a]	24 min	0.002	39h	0	–	0	–
4	0.91	14 min	0.04	25 h 28 min	0.08	88 min	0	–
5	0.99	6 min	0.20	1 h 4 min	0.38	102 min	0	–
10	–	–	–	–	–	–	0.07	0.04 min
15	–	–	–	–	–	–	0.54	0.19 min

[a] We use preselecting technique only for $u = 3$. In fact, more than 3 traces are enough to recover the key with probability > 0.5.

Effect of Preselecting: Via selecting the traces according to Subsect. 4.2, we are able to confine the dimension of EHNP instances we build, thus controlling the hardness. Contrary to the intuitive idea, traces with smaller weight won't contribute to the success probability, while heavier traces add to the success rate. This is a surprising result, for [8] indicates that smaller traces are desired for all attacks. As we discussed in Sect. 4.2, fewer merged digits lead to higher scores for an average trace. As the results show, the value of T must balance the running time and the success rate. For the algorithm we use, the success rate is higher when $T \in (105, 110]$. However, the time cost decreases with smaller T. The results also illustrate that the computation is mostly consumed by sieving. Recall that previous EHNP attacks only use BKZ as the SVP solver. Compared with the 0.002 probability of success, our sieve attack is more efficient.

6.2 Attacking with More Traces

When we use more than 3 traces to attack ECDSA, we also enjoy an advantage compared with previous attacks. As the results show, with more information, the probability of success rises. In particular, with 5 traces the probability is close to 1, far more than the probability that previous attacks can reach with 7 or 8 traces. Table 2 shows our new result.

The total time is the average time of a single attack multiplied by the number of trials necessary to recover the key. Recall that De Micheli et al.'s attack can reach the maximum success probability 0.45 with 7 traces while Fan et al. can reach the probability 0.68 with 7 traces. When attacking with more than 3 traces, we did not implement the preselecting technique. In fact, using randomly generated traces proves enough to recover the key k. Our method is able to get a significantly improved success rate with a smaller number of traces. It also requires less time compared with other attacks. On average, the running time of the new approach is 97% shorter than De Micheli's attack.

6.3 Handling Errors

It is expected to obtain traces with errors in practice. The errors usually occur when an "A" in the trace is wronged as "D" or "D" wronged as "A". Figure 3(a) shows the result of attacks with different number of errors. In the experiments we set $d' = 70$ when calling Subsieve. The two experiments use the same setting of block size and free dimensions. When 5 traces are used, the success rate is close to 1 with no more than 4 errors. When 5 or more errors are added, the success rate significantly drops. Attacking with 4 traces is slightly better when handling more errors, for the dimension of the lattice is still not too large.

Changing Parameters: With more errors, the algorithm needs to be optimized. For example, our attack relies on the "dimensions for free" technique [9] to save computational resources. In the existence of errors, however, the free dimension should decrease to maximize the success probability. Figure 4 shows

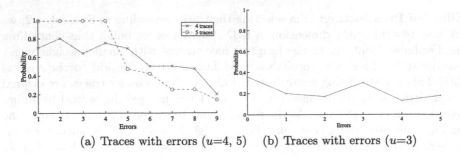

(a) Traces with errors (u=4, 5)   (b) Traces with errors (u=3)

Fig. 3. New estimation of $\|\mathbf{z}\|$

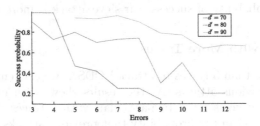

Fig. 4. Result of attacks on 5 traces with errors

the result of attacking 5 traces with different settings. The algorithm is stronger when d' increases, and the attack is more likely to succeed.

Figure 4 illustrates the result of attacking 5 erroneous traces with different settings for sieving. When d' increases, the attack is able to reach a higher probability of success.

We also carry out experiments of attacking 3 traces with errors. The results are shown in Fig. 3(b). For the attack we preselect the traces to make $T \in$ [95, 105]. This case is more likely to appear in practical scenario. Adding errors to the traces has an explicit influence on the success rate, which is not very high even without errors.

7   Conclusion

Previous EHNP attacks of ECDSA already gain remarkable advantage against the HNP method. In this work, we continue to improve the success probability to nearly 100% with only 4 or 5 traces from FLUSH+RELOAD attack, while previous EHNP attacks need 7 traces to reach similar result. With 3 traces, we significantly improve the success probability by more than 400 times. The attack also recovers the key with 3 traces when attacking with erroneous information, at the cost of success probability.

The new attack is based on the analysis and observation of the ECDSA-EHNP problem. Using a more accurate expected value of the target vector, we can decide the condition for successful attacks. The attack algorithm combines BKZ reduction and sieve. Unlike previous works, in this attack, BKZ serves as preprocessing, and sieve is the main SVP solver. With suitable parameters, the target vector will appear in the output set of vectors. The attack is tested on the **secp256k1** curve in experiments, but the attack does not rely on special structure of curves and can be mounted on any curve.

To avoid being attacked by this kind of technique, one can simply choose a new key every transaction. This would prevent the attacker from obtaining enough information of the changing key. Another possible way is to switch to other scalar multiplications to mitigate side-channel leakage. For example, new versions of OpenSSL libraries have use constant-time implementations for curves such as **secp256k1**.

Acknowledgments. This work was supported by the National Natural Science Foundation of China (Nos. 61872449, 62125205).

References

1. Albrecht, M.R., Ducas, L., Herold, G., Kirshanova, E., Postlethwaite, E.W., Stevens, M.: The general sieve kernel and new records in lattice reduction. In: Ishai, Y., Rijmen, V. (eds.) EUROCRYPT 2019. LNCS, vol. 11477, pp. 717–746. Springer, Cham (2019). https://doi.org/10.1007/978-3-030-17656-3_25

2. Albrecht, M.R., Göpfert, F., Virdia, F., Wunderer, T.: Revisiting the expected cost of solving uSVP and applications to LWE. In: Takagi, T., Peyrin, T. (eds.) ASIACRYPT 2017. LNCS, vol. 10624, pp. 297–322. Springer, Cham (2017). https://doi.org/10.1007/978-3-319-70694-8_11

3. Albrecht, M.R., Heninger, N.: On bounded distance decoding with predicate: breaking the "lattice barrier" for the hidden number problem. In: Canteaut, A., Standaert, F.-X. (eds.) EUROCRYPT 2021. LNCS, vol. 12696, pp. 528–558. Springer, Cham (2021). https://doi.org/10.1007/978-3-030-77870-5_19

4. Boneh, D., Venkatesan, R.: Hardness of computing the most significant bits of secret keys in Diffie-Hellman and related schemes. In: Koblitz, N. (ed.) CRYPTO 1996. LNCS, vol. 1109, pp. 129–142. Springer, Heidelberg (1996). https://doi.org/10.1007/3-540-68697-5_11

5. Breitner, J., Heninger, N.: Biased nonce sense: lattice attacks against weak ECDSA signatures in cryptocurrencies. In: Goldberg, I., Moore, T. (eds.) FC 2019. LNCS, vol. 11598, pp. 3–20. Springer, Cham (2019). https://doi.org/10.1007/978-3-030-32101-7_1

6. Dachman-Soled, D., Ducas, L., Gong, H., Rossi, M.: LWE with side information: attacks and concrete security estimation. In: Micciancio, D., Ristenpart, T. (eds.) CRYPTO 2020. LNCS, vol. 12171, pp. 329–358. Springer, Cham (2020). https://doi.org/10.1007/978-3-030-56880-1_12

7. Dall, F., et al.: Cachequote: efficiently recovering long-term secrets of SGX EPID via cache attacks (2018)

8. De Micheli, G., Piau, R., Pierrot, C.: A tale of three signatures: practical attack of ECDSA with wNAF. In: Nitaj, A., Youssef, A. (eds.) AFRICACRYPT 2020. LNCS, vol. 12174, pp. 361–381. Springer, Cham (2020). https://doi.org/10.1007/978-3-030-51938-4_18

9. Ducas, L.: Shortest vector from lattice sieving: a few dimensions for free. In: Nielsen, J.B., Rijmen, V. (eds.) EUROCRYPT 2018. LNCS, vol. 10820, pp. 125–145. Springer, Cham (2018). https://doi.org/10.1007/978-3-319-78381-9_5

10. Fan, S., Wang, W., Cheng, Q.: Attacking OpenSSL implementation of ECDSA with a few signatures. In: Proceedings of the 2016 ACM SIGSAC Conference on Computer and Communications Security, pp. 1505–1515 (2016)

11. Genkin, D., Pachmanov, L., Pipman, I., Tromer, E., Yarom, Y.: ECDSA key extraction from mobile devices via nonintrusive physical side channels. In: Proceedings of the 2016 ACM SIGSAC Conference on Computer and Communications Security, CCS 2016, pp. 1626–1638. Association for Computing Machinery, New York (2016). https://doi.org/10.1145/2976749.2978353

12. Hai, H., Ning, N., Lin, X., Zhiwei, L., Bin, Y., Shilei, Z.: An improved wNAF scalar-multiplication algorithm with low computational complexity by using prime precomputation. IEEE Access 9, 31546–31552 (2021)

13. Hlaváč, M., Rosa, T.: Extended hidden number problem and its cryptanalytic applications. In: Biham, E., Youssef, A.M. (eds.) SAC 2006. LNCS, vol. 4356, pp. 114–133. Springer, Heidelberg (2007). https://doi.org/10.1007/978-3-540-74462-7_9

14. Howgrave-graham, N.A., Smart, N.P.: Lattice attacks on digital signature schemes. Des. Codes Crypt. 23, 283–290 (2001)

15. Jancar, J., Sedlacek, V., Svenda, P., Sys, M.: Minerva: the curse of ECDSA nonces systematic analysis of lattice attacks on noisy leakage of bit-length of ECDSA nonces. IACR Trans. Cryptogr. Hardw. Embed. Syst. 2020(4), 281–308 (2020). https://doi.org/10.13154/tches.v2020.i4.281-308. https://tches.iacr.org/index.php/TCHES/article/view/8684

16. Kocher, P., Jaffe, J., Jun, B.: Differential power analysis. In: Wiener, M. (ed.) CRYPTO 1999. LNCS, vol. 1666, pp. 388–397. Springer, Heidelberg (1999). https://doi.org/10.1007/3-540-48405-1_25

17. Micciancio, D., Regev, O.: Lattice-based cryptography. In: Bernstein, D.J., Buchmann, J., Dahmen, E. (eds.) Post-Quantum Cryptography, pp. 147–191. Springer, Heidelberg (2009). https://doi.org/10.1007/978-3-540-88702-7_5

18. Micciancio, D., Walter, M.: Practical, predictable lattice basis reduction. In: Fischlin, M., Coron, J.-S. (eds.) EUROCRYPT 2016. LNCS, vol. 9665, pp. 820–849. Springer, Heidelberg (2016). https://doi.org/10.1007/978-3-662-49890-3_31

19. Nguyen, P.Q., Shparlinski, I.E.: The insecurity of the elliptic curve digital signature algorithm with partially known nonces. Des. Codes Crypt. 30(2), 201–217 (2003)

20. Nguyen, P.Q., Vallée, B.: The LLL algorithm: survey and applications. Information Security and Cryptography. Springer, Heidelberg (2010). https://doi.org/10.1007/978-3-642-02295-1. https://hal.archives-ouvertes.fr/hal-01141414

21. van de Pol, J., Smart, N.P., Yarom, Y.: Just a little bit more. In: Nyberg, K. (ed.) CT-RSA 2015. LNCS, vol. 9048, pp. 3–21. Springer, Cham (2015). https://doi.org/10.1007/978-3-319-16715-2_1

22. The FPLLL development team: fplll, a lattice reduction library, Version: 5.4.1 (2021). https://github.com/fplll/fplll

23. The FPLLL development team: fpylll, a Python wraper for the fplll lattice reduction library, Version: 0.5.6 (2021). https://github.com/fplll/fpylll

24. The FPLLL development team: The general sieve kernel (g6k) (2021). https://github.com/fplll/fpylll
25. Yarom, Y., Benger, N.: Recovering openssl ECDSA nonces using the flush+ reload cache side-channel attack. IACR Cryptol. ePrint Arch. **2014**, 140 (2014)
26. Yarom, Y., Falkner, K.: Flush+reload: a high resolution, low noise, L3 cache side-channel attack. In: 23rd USENIX Security Symposium (USENIX Security 2014), pp. 719–732 (2014)

Hybrid Dual and Meet-LWE Attack

Lei Bi[1,2(✉)], Xianhui Lu[1,2,3], Junjie Luo[4], and Kunpeng Wang[1,2]

[1] KLOIS, Institute of Information Engineering, CAS, Beijing 100093, China
{bilei,luxianhui,wangkunpeng}@iie.ac.cn
[2] School of Cyber Security, University of Chinese Academy of Sciences,
Beijing 100049, China
[3] State Key Laboratory of Cryptology, P.O. Box 5159, Beijing 100878, China
[4] Nanyang Technological University, Singapore 639798, Singapore
junjie.luo@ntu.edu.sg

Abstract. The Learning with Errors (LWE) problem is one of the most prominent problems in lattice-based cryptography. Many practical LWE-based schemes, including Fully Homomorphic encryption (FHE), use sparse ternary secret for the sake of efficiency. Several (hybrid) attacks have been proposed that benefit from such sparseness, thus researchers believe the security of the schemes with sparse ternary secrets is not well-understood yet. Recently, May [Crypto 2021] proposed an efficient meet-in-the-middle attack named Meet-LWE for LWE with ternary secret, which significantly improves Odlyzko's algorithm. In this work, we generalize May's Meet-LWE and then introduce a new hybrid attack which combines Meet-LWE with lattice dual attack. We implement our algorithm to FHE-type parameters of LWE problem and compare it with the previous hybrid dual attacks. The result shows that our attack outperforms other attacks in a large range of parameters. We note that our attack has no impact on the LWE-based schemes in the PQC Standardization held by NIST as their secrets are not sparse and/or ternary.

Keywords: LWE · Meet-in-the-middle · Dual attack · Hybrid attack

1 Introduction

For decades, the Learning with Errors (LWE) problem [28] has brought large number of cryptographic applications in lattice-based cryptography, from public-key encryptions [6,17] and digital signatures [5,18] to homomorphic encryptions (HE) [15,22,29]. Informally, for a fixed secret $\mathbf{s}$ sampled from some fixed distribution over $\mathbb{Z}_q^n$, a set of LWE instances is defined as $(\mathbf{A}, \mathbf{b} = \mathbf{A}\mathbf{s} + \mathbf{e} \bmod q) \in \mathbb{Z}_q^{m \times n} \times \mathbb{Z}_q^m$, where $\mathbf{A}$ is uniformly sampled from $\mathbb{Z}_q^{m \times n}$ and $\mathbf{e}$ is a short error vector sampled from a small discrete Gaussian distribution. The search-version LWE is to recover $\mathbf{s}$ given the instances above and the decision-version LWE asks to distinguish LWE instances from uniform ones.

The secret in originally proposed LWE-based schemes is uniform over $\mathbb{Z}_q^n$, while recently many practical constructions diverted the choice of secret distribution for the sake of efficiency. For instance, as one of the most popular

K. Nguyen et al. (Eds.): ACISP 2022, LNCS 13494, pp. 168–188, 2022.
https://doi.org/10.1007/978-3-031-22301-3_9

implementation of LWE, most HE schemes including HElib [22], SEAL [29] and HEAAN [15] use ternary secret. Even more, the fully HE (FHE) schemes [11, 12,14,21,23] use sparse ternary secrets as it depends on a key technique named bootstrapping which needs the sparsity of the secret. Another well-known lattice-based hard problem NTRU [9] also uses small/sparse[1] secrets.

The concrete security of these LWE-based (NTRU-based) schemes with small/sparse secrets is still not well-understood [1]. Many works [2,4,16] show that they are less secure than those with non-small/sparse secrets, but it is still inconclusive whether they are unsafe.

Recently, May [27] introduced a new combinatorial attack, named Meet-LWE, on ternary LWE that significantly improves over Odlyzko's Meet-in-the-Middle (MitM) attack [24]. Compared with Odlyzko's algorithm of runtime $S^{0.5}$, Meet-LWE runs in time roughly $S^{0.25}$, where S is the size of the search-space.

The main open problem proposed by May [27] is whether Meet-LWE can improve lattice hybrid attacks. We remark that the "lattice hybrid attack" in [27] means specifically *hybrid decoding attack* that combines the Nearest Plane (NP) algorithm [7] used in decoding attack and exhaustive-search, which is initialed by Howgrave-Graham [25] against NTRU. From the point of view of attacks against NTRU, hybrid decoding attack is presumably the best-known attack.

For FHE schemes, which are based on LWE with sparse ternary secret, there are two types of hybrid attacks that are usually better than hybrid decoding attack: hybrid primal attack [20,30,31,33,34] and hybrid dual attack [2,10,16, 19,32]. We note that hybrid primal attack is essentially the same as hybrid decoding attack as it also needs NP algorithm to solve a decoding problem (in a different lattice), while hybrid dual attack is different from them.

Therefore, except for the open problem proposed by May [27], another problem follows from [27] is whether Meet-LWE can be used to improve *hybrid dual attack* for LWE with sparse ternary secret. We study this problem in this paper.

1.1   Related Work

Hybrid dual attack is an efficient attack against LWE, especially LWE with small/sparse secrets. Albrecht [2] introduced the first hybrid dual attack on LWE with small/sparse secret, which is a combination of dual attack and exhaustive-search. Accordingly, the hybrid dual attack consists of two phases, which we name them as the *lattice-phase* and the *guess-phase*, where the first phase uses dual attack to construct a new LWE instance and the second phase uses exhaustive-search to solve the new instance.

The works following [2] improve the attack by accelerating the guess-phase. Espitau-Joux-Kharchenko [19] proposed an efficient matrix multiplication method to accelerate exhaustive-search. Bi-Lu-Luo-Wang-Zhang [10] generalized Albrecht's hybrid dual attack to arbitrary secret and error by using both optimal

---

[1] In this paper, when we refer to "small", we mean that the secret is binary/ternary and has no fixed Hamming weight, i.e., uniform in $\{0,1\}$ or $\{0,\pm1\}$. While for "sparse", we mean that the secret is binary/ternary with a small fixed Hamming weight w.

pruning and generalized efficient matrix multiplication. Cheon-Hhan-Hong-Son [16] replaced the exhaustive-search with MitM technique in [25] and showed that the resulting hybrid attack outperforms other attacks for sparse ternary LWE with large modulus. Our attack follows a similar strategy as in [16] but we replace the exhaustive-search with the more efficient algorithm Meet-LWE.

1.2 Contributions

In this paper, we combine Meet-LWE with dual attack and introduce a new hybrid dual attack, which we call hybrid dual Meet-LWE attack. The idea is to replace the exhaustive-search for sub-secret in hybrid dual attack by Meet-LWE. One key step in Meet-LWE is to guess k coordinates of error $\mathbf{e}$ such that we can get k LWE equations without error. These equations will then be used to decrease the size of the candidate set of secrets in the MitM step. The main difficulty in replacing the exhaustive-search by Meet-LWE in *hybrid decoding attacks* (and also hybrid primal attacks) is that we cannot use the k error-free LWE equations on the projected sub-secret anymore [27].

w	64	128	192	64	128	192	64	128	192	64	128	192
200										103	120	131
160		Ours								117	146	161
120		Hybrid1								136	182	202
100		Hybrid2					102	124	133	147	199	230
80							119	146	162	162	225	276
60				90	106	111	134	179	207			
50				101	126	133	146	202	241			
40	76	83	86	115	153	166	163	234	287			
30	95	110	115	138	193	217						
20	128	161	175									
15	153	205	230									
log q / w	64	128	192	64	128	192	64	128	192	64	128	192
log n	10			11			12			13		

Fig. 1. Comparison of our attack, HYBRID1 [10], HYBRID2 [16] for different LWE parameters settings $(\log n, \log q, w)$. For each case, the color indicates the best attack and its bit security.

However, this is not a problem for *hybrid dual attacks*, since we can view the lattice-phase of hybrid dual attacks as a dimension-error trade-off, as observed by Albrecht [2]. More precisely, in hybrid dual attacks, the lattice-phase produces a new LWE instance that has a smaller dimension but a larger error. Our attack solves the new LWE instance by a generalized version of Meet-LWE. One feature of this generalization is that the secret of the new LWE instance follows an atypical ternary distribution while the original Meet-LWE is performed on ternary secret with exactly $w/2$ entries of 1 and $w/2$ entries of -1. In addition, the large error of the new LWE instance makes the analysis of Meet-LWE different from the original setting. We generalize Meet-LWE for the new setting in hybrid dual attacks and give a rigorous analysis for it.

We also compare our attack with previous hybrid dual attacks on sparse ternary LWE problems with FHE-type parameters and find out that our attack outperforms those attacks in a large range of parameters, especially when the Hamming weight of secret is small and the modulus q is not too large. See Fig. 1 for an overview of the comparison. The main advantage of our attack is its high efficiency in the guess-phase due to Meet-LWE.

We remark that our result does not invalidate the security claims of the schemes in PQC Standardization held by NIST since their secrets are not sparse/ternary or they use large enough Hamming weight.

1.3   Roadmap

In Sect. 2, we give some notations and a brief introduction of lattice reduction algorithms and LWE problem. We recall May's Meet-LWE in Sect. 3 and recall previous hybrid dual attacks in Sect. 4. Our new hybrid dual Meet-LWE attack is given in Sect. 5. In Sect. 6, we compare the complexity of our algorithm with previous hybrid dual attacks on LWE problem with FHE-type parameters. Finally, in Sect. 7 we present the conclusion of this paper.

2   Preliminaries

2.1   Notations

Denote log short for $\log_2$ and denote ln for the natural logarithm. Denote vectors in bold, e.g. $\mathbf{v}$. The Euclidean norm of $\mathbf{v}$ is $||\mathbf{v}||$. Denote $\langle \cdot, \cdot \rangle$ the product of two vectors. Matrices are denoted in upper-case bold, e.g. $\mathbf{A}$. Denote $hm(\cdot)$ the Hamming weight of a vector. For a compact set $S \in \mathbb{R}^n$, denote $\mathcal{U}(S)$ the uniform distribution over S. Denote $\mathcal{G}_{\mathbf{c},s}$ the Gaussian distribution of center $\mathbf{c}$ and deviation s, and denote $\mathcal{G}_s$ short for $\mathcal{G}_{0,s}$. Denote the combinatorial number $\binom{M}{N_1}\binom{M-N_1}{N_2}$ as $\binom{M}{N_1,N_2}$.

2.2   Lattice and Lattice Reduction

Lattice. A lattice of *dimension* m is a discrete additive subgroup of $\mathbb{R}^m$ for some $m \in \mathbb{N}$. A basis $\mathbf{B}$ of a lattice Λ is a set of n linearly independent vectors $\{\mathbf{b}_1, \dots, \mathbf{b}_n\} \subset \mathbb{R}^m$ satisfies $\Lambda = \Lambda(\mathbf{B}) = \mathbf{B} \cdot \mathbb{Z}^m = \left\{ \sum_{i \in [n]} z_i \cdot \mathbf{b}_i : z_i \in \mathbb{Z} \right\}$. We call n the *rank* of the lattice. If $n = m$, Λ is called a *full-rank lattice*. Denote $\det(\Lambda) = \sqrt{\det(\mathbf{B}^T\mathbf{B})}$ the determinant of $\Lambda = \Lambda(\mathbf{B})$. The *shortest vector* of Λ is a non-zero vector in a lattice Λ that has the minimum norm. Denote $\lambda_1(\Lambda)$

the norm of the shortest non-zero vector, i.e., $\lambda_1(\Lambda) = \min_{\mathbf{v} \in \Lambda, \mathbf{v} \neq 0} ||\mathbf{v}||$.

Lattice Reduction Algorithm. Given a basis of a lattice as input, the lattice reduction algorithm outputs a new basis of the lattice that consists of relatively shorter and relatively pairwise not so skew vectors. The quality of basis outputted by a lattice reduction algorithm is characterized by the *root-Hermite factor* δ_0 which satisfies $\delta_0^m = \frac{||\mathbf{b}_1||}{\det(\Lambda)^{\frac{1}{m}}}$, where $\mathbf{b}_1$ is the first and shortest vector in the output basis.

The BKZ algorithm [13], which is a successful generalization of the famous LLL algorithm, is now a commonly used lattice reduction algorithm. The most important parameter for BKZ is the blocksize β, whose relation with δ_0 is given in the following heuristic.

Heuristic 1. *BKZ with blocksize β yields a basis with root-Hermite factor*

$$\delta_0 \approx \left(\frac{\beta}{2\pi e} (\pi \beta)^{\frac{1}{\beta}} \right)^{\frac{1}{2(\beta-1)}}.$$

This heuristic is experimentally verified by Chen [13].

2.3   The Learning with Errors Problem

Definition 1 (LWE [28]). *Let $n, q \in \mathbb{N}$. $\mathcal{S}$ is the secret distribution over $\mathbb{Z}_q^n$ and χ is a small error distribution over $\mathbb{Z}$. For a secret $\mathbf{s} \leftarrow \mathcal{S}$, denote $LWE_{n,q,\mathbf{s},\chi}$ the probability distribution on $\mathbb{Z}_q^n \times \mathbb{Z}_q$ obtained by sampling $\mathbf{a} \in \mathbb{Z}_q^n$ uniformly random, sampling $e \xleftarrow{\$} \chi$ and returning $(\mathbf{a}, \langle \mathbf{a}, \mathbf{s} \rangle + e) \in \mathbb{Z}_q^n \times \mathbb{Z}_q$. Given access to the outputs from $LWE_{n,q,\mathbf{s},\chi}$, we define two versions of LWE problem:*

- *Decision-LWE. Given m instances, distinguish $LWE_{n,q,\mathbf{s},\chi}$ from $\mathcal{U}(\mathbb{Z}_q^n \times \mathbb{Z}_q)$ for a fixed $\mathbf{s} \leftarrow \mathcal{S}$.*
- *Search-LWE. Given m instances sampled from $LWE_{n,q,\mathbf{s},\chi}$ with a fixed $\mathbf{s} \leftarrow \mathcal{S}$, recover $\mathbf{s}$.*

The LWE instances can be rewrite in matrix form as follows:

$$(\mathbf{A}, \mathbf{b} = \mathbf{A}\mathbf{s} + \mathbf{e} \bmod q)$$

with $\mathbf{s} \leftarrow \mathcal{S}, \mathbf{A} \xleftarrow{\$} \mathbb{Z}_q^{m \times n}, \mathbf{e} \xleftarrow{\$} \chi^m, \mathbf{b} \in \mathbb{Z}_q^m$.

In this paper, we focus on LWE with sparse ternary secrets. We consider three different distributions of sparse ternary $\mathbf{s}$, where the last type of distribution characterizes the error of the new LWE instance in the guess-phase of hybrid dual attacks.

- Ternary-0: $\mathcal{T}_0^n(w) = \left\{ \mathbf{s} \in \{0, \pm 1\}^n : \mathbf{s} \text{ has } \frac{w}{2}(\pm 1)\text{-entries each} \right\}$
- Ternary-1: $\mathcal{T}_1^n(w) = \left\{ \mathbf{s} \in \{0, \pm 1\}^n : \mathbf{s} \text{ has } w \text{ non-zero entries} \right\}$
- Ternary-2: $\mathcal{T}_2^n(w) = \sum_{h=0}^{w} p_s(h) \mathcal{T}_1^n(h)$, where $\sum_{h=0}^{w} p_s(h) = 1$, i.e., $\mathcal{T}_2^n(w)$ is a mixture distribution of $\mathcal{T}_1^n(h)$ with weight $p_s(h)$ for $h \leq w$.

2.4 Lemma

Lemma 1 ([8]). *For any real $s > 0$ and $C > 0$, and any $\mathbf{x} \in \mathbb{R}^d$, we have*

$$\Pr\left[|\langle \mathbf{x}, \mathcal{G}_s \rangle| \geq C \cdot s ||\mathbf{x}||\right] < 2 \cdot \exp\left(-\frac{C^2}{2}\right).$$

3   May's Meet-LWE Attack

In this section, we review May's Meet-LWE [27] attack on LWE with $\mathbf{s} \in T_0^n(w)$ and $\mathbf{e} \in \{0, \pm 1\}^m$, and show that it can be straightforwardly generalized to the case with $\mathbf{s} \in T_1^n(w)$.

3.1   Ternary-0

We recall May's Meet-LWE in its simplest form (Rep-0 in [27]). Given LWE instance $(\mathbf{A}, \mathbf{b} = \mathbf{As} + \mathbf{e} \bmod q) \in \mathbb{Z}_q^{m \times n} \times \mathbb{Z}_q^m$, where $\mathbf{s} \in T_0^n(w)$ and $\mathbf{e} \in \{0, \pm 1\}^m$, a typical MitM works by splitting the secret into $\mathbf{s} = \mathbf{s}_1 + \mathbf{s}_2$, rewriting the LWE equation as

$$\mathbf{As}_1 = \mathbf{b} - \mathbf{As}_2 - \mathbf{e} \bmod q,$$

and hashing $\mathbf{As}_1$ and $\mathbf{b} - \mathbf{As}_2$ for all enumerated $\mathbf{s}_1, \mathbf{s}_2 \in T_0^n(w/2)$. Then for each pair of $\mathbf{s}_1$ and $\mathbf{s}_2$ with colliding hash values, we check whether

$$\mathbf{b} - \mathbf{A}(\mathbf{s}_1 + \mathbf{s}_2) \bmod q \in \{0 \pm 1\}^m.$$

In order to reduce the number of doing hash, which is the main runtime of the process, Meet-LWE chooses only a subset of $T_0^n(w/2)$ for $\mathbf{s}_1$ and $\mathbf{s}_2$ as follows.

Notice that the number of *representations* $\mathbf{s} = \mathbf{s}_1 + \mathbf{s}_2$ is $R = \binom{w/2}{w/4}^2$. We define the mapping

$$\pi_k^m : \mathbb{Z}_q^m \to \mathbb{Z}_q^k, \mathbf{x} = (x_1, \cdots, x_m) \to (x_1, \cdots, x_k)$$

and fix a random target $\mathbf{t} \in \mathbb{Z}_q^k$ and then look for $\mathbf{s}_1$ and $\mathbf{s}_2$ satisfying

$$\pi_k^m(\mathbf{As}_1 + \mathbf{e}_1) = \mathbf{t} \bmod q \text{ and } \pi_k^m(\mathbf{b} - \mathbf{As}_2 + \mathbf{e}_2) = \mathbf{t} \bmod q, \qquad (1)$$

where $\mathbf{e}_1, \mathbf{e}_2 \in \{0, \pm 1\}^m$ satisfies $\mathbf{e}_1 - \mathbf{e}_2 = \mathbf{e}$. To ensure that there is at least one couple of $\mathbf{s}_1$ and $\mathbf{s}_2$ satisfying Eq. (1), we choose k such that $k = \lfloor \log_q R \rfloor$ and therefore we have $q^k \leq R$. Note that the probability that Eq. (1) holds for at least one representation of $\mathbf{s}_1 + \mathbf{s}_2$ is $p_\pi = \left(1 - \frac{1}{q^k}\right)^R \approx \frac{1}{e}$. In order to find such $\mathbf{s}_1$ and $\mathbf{s}_2$, we make up two lists

$$L_1^{(1)} = \{(\mathbf{s}_1, \varphi(\mathbf{As}_1)) : \pi_k^m(\mathbf{As}_1 + \mathbf{e}_1) = \mathbf{t} \bmod q\},$$

$$L_2^{(1)} = \{(\mathbf{s}_2, \varphi(\mathbf{b} - \mathbf{As}_2)) : \pi_k^m(\mathbf{b} - \mathbf{As}_2 + \mathbf{e}_2) = \mathbf{t} \bmod q\},$$

where the hash function $\varphi : \mathbb{Z}_q^m \to \{0, 1\}^m$ is defined as

Algorithm 1. Meet-LWE on LWE with Ternary-0 Secret

Require: $(\mathbf{A}, \mathbf{b} = \mathbf{A}\mathbf{s} + \mathbf{e} \bmod q) \in \mathbb{Z}_q^{m \times n} \times \mathbb{Z}_q^m$ with $\mathbf{s} \in \mathcal{T}_0^n(w)$ and $\mathbf{e} \in \{0, \pm 1\}^m$
Ensure: $\mathbf{s} \in \mathcal{T}_0^n(w)$ satisfying $\mathbf{A}\mathbf{s} - \mathbf{b} \bmod q \in \{0, \pm 1\}^m$

1: compute the number R of representations of $\mathbf{s} = \mathbf{s}_1 + \mathbf{s}_2$ where $\mathbf{s}_1, \mathbf{s}_2 \in \mathcal{T}_0^n(w/2)$
2: compute $k = \lfloor \log_q(R) \rfloor$
3: sample a random $\mathbf{t} \in \mathbb{Z}_q^k$
4: **for** all $\pi_k^m(\mathbf{e}_1) \in \{0, \pm 1\}^{k/2} \times 0^{k/2}$ **do**
5:    construct $L_1^{(1)} = \{(\mathbf{s}_1, \varphi(\mathbf{A}\mathbf{s}_1)) : \pi_k^m(\mathbf{A}\mathbf{s}_1 + \mathbf{e}_1) = \mathbf{t} \bmod q\}$ via a standard MitM
     on $\mathbf{u}_1 \in \mathcal{T}_0^{n/2}(w/4) \times 0^{n/2}$ and $\mathbf{u}_2 \in 0^{n/2} \times \mathcal{T}_0^{n/2}(w/4)$.
6: **for** all $\pi_k^m(\mathbf{e}_2) \in 0^{k/2} \times \{0, \pm 1\}^{k/2}$ **do**
7:    construct $L_2^{(1)} = \{(\mathbf{s}_2, \varphi(\mathbf{b} - \mathbf{A}\mathbf{s}_2)) : \pi_k^m(\mathbf{b} - \mathbf{A}\mathbf{s}_2 + \mathbf{e}_2) = \mathbf{t} \bmod q\}$ analogously
8: **for** all matched of $(\mathbf{s}_1, \cdot)$ and $(\mathbf{s}_2, \cdot)$ in the second component of $L_1^{(1)}$ and $L_2^{(2)}$ **do**
9:    **if** $\mathbf{s} = \mathbf{s}_1 + \mathbf{s}_2 \in \{\pm 1, 0\}^n$ has weight w and $\mathbf{A}\mathbf{s} - \mathbf{b} \bmod q \in \{0, \pm 1\}^m$ **then**
10:      **return** $\mathbf{s}$

$$\varphi(\mathbf{x})_i = \begin{cases} 0 & \text{if } x_i \in \left[-\frac{q}{2}, -1\right) \\ 1 & \text{if } x_i \in \left[0, \frac{q}{2} - 1\right) \\ 0, 1 & \text{if } x_i \in [-1, 0) \cup \left[\frac{q}{2} - 1, \frac{q}{2}\right) \end{cases}.$$

Notice that for entries in the two border ranges $[-1, 0)$ and $\left[\frac{q}{2} - 1, \frac{q}{2}\right)$, we assign both 0 and 1 to them. The lists $L_1^{(1)}, L_2^{(1)}$ can be constructed in a standard MitM manner, i.e., enumerate $\mathbf{s}_1$ as the sum of $\mathbf{u}_1 \in \mathcal{T}_0^{n/2}(w/4) \times 0^{n/2}$ and $\mathbf{u}_2 \in 0^{n/2} \times \mathcal{T}_0^{n/2}(w/4)$. Analogously, we proceed with $\mathbf{s}_2 = \mathbf{u}_3 + \mathbf{u}_4$.

To summarize, we first compute a number k based on the number of representations R. Next for each enumeration of the first k coordinates of $\mathbf{e}$ (via some standard MitM approach as $\mathbf{e} = \mathbf{e}_1 + \mathbf{e}_2$), we construct lists $L_1^{(1)}$ and $L_2^{(1)}$ and then search for a representation $\mathbf{s}_1 + \mathbf{s}_2$ of $\mathbf{s}$ based on the second component of $L_1^{(1)}$ and $L_2^{(1)}$. The full algorithm is listed in Algorithm 1.

Analysis. The size of lists $L_1^{(1)}$ and $L_2^{(1)}$ is $L^{(1)} = \frac{S^{(1)}}{q^k} \approx \frac{S^{(1)}}{R} = \binom{n}{w/4, w/4} \binom{w/2}{w/4}^{-2}$, where $S^{(1)} = \binom{n}{w/4, w/4}$ is the search-space of $\mathbf{s}_1$ and $\mathbf{s}_2$. Notice that $L^{(1)}$ is much smaller than $S^{(1)}$ and this is the main advantage of Meet-LWE. We remark that here we only count one in $L^{(1)}$ for each element in the lists $L_1^{(1)}$ and $L_2^{(1)}$, and omit possible multiple labels for elements, since the expected number of labels for each element is $\frac{2}{q} \cdot m = \Theta(1)$. However, in Sect. 5 when we study our hybrid attack we cannot omit this as the error becomes much larger. We will discuss this in more detail in Sect. 5. The size of the four lists for $\mathbf{u}_1, \mathbf{u}_2, \mathbf{u}_3, \mathbf{u}_4$ is $L^{(2)} = S^{(2)} = \binom{n/2}{w/8, w/8}$, where $S^{(2)}$ is the search-space of $\mathbf{u}_1, \mathbf{u}_2, \mathbf{u}_3, \mathbf{u}_4$.

The time $T^{(1)}$ to construct list $L_1^{(1)}$ (respectively $L_2^{(1)}$) is

$$T^{(1)} = \max\left\{L^{(1)}, L^{(2)}\right\}.$$

Finding a representation $\mathbf{s}_1 + \mathbf{s}_2$ from $L_1^{(1)}$ and $L_2^{(1)}$ can be realized via Odlyzko's hash function on the $m - k$ coordinates in time

$$T^{(0)} = \max\left\{ L^{(1)}, 2^{-(m-k)}\left(L^{(1)} \right)^2 \right\} = L^{(1)}.$$

Here we assume that $L^{(1)} \leq 2^{m-k}$, otherwise we can modify Odlyzko's hash function by assigning more than two labels to ensure this.

Then the time complexity of list construction is $T_s = \max\{T^{(1)}, T^{(0)}\} = \max\{L^{(1)}, L^{(2)}\}$. In addition, the time of enumerating

$$\pi_k^m(\mathbf{e}_1) \in \{0, \pm 1\}^{k/2} \times 0^{k/2} \text{ and } \pi_k^m(\mathbf{e}_2) \in 0^{k/2} \times \{0, \pm 1\}^{k/2}$$

is $T_e = 3^{k/2}$. We summarize these results in Lemma 2.

Lemma 2. *The runtime of Meet-LWE attack on LWE with Ternary-0 secret shown in Algorithm 1 is computed as*

$$T_{MitM\text{-}0} = T_s \cdot T_e = \max\left\{ \binom{n}{w/4, w/4}\binom{w/2}{w/4}^{-2}, \binom{n/2}{w/8, w/8} \right\} \cdot 3^{k/2},$$

and the success probability is $p_{MitM\text{-}0} = p_\pi = \frac{1}{e}$.

3.2 Ternary-1

Recall that $\mathcal{T}_1^n(w)$ contains $\mathbf{s} \in \{0, \pm 1\}^n$ with w non-zero entries. This type of secret is very similar to Ternary-0. Given LWE instance with secret $\mathbf{s} \in \mathcal{T}_1^n(w)$, we can split $\mathbf{s}$ into $\mathbf{s}_1 + \mathbf{s}_2$ with $\mathbf{s}_1, \mathbf{s}_2 \in \mathcal{T}_1^n(w/2)$. The number of representations is $R = \binom{w}{w/2}$. The two levels of lists is constructed similarly as Sect. 3.1. Accordingly, we can compute the size of the lists as $L^{(1)} = \frac{S^{(1)}}{R} = \binom{n}{w/2} \cdot 2^{w/2} / \binom{w}{w/2}$ and $L^{(2)} = S^{(2)} = \binom{n/2}{w/4} \cdot 2^{w/4}$. The total runtime is

$$T_{\text{MitM-1}} = T_s \cdot T_e = \max\left\{ \binom{n}{w/2} \cdot 2^{w/2} / \binom{w}{w/2}, \binom{n/2}{w/4} \cdot 2^{w/4} \right\} \cdot 3^{k/2},$$

where $k = \lfloor \log_q R \rfloor$, and the success probability is also $p_{\text{MitM-1}} = p_\pi = \frac{1}{e}$.

4 Hybrid Dual Attacks

In this section, we review previous hybrid dual attacks [2,10,16,19]. Hybrid dual attacks have two phases: the lattice-phase and the guess-phase. The lattice-phase is the same for all hybrid dual attacks and we can view it as a dimension-error trade-off, i.e., after the first phase, we get a new decision-LWE instance with a smaller dimension but a larger error. In the guess-phase, there are two different approaches to solve the new instance. A detailed description follows.

Lattice-Phase. In order to distinguish whether the given instance $(\mathbf{A}, \mathbf{b})$ is sampled from $\mathcal{U}(\mathbb{Z}_q^{m \times n} \times \mathbb{Z}_q^m)$ or $\mathrm{LWE}_{n,q,\mathbf{s},\mathcal{G}_\sigma}$ with $\mathbf{s} \in \mathcal{T}_1^n(w)$, we divide $\mathbf{A}$ into two parts: $\mathbf{A} = (\mathbf{A}_1, \mathbf{A}_2) \in \mathbb{Z}_q^{m \times r} \times \mathbb{Z}_q^{m \times (n-r)}$. Accordingly, we also divide $\mathbf{s}$ into two parts: $\mathbf{s} = (\mathbf{s}_1, \mathbf{s}_2) \in \{0, \pm 1\}^r \times \{0, \pm 1\}^{n-r}$. In this phase, the attack constructs the dual lattice over $\mathbf{A}_2$:

$$\Lambda(\mathbf{A}_2) = \left\{ (\mathbf{w}, \mathbf{v}) \in \mathbb{Z}^m \times \left(\frac{1}{c} \cdot \mathbb{Z}\right)^{n-r} : \mathbf{w} \cdot \mathbf{A}_2 = c \cdot \mathbf{v} \bmod q \right\}$$

with scale factor $c = \sigma \cdot \sqrt{\frac{m}{w_{n-r}}}$, where w_{n-r} is the expected hamming weight of $\mathbf{s}_2$. If the given instance follows $\mathrm{LWE}_{n,q,\mathbf{s},\mathcal{G}_\sigma}$, by obtaining short vector $(\mathbf{w}, \mathbf{v})$ from $\Lambda(\mathbf{A}_2)$, we compute $\langle \mathbf{w}, \mathbf{b} \rangle \bmod q$ as

$$\langle \mathbf{w}, \mathbf{b} \rangle = \mathbf{w}(\mathbf{A}\mathbf{s} + \mathbf{e})$$
$$= \mathbf{w}\mathbf{A}_1\mathbf{s}_1 + \mathbf{w}\mathbf{A}_2\mathbf{s}_2 + \langle \mathbf{w}, \mathbf{e} \rangle$$
$$= \mathbf{w}\mathbf{A}_1\mathbf{s}_1 + c \cdot \langle \mathbf{v}, \mathbf{s}_2 \rangle + \langle \mathbf{w}, \mathbf{e} \rangle \bmod q.$$

This can be viewed as a new LWE instance $(\bar{\mathbf{a}}, \bar{b} = \langle \bar{\mathbf{a}}, \mathbf{s}_1 \rangle + \bar{e} \bmod q)$, where

$$\bar{b} = \langle \mathbf{w}, \mathbf{b} \rangle \bmod q,$$
$$\bar{\mathbf{a}} = \mathbf{w}\mathbf{A}_1 \bmod q, \tag{2}$$
$$\bar{e} = c \cdot \langle \mathbf{v}, \mathbf{s}_2 \rangle + \langle \mathbf{w}, \mathbf{e} \rangle \bmod q.$$

Denote M the number of short vectors $(\mathbf{w}, \mathbf{v}) \in \Lambda(\mathbf{A}_2)$. We write Eq. (2) in the matrix form as $\bar{\mathbf{b}} = \bar{\mathbf{A}}\mathbf{s}_1 + \bar{\mathbf{e}} \bmod q$, where $\bar{\mathbf{b}}, \bar{\mathbf{e}} \in \mathbb{Z}_q^M$ and $\bar{\mathbf{A}} \in \mathbb{Z}_q^{M \times r}$. This instance follows distribution $\mathrm{LWE}_{r,q,\mathbf{s}_1,\mathcal{G}_\rho}$ with $\rho = \ell\sigma$ where $\ell = \|(\mathbf{w}, \mathbf{v})\|$ [6]. If the given instance is from $\mathcal{U}\left(\mathbb{Z}_q^{m \times n} \times \mathbb{Z}_q^m\right)$, then the new instance $(\bar{\mathbf{A}}, \bar{\mathbf{b}})$ is also uniform over $\mathbb{Z}_q^{M \times r} \times \mathbb{Z}_q^M$. So next we are going to solve this new decision-LWE instance in the second phase.

Guess-Phase. The difference between different hybrid dual attacks is the method of solving the new instance in this phase.

The first method works by checking the distribution of $\bar{\mathbf{b}} - \bar{\mathbf{A}}\tilde{\mathbf{s}}_1 \bmod q$, where $\tilde{\mathbf{s}}_1$ is some guessed candidate of $\mathbf{s}_1$. By enumerating $\tilde{\mathbf{s}}_1$ in some way, we can compute $\bar{\mathbf{b}} - \bar{\mathbf{A}}\tilde{\mathbf{s}}_1 \bmod q$. It equals to a Gaussian error $\bar{\mathbf{e}}$ if $(\bar{\mathbf{A}}, \bar{\mathbf{b}}) \sim \mathrm{LWE}_{r,q,\mathbf{s}_1,\mathcal{G}_\rho}$, otherwise it is uniform over $\mathbb{Z}_q^M$. We can compute the statistical distance to distinguish $\mathrm{LWE}_{n,q,\mathbf{s}_1,\mathcal{G}_\rho}$ from $\mathcal{U}\left(\mathbb{Z}_q^{M \times r} \times \mathbb{Z}_q^M\right)$. This method is used in the first hybrid dual attack [2] and also in [10,19]. Note that [19] defined the distance by themselves instead of using statistical distance while the results are similar.

The second method is to check whether all entries of $\bar{\mathbf{b}} - \bar{\mathbf{A}}\tilde{\mathbf{s}}_1 \bmod q$ are in some range $[-B, B]$ for a chosen B. If this holds for one enumerated $\tilde{\mathbf{s}}_1$, we decide the original instance is from $\mathrm{LWE}_{n,q,\mathbf{s},\mathcal{G}_\sigma}$. The hybrid dual attack in [16] uses this method and it additionally accelerates the guessing of $\mathbf{s}_1$ by a MitM approach. Notice that compared with the first method, the second method has a stricter requirement on the error size of the new LWE instance, and thus shorter vectors from the dual lattice are required in the lattice-phase.

5   Combine Meet-LWE with Dual Attack

We are now ready to present our hybrid dual Meet-LWE attack. The idea is to replace the exhaustive-search in the guess-phase of hybrid dual attacks by Meet-LWE. That is, in the guess-phase, we use generalized Meet-LWE to solve the new instance $(\bar{\mathbf{A}}, \bar{\mathbf{b}}) \in \mathbb{Z}_q^{M \times r} \times \mathbb{Z}_q^M$.

There are two problems we need to overcome when applying Meet-LWE to the new setting. The first one is that the secret of the new LWE instance has a different distribution, which will influence the choices of k and the analysis of success probability. The second one is that the error of the new LWE instance becomes large. For this we need to re-analyze the runtime of Meet-LWE as some constant omitted in the original setting with ternary error now becomes too large to be omitted. We solve these two problems in Sect. 5.1 and Sect. 5.2 respectively, and then present the complete algorithm and analysis in Sect. 5.3.

5.1   Meet-LWE on Ternary-2 LWE

We first consider the secret distribution of the new instance $(\bar{\mathbf{A}}, \bar{\mathbf{b}} = \bar{\mathbf{A}}\mathbf{s}_1 + \bar{\mathbf{e}} \mod q) \in \mathbb{Z}_q^{M \times r} \times \mathbb{Z}_q^M$. Note that in this subsection, we follow May [27] to set the error ternary and defer the discussion of the Gaussian error to the next subsection.

As the secret $\mathbf{s}_1 \in \{0, \pm 1\}^r$ is part of the original secret $\mathbf{s}$, we have $hm(\mathbf{s}_1) \le w_r := \min(r, w)$. Thus $\mathbf{s}_1 \in \mathcal{T}_2^r(w_r)$ and for each $h \le w_r$ the probability $p_s(h)$ for $\mathbf{s}_1$ to have weight h is $p_s(h) = \frac{\binom{w}{h}\binom{n-w}{r-h}}{\binom{n}{r}}$.

To apply Meet-LWE attack to this type of secret, we first need to choose a weight parameter $\hat{w} \le w_r$ and use $\mathbf{u}_1, \mathbf{u}_2 \in \mathcal{T}_1^r(\hat{w}/2)$ to form $\mathbf{s}_1$. Then the search-space of $\mathbf{u}_1, \mathbf{u}_2$ is $S^{(1)} = \binom{r}{\hat{w}/2} \cdot 2^{\hat{w}/2}$. Notice that for a fixed parameter $\hat{w}$, we can only form the secrets in $\bigcup_{h=0}^{\hat{w}/2} \mathcal{T}_1^r(2h)$, and hence the success probability is at most $\sum_{h=0}^{\hat{w}/2} p_s(2h)$.

The next step is to identify the dimension k of the random target $\mathbf{t} \in \mathbb{Z}_q^k$. Recall that in Sect. 3.1 and Sect. 3.2, we just set $k = \lfloor \log_q R \rfloor$ based on the number of representations R. However, for $\mathcal{T}_2^r(w_r)$ we cannot identify k directly as we have different number of representations for different cases of $\mathbf{s}_1$ with different weights. More precisely, for each $h \le \hat{w}/2$, the number of representations of $\mathbf{u}_1 + \mathbf{u}_2$ for $\mathbf{s}_1$ with $hm(\mathbf{s}_1) = 2h$ is $R(h) = \binom{2h}{h}\binom{r-2h}{\hat{w}/2-h} \cdot 2^{\hat{w}/2-h}$. Notice that since $hm(\mathbf{s}_1) = 2h$ and $\mathbf{u}_1, \mathbf{u}_2 \in \mathcal{T}_1^r(\hat{w}/2)$, there are $\hat{w}/2 - h$ non-zero entries of $\mathbf{u}_1$ and $\hat{w}/2 - h$ non-zero entries of $\mathbf{u}_2$ that cancel each other out among the $r - 2h$ 0-entries of $\mathbf{s}_1$, and for each cancel out entry, we have two possibilities $1+(-1) = 0$ or $(-1)+1 = 0$. This gives us $\binom{r-2h}{\hat{w}/2-h} \cdot 2^{\hat{w}/2-h}$. For the $2h$ non-zero entries of $\mathbf{s}_1$, there are $\hat{w}/2 - (\hat{w}/2 - h) = h$ entries from $\mathbf{u}_1$ and $\mathbf{u}_2$ respectively, which gives us $\binom{2h}{h}$.

For each $R(h)$, let $k(h) = \lfloor \log_q(R(h)) \rfloor$. Thus we need to choose

$$k \in [\min_h(k(h)), \max_h(k(h))].$$

Algorithm 2. Generalized Meet-LWE on LWE with Ternary-2 Secret

---

Require: $(\bar{\mathbf{A}}, \bar{\mathbf{b}}) \in \mathbb{Z}_q^{M \times r} \times \mathbb{Z}_q^M, \hat{w}$

Ensure: $\mathbf{s}_1 \in T_2^r(\hat{w})$ satisfying $\bar{\mathbf{A}}\mathbf{s}_1 - \bar{\mathbf{b}} \bmod q \in \{0, \pm 1\}^M$ or $\perp$

1: **for** each $h \in [0, \hat{w}/2]$ **do**
2:    compute the number $R(h)$ of representations of $\mathbf{s}_1 = \mathbf{u}_1 + \mathbf{u}_2$ where $\mathbf{u}_1, \mathbf{u}_2 \in T_1^r(\hat{w}/2)$
3:    compute $k(h) = \lfloor \log_q(R) \rfloor$
4: choose a $k \in [\min_h(k(h)), \max_h(k(h))]$ (we will brute-force all possible values for k and choose the optimal one in Section 6)
5: sample a random $\mathbf{t} \in \mathbb{Z}_q^k$
6: **for** all $\pi_k^M(\mathbf{e}_1) \in \{0, \pm 1\}^{k/2} \times 0^{k/2}$ **do**
7:    construct $L_1^{(1)} = \{(\mathbf{u}_1, \varphi(\bar{\mathbf{A}}\mathbf{u}_1)) : \pi_k^M(\bar{\mathbf{A}}\mathbf{u}_1 + \mathbf{e}_1) = \mathbf{t} \bmod q\}$ via a standard MitM
8: **for** all $\pi_k^M(\mathbf{e}_2) \in 0^{k/2} \times \{0, \pm 1\}^{k/2}$ **do**
9:    construct $L_2^{(1)} = \{(\mathbf{u}_2, \varphi(\bar{\mathbf{b}} - \bar{\mathbf{A}}\mathbf{u}_2)) : \pi_k^M(\bar{\mathbf{b}} - \bar{\mathbf{A}}\mathbf{u}_2 + \mathbf{e}_2) = \mathbf{t} \bmod q\}$ analogously
10: **for** all matched of $(\mathbf{u}_1, \cdot)$ and $(\mathbf{u}_2, \cdot)$ in the second component of $L_1^{(1)}$ and $L_2^{(1)}$ **do**
11:    **if** $\mathbf{s}_1 = \mathbf{u}_1 + \mathbf{u}_2 \in T_2^r(\hat{w})$ and $\bar{\mathbf{A}}\mathbf{s}_1 - \bar{\mathbf{b}} \bmod q \in \{0, \pm 1\}^M$ **then**
12:        **return** $\mathbf{s}_1$
13: **return** $\perp$

For a fixed k, if $hm(\mathbf{s}_1) = 2h$, then

$$\pi_k^M(\bar{\mathbf{A}}\mathbf{u}_1 + \mathbf{e}_1) = \mathbf{t} \bmod q \text{ and } \pi_k^M(\bar{\mathbf{b}} - \bar{\mathbf{A}}\mathbf{u}_2 + \mathbf{e}_2) = \mathbf{t} \bmod q$$

holds with probability $p_\pi(h) = 1 - \left(1 - \frac{1}{q^k}\right)^{R(h)}$, where $\bar{\mathbf{e}} = \mathbf{e}_1 - \mathbf{e}_2$. Then overall success probability is

$$\sum_{h=0}^{\hat{w}/2} p_s(2h) \cdot p_\pi(h) = \sum_{h=0}^{\hat{w}/2} p_s(2h) \cdot \left(1 - \left(1 - \frac{1}{q^k}\right)^{R(h)}\right). \tag{3}$$

The remaining part of the algorithm is the same as before. We give the pseudo-code of the generalized Meet-LWE on LWE with Ternary-2 Secret in Algorithm 2.

Analysis. The runtime analysis is similarly as before. The sizes of the lists are $L^{(1)} = \frac{S^{(1)}}{q^k}$ and $L^{(2)} = S^{(2)} = \binom{r/2}{\hat{w}/4} \cdot 2^{\hat{w}/4}$. The time $T^{(1)}$ to construct list $L_1^{(1)}$, respectively $L_2^{(1)}$, is $T^{(1)} = \max\{L^{(1)}, L^{(2)}\}$, and the time $T^{(0)}$ of approximately matching on the $M - k$ coordinates via Odlyzko's hash function is $T^{(0)} = \max\{L^{(1)}, 2^{-(M-k)}(L^{(1)})^2\} = L^{(1)}$. The time of list construction is

$$T_s = \max\{T^{(1)}, T^{(0)}\} = \max\{L^{(1)}, L^{(2)}\}.$$

The time of enumerating $\pi_k^M(\mathbf{e}_1)$ and $\pi_k^M(\mathbf{e}_2)$ is $T_e = 3^{k/2}$.

Combining the runtime and the success probability given in Eq. (3), we conclude with the following lemma.

Lemma 3. *The runtime of Meet-LWE algorithm in Algorithm 2 is*

$$T_{MitM\text{-}2} = T_s \cdot T_e = \max\left\{\binom{r}{\hat{w}/2} \cdot 2^{\hat{w}/2}/q^k, \binom{r/2}{\hat{w}/4} \cdot 2^{\hat{w}/4}\right\} \cdot 3^{k/2},$$

and the success probability is $p_{MitM\text{-}2} = \sum_{h=0}^{\hat{w}/2} p_s(2h) \cdot p_\pi(h)$.

5.2   The Larger Error

When performing Meet-LWE in the guess-phase of hybrid dual attack, the error of the new LWE instance is Gaussian instead of in $\{0,\pm1\}^M$. In this case, we need to reconsider the runtime of the attack. We first choose a boundary B to cover the new error with a high probability[2] as in the following lemma, which can be proved by using Lemma 1.

Lemma 4. *Error $\bar{e}$ of the new LWE instance given in Eq. (2) satisfies*

$$\Pr\left[|\bar{e}| < B\right] \geq 1 - 2 \cdot \exp(-4\pi),$$

where $B = (2\sqrt{2\pi} + 1) \cdot \sqrt{\frac{m}{m+n-r}} \cdot \ell\sigma$ *and ℓ is the length of* $(\mathbf{w},\mathbf{v}) \in \Lambda(\mathbf{A}_2)$. *Thus, we have that*

$$p_M := \Pr\left[\bar{\mathbf{e}} \in [-B, B]^M\right] \geq (1 - 2 \cdot \exp(-4\pi))^M.$$

Now we have to enumerate $\pi_k^M(\mathbf{e}_1)$ and $\pi_k^M(\mathbf{e}_2)$ in a larger range $[-B, B]$ using time $T_e = (2B + 1)^{k/2}$.

Note that for the estimation in Sect. 6 we usually have $k = 1$ as q and B are large. In this case we can still use MitM for $\pi_1^M(\mathbf{e}_1)$ and $\pi_1^M(\mathbf{e}_2)$ in one dimension to get time T_e. We note that this case is not considered in [27] as the parameter k in [27] is large, which is different from ours.

Specifically, now we can use

$$\pi_1^M(\mathbf{e}_1) \in [0, c) \text{ and } \pi_1^M(\mathbf{e}_2) \in \{c \cdot i - B \mid i \in [0, c)\}$$

to form $\pi_1^M(\bar{\mathbf{e}}) \in [-B, B]$, where $c = \lceil\sqrt{2B+1}\rceil$. For example, to enumerate $e \in [-40, 40]$ we can split it into $e = e_1 + e_2$ by taking $e_1 \in [0, 9)$ and $e_2 \in \{9 \cdot i - 40 \mid i \in [0, 9)\}$ where $9 = \lceil\sqrt{40 \times 2 + 1}\rceil$. This method can also be used to deal with the situation when k is odd.

---

[2] In Lemma 4, we follow [16] to choose the value of B such that the probability for $|\bar{e}| < B$ is close to 1. Our experimental results show that the overall attack complexity is not sensitive on B and the current choice of B in Lemma 4 is almost optimal.

The second difference is that when constructing lists

$$L_1^{(1)} = \left\{ (\mathbf{u}_1, \varphi\left(\bar{\mathbf{A}}\mathbf{u}_1\right)) : \pi_k^M\left(\bar{\mathbf{A}}\mathbf{u}_1 + \mathbf{e}_1\right) = \mathbf{t} \bmod q \right\},$$
$$L_2^{(1)} = \left\{ (\mathbf{u}_2, \varphi\left(\bar{\mathbf{b}} - \bar{\mathbf{A}}\mathbf{u}_2\right)) : \pi_k^M\left(\bar{\mathbf{b}} - \bar{\mathbf{A}}\mathbf{u}_2 + \mathbf{e}_2\right) = \mathbf{t} \bmod q \right\},$$

we will use a different hash function $\varphi : \mathbb{Z}_q^M \to \{0,1\}^M$ defined as

$$\varphi(\mathbf{x})_i = \begin{cases} 0 & \text{if } x_i \in \left[-\frac{q}{2}, -B\right) \\ 1 & \text{if } x_i \in \left[0, \frac{q}{2} - B\right) \\ 0,1 & \text{if } x_i \in [-B, 0) \cup \left[\frac{q}{2} - B, \frac{q}{2}\right) \end{cases}.$$

Recall that in Sect. 3.1, when we compute the size $L^{(1)}$ of lists $L_1^{(1)}$ and $L_2^{(1)}$, we count each element once in $L^{(1)}$ as each element has only a constant number of labels in expectation. However, this does not hold for the current setting, since now the expected number of labels for each element is $\frac{2B+1}{q}M$, which is not small anymore if B is large.

To figure out this difference, we introduce a new notation $\overline{L^{(1)}}$ to represent the overall number of labels for all elements in lists $L_1^{(1)}$ and $L_2^{(1)}$, and we still use $L^{(1)}$ to represent the number of elements in the lists. For a given M, we have

$$\overline{L^{(1)}} = L^{(1)} \cdot 2^{\frac{2B+1}{q}M}.$$

Since $\overline{L^{(1)}}$ will influence the runtime, we need to be careful when choosing the dimension M for the new LWE instance to optimize the runtime of Meet-LWE.

5.3 Our Attack

Now we are ready to give our attack. For given guessing dimension r, blocksize β and weight parameter $\hat{w} \leq w_r$, the pseudo-code of our attack is shown in Algorithm 3. Line 1–4 is the lattice-phase of our attack, which is the same as other hybrid dual attacks. After this phase, we get a new instance $(\bar{\mathbf{A}}, \bar{\mathbf{b}}) \in \mathbb{Z}_q^{M \times r} \times \mathbb{Z}_q^M$ and solve it by using Algorithm 4. Then according to the output of Algorithm 4, Algorithm 3 outputs the result of the decision-LWE problem.

Note that Algorithm 4 is essentially the same as Algorithm 2, except that in Algorithm 4, the scope of exhaustive-searching $\pi_k^M(\mathbf{e}_1), \pi_k^M(\mathbf{e}_2)$ in line 6, 8 and the final judgment condition in line 11 are both changed to adapt to the situation of large error in hybrid dual attack.

Analysis. We represent $\mathbf{s}_1 = \mathbf{u}_1 + \mathbf{u}_2$ with $\mathbf{u}_1, \mathbf{u}_2 \in T_1^r(\hat{w}/2)$. The sizes of the two level lists are $L^{(1)} = \frac{S^{(1)}}{q^k} = \binom{r}{\hat{w}/2} \cdot 2^{\hat{w}/2} \cdot \frac{1}{q^k}$, $L^{(2)} = S^{(2)} = \binom{r/2}{\hat{w}/4} \cdot 2^{\hat{w}/4}$. Then the time $T^{(1)}$ to construct list $L_1^{(1)}$ (respectively $L_2^{(1)}$) is computed as $T^{(1)} = \max\left\{L^{(1)}, L^{(2)}\right\}$. Finding a representation $\mathbf{u}_1 + \mathbf{u}_2$ from $L_1^{(1)}$ and $L_2^{(1)}$ can be realized via Odlyzko's hash function on the $M - k$ coordinates in time

Algorithm 3. Hybrid Dual Meet-LWE Attack
***
Require: $(\mathbf{A}, \mathbf{b}) \in \mathbb{Z}_q^{m \times n} \times \mathbb{Z}_q^m, r, \beta, \hat{w}, \sigma$
Ensure: LWE or Uniform
1: divide $\mathbf{A}$ into two parts $(\mathbf{A}_1, \mathbf{A}_2) \in \mathbb{Z}_q^{m \times r} \times \mathbb{Z}_q^{m \times (n-r)}$
2: construct lattice $\Lambda(\mathbf{A}_2) = \{(\mathbf{w}, \mathbf{v}) \in \mathbb{Z}^m \times \mathbb{Z}^{n-r} : \mathbf{w} \cdot \mathbf{A}_2 = \mathbf{v} \bmod q\}$
3: perform BKZ algorithm with blocksize β on $\Lambda(\mathbf{A}_2)$ to obtain M short vectors $(\mathbf{w}, \mathbf{v})$ of length ℓ
4: construct new instance $(\bar{\mathbf{A}}, \bar{\mathbf{b}}) \in \mathbb{Z}_q^{M \times r} \times \mathbb{Z}_q^M$ by computing each row/entry of $\bar{\mathbf{A}}$ and $\bar{\mathbf{b}}$ as $\bar{\mathbf{a}} = \mathbf{w}\mathbf{A}_1 \bmod q$ and $\bar{b} = \langle \mathbf{w}, \mathbf{b} \rangle \bmod q$
5: set B as Lemma 4
6: run Algorithm 4 on input $(\bar{\mathbf{A}}, \bar{\mathbf{b}}), B$ and $\hat{w}$
7: **if** Algorithm 4 outputs a secret vector **then**
8:     **return** LWE
9: **else**
10:     **return** Uniform
***

$$T^{(0)} = \max\left\{\overline{L^{(1)}}, 2^{-(M-k)}\left(\overline{L^{(1)}}\right)^2\right\} \text{ where } \overline{L^{(1)}} = L^{(1)} \cdot 2^{\frac{2B+1}{q}M}. \text{ Then the time}$$

of list construction is

$$T_s = \max\left\{T^{(1)}, T^{(0)}\right\}. \tag{4}$$

And the time of enumerating $\pi_k^M(\mathbf{e}_1)$ and $\pi_k^M(\mathbf{e}_2)$ is

$$T_e = (2B+1)^{k/2}. \tag{5}$$

Combining Eq. (4), Eq. (5) and Lemma 4, we get the following theorem.

Theorem 1. *The runtime of our hybrid dual Meet-LWE attack in Algorithm 3 is*

$$T_{DUAL\text{-}MEET} = T_{reduction} + T_{meet},$$

where $T_{reduction} = T_{BKZ}(\beta)$, $T_{meet} = T_s \cdot T_e$ and T_s, T_e are defined as Eq. (4), Eq. (5) respectively. The success probability of the attack is

$$p_{DUAL\text{-}MEET} = p_{MitM\text{-}2} \cdot p_M,$$

where $p_{MitM\text{-}2} = \sum_{h=0}^{\hat{w}/2} p_s(2h) \cdot p_\pi(h)$, and $p_M = (1 - 2 \cdot \exp(-4\pi))^M$.

6   Complexity Estimation and Comparison

In this section, we present a detailed comparison of our attack with the other two hybrid dual attacks in [10] and [16][3] (we refer to them as HYBRID1 and HYBRID2 respectively) by estimating the bit-security of various parameter settings of sparse ternary LWE.

***

[3] Notice that [10] and [16] are the representatives of existing two different categories of hybrid dual attacks and [10] improves the attack in [2] with additional tricks.

Algorithm 4. Generalized Meet-LWE on LWE with Ternary-2 Secret and large error

---

Require: $(\bar{\mathbf{A}}, \bar{\mathbf{b}}) \in \mathbb{Z}_q^{M \times r} \times \mathbb{Z}_q^M, B, \hat{w}$

Ensure: $\mathbf{s}_1 \in \mathcal{T}_2^r(\hat{w})$ satisfying $\bar{\mathbf{A}}\mathbf{s}_1 - \bar{\mathbf{b}} \bmod q \in \{0, \cdots, \pm B\}^M$ or $\perp$

1: **for** each $h \in [0, \hat{w}/2]$ **do**
2:     compute the number $R(h)$ of representations of $\mathbf{s}_1 = \mathbf{u}_1 + \mathbf{u}_2$ where $\mathbf{u}_1, \mathbf{u}_2 \in \mathcal{T}_1^r(\hat{w}/2)$
3:     compute $k(h) = \lfloor \log_q(R) \rfloor$
4:     choose a $k \in [\min_h(k(h)), \max_h(k(h))]$ (we will choose the optimal value of k to optimize the complexity in Section 6)
5:     sample a random $\mathbf{t} \in \mathbb{Z}_q^k$
6: **for** all $\pi_k^M(\mathbf{e}_1) \in \{0, \cdots, \pm B\}^{k/2} \times 0^{k/2}$ **do**
7:     construct $L_1^{(1)} = \left\{ (\mathbf{u}_1, \varphi(\bar{\mathbf{A}}\mathbf{u}_1)) : \pi_k^M(\bar{\mathbf{A}}\mathbf{u}_1 + \mathbf{e}_1) = \mathbf{t} \bmod q \right\}$ via a standard MitM
8: **for** all $\pi_k^M(\mathbf{e}_2) \in 0^{k/2} \times \{0, \cdots, \pm B\}^{k/2}$ **do**
9:     construct $L_2^{(1)} = \left\{ (\mathbf{u}_2, \varphi(\bar{\mathbf{b}} - \bar{\mathbf{A}}\mathbf{u}_2)) : \pi_k^M(\bar{\mathbf{b}} - \bar{\mathbf{A}}\mathbf{u}_2 + \mathbf{e}_2) = \mathbf{t} \bmod q \right\}$ analogously
10: **for** all matched of $(\mathbf{u}_1, \cdot)$ and $(\mathbf{u}_2, \cdot)$ in the second component of $L_1^{(1)}$ and $L_2^{(1)}$ **do**
11:     **if** $\mathbf{s}_1 = \mathbf{u}_1 + \mathbf{u}_2 \in \mathcal{T}_2^r(\hat{w})$ and $\bar{\mathbf{A}}\mathbf{s}_1 - \bar{\mathbf{b}} \bmod q \in \{0, \cdots, \pm B\}^M$ **then**
12:         **return** $\mathbf{s}_1$
13: **return** $\perp$

Our estimators take LWE parameters as input and find optimal parameters for the attack to get the optimal (lowest) bit-security. The estimation of bit-security is computed as $\log T_{\text{attack}} - \log p_{\text{attack}}$ [4]. The concrete formulas for our attack are given in Theorem 1.

The runtime of each hybrid attack T_{attack} consists of two parts: $T_{\text{reduction}}$ and T_{guess}, where $T_{\text{reduction}}$ is the time of lattice reduction, and T_{guess} corresponds to the guess-phase for searching the correct sub-secret in dimension r (which is denoted as T_{meet} in our attack as we use MitM technique to accelerate guessing). Under the optimal parameters we usually have $T_{\text{reduction}} \approx T_{\text{guess}}$. The main parameter to balance $T_{\text{reduction}}$ and T_{guess} is the dimension r. Since we focus on sparse ternary LWE problems, in the guess-phase we usually only cover part of the search-space, which incurs a loss in p_{attack} but reduces T_{guess}. The final estimation is a trade-off between the three components: $T_{\text{reduction}}$, T_{guess}, and p_{attack}. Note that in this paper we assume that $T_{\text{BKZ}}(d, \beta) = 8d \cdot 2^{0.292\beta + 16.4}$, where d is the dimension of the lattice and β is the blocksize of BKZ, and use the amortizing model [2] for BKZ performed in dual attack.

We perform the attacks on LWE with FHE-type parameters. Before presenting the complete picture of the comparison, we first analyze 3 typical cases in detail to get a close look into the inner parts of the attacks.

Table 1. $\log n = 12,\ \log q = 50,\ w = 128,\ \sigma = 3.2$

Attack		Dual	HYBRID1	HYBRID2	OURS
Cost (bit)	attack	302	215	221	202
	reduction	302	166	183	172
	guess	–	166	181	170 = 147+23
	prob.	–	49	38	30
Parameter	r	–	1839	2247	2245
	β	925	460	520	483
	k	–	–	–	1

Table 2. $\log n = 10,\ \log q = 20,\ w = 192,\ \sigma = 3.2$

Attack		Dual	HYBRID1	HYBRID2	OURS
Cost (bit)	attack	188	175	285	220
	reduction	188	169	267	204
	guess	–	169	267	203 = 156 + 47
	prob.	–	5	19	16
Parameter	r		161	357	432
	b	539	475	810	595
	k	–	–	–	5

Table 3. $\log n = 13,\ \log q = 200,\ w = 128,\ \sigma = 3.2$

Attack		Dual	HYBRID1	HYBRID2	OURS
Cost (bit)	attack	140	124	120	206
	reduction	140	112	112	198
	guess	–	110	112	199 = 120 + 79
	prob.	–	12	9	7
Parameter	r	–	1650	2050	1637
	b	365	270	269	563
	k	–	–	–	1

6.1   Case 1

We begin with a case for which our attack works the best. We set $\log n = 12$, $\log q = 50$, $w = 128$, $\sigma = 3.2$. The results for the standalone dual attack, HYBRID1, HYBRID2, and our attack are shown in Table 1. In addition to $\log T_{\text{reduction}}$, $\log T_{\text{guess}}$, and $-\log p_{\text{attack}}$, we also give the guessing dimension

r and blocksize β for each attack. For our attack, we additionally give the enumeration dimension k for the error and we split T_{guess} into T_s and T_e.

All three hybrid attacks achieve lower complexity than the standalone dual attack due to the sparse ternary secret. Our attack achieves the lowest complexity due to its high efficiency in the guessing. Compared with HYBRID1, our attack guesses in a larger dimension (2245 vs 1839) in a slightly longer time (170 vs 166) but achieves a much higher success probability (30 vs 49). Compared with HYBRID2, our attack guesses in a similar dimension with a shorter time (170 vs 181) and achieves a higher success probability (30 vs 38).

Notice that the time of guessing T_{guess} for our attack is close to HYBRID1 and shorter than HYBRID2 even if the time $T_e = 2^{23}$ for enumerating $\mathbf{e}_1, \mathbf{e}_2$ is included. Recall that reference [27] deals with schemes with ternary secrets and the time for enumeration is $T_e = 3^{k/2}$. For us, the new LWE instance after the lattice-phase has a large error range B, which could make $T_e = (2B + 1)^{k/2}$ very large. At first glance, it may look strange that here our T_e is still so small. However, notice that in our case q is large enough for the number of representations R such that we just need to fix a random target $\mathbf{t}$ in one dimension, i.e., $k = 1$, thus $T_e = (2B + 1)^{0.5}$ is not too large.

6.2   Case 2

Next, we look at a different case with a larger weight ratio $\frac{w}{n}$, where HYBRID1 works the best. We choose $\log n = 10$, $\log q = 20$, $w = 192$, $\sigma = 3.2$. The results are shown in Table 2. Different from the first case, now HYBRID1 achieves the lowest complexity. The main reason for the bad performance of our attack is the larger $T_e = 2^{47}$ due to the larger weight ratio $\frac{w}{n} \approx 0.177$. Recall that for case 1 we have $\frac{w}{n} \approx 0.031$. The large weight ratio results in a larger number R of representations, which increases the dimension k for the random target $\mathbf{t}$ and then increases T_e.

It may look weird that our attack and HYBRID2, which use the MitM technique, are even worse than the standalone dual attack. This is due to the fundamental difference between the two different categories of hybrid dual attacks discussed in Sect. 4. For dual attack and HYBRID1, they need to find short vectors in the lattice-phase such that in the guess-phase the distribution of the new error with range B can be differentiated from the uniform distribution. While for our attack and HYBRID2, we have to guarantee a smaller $\frac{B}{q}$ such that we can recognize the correct solution by checking each entry of $\bar{\mathbf{b}} - \bar{\mathbf{A}}\mathbf{s}_1 \bmod q$. Therefore, we have to find shorter vectors in the lattice-phase, which makes $T_{\text{reduction}}$ large, especially when $\frac{w}{n}$ is large.

6.3   Case 3

We consider the last case with a very large $q = 2^{200}$, with which HYBRID2 works best. We set $\log n = 13$, $\log q = 200$, $w = 128$, and $\sigma = 3.2$. The results are shown in Table 3. We can see that HYBRID1 and HYBRID2 have similar complexity that are smaller than dual attack, while our attack has a much larger complexity than all of them since we have a very large $T_e = 2^{79}$. Since $k = 1$, the main reason for the large $T_e = (2B + 1)^{k/2}$ is that when q is large, the range B of the error after the lattice reduction also becomes large. On the other hand, HYBRID1 and HYBRID2 are mainly influenced by the relative value of $\frac{B}{q}$ instead of the absolute value of B. Notice that in this case with large q and small $\frac{w}{n}$, HYBRID2 outperforms HYBRID1 while in the first two cases HYBRID2 cannot compete with HYBRID1.

6.4 Overview

To summarize, our attack outperforms HYBRID1 and HYBRID2 when the weight ratio $\frac{w}{n}$ is small and q is not too large. When the ratio $\frac{w}{n}$ is large, our attack and HYBRID2 are both worse than HYBRID1, sometimes even worse than dual attack. When q is very large, our attack suffers from the large T_e, and HYBRID2 achieves the best performance if the ratio $\frac{w}{n}$ is small enough.

To give an overview of the different advantages of the three hybrid dual attacks, we consider a series of sparse ternary LWE problems with FHE-type parameters. For each $\log n = 10, 11, 12, 13$, we choose appropriate q such the corresponding scheme with ternary secret has bit-security around 128 to 256. For each considered case of n and q, we consider three different values of $w = 64, 128, 192$ and fix $\sigma = 8/\sqrt{2\pi} \approx 3.2$.

The comparison results are shown in Fig. 1. For each case we give the estimation result of the best attack together with a color indicating the best attack for this case. The figure can be roughly partitioned into three regions, corresponding to the three cases considered above. Our attack is the best for most cases when $\log n = 12$. For $\log n = 10, 11$, as the weight ratio $\frac{w}{n}$ becomes larger, HYBRID1 is the best for most cases and our attack is the best for cases with small weight (e.g., all cases for $w = 64$ and $\log n = 11$). When $\log n = 13$, the corresponding values of q become large. In this case, HYBRID2 becomes the best attack for most cases while our attack is the best for cases with smaller q.

Based on Fig. 1, some FHE implementations (e.g., HElib [22] and HEAAN [15]) with parameters that fall within the advantage area of our attack should re-estimate their parameters. Our results do not make any impact on the schemes in Round 3 of Post-Quantum Cryptography Standardization held by NIST since for the LWE-based schemes, they do not adopt sparse ternary secret terms (except for NTRULPrime, however for these schemes, HYBRID1 works better), and for NTRU-based schemes, dual attacks cannot be applied to estimate the bit-security of them [3].

Remark 1. We do not include dual attack as HYBRID1 always works no worse than dual attack [10]. In addition, we also compare these three attacks with the primal attack and the comparison shows that the hybrid dual attacks work better than the primal attack in most cases. Due to the space limitation, we do not give the specific comparison results here.

7 Conclusion

In this work, we introduce and analyze a new hybrid dual attack named hybrid dual Meet-LWE attack, which combines dual attack and a generalization of Meet-LWE attack [27]. We compare our attack with previous hybrid dual attacks on LWE with FHE-type parameters. The result shows that our attack outperforms those attacks in a large range of parameters. According to our results, some FHE implementations should update their parameters.

For future works, we note that the main drawback of our attack is the additional time of guessing k coordinates of the errors, which increases with q. Recently, [26] introduced a locality sensitive hashing (LSH) technique that avoids the guessing of the errors in Meet-LWE. It is interesting to study whether this technique can improve the performance of our attack.

Acknowledgement. This work is supported by the National Natural Science Foundation of China (No. 61972391) and the Open Project Program of State Key Laboratory of Cryptology (MMKFKT201810).

References

1. Albrecht, M., et al.: Homomorphic encryption standard (2018)
2. Albrecht, M.R.: On dual lattice attacks against small-secret LWE and parameter choices in HElib and SEAL. In: Coron, J.-S., Nielsen, J.B. (eds.) EUROCRYPT 2017. LNCS, vol. 10211, pp. 103–129. Springer, Cham (2017). https://doi.org/10.1007/978-3-319-56614-6_4
3. Albrecht, M.R., Curtis, B.R., Deo, A., Davidson, A., Player, R., Postlethwaite, E.W., Virdia, F., Wunderer, T.: Estimate all the LWE, NTRU schemes! In: Catalano, D., De Prisco, R. (eds.) SCN 2018. LNCS, vol. 11035, pp. 351–367. Springer, Cham (2018). https://doi.org/10.1007/978-3-319-98113-0_19
4. Albrecht, M.R., Player, R., Scott, S.: On the concrete hardness of learning with errors. J. Math. Cryptol. **9**(3), 169–203 (2015)
5. Alkim, E., Barreto, P.S.L.M., Bindel, N., Krämer, J., Longa, P., Ricardini, J.E.: The lattice-based digital signature scheme qtesla. In: ACNS (2020)
6. Alkim, E., Ducas, L., Pöppelmann, T., Schwabe, P.: Post-quantum key exchange - a new hope. In: 25th USENIX, pp. 327–343 (2016)
7. Babai, L.: On lovász'lattice reduction and the nearest lattice point problem. Combinatorica **6**(1), 1–13 (1986)
8. Banaszczyk, W.: Inequalities for convex bodies and polar reciprocal lattices in $r \wedge n$ II: application of k-convexity. Discret. Comput. Geom. (1996)
9. Bernstein, D.J., Chuengsatiansup, C., Lange, T., van Vredendaal, C.: NTRU prime: reducing attack surface at low cost. In: Adams, C., Camenisch, J. (eds.) SAC 2017. LNCS, vol. 10719, pp. 235–260. Springer, Cham (2018). https://doi.org/10.1007/978-3-319-72565-9_12
10. Bi, L., Lu, X., Luo, J., Wang, K., Zhang, Z.: Hybrid dual attack on LWE with arbitrary secrets. IACR Cryptol. ePrint Arch. **2021**, 152 (2021)
11. Chen, H., Chillotti, I., Song, Y.: Improved bootstrapping for approximate homomorphic encryption. In: Ishai, Y., Rijmen, V. (eds.) EUROCRYPT 2019. LNCS, vol. 11477, pp. 34–54. Springer, Cham (2019). https://doi.org/10.1007/978-3-030-17656-3_2

12. Chen, H., Han, K.: Homomorphic lower digits removal and improved FHE boot-strapping. In: Nielsen, J.B., Rijmen, V. (eds.) EUROCRYPT 2018. LNCS, vol. 10820, pp. 315–337. Springer, Cham (2018). https://doi.org/10.1007/978-3-319-78381-9_12

13. Chen, Y.: Réduction de réseau et sécurité concrete du chiffrement completement homomorphe. Ph.D. thesis, Paris 7 (2013)

14. Cheon, J.H., Han, K., Kim, A., Kim, M., Song, Y.: Bootstrapping for approximate homomorphic encryption. In: Nielsen, J.B., Rijmen, V. (eds.) EUROCRYPT 2018. LNCS, vol. 10820, pp. 360–384. Springer, Cham (2018). https://doi.org/10.1007/978-3-319-78381-9_14

15. Cheon, J.H., Han, K., Kim, A., Kim, M., Song, Y.: Snucrypto HEAAN (2019). http://github.com/homenc/HElib

16. Cheon, J.H., Hhan, M., Hong, S., Son, Y.: A hybrid of dual and meet-in-the-middle attack on sparse and ternary secret LWE. IEEE Access (2019)

17. Cheon, J.H., Kim, D., Lee, J., Song, Y.: Lizard: cut off the tail! a practical post-quantum public-key encryption from LWE and LWR. In: Catalano, D., De Prisco, R. (eds.) SCN 2018. LNCS, vol. 11035, pp. 160–177. Springer, Cham (2018). https://doi.org/10.1007/978-3-319-98113-0_9

18. Ducas, L., Kiltz, E., Lepoint, T., Lyubashevsky, V., Schwabe, P., Seiler, G., Stehlé, D.: Crystals-dilithium: a lattice-based digital signature scheme. IACR Trans. Cryptogr. Hardw. Embed. Syst. **2018**(1), 238–268 (2018)

19. Espitau, T., Joux, A., Kharchenko, N.: On a dual/hybrid approach to small secret LWE. In: Bhargavan, K., Oswald, E., Prabhakaran, M. (eds.) INDOCRYPT 2020. LNCS, vol. 12578, pp. 440–462. Springer, Cham (2020). https://doi.org/10.1007/978-3-030-65277-7_20

20. Göpfert, F., van Vredendaal, C., Wunderer, T.: A hybrid lattice basis reduction and quantum search Attack on LWE. In: Lange, T., Takagi, T. (eds.) PQCrypto 2017. LNCS, vol. 10346, pp. 184–202. Springer, Cham (2017). https://doi.org/10.1007/978-3-319-59879-6_11

21. Halevi, S., Shoup, V.: Bootstrapping for HElib. In: Oswald, E., Fischlin, M. (eds.) EUROCRYPT 2015. LNCS, vol. 9056, pp. 641–670. Springer, Heidelberg (2015). https://doi.org/10.1007/978-3-662-46800-5_25

22. Halevi, S., Shoup, V.: (2019). https://github.com/homenc/HElib

23. Han, K., Ki, D.: Better bootstrapping for approximate homomorphic encryption. In: Jarecki, S. (ed.) CT-RSA 2020. LNCS, vol. 12006, pp. 364–390. Springer, Cham (2020). https://doi.org/10.1007/978-3-030-40186-3_16

24. Hoffstein, J., Pipher, J., Silverman, J.H.: NTRU: a ring-based public key cryptosystem. In: ANTS (1998)

25. Howgrave-Graham, N.: A hybrid lattice-reduction and meet-in-the-middle attack against NTRU. In: Menezes, A. (ed.) CRYPTO 2007. LNCS, vol. 4622, pp. 150–169. Springer, Heidelberg (2007). https://doi.org/10.1007/978-3-540-74143-5_9

26. Kirshanova, E., May, A.: How to find ternary LWE keys using locality sensitive hashing. In: Paterson, M.B. (ed.) IMACC 2021. LNCS, vol. 13129, pp. 247–264. Springer, Cham (2021). https://doi.org/10.1007/978-3-030-92641-0_12

27. May, A.: How to meet ternary LWE keys. In: Malkin, T., Peikert, C. (eds.) CRYPTO 2021. LNCS, vol. 12826, pp. 701–731. Springer, Cham (2021). https://doi.org/10.1007/978-3-030-84245-1_24

28. Regev, O.: On lattices, learning with errors, random linear codes, and cryptography. J. ACM (JACM) (2009)

29. Microsoft SEAL: (2019). https://github.com/Microsoft/SEAL

30. Son, Y., Cheon, J.H.: Revisiting the hybrid attack on sparse secret LWE and application to HE parameters. In: WAHC@CCS 2019, pp. 11–20 (2019)
31. Wunderer, T.: Revisiting the hybrid attack: improved analysis and refined security estimates. IACR Cryptol. ePrint Arch. **2016**, 733 (2016)
32. Wunderer, T.: On the Security of Lattice-Based Cryptography Against Lattice Reduction and Hybrid Attacks. Ph.D. thesis, Darmstadt University of Technology, Germany (2018)
33. Wunderer, T.: A detailed analysis of the hybrid lattice-reduction and meet-in-the-middle attack. J. Math. Cryptol. **13**(1), 1–26 (2019)
34. Wunderer, T., Burger, M., Nguyen, G.N.: Parallelizing the hybrid lattice-reduction and meet-in-the-middle attack. In: CSE 2018, pp. 185–193 (2018)

Cryptanalysis and Repair of a Gabidulin Code Based Cryptosystem from ACISP 2018

Wenshuo Guo[(✉)] and Fang-Wei Fu

Chern Institute of Mathematics and LPMC, Nankai University, Tianjin, China
ws_guo@mail.nankai.edu.cn, fwfu@nankai.edu.cn

Abstract. This paper presents a key recovery attack on a rank metric based cryptosystem proposed by Lau and Tan at ACISP 2018, which uses Gabidulin codes as the underlying decodable code. This attack is shown to cost polynomial time and therefore completely breaks the cryptosystem. Specifically, we convert the problem of recovering the private key into solving a multivariate linear system over the base field. We then present a simple repair for this scheme, which is shown to require exponential complexity for the proposed attack. Additionally, we apply this attack to cryptanalyze another Gabidulin code based cryptosystem proposed by Loidreau at PQCrypto 2017, and improve Loidreau's result in a talk at CBCrypto 2021.

Keywords: Post-quantum cryptography · Code-based cryptography · Gabidulin codes · Key recovery attack

1 Introduction

In post-quantum era, public key cryptosystems based on number theoretic problems will suffer serious security threat due to Shor's algorithm [37]. To prevent attacks from quantum computers, people have paid much attention to seeking alternatives for future use. Among these alternatives, code-based cryptography is one of the most promising candidates, whose security depends on the NP-completeness of decoding general linear codes [8]. The first cryptosystem of this type was proposed by McEliece [30] in 1978 using Goppa codes as the underlying linear code, which is now known as the McEliece cryptosystem. Although this scheme remains secure, it has never been used in practical situations due to the drawback of large key size. To tackle this problem, various improvements have been proposed one after another. In general, these variants can be divided into

This research was supported by the National Key Research and Development Program of China (Grant No. 2018YFA0704703), the National Natural Science Foundation of China (Grant No. 61971243), the Natural Science Foundation of Tianjin (20JCZDJC00610), and the Fundamental Research Funds for the Central Universities of China (Nankai University).

K. Nguyen et al. (Eds.): ACISP 2022, LNCS 13494, pp. 189–205, 2022.
https://doi.org/10.1007/978-3-031-22301-3_10

two categories: one is to replace Goppa codes with other Hamming metric codes [1,4,23,31], the other is to use codes endowed with other metric [2,22].

In 1991, Gabidulin et al. [15] proposed an encryption scheme based on rank metric codes, namely the GPT cryptosystem based on Gabidulin codes. The greatest advantage of rank metric based cryptosystems consists in their compact representation of public keys. Some representative variants based on Gabidulin codes can be found in [7,12,14,24,27,35]. Unfortunately, most of these variants have been completely or partially broken due to the inherent structural weakness of Gabidulin codes [9,11,16,20,32,34].

In [25], Lau and Tan proposed a public key cryptosystem based on Gabidulin codes, which was later published in [26] with an extended version. In this proposal, the public key consists of two parts, namely a generator matrix of the disturbed Gabidulin code by a random code that has maximum rank weight n and a vector of rank weight n. This technique of masking the structure of Gabidulin codes, as claimed by Lau and Tan, can prevent some existing attacks such as Frobenius weak attack [19], reduction attack [32], and Overbeck's attack [34]. Additionally, the recent Coggia-Couvreur attack [11] and Ghatak's attack [18] designed for Loidreau's cryptosystem [27] do not work on this scheme either.

Our Contributions. Firstly, we show that all the generating vectors of a Gabidulin code, together with the zero vector, form a 1-dimensional linear space. In other words, for a fixed generating vector g of a Gabidulin code $\mathcal{G} \subseteq \mathbb{F}_{q^m}^n$, any other generating vector must be of the form γg for some $\gamma \in \mathbb{F}_{q^m}^*$. This suggests that there are totally $q^m - 1$ generating vectors for a Gabidulin code over $\mathbb{F}_{q^m}$. Secondly, we introduce a different approach from the one in [20] to compute the generating vector of Gabidulin codes from an arbitrary generator matrix. Thirdly, this paper presents a simple yet efficient key recovery attack on the Lau-Tan cryptosystem. Fourthly, we give a simple but effective repair for this system, which is shown to be secure against the existing structural attacks and have larger information transfer rate. Lastly, when applying this attack to analyze Loidreau's cryptosystem, we get a reduction in the complexity of recovering an equivalent private key.

The rest of this paper is organized as follows. Section 2 introduces basic notions used throughout this paper, as well as the concept of Moore matrices and Gabidulin codes. Section 3 gives a simple description of the Lau-Tan cryptosystem. Section 4 mainly describes the principle of our attack. Specifically, we first present some further results about Gabidulin codes that will be helpful for explaining why our attack works. Then a detailed description of this attack will be given in two steps. Lastly, we give a complexity analysis of this attack and some experimental results. In Sect. 5, we propose a modification for this scheme, investigate its security and give some practical parameters. In Sect. 6, we apply this attack to cryptanalyze Loidreau's cryptosystem. Section 7 concludes this paper.

2   Preliminaries

In this section, we first introduce some notations and basic concepts in coding theory. After that, we recall the concept of Gabidulin codes, and present some related results in the meanwhile.

2.1   Notations and Basic Concepts

For a prime power q, we denote by $\mathbb{F}_q$ the finite field with q elements, and $\mathbb{F}_{q^m}$ an extension field of $\mathbb{F}_q$ of degree m. Note that $\mathbb{F}_{q^m}$ can be seen as a linear space over $\mathbb{F}_q$ of dimension m. A vector $\boldsymbol{a} \in \mathbb{F}_{q^m}^m$ is called a basis vector if the components of $\boldsymbol{a}$ form a basis of $\mathbb{F}_{q^m}$ over $\mathbb{F}_q$. Particularly, we call $\boldsymbol{a}$ a normal basis vector if $\boldsymbol{a}$ has the form $(\alpha^{q^{m-1}}, \alpha^{q^{m-2}}, \ldots, \alpha)$ for some $\alpha \in \mathbb{F}_{q^m}^* = \mathbb{F}_{q^m} \backslash \{0\}$. For two positive integers k and n, denote by $\mathcal{M}_{k,n}(\mathbb{F}_q)$ the space of all $k \times n$ matrices over $\mathbb{F}_q$, and by $\mathrm{GL}_n(\mathbb{F}_q)$ the set of all invertible matrices in $\mathcal{M}_{n,n}(\mathbb{F}_q)$. For a matrix $M \in \mathcal{M}_{k,n}(\mathbb{F}_q)$, denote by $\langle M \rangle_q$ the linear space spanned by the rows of M over $\mathbb{F}_q$.

An $[n, k]$ linear code $\mathcal{C}$ over $\mathbb{F}_{q^m}$ is a k-dimensional subspace of $\mathbb{F}_{q^m}^n$, and any element in $\mathcal{C}$ is called a codeword of $\mathcal{C}$. The dual code of $\mathcal{C}$, denoted by $\mathcal{C}^\perp$, is the orthogonal space of $\mathcal{C}$ under the usual inner product over $\mathbb{F}_{q^m}^n$. A $k \times n$ matrix G is called a generator matrix of $\mathcal{C}$ if its row vectors form a basis of $\mathcal{C}$ over $\mathbb{F}_{q^m}$. A generator matrix H of $\mathcal{C}^\perp$ is called a parity-check matrix of $\mathcal{C}$. For a codeword $\boldsymbol{c} \in \mathcal{C}$, the rank support of $\boldsymbol{c}$, denoted by $\mathrm{Supp}(\boldsymbol{c})$, is the linear space spanned by the components of $\boldsymbol{c}$ over $\mathbb{F}_q$. The rank weight of $\boldsymbol{c}$ with respect to $\mathbb{F}_q$, denoted by $\mathrm{rk}(\boldsymbol{c})$, is defined to be the dimension of $\mathrm{Supp}(\boldsymbol{c})$ over $\mathbb{F}_q$. The minimum rank distance of $\mathcal{C}$, denoted by $\mathrm{rk}(\mathcal{C})$, is defined to be the minimum rank weight of all nonzero codewords in $\mathcal{C}$. For a matrix $M \in \mathcal{M}_{k,n}(\mathbb{F}_{q^m})$, the rank support of M, denoted by $\mathrm{Supp}(M)$, is defined to be the linear space spanned by entries of M over $\mathbb{F}_q$. The rank weight of M with respect to $\mathbb{F}_q$, denoted by $\mathrm{rk}(M)$, is defined as the dimension of $\mathrm{Supp}(M)$ over $\mathbb{F}_q$.

2.2   Gabidulin Codes

This section recalls the concept of Gabidulin codes. Before doing this, we first introduce the definition of Moore matrices and some related results.

Definition 1 (Moore matrices). *For an integer i and $\alpha \in \mathbb{F}_{q^m}$, we define $\alpha^{[i]} = \alpha^{q^i}$ to be the i-th Frobenius power of α. For a vector $\boldsymbol{a} = (\alpha_1, \alpha_2, \ldots, \alpha_n) \in \mathbb{F}_{q^m}^n$, we define $\boldsymbol{a}^{[i]} = (\alpha_1^{[i]}, \alpha_2^{[i]}, \ldots, \alpha_n^{[i]})$ to be the i-th Frobenius power of $\boldsymbol{a}$. For positive integers $k \leqslant n$, a $k \times n$ Moore matrix generated by $\boldsymbol{a}$ is defined as*

$$
\mathrm{Mr}_k(\boldsymbol{a}) = \begin{pmatrix} \alpha_1 & \alpha_2 & \cdots & \alpha_n \\ \alpha_1^{[1]} & \alpha_2^{[1]} & \cdots & \alpha_n^{[1]} \\ \vdots & \vdots & & \vdots \\ \alpha_1^{[k-1]} & \alpha_2^{[k-1]} & \cdots & \alpha_n^{[k-1]} \end{pmatrix}.
$$

For a positive integer l and a matrix $M = (M_{ij}) \in \mathcal{M}_{k,n}(\mathbb{F}_{q^m})$, we denote by $M^{[l]} = (M_{ij}^{[l]})$ the l-th Frobenius power of M. For a set $\mathcal{V} \subseteq \mathbb{F}_{q^m}^n$, we denote by $\mathcal{V}^{[l]} = \{v^{[l]} : v \in \mathcal{V}\}$ the l-th Frobenius power of $\mathcal{V}$. Particularly, for a linear code $\mathcal{C} \subseteq \mathbb{F}_{q^m}^n$, it is easy to verify that $\mathcal{C}^{[l]}$ is also a linear code over $\mathbb{F}_{q^m}$.

The following proposition presents simple properties of Moore matrices.

Proposition 1. *(1) For two $k \times n$ Moore matrices $A, B \in \mathcal{M}_{k,n}(\mathbb{F}_{q^m})$, the sum $A + B$ is also a $k \times n$ Moore matrix.*

(2) For a Moore matrix $M \in \mathcal{M}_{k,n}(\mathbb{F}_{q^m})$ and a matrix $Q \in \mathcal{M}_{n,l}(\mathbb{F}_q)$, the product MQ forms a $k \times l$ Moore matrix.

(3) For a vector $a \in \mathbb{F}_{q^m}^n$ with $\mathrm{rk}(a) = l$, there exist $a' \in \mathbb{F}_{q^m}^l$ with $\mathrm{rk}(a') = l$ and $Q \in \mathrm{GL}_n(\mathbb{F}_q)$ such that $a = (a'\|0)Q$. Furthermore, let $A = \mathrm{Mr}_k(a)$ and $A' = \mathrm{Mr}_k(a')$, then $A = [A'|0]Q$.

(4) For positive integers $k \leqslant n \leqslant m$, let $a \in \mathbb{F}_{q^m}^n$ be a vector such that $\mathrm{rk}(a) = n$, then the Moore matrix $\mathrm{Mr}_k(a)$ has rank k.

Proof. Statements (1), (2) and (3) are trivial and the proof is omitted here.

(4) Let $a = (\alpha_1, \ldots, \alpha_n) \in \mathbb{F}_{q^m}^n$. If $\mathrm{Rank}(\mathrm{Mr}_k(a)) < k$, then there exists $\boldsymbol{\lambda} = (\lambda_0, \ldots, \lambda_{k-1}) \in \mathbb{F}_{q^m}^k \setminus \{\mathbf{0}\}$ such that $\boldsymbol{\lambda}\mathrm{Mr}_k(a) = \mathbf{0}$. Let $f(x) = \sum_{j=0}^{k-1} \lambda_j x^{[j]} \in \mathbb{F}_{q^m}[x]$, then $f(\alpha_i) = 0$ holds for any $1 \leqslant i \leqslant n$. It follows that $f(\alpha) = 0$ for any $\alpha \in \langle \alpha_1, \ldots, \alpha_n \rangle_q$, which conflicts with the fact that $f(x) = 0$ admits at most q^{k-1} roots.

In particular, we have the following proposition, which was once exploited by Loidreau in [28] to cryptanalyze an encryption scheme [27] based on Gabidulin codes.

Proposition 2 (Moore matrix decomposition). *Let a be a basis vector of $\mathbb{F}_{q^m}$ over $\mathbb{F}_q$. For a positive integer $k \leqslant m$, let $M = \mathrm{Mr}_k(a)$ be a Moore matrix generated by a. Then for any $k \times n$ Moore matrix $M' \in \mathcal{M}_{k,n}(\mathbb{F}_{q^m})$, there exists $Q \in \mathcal{M}_{m,n}(\mathbb{F}_q)$ such that $M' = MQ$.*

Now we formally introduce the definition of Gabidulin codes.

Definition 2 (Gabidulin codes). *For positive integers $k < n \leqslant m$, let $a \in \mathbb{F}_{q^m}^n$ such that $\mathrm{rk}(a) = n$. The $[n, k]$ Gabidulin code generated by a, denoted by $\mathrm{Gab}_{n,k}(a)$, is defined as the linear space spanned by the rows of $\mathrm{Mr}_k(a)$ over $\mathbb{F}_{q^m}$. $\mathrm{Mr}_k(a)$ is called a canonical generator matrix of $\mathrm{Gab}_{n,k}(a)$, and a a generating vector respectively.*

Remark 1. Gabidulin codes can be seen as a rank metric counterpart of generalized Reed-Solomon (GRS) codes, both of which admit good algebraic properties. The dual of an $[n, k]$ Gabidulin code is an $[n, n-k]$ Gabidulin code [16]. An $[n, k]$ Gabidulin code has minimum rank distance $n-k+1$ [21] and can therefore correct up to $\lfloor \frac{n-k}{2} \rfloor$ rank errors in theory. Efficient decoding algorithms for Gabidulin codes can be found in [13,29,36].

To reduce the public key size, Lau and Tan exploited the so-called partial circulant matrix in the cryptosystem, which is defined as follows.

Definition 3 (Partial circulant matrices). *For $a = (\alpha_1, \alpha_2, \ldots, \alpha_n) \in \mathbb{F}_{q^m}^n$, the circulant matrix generated by a, denoted by $\mathrm{Cir}_n(a)$, is defined to be a matrix whose first row is a and i-th row is obtained by cyclically right shifting the $i-1$-th row for $2 \leqslant i \leqslant n$. The $k \times n$ partial circulant matrix generated by a, denoted by $\mathrm{Cir}_k(a)$, is defined to be the first k rows of $\mathrm{Cir}_n(a)$.*

Remark 2. Let a be a normal basis vector of $\mathbb{F}_{q^m}$ over $\mathbb{F}_q$, then it is easy to verify that the $k \times m$ partial circulant matrix generated by a is exactly the $k \times m$ Moore matrix generated by a. In other words, we have $\mathrm{Cir}_k(a) = \mathrm{Mr}_k(a)$.

3 Lau-Tan Cryptosystem

In this section, we mainly give a simple description of the Lau-Tan cryptosystem that uses Gabidulin codes as the underlying decodable code. For a given security level, choose positive integers $m > n > k > k'$ and r such that $k' = \lfloor \frac{k}{2} \rfloor$ and $r = \lfloor \frac{n-k}{2} \rfloor$. The Lau-Tan cryptosystem consists of the following three algorithms.

– Key Generation

Let $\mathcal{G}$ be an $[n, k]$ Gabidulin code over $\mathbb{F}_{q^m}$, and $G \in \mathcal{M}_{k,n}(\mathbb{F}_{q^m})$ be a generator matrix of $\mathcal{G}$ of canonical form. Randomly choose matrices $S \in \mathrm{GL}_k(\mathbb{F}_{q^m})$ and $T \in \mathrm{GL}_n(\mathbb{F}_q)$. Randomly choose $u \in \mathbb{F}_{q^m}^n$ such that $\mathrm{rk}(u) = n$ and set $U = \mathrm{Cir}_k(u)$. Let $G_{pub} = SG + UT$, then we publish (G_{pub}, u) as the public key, and keep (S, G, T) as the private key.

– Encryption

For a plaintext $m \in \mathbb{F}_{q^m}^{k'}$, randomly choose a vector $m_s \in \mathbb{F}_{q^m}^{k-k'}$ such that $\mathrm{rk}((m\|m_s)U) > \lceil \frac{3}{4}(n-k) \rceil$. Randomly choose $e_1, e_2 \in \mathbb{F}_{q^m}^n$ such that $\mathrm{rk}(e_1) \leqslant \frac{r}{2}$ and $\mathrm{rk}(e_2) \leqslant \frac{r}{2}$. Compute $c_1 = (m\|m_s)U + e_1$ and $c_2 = (m\|m_s)G_{pub} + e_2$. Then the ciphertext is $c = (c_1, c_2)$.

– Decryption

For a ciphertext $c = (c_1, c_2) \in \mathbb{F}_{q^m}^{2n}$, compute $c' = c_2 - c_1 T = (m\|m_s)SG + e_2 - e_1 T$. Note that $\mathrm{rk}(e_2 - e_1 T) \leqslant \mathrm{rk}(e_2) + \mathrm{rk}(e_1 T) \leqslant r$, decoding c' with the fast decoder of $\mathcal{G}$ will lead to $m' = (m\|m_s)S$, then by computing $m'S^{-1}$ one can recover the plaintext m.

4 Key Recovery Attack

This section discusses how to efficiently recover an equivalent private key of the Lau-Tan cryptosystem. We point out that the knowledge of T is of great importance for the security of the whole cryptosystem. Specifically, if one can find the private T, then one is able to recover everything needed to decrypt an arbitrary ciphertext in polynomial time. Before describing this attack, we first introduce some further results about Gabidulin codes.

4.1 Further Results About Gabidulin Codes

Similar to GRS codes in the Hamming metric, Gabidulin codes also have good algebraic structure. For instance, if $\mathcal{G}$ is a Gabidulin code over $\mathbb{F}_{q^m}$, then its l-th Frobenius power is also a Gabidulin code. Formally, we introduce the following proposition.

Proposition 3. *Let $\mathcal{G}$ be an $[n,k]$ Gabidulin code over $\mathbb{F}_{q^m}$, with $G \in \mathcal{M}_{k,n}(\mathbb{F}_{q^m})$ as a generator matrix. For any positive integer l, $G^{[l]}$ is also an $[n,k]$ Gabidulin code and has $G^{[l]}$ as a generator matrix.*

Proof. Trivial from a straightforward verification.

For a proper positive integer l, the intersection of a Gabidulin code and its l-th Frobenius power is still a Gabidulin code, as described in the following proposition.

Proposition 4. *For an $[n,k]$ Gabidulin code $\mathcal{G}$ over $\mathbb{F}_{q^m}$, let $\boldsymbol{g} \in \mathbb{F}_{q^m}^n$ be a generating vector of $\mathcal{G}$. For a positive integer $l \leqslant \min\{k-1, n-k\}$, the intersection of $\mathcal{G}$ and its l-th Frobenius power is an $[n, k-l]$ Gabidulin code with $\boldsymbol{g}^{[l]}$ as a generating vector. In other words, we have the following equality*

$$\mathcal{G} \cap \mathcal{G}^{[l]} = \mathrm{Gab}_{n,k-l}(\boldsymbol{g}^{[l]}).$$

Proof. By Definition 2, $\mathcal{G}$ is an $\mathbb{F}_{q^m}$-span of $\boldsymbol{g}, \ldots, \boldsymbol{g}^{[k-1]}$, i.e. $\mathcal{G} = \langle \boldsymbol{g}, \ldots, \boldsymbol{g}^{[k-1]} \rangle_{q^m}$. By Proposition 3, we have $\mathcal{G}^{[l]} = \langle \boldsymbol{g}^{[l]}, \ldots, \boldsymbol{g}^{[k+l-1]} \rangle_{q^m}$. Note that $l \leqslant \min\{k-1, n-k\}$, then $k+l \leqslant n$ and $\boldsymbol{g}, \ldots, \boldsymbol{g}^{[k+l-1]}$ are linearly independent over $\mathbb{F}_{q^m}$. It follows that $\mathcal{G} \cap \mathcal{G}^{[l]} = \langle \boldsymbol{g}^{[l]}, \ldots, \boldsymbol{g}^{[k-1]} \rangle_{q^m}$ forms an $[n, k-l]$ Gabidulin code, having $\boldsymbol{g}^{[l]}$ as a generating vector. This completes the proof.

Proposition 5. *For positive integers $k < n \leqslant m$, let $\mathcal{G} \subset \mathbb{F}_{q^m}^n$ be an $[n,k]$ Gabidulin code, and $A \in \mathcal{M}_{k,n}(\mathbb{F}_{q^m})$ a nonzero Moore matrix. If all the row vectors of A are codewords in $\mathcal{G}$, then A forms a generator matrix of $\mathcal{G}$.*

Proof. It suffices to prove $\mathrm{Rank}(A) = k$. Suppose that A is generated by $\boldsymbol{a} \in \mathbb{F}_{q^m}^n$, i.e. $A = \mathrm{Mr}_k(\boldsymbol{a})$. Let $l = \mathrm{rk}(\boldsymbol{a})$, then there exist $\boldsymbol{a}' \in \mathbb{F}_{q^m}^l$ with $\mathrm{rk}(\boldsymbol{a}') = l$ and $Q \in \mathrm{GL}_n(\mathbb{F}_q)$ such that $\boldsymbol{a} = (\boldsymbol{a}'\|\boldsymbol{0})Q$. Let $A' \in \mathcal{M}_{k,l}(\mathbb{F}_{q^m})$ be a Moore matrix generated by $\boldsymbol{a}'$, then it follows immediately that $A = [A'|0]Q$. If $l > k$, then $\mathrm{Rank}(A) = \mathrm{Rank}(A') = k$ due to Proposition 1 and therefore the conclusion is proved. Otherwise, there will be $\langle A' \rangle_{q^m} = \mathbb{F}_{q^m}^l$. From this we can deduce that the minimum rank distance of $\mathcal{G}$ will be 1, which conflicts with the fact that $\mathrm{rk}(\mathcal{G}) = n - k + 1 \geqslant 2$. Hence $l > k$ and $\mathrm{Rank}(A) = k$. This completes the proof.

By Definition 2, a Gabidulin code is uniquely determined by its generating vector. Naturally, it is important to make clear what all these vectors look like and how many generating vectors there exist for a Gabidulin code.

Proposition 6. *Let $\mathcal{G}$ be an $[n,k]$ Gabidulin code over $\mathbb{F}_{q^m}$, with $\boldsymbol{g} \in \mathbb{F}_{q^m}^n$ as a generating vector. Let $\boldsymbol{g}' \in \mathbb{F}_{q^m}^n$ be a codeword in $\mathcal{G}$, then $\boldsymbol{g}'$ forms a generating vector if and only if there exists $\gamma \in \mathbb{F}_{q^m}^*$ such that $\boldsymbol{g}' = \gamma\boldsymbol{g}$.*

Proof. Assume that $g = (\alpha_1, \ldots, \alpha_n)$ and $g' = (\alpha'_1, \ldots, \alpha'_n)$, let $G = \text{Mr}_k(g)$ and $G' = \text{Mr}_k(g')$. The conclusion is trivial if $g = g'$. Otherwise, without loss of generality we assume that $\alpha'_1 \neq \alpha_1$, then there exists $\gamma \in \mathbb{F}^*_{q^m} \backslash \{1\}$ such that $\alpha'_1 = \gamma\alpha_1$. Let

$$S = \begin{pmatrix} \gamma & 0 & \cdots & 0 \\ 0 & \gamma^{[1]} & \cdots & 0 \\ \vdots & \vdots & & \vdots \\ 0 & 0 & \cdots & \gamma^{[k-1]} \end{pmatrix},$$

then $SG = \text{Mr}_k(\gamma g)$. Let $g^* = \gamma g - g' = (0, \gamma\alpha_2 - \alpha'_2, \ldots, \gamma\alpha_n - \alpha'_n)$ and $G^* = \text{Mr}_k(g^*)$, then $G^* = SG - G'$. Apparently all the row vectors of G^* are codewords in $\mathcal{G}$. If $g^* \neq 0$, then G^* forms a generator matrix of $\mathcal{G}$ of canonical form due to Proposition 5. Together with $\text{rk}(g^*) \leqslant n - 1$, easily we can deduce that $\text{rk}(c) \leqslant n-1$ for any $c \in \mathcal{G}$, which clearly contradicts the fact that $\text{rk}(g) = n$. Therefore there must be $g^* = 0$, or equivalently $g' = \gamma g$. The opposite is obvious from a straightforward verification.

The following corollary is drawn immediately from Proposition 6.

Corollary 1. *An $[n, k]$ Gabidulin code over $\mathbb{F}_{q^m}$ admits $q^m - 1$ generator matrices of canonical form, or equivalently $q^m - 1$ generating vectors.*

Remark 3. Let $\mathcal{G} \subseteq \mathbb{F}^n_{q^m}$ be an $[n, k]$ Gabidulin code, and $M \in \mathcal{M}_{k,m}(\mathbb{F}_{q^m})$ a Moore matrix generated by a basis vector of $\mathbb{F}_{q^m}$ over $\mathbb{F}_q$. By Proposition 2, for any canonical generator matrix G, there exists a unique $Q \in \mathcal{M}_{m,n}(\mathbb{F}_q)$ such that $G = MQ$. For a fixed M, there exist $q^m - 1$ Q's in $\mathcal{M}_{m,n}(\mathbb{F}_q)$ such that MQ forms a canonical generator matrix of $\mathcal{G}$. Furthermore, all these Q's together with the zero matrix form an $\mathbb{F}_q$-linear space of dimension m.

4.2   Recovering the Private T

This section mainly describes an efficient algorithm for recovering the private T. The technique we adopt here is to convert the problem of recovering T into solving a multivariate linear system, which clearly costs polynomial time. Before doing this, we first introduce the so-called subfield expanding transform.

Subfield Expanding Transform. For $\beta_1, \ldots, \beta_n \in \mathbb{F}_{q^m}$, we construct an equation as

$$\sum_{j=1}^n x_j\beta_j = 0, \tag{1}$$

where x_j's are underdetermined variables in $\mathbb{F}_q$. Let a be a basis vector of $\mathbb{F}_{q^m}$ over $\mathbb{F}_q$. For each $1 \leqslant j \leqslant n$, there exists $b_j \in \mathbb{F}^m_q$ such that $\beta_j = b_j a^T$. It follows that $\sum_{j=1}^n x_j\beta_j = \sum_{j=1}^n x_j(b_j a^T) = (\sum_{j=1}^n x_j b_j)a^T$, and moreover, (1) holds if and only if

$$\sum_{j=1}^n x_j b_j = \mathbf{0}. \tag{2}$$

Obviously, the linear systems (1) and (2) share the same solution space. A transform that derives (2) from (1) is called a subfield expanding transform (SET for short).

In the Lau-Tan cryptosystem, let $H \in \mathcal{M}_{n-k,n}(\mathbb{F}_{q^m})$ be a parity-check matrix of $\mathcal{G}$ of canonical form. Let $M \in \mathcal{M}_{n-k,m}(\mathbb{F}_{q^m})$ be a Moore matrix generated by a basis vector of $\mathbb{F}_{q^m}$ over $\mathbb{F}_q$, then there exists an underdetermined matrix $X \in \mathcal{M}_{m,n}(\mathbb{F}_q)$ such that $H = MX$. On the other hand, there exists another underdetermined matrix $T^* \in \mathrm{GL}_n(\mathbb{F}_q)$ such that $G_{pub} - UT^*$ forms a generator matrix of $\mathcal{G}$. This leads to a parity-check matrix equation as follows

$$(G_{pub} - UT^*)(MX)^T = G_{pub}X^T M^T - UT^* X^T M^T = 0. \tag{3}$$

We therefore obtain a system of $k(n-k)$ multivariate quadratic equations, with $n(m+n)$ variables in $\mathbb{F}_q$. This system admits at least q^m solutions. Specifically, we introduce the following proposition.

Proposition 7. *The linear system* (3) *has at least* q^m *solutions.*

Proof. If $T^* = T$, then we can deduce from (3) that

$$(G_{pub} - UT^*)(MX)^T = (SG + UT - UT^*)(MX)^T = SG(MX)^T = 0.$$

Note that $SG \in \mathcal{M}_{k,n}(\mathbb{F}_{q^m})$ forms a generator matrix of $\mathcal{G}$. By $SG(MX)^T = 0$, all the row vectors of MX are contained in $\mathcal{G}^\perp$, which is an $[n, n-k]$ Gabidulin code. On the other hand, it is clear that MX forms an $(n-k) \times n$ Moore matrix. By Proposition 5, MX forms a canonical generator matrix of $\mathcal{G}^\perp$ for a nonzero X. Then the conclusion is immediately proved from Corollary 1. Furthermore, we have that X is an $m \times n$ matrix of full rank.

Note that solving a multivariate quadratic system generally requires exponential time. Instead of solving the system (3) directly, the technique we exploit here is to consider each entry of $T^* X^T$ as a new variable in $\mathbb{F}_q$ and set $Y = XT^{*T}$. In other words, we rewrite (3) into a matrix equation as follows

$$G_{pub}X^T M^T - UY^T M^T = 0. \tag{4}$$

This leads to a linear system of $k(n-k)$ equations, with coefficients in $\mathbb{F}_{q^m}$ and $2mn$ variables in $\mathbb{F}_q$. To solve the system (4), we usually convert this problem into an instance over the base field $\mathbb{F}_q$. Applying SET to (4) leads to a linear system of $mk(n-k)$ equations over $\mathbb{F}_q$, with $2mn$ variables to be determined. For cryptographic use, generally we have $mk(n-k) \geqslant 2mn$.

Remark 4. With each solution (X, T^*) of (3), one can obtain a solution of (4) by computing $Y = XT^{*T}$, which implies that (4) also has at least q^m solutions. Conversely, if (4) has exactly q^m solutions, then these solutions must correspond to those of (3) where $T^* = T$. In this situation, solving (4) for any nonzero solution (X, Y) enables us to recover the private T by solving the matrix equation $Y = XT^{*T}$.

As for whether or not the system (4) has other types of solutions, we make an **Assumption** that the answer is negative. According to our experimental results in MAGMA [10], this assumption holds with high probability. To make it easier, a simplified version of this problem is considered. Let G be an arbitrary generator matrix of an $[n, k]$ Gabidulin code and $\boldsymbol{u} \in \mathbb{F}_{q^m}^n$ such that $\mathrm{rk}(\boldsymbol{u}) = n$. We then construct a matrix equation as

$$GX^T M^T + \mathrm{Cir}_k(\boldsymbol{u}) Y^T M^T = 0,$$

where $M \in \mathcal{M}_{n-k,m}(\mathbb{F}_{q^m})$ is a Moore matrix generated by a basis vector of $\mathbb{F}_{q^m}$ over $\mathbb{F}_q$ and $X, Y \in \mathcal{M}_{m,n}(\mathbb{F}_q)$ are two underdetermined matrices. By applying SET to this system above, we obtain a new system over $\mathbb{F}_q$. By Remark 4, if this newly obtained system admits a solution space of dimension m, then there must be $Y = 0$. Finally, we ran 1000 random tests for $q = 2, m = 25, n = 23, k = 10$, and for $q = 3, m = 18, n = 15, k = 7$ respectively. It turns out that this assumption holds in all of these random instances.

Algorithm 1 : T-Recovering Algorithm

Input: (G_{pub}, U)
Output: T

1: Let $\boldsymbol{a}$ be a basis vector of $\mathbb{F}_{q^m}$ over $\mathbb{F}_q$ and set $M = \mathrm{Mr}_{n-k}(\boldsymbol{a})$
2: Let $X, Y \in \mathcal{M}_{m,n}(\mathbb{F}_q)$ be two underdetermined matrices and set

$$G_{pub} X^T M^T - U Y^T M^T = 0 \tag{5}$$

3: Apply SET to (5) to obtain a linear system over $\mathbb{F}_q$
4: Solve the system from Step 3 for any nonzero (X, Y)
5: Solve the matrix equation $Y = X T^{*T}$ for T^*
6: **return** $T = T^*$

4.3   Finding an Equivalent (S', G')

In Sect. 4.2, we have discussed how to efficiently recover T from (G_{pub}, U). With the knowledge of T, one can recover SG by computing $SG = G_{pub} - UT$, which forms a generator matrix of $\mathcal{G}$. To decrypt a ciphertext as the legitimate receiver does, one needs to recover a generator matrix G' of $\mathcal{G}$ of canonical form and an invertible matrix S' such that $S'G' = SG$, where (S', G') is called an equivalent form of (S, G). Once such a G' is obtained, then one can recover S' by solving a matrix equation.

Now we investigate how to derive a canonical generator matrix of a Gabidulin code, or equivalently a generating vector, from an arbitrary generator matrix. In [20] the authors presented an iterative method of computing the generating vector. Here in this paper we present a different approach to do this.

An Approach to Compute the Generating Vector. For an $[n, k]$ Gabidulin code $\mathcal{G}$ over $\mathbb{F}_{q^m}$, let $G \in \mathcal{M}_{k,n}(\mathbb{F}_{q^m})$ be an arbitrary generator matrix of $\mathcal{G}$. We first compute a parity-check matrix of $\mathcal{G}$ from G, say H. Let $M \in \mathcal{M}_{k,m}(\mathbb{F}_{q^m})$ be a Moore matrix generated by a basis vector of $\mathbb{F}_{q^m}$ over $\mathbb{F}_q$, then there exists an underdetermined matrix $X \in \mathcal{M}_{m,n}(\mathbb{F}_q)$ such that MX forms a canonical generator matrix of $\mathcal{G}$. By setting $(MX)H^T = 0$, we obtain a linear system of $k(n-k)$ equations, with coefficients in $\mathbb{F}_{q^m}$ and mn variables in $\mathbb{F}_q$. Applying SET to this system leads to a new linear system over the base field $\mathbb{F}_q$, with $mk(n-k)$ equations and mn variables. For cryptographic use, generally we have $mk(n-k) \geqslant mn$. By Corollary 1, this newly obtained system admits $q^m - 1$ nonzero solutions. And for any nonzero solution, say X, the first row of MX will be a generating vector of $\mathcal{G}$.

Algorithm 2 : (S', G')-Recovering Algorithm

Input: (G_{pub}, U, T)
Output: (S', G')

1: Let $\boldsymbol{a}$ be a basis vector of $\mathbb{F}_{q^m}$ over $\mathbb{F}_q$ and set $M = \mathrm{Mr}_k(\boldsymbol{a})$
2: Compute $SG = G_{pub} - UT$ and let $\mathcal{G} = \langle SG \rangle_{q^m}$
3: Let $H \in \mathcal{M}_{n-k,n}(\mathbb{F}_{q^m})$ be a parity-check matrix of $\mathcal{G}$
4: Let $X \in \mathcal{M}_{m,n}(\mathbb{F}_q)$ be an underdetermined matrix and set

$$(MX)H^T = 0 \qquad (6)$$

5: Apply SET to (5) to obtain a linear system over $\mathbb{F}_q$
6: Solve the system from Step 5 for any nonzero X
7: Compute $G' = MX$
8: Compute $S' \in \mathrm{GL}_k(\mathbb{F}_{q^m})$ such that $S'G' = SG$
9: **return** (S', G')

4.4   Complexity of the Attack

Our attack consists of two phases: firstly, we manage to recover the private T from the published information, as described in Algorithm 1; secondly, with the knowledge of T and the public key, we compute a canonical generator matrix G' of the secret Gabidulin code and an invertible matrix S', as described in Algorithm 2. Hence the complexity analysis is done in the following two aspects.

Complexity of Algorithm 1. In Step 1 we construct a Moore matrix $M \in \mathcal{M}_{n-k,m}(\mathbb{F}_{q^m})$ whose first row forms a basis vector of $\mathbb{F}_{q^m}$ over $\mathbb{F}_q$. To avoid executing the Frobenius operation, here we choose $\boldsymbol{a}$ to be a normal basis vector, then we set $M = \mathrm{Cir}_{n-k}(\boldsymbol{a})$. In Step 2 we construct a multivariate linear system by performing matrix multiplication, requiring $\mathcal{O}(mn^3)$ operations in $\mathbb{F}_{q^m}$. The subfield expanding transform performed to (5) requires $\mathcal{O}(m^3n^3)$ operations in $\mathbb{F}_{q^m}$. Step 4 requires $\mathcal{O}(m^3n^3)$ operations to solve the linear system over $\mathbb{F}_q$ and Step 5 requires $\mathcal{O}(n^3)$ operations in $\mathbb{F}_q$. The total complexity of Algorithm 1 consists of $\mathcal{O}(m^3n^3 + mn^3)$ operations in $\mathbb{F}_{q^m}$ and $\mathcal{O}(m^3n^3 + n^3)$ operations in $\mathbb{F}_q$.

Complexity of Algorithm 2. In Step 1 we still choose a normal basis vector to construct M. To compute SG, we perform matrix addition and multiplication with $\mathcal{O}(n^3)$ operations in $\mathbb{F}_{q^m}$. Step 3 computes a parity-check H of $\mathcal{G}$ from SG, requiring $\mathcal{O}(n^3)$ operations in $\mathbb{F}_{q^m}$. Then we construct a linear system in Step 4, which costs $\mathcal{O}(mn^3)$ operations in $\mathbb{F}_{q^m}$. In Step 5 we apply SET to (6) to obtain a new system over $\mathbb{F}_q$, requiring $\mathcal{O}(m^3n^3)$ operations in $\mathbb{F}_{q^m}$. Solving this new system in Step 6 costs $\mathcal{O}(m^3n^3)$ operations in $\mathbb{F}_q$, and computing $G' = MX$ in Step 7 requires $\mathcal{O}(mn^2)$ operations in $\mathbb{F}_{q^m}$. In Step 8, we shall compute S' from $S'G'$ with $\mathcal{O}(n^3)$ operations. The total complexity of Algorithm 2 consists of $\mathcal{O}(m^3n^3 + mn^3 + n^3)$ operations in $\mathbb{F}_{q^m}$ and $\mathcal{O}(m^3n^3)$ operations in $\mathbb{F}_q$.

Finally, the total complexity of the attack is $\mathcal{O}(m^3n^3 + mn^3 + n^3)$ in $\mathbb{F}_{q^m}$ plus $\mathcal{O}(m^3n^3 + n^3)$ in $\mathbb{F}_q$.

4.5 Implementation

This attack has been implemented in MAGMA and permits to recover the private T. We tested this attack on a personal computer and succeeded for parameters as illustrated in Table 1. For each parameter set, this attack has been run 100 times and the last column gives the average timing (in seconds). Our implementation is just a proof of feasibility of this attack and does not consider the proposed parameters in [25,26].

Table 1. These tests were performed using MAGMA V2.11-1 on 11th Gen Intel[R] Core[TM] i7-11700 @ 2.5 GHz processor with 16 GB of memory.

q	m	n	k	t
2	22	18	9	8.6
2	28	22	9	40.7
2	35	26	12	173.2

5 A Repair

To prevent the proposed attack, we give a simple repair for the Lau-Tan cryptosystem in this section. Then we explain why this repair can resist the existing structural attacks, as well as the key recovery attack described in Sect. 4. After that, practical security of this repair against generic attacks is investigated. Following this, we suggest parameters for the security of at least 128 bits, 192 bits, and 256 bits. Public key sizes under these parameters are also given.

5.1 Description of the Repair

For a given security level, choose a field $\mathbb{F}_q$ and positive integers $m, n, k, \lambda, r_1, r_2$ such that $r = \lfloor \frac{n-k}{2} \rfloor$ and $r_1 + \lambda r_2 \leqslant r$. Our repair consists of the following three procedures.

- Key Generation

  Let $\mathcal{G}$ be an $[n, k]$ Gabidulin code over $\mathbb{F}_{q^m}$, and $G \in \mathcal{M}_{k,n}(\mathbb{F}_{q^m})$ a generator matrix of $\mathcal{G}$ of canonical form. Randomly choose matrices $S \in GL_k(\mathbb{F}_{q^m})$ and $T \in GL_n(\mathcal{V})$, where $\mathcal{V} \subseteq \mathbb{F}_{q^m}$ is a randomly chosen $\mathbb{F}_q$-linear space of dimension λ. Randomly choose $\boldsymbol{u} \in \mathbb{F}_{q^m}^n$ such that $rk(\boldsymbol{u}) = n$ and set $U = Cir_k(\boldsymbol{u})$. Let $G_{pub} = (SG + U)T^{-1}$, then we publish $(G_{pub}, \boldsymbol{u})$ as the public key, and keep (S, G, T) as the private key.

- Encryption

  For a plaintext $\boldsymbol{m} \in \mathbb{F}_{q^m}^k$, randomly choose $\boldsymbol{e}_1 \in \mathbb{F}_{q^m}^n$ with $rk(\boldsymbol{e}_1) = r_1$ and $\boldsymbol{e}_2 \in \mathbb{F}_{q^m}^n$ with $rk(\boldsymbol{e}_2) = r_2$. Compute $\boldsymbol{c}_1 = \boldsymbol{m}U + \boldsymbol{e}_1$ and $\boldsymbol{c}_2 = \boldsymbol{m}G_{pub} + \boldsymbol{e}_2$, then the ciphertext is $\boldsymbol{c} = (\boldsymbol{c}_1, \boldsymbol{c}_2)$.

- Decryption

  For a ciphertext $\boldsymbol{c} = (\boldsymbol{c}_1, \boldsymbol{c}_2) \in \mathbb{F}_{q^m}^{2n}$, compute $\boldsymbol{c}' = \boldsymbol{c}_2 T - \boldsymbol{c}_1 = \boldsymbol{m}SG + \boldsymbol{e}_2 T - \boldsymbol{e}_1$. Note that $rk(\boldsymbol{e}_2 T - \boldsymbol{e}_1) \leqslant rk(\boldsymbol{e}_2 T) + rk(\boldsymbol{e}_1) \leqslant \lambda r_2 + r_1 \leqslant r$. Decoding $\boldsymbol{c}'$ with the decoder of $\mathcal{G}$ leads to $\boldsymbol{m}' = \boldsymbol{m}S$, then by computing $\boldsymbol{m}'S^{-1}$ one can recover the plaintext $\boldsymbol{m}$.

Remark 5. It is clear that the public key will degenerate into an instance of the original system if $\lambda = 1$ and $\mathcal{V} = \mathbb{F}_q$, which has been completely broken in the present paper. To achieve the IND-CPA security, the original encryption procedure chooses an extra vector $\boldsymbol{m}_s$ to concatenate $\boldsymbol{m}$, which greatly reduces the information transfer rate. To avoid this defect, we remove the use of $\boldsymbol{m}_s$ in the encrypting process. Consequently, a problem arises that the repaired scheme only satisfies the security notion of One-Wayness. However, we can follow the approach in [24] to convert this repair into an IND-CCA2 secured encryption scheme.

5.2   Security Analysis

Now we investigate the security of this repair in the following three aspects.

Structural Attacks. Resistance of our repair against the existing structural attacks [11,18,19,32,34] is apparent. In what follows, therefore, we only consider the key recovery attack presented in Sect. 4. With a similar analysis, we construct a matrix equation as follows

$$G_{pub}Y^T M^T - UX^T M^T = 0. \tag{7}$$

What differs from (4) is that $X \in \mathcal{M}_{m,n}(\mathbb{F}_q)$ and $Y \in \mathcal{M}_{m,n}(\mathbb{F}_{q^m})$ is taken in an $\mathbb{F}_q$-linear space of dimension λ. Applying SET to (7) will lead to a linear system over $\mathbb{F}_q$, with $k(n - k)m$ equations and $(\lambda + 1)mn$ variables. Solving this system generally requires $\mathcal{O}((\lambda + 1)^3 m^3 n^3)$ operations. Note that we cannot presuppose $\mathbb{F}_q \subseteq \mathcal{V}$ because of the additive structure, which suggests that one has to enumerate λ-dimensional $\mathbb{F}_q$-subspaces of $\mathbb{F}_{q^m}$ with a complexity of $\mathcal{O}(q^{\lambda(m-\lambda)})$. Finally the whole complexity of our attack on this repair can be evaluated as $\mathcal{O}((\lambda + 1)^3 m^3 n^3 q^{\lambda(m-\lambda)})$. It is easy to see that this repair can easily reach the desired security for parameters of proper size.

Generic Attacks. We first introduce the so-called rank syndrome decoding (RSD) problem on which the security of most code-based cryptosystems relies. An RSD problem with parameters (q, m, n, k, t) is to search for a vector $e \in \mathbb{F}_{q^m}^n$ such that $\mathrm{rk}(e) = t$ and $s = eH^T$, where $H \in \mathcal{M}_{n-k,n}(\mathbb{F}_{q^m})$ is a matrix of full rank and $s \in \mathbb{F}_{q^m}^{n-k}$. Generic attacks on the RSD problem can be divided into two categories, namely the combinatorial attacks as listed in Table 2 and the algebraic attacks as listed in Table 3. The security of a code-based cryptosystem under these attacks only relate to the practical parameters, and does not rely on the algebraic structure of the underlying code.

Table 2. Best known combinatorial attacks on the RSD problem.

Attack	Complexity
[33]	$\mathcal{O}\left(\min\left\{ m^3 t^3 q^{(t-1)(k+1)}, (k+t)^3 t^3 q^{(t-1)(m-t)} \right\} \right)$
[17]	$\mathcal{O}\left((n-k)^3 m^3 q^{\min\left\{ t\lceil \frac{mk}{n} \rceil, (t-1)\lceil \frac{m(k+1)}{n} \rceil \right\}} \right)$
[3]	$\mathcal{O}\left((n-k)^3 m^3 q^{t\lceil \frac{m(k+1)}{n} \rceil - m} \right)$

Table 3. Best known algebraic attacks on the RSD problem.

Attack	Condition	Complexity
[17]	$\left\lceil \frac{(t+1)(k+1)-(n+1)}{t} \right\rceil \leqslant k$	$\mathcal{O}\left(k^3 t^3 q^{t\left\lceil \frac{(t+1)(k+1)-(n+1)}{t} \right\rceil} \right)$
[6]	$m\binom{n-k-1}{t} \geqslant \binom{n}{t} - 1$	$\mathcal{O}\left(m\binom{n-p-k-1}{t} \binom{n-p}{t}^{\omega-1} \right)$, where $\omega = 2.81$ and $p = \min\{1 \leqslant i \leqslant n : m\binom{n-i-k-1}{t} \geqslant \binom{n-i}{t} - 1\}$
[5]		$\mathcal{O}\left(\left(\frac{((m+n)t)^t}{t!} \right)^\omega \right)$
[6]	$m\binom{n-k-1}{t} < \binom{n}{t} - 1$	$\mathcal{O}\left(q^{at} m\binom{n-k-1}{t} \binom{n-a}{t}^{\omega-1} \right)$, where $a = \min\{1 \leqslant i \leqslant n : m\binom{n-k-1}{t} \geqslant \binom{n-i}{t} - 1\}$
[5]		$\mathcal{O}\left(\left(\frac{((m+n)t)^{t+1}}{(t+1)!} \right)^\omega \right)$

Proposed Parameters. Now we consider the practical security of this repair and propose some parameters for the security of at least 128 bits, 192 bits, and 256 bits. As illustrated in Table 4, we consider $m = n$ and $r_1 = r_2 = t = \lfloor \frac{n-k}{2(\lambda+1)} \rfloor$. The ciphertext of our repair consists of the following two parts

$$c_1 = mU + e_1, c_2 = mG_{pub} + e_2,$$

which lead to an RSD instance of parameters (q, m, n, k, t). Meanwhile, it is easy to see that

$$(c_1 || c_2) = m[U | G_{pub}] + (e_1 || e_2),$$

and this results in another RSD instance of parameters $(q, m, 2n, k, 2t)$. Additionally, we also consider the proposed key recovery attack described above, which requires $\mathcal{O}((\lambda + 1)^3 m^3 n^3 q^{\lambda(m-\lambda)})$ operations in $\mathbb{F}_q$. Finally we give some suggested parameters in Table 4, as well as the corresponding public-key sizes.

Table 4. Parameters and public-key size (in bytes).

Parameters							Public-Key Size	Security
q	m	n	k	λ	r_1	r_2		
2	79	79	37	2	7	7	29645	128
2	91	91	43	2	8	8	45546	193
2	110	110	50	2	10	10	77138	265

6   Cryptanalysis of Loidreau's Cryptosystem

The success of our attack on the Lau-Tan cryptosystem relies on four points. One is the fact of Moore matrix decomposition as described in Proposition 2, the second is to construct a system of equations from the parity-check matrix equation, the third is to reduce the problem of solving a multivariate quadratic system into solving a multivariate linear system, and the last is any nonzero solution of this linear system leads to an equivalent private key.

Based on Points 1, 2, and 4 described above, we provide another perspective on the security of Loidreau's cryptosystem [27], which has been completely broken for specific parameters [11,18]. Firstly, we give a simple description for the principle of Loidreau's cryptosystem. The public key in this cryptosystem is published as $G_{pub} = GP^{-1}$, where G is a generator matrix of an $[n, k]$ Gabidulin code $\mathcal{G} \subseteq \mathbb{F}_{q^m}$ and $P \in \mathrm{GL}_n(\mathbb{F}_{q^m})$ with entries contained in a small λ-dimensional $\mathbb{F}_q$-linear space $\mathcal{V} \subseteq \mathbb{F}_{q^m}$. To encrypt a plaintext $m \in \mathbb{F}_{q^m}^k$, one first encodes m by computing mG_{pub}, then disguises this codeword by adding an error vector $e \in \mathbb{F}_{q^m}^n$ with $\mathrm{rk}(e) = \lfloor \frac{n-k}{2\lambda} \rfloor$. To decrypt a ciphertext $c = mG_{pub} + e$, one first computes $c' = cP$, then decodes c' with the decoder of $\mathcal{G}$ to recover eP due to $\mathrm{rk}(eP) \leqslant \lfloor \frac{n-k}{2} \rfloor$. Then one can obtain m by solving the linear system $mG = c' - eP$.

In a talk [28] at CBCrypto 2021, Loidreau proposed an attack to recover a polynomial-time decoder of the public code with a complexity of $\mathcal{O}((\lambda n + (n-k)^2)^3 m^3 q^{(\lambda-1)m})$ for $q = 2$, which can be easily generalized to any field $\mathbb{F}_q$. Loidreau's attack manages to recover $Y \in \mathcal{M}_{m,n}(\mathcal{V})$ such that $G_{pub}(MY)^T = 0$, where $M \in \mathcal{M}_{n-k,m}(\mathbb{F}_{q^m})$ is a Moore matrix generated by a basis vector of $\mathbb{F}_{q^m}$ over $\mathbb{F}_q$. Then with the knowledge of Y, one can decrypt any ciphertext in polynomial time. Specifically, let $c = mG_{pub} + e$ be the received ciphertext, then one computes $s = c(MY)^T = eY^T M^T$. Note that $\mathrm{rk}(eY^T) \leqslant \lfloor \frac{n-k}{2} \rfloor$, then one can recover $e' = eY^T$ by using the syndrome decoder of an $[m, m - n + k]$ Gabidulin code that has M as a parity-check matrix. After that, one can recover e by solving the linear system $e' = eY^T$.

Now we apply the proposed attack to Loidreau's cryptosystem. Let $H \in \mathcal{M}_{n-k,n}(\mathbb{F}_{q^m})$ be a canonical parity-check matrix of $\mathcal{G}$, and $\mathcal{G}_{pub} = \langle G_{pub} \rangle_{q^m}$ the public code. It is clear that $H_{pub} = HP^T$ forms a parity-check matrix of $\mathcal{G}_{pub}$. Let $M \in \mathcal{M}_{n-k,m}(\mathbb{F}_{q^m})$ be a Moore matrix generated by a basis vector of $\mathbb{F}_{q^m}$ over $\mathbb{F}_q$, then there exists $Y^* \in \mathcal{M}_{m,n}(\mathbb{F}_q)$ such that $H = MY^*$. Let $Y = Y^*P^T$, then one can construct a linear system from the parity-check matrix equation $G_{pub}H_{pub}^T = 0$, which is equivalent to

$$G_{pub}(MY)^T = G_{pub}Y^T M^T = 0. \tag{8}$$

While in Loidreau's attack, the corresponding linear system is constructed from $SH_{pub} = MY$, which introduces extra variables from an underdetermined matrix $S \in \mathrm{GL}_{n-k}(\mathbb{F}_{q^m})$. Applying SET to (8) leads to a linear system over $\mathbb{F}_q$ of $k(n-k)m$ equations and λmn variables. For cryptographic use, $k(n-k)m \geqslant \lambda mn$ always holds in practical situations. And this system admits q^m solutions when $\mathcal{V}$ is correctly guessed, which has been validated through numerous experiments. Solving this system for any nonzero solution permits us to obtain $Y' \in \mathcal{M}_{m,n}(\mathcal{V})$ such that $G_{pub}(MY')^T = 0$. On the other hand, one can always presuppose $1 \in \mathcal{V}$ since $G_{pub} = \alpha^{-1}G(\alpha^{-1}P)^{-1}$ for any nonzero $\alpha \in \mathcal{V}$. Finally this attack requires a complexity of $\mathcal{O}(\lambda^3 n^3 m^3 q^{(\lambda-1)m})$ in $\mathbb{F}_q$, which is clearly lower than Loidreau's attack.

7   Conclusion

Our attack has revealed the structural weakness of the Lau-Tan cryptosystem. Although the first part of the public key hides the structure of Gabidulin codes nicely, the second part reveals important information that can be used to design a key recovery attack. Specifically, we convert the problem of recovering the private key into solving a multivariate linear system over the base field. Extensive experiments have been performed and the results accord with our theoretical expectations. To prevent this attack, we give a simple but effective repair for this cryptosystem, which is shown to be secure against all the existing structural attacks. Furthermore, when applying this attack to analyze Loidreau's cryptosystem, we reduce the complexity of recovering a polynomial-time decoder of the public code.

References

1. Aguilar-Melchor, C., Blazy, O., Deneuville, J.-C., Gaborit, P., Zémor, G.: Efficient encryption from random quasi-cyclic codes. IEEE Trans. Inform. Theory **64**(5), 3927–3943 (2018)
2. Aragon, N., Gaborit, P., Hauteville, A., Ruatta, O., Zémor, G.: Low rank parity check codes: new decoding algorithms and applications to cryptography. IEEE Trans. Inform. Theory **65**(12), 7697–7717 (2019)

3. Aragon, N., Gaborit, P., Hauteville, A., Tillich, J.-P.: A new algorithm for solving the rank syndrome decoding problem. In: Proceedings of 2018 IEEE International Symposium on Information Theory (ISIT 2018), pp. 2421–2425. IEEE (2018)

4. Baldi, M., Chiaraluce, F., Garello, R.: On the usage of quasi-cyclic low-density parity-check codes in the McEliece cryptosystem. In: Proceedings of 2007 IEEE International Conference on Communications (ICC 2007), pp. 951–956. IEEE (2007)

5. Bardet, M., Briaud, P., Bros, M., Gaborit, P., Neiger, V., Ruatta, O., Tillich, J.-P.: An algebraic attack on rank metric code-based cryptosystems. In: Canteaut, A., Ishai, Y. (eds.) EUROCRYPT 2020. LNCS, vol. 12107, pp. 64–93. Springer, Cham (2020). https://doi.org/10.1007/978-3-030-45727-3_3

6. Bardet, M., Bros, M., Cabarcas, D., Gaborit, P., Perlner, R., Smith-Tone, D., Tillich, J.-P., Verbel, J.: Improvements of algebraic attacks for solving the rank decoding and MinRank problems. In: Moriai, S., Wang, H. (eds.) ASIACRYPT 2020. LNCS, vol. 12491, pp. 507–536. Springer, Cham (2020). https://doi.org/10.1007/978-3-030-64837-4_17

7. Berger, T., Loidreau, P.: Designing an efficient and secure public-key cryptosystem based on reducible rank codes. In: Canteaut, A., Viswanathan, K. (eds.) INDOCRYPT 2004. LNCS, vol. 3348, pp. 218–229. Springer, Heidelberg (2004). https://doi.org/10.1007/978-3-540-30556-9_18

8. Berlekamp, E.R., McEliece, R.J., Van Tilborg, H.: On the inherent intractability of certain coding problems. IEEE Trans. Inform. Theory $24(3)$, 384–386 (1978)

9. Bombar, M., Couvreur, A.: Decoding supercodes of gabidulin codes and applications to cryptanalysis. In: Cheon, J.H., Tillich, J.-P. (eds.) PQCrypto 2021 2021. LNCS, vol. 12841, pp. 3–22. Springer, Cham (2021). https://doi.org/10.1007/978-3-030-81293-5_1

10. Bosma, W., Cannon, J., Playoust, C.: The MAGMA algebra system I: the user language. J. Symbolic Comput. $24(3-4)$, 235–265 (1997)

11. Coggia, D., Couvreur, A.: On the security of a Loidreau rank metric code based encryption scheme. Des. Codes Crypt. $88(9)$, 1941–1957 (2020). https://doi.org/10.1007/s10623-020-00781-4

12. Faure, C., Loidreau, P.: A new public-key cryptosystem based on the problem of reconstructing p–polynomials. In: Ytrehus, Ø. (ed.) WCC 2005. LNCS, vol. 3969, pp. 304–315. Springer, Heidelberg (2006). https://doi.org/10.1007/11779360_24

13. Gabidulin, E.M.: Theory of codes with maximum rank distance. Prob. Peredachi Inf. $21(1)$, 3–16 (1985)

14. Gabidulin, E.M., Ourivski, A.V., Honary, B., Ammar, B.: Reducible rank codes and their applications to cryptography. IEEE Trans. Inform. Theory $49(12)$, 3289–3293 (2003)

15. Gabidulin, E.M., Paramonov, A.V., Tretjakov, O.V.: Ideals over a non-commutative ring and their application in cryptology. In: Davies, D.W. (ed.) EUROCRYPT 1991. LNCS, vol. 547, pp. 482–489. Springer, Heidelberg (1991). https://doi.org/10.1007/3-540-46416-6_41

16. Gaborit, P., Otmani, A., Kalachi, H.T.: Polynomial-time key recovery attack on the Faure-Loidreau scheme based on Gabidulin codes. Des. Codes Cryptogr. $86(7)$, 1391–1403 (2018)

17. Gaborit, P., Ruatta, O., Schrek, J.: On the complexity of the rank syndrome decoding problem. IEEE Trans. Inf. Theory $62(2)$, 1006–1019 (2016)

18. Ghatak, A.: Extending Coggia-Couvreur attack on Loidreau's rank-metric cryptosystem. Des. Codes Cryptogr. 90, 215–238 (2022)

19. Horlemann-Trautmann, A.-L., Marshall, K., Rosenthal, J.: Considerations for rank-based cryptosystems. In: Proceedings of 2016 IEEE International Symposium on Information Theory (ISIT 2016), pp. 2544–2548. IEEE (2016)

20. Horlemann-Trautmann, A.-L., Marshall, K., Rosenthal, J.: Extension of overbeck's attack for Gabidulin-based cryptosystems. Des. Codes Cryptogr. **86**(2), 319–340 (2018)

21. Horlemann-Trautmann, A.-L., Marshall, K.: New criteria for MRD and Gabidulin codes and some rank-metric code constructions. arXiv:1507.08641 [cs.IT] (2015)

22. Horlemann-Trautmann, A.-L., Werger, V.: Information set decoding in the Lee metric with applications to cryptography. Adv. Math. Commun. **15**(4), 677–699 (2021)

23. Janwa, H., Moreno, O.: McEliece public key cryptosystems using algebraic-geometric codes. Des. Codes Cryptogr. **8**(3), 293–307 (1996)

24. Lau, T.S.C., Tan, C.H.: New rank codes based encryption scheme using partial circulant matrices. Des. Codes Crypt. **87**(12), 2979–2999 (2019). https://doi.org/10.1007/s10623-019-00659-0

25. Lau, T.S.C., Tan, C.H.: A new encryption scheme based on rank metric codes. In: Susilo, W., Yang, G. (eds.) ACISP 2018. LNCS, vol. 10946, pp. 750–758. Springer, Cham (2018). https://doi.org/10.1007/978-3-319-93638-3_43

26. Lau, T.S.C., Tan, C.H.: A new technique in rank metric code-based encryption. Cryptography **2**(4), 32 (2018)

27. Loidreau, P.: A new rank metric codes based encryption scheme. In: Lange, T., Takagi, T. (eds.) PQCrypto 2017. LNCS, vol. 10346, pp. 3–17. Springer, Cham (2017). https://doi.org/10.1007/978-3-319-59879-6_1

28. Loidreau, P.: Analysis of a rank metric codes based encryption scheme. https://drive.google.com/file/d/1FuMgqm0NfGMJOxaZyrIrI1OWn0UICwPo/view. Accessed 1 July 2021

29. Loidreau, P.: A welch–berlekamp like algorithm for decoding gabidulin codes. In: Ytrehus, Ø. (ed.) WCC 2005. LNCS, vol. 3969, pp. 36–45. Springer, Heidelberg (2006). https://doi.org/10.1007/11779360_4

30. McEliece, R.J.: A public-key cryptosystem based on algebraic coding theory. Jet Propuls. Lab. DSN Progr. Rep. **42–44**, 114–116 (1978)

31. Niederreiter, H.: Knapsack-type cryptosystems and algebraic coding theory. Prob. Contr. Inform. Theory **15**(2), 157–166 (1986)

32. Otmani, A., Kalachi, H.T., Ndjeya, S.: Improved cryptanalysis of rank metric schemes based on Gabidulin codes. Des. Codes Cryptogr. **86**(9), 1983–1996 (2018)

33. Ourivski, A.V., Johansson, T.: New technique for decoding codes in the rank metric and its cryptography applications. Problems Inform. Transm. **38**(3), 237–246 (2002)

34. Overbeck, R.: Structural attacks for public key cryptosystems based on Gabidulin codes. J. Cryptology **21**(2), 280–301 (2008)

35. Renner, J., Puchinger, S., Wachter-Zeh, A.: LIGA: a cryptosystem based on the hardness of rank-metric list and interleaved decoding. Des. Codes Cryptogr. **89**(6), 1279–1319 (2021). Springer

36. Richter, G., Plass, S.: Error and erasure decoding of rank-codes with a modified Berlekamp-Massey algorithm. ITG FACHBERICHT, pp. 203–210 (2004)

37. Shor, P.W.: Polynomial-time algorithms for prime factorization and discrete logarithms on a quantum computer. SIAM Rev. **41**(2), 303–332 (1994)

Public-Key Cryptography

Chosen Ciphertext Secure Keyed Two-Level Homomorphic Encryption

Yusaku Maeda[1] and Koji Nuida[2,3(✉)]

[1] The University of Tokyo, Tokyo, Japan
[2] Institute of Mathematics for Industry (IMI), Kyushu University, Fukuoka, Japan
nuida@imi.kyushu-u.ac.jp
[3] National Institute of Advanced Industrial Science and Technology (AIST),
Tokyo, Japan

Abstract. Homomorphic encryption (HE) is a useful variant of public key encryption (PKE), but it has a drawback that HE cannot fully achieve IND-CCA2 security, a standard security notion for PKE. Emura et al. (PKC 2013) proposed a "keyed" version of HE, called KH-PKE, which introduces a separate key for homomorphic evaluation and then achieves security close to IND-CCA2. Current KH-PKE schemes are classified into ones supporting only a single kind of homomorphic operation (addition or multiplication) and others that are fully homomorphic but are consequently not very efficient; no intermediate schemes with both efficiency and richer functionality are known so far. In this paper, we propose a "two-level" KH-PKE scheme for evaluating degree-two polynomials, by cleverly combining Emura et al.'s generic framework with a recent efficient two-level HE by Attrapadung et al. (ASIACCS 2018).

1 Introduction

1.1 Background

Homomorphic encryption (HE) is a cryptographic primitive first introduced in [16], which allows one to compute on encrypted data without a secret key. The most basic and efficient HE are additively HE (AHE), which only allows addition between ciphertexts, and multiplicative HE, which only allows multiplication. On the other hand, fully homomorphic encryption (FHE) can carry out arbitrary computations on encrypted data, but efficiency of FHE is still not sufficiently practical. To take the advantages of both types of HE, somewhat homomorphic encryption (SHE) allows one to compute unlimited number of addition and a limited number of multiplication. Among them, two-level homomorphic encryption (2LHE) schemes [3,5,11], which enables a single multiplication (as well as unlimited number of addition), have significantly better efficiency. The state-of-the-art 2LHE scheme at the present is the one by Attrapadung et al. in 2018 [3] based on prime-order pairing group and practical computational assumption (SXDH assumption).

Although HE is useful, it has a drawback that an HE scheme cannot in principle satisfy IND-CCA2 security, a standard security notion for public key

K. Nguyen et al. (Eds.): ACISP 2022, LNCS 13494, pp. 209–228, 2022.
https://doi.org/10.1007/978-3-031-22301-3_11

encryption (PKE). Roughly speaking, this is because enabling computation over ciphertexts is equivalent to allowing alteration of ciphertexts, the latter being contradictory to IND-CCA2 security. To overcome this issue, Emura et al. pointed out that the property that anyone could perform homomorphic operation was the main obstacle for achieving IND-CCA2 security, and proposed keyed-homomorphic PKE (KH-PKE) [9,10][1]. In KH-PKE, the homomorphic operation is administrated by an evaluation key ek. They also proposed a new security notion called KH-CCA security for KH-PKE. KH-CCA security achieves IND-CCA1 security against adversaries possessing ek from the beginning, and IND-CCA2 security against those not possessing ek at all (and some intermediate security if ek is leaked during the security game). They also gave a concrete construction of KH-PKE schemes using hash proof systems (HPSs) [7,8].

Emura et al.'s KH-PKE scheme is practically efficient, but it realizes the functionality of AHE only. There are also other KH-PKE schemes with single kind of functionality [12,14]. On the other hand, fully homomorphic KH-PKE schemes are proposed in [13] using indistinguishability obfuscation ($i\mathcal{O}$) and recently in [17] without $i\mathcal{O}$; but these are not very efficient similarly to ordinary (i.e., non-keyed) FHE. In contrast to ordinary HE, the existing KH-PKE schemes in the literature have no counterparts of SHE (such as 2LHE) that have stronger functionality than [9,10,12,14] and are significantly more efficient than [13,17].

1.2   Our Contributions

In this paper, we introduce new type of KH-PKE named *keyed two-level homomorphic encryption (Keyed-2LHE)*, which can handle unlimited number of addition and a single multiplication over ciphertexts administrated by an evaluation key. We also give a concrete construction of Keyed-2LHE schemes. Although our Keyed-2LHE scheme has some overhead compared to the KH-PKE scheme by Emura et al. [9,10] and to the 2LHE scheme by Attrapadung et al. [3], the underlying setting (prime-order pairing groups and SXDH assumption) is the same as [3] and the overhead is within a feasible range (e.g., our public key and ciphertext sizes are only up to four times larger than those of [3]). This is the first KH-PKE that allows both addition and multiplication with practical efficiency.

The very first idea for constructing our Keyed-2LHE scheme is simple; it is a kind of abstraction of Attrapadung et al.'s 2LHE scheme that can then be interpreted in the context of Emura et al.'s generic framework for realizing KH-PKE. We emphasize, however, that it was never a straightforward task to successfully combine the two schemes. In detail, the generic construction by Emura et al. uses three kinds of HPSs P, $\widehat{P}$, and $\widetilde{P}$. Here P is for masking the plaintext, and $\widetilde{P}$ is for achieving IND-CCA2 security when the evaluation key is not used. The role of $\widehat{P}$ is most complicated; it should simultaneously

---

[1] The notion of KH-PKE was proposed in 2013 [10]. A construction for concrete KH-PKE schemes was also given in that paper, but its security proof was not correct and their scheme was actually not secure. The issue was then fixed in 2018 [9] by modifying the construction as well as the security proof.

take care of having (additive) homomorphic property and achieving IND-CCA1 security when the evaluation key is available. In our proposed scheme, there are two levels of ciphertexts, and hence $3 \times 2 = 6$ HPSs are used in total. Among them, the constructions of five HPSs except $\widehat{P}$ for level-2 ciphertexts are relatively simple; these are, in some sense, direct products of HPSs where the underlying HPSs follow known constructions already used by Emura et al. [9]. On the other hand, for the $\widehat{P}$ in level-2 part, it is not sufficient to take care of additive homomorphic property and IND-CCA1 security; it should also be related in an appropriate manner to the HPSs in level-1 part in order to realize multiplicative homomorphic property. For simultaneously achieving these three requirements, the known construction of HPSs used in [9] was not enough, and we had to develop a new tailor-made HPS to fill in the last piece of our construction. We also note that our resulting scheme fortunately shares a key property (called source ciphertext hiding property) with Emura et al.'s construction, which makes the security proof of our proposed scheme just analogous to the proof in [9].

1.3   Related Work

There are also several researches on achieving security close to IND-CCA2 while allowing computation over ciphertexts [2,6,15]. However, they differ from KH-PKE in that they are not equipped with an evaluation key and they only achieve security strictly weaker than IND-CCA2 (in contrast to our scheme achieving IND-CCA2 security against adversaries not possessing the evaluation key).

1.4   Organization of the Paper

In Sect. 2, we review some basic notions and prepare notations. In Sect. 3, we describe hash proof systems. In Sect. 4, we define syntax and security notion for Keyed-2LHE, and give a concrete description of our proposed scheme. Finally, we evaluate the efficiency of our proposed scheme in Sect. 5.

2   Preliminaries

Throughout the paper, "PPT" stands for "probabilistic polynomial-time". For a probabilistic algorithm $\mathcal{A}$, we write $a \leftarrow \mathcal{A}$ to represent that a is obtained as an output of $\mathcal{A}$. Similarly, for a set A, we write $a \leftarrow A$ to represent that a is chosen from A uniformly at random. We say that a non-negative function $f(\lambda)$ in an integer λ is *negligible* if $f(\lambda) \in \lambda^{-\omega(1)}$. We write $\mathbb{Z}/N\mathbb{Z}$ simply as $\mathbb{Z}_N$.

Let $X = \{X_n\}_{n \in \mathbb{N}}$ and $Y = \{Y_n\}_{n \in \mathbb{N}}$ be families of random variables defined on a finite set Ω. X and Y are said to be *ε-close* if the statistical distance satisfies

$$\Delta(X_n, Y_n) = \frac{1}{2} \sum_{\omega \in \Omega} |\Pr[X_n = \omega] - \Pr[Y_n = \omega]| \leq \varepsilon .$$

Furthermore, when $\varepsilon = \varepsilon(n)$ is negligible in n, we say that X and Y are *statistically indistinguishable*, denoted by $X \overset{s}{\approx} Y$. On the other hand, X and Y are said to be *computationally indistinguishable*, denoted by $X \overset{c}{\approx} Y$, if for any PPT algorithm $\mathcal{A}$, we have $|\Pr[\mathcal{A}(X_n) = 1] - \Pr[\mathcal{A}(Y_n) = 1]| \leq \mathrm{negl}(n)$ where $\mathrm{negl}(n)$ denotes a negligible function in n.

Definition 1 (approximate samplability). *For a finite set B_n and its subset B'_n indexed by $n \in \mathbb{N}$, we say B'_n is approximately samplable relative to B_n if there exists a sequence of random variables on B_n that is statistically indistinguishable from the uniform distribution on B'_n and polynomial-time samplable.*

Definition 2 (collision resistant hash function).. *Let $\{f_i\}_{i \in I}$ be a family of hash functions indexed by $i \in I$, specified by the security parameter 1^ℓ. $\{f_i\}_{i \in I}$ is said to be* collision resistant (CR) *if for any PPT algorithm $\mathcal{A}$, the probability*

$$\Pr[x \neq x^* \wedge f_i(x) = f_i(x^*) \mid i \leftarrow I; (x, x^*) \leftarrow \mathcal{A}(1^\ell, i)]$$

is negligible in ℓ.

2.1 Pairings

Definition 3 (bilinear group generation algorithm). *A bilinear group generation algorithm* GenBG *takes a security parameter 1^ℓ as input, and outputs $(p, \mathbb{G}_1, \mathbb{G}_2, \mathbb{G}_T, g_1, g_2, e)$. Here, $\mathbb{G}_1, \mathbb{G}_2$, and $\mathbb{G}_T$ are cyclic groups of prime order $p = \Theta(2^\ell)$, while g_1, g_2 are generators of $\mathbb{G}_1, \mathbb{G}_2$, respectively, and $e \colon \mathbb{G}_1 \times \mathbb{G}_2 \to \mathbb{G}_T$ is a non-degenerate bilinear map called pairing.*

Definition 4 (SXDH assumption). *We say that Symmetric External Diffie–Hellman (SXDH) assumption holds in* GenBG*, when for* pp $=$ $(p, \mathbb{G}_1, \mathbb{G}_2, \mathbb{G}_T, g_1, g_2, e) \leftarrow$ GenBG(1^ℓ) *and $i = 1, 2$, we have*

$$\{(\mathrm{pp}, g_i^\alpha, g_i^\beta, g_i^{\alpha\beta}) \mid \alpha, \beta \leftarrow \mathbb{Z}_p\} \overset{c}{\approx} \{(\mathrm{pp}, g_i^\alpha, g_i^\beta, g_i^\gamma) \mid \alpha, \beta, \gamma \leftarrow \mathbb{Z}_p\}.$$

2.2 Notation

From now on, all operations on cyclic groups will be written additively, unless otherwise noted. Also for simplicity, for $x \in \mathbb{G}_1$ and $y \in \mathbb{G}_2$, we write $x \otimes y := e(x, y)$. We will extend this notation to matrices in the following manner. We define the tensor product between $x \in \mathbb{G}_1$ and a matrix $Y = (y_{ij}) \in \mathbb{G}_2^{k \times \ell}$ as

$$x \otimes Y := \begin{bmatrix} x \otimes y_{11} & \cdots & x \otimes y_{1\ell} \\ \vdots & \ddots & \vdots \\ x \otimes y_{k1} & \cdots & x \otimes y_{k\ell} \end{bmatrix} \in \mathbb{G}_T^{k \times \ell}$$

and for a matrix $X = (x_{ij}) \in \mathbb{G}_1^{m \times n}$, we define the tensor product between X and Y as

$$X \otimes Y := \begin{bmatrix} x_{11} \otimes Y & \cdots & x_{1n} \otimes Y \\ \vdots & \ddots & \vdots \\ x_{m1} \otimes Y & \cdots & x_{mn} \otimes Y \end{bmatrix} \in \mathbb{G}_T^{mk \times n\ell}.$$

Note that this definition satisfies $(X \otimes Y)^\top = X^\top \otimes Y^\top$, where $\top$ represents the trasposition of a matrix.

Furthermore, we define the tensor product between two elements $a, b \in \mathbb{Z}_p$ as $a \otimes b := ab$, and extend it to matrices over $\mathbb{Z}_p$ in a similar manner as above. Also, multiplication of a matrix over $\mathbb{Z}_p$ to a matrix with components in $\mathbb{G}_1$, $\mathbb{G}_2$, or $\mathbb{G}_T$ is defined in the same way as the usual matrix multiplication where the scalar multiplication to group elements plays the role of multiplication between matrix components. Note that these definitions satisfy $(AX) \otimes (BY) = (A \otimes B)(X \otimes Y)$ (assuming that the matrix sizes are consistent to multiplication), where A and B are matrices over $\mathbb{Z}_p$, X is a matrix over $\mathbb{G}_1$, and Y is a matrix over $\mathbb{G}_2$.

Under the notations, SXDH assumption can be rewritten as follows.

Proposition 1. *SXDH assumption is equivalent to the following statement: for* $\mathsf{pp} = (p, \mathbb{G}_1, \mathbb{G}_2, \mathbb{G}_T, g_1, g_2, e) \leftarrow \mathsf{GenBG}(1^\ell)$, $g_1' \leftarrow \mathbb{G}_1$, $g_2' \leftarrow \mathbb{G}_2$, $\boldsymbol{g}_1 = (g_1, g_1') \in \mathbb{G}_1^2$, *and* $\boldsymbol{g}_2 = (g_2, g_2') \in \mathbb{G}_2^2$, *we have for both* $i = 1, 2$

$$\{(\mathsf{pp}, \boldsymbol{g}_i, \boldsymbol{x}) \mid \boldsymbol{x} \leftarrow \langle \boldsymbol{g}_i \rangle\} \overset{c}{\approx} \{(\mathsf{pp}, \boldsymbol{g}_i, \boldsymbol{x}) \mid \boldsymbol{x} \leftarrow \mathbb{G}_i^2\} \ .$$

Proof. Two distributions in the statement can be rewritten as

$$\{(\mathsf{pp}, \boldsymbol{g}_i, \boldsymbol{x}) \mid \boldsymbol{x} \leftarrow \langle \boldsymbol{g}_i \rangle\} = \{(\mathsf{pp}, (g_i, \alpha g_i), (\beta g_i, \alpha\beta g_i)) \mid \alpha, \beta \leftarrow \mathbb{Z}_p\} \ ,$$

$$\{(\mathsf{pp}, \boldsymbol{g}_i, \boldsymbol{x}) \mid \boldsymbol{x} \leftarrow \mathbb{G}_i^2\} = \{(\mathsf{pp}, (g_i, \alpha g_i), (\beta g_i, \gamma g_i)) \mid \alpha, \beta, \gamma \leftarrow \mathbb{Z}_p\} \ ,$$

which are obviously equivalent to the distributions in Definition 4. □

3   Hash Proof Systems

Definition 5 (hash proof system). *Let* X, Π *be finite sets and* $\emptyset \neq L \subset X$. *We assume that any* $x \in L$ *has a witness* w *to ensure that* $x \in L$, *and that a random element of* L *can be efficiently sampled together with its witness. Then Hash Proof System (HPS)* $\boldsymbol{P} = (X, L, \Pi)$ *consists of the following five algorithms.*

- *SetUp(1^ℓ), with security parameter 1^ℓ, outputs public parameter pp, which includes descriptions of sets X and L.*
- *HashKG(pp) outputs a secret key hk.*
- *ProjKG(hk) outputs the corresponding public key hp.*
- *Hash(hk, x), with $x \in X$, outputs the corresponding hash value $\pi \in \Pi$.*
- *ProjHash(hp, x, w), with $x \in L$ and its witness w, outputs the corresponding hash value $\pi \in \Pi$.*

We define W, K, S *to be the sets consisting of all the possible values of witness* w, *secret keys* hk, *and public keys* hp, *respectively.*

We may omit input hk in the algorithm Hash or inputs hp, w in ProjHash when they are obvious from the context. Also, when we give concrete constructions of the above algorithms, we may omit the description on SetUp if it is obvious.

HPS is required to satisfy the correctness: for pp $\leftarrow$ SetUp(1^ℓ), hk $\leftarrow$ HashKG(pp), hp $\leftarrow$ ProjKG(hk), and for any $x \in L$ and its witness w, we have Hash(hk, x) = ProjHash(hp, x, w).

Definition 6 (smoothness). *HPS is said to be ε-smooth relative to $X' \subset X$ if for* pp $\leftarrow$ SetUp(1^ℓ), hk $\leftarrow$ HashKG(pp), *and* hp $\leftarrow$ ProjKG(hk), *the following two distributions*

$$\{(\mathsf{hp}, x, \mathsf{Hash}(x)) \mid x \leftarrow X' \setminus L\}, \quad \{(\mathsf{hp}, x, \pi) \mid x \leftarrow X' \setminus L, \pi \leftarrow \Pi\}$$

are ε-close. When ε is negligible in ℓ, we simply say that the HPS is smooth.

Definition 7 (universal$_1$). *HPS is said to be ε-universal$_1$ if for any* hp $\in S$, $x \in X \setminus L$, *and $\pi \in \Pi$, we have*

$$\Pr_{\mathsf{hk} \leftarrow K}[\mathsf{Hash}(\mathsf{hk}, x) = \pi \wedge \mathsf{ProjKG}(\mathsf{hk}) = \mathsf{hp}] \le \varepsilon \cdot \Pr_{\mathsf{hk} \leftarrow K}[\mathsf{ProjKG}(\mathsf{hk}) = \mathsf{hp}] .$$

When ε is negligible in ℓ, we simply say that the HPS is universal$_1$.

Definition 8 (universal$_2$). *HPS is said to be (information-theoretically) ε-universal$_2$ if for any* hp $\in S$, $x, x^* \in X \setminus L$ *($x \neq x^*$), and $\pi, \pi^* \in \Pi$, we have*

$$\Pr_{\mathsf{hk} \leftarrow K}[\mathsf{Hash}(\mathsf{hk}, x) = \pi \wedge \mathsf{Hash}(\mathsf{hk}, x^*) = \pi^* \wedge \mathsf{ProjKG}(\mathsf{hk}) = \mathsf{hp}]$$
$$\le \varepsilon \cdot \Pr_{\mathsf{hk} \leftarrow K}[\mathsf{Hash}(\mathsf{hk}, x^*) = \pi^* \wedge \mathsf{ProjKG}(\mathsf{hk}) = \mathsf{hp}] .$$

When ε is negligible in ℓ, we simply say that the HPS is universal$_2$.

Its computational variant was also defined in [9] as follows.

Definition 9 (first-adaptive computationally universal$_2$). *Let P be a HPS. We define the following game between a challenger and an adversary $\mathcal{A}$:*

1. *The challenger randomly picks* pp $\leftarrow$ SetUp(1^ℓ) *and* hk $\leftarrow K$, *computes* hp $\leftarrow$ ProjKG(hk), *and sends* pp, hp *to $\mathcal{A}$.*
2. *$\mathcal{A}$ queries to* Hash *oracle. Hash oracle takes $x \in X$ as input and returns* Hash(hk, x) *if $x \in L$, and returns $\perp$ otherwise.*
3. *At an arbitrary point of the game, $\mathcal{A}$ submits $x^* \in X$ to the challenger. The challenger responds by sending $\pi^* =$ Hash(hk, x^*) back to $\mathcal{A}$. $\mathcal{A}$ is allowed to continue* Hash *queries even after the submission.*
4. *$\mathcal{A}$ outputs $x \in X \setminus L$ and $\pi \in \Pi$.*

$\mathcal{A}$ wins the game if the output of the game satisfies $x \neq x^*$ and Hash(hk, x) = π. *We say that P is* first-adaptive computationally universal$_2$, *if the probability for winning the game is negligible in ℓ for any PPT algorithm $\mathcal{A}$.*

Definition 10 (hardness of a subset membership problem). *We say that subset membership problem of the HPS is* hard *relative to $X' \subset X$ if for* pp $\leftarrow$ SetUp(1^ℓ), *we have* $\{(\mathsf{pp}, x) \mid x \leftarrow L\} \overset{c}{\approx} \{(\mathsf{pp}, x) \mid x \leftarrow X' \setminus L\}$.

This intuitively means that an element of L and an element of $X' \backslash L$ cannot be distinguished in polynomial time. We note that there are cases where distinction is possible given an additional information, formalized as follows.

Definition 11 (trapdoor subset membership problem). *When HPS has the following two PPT algorithms in addition to the five algorithms in Definition 5, we say that the subset membership problem associated to the HPS has a trapdoor:*

- TrapdoorSetUp(1^ℓ) *takes security parameter 1^ℓ as input, and outputs public parameter* pp *together with a trapdoor τ.*
- Distinguish(x, τ) *takes $x \in X$ and a trapdoor τ as inputs and decides whether $x \in L$ or not.*

3.1 Construction of HPS Based on Diverse Vector Space

As a generic construction of HPS, a construction based on a diverse group system is proposed in [8]. However, since we only deal with the construction based on cyclic groups, it is more convenient to think about the special case of diverse group system called diverse vector space [1,4]. All the HPSs used for our proposed scheme are based on this framework.

The definition of a diverse vector space is given below, which is slightly modified from the definition in [1] in order to make our argument simpler.

Definition 12 (diverse vector space). *Let $\mathbb{G}$ be a cyclic group of prime order p, $X = \mathbb{G}^n$, and $L = \langle g_1, \ldots, g_d \rangle \subset X$. Now any homomorphism $\phi \colon X \to \Pi = \mathbb{G}$ can be represented as $\phi(x) = k^\top x$ for some $k \in \mathbb{Z}_p^n$. Therefore, $\mathrm{Hom}(X, \Pi)$ can be identified with $K = \mathbb{Z}_p^n$. We call the tuple (K, X, L, Π) a diverse vector space.*

In the remaining part of this section, we assume $d = 1$ for simplicity.

Given a diverse vector space (K, X, L, Π), we can construct an HPS as follows. Note that the witness for $x \in L$ can be set as $w \in \mathbb{Z}_p$ that satisfies $x = wg$.

- HashKG(pp), with public parameter pp, outputs hk $= k \leftarrow K$.
- ProjKG(hk), with secret key hk $= k$, outputs a public key hp $= s := k^\top g$.
- Hash(hk, x), with hk $= k$ and $x \in X$, outputs a hash value $\pi = k^\top x$.
- ProjHash(hp, x, w), with public key hp $= s$ and $x \in L$ together with its witness w, outputs a hash value $\pi = ws$.

The correctness of the above construction can be shown by checking

$$\mathsf{Hash}(x) = k^\top x = k^\top (wg) = w(k^\top g) = ws = \mathsf{ProjHash}(x, w).$$

Proposition 2. *The above HPS is 0-smooth and $(1/p)$-universal$_1$. Also, the subset membership problem associated to the HPS has a trapdoor.*

Proof. The smoothness and the universal$_1$ property follow from Example 1 in Section 7.4.1 of [8]. On the other hand, we can check that the subset membership problem has a trapdoor, by giving two algorithms in Definition 11 as follows:

- TrapdoorSetUp(1^ℓ) generates a generator g of L by calculating

$$\boldsymbol{g} = (g, \tau_1 \cdot g, \tau_2 \cdot g, \ldots, \tau_{n-1} \cdot g) \text{ where } g \leftarrow \mathbb{G} \setminus \{0\}, \tau_1, \ldots, \tau_{n-1} \leftarrow \mathbb{Z}_p$$

and outputs $\tau := (\tau_1, \ldots, \tau_{n-1})$ as a trapdoor.
- Distinguish($\boldsymbol{x}, \tau$) takes $\boldsymbol{x} = (x_0, \ldots, x_{n-1}) \in X$ and $\tau = (\tau_1, \ldots, \tau_{n-1})$ as inputs, and check if $x_i = \tau_i \cdot x_0$ holds for $i = 1, \ldots, n-1$. If all the conditions are satisfied, the algorithm decides $\boldsymbol{x} \in L$, and otherwise decides $\boldsymbol{x} \notin L$.

Hence the claim holds. □

Also, we can construct universal$_2$ HPS by combining the above construction with a hash function. Let E be a finite set, and modify the definitions of X and L by $X = \mathbb{G}^n \times E$, $L = \langle \boldsymbol{g} \rangle \times E$. In addition, let $\Gamma \colon X \to \mathbb{Z}_p^m$ be a hash function.

- HashKG(pp) outputs hk $= (\boldsymbol{k}_0, \ldots, \boldsymbol{k}_m) \leftarrow (\mathbb{Z}_p^n)^{m+1}$.
- ProjKG(hk) outputs hp $= (s_0, \ldots, s_m) := (\boldsymbol{k}_0^\top \boldsymbol{g}, \ldots, \boldsymbol{k}_m^\top \boldsymbol{g})$.
- Hash(hk, $(\boldsymbol{x}, e)$), with $(\boldsymbol{x}, e) \in X$, calculates $\Gamma(\boldsymbol{x}, e) = (\gamma_1, \ldots, \gamma_m)$ and outputs

$$\pi = \boldsymbol{k}_0^\top \boldsymbol{x} + \sum_{i=1}^m \gamma_i \boldsymbol{k}_i^\top \boldsymbol{x} \ .$$

- ProjHash(hp, $(\boldsymbol{x}, e), w$) with $(\boldsymbol{x}, e) \in L$ and the corresponding witness w, calculates $\Gamma(\boldsymbol{x}, e) = (\gamma_1, \ldots, \gamma_m)$ and outputs

$$\pi = w s_0 + \sum_{i=1}^m \gamma_i w s_i \ .$$

Proposition 3. *For the HPS above, if Γ is injective, then the HPS is information-theoretically universal$_2$. If Γ is sampled from a family of collision resistant hash functions, then the HPS is first-adaptive computationally universal$_2$.*

Proof. The statement follows immediately from Proposition 1 of [9]. □

3.2   Direct Product of HPS

In this section, we define direct product of HPS, and describe some properties. We note that a notion of direct product of HPS is also defined in [1], but their definition slightly differs from ours.

Suppose that two HPSs $P_1 = (X_1, L_1, \Pi_1)$, $P_2 = (X_2, L_2, \Pi_2)$ are given. We denote algorithms and sets related to each HPS by putting the corresponding subscript. In this situation, we can construct a new HPS $P = (X_1 \times X_2, L_1 \times L_2, \Pi_1 \times \Pi_2)$ in the following manner.

- HashKG(pp) calculates hk$_i \leftarrow$ HashKG$_i$(pp) ($i = 1, 2$), and outputs hk $= $ (hk$_1$, hk$_2$).
- ProjKG(hk) takes hk $= $ (hk$_1$, hk$_2$) as input, calculates hp$_i \leftarrow$ ProjKG$_i$(hk$_i$) ($i = 1, 2$), and outputs hp $= $ (hp$_1$, hp$_2$).

- Hash(hk, x) takes hk = (hk$_1$, hk$_2$) and $x = (x_1, x_2) \in X_1 \times X_2$ as inputs, calculates $\pi_i \leftarrow$ Hash$_i$(hk$_i$, x_i) ($i = 1, 2$), and outputs $\pi = (\pi_1, \pi_2)$.
- ProjHash(hp, x, w) takes hp = (hp$_1$, hp$_2$), $x = (x_1, x_2) \in L_1 \times L_2$ and the pair of the corresponding witnesses $w = (w_1, w_2)$ as inputs, calculates $\pi_i \leftarrow$ ProjHash$_i$(hp$_i$, x_i, w_i) ($i = 1, 2$), and outputs $\pi = (\pi_1, \pi_2)$.

Proposition 4. *The HPS $\boldsymbol{P}$ constructed as above satisfies the following:*

1. *If $\boldsymbol{P}_1$ and $\boldsymbol{P}_2$ are smooth, then $\boldsymbol{P}$ is smooth relative to $X' = (X_1 \setminus L_1) \times (X_2 \setminus L_2)$.*
2. *If $\boldsymbol{P}_1$ and $\boldsymbol{P}_2$ are universal$_1$, then $\boldsymbol{P}$ is universal$_1$.*
3. *If $\boldsymbol{P}_1$ and $\boldsymbol{P}_2$ are universal$_2$, then $\boldsymbol{P}$ is universal$_2$.*

Proof (Sketch). For Part 1, for pp $\leftarrow$ SetUp(1^ℓ), hk $\leftarrow$ HashKG(pp), and hp $\leftarrow$ ProjKG(hk), the two components of Hash(x) = (Hash$_1$(x_1), Hash$_2$(x_2)) given hp and $x \leftarrow X' \setminus L$ can be replaced in a statistically indistinguishable manner with random elements of Π_1 and Π_2 owing to the smoothness of $\boldsymbol{P}_1$ and $\boldsymbol{P}_2$, respectively. This implies the smoothness of $\boldsymbol{P}$.

For Part 2, if $x = (x_1, x_2) \in X \setminus L$, then we have $x_i \in X_i \setminus L_i$ for at least one $i \in \{1, 2\}$. Now the desired bound for the probability of Hash(x) = (π_1, π_2) is given by a bound for the probability of Hash$_i$(x_i) = π_i implied by the universal$_1$ property for $\boldsymbol{P}_i$. This implies the universal$_1$ property for $\boldsymbol{P}$. The case of Part 3 is similar.   □

Proposition 5. *If both $\boldsymbol{P}_1$ and $\boldsymbol{P}_2$ are first-adaptive computationally universal$_2$ and the subset membership problem for each of $\boldsymbol{P}_1$ and $\boldsymbol{P}_2$ has a trapdoor, then $\boldsymbol{P}$ is first-adaptive computationally universal$_2$ and its subset membership problem also has a trapdoor.*

Proof (Sketch). The statement for the existence of a trapdoor for $\boldsymbol{P}$ holds obviously. For the first-adaptive computationally universal$_2$ property, intuitively speaking, if a PPT adversary were able to break this property for $\boldsymbol{P}$, then the adversary could also break this property for either $\boldsymbol{P}_1$ or $\boldsymbol{P}_2$.   □

4 Keyed Two-Level Homomorphic Encryption

4.1 Syntax and Security Notion

The syntax and security notion for KH-PKE defined in [9,10] can be naturally extended to the case of 2LHE as follows.

Definition 13 (syntax of Keyed-2LHE). *Let $\mathcal{M}$ be a message space of the form $\mathcal{M} = \{(i, m) \mid i \in \{1, 2\}, m \in \mathcal{M}'\}$, where $\mathcal{M}'$ is a ring. We set $\mathcal{M}_i = \{i\} \times \mathcal{M}'$ for $i = 1, 2$. A keyed two-level homomorphic encryption (Keyed-2LHE) is defined by five algorithms below.*

- ParamGen(1^ℓ), *with security parameter 1^ℓ, outputs public parameter* pp.
- KeyGen(pp) *takes* pp *as input and outputs three keys* (pk, sk, ek).

- Enc(pk, m) *takes* pk *and* $m \in \mathcal{M}$ *as inputs and outputs ciphertext* C.
- Dec(sk, C) *takes* sk *and a ciphertext* C *as inputs and outputs plaintext* $m \in \mathcal{M}$ *or* $\perp$, *which represents a failure of decryption.*
- Eval(ek, f, C, C') *takes evaluation key* ek, *operation* $f: \mathcal{M}^2 \to \mathcal{M}$ *and two ciphertexts* C, C' *as inputs and outputs a ciphertext* C'' *or* $\perp$, *which represents a failure of evaluation. Here* f *is one of* Add$^{(1)}: \mathcal{M}_1^2 \to \mathcal{M}_1$, Add$^{(2)}: \mathcal{M}_2^2 \to \mathcal{M}_2$, *and* Mult: $\mathcal{M}_1^2 \to \mathcal{M}_2$, *which represent the following operations:*

$$\text{Add}^{(i)}: (i, m), (i, m') \mapsto (i, m + m') \text{ for } i \in \{1, 2\},$$
$$\text{Mult} \ : (1, m), (1, m') \mapsto (2, mm').$$

In a Keyed-2LHE scheme, we refer to a ciphertext corresponding to a plaintext with $i = 1$ as level-1 ciphertext. Level-2 ciphertext is defined similarly.

Definition 14 (KH-CCA secure Keyed-2LHE). *We say that a Keyed-2LHE scheme is KH-CCA secure if for any PPT adversary* $\mathcal{A}$, *its advantage given by*

$$\left| \Pr[\text{pp} \leftarrow \text{ParamGen}(1^\ell); (\text{pk}, \text{sk}, \text{ek}) \leftarrow \text{KeyGen}(\text{pp}); (i^*, m_0^*, m_1^*, \text{st}) \leftarrow \mathcal{A}^{\mathcal{O}}(\text{find}, \text{pk}); \right.$$

$$\left. b \leftarrow \{0, 1\}; C^* \leftarrow \text{Enc}(\text{pk}, (i^*, m_b^*)); b' \leftarrow \mathcal{A}^{\mathcal{O}}(\text{guess}, \text{st}, C^*): b = b'] - \frac{1}{2} \right|$$

is negligible in ℓ. *Here* $\mathcal{O}$ *denotes oracles* RevEK, Dec, Eval *described below, and we suppose that a list* List *is used throughout the KH-CCA game, which is set to* $\emptyset$ *in the* find *stage and set to* List $= (C^*)$ *at the beginning of the* guess *stage.*

- RevEK *returns evaluation key* ek.
- Dec *takes a ciphertext* C *as input and returns* $\perp$ *if* $C \in$ List, *and* Dec(sk, C) *if* $C \notin$ List.
- Eval *takes two ciphertexts* C, C' *and an operation* f *as inputs and returns* $C'' = $ Eval(ek, f, C, C'). *If* $C'' \neq \perp$ *and either* C *or* C' *is in* List, Eval *appends* C'' *to* List.

We also have the following constraints: RevEK *can be queried only once;* Eval *cannot be queried after* RevEK *has been queried; and* Dec *cannot be queried if* RevEK *is already queried and* $\mathcal{A}$ *has already received* C^* *from the challenger.*

As in the original KH-CCA security in [9,10], the list List was introduced for avoiding the following trivial attack: generate a ciphertext C' from the challenge ciphertext C^* by using Eval, send C' to the oracle Dec, and determine the plaintext of C^* by using its relation to the plaintext of C'.

4.2 Overview of Our Construction

When focusing on each level, our scheme mostly follows the generic construction in [10], i.e., there are three HPSs (corresponding to $P, \hat{P}, \tilde{P}$ in [10]) for each level. Therefore, we require six HPSs in total to construct our scheme.

Intuitively, $\boldsymbol{P}$ is used to hide information of the plaintext. The smoothness and the hardness of the subset membership problem of $\boldsymbol{P}$ guarantee that the hash value used to mask the plaintext is indistinguishable from a uniformly random value. Also, $\widehat{\boldsymbol{P}}$ guarantees security against an adversary who has ek, and $\widetilde{\boldsymbol{P}}$ guarantees security against an adversary who does not have ek. The universal property of $\widehat{\boldsymbol{P}}$ and $\widetilde{\boldsymbol{P}}$ means that the adversary cannot forge a hash value for a ciphertext calculated in a correct manner.

Compared to the construction in [10], the message space in our scheme is changed to $\mathcal{M}' = \mathbb{Z}_p$, and the construction of the ciphertext is slightly modified (in a way similar to so-called lifted-ElGamal cryptosystem). To apply this modification, a restriction on the message space is required; see Remark 1 below. Another difference is that for HPSs $\boldsymbol{P}$ and $\widehat{\boldsymbol{P}}$, key generation algorithms HashKG, ProjKG are common in both levels, and a hash value for the level-2 HPS can be calculated from those for the level-1 HPS by applying pairings. These properties are necessary for computing multiplications.

From now on, when we want to specify levels of HPS or the corresponding sets and algorithms, we denote this by using superscripts "(1)" and "(2)".

4.3   Construction of Hash Proof System

In this section, we give concrete constructions of HPSs for the proposed scheme.

All the HPSs described here computes $(p, \mathbb{G}_1, \mathbb{G}_2, \mathbb{G}_T, g_1, g_2, e) \leftarrow \mathsf{GenBG}(1^\ell)$, chooses $g_1' \leftarrow \mathbb{G}_1$, $g_2' \leftarrow \mathbb{G}_2$ and sets $\boldsymbol{g}_1 := (g_1, g_1') \in \mathbb{G}_1^2$, $\boldsymbol{g}_2 := (g_2, g_2') \in \mathbb{G}_2^2$. Then, as pp, $\mathsf{SetUp}(1^\ell)$ outputs these together with $g_T := g_1 \otimes g_2$, $\boldsymbol{h}_1 := \boldsymbol{g}_1 \otimes g_2$, $\boldsymbol{h}_2 := g_1 \otimes \boldsymbol{g}_2$, and $\boldsymbol{h}_3 := \boldsymbol{g}_1 \otimes \boldsymbol{g}_2$. For universal$_2$ HPSs, we assume that the setup algorithm also outputs hash functions necessary for the construction.

HPS (Level-1). Let $X = \mathbb{G}_1^2 \times \mathbb{G}_2^2$ and $L = \langle \boldsymbol{g}_1 \rangle \times \langle \boldsymbol{g}_2 \rangle$. The witness for $x = (\boldsymbol{x}_1, \boldsymbol{x}_2) \in L$ is $w = (w_1, w_2) \in \mathbb{Z}_p^2$ that satisfies $(\boldsymbol{x}_1, \boldsymbol{x}_2) = (w_1 \boldsymbol{g}_1, w_2 \boldsymbol{g}_2)$. Furthermore, let $X' = (\mathbb{G}_1^2 \setminus \langle \boldsymbol{g}_1 \rangle) \times (\mathbb{G}_2^2 \setminus \langle \boldsymbol{g}_2 \rangle)$, $\Pi = \widehat{\Pi} = \widetilde{\Pi} = \mathbb{G}_1 \times \mathbb{G}_2$. In this situation, we define three HPSs for level-1 ciphertexts $\boldsymbol{P}^{(1)} = (X, L, \Pi)$, $\widehat{\boldsymbol{P}}^{(1)} = (X, L, \widehat{\Pi})$, $\widetilde{\boldsymbol{P}}^{(1)} = (X \times \Pi \times \widehat{\Pi}, L \times \Pi \times \widehat{\Pi}, \widetilde{\Pi})$ as in Fig. 1.

Proposition 6. $\boldsymbol{P}^{(1)}$ *satisfies the following:*

1. $\boldsymbol{P}^{(1)}$ *is smooth relative to* X'.
2. *Under SXDH assumption, the subset membership problem of* $\boldsymbol{P}^{(1)}$ *is hard relative to* X' *and has a trapdoor.*
3. $X' \setminus L$ *is approximately samplable relative to* X.

Proof. Since $\boldsymbol{P}^{(1)}$ can be interpreted as the direct product of two HPSs constructed via generic construction based on a diverse vector space, the smoothness follows from Proposition 4. The hardness of the subset membership problem and the trapdoor property follow from Propositions 1 and 2, respectively.

The approximate samplability can be deduced from the fact that the uniform distribution on $X' \setminus L$ is statistically indistinguishable from the uniform distribution on X, as $|X' \setminus L| = p^2(p-1)^2$ and $|X| = p^4$. $\square$

$P^{(1)}$	$\widehat{P}^{(1)}$	$\widetilde{P}^{(1)}$
HashKG(pp): $k_i \leftarrow \mathbb{Z}_p^2$ $(i=1,2)$ Output hk $= (k_1, k_2)$	$\widehat{\text{HashKG}}$(pp): $\widehat{k}_i \leftarrow \mathbb{Z}_p^2$ $(i=1,2)$ Output $\widehat{\text{hk}} = (\widehat{k}_1, \widehat{k}_2)$	$\widetilde{\text{HashKG}}$(pp): $(\widetilde{k}_{ij})_{j=0}^n \leftarrow (\mathbb{Z}_p^2)^{n+1}$ $(i=1,2)$ Output $\widetilde{\text{hk}} = ((\widetilde{k}_{1j})_{j=0}^n, (\widetilde{k}_{2j})_{j=0}^n)$
ProjKG(hk): $s_i = k_i^\top g_i$ $(i=1,2)$ Output hp $= (s_1, s_2)$	$\widehat{\text{ProjKG}}(\widehat{\text{hk}})$: $\widehat{s}_i = \widehat{k}_i^\top g_i$ $(i=1,2)$ Output $\widehat{\text{hp}} = (\widehat{s}_1, \widehat{s}_2)$	$\widetilde{\text{ProjKG}}(\widetilde{\text{hk}})$: $\widetilde{s}_{ij} = \widetilde{k}_{ij}^\top g_i$ $(i=1,2,\ j=0,\dots,n)$ Output $\widetilde{\text{hp}} = ((\widetilde{s}_{1j})_{j=0}^n, (\widetilde{s}_{2j})_{j=0}^n)$
Hash(hk, x): $\pi_i = k_i^\top x_i$ $(i=1,2)$ Output $\pi = (\pi_1, \pi_2)$	$\widehat{\text{Hash}}(\widehat{\text{hk}}, x)$: $\widehat{\pi}_i = \widehat{k}_i^\top x_i$ $(i=1,2)$ Output $\widehat{\pi} = (\widehat{\pi}_1, \widehat{\pi}_2)$	$\widetilde{\text{Hash}}(\widetilde{\text{hk}}, (x, e, \widehat{\pi}))$: $(\gamma_{ij})_{j=1}^n = \Gamma_i(x_i, e_i, \widehat{\pi}_i)$ $(i=1,2)$ $\widetilde{\pi}_i = \widetilde{k}_{i0}^\top x_i + \sum_{j=1}^n \gamma_{ij} \widetilde{k}_{ij}^\top x_i$ $(i=1,2)$ Output $\widetilde{\pi} = (\widetilde{\pi}_1, \widetilde{\pi}_2)$
ProjHash(hp, x, w): $\pi_i = w_i s_i$ $(i=1,2)$ Output $\pi = (\pi_1, \pi_2)$	$\widehat{\text{ProjHash}}(\widehat{\text{hp}}, x, w)$: $\widehat{\pi}_i = w_i \widehat{s}_i$ $(i=1,2)$ Output $\widehat{\pi} = (\widehat{\pi}_1, \widehat{\pi}_2)$	$\widetilde{\text{ProjHash}}(\widetilde{\text{hp}}, (x, e, \widehat{\pi}), w)$: $(\gamma_{ij})_{j=1}^n = \Gamma_i(x_i, e_i, \widehat{\pi}_i)$ $(i=1,2)$ $\widetilde{\pi}_i = w_i \widetilde{s}_{i0} + w_i \sum_{j=1}^n \gamma_{ij} \widetilde{s}_{ij}$ $(i=1,2)$ Output $\widetilde{\pi} = (\widetilde{\pi}_1, \widetilde{\pi}_2)$

Fig. 1. HPSs for level-1 ciphertexts, where $\Gamma_1 \colon \mathbb{G}_1^4 \to \mathbb{Z}_p^n$ and $\Gamma_2 \colon \mathbb{G}_2^4 \to \mathbb{Z}_p^n$ are hash functions

Proposition 7. $\widehat{P}^{(1)}$ *is universal₁.*

Proof. Since $\widehat{P}^{(1)}$ can be interpreted as the direct product of two $(1/p)$-universal₁ HPSs constructed by applying generic construction based on a diverse vector space, the statement follows from Proposition 4. □

Proposition 8. $\widetilde{P}^{(1)}$ *satisfies the following:*

1. *If Γ_1 and Γ_2 are injective, then $\widetilde{P}^{(1)}$ is information-theoretically universal₂.*
2. *If Γ_1 and Γ_2 are sampled from a family of collision resistant hash functions, then $\widetilde{P}^{(1)}$ is first-adaptive computationally universal₂.*

Proof. Since $\widetilde{P}^{(1)}$ can be interpreted as the direct product of two HPSs constructed by applying generic construction based on a diverse vector space, the statement follows from Propositions 4 and 5. □

HPS (Level-2). Let $X = \mathbb{G}_T^4 \times \mathbb{G}_T^2 \times \mathbb{G}_T^2$ and $L = \langle h_1 \rangle \times \langle h_2 \rangle \times \langle h_3 \rangle$. A witness for $x = (x_1, x_2, x_3) \in L$ is $w = (w_1, w_2, w_3) \in \mathbb{Z}_p^3$ satisfying $(x_1, x_2, x_3) = (w_1 h_1, w_2 h_2, w_3 h_3)$. Moreover, let $X' = \langle h_1 \rangle \times \langle h_2 \rangle \times \mathbb{G}_T^2 \subset X$, $\Pi = \mathbb{G}_T$, $\widehat{\Pi} = \widetilde{\Pi} = \mathbb{G}_T^3$. Now we define three HPSs for level-2 ciphertexts $P^{(2)} = (X, L, \Pi)$, $\widehat{P}^{(2)} = (X, L, \widehat{\Pi})$, $\widetilde{P}^{(2)} = (X \times \Pi \times \widehat{\Pi}, L \times \Pi \times \widehat{\Pi}, \widetilde{\Pi})$ as in Fig. 2.

$\boldsymbol{P}^{(2)}$	$\widehat{\boldsymbol{P}}^{(2)}$	$\widetilde{\boldsymbol{P}}^{(2)}$
HashKG(pp): $\quad \boldsymbol{k}_i \leftarrow \mathbb{Z}_p^2 \ (i=1,2)$ $\quad$ Output hk $= (\boldsymbol{k}_1, \boldsymbol{k}_2)$	$\widehat{\text{HashKG}}$(pp): $\quad \widehat{\boldsymbol{k}}_i \leftarrow \mathbb{Z}_p^2 \ (i=1,2)$ $\quad$ Output $\widehat{\text{hk}} = (\widehat{\boldsymbol{k}}_1, \widehat{\boldsymbol{k}}_2)$	$\widetilde{\text{HashKG}}$(pp): $\quad (\widetilde{\boldsymbol{k}}_{1j})_{j=0}^n \leftarrow (\mathbb{Z}_p^4)^{n+1}$, $\quad (\widetilde{\boldsymbol{k}}_{2j})_{j=0}^n, (\widetilde{\boldsymbol{k}}_{3j})_{j=0}^n \leftarrow (\mathbb{Z}_p^2)^{n+1}$ $\quad$ Output $\widetilde{\text{hk}} = ((\widetilde{\boldsymbol{k}}_{1j})_{j=0}^n, (\widetilde{\boldsymbol{k}}_{2j})_{j=0}^n, (\widetilde{\boldsymbol{k}}_{3j})_{j=0}^n)$
ProjKG(hk): $\quad s_i = \boldsymbol{k}_i^\top \boldsymbol{g}_i \ (i=1,2)$ $\quad$ Output hp $= (s_1, s_2)$	$\widehat{\text{ProjKG}}(\widehat{\text{hk}})$: $\quad \widehat{s}_i = \widehat{\boldsymbol{k}}_i^\top \boldsymbol{g}_i \ (i=1,2)$ $\quad$ Output $\widehat{\text{hp}} = (\widehat{s}_1, \widehat{s}_2)$	$\widetilde{\text{ProjKG}}(\widetilde{\text{hk}})$: $\quad \widetilde{s}_{ij} = \widetilde{\boldsymbol{k}}_{ij}^\top \boldsymbol{h}_i \ (i=1,2,3, \ j=0,\ldots,n)$ $\quad$ Output $\widetilde{\text{hp}} = ((\widetilde{s}_{1j})_{j=0}^n, (\widetilde{s}_{2j})_{j=0}^n, (\widetilde{s}_{3j})_{j=0}^n)$
Hash(hk, x): $\quad \pi_1 = (\boldsymbol{k}_1 \otimes \boldsymbol{k}_2)^\top \boldsymbol{x}_1$ $\quad \pi_2 = \boldsymbol{k}_1^\top \boldsymbol{x}_2, \pi_3 = \boldsymbol{k}_2^\top \boldsymbol{x}_3$ $\quad$ Output $\pi = -\pi_1 + \pi_2 + \pi_3$	$\widehat{\text{Hash}}(\widehat{\text{hk}}, x)$: $\quad \widehat{\pi}_1 = (\widehat{\boldsymbol{k}}_1 \otimes \widehat{\boldsymbol{k}}_2)^\top \boldsymbol{x}_1$ $\quad \widehat{\pi}_2 = \widehat{\boldsymbol{k}}_1^\top \boldsymbol{x}_2, \widehat{\pi}_3 = \widehat{\boldsymbol{k}}_2^\top \boldsymbol{x}_3$ $\quad$ Output $\widehat{\pi} = (\widehat{\pi}_1, \widehat{\pi}_2, \widehat{\pi}_3)$	$\widetilde{\text{Hash}}(\widetilde{\text{hk}}, (x, e, \widehat{\pi}))$: $\quad (\gamma_{ij})_{j=1}^n = \Gamma_i(\boldsymbol{x}_i, e, \widehat{\pi}_i) \ (i=1,2,3)$ $\quad \widetilde{\pi}_i = \widetilde{\boldsymbol{k}}_{i0}^\top \boldsymbol{x}_i + \sum_{j=1}^n \gamma_{ij} \widetilde{\boldsymbol{k}}_{ij}^\top \boldsymbol{x}_i \ (i=1,2,3)$ $\quad$ Output $\widetilde{\pi} = (\widetilde{\pi}_1, \widetilde{\pi}_2, \widetilde{\pi}_3)$
ProjHash(hp, x, w): $\quad \pi_1 = w_1(\widehat{s}_1 \otimes s_2)$ $\quad \pi_2 = w_2(s_1 \otimes g_2)$ $\quad \pi_3 = w_3(g_1 \otimes s_2)$ $\quad$ Output $\pi = -\pi_1 + \pi_2 + \pi_3$	$\widehat{\text{ProjHash}}(\widehat{\text{hp}}, x, w)$: $\quad \widehat{\pi}_1 = w_1(\widehat{s}_1 \otimes \widehat{s}_2)$ $\quad \widehat{\pi}_2 = w_2(\widehat{s}_1 \otimes g_2)$ $\quad \widehat{\pi}_3 = w_3(g_1 \otimes \widehat{s}_2)$ $\quad$ Output $\widehat{\pi} = (\widehat{\pi}_1, \widehat{\pi}_2, \widehat{\pi}_3)$	$\widetilde{\text{ProjHash}}(\widetilde{\text{hp}}, (x, e, \widehat{\pi}), w)$: $\quad (\gamma_{ij})_{j=1}^n = \Gamma_i(\boldsymbol{x}_i, e, \widehat{\pi}_i) \ (i=1,2,3)$ $\quad \widetilde{\pi}_i = w_i \widetilde{s}_{i0} + w_i \sum_{j=1}^n \gamma_{ij} \widetilde{s}_{ij} \ (i=1,2,3)$ $\quad$ Output $\widetilde{\pi} = (\widetilde{\pi}_1, \widetilde{\pi}_2, \widetilde{\pi}_3)$

Fig. 2. HPSs for level-2 ciphertexts, where $\Gamma_1 : \mathbb{G}_T^6 \to \mathbb{Z}_p^n$, $\Gamma_2 : \mathbb{G}_T^4 \to \mathbb{Z}_p^n$, and $\Gamma_3 : \mathbb{G}_T^4 \to \mathbb{Z}_p^n$ are hash functions

Proposition 9. $\boldsymbol{P}^{(2)}$ *satisfies the following:*

1. $\boldsymbol{P}^{(2)}$ *is smooth relative to* X'.
2. *Under SXDH assumption, the subset membership problem of* $\boldsymbol{P}^{(2)}$ *is hard relative to* X' *and has a trapdoor.*
3. $X' \setminus L$ *is approximately samplable relative to* X.

Proof. **Smoothness:** For pp $\leftarrow$ SetUp(1^ℓ), hk $\leftarrow$ HashKG(pp), and any fixed hp $= (s_1, s_2) \leftarrow$ ProjKG(hk), we have

$$\{(x, \text{Hash}(\text{hk}, x)) \mid x \leftarrow X' \setminus L\}$$
$$= \{((\boldsymbol{x}_1, \boldsymbol{x}_2, \boldsymbol{x}_3), -(\boldsymbol{k}_1 \otimes \boldsymbol{k}_2)^\top \boldsymbol{x}_1 + \boldsymbol{k}_1^\top \boldsymbol{x}_2 + \boldsymbol{k}_2^\top \boldsymbol{x}_3) \mid \boldsymbol{x}_1 \leftarrow \langle \boldsymbol{h}_1 \rangle, \boldsymbol{x}_2 \leftarrow \langle \boldsymbol{h}_2 \rangle, \boldsymbol{x}_3 \leftarrow \mathbb{G}_T^2 \setminus \langle \boldsymbol{h}_3 \rangle\}$$
$$= \{((w_1 \boldsymbol{h}_1, w_2 \boldsymbol{h}_2, g_1 \otimes \boldsymbol{x}_2'), -w_1(s_1 \otimes s_2) + w_2(s_1 \otimes g_2) + (g_1 \otimes \boldsymbol{k}_2^\top \boldsymbol{x}_2'))$$
$$\mid w_1, w_2 \leftarrow \mathbb{Z}_p, \boldsymbol{x}_2' \leftarrow \mathbb{G}_2^2 \setminus \langle g_2 \rangle\}$$
$$= \{((w_1 \boldsymbol{h}_1, w_2 \boldsymbol{h}_2, g_1 \otimes \boldsymbol{x}_2'), -w_1(s_1 \otimes s_2) + w_2(s_1 \otimes g_2) + (g_1 \otimes \pi_2'))$$
$$\mid w_1, w_2 \leftarrow \mathbb{Z}_p, \boldsymbol{x}_2' \leftarrow \mathbb{G}_2^2 \setminus \langle g_2 \rangle, \pi_2' \leftarrow \mathbb{G}_2\}$$

(as the conditional distribution of $\boldsymbol{k}_2^\top \boldsymbol{x}_2'$ conditioned on a given $s_2 = \boldsymbol{k}_2^\top \boldsymbol{g}_2$ is uniformly random over $\mathbb{G}_2$, by the linear independence of $\boldsymbol{g}_2$ and $\boldsymbol{x}_2'$)

$$= \{((\boldsymbol{x}_1, \boldsymbol{x}_2, \boldsymbol{x}_3), \pi) \mid \boldsymbol{x}_1 \leftarrow \langle \boldsymbol{h}_1 \rangle, \boldsymbol{x}_2 \leftarrow \langle \boldsymbol{h}_2 \rangle, \boldsymbol{x}_3 \leftarrow \mathbb{G}_T^2 \setminus \langle \boldsymbol{h}_3 \rangle, \pi \leftarrow \mathbb{G}_T\}$$
$$= \{(x, \pi) \mid x \leftarrow X' \setminus L, \pi \leftarrow \Pi\} .$$

Hardness of the Subset Membership Problem: For any given pp $\leftarrow$ SetUp(1^ℓ), a uniformly random element of L is of the form $x = (\boldsymbol{x}_1, \boldsymbol{x}_2, \boldsymbol{x}_3)$ with each $\boldsymbol{x}_j \leftarrow \langle \boldsymbol{h}_j \rangle$. Now the component $\boldsymbol{x}_3$ is equivalent to $g_1 \otimes \boldsymbol{x}_2'$ with $\boldsymbol{x}_2' \leftarrow \langle \boldsymbol{g}_2 \rangle$, which is computationally indistinguishable from choosing $\boldsymbol{x}_2' \leftarrow \mathbb{G}_2^2 \setminus \langle \boldsymbol{g}_2 \rangle$ owing to the SXDH assumption. For the latter, $\boldsymbol{x}_3$ becomes uniformly random over $\mathbb{G}_T^2 \setminus \langle \boldsymbol{h}_3 \rangle$, therefore x becomes uniformly random over $X' \setminus L$.

Trapdoor of the Subset Membership Problem: This is deduced by defining two algorithms in Definition 11 in the following manner:

- TrapdoorSetUp(1^ℓ) chooses $\boldsymbol{g}_1, \boldsymbol{g}_2$ in the SetUp by computing $\boldsymbol{g}_1 = (g_1, \tau_1 \cdot g_1)$, $\boldsymbol{g}_2 = (g_2, \tau_2 \cdot g_2)$ where $\tau_1, \tau_2 \leftarrow \mathbb{Z}_p$ and outputs $\tau = (\tau_1, \tau_2)$ as a trapdoor.
- Distinguish(x, τ) takes $x = (\boldsymbol{x}_1, \boldsymbol{x}_2, \boldsymbol{x}_3) \in X$ and $\tau = (\tau_1, \tau_2)$ as inputs. For $\boldsymbol{x}_1 = (x_{11}, x_{12}, x_{13}, x_{14})$, $\boldsymbol{x}_2 = (x_{21}, x_{22})$, and $\boldsymbol{x}_3 = (x_{31}, x_{32})$, if all of

$$x_{12} = \tau_2 \cdot x_{11}, \ x_{13} = \tau_1 \cdot x_{11}, \ x_{14} = \tau_1 \tau_2 \cdot x_{11}, \ x_{22} = \tau_1 \cdot x_{21}, \ x_{32} = \tau_2 \cdot x_{31}$$

hold, then the algorithm decides that $\boldsymbol{x} \in L$; otherwise decides that $\boldsymbol{x} \notin L$.

Approximate Samplability: This follows from the fact that the uniform distributions over $X' \setminus L$ and over X' are statistically indistinguishable, and the fact that the elements of X' are efficiently samplable. $\qquad\square$

Proposition 10. $\widetilde{\boldsymbol{P}}^{(2)}$ *satisfies the following:*

1. *If Γ_1, Γ_2, and Γ_3 are injective, then $\widetilde{\boldsymbol{P}}^{(2)}$ is information-theoretically universal$_2$.*
2. *If Γ_1, Γ_2, and Γ_3 are sampled from a family of collision resistant hash functions, then $\widetilde{\boldsymbol{P}}^{(2)}$ is first-adaptive computationally universal$_2$.*

Proof. $\widetilde{\boldsymbol{P}}^{(2)}$ can be represented as the direct product of three HPSs based on diverse vector spaces (except that the set E is common in all three HPSs). Hence the universal$_2$ property can be shown similarly to Propositions 4 and 5. $\qquad\square$

Proposition 11. $\widehat{\boldsymbol{P}}^{(2)}$ *is $((2p-1)/p^2)$-universal$_1$.*

Proof. Let $\widehat{\mathsf{hp}} = (\widehat{s}_1, \widehat{s}_2) \in \mathbb{G}_1 \times \mathbb{G}_2$, $x = (\boldsymbol{x}_1, \boldsymbol{x}_2, \boldsymbol{x}_3) \in X \setminus L$, and $\widehat{\pi} = (\widehat{\pi}_1, \widehat{\pi}_2, \widehat{\pi}_3) \in \mathbb{G}_T^3$ be chosen randomly. The goal of the proof is to show that

$$\Pr_{\widehat{\mathsf{hk}} \leftarrow \widehat{K}} [\widehat{\mathsf{Hash}}(x) = \widehat{\pi} \mid \widehat{\mathsf{ProjKG}}(\widehat{\mathsf{hk}}) = \widehat{\mathsf{hp}}]$$

is at most $(2p-1)/p^2$. Here, x can be represented as

$$\boldsymbol{x}_1 = w_1(\boldsymbol{g}_1 \otimes \boldsymbol{g}_2) + w_1'(\boldsymbol{g}_1 \otimes \boldsymbol{g}_2') + w_1''(\boldsymbol{g}_1' \otimes \boldsymbol{g}_2) + w_1'''(\boldsymbol{g}_1' \otimes \boldsymbol{g}_2') ,$$
$$\boldsymbol{x}_2 = w_2(\boldsymbol{g}_1 \otimes \boldsymbol{g}_2) + w_2'(\boldsymbol{g}_1' \otimes \boldsymbol{g}_2) ,$$
$$\boldsymbol{x}_3 = w_3(\boldsymbol{g}_1 \otimes \boldsymbol{g}_2) + w_3'(\boldsymbol{g}_1 \otimes \boldsymbol{g}_2') ,$$

where elements $\boldsymbol{g}_1'$ and $\boldsymbol{g}_2'$ are linearly independent from $\boldsymbol{g}_1$ and $\boldsymbol{g}_2$, respectively. We note that at least one of w_1', w_1'', w_1''', w_2', and w_3' is non-zero, since $x \in X \setminus L$.

Under the condition that $\widehat{\mathsf{ProjKG}}(\widehat{\mathsf{hk}}) = \widehat{\mathsf{hp}}$, i.e., $(\widehat{k}_1^\top g_1, \widehat{k}_2^\top g_2) = (\widehat{s}_1, \widehat{s}_2)$, the condition $\widehat{\mathsf{Hash}}(x) = \widehat{\pi}$ is equivalent to

$$w_1(\widehat{s}_1 \otimes \widehat{s}_2) + w_1'(\widehat{s}_1 \otimes \widehat{k}_2^\top g_2') + w_1''(\widehat{k}_1^\top g_1' \otimes \widehat{s}_2) + w_1'''(\widehat{k}_1^\top g_1' \otimes \widehat{k}_2^\top g_2') = \widehat{\pi}_1 \ ,$$

$$w_2(\widehat{s}_1 \otimes g_2) + w_2'(\widehat{k}_1^\top g_1' \otimes g_2) = \widehat{\pi}_2 \ ,$$

$$w_3(g_1 \otimes \widehat{s}_2) + w_3'(g_1 \otimes \widehat{k}_2^\top g_2') = \widehat{\pi}_3 \ .$$

Moreover, since g_1', g_2' are linearly independent from g_1, g_2, respectively, $\widehat{k}_1^\top g_1'$ and $\widehat{k}_2^\top g_2'$ take uniformly random values over $\mathbb{G}_1$ and $\mathbb{G}_2$ independently from $\widehat{s}_1$ and $\widehat{s}_2$, respectively, assuming $\widehat{k}_1, \widehat{k}_2 \leftarrow \mathbb{Z}_p^2$. If we write these values as π_1', π_2', the conditions above can be rewritten as

$$w_1(\widehat{s}_1 \otimes \widehat{s}_2) + w_1'(\widehat{s}_1 \otimes \pi_2') + w_1''(\pi_1' \otimes \widehat{s}_2) + w_1'''(\pi_1' \otimes \pi_2') = \widehat{\pi}_1 \ , \tag{1}$$

$$w_2(\widehat{s}_1 \otimes g_2) + w_2'(\pi_1' \otimes g_2) = \widehat{\pi}_2 \ , \tag{2}$$

$$w_3(g_1 \otimes \widehat{s}_2) + w_3'(g_1 \otimes \pi_2') = \widehat{\pi}_3 \ . \tag{3}$$

Now if $(w_1', w_1'') \neq (0,0)$ (respectively, $w_2' \neq 0$, or $w_3' \neq 0$), then as π_1', π_2' are uniformly random, the left-hand side of Equation (1) (respectively, (2), or (3)) takes a uniformly random value, therefore the condition above holds with probability at most $1/p \leq (2p-1)/p^2$. In the remaining case, we have $w_1''' \neq 0$. In this case, Eq. (1) can be rewritten as $(\pi_1' + v_1'\widehat{s}_1) \otimes (\pi_2' + v_1''\widehat{s}_2) = \widehat{\pi}_1'$, where $v_1' := w_1'w_1'''^{-1}$, $v_1'' := w_1''w_1'''^{-1}$, and $\widehat{\pi}_1' := w_1'''^{-1}(\widehat{\pi}_1 - w_1(\widehat{s}_1 \otimes \widehat{s}_2)) + v_1'v_1''(\widehat{s}_1 \otimes \widehat{s}_2)$. Furthermore, as π_1', π_2' are uniformly random, $\pi_1'' := \pi_1' + v_1'\widehat{s}_1$ and $\pi_2'' := \pi_2' + v_1'\widehat{s}_2$ are also uniformly random. Now the given condition is equivalent to $\pi_1'' \otimes \pi_2'' = \widehat{\pi}_1'$. This holds with probability at most $1/p$ when $\widehat{\pi}_1' \neq 0$, and with probability $(2p-1)/p^2$ when $\widehat{\pi}_1' = 0$. Hence the statement also holds in this case. □

4.4 Concrete Construction of the Proposed Scheme

Our proposed scheme except the multiplication, which mostly follows the generic construction in [10], is given in Fig. 3.

For the multiplication algorithm taking ek, $f = \mathsf{Mult}$, and level-1 ciphertexts $C = (1, x, e, \widehat{\pi}, \widetilde{\pi})$, $C' = (1, x', e', \widehat{\pi}', \widetilde{\pi}')$ as inputs, it computes the following:

1. If $\widetilde{\pi} \neq \widehat{\mathsf{Hash}}^{(1)}(x, e, \widehat{\pi})$ or $\widetilde{\pi}' \neq \widehat{\mathsf{Hash}}^{(1)}(x', e', \widehat{\pi}')$, output $\perp$.
2. Sample $x_0 \in L^{(2)}$ together with its witness w_0.
3. Set $x'' = (\boldsymbol{x}_1 \otimes \boldsymbol{x}_2', \boldsymbol{x}_1 \otimes e_2', e_1 \otimes \boldsymbol{x}_2') + x_0$.
4. Set $e'' \leftarrow e_1 \otimes e_2' + \mathsf{ProjHash}^{(2)}(x_0, w_0)$.
5. Set $\widehat{\pi}'' \leftarrow (\widehat{\pi}_1 \otimes \widehat{\pi}_2', \widehat{\pi}_1 \otimes e_2', e_1 \otimes \widehat{\pi}_2') + \widehat{\mathsf{ProjHash}}^{(2)}(x_0, w_0)$.
6. Set $\widetilde{\pi}'' \leftarrow \widehat{\mathsf{Hash}}^{(2)}(x'', e'', \widehat{\pi}'')$.
7. Output $(2, x'', e'', \widehat{\pi}'', \widetilde{\pi}'')$.

KeyGen(1^ℓ):	Dec(sk, C): $C = (i, x, e, \widehat{\pi}, \widetilde{\pi})$
$\quad$ hk $\leftarrow$ HashKG(pp), hp $\leftarrow$ ProjKG(hk)	$\quad$ If $\widehat{\pi} \neq \widehat{\text{Hash}}^{(i)}(x)$, output $\bot$
$\quad \widehat{\text{hk}} \leftarrow \widehat{\text{HashKG}}(\text{pp})$, $\widehat{\text{hp}} \leftarrow \widehat{\text{ProjKG}}(\widehat{\text{hk}})$	$\quad$ If $\widetilde{\pi} \neq \widetilde{\text{Hash}}^{(i)}(x, e, \widehat{\pi})$, output $\bot$
$\quad \widetilde{\text{hk}}^{(i)} \leftarrow \widetilde{\text{HashKG}}^{(i)}(\text{pp})$ $(i = 1, 2)$	$\quad \pi \leftarrow \text{Hash}^{(i)}(x)$
$\quad \widetilde{\text{hp}}^{(i)} \leftarrow \widetilde{\text{ProjKG}}^{(i)}(\widetilde{\text{hk}}^{(i)})$ $(i = 1, 2)$	$\quad$ When $i = 1$, output $m = (e_1 - \pi_1)/g_1$
$\quad \text{pk} = (\text{hp}, \widehat{\text{hp}}, \widetilde{\text{hp}}^{(1)}, \widetilde{\text{hp}}^{(2)})$	$\quad$ When $i = 2$, output $m = (e - \pi)/g_T$
$\quad \text{sk} = (\text{hk}, \widehat{\text{hk}}, \widetilde{\text{hk}}^{(1)}, \widetilde{\text{hk}}^{(2)})$, $\text{ek} = (\widehat{\text{hk}}^{(1)}, \widehat{\text{hk}}^{(2)})$	
$\quad$ Output (pk, sk, ek)	Eval(ek, Add$^{(i^*)}$, C, C'):
	$\quad C = (i, x, e, \widehat{\pi}, \widetilde{\pi})$, $C' = (i', x', e', \widehat{\pi}', \widetilde{\pi}')$
	$\quad$ If not $i = i' = i^*$, output $\bot$
Enc(pk, (i, m)):	$\quad$ If $\widetilde{\pi} \neq \widetilde{\text{Hash}}^{(i)}(x, e, \widehat{\pi})$, output $\bot$
$\quad$ Sample $x \in L^{(i)}$ together with its witness w	$\quad$ If $\widetilde{\pi}' \neq \widetilde{\text{Hash}}^{(i)}(x', e', \widehat{\pi}')$, output $\bot$
$\quad \pi \leftarrow \text{ProjHash}^{(i)}(x, w)$	$\quad$ Sample $x_0 \in L^{(i)}$ together with its witness w_0
$\quad$ When $i = 1$, $e = (mg_1, mg_2) + \pi$	$\quad x'' = x + x' + x_0$, $e'' = e + e' + \text{ProjHash}^{(i)}(x_0, w_0)$
$\quad$ When $i = 2$, $e = mg_T + \pi$	$\quad \widehat{\pi}'' = \widehat{\pi} + \widehat{\pi}' + \widehat{\text{ProjHash}}^{(i)}(x_0, w_0)$
$\quad \widehat{\pi} \leftarrow \widehat{\text{ProjHash}}^{(i)}(x, w)$	$\quad \widetilde{\pi}'' \leftarrow \widetilde{\text{Hash}}^{(i)}(x'', e'', \widehat{\pi}'')$
$\quad \widetilde{\pi} \leftarrow \widetilde{\text{ProjHash}}^{(i)}((x, e, \widehat{\pi}), w)$	$\quad$ Output $C'' = (i, x'', e'', \widehat{\pi}'', \widetilde{\pi}'')$
$\quad$ Output $C = (i, x, e, \widehat{\pi}, \widetilde{\pi})$	

Fig. 3. Proposed Keyed-2LHE scheme (except homomorphic multiplication)

Let us confirm the correctness of the multiplication. Let C and C' be level-1 ciphertexts of plaintexts m and m', respectively. The operation of adding x_0 or its hash values does not affect correctness (since it is just for rerandomization), therefore we ignore it here. In Steps 3 and 4, the second and the third components of x'' and the value of e'' can be represented as

$$x_1 \otimes e'_2 = x_1 \otimes (m'g_2 + k_2^\top x'_2) ,$$
$$e_1 \otimes x'_2 = (mg_1 + k_1^\top x_1) \otimes x'_2 ,$$
$$e_1 \otimes e'_2 = (mg_1 + k_1^\top x_1) \otimes (m'g_2 + k_2^\top x'_2) .$$

Hence, when we apply Dec to the evaluated ciphertext, we indeed obtain

$$(e'' - \text{Hash}^{(2)}(x_1 \otimes x'_2, x_1 \otimes e'_2, e_1 \otimes x'_2))/g_T$$
$$= (e_1 \otimes e'_2 + (k_1 \otimes k_2)^\top (x_1 \otimes x'_2) - k_1^\top (x_1 \otimes e'_2) - k_2^\top (e_1 \otimes x'_2))/g_T$$
$$= ((mg_1 + k_1^\top x_1) \otimes (m'g_2 + k_2^\top x'_2) + (k_1^\top x_1) \otimes (k_2^\top x'_2)$$
$$\qquad - (k_1^\top x_1) \otimes (m'g_2 + k_2^\top x'_2) - (mg_1 + k_1^\top x_1) \otimes (k_2^\top x'_2))/g_T$$
$$= ((mg_1) \otimes (m'g_2))/g_T = mm' .$$

The remaining task to confirm the correctness is to see that $\widehat{\pi}''$ is a correct hash value, and this can be checked from

$$\widehat{\pi}_1 \otimes \widehat{\pi}'_2 = (\widehat{k}_1^\top x_1) \otimes (\widehat{k}_2^\top x'_2) = (\widehat{k}_1 \otimes \widehat{k}_2)^\top (x_1 \otimes x'_2) ,$$
$$\widehat{\pi}_1 \otimes e'_2 = (\widehat{k}_1^\top x_1) \otimes e'_2 = \widehat{k}_1^\top (x_1 \otimes e'_2) ,$$
$$e_1 \otimes \widehat{\pi}'_2 = e_1 \otimes (\widehat{k}_2^\top x'_2) = \widehat{k}_2^\top (e_1 \otimes x'_2) .$$

Remark 1. In our Dec algorithm, we need to compute division by group element g_1 or g_T, which corresponds to computing the discrete logarithm when the groups are written multiplicatively. To execute decryption efficiently, restriction of the plaintext space for input ciphertexts is essential (which also was the case with 2LHE in [3] and DDH-based KH-PKE in [9]). For the concrete method regarding the discrete logarithm computation, we refer to the previous paper [3].

Theorem 1. *The Keyed-2LHE scheme constructed above is KH-CCA secure under SXDH assumption.*

Proof (Sketch). The underlying idea of the security proof is the same as the one in [9]; we basically want to perform the following game-hopping:

1. For the challenge ciphertext $C^* = (i^*, x^*, e^*, \widehat{\pi}^*, \widetilde{\pi}^*)$, replace the component $x^* \leftarrow L$ with $x^* \leftarrow X' \setminus L$ (owing to the hardness of the subset membership problem relative to $X' \subset X$).
2. Replace the component e^* with a uniformly random element (owing to the smoothness of $\boldsymbol{P}$ relative to $X' \subset X$).
3. Replace $x^* \leftarrow X' \setminus L$ back to $x^* \leftarrow L$ (owing to the hardness of the subset membership problem relative to $X' \subset X$).

If this is successfully done, the challenge ciphertext C^* in the resulting game will be independent of the challenge plaintext m^*, which will imply the security of the scheme. However, the use of decryption/evaluation oracles may be an obstacle to Step 2 of the game-hopping.

For explanation, we suppose that given the challenge ciphertext C^*, the adversary uses oracle $\mathsf{Eval}(C^*, C)$ with another valid ciphertext C to obtain a resulting ciphertext $C^\dagger$ and no more oracles are used. When the component x^* of C^* is changed to $x^* \leftarrow X' \setminus L$, the response $C^\dagger$ to the query $\mathsf{Eval}(C^*, C)$ may leak some information on secret keys for HPSs, which is not suitable for Step 2 of the game-hopping. The idea in [9] to resolve this issue is to perform another game-hopping before the main game-hopping above, which changes the response to the query $\mathsf{Eval}(C^*, C)$ in a way that the oracle first generates a fresh ciphertext $\overline{C^*}$ of m^* (independent of C^*) and then return the result $C^\dagger$ of $\mathsf{Eval}(\overline{C^*}, C)$. In the case of [9], a certain "source ciphertext hiding property" shown in [9] guarantees that this preliminary game-hopping does not change the distribution of $C^\dagger$. And after the preliminary game-hopping, the ciphertext $C^\dagger$ is not dependent on C^* anymore, therefore the change of x^* to $x^* \leftarrow X' \setminus L$ causes no leakage of information on secret keys of HPSs (where the precise proof requires universal properties of $\widehat{\boldsymbol{P}}$ and $\widetilde{\boldsymbol{P}}$), as desired. We note that similar recursive replacements of challenge ciphertext by fresh ciphertexts (like $\overline{C^*}$ above) have to be performed when the list of oracle queries by the adversary is more complicated.

In the case of our proposed scheme, we can extend the source ciphertext hiding property, which was the key property in the case of [9], to the present case as follows. For a ciphertext $C = (i, x, e, \widehat{\pi}, \widetilde{\pi})$, we say that C is $\widetilde{\boldsymbol{P}}^{(i)}$-*consistent*, if $\widetilde{\pi} = \widetilde{\mathsf{Hash}}^{(i)}(x, e, \widehat{\pi})$ holds. (Similarly for $\widehat{\boldsymbol{P}}^{(i)}$.)

Lemma 1 (source ciphertext hiding property). *Let $i \in \{1,2\}$. Assume that level-i ciphertexts $C = (i, x, e, \widehat{\pi}, \widetilde{\pi})$ and $C' = (i, x', e', \widehat{\pi}', \widetilde{\pi}')$ satisfy:*

(*) *C and C' are $\widehat{P}^{(i)}$-consistent and $\widetilde{P}^{(i)}$-consistent ciphertexts for the same plaintext, and the distributions of C and C' are identical and independent with each other.*

Moreover, let $C'' = (i, x'', e'', \widehat{\pi}'', \widetilde{\pi}'')$ be a $\widehat{P}^{(i)}$-consistent and $\widetilde{P}^{(i)}$-consistent level-i ciphertext. Under these assumptions, for any operation $f \in \{\mathsf{Add}^{(1)}, \mathsf{Add}^{(2)}, \mathsf{Mult}\}$, the outputs of $\mathsf{Eval}(f, C, C'')$ and $\mathsf{Eval}(f, C', C'')$ satisfy the condition (*) (unless the evaluation is not rejected).

Based on this property, the security of our proposed scheme is proved in a way analogous to [9] as outlined above. (See the full version for the details.)   □

Remark 2. In our scheme, if a party has only the part $\widetilde{\mathsf{hk}}^{(1)}$ of the evaluation key $\mathsf{ek} = (\widetilde{\mathsf{hk}}^{(1)}, \widetilde{\mathsf{hk}}^{(2)})$, then the party can only compute addition between level-1 ciphertexts but not the other homomorphic operations. This feature to partially allow operations by giving the evaluation key partially is a new feature that previous schemes did not possess, though we are leaving the formal definition for security with such partial key exposure as a future research topic.

Table 1. Comparison of key and ciphertext sizes (numbers of elements in $\mathbb{Z}_p$, $\mathbb{G}_1$, $\mathbb{G}_2$, $\mathbb{G}_T$ in this order)

	Ours	2LHE [3]	KH-PKE [9]
sk	32, 0, 0, 0	2, 0, 0, 0	8, 0, 0, 0
pk	0, 4, 4, 9	0, 2, 2, 4	0, 4, −, −
ek	0, 2, 2, 6	-	0, 2, −, −
Level-1 Ciphertext	0, 5, 5, 0	0, 2, 2, 0	0, 5, −, −
Level-2 Ciphertext	0, 0, 0, 15	0, 0, 0, 4	-

Table 2. Numbers of operations in our proposed scheme; here "Op" and "Exp" denote addition and scalar multiplication, respectively, over additive groups $\mathbb{G}_1$, $\mathbb{G}_2$, $\mathbb{G}_T$ in this order, and "DL" denotes computation of discrete logarithm (with restricted exponent)

		Op	Exp	Pairing	DL
KeyGen		4, 4, 15	8, 8, 24	0	0
Enc	Level-1	2, 2, 0	7, 7, 0	0	0
	Level-2	0, 0, 6	0, 0, 21	0	0
Dec	Level-1	4, 2, 0	6, 4, 0	0	1
	Level-2	0, 0, 18	0, 0, 24	0	1
Eval	$\mathsf{Add}^{(1)}$	11, 11, 0	10, 10, 0	0	0
	$\mathsf{Add}^{(2)}$	0, 0, 41	0, 0, 38	0	0
	Mult	2, 2, 19	4, 4, 22	12	0

5   Efficiency Evaluations

In this section, we evaluate the efficiency of our proposed scheme for the case where hash functions Γ in $\widetilde{\boldsymbol{P}}^{(1)}$ and $\widetilde{\boldsymbol{P}}^{(2)}$ are collision resistant (i.e., the case where $\widetilde{\boldsymbol{P}}$ is first-adaptive computationally universal$_2$), and the case where $n = 1$ in $\widetilde{\boldsymbol{P}}^{(1)}$ and $\widetilde{\boldsymbol{P}}^{(2)}$ (similarly to the DDH-based instantiation of KH-PKE in [9]). Also, we assume that all the necessary values of pairings between secret keys, public keys, or public parameters are computed in advance during the key generation, and the resulting values are involved in secret keys or public keys.

A comparison of key and ciphertext sizes among our scheme, the state-of-the-art 2LHE scheme [3], and the original KH-PKE scheme [9] (precisely, its DDH-based instantiation in Section 5.3 of [9]) is shown in Table 1. The four numbers in each cell denote the numbers of elements in $\mathbb{Z}_p$, $\mathbb{G}_1$, $\mathbb{G}_2$, and $\mathbb{G}_T$, respectively. It is natural that our scheme is less efficient than the other two schemes, since our scheme achieves stronger security than [3] and realizes stronger functionality than [9]. We expect that the overhead of our scheme compared to the other two schemes is within an acceptable range from practical viewpoints.

Table 2 shows the numbers of addition and scalar multiplication (note that now $\mathbb{G}_1$, $\mathbb{G}_2$, and $\mathbb{G}_T$ are regarded as additive groups), pairing, and computation of discrete logarithm (with restricted exponent; see Remark 1) in each algorithm for our proposed scheme. Here the three numbers in each cell for "Op" and "Exp" are those for $\mathbb{G}_1$, $\mathbb{G}_2$, and $\mathbb{G}_T$. Note that operations on $\mathbb{Z}_p$ are omitted here, since they are much faster than operations over $\mathbb{G}_1$, $\mathbb{G}_2$, and $\mathbb{G}_T$.

Acknowledgement. This research was partially supported by the Ministry of Internal Affairs and Communications SCOPE Grant Number 182103105, JST CREST JPMJCR19F6, and JSPS KAKENHI Grant Number 19H01109.

References

1. Abdalla, M., Benhamouda, F., Pointcheval, D.: Disjunctions for hash proof systems: new constructions and applications. In: Oswald, E., Fischlin, M. (eds.) EUROCRYPT 2015. LNCS, vol. 9057, pp. 69–100. Springer, Heidelberg (2015). https://doi.org/10.1007/978-3-662-46803-6_3
2. An, J.H., Dodis, Y., Rabin, T.: On the security of joint signature and encryption. In: Knudsen, L.R. (ed.) EUROCRYPT 2002. LNCS, vol. 2332, pp. 83–107. Springer, Heidelberg (2002). https://doi.org/10.1007/3-540-46035-7_6
3. Attrapadung, N., Hanaoka, G., Mitsunari, S., Sakai, Y., Shimizu, K., Teruya, T.: Efficient two-level homomorphic encryption in prime-order bilinear groups and A fast implementation in WebAssembly. In: Proceedings of AsiaCCS 2018, pp. 685–697. ACM (2018)
4. Benhamouda, F., Blazy, O., Chevalier, C., Pointcheval, D., Vergnaud, D.: New techniques for SPHFs and efficient one-round PAKE protocols. In: Canetti, R., Garay, J.A. (eds.) CRYPTO 2013. LNCS, vol. 8042, pp. 449–475. Springer, Heidelberg (2013). https://doi.org/10.1007/978-3-642-40041-4_25

5. Boneh, D., Goh, E.-J., Nissim, K.: Evaluating 2-DNF formulas on ciphertexts. In: Kilian, J. (ed.) TCC 2005. LNCS, vol. 3378, pp. 325–341. Springer, Heidelberg (2005). https://doi.org/10.1007/978-3-540-30576-7_18

6. Canetti, R., Krawczyk, H., Nielsen, J.B.: Relaxing chosen-ciphertext security. In: Boneh, D. (ed.) CRYPTO 2003. LNCS, vol. 2729, pp. 565–582. Springer, Heidelberg (2003). https://doi.org/10.1007/978-3-540-45146-4_33

7. Cramer, R., Shoup, V.: A practical public key cryptosystem provably secure against adaptive chosen ciphertext attack. In: Krawczyk, H. (ed.) CRYPTO 1998. LNCS, vol. 1462, pp. 13–25. Springer, Heidelberg (1998). https://doi.org/10.1007/BFb0055717

8. Cramer, R., Shoup, V.: Universal hash proofs and a paradigm for adaptive chosen ciphertext secure public-key encryption. In: Knudsen, L.R. (ed.) EUROCRYPT 2002. LNCS, vol. 2332, pp. 45–64. Springer, Heidelberg (2002). https://doi.org/10.1007/3-540-46035-7_4

9. Emura, K., Hanaoka, G., Nuida, K., Ohtake, G., Matsuda, T., Yamada, S.: Chosen ciphertext secure keyed-homomorphic public-key cryptosystems. Des. Codes Cryptogr. **86**(8), 1623–1683 (2018)

10. Emura, K., Hanaoka, G., Ohtake, G., Matsuda, T., Yamada, S.: Chosen ciphertext secure keyed-homomorphic public-key encryption. In: Kurosawa, K., Hanaoka, G. (eds.) PKC 2013. LNCS, vol. 7778, pp. 32–50. Springer, Heidelberg (2013). https://doi.org/10.1007/978-3-642-36362-7_3

11. Freeman, D.M.: Converting pairing-based cryptosystems from composite-order groups to prime-order groups. In: Gilbert, H. (ed.) EUROCRYPT 2010. LNCS, vol. 6110, pp. 44–61. Springer, Heidelberg (2010). https://doi.org/10.1007/978-3-642-13190-5_3

12. Jutla, C.S., Roy, A.: Dual-system simulation-soundness with applications to UC-PAKE and more. In: Iwata, T., Cheon, J.H. (eds.) ASIACRYPT 2015. LNCS, vol. 9452, pp. 630–655. Springer, Heidelberg (2015). https://doi.org/10.1007/978-3-662-48797-6_26

13. Lai, J., Deng, R.H., Ma, C., Sakurai, K., Weng, J.: CCA-secure keyed-fully homomorphic encryption. In: Cheng, C.-M., Chung, K.-M., Persiano, G., Yang, B.-Y. (eds.) PKC 2016. LNCS, vol. 9614, pp. 70–98. Springer, Heidelberg (2016). https://doi.org/10.1007/978-3-662-49384-7_4

14. Libert, B., Peters, T., Joye, M., Yung, M.: Non-malleability from malleability: simulation-sound quasi-adaptive NIZK proofs and CCA2-secure encryption from homomorphic signatures. In: Nguyen, P.Q., Oswald, E. (eds.) EUROCRYPT 2014. LNCS, vol. 8441, pp. 514–532. Springer, Heidelberg (2014). https://doi.org/10.1007/978-3-642-55220-5_29

15. Prabhakaran, M., Rosulek, M.: Homomorphic encryption with CCA security. In: Aceto, L., Damgård, I., Goldberg, L.A., Halldórsson, M.M., Ingólfsdóttir, A., Walukiewicz, I. (eds.) ICALP 2008. LNCS, vol. 5126, pp. 667–678. Springer, Heidelberg (2008). https://doi.org/10.1007/978-3-540-70583-3_54

16. Rivest, R.L., Adleman, L., Dertouzos, M.L.: On data banks and privacy homomorphisms. Found. Secure Comput. **4**(11), 169–180 (1978)

17. Sato, S., Emura, K., Takayasu, A.: Keyed-fully homomorphic encryption without indistinguishability obfuscation. In ACNS 2022 (to appear)

Structure-Preserving Linearly Homomorphic Signature with Designated Combiner for Subspace

Yumei Li[1]([envelope]) [ID], Mingwu Zhang[1,3,4], and Futai Zhang[2]

[1] Hubei University of Technology, Wuhan 430068, China
leamergo@gmail.com
[2] Fujian Normal University, Fuzhou 350117, China
[3] Guangxi Key Laboratory of Cryptography and Information Security, Guilin, China
[4] Xiangyang Industrilal Institute of Hubei University of Technology,
Xiangyang, China

Abstract. Linearly homomorphic signature allows signature holders to perform arbitrary linear computation on signed vectors. The special "function" makes linearly homomorphic signature suitable for many applications. However, publicly combinable is not advisable in some specific scenarios. Although some schemes with designated combiners have been proposed, they break the homomorphism of the combined signature. The combined vectors cannot be combined again. In this paper, we put forth the notion of structure-preserving linearly homomorphic signatures with the designated combiner. The combined signature is indistinguishable from signatures generated by the signer. Only the signer and the designated entity can generate a valid signature for any combined vector. Finally, we prove our scheme is secure under the CDH problem assumption and show it is efficient.

Keywords: Structure-preserving and linearly homomorphic signature · Designated combiner

1 Introduction

Digital signature is a cryptographic tool that can be used to guarantee the authenticity and integrity of messages. However, some extra properties should be added to satisfy the requirements in specific scenarios, such as network coding and cloud auditing. Composability is an important cryptographic design notion for building systems and protocols. Homomorphic signature as a class of special digital signatures, provides a special function called "Combine", which allows any entity with the signer's public key to compute on the signed messages. The function is very useful in network coding and cloud storage auditing.

A secure traditional digital signature scheme requires that the adversary must be unable to generate even one signature on a message unsigned by the signer. Unlike the traditional digital signatures, the signature object of homomorphic signature is the linear vector space. A valid vector signature either comes directly from the signer or is derived from the signed vectors. Therefore, the security requirement of this technique is that the adversary cannot forge a signature on a vector unsigned by the signer, an additional condition is that the vector cannot be derived from the signed vector.

Linearly homomorphic signature (LHS) [3] allows any entity to evaluate linear functions over the signed messages. It is used to prevent pollution attacks in the network coding routing mechanisms [7,20,23]. Any entity with the signer's public key can generate a valid combined signature from some signed message by linear homomorphic operation. However, in some specific mechanisms, such as cloud computing, the signer wants the server to be the only entity that can combine the signatures. An intuitive method is that the signer sends vector/signature pair to a designed server via a reliable secret channel. It is obviously unreasonable. Some related works have been proposed to solve this problem [17,18]. However, the existing schemes only support a one-time homomorphic combination, where a combined vector cannot be an input of the combine algorithm. The reason is that the structure of the signature has been changed. Besides, to achieve public verification, the combine algorithm in [18] needs to compute at least l (the number of vectors to be combined) times of hash to group and bilinear map operations which will require a significant cost overhead.

This paper considers structure-preserving linearly homomorphic schemes with the designated combiner (SPS-LHSDC) and all vectors (generated by the signer or combiner) to support public verification. In 2010, Abe et al. proposed the first instantiation of structure-preserving signatures [1]. In their definitions, *structure-preserving* means its verification keys, signatures, and messages are elements in a bilinear group, and the verification equation is a conjunction of pairing-product equations. Unlike the definition proposed by Abe et al., in our work, structure-preserving is mainly used to illustrate the structure of signatures generated by the signer and the designated combiner are the same. Besides, our construction does not require these elements (including verification keys, signatures, and messages) in a bilinear group.

1.1 Our Contribution

In this paper, we put forth the notion of structure-preserving linearly homomorphic signatures with the designated combiner. The combined signature is indistinguishable from the signature generated by the signer, i.e., both signatures can be verified by the verifier using the verification algorithm. That is to say, the structure of the signature keeps unchanged after being combined. Besides, this work only allows the designated entity to compute a combined signature on signed vectors (basis vectors or combined vectors). Other entities except for the signer and the designated entity cannot generate a valid signature for any vector. Finally, we propose a detailed SPS-LHSDC scheme and prove it is secure under the CDH problem assumption. Analysis shows that the combine algorithm in our scheme is efficient.

1.2   Related Work

The notion of the homomorphic signature can be traced back to Desmedt [10]. Its formal definition has not been proposed until the work of Jonson et al. [14]. After that, various homomorphic signature schemes have been proposed. For instance, linearly homomorphic signature schemes [3,8,15,19,21], polynomial homomorphic signature schemes [5,6], fully homomorphic signature schemes [13] and the homomorphic aggregate signature schemes [22]. Significantly, linearly homomorphic signature schemes are particularly useful in many applications such as network coding or proof of storage.

The linearly homomorphic signature is at first proposed to prevent pollution attacks in network coding. Boneh et al. [3] in 2009 first introduced the formal definition and security model of linearly homomorphic signature, and proposed two different instantiations. In their scheme, the computational cost of signature generation and verification depends on the size of the vector. In 2010, Gennaro et al. [12] proposed a linearly homomorphic signature scheme based on the RSA assumption. The scheme requires low computational overhead since the linear combination can be achieved by choosing smaller integer coefficients. Boneh et al. [4] proposed the first lattice-based linearly homomorphic signature scheme, which verifies vectors in the binary domain and is resistant to quantum attacks. In 2011, Attrapadung et al. [2] first proposed a linearly homomorphic signature scheme that is secure under the standard model, which allows a single vector to be dynamically signed with a constant length of the signature. Attrapadung et al. [3] proposed a linearly homomorphic signature scheme that can achieve complete content hiding under the standard model. Li et al. [16] proposed an efficient identity-based linearly homomorphic network coding signature scheme. The signature cost of this scheme is independent of the size of the vector.

Inspired by the open problem proposed by Rivest in 2000, Lin et al. [17] proposed a linearly homomorphic signature scheme with designated entities based on the idea of key agreement. Only the designated combiner can perform homomorphic operations, and only the designated verifier can verify the integrity and authenticity of the signature. In 2021, Lin et al. [18] proposed a linearly homomorphic signature scheme with designated combiner that supports public verification. Fuchsbauer et al. [11] used the idea of equivalence class to construct a randomization structure-preserving homomorphic signature scheme, the signature of any message is indistinguishable from the signature generated by randomization of the signature.

1.3   Organization

The overall structure of the rest of this paper is as follows. In Sect. 2, we present some preliminaries as well as the formal definition and security model of SPS-LHSDC. Then, we present a specific SPS-LHSDC in Sect. 3 and prove its security in Sect. 4. Subsequently, we give the theoretical evaluation in Sect. 5. Finally, we conclude this paper in Sect. 6.

2   Preliminaries and Definitions

2.1   Mathematic Background

Definition 1 [Bilinear map]. *Suppose* $\mathbb{G}_1, \mathbb{G}_2$ *are cyclic groups with sizeable prime order* q. *A map* $e : \mathbb{G}_1 \times \mathbb{G}_1 \rightarrow \mathbb{G}_2$ *is called a bilinear map if it satisfies the following properties:*

1. *Bilinearity: for any* $a, b \in \mathbb{Z}_q$ *and* $g \in \mathbb{G}_1$, *we have* $e(g^a, g^b) = e(g, g)^{ab}$.
2. *Non-degeneracy: if* g *is a generator of* $\mathbb{G}_1$, *then* $e(g, g)$ *is a generator of* $\mathbb{G}_2$.
3. *Computability: for any* $g \in \mathbb{G}_1$, $e(g, g)$ *is efficiently computable.*

Definition 2 [Computational Diffie-Hellman Problem (CDH)]. *Suppose* $\mathbb{G}_1$ *is a cyclic group with sizeable prime order* q. *Given* $g, g^a, g^b \in \mathbb{G}_1$, *the* CDH *problem is to compute* g^{ab} *for some randomly chosen* $a, b \in \mathbb{Z}_q^*$.

The advantage of an algorithm $\mathcal{A}$ *in solving CDH problem in* $\mathbb{G}_1$ *is defined as*

$$\Pr[\mathcal{A}(g, g^a, g^b) = g^{ab} : a, b \in \mathbb{Z}_q^*]$$

Definition 3 [CDH Assumption]. *We say that the* CDH *assumption holds in* $\mathbb{G}_1$ *if there is no probabilistic polynomial-time algorithm can solve the* CDH *problem in* $\mathbb{G}_1$ *with non-negligible advantage.*

2.2   The Augmented Basis Vectors

A linearly homomorphic signature scheme is a technique that signs a subspace $V \subset \mathbb{F}_q^N$, so that only vectors $\mathbf{w} \in V$ can be accepted as valid. To sign a subspace V described with a set of basis vectors, the signer only needs to sign these basis vectors and other vectors' signatures can be derived from these basis vectors' signatures. Before signing, a file can be divided into an ordered sequence of n-dimensional vectors $\bar{\mathbf{m}}_1, \ldots, \bar{\mathbf{m}}_k \in \mathbb{F}_q^n$. In order to guarantee these vectors linearly independent, the signer augments $\bar{\mathbf{m}}_1, \ldots, \bar{\mathbf{m}}_k$ and makes them just like basis vectors. The signer appends a unit vector of length k to the vectors $\mathbf{m}_i$ before signing them. Let $N = n + k$, the k original vectors $\bar{\mathbf{m}}_1, \ldots, \bar{\mathbf{m}}_k$ are transformed into k augmented vectors $\mathbf{m}_1, \ldots, \mathbf{m}_k$ as follows:

$$\mathbf{m}_l = (-\bar{\mathbf{m}}_l-, m_{l(n+1)}, \ldots, m_{lN})$$

where

$$m_{l(n+j)} = \begin{cases} 1, l = j \\ 0, l \neq j \end{cases} \quad l, j = 1, 2, \ldots, k$$

The data component of the vector $\mathbf{m}_i$ is its left-most n items and the augmentation component of $\mathbf{m}_i$ is the right-most k items. The augmented vectors $\mathbf{m}_1, \ldots, \mathbf{m}_k$ are clearly independent and can be viewed as a basis of a k-dimensional subspace $V \subset \mathbb{F}_q^N$.

2.3   The Formal Definition

A structure-preserving linearly homomorphic signature scheme with designed combiner (SPS-LHSDC) consists of a set of probabilistic polynomial-time algorithms (Setup, KeyGen, Sign, Verify) with the following functionality:

- **Setup** $(1^\lambda, N) \to pp$. On input security parameters 1^λ and an integer N denoting the dimension of vectors to be signed, this algorithm outputs the public parameters pp. The public parameters pp include a prime field $\mathbb{F}_q$ which the vector subspace for signing is based on.
- **KeyGen** $(pp) \to (sk, pk)$. On input the public parameters pp, this algorithm outputs a private key sk and the corresponding public key pk.
- **Sign** $(pp, sk_u, pk_c, id, \mathbf{m}) \to (\tau, \sigma)$. On input the public parameters pp, a signer's private key sk_u, a combiner's public key pk_c, a subspace identifier $id \in \{0,1\}^\lambda$ and a vector $\mathbf{m} = (m_1, \dots, m_N) \in \mathbb{F}_q^N$, this algorithm outputs the tag $\tau = (id, pk_c)$ of the subspace and the signature σ of $\mathbf{m}$. (Note that to sign a subspace V, the signer should generate all signatures for a set of basis vectors $\mathbf{m}_1, \dots, \mathbf{m}_k \in V$.)
- **Combine** $(pp, pk_u, sk_c, \tau, \{\beta_l, \mathbf{m}_l, \sigma_l\}_{l=1}^k) \to (\hat{\mathbf{m}}, \hat{\sigma})$. On input the public parameters pp, a signer's public key pk_u, a combiner's secret key sk_c, a tag τ of the subspace, and a tuple $\{\beta_l, \mathbf{m}_l, \sigma_l\}_{l=1}^k$ with $\beta_l \in \mathbb{F}_q$, this algorithm outputs a vector/signature pair $(\hat{\mathbf{m}}, \hat{\sigma})$.
- **Verify** $(pp, pk_u, \tau, \mathbf{w}, \sigma) \to 0$ or 1. On input the public parameters pp, a user public key pk_u, a tag τ of subspace V, a vector $\mathbf{w} \in V$ and its signature σ, this algorithm outputs either 0 (reject) or 1 (accept).

A secure SPS-LHSDC scheme must satisfy the following requirement of correctness. For each output pp by the **Setup** algorithm and (sk, pk) by the **KeyGen**, it holds that:

- For all τ and all $\mathbf{w} \in \mathbb{F}_q^N$, if $\upsilon \leftarrow$ **Sign**$(pp, sk_u, pk_c, id, \mathbf{w})$ then **Verify** $(pp, pk_u, \tau, \mathbf{w}, \sigma) = 1$.
- For all $id \in \{0,1\}^\lambda$ and all sets of triples $\{\beta_l, \mathbf{m}_l, \sigma_l\}_{l=1}^k$, for all l, if **Verify** $(pp, pk_u, \tau, \mathbf{m}_l, \sigma_l) = 1$, then

$$\text{\textbf{Verify}}(pp, pk_u, \tau, \text{\textbf{Combine}}(pp, pk_u, sk_c, \tau, \{\beta_l, \mathbf{m}_l, \sigma_l\}_{l=1}^k)) = 1.$$

2.4   Security Model

We analyze the ability of an adversary $\mathcal{A}$ and define security of a SPS-LHSDC scheme. In a SPS-LHSDC scheme, a successful attack means that an adversary $\mathcal{A}$ outputs a successful forgery that pass the verification. A forgery is successful if it belongs to one of the following three types of forgery.

- **Type 1 forgery:** $\mathcal{A}$ never queried the signature of vector subspace V and generates a valid signature for a non-zero vector $\mathbf{w}^* \in V$.

- **Type 2 forgery:** $\mathcal{A}$ never queried the signature of vector subspace V with the tag τ^* and generates a valid signature for a non-zero vector $\mathbf{w}^* \in V$, but $\mathcal{A}$ has queried the signature of vector subspace V marked by the same tag τ^*.
- **Type 3 forgery:** $\mathcal{A}$ has queried the signature of vector subspace V and generates a combined signature by the basis vectors' signatures, while the combiner's secret key is unknown to $\mathcal{A}$.

Definition 4. *A SPS-LHSDC scheme $\Omega = $ (Setup, KeyGen, Sign, Combine, Verify) is secure if the advantage of any probabilistic, polynomial-time adversary $\mathcal{A}$ in the following security game is negligible in the security parameter λ:*

Initialization: The challenger $\mathcal{C}$ chooses a positive integer N and runs **Setup** $(1^\lambda, N)$ to obtain pp, and **KeyGen** (pp) to get pk_u. $\mathcal{C}$ sends pp, pk_u to $\mathcal{A}$.

Queries: $\mathcal{A}$ adaptively issues the following queries.

- Combiner-Key Generation Query: Proceeding adaptively, on receiving a combiner-key generation query from $\mathcal{A}$, $\mathcal{C}$ runs **KeyGen** algorithm to produce the public key pk_c and private key sk_c for a new combiner, and sends the public key to $\mathcal{A}$.
- Combiner Corruption Query: Proceeding adaptively, $\mathcal{C}$ is given a combiner's public pk_c, and returns the corresponding private key sk_c to $\mathcal{A}$.
- **Sign Query:** Proceeding adaptively, $\mathcal{A}$ specifies a sequence of vector subspace $V_i \subset \mathbb{F}_q^N$ described by basis vector $\mathbf{m}_{i1}, \dots, \mathbf{m}_{ik}$, $\mathcal{C}$ does as follows:
    1. Chooses an identifier $id_i \in \{0,1\}^\lambda$ at randomly, and sets the tag $\tau_i = (id_i, pk_c)$ for the subspace V_i.
    2. Generates basis vectors' signatures $\sigma_{i1}, \dots, \sigma_{ik}$ by running **Sign** algorithm.
    3. Sends the tag τ_i and basis vectors' signatures $\sigma_{i1}, \dots, \sigma_{ik}$ to $\mathcal{A}$.
- **Combine Query:** Proceeding adaptively, $\mathcal{C}$ is given $\tau_i, \{\beta_{il}, \mathbf{m}_{il}, \sigma_{il}\}_{l=1}^k$, and runs **Combine** $(pp, pk_u, sk_c, \tau_i, \{\beta_{il}, \mathbf{m}_{il}, \sigma_{il}\}_{l=1}^k)$ to generate a vector/signature pair $(\hat{\mathbf{m}}_i, \hat{\sigma}_i)$, where $\hat{\mathbf{m}}_i = \sum_{l=1}^k \beta_{il} \mathbf{m}_{il}$.

Output: $\mathcal{A}$ outputs the signer's public key pk_u^*, the combiner's public key pk_c^*, a tag τ^*, a non-zero vector $\mathbf{w}^* \in \mathbb{F}_q^N$, and a signature σ^*.

The adversary $\mathcal{A}$ wins if **Verify** $(pp, pk_u^*, \tau^*, \mathbf{w}^*, \sigma^*) = 1$, and either(1) $\tau^* \neq \tau_i$ for any i (Type 1 forgery), or (2) $\tau^* = \tau_i$ for some i but $\mathbf{w}^* \notin V_i$ (Type 2 forgery), or (3) $\tau^* = \tau_i$ for some i but $\mathbf{w}^* \in V_i - \{\mathbf{m}_{i1}, \dots, \mathbf{m}_{ik}\}$, and $\mathcal{A}$ knows nothing about the combiner's secret key sk_c^* (Type 3 forgery). We require $\mathcal{A}$ to output a non-zero vector $\mathbf{w}^*$ since the zero vector lies in every linear subspace.

3   Our Construction

This section shows the construction of a structure-preserving linearly homomorphic signature scheme with the designated combiner. The construction is based on the network coding signature schemes proposed by Boneh et al. [3] and Lin et al. [18].

- **Setup** $(1^\lambda) \rightarrow (pp)$. Given security parameter 1^λ and a positive integer N, this algorithm works as follows:
    1. Generates two cyclic groups $\mathbb{G}_1, \mathbb{G}_2$ with prime order $q > 2^\lambda$ and a symmetric bilinear map $e : \mathbb{G}_1 \times \mathbb{G}_1 \rightarrow \mathbb{G}_2$.
    2. Chooses generators $g, g_1, \ldots, g_N \in \mathbb{G}_1 \backslash \{1\}$ randomly.
    3. Lets $H_1 : \{0,1\}^* \rightarrow \mathbb{G}_1$.
    4. Outputs the public parameters $pp = (q, \mathbb{G}_1, \mathbb{G}_2, e, g, g_1, \ldots, g_N, H_1)$.
- **KeyGen** $(pp) \rightarrow (sk, pk)$. Given the public parameters pp, the signer randomly picks a private key $sk_u = x \in \mathbb{Z}_q^*$ and sets $pk_u = g^x$ as his/her public key. Similarly, the $(sk_c = y, pk_c = g^y)$ is the private/public key pair of the designated combiner.
- **Sign** $(pp, sk_u, pk_c, id, \mathbf{m}) \rightarrow \sigma$. Taking the public parameters pp, a signer's private key sk_u, a combiner's public key pk_c, an identifier $id \in \{0,1\}^\lambda$ and a vector $\mathbf{m} = (m_1, \cdots, m_N) \in V$ as input, the signer sets the tag $\tau = (id, pk_c)$ of the subspace and computes the signature

$$\sigma = (\prod_{j=1}^{k} H_1(j, \tau)^{m_{n+j}} \prod_{i=1}^{n} g_i^{m_i} \cdot pk_c)^x$$

  where $N = n + k$, and n is data component's length and k is the augmentation component's length.
- **Combine** $(pp, \tau, pk_u, sk_c, id, \{\beta_l, \mathbf{m}_l, \sigma_l\}_{l=1}^{k}) \rightarrow (\hat{\mathbf{m}}, \hat{\sigma})$. Given a public parameters pp, a signer's public key pk_u, a combiner's private key sk_c, a tag τ of subspace and $\{\beta_l, \mathbf{m}_l, \sigma_l\}_{l=1}^{k}$ with $\beta_l \in \mathbb{Z}_q^*$, the combiner computes $r = y(\sum_{l=1}^{k} \beta_l - 1) \mod q, R = pk_u^r$, and outputs:

$$\hat{\mathbf{m}} = \sum_{l=1}^{k} \beta_l \mathbf{m}_l = (\hat{m}_1, ..., \hat{m}_N) \in V,$$

$$\sigma = \prod_{l=1}^{k} \sigma_l^{\beta_l} / R$$

- **Verify** $(pp, pk_u, \tau, \mathbf{w}, \sigma) \rightarrow (0, 1)$. Given public parameters pp, a signer's public key pk_u, a tag $\tau = (id, pk_c)$ of subspace, a vector $\mathbf{w}$ and a signature σ, if

$$e(\sigma, g) = e(\prod_{j=1}^{k} H_1(j, \tau)^{w_{n+j}} \prod_{i=1}^{n} g_i^{w_i} \cdot pk_c, pk_u),$$

  the algorithm outputs 1; otherwise it outputs 0.

4   Correctness and Security Analysis

4.1   Correctness Analysis

Assuming that all the entities faithfully follow the above algorithms, the correctness of the signature can be checked from the following two aspects.

1. For the signature σ generated by **Sign** algorithm, we have:

$$
e\,(\sigma, g) = e((\prod_{j=1}^{k} H_1(j, \tau)^{m_{n+j}} \prod_{i=1}^{n} g_i^{m_i} \cdot pk_c)^x, g)
$$

$$
= e(\prod_{j=1}^{k} H_1(j, \tau)^{m_{n+j}} \prod_{i=1}^{n} g_i^{m_i} \cdot pk_c, pk_u)
$$

2. For the vector/signature pair $(\hat{\mathbf{m}}, \hat{\sigma})$ with the tag τ generated by the algorithm **Combine**, we have $\hat{\sigma}$ is equivalent to the output of **Sign** algorithm, that is:

$$
U = \prod_{l=1}^{k} \sigma_l^{\beta_l}
$$

$$
= \prod_{l=1}^{k}((\prod_{j=1}^{k} H_1(ID, j)^{m_{l(n+j)}} \prod_{i=1}^{n} g_i^{m_{li}} \cdot pk_c)^x)^{\beta_l}
$$

$$
= \prod_{l=1}^{k}(\prod_{j=1}^{k} H_1(ID, j)^{(\beta_l m_{l(n+j)})} \prod_{i=1}^{n} g_i^{\beta_l m_{li}} \cdot pk_c^{\beta_l})^x
$$

$$
= (\prod_{j=1}^{k} H_1(ID, j)^{\sum_{l=1}^{k} \beta_l m_{l(n+j)}} \prod_{i=1}^{n} g_i^{\sum_{l=1}^{k} \beta_l m_{li}} \cdot pk_c^{\sum_{l=1}^{k} \beta_l})^x
$$

$$
= (\prod_{j=1}^{k} H_1(ID, j)^{\hat{m}_{n+j}} \prod_{i=1}^{n} g_i^{\hat{m}_i} \cdot pk_c^{\sum_{l=1}^{k} \beta_l})^x
$$

$$
\Rightarrow \hat{\sigma} = U/R
$$

$$
= (\prod_{j=1}^{k} H_1(ID, j)^{\hat{m}_{n+j}} \prod_{i=1}^{n} g_i^{\hat{m}_i} \cdot pk_c^{\sum_{l=1}^{k} \beta_l})^x / pk_u^{y(\sum_{l=1}^{k} \beta_l - 1)}
$$

$$
= (\prod_{j=1}^{k} H_1(ID, j)^{\hat{m}_{n+j}} \prod_{i=1}^{n} g_i^{\hat{m}_i} \cdot pk_c^{\sum_{l=1}^{k} \beta_l})^x / pk_c^{x(\sum_{l=1}^{k} \beta_l - 1)}
$$

$$
= (\prod_{j=1}^{k} H_1(ID, j)^{\hat{m}_{n+j}} \prod_{i=1}^{n} g_i^{\hat{m}_i} \cdot pk_c)^x
$$

$$
= \mathbf{Sign}(pp, sk_u, pk_c, id, \hat{\mathbf{m}}).
$$

4.2   Security Analysis

Theorem 1. *If the adversary can break the proposed scheme with non-negligible advantage ϵ, the CDH problem can be solved with non-negligible advantage $\epsilon' \geq e^2(1 - \frac{1}{q_s \cdot q_h})(1 - \frac{1}{q})\epsilon$, where q_h, q_s are the times of queries made to the H_1 **Query** and **Sign Query**.*

Proof. Given some public parameters $pp = (q, \mathbb{G}_1, \mathbb{G}_2, e, g)$. Suppose there is an adversary $\mathcal{A}$, we construct another polynomial-time algorithm $\mathcal{B}$ to solve the CDH problem by interacting with $\mathcal{A}$.

Let $a, b \in \mathbb{Z}_q^*$ be a random input of CDH problem instance g^a, g^b, the algorithm $\mathcal{B}$ is required to output g^{ab}.

Initialization. $\mathcal{B}$ chooses a positive integer N, then does the following:

1. Chooses $s_j \in \mathbb{Z}_q^*$ and sets $g_j = (g^b)^{s_j}$ for $j \in [1, N]$.
2. Lets $pk_u = g^a$, and $pp = (q, \mathbb{G}_1, \mathbb{G}_2, e, g, g_1, \ldots, g_N)$.
3. Sends the public parameters pp and the user public key pk_u to $\mathcal{A}$.

Combiner-Key Generation Query. Suppose $\mathcal{A}$ issues at most q_k combiner-key generation queries. $\mathcal{B}$ denotes t-th combiner-key generation query as $(pk_c^{(t)}, sk_c^{(t)})$, and guesses the T-th query is the challenge designated combiner, where $T \in [1, q_k]$. $\mathcal{B}$ maintains a list L_k that consists of tuples $(t, sk_c^{(t)}, pk_c^{(t)})$, then does:

1. If $t \neq T$, $\mathcal{B}$ selects a random value $y_t \in \mathbb{Z}_q^*$ as the private key $sk_c^{(t)}$ and computes the public key $pk_c^{(t)} = g^{y_t}$.
2. If $t = T$, $\mathcal{B}$ selects a random value y_t and sets the combiner's public key $pk_c^{(t)} = g^{by_t}$. The private key $sk_c^{(T)}$ is unknown to both $\mathcal{B}$ and $\mathcal{A}$.

$\mathcal{B}$ inserts $(t, sk_c^{(t)}, pk_c^{(t)})$ into the list L_k and returns $pk_c^{(t)}$ to $\mathcal{A}$.

Combiner Corruption Query. $\mathcal{B}$ is given a combiner's public key $pk_c^{(t)}$, $\mathcal{B}$ aborts the simulation if $t = T$, otherwise, $\mathcal{B}$ looks up the list L_k and returns the corresponding private key $sk_c^{(t)}$ to $\mathcal{A}$.

H_1 **Query.** $\mathcal{B}$ maintains a list L_H that consists of tuples $(\tau, \{\zeta_i, H_1(i, \tau)\}_{i=1}^k)$. When $\mathcal{A}$ requests the value of $H_1(i, \tau)$, $\mathcal{B}$:

1. If τ has already been queried, $\mathcal{B}$ returns $H_1(i, \tau), i \in [1, k]$.
2. Otherwise, $\mathcal{B}$ randomly chooses $\zeta_i \in \mathbb{Z}_q^*$, computes $H_1(i, \tau) = (g^b)^{\zeta_i}$, adds $(\tau, \{\zeta_i, H_1(i, \tau)\}_{i=1}^k)$ into the L_H list and returns $\{H_1(i, \tau)\}_{i=1}^k$ to $\mathcal{A}$.

Sign Query. $\mathcal{A}$ requests the signature on the vector subspace $V \subset \mathbb{Z}_q^N$, described by properly augmented basis vectors $\mathbf{m}_1, \ldots, \mathbf{m}_k \in \mathbb{Z}_q^N$ ($\mathbf{m}_i = (m_1, \ldots, m_N)$). The algorithm $\mathcal{B}$ does the following:

1. Chooses a random $id \leftarrow \{0, 1\}^\lambda$ and sets the tag $\tau = (id, pk_c^{(t)})$ for subspace. If $H_1(\cdot, \tau)$ has already been queried, the simulation is aborted.

2. Lets $k = N - n$, computes $\zeta_i = -\sum_{j=1}^{n} s_j m_{ij}$ for $i = 1, \ldots, k$.

3. Chooses a random value $z_i \in \mathbb{Z}_q^*$, and sets $H_1(i, \tau) = \frac{g^{z_i} \cdot (g^b)^{\zeta_i} \,(t)}{pk_c}$.

4. Computes
$$\sigma_i = (g^a)^{z_i}$$

5. Outputs the tag τ and signatures $(\sigma_1, \ldots \sigma_k)$.

Combine Query. When $\mathcal{A}$ submits $(pk_c^{(t)}, \tau, \{\beta_i, \mathbf{m}_i, \sigma_i\}_{i=1}^k)$, $\mathcal{B}$ aborts the simulation if $t = T$. Otherwise, $\mathcal{B}$ checks whether the tag τ already appears in the sign queries, then $\mathcal{B}$ proceeds as follows:

1. Computes $r = y_t(\sum_{i=1}^{k} \beta_i - 1) \mod q$ and $R = pk_u^r$.
2. Computes $\hat{\mathbf{m}} = \sum_{i=1}^{k} \beta_i \mathbf{m}_i = (\hat{m}_1, \ldots, \hat{m}_N)$.
3. Computes $\hat{\sigma} = \prod_{i=1}^{k} \sigma_i^{\beta_i} / R$.
4. Outputs the tag τ and vector/signature pair $(\hat{\mathbf{m}}, \hat{\sigma})$

Output. If $\mathcal{B}$ does not abort, then $\mathcal{A}$ outputs a combiner's public key pk_c^*, a tag τ^*, a non-zero vector $\mathbf{w}^*$ and a valid signature σ^*.

If τ^* is not the tag used to answer a previous signature query, then $\mathcal{B}$ computes $H_1(\cdot, \tau^*)$ as above, in this case $H_1(i, \tau^*) = (g^b)^{\zeta_i}$ for $i = 1, \ldots, k$. $\mathcal{B}$ computes $\omega = (\frac{\sigma^*}{g^{ay}})^{\frac{1}{\mathbf{s} \cdot \mathbf{w}^*}}$, and outputs ω, where $\mathbf{s} = (s_1, \ldots s_n, \zeta_1, \ldots, \zeta_k)$.

The responses to all hash queries are independent and uniformly random in $\mathbb{G}_1$. We also observe that $g_1, \ldots, g_N$ are random group elements, and the public key pk_u output by $\mathcal{B}$ is distributed identically to the public key produced by the real **KeyGen** algorithm.

Next, we show that the signature σ output by $\mathcal{B}$ is identical to the signature that would be produced by the real **Sign** algorithm computed by $\mathcal{B}$. In fact, setting the public key pk_u and hash query as above, we have

$$\sigma = (\prod_{i=1}^{k} (H_1(i, \tau))^{m_{n+i}} \prod_{j=1}^{n} g_j^{m_j} \cdot pk_c^{(t)})^a = (g^a)^z$$

where $\sigma = (\prod_{i=1}^{k} (H_1(i, \tau))^{m_{n+i}} \prod_{j=1}^{n} g_j^{m_j} \cdot pk_c^{(t)})^a$ is the "real" signature and $\sigma = (g^a)^z$ is the signature computed by $\mathcal{B}$. The "real" signature is equal to

$$\sigma = (\frac{g^z \cdot (g^b)^{\zeta}}{pk_c} \cdot \prod_{j=1}^{n} g_j^{m_j} \cdot pk_c)^a = g^{az} \cdot g^{ab(\mathbf{s} \cdot \mathbf{m})}$$

From the construction of ζ in signature, we have $\mathbf{s} \cdot \mathbf{m} = 0$, and $\sigma = g^{az}$. Therefore, the **Sign** algorithm has been correctly simulated by $\mathcal{B}$.

Probability Analysis. We next analyze the probability that $\mathcal{B}$ does not abort the simulation. Let q_k, q_r, q_h, q_s, q_c be the times of queries made to the **Combiner-Key Generation Query, Combiner corruption Query,** H_1

Query, **Sign Query** and **Combine Query**, respectively. The conditions that $\mathcal{B}$ does not abort the simulation includes the following three aspects: (1) $\mathcal{A}$ has never issued a combiner corruption query on the challenge combiner. This probability is $(1 - \frac{1}{q_k})^{q_r}$. (2) $\mathcal{A}$ has never issued a combine corruption query on the challenge combiner. This probability is $(1 - \frac{1}{q_k})^{q_c}$. (3) $\mathcal{B}$ never aborts the simulation in sign query phase. This probability is $1 - \frac{1}{q_s \cdot q_h}$.

The probability of the simulation does not abort is $(1 - \frac{1}{q_k})^{q_r}(1 - \frac{1}{q_k})^{q_c}(1 - \frac{1}{q_s \cdot q_h}) \geq e^2(1 - \frac{1}{q_s \cdot q_h})$. Besides, we assume that the probability that of $\mathcal{A}$ outputs a valid signature successfully is ϵ.

Suppose the simulation is not aborted and $\mathcal{A}$ outputs a tag τ^*, a non-zero vector $\mathbf{w}^*$ and a signature σ^*. If $\mathbf{Verify}(pp, pk_u, \mathbf{w}^*, w^*, \sigma^*) = 1$, we have

$$e(\sigma^*, g) = e(\prod_{i=1}^{k} H_1(i, \tau)^{w_{n+i}} \prod_{j=1}^{n} g_j^{w_j} \cdot pk_c^{(t)}, pk_u)$$

Because of the same reasoning as above, we have

$$e(g^{b(\sum_{j=1}^{k} \zeta_j w_{n+j} + \sum_{i=1}^{n} s_j w_j) + y}, pk_u) = e(g^{ab(\mathbf{s} \cdot \mathbf{w}^*)} \cdot g^{ay}, g)$$

According to the non-degeneracy property of e, we have

$$\sigma^* = g^{ab(\mathbf{s} \cdot \mathbf{w}^*)} \cdot g^{ay}$$

It follows that if $\mathbf{s} \cdot \mathbf{w}^* \neq 0 \mod q$ then the element $\omega = (\frac{\sigma^*}{g^{ay}})^{\frac{1}{\mathbf{s} \cdot \mathbf{w}^*}}$ output by $\mathcal{B}$ is equal to g^{ab}.

$\mathcal{B}$ cannot compute g^{ab} if $\mathbf{s} \cdot \mathbf{w}^* = 0 \mod q$ even if the forgery belongs to one of the three types of forgery. In the following cases, the probability of $\mathbf{s} \cdot \mathbf{w}^* = 0 \mod q$ is as follows: (1) $\mathcal{A}$ has not queried the signature with the tag τ^*. All elements of the vector $\mathbf{s}$ are uniformly distributed over $\mathbb{Z}_q$ and $\mathcal{A}$ knows nothing about them. Since the vector $\mathbf{w}^*$ is a non-zero vector, $\mathbf{s} \cdot \mathbf{w}^*$ is uniformly distributed over $\mathbb{Z}_q$, which indicates that the probability of $\mathbf{s} \cdot \mathbf{w}^* = 0$ is at most $1/q$. (2) $\mathcal{A}$ has queried a signature query under the tag τ, but the vector $\mathbf{w}^* \notin V$. All elements of the vector $\mathbf{s}$ above are uniformly distributed over $\mathbb{Z}_q$, implying that $\mathbf{s}$ is uniformly distributed over $V^\perp$. Therefore, for any $\mathbf{w}^* \notin V$, $\mathbf{s} \cdot \mathbf{w}^*$ is uniformly distributed over $\mathbb{Z}_q$. Obviously, the probability of $\mathbf{s} \cdot \mathbf{w}^* = 0$ is also at most $1/q$. (3) $\mathcal{A}$ has queried a signature query under the tag τ, the vector $\mathbf{w}^* \in V - \{\mathbf{m}_1, \ldots, \mathbf{m}_k\}$. Since $\mathbf{m}_1, \ldots, \mathbf{m}_k$ is a set of basis vectors of V, all of them are none-zero vectors. All elements of the vector $\mathbf{s}$ above uniformly distributed over $\mathbb{Z}_q$, implying that $\mathbf{s}$ is uniformly distributed in V. For any $\mathbf{m}_i, i \in [1, k]$ we see that $\mathbf{s} \cdot \mathbf{m}_i$ satisfies uniformly distributed over $\mathbb{Z}_q$. Thus, for any $\mathbf{w}^* \notin V - \{\mathbf{m}_1, \ldots, \mathbf{m}_k\}$, $\mathbf{s} \cdot \mathbf{w}^*$ is uniformly distributed over $\mathbb{Z}_{q-k}$. Obviously, the probability of $\mathbf{s} \cdot \mathbf{w}^* = 0$ is $\frac{1}{q-k}$. Since $q >> k$, the probability of $\mathbf{s} \cdot \mathbf{w}^* = 0$ is close to $1/q$.

According to the three above situations, the probability of $\mathbf{s} \cdot \mathbf{w}^* \neq 0 \mod q$ is $1 - \frac{1}{q}$. Overall, the simulator $\mathcal{B}$ can output $\omega = g^{ab}$ with the probability

$$\epsilon' \geq e^2(1 - \frac{1}{q_s \cdot q_h})(1 - \frac{1}{q})\epsilon.$$

Since the CDH assumption holds, the advantage of solving the CDH problem is negligible, i.e. ϵ' is negligible, we say the probability ϵ of $\mathcal{A}$ forging a valid signature is negligible. Therefore, there exists no probabilistic polynomial-time adversary $\mathcal{A}$ that can break the proposed scheme.

The proof is completed.

5   Theoretical Analysis

Table 2 shows the comparison among our SPS-LHSDC scheme, Boneh et al.'s [3] NCS_1 scheme and Lin et al.'s [18] scheme over signature generation, combination and verification.

Computation Cost: Using a personal computer (PC) with an Intel i5 3.2 GHz quad-cores processor, 4 GB RAM, we evaluate each operation under the Java Pairing-Based Cryptography Library (JPBC) [9]. The parameter $a.param$ provides a symmetric pairing. The running time of different pairing-based operations is listed in Table 1. We omit the map to $\mathbb{Z}_q$ hash operation and additive operation in $\mathbb{Z}_q$, since the cost of these operations is negligible.

Table 1. Operations and time consumption

	Operation	Time
T_E	Exponential operation in $\mathbb{G}_1$	9 ms
T_P	Bilinear map operation	6 ms
T_H	Map-to-point hash operation	21 ms
T_M	Multiplicative operation in $\mathbb{G}_1$	5×10^{-2} ms
T_I	Inverse operation in $\mathbb{G}_1$	5×10^{-3} ms

Table 2. Comparison of computation cost

Scheme			
Algorithm	[3]	[18]	Our scheme
Sign	$(n+2)T_E + 1T_H + nT_M \approx 9n + 39\ ms$	$(n+2)T_E + 1T_P + 3T_H + (n+1)T_M \approx 9n + 87\ ms$	$(n+2)T_E + 1T_H + (n+1)T_M \approx 9n + 39\ ms$
Combine	$kT_E + (k-1)T_M \approx 9k\ ms$	$(k+3)T_E + 1T_P + 1T_H + kT_I + 2kT_M \approx 9k + 54\ ms$	$(k+1)T_E + (k-1)T_M \approx 9k + 9\ ms$
Verify	$NT_E + 2T_P + kT_H + (N-1)T_M \approx 9N + 21k + 12\ ms$	$(N+1)T_E + 2T_P + (k+1)T_H + 1T_I + NT_M \approx 9N + 21k + 42\ ms$	$NT_E + 2T_P + kT_H + NT_M \approx 9N + 21k + 12\ ms$
Designated combiner	No	Yes	Yes

In order to facilitate comparison, we assume that there are k vectors and each vector has n sectors. Let $N = (n + k)$ is the dimension of the augmented vector. From Table 2, we see that our scheme requires lower computation cost than Lin et al.'s [18] scheme, and slightly higher computation cost than Boneh et al.'s [3] scheme in signature generation, combination and verification phases.

6   Conclusion

In this paper, we formalize the definition as well as the security model for structure-preserving linearly homomorphic signature scheme with designated combiner for subspace. In this work, the combined signature is indistinguishable from signatures generated by the signer, and only the designated entity can run the combine algorithm. Other entities except for the signer and the designated entity cannot generate a valid signature for any vector in the signed subspace. Finally, we propose an efficient structure-preserving linearly homomorphic signature scheme with designated combiner and prove it is secure under the CDH problem assumption. The theoretical analysis shows that the combine algorithm in our scheme needs a lower cost compared to other schemes with designated combiner.

Acknowledgement. We thank the anonymous reviewers of ACISP 2022 for their useful comments. This work is supported by the National Natural Science Foundation of China under grants (62172096, 62072134, U2001205), and the Key projects of Guangxi Natural Science Foundation under grant 2019JJD170020, and the Key Research and Development Program of Hubei Province under Grant 2021BEA163.

References

1. Abe, M., Fuchsbauer, G., Groth, J., Haralambiev, K., Ohkubo, M.: Structure-preserving signatures and commitments to group elements. In: Rabin, T. (ed.) CRYPTO 2010. LNCS, vol. 6223, pp. 209–236. Springer, Heidelberg (2010). https://doi.org/10.1007/978-3-642-14623-7_12
2. Attrapadung, N., Libert, B.: Homomorphic network coding signatures in the standard model. In: Catalano, D., Fazio, N., Gennaro, R., Nicolosi, A. (eds.) PKC 2011. LNCS, vol. 6571, pp. 17–34. Springer, Heidelberg (2011). https://doi.org/10.1007/978-3-642-19379-8_2
3. Attrapadung, N., Libert, B., Peters, T.: Efficient completely context-hiding quotable and linearly homomorphic signatures. In: Kurosawa, K., Hanaoka, G. (eds.) PKC 2013. LNCS, vol. 7778, pp. 386–404. Springer, Heidelberg (2013). https://doi.org/10.1007/978-3-642-36362-7_24
4. Boneh, D., Freeman, D.M.: Linearly homomorphic signatures over binary fields and new tools for lattice-based signatures. In: Catalano, D., Fazio, N., Gennaro, R., Nicolosi, A. (eds.) PKC 2011. LNCS, vol. 6571, pp. 1–16. Springer, Heidelberg (2011). https://doi.org/10.1007/978-3-642-19379-8_1
5. Boneh, D., Freeman, D., Katz, J., Waters, B.: Signing a linear subspace: signature schemes for network coding. In: Jarecki, S., Tsudik, G. (eds.) PKC 2009. LNCS, vol. 5443, pp. 68–87. Springer, Heidelberg (2009). https://doi.org/10.1007/978-3-642-00468-1_5

6. Catalano, D., Fiore, D., Warinschi, B.: Homomorphic signatures with efficient verification for polynomial functions. In: Garay, J.A., Gennaro, R. (eds.) CRYPTO 2014. LNCS, vol. 8616, pp. 371–389. Springer, Heidelberg (2014). https://doi.org/10.1007/978-3-662-44371-2_21

7. Chang, J., Ji, Y., Shao, B., Xu, M., Xue, R.: Certificateless homomorphic signature scheme for network coding. IEEE/ACM Trans. Netw. 28(6), 2615–2628 (2020)

8. Cheng, C., Lee, J., Jiang, T., Takagi, T.: Security analysis and improvements on two homomorphic authentication schemes for network coding. IEEE Trans. Inf. Forensics Secur. 11(5), 993–1002 (2016)

9. De Caro, A., Iovino, V.: jPBC: Java pairing based cryptography. In: Proceedings of the 16th IEEE Symposium on Computers and Communications, ISCC 2011, pp. 850–855. IEEE (2011)

10. Desmedt, Y.: Computer security by redefining what a computer is. In: Proceedings on the 1992–1993 Workshop on New Security Paradigms, pp. 160–166. ACM (1993)

11. Fuchsbauer, G., Hanser, C., Slamanig, D.: Structure-preserving signatures on equivalence classes and constant-size anonymous credentials. J. Cryptol. 32(2), 498–546 (2019). https://doi.org/10.1007/s00145-018-9281-4

12. Gennaro, R., Katz, J., Krawczyk, H., Rabin, T.: Secure network coding over the integers. In: Nguyen, P.Q., Pointcheval, D. (eds.) PKC 2010. LNCS, vol. 6056, pp. 142–160. Springer, Heidelberg (2010). https://doi.org/10.1007/978-3-642-13013-7_9

13. Gorbunov, S., Vaikuntanathan, V., Wichs, D.: Leveled fully homomorphic signatures from standard lattices. In: Proceedings of the Forty-Seventh Annual ACM on Symposium on Theory of Computing, STOC 2015, pp. 469–477. ACM (2015)

14. Johnson, R., Molnar, D., Song, D., Wagner, D.: Homomorphic signature schemes. In: Preneel, B. (ed.) CT-RSA 2002. LNCS, vol. 2271, pp. 244–262. Springer, Heidelberg (2002). https://doi.org/10.1007/3-540-45760-7_17

15. Li, T., Chen, W., Tang, Y., Yan, H.: A homomorphic network coding signature scheme for multiple sources and its application in IoT. Secur. Commun. Netw. 2018, 9641273:1–9641273:6 (2018)

16. Li, Y., Zhang, F., Liu, X.: Secure data delivery with identity-based linearly homomorphic network coding signature scheme in IoT. IEEE Trans. Serv. Comput. 15(4), 2202–2212 (2022). https://doi.org/10.1109/TSC.2020.3039976

17. Lin, C.-J., Huang, X., Li, S., Wu, W., Yang, S.-J.: Linearly homomorphic signatures with designated entities. In: Liu, J.K., Samarati, P. (eds.) ISPEC 2017. LNCS, vol. 10701, pp. 375–390. Springer, Cham (2017). https://doi.org/10.1007/978-3-319-72359-4_22

18. Lin, C., Xue, R., Huang, X.: Linearly homomorphic signatures with designated combiner. In: Huang, Q., Yu, Yu. (eds.) ProvSec 2021. LNCS, vol. 13059, pp. 327–345. Springer, Cham (2021). https://doi.org/10.1007/978-3-030-90402-9_18

19. SadrHaghighi, S., Khorsandi, S.: An identity-based digital signature scheme to detect pollution attacks in intra-session network coding. In: 13th International Iranian Society of Cryptology Conference on Information Security and Cryptology, ISCISC 2016, pp. 7–12. IEEE (2016)

20. Yu, H., Li, W.: A certificateless signature for multi-source network coding. J. Inf. Secur. Appl. 55, 102655 (2020)

21. Yu, Z., Wei, Y., Ramkumar, B., Guan, Y.: An efficient signature-based scheme for securing network coding against pollution attacks. In: INFOCOM 2008. 27th IEEE International Conference on Computer Communications, Joint Conference of the IEEE Computer and Communications Societies, pp. 1409–1417. IEEE (2008)

22. Zhang, P., Yu, J., Wang, T.: A homomorphic aggregate signature scheme based on lattice. Chin. J. Electron. **21**(4), 701–704 (2012)
23. Zhang, Y., Jiang, Y., Li, B., Zhang, M.: An efficient identity-based homomorphic signature scheme for network coding. In: Barolli, L., Zhang, M., Wang, X.A. (eds.) EIDWT 2017. LNDECT, vol. 6, pp. 524–531. Springer, Cham (2018). https://doi. org/10.1007/978-3-319-59463-7_52

TIDE: A Novel Approach to Constructing Timed-Release Encryption

Angelique Faye Loe[1]([✉]), Liam Medley[1], Christian O'Connell[2],
and Elizabeth A. Quaglia[1]

[1] Royal Holloway, University of London, Egham, UK
angelique.loe.2016@live.rhul.ac.uk
[2] Egham, UK

Abstract. In ESORICS 2021, Chvojka et al. introduced the idea of taking a time-lock puzzle and using its solution to generate the keys of a public key encryption (PKE) scheme [12]. They use this to define a timed-release encryption (TRE) scheme, in which the secret key is encrypted 'to the future' using a time-lock puzzle, whilst the public key is published. This allows multiple parties to encrypt a message to the public key of the PKE scheme. Then, once a solver has spent a prescribed length of time evaluating the time-lock puzzle, they obtain the secret key and hence can decrypt all of the messages.

In this work we introduce TIDE (TIme Delayed Encryption), a novel approach to constructing timed-release encryption based upon the RSA cryptosystem, where instead of directly encrypting the secret key to the future, we utilise number-theoretic techniques to allow the solver to factor the RSA modulus, and hence derive the decryption key. We implement TIDE on a desktop PC and on Raspberry Pi devices validating that TIDE is both efficient and practically implementable. We provide evidence of practicality with an extensive implementation study detailing the source code and practical performance of TIDE.

Keywords: Auctions · Time-lock puzzle · Timed-release encryption · Public key cryptography

1 Introduction

In 1996, Rivest et al. introduced the notion of sending a message 'to the future' using a time-lock puzzle [35]. This seminal paper is the basis of modern-day delay-based cryptography. Delay-based cryptography is a prominent and wide-ranging subject built around the notion of associating standard 'wall-clock time' with an iterated sequential computation. In modern times, delay-based cryptography is used in the classical sense of encrypting a message to the future using various primitives such as time-lock puzzles [18,29], timed-release encryption [11,12] and delay encryption [10]; as well as in alternative applications such as

Independent.

providing a computational proof-of-age of a document, and building a public randomness beacon [8,32,38].

In this paper, we introduce TIDE, a novel construction of timed-release encryption. TIDE is particularly suited to the application of sealed-bid auctions, providing a practical and efficient solution to Vickrey auctions, as we shall explore next.

1.1 Sealed-Bid Auctions

Sealed-bid auctions allow bidders to secretly submit a bid for some goods without learning the bids of any other party involved until the end of the auction. In a sealed-bid second-price auction, known as a Vickrey auction, the highest bidder wins the goods but pays the price of the second highest bid [1,6,37]. The challenge of building a fair, efficient, and cryptographically secure Vickrey auction has been of interest for decades [4,9,10,21,25]. A common approach to constructing sealed-bid auctions is to implement a *commit and reveal* solution using an append-only bulletin board, e.g., a blockchain [21]. Such solutions consist of two phases: a bidding phase, where parties commit to a bid and post their commitment on the bulletin board; and an opening phase where parties reveal their bids. However, the main drawback of this approach is that parties are not obliged to open their bids, which is particularly problematic in the example of Vickrey auctions as it is necessary to learn the second highest bid as well as the first [1,6]. For an auction to be transparent and fair it is desirable that each party must open their commitments to the bid once the bidding phase has ended.

By replacing the commitments with time-lock puzzles one can obtain an elegant method of solving this problem [35]. Each party encrypts their bid as the solution to a time-lock puzzle. Therefore, in the opening phase if a party does not reveal their bid it can instead be opened by computing the solution to the puzzle. However, this method does not scale well becaue it leads to many different time-lock puzzles being solved, which is computationally expensive. Recently there has been research into solving this problem more efficiently.

At CRYPTO 2019 [29], Malavolta et al. suggest that each party encrypts their bid as a time-lock puzzle, as in the classical method suggested by Rivest et al. Their insight is that the tallyer then uses techniques from homomorphic encryption to evaluate a computation over the set of puzzles to determine the winning bidder. This leads to only the relevant puzzle being solved rather than the entire set of puzzles. Whilst this is a very elegant solution the application relies on fully homomorphic TLP constructions and all current constructions of homomorphic TLPs are based on indistinguishability obfuscation (IO) [10,29]. IO aims to obfuscate programs to make them unintelligible whilst retaining their original functionality [2]. However, IO is known to be impractical with no construction efficiently implementable at the time of writing [24].

At EUROCRYPT 2021 Burdges et al. introduce Delay Encryption [10], a primitive which offers an alternative approach to solving this problem, using a delay-based analogue to identity-based encryption. Where time-lock puzzles require each bidder to encrypt their bid against a unique time-lock puzzle, Delay Encryption instead requires bidders to encrypt their bid to a public *session ID*.

This session ID acts as a bulletin board, meaning anyone who knows this session ID can efficiently encrypt messages to it. All messages encrypted to the session ID can be efficiently decrypted by any party who knows a secret *session key*. The key feature of DE is a slow and sequential Extract algorithm, which outputs a session key after a prescribed amount of time. This time delay defines the bidding phase of the auction in which parties may encrypt bids to the session ID. Once the session key has been extracted all bids can be decrypted, thus replacing the opening phase described in the commit-and-reveal paradigm. This works well in the context of auctions as in the opening phase. In DE rather than solving multiple time-lock puzzle the Extract algorithm is run once which outputs a *session key*.

This seems to be an ideal solution, however the construction of DE presented in [10] comes with two significant practical disadvantages: (i) The storage requirements needed to compute the decryption key is huge - a delay of one hour requires 12 TiB of storage; (ii) The time taken to run setup grows proportionally to the delay, which is very expensive. These two factors make this construction problematic from a practical standpoint.

The goal of the approaches outlined above is to utilise a time-delay to solve the auction problem in a scalable manner. This improves upon the efficiency of Rivest's solution by ensuring that at most two sequential computation (namely the puzzles containing the two highest bids in [29], and Extract in [10]) needs to be run, rather than one for each bid. However, the approaches so far have practical problems with the instantiation of their proposed candidate.

At ESORICS 2021 Chvojka et al. introduce the idea of taking a TLP and using its solution in the key generation of a public key encryption (PKE) scheme [12]. They use this to define a timed-release encryption (TRE) scheme where multiple parties encrypt a message to the public key of the PKE scheme. Then upon solving the puzzle they can reconstruct the secret key and decrypt all of the messages. The authors explain how to achieve this generically using standard TLP and PKE primitives, but no concrete instantiation is provided.

In this work we present TIDE, a novel, efficient and easily implementable approach to building a TRE scheme to solve the scalability problems in Vickrey auctions. TIDE seamlessly integrates RSA encryption into a TLP using powerful results from number theory. On top of being a concrete construction, TIDE subtly differs in its approach to that in [12] in the way the secret key is derived. We provide further insights on how TIDE works next.

1.2   Technical Overview

TIDE relies on the RSW time-lock assumption, which states that it is hard to compute $x^{2^t} \bmod N$ in fewer than t sequential steps [35], for an RSA modulus N. This assumption was first introduced in 1996 by Rivest et al. [35], and has been used to build a variety of cryptographic constructions [8,18,29,32,38]. TIDE deviates from previous literature by using number theoretic techniques to utilise the output $x^{2^t} \bmod N$ in a novel way. Previous approaches used squaring solely for its sequential properties, i.e., the final output is used only to guarantee a delay. For example, in time-lock puzzles, the solution to the puzzle is precomputed using a trapdoor, in order to hide a message as the product of the solution and the message [18,29,35]. This allows one to trivially obtain the message upon computing the delay, and hence solving the puzzle.

In the context of verifiable delay functions, the RSW assumption is used to prove that a certain amount of clock time has taken place. This is achieved by the solver computing repeated squarings upon a randomly sampled element of $\mathbb{Z}_N^*$, and computing a proof in order to mathematically prove to a verifier that t squarings have taken place [8,32,38].

In TIDE the output of the computation expands beyond guaranteeing a delay. Namely TIDE provides exactly the information required to factor the RSA modulus N. TIDE achieves this by incorporating a theorem of Fermat and Rabin, which states that if x and x' are known such that $x^2 \equiv x'^2 \bmod N$, where $x \not\equiv \pm x' \bmod N$, then the non-trivial factors of N can be recovered in polynomial time [33]. By carefully setting up the system we provide the user with value x and ensure that the output of the squaring reveals x'. Therefore knowledge of x and x' can be used to factor N in polynomial time. Then we combine this with a standard RSA encryption scheme using N and a encryption exponent as the public key. Once a solving party computes the delay they can derive the secret key and hence can decrypt all messages. Therefore, our construction can be seen as a natural integration of an RSW-based time-lock puzzle and the RSA encryption scheme. We formalise this in terms of syntax and security definitions in Sect. 4, where we follow the definition of TRE by Chvojka et al. [12].

The key insight of TIDE is contained in the generation of the public key and puzzle, as this allows us to use the relevant theorem of Rabin [33]. N is chosen to be a particular class of RSA modulus known as a Blum integer $N = pq$, which has the property that $p \equiv q \equiv 3 \bmod 4$. The puzzle consists of three different elements, $P = (x, x_0, x_{-t})$. First, the element x is efficiently sampled such that $\mathcal{J}_N(x) = -1$, where $\mathcal{J}_N(x)$ is the Jacobi symbol [26]. Next, the seed x_0 is calculated as $x_0 \equiv x^2 \bmod N$. Crucial to TIDE is the term x_{-t}, where $x_{-t}^2 \equiv x_0 \bmod N$.

Now, any party wishing to solve the puzzle sequentially calculates the term $x_{-1} := x' \equiv \sqrt{x_0}$ by repeated squaring. The term x' has the property $\mathcal{J}_N(x') = +1$. This is crucial, as in Gen x was chosen such that $\mathcal{J}_N(x) = -1$. Therefore, the solving party obtains the term $x^2 \equiv x'^2 \equiv x_0 \bmod N$, where $x \neq x' \bmod N$. Thus, the party obtains all four square roots of x_0. Therefore, Solve can recover the non-trivial factors of N in polynomial time using the result from Rabin [33].

The simplicity of RSA encryption and decryption makes TIDE a conceptually simple approach to sealed-bid auctions, whilst the underlying number theoretic techniques allow the functionality to be very efficient and practical.

1.3   Related Work

Alternatives to Vickrey Auctions. The most common style of auction is the sealed first-bid auction in which the highest bidder wins and pays the amount they bid for the goods. From a cryptographic perspective this is more straightforward to implement, making it easier to include additional properties in such schemes. For example, research has been done into sealed first-bid auction schemes where the bids of losers remain hidden, by requiring bidders to run a protocol computing the highest bid, and ensuring that only the highest bid is opened [4, 36].

In a well-known paper 'Secure Multiparty Computation Goes Live' [7], techniques from multi-party computation were used to implement a nation wide double auction in Denmark. In a double auction, sellers indicate how much of an item they are willing to sell at certain price points, whilst buyers indicate how much of the same item they are willing to buy at each price point. Using this information, the *market clearing price*, i.e., the price per unit of this item is computed, allowing transactions to be made at this price point.

Both of these examples rely on a very different framework to that of TIDE: they requires multiple parties being online at the same time carrying out a protocol. As such, whilst linked by the application of auctions, we view such work as tangential. We now turn our attention to delay-based cryptography which is more closely related to our work.

Encrypting a Message to the Future. Time-lock puzzles (TLPs) were first introduced in the seminal paper of Rivest et al. [35] as a way to encrypt messages to the future. They suggested various applications for this, including sealed-bid auctions and key escrow schemes. The method they use to build the delay is sequentially squaring in a finite group of unknown order, which is known as the RSW time-lock assumption. Recently, there have been some alternative approaches to building TLPs. Rather than using repeated squaring new TLPs include using witness encryption and bitcoin [27], randomised encodings [3], and random isogeny walks over elliptic curves [17].

The RSW time-lock assumption has been used as the base of various constructions of *verifiable delay functions* (VDFs) [8, 32, 38]. In a VDF a solver computes a delay similarly to a time-lock puzzle, but rather than decrypting a message at the end, the solver instead proves that they have spent the prescribed amount of time on the computation. This proof of elapsed time has primarily found use in randomness beacons which are used in blockchain design [13].

In 2019 De Feo et al. introduced a VDF based upon isogeny walks [17], which in 2021 they extended to a *delay encryption* (DE) scheme. DE is similar to a time-lock puzzle, but rather than proving that time has elapsed, instead a *session key* is derived. This can be seen as similar to the decryption key described in the technical overview of TIDE, in Sect. 1.2. Indeed DE as a primitive is very similar to the notion of timed-release encryption where we align our TIDE construction. The key difference between the two primitives is that DE uses notions from identity-based encryption and thus avoids using a trapdoor in the setup phase.

Recall in Sect. 1.1 that timed-release encryption (TRE) is another delay-based primitive, whose traditional definition combines public-key encryption with a time-server [11, 30]. Messages can be encrypted to a public key and decryption requires a trapdoor which is kept confidential by a time-server until at an appointed time. In a recent paper by Chvojka et al. [12] TRE was defined generically with a view to improving versatility and functionality. Whilst we build a timed-release encryption scheme following the definitions of Chvojka et al., our scheme does not require a time-server.

1.4 Contributions

In our work we design a novel and theoretically efficient variant of a time-lock puzzle by utilising RSA encryption and decryption to obtain a simple and efficient construction. We provide a security and efficiency analysis of our construction, proving that TIDE is cryptographically secure under the TRE notions [12]. We analyse the theoretical and practical efficiency of our scheme, proving that it has concrete theoretical advantages over the alternative proposals for Vickrey auctions and demonstrate that it is significantly more practical than current candidates. We present evidence of the practicality of our scheme by providing an implementation study using Raspberry Pi devices and a desktop PC, showing that TIDE can be run efficiently on consumer grade hardware. In particular, we show that when using a 2048-bit modulus, TIDE takes approximately one second to setup on a desktop PC and 30 s on a Raspberry Pi.

2 Preliminaries: Assumptions and Number Theory

In this section we review the time-lock assumption and number theory required to construct TIDE. For well-known theorems we refer to the relevant sources and we prove the other theorems in Sect. 4 and Appendix B of our full paper [28].

The RSW time-lock assumption [35] is core to a number of notable constructions using a cryptographic delay in the latest literature [8,16,18,29,32,38].

**Definition 1. *RSW time-lock assumption:* **Let $N = pq$ where p and q are distinct odd primes. Uniformly select $x \in \mathbb{Z}_N^*$, where $\mathbb{Z}_N^* = \{x \mid x \in (0, N) \wedge gcd(x, N) = 1\}$. Then set the seed term as $x_0 := x^2 \bmod N$. If a probabilistic polynomial time (PPT) adversary $\mathcal{A}$ does not know the factorisation of N or group order $\phi(N)$ then calculating $x_t \equiv x_0^{2^t} \bmod N$ is a non-parallelizable calculation that will require t sequential modular exponentiations calculated with the Algorithm 2.1 Square and Multiply [35].

Secondly we note that the modulus used in our TIDE will be a Blum integer [5]. A Blum integer $N = pq$, is the product of two Gaussian primes. A Gaussian prime has the property $p \equiv 3 \bmod 4$.

Next, we provide the definition of quadratic residues.

**Definition 2. *Quadratic Residues* **in $\mathbb{Z}_N^*$ are numbers r that satisfy congruences of the form:

$$x^2 \equiv r \mod N \tag{1}$$

If an integer x exists such that the preceding congruence is satisfied, we say that r is a quadratic residue of N. If no such x exists we say that r is a quadratic non-residue of N.

Algorithm 2.1: Square and Multiply [14]

    input : (a, b, N), $//$ $a, b, N \in \mathbb{N}$, $a^b \bmod N$

1 $d := 1$
2 $B := \text{bin}(b)$ $//$ b `in binary`
3 **for** $j \in B$ **do**
4      $d := d^2 \bmod N$
5   **if** $j = 1$ **then**
6        $\mid$ $d := da \bmod N$
7   **end**
8 **end**
    output: d

The Jacobi symbol, denoted $\mathcal{J}_N(r)$, is a function which defines the quadratic character of r in Eq. 1. The Jacobi Symbol can be calculated in polynomial time using Euler's Criterion.

Theorem 1. *Euler's Criterion can be used to calculate the Jacobi Symbol of the number r in Eq. 1 for a prime modulus p. If $\gcd(r, p) = 1$, then:*

$$\mathcal{J}_p(r) = r^{\frac{p-1}{2}} = \begin{cases} +1, \text{if } r \in \mathcal{QR}_p \\ -1, \text{if } r \in \mathcal{QNR}_p \end{cases} \tag{2}$$

where $r \in \mathcal{QR}_p$ indicates that r is a quadratic residue of p and $r \in \mathcal{QNR}_p$ indicates that r is a quadratic non-residue of p.

When the modulus is a prime number if the Jacobi symbol evaluates to $+1$ then r is always a quadratic residue and if the Jacobi symbol evaluates to -1 then r is always a quadratic non-residue. The Jacobi symbol is more complex when the modulus is a composite number $N = pq$.

Corollary 1 *(of Theorem 1). Euler's Criterion can be used to calculate the Jacobi Symbol of the number r in Eq. 1 for a composite modulus N if the factorisation of N is known.*

Algorithm 2.2 shows how to determine the quadratic character of r for composite N using Theorem 1 and Corollary 1. When N is composite the quadratic character of r can take three formats. If the Jacobi symbol evaluates to -1 then r is always a quadratic non-residue, denoted $\mathcal{QNR}_N^{-1}$. However, if the Jacobi symbol evaluates to $+1$ then r can either be a quadratic residue, denoted $\mathcal{QR}_N$ or a quadratic non-residue denoted $\mathcal{QNR}_N^{+1}$.

Quadratic residues and quadratic non-residues for composite N have a distinct distribution in $\mathbb{Z}_N^*$.

Algorithm 2.2: Calculating $\mathcal{J}_N(r)$ for composite N.

---

    input : (r, p, q)

1 $\mathcal{J}_p(r) := r^{\frac{p-1}{2}} \bmod p$

2 $\mathcal{J}_q(r) := r^{\frac{q-1}{2}} \bmod q$

3 **if** $\mathcal{J}_p(r) = 1 \wedge \mathcal{J}_q(r) = 1$ **then**

4 | $x := \mathcal{QR}_N$

5 **else if** $\mathcal{J}_p(r) = -1 \wedge \mathcal{J}_q(r) = -1$ **then**

6 | $x := \mathcal{QNR}_N^{+1}$

7 **else**

8 | $x := \mathcal{QNR}_N^{-1}$

9 **end**

    output: x

Theorem 2. *The cardinality of $\mathcal{QR}_N$, $\mathcal{QNR}_N^{+1}$, and $\mathcal{QNR}_N^{-1}$ for composite $N = pq$, where p and q are distinct primes is as follows:*

$$|\mathcal{QR}_N| = \frac{|\mathbb{Z}_N^*|}{4} = \frac{\phi(N)}{4}.$$

$$|\mathcal{QNR}_N^{+1}| = \frac{|\mathbb{Z}_N^*|}{4} = \frac{\phi(N)}{4}. \tag{3}$$

$$|\mathcal{QNR}_N^{-1}| = \frac{|\mathbb{Z}_N^*|}{2} = \frac{\phi(N)}{2}.$$

where, $|\mathbb{Z}_N^*| = \phi(N) = (p-1)(q-1)$, and $\phi(N)$ is Euler's totient function.

Next, we discuss how to calculate preceding terms of the seed term $x_0 \in \mathcal{QR}_N$ in an RSW time-lock sequence. To calculate the subsequent term of x_0 in the sequence evaluate $x_1 \equiv x_0^{2^1} \bmod N$ by inputting $(x_0, 2^1, N)$ into Algorithm 2.1.

If the factorisation of N is known Theorem 1 can be used in conjunction with the Chinese Remainder Theorem (CRT) to calculate the term x_{-1} in polynomial time. The CRT can be found in our Auxiliary material.

Theorem 3. *Let p be a Gaussian prime. For any $r \in \mathbb{Z}_p^*$, if $\mathcal{J}_p(r) = +1$, then finding α such that $\alpha \equiv \sqrt{r} \bmod p$ can be found by calculating $\alpha \equiv r^{\frac{p+1}{4}} \bmod p$.*

Example 1. Let $N = 67 \cdot 139 = pq = 9313$. Given the seed $x_0 = 776 \in \mathcal{QR}_N$, the square root of $x_0 \bmod N$, denoted by $x_{-1} = \sqrt{x_0}$, can be found as follows:

– calculate $\alpha \equiv x_0^{\frac{p+1}{4}} \equiv x_0^{17} \equiv 21 \bmod p$

– calculate $\beta \equiv x_0^{\frac{q+1}{4}} \equiv x_0^{35} \equiv 9 \bmod q$

– calculate $x_{-1} = \alpha q(q^{-1} \bmod p) + \beta p(p^{-1} \bmod q) = 128862$

Then α and β are calculated using Theorem 3 and x_{-1} is calculated using the CRT. Note that $(q^{-1} \bmod p)$ and $(p^{-1} \bmod q)$ are calculated using Euclid's Extended Algorithm. To verify correctness, note that $128862^2 \equiv 776 \equiv x_0 \bmod N$. We provide formal analysis of this in Sect. 4.

If $r \in \mathcal{QR}_N$ then the CRT implies that there are four distinct solutions to Eq. 1.

Theorem 4. *For all $N = pq$, where p and q are distinct odd primes, each $r \in \mathcal{QR}_N$ has four distinct solutions.*

If N is a Blum integer, then the four square roots of each $r \in \mathcal{QR}_N$ has specific properties. That is, two of the square roots of r are quadratic non-residues with Jacobi symbol -1, one square root is a quadratic non-residue with Jacobi symbol $+1$, and one square root is a quadratic residue.

Theorem 5. *Let N be a Blum integer. Then for all $r \in \mathcal{QR}_N$, if $x^2 \equiv x'^2 \equiv r \bmod N$, where $x \neq \pm x'$, then without loss of generality $\mathcal{J}_N(\pm x) = -1$, and $\mathcal{J}_N(\pm x') = +1$. That is $\pm x \in \mathcal{QNR}_N^{-1}$, $x' \in \mathcal{QR}_N$ and $-x' \in \mathcal{QNR}_N^{+1}$. We refer to $x' \in \mathcal{QR}_N$ as the principal square root of $r \bmod N$.*

Finally, we discuss a method to factor a Blum integer N in polynomial time if specific information is provided.

Fermat's factorisation method is a technique to factor an odd composite number $N = pq$ in exponential time [15]. The method requires finding x and x' such that $x^2 - x'^2 = N$ is satisfied. Then the left-hand side can be expressed as a difference of squares $(x - x')(x + x') = N$.

Fermat's method can be extended to finding x and x' to satisfy the following weaker congruence of squares condition $x^2 \equiv x'^2 \bmod N$, where $x \neq \pm x'$. This congruence can be expressed as $(x-x')(x+x') \equiv 0 \bmod N$. Finding a congruence of squares forms the basis for several sub-exponential sieving-based factorisation algorithms [15]. However, if x and x' in a congruence of squares are known, then factoring N can be done in polynomial time.

Theorem 6. *Let N be a Blum integer. If x and x' are known such that $x^2 \equiv x'^2 \bmod N$, where $x \not\equiv \pm x' \bmod N$, then the non-trivial factors of N can be recovered in polynomial time.*

Proof. Proofs for Theorems 1, 2, 4, and Corollary 1 can be found in [26]. Proofs for Theorems 3 and 6 can be found in Sect. 4. The proof for Theorem 5 can be found in Appendix B of our full paper [28].

3   Our Construction

In this section we give the concrete details of our construction TIDE. Formally, TIDE is a TRE scheme and we provide a formal exposition of its security properties in Sect. 4. In our TRE scheme $\mathcal{C}$ is the Challenger, $\mathcal{S}$ is the Solver, and $\mathcal{A}$ is the Adversary. In the context of Vickery auctions, $\mathcal{C}$ can be though of as the auctioneer and $\mathcal{S}$ can be thought of as a Bidder. As is customary, multiple bidders are participate in an auction.

A TRE scheme consists of four algorithms: Gen, Solve, Encrypt, Decrypt. Gen and Solve provide the time-lock element of the scheme: Gen generates a secret key, public key and a puzzle, Solve takes the puzzle and recovers the corresponding secret key. Encrypt can be ran by multiple parties (bidders) simultaneously using the public key. Solve can be run by any party i.e. any bidder or third party can run this algorithm. Once Solve has terminated, the Solver can then use the secret key to decrypt all of the bids encrypted with Encrypt by using the Decrypt algorithm. We now outline the details of the four TIDE algorithms.

- $(\mathsf{sk}, \mathsf{pk}, P, t) \leftarrow \mathsf{Gen}(1^\kappa, t)$ takes as input a security parameter 1^κ and time parameter t and ouputs a secret key sk, public key pk, puzzle P, and time parameter. The secret key consists of the factors of $\mathsf{sk} := (p, q)$ and the public key consists of an RSA modulus N and fixed encryption exponent $e := 2^{16} + 1 = 65537$. The puzzle is set to $P := (x, x_0, x_{-t})$, where $x^2 \equiv x_0 \bmod N$, $\mathcal{J}_N(x) = -1$, and where $x_{-t}^{2^t} \equiv x_0 \bmod N$.
- $\mathsf{sk} \leftarrow \mathsf{Solve}(\mathsf{pk}, P, t)$ takes as input the public key pk, puzzle P, and time parameter t and outputs the secret key $\mathsf{sk} := (p, q)$, where $N = pq$.
- $c \leftarrow \mathsf{Encrypt}(\mathsf{pk}, m)$ takes as input a public key $\mathsf{pk} := (N, e)$ and a message m and outputs a ciphertext c.
- $\{m, \bot\} \leftarrow \mathsf{Decrypt}(\mathsf{sk}, c)$ takes as input the secret key $\mathsf{sk} := (p, q)$ and a ciphertext c as input and outputs a message m or error $\bot$.

Algorithm 3.1: Gen run on security parameter 1^κ and time parameter t to create the secret key sk, public key pk and puzzle P.

input : $1^\kappa, t$
1 $p, q := 1$
2 while $p = q$ do
3 $\quad p := \mathbf{prime}(\frac{\kappa}{2})$
4 $\quad q := \mathbf{prime}(\frac{\kappa}{2})$
5 end
6 $N := pq$
7 $\mathcal{J}_p(x), \mathcal{J}_q(x) := 1$
8 while $\neg(\mathcal{J}_p(x) = 1 \wedge \mathcal{J}_q(x) \neq 1) \wedge \neg(\mathcal{J}_p(x) \neq 1 \wedge \mathcal{J}_q(x) = 1)$ do
9 $\quad x := \mathcal{U}(2, N)$
10 $\quad \mathcal{J}_p(x) := x^{\frac{p-1}{2}} \bmod p$
11 $\quad \mathcal{J}_q(x) := x^{\frac{q-1}{2}} \bmod q$
12 end
13 $x_0 := x^2 \bmod N$
14 $\alpha_t := x_0^{\frac{p+1}{4}^t \bmod p-1} \bmod p$
15 $\beta_t := x_0^{\frac{q+1}{4}^t \bmod q-1} \bmod q$
16 $x_{-t} := \alpha_t q(q^{-1} \bmod p) + \beta_t p(p^{-1} \bmod q) \bmod N$
17 $P := (x, x_0, x_{-t})$
output: $(\mathsf{sk}, \mathsf{pk}, P, t)$

1) $\mathcal{C}$ runs $(\mathsf{sk}, \mathsf{pk}, P, t) \leftarrow_{\text{R}} \mathsf{Gen}(1^\kappa, t)$ to generate the secret key, public key, and puzzle as seen on Algorithm 3.1 Gen. The function $\mathsf{prime}(j)$ on lines 3 and 4 is the Miller-Rabin Monte Carlo algorithm [31] which generates j bit Gaussian primes. That is, $p \leftarrow_{\text{R}} \mathsf{prime}(j)$. This guarantees that N, which is calculated on line 6, is a Blum integer. Gen then enters a while loop. The purpose of the while loop is to find an x such that $x \in \mathcal{QNR}_N^{-1}$. The logic statement on line 8 condenses the conditional statements in lines $3, 5$ and 7 of Algorithm 2.2 using De Morgan's laws [22]. Once a suitable x is found x_0 is set to $x^2 \bmod N$. Once x is sampled and x_0 is computed the term x_{-t} is calculated, where $x_{-t}^{2^t} \equiv x_0 \bmod N$. To calculate x_{-t} in polynomial time, Euler's Criterion, the Fermat-Euler Theorem and the Chinese Remainder Theorem (CRT) must be applied.

Next, α_t is calculated, where α_t is the tth square root of $x_0 \bmod p$. To complete the calculation of the term x_{-t}, the CRT is used on line 16, where the terms $(q^{-1} \bmod p)$ and $(p^{-1} \bmod q)$ are calculated using Euclid's Extended Algorithm (EEA). Theorem 3 tells us that $\alpha \equiv \sqrt{x_0} \equiv x_0^\omega \bmod p$, where $\omega = \frac{p+1}{4}$. Let α_t be the tth square root of $x_0 \bmod p$. For example, if $t = 2$, then $\alpha_2 \equiv \sqrt{\sqrt{x_0}} \equiv (x_0^\omega)^\omega \equiv x_0^{\omega^2}$. Therefore, $\alpha_t \equiv x_0^{\omega^t} \bmod p$. Note that the exponent ω^t, for large t will make calculating $x_0^{\omega^t} \bmod p$ computationally infeasible. Therefore, the Fermat-Euler Theorem is used so the exponent ω^t can be reduced $\bmod(p-1)$. Next, β_t is calculated, where β_t is the tth square root of $x_0 \bmod q$. β_t is calculated in a similar fashion as α_t, except ω is set to $\frac{q+1}{4}$.

The puzzle P is set to the tuple (x, x_0, x_{-t}) and then $\mathcal{C}$ securely stores sk and passes (pk, P, t) to $\mathcal{S}$ who must solve:

Given $(\mathsf{pk} := (N, e), P := (x, x_0, x_{-t}), t)$, find the factors of N.

Algorithm 3.2: Solve runs on the public key, puzzle, and time parameter pk, P, t to recover the secret key sk.

---

    input : $\mathsf{pk} := (N, e), P = (x, x_0, x_{-t}), t$

1   $x' := x_{-t}^{2^{t-1}} \bmod N$

2   $p' := \gcd(x - x', N)$

3   $q' := \frac{N}{p'}$

4   $\mathsf{sk} := (p', q')$

    output: sk

---

2) $\mathcal{S}$ (or any party) runs $\mathsf{sk} \leftarrow \mathsf{Solve}(\mathsf{pk}, P, t)$ to solve the challenge, as seen on Algorithm 3.2 Solve. First Solve calculates the term x' in $t-1$ sequential steps by evaluating $x_{-t}^{2^{t-1}} \bmod N$. This is where the sequential calculation takes place using Algorithm 2.1 with inputs $(x_{-t}, 2^{t-1}, N)$. The term x' is guaranteed to be in $\mathcal{QR}_N$ by Definition 2. $\mathcal{S}$ now has $x \in \mathcal{QNR}_N^{-1}$ and $x' \in \mathcal{QR}_N$. Therefore, x must be distinct from x', and we have $x^2 \equiv x'^2 \equiv x_0 \bmod N$. Finally, using the result from Theorem 6, Solve calculates $\gcd(x - x', N)$ to recover one factor p' of

N using Euclid's Extended Algorithm. Next, $\frac{N}{\gcd(x-x',N)}$ is calculated to recover the other factor q'.

3) $\mathcal{S}$ runs $c \leftarrow$ Encrypt(pk, m) as seen in Algorithm 3.3 Encrypt. Encrypt inputs the public key pk $:= (N, e)$ and encrypts a message m using RSA-OEAP encryption and outputs the ciphertext c. First Encrypt outputs the RSA-OAEP parameters k_0, k_1, G, H, where k_0 and k_1 are constants used for padding and G and H are hashing algorithms modelled as random oracles. Using RSA-OAEP, parties can encrypt messages to this modulus and encryption exponent. This means that messages can only be decrypted using the Decrypt algorithm only after Solve has recovered the secret key sk. Note that the Solve and Encrypt algorithms are not sequential. The Encrypt algorithm can be run by any Solver (Bidder) using pk prior to the Solve algorithm recovering the sk.

Algorithm 3.3: Encrypt runs on a message public key pk and message m, to produce ciphertext c.

> **input** : pk $:= (N, e), m$
> 1 $k_0, k_1, G, H \leftarrow$ **params**(1^κ) // OAEP parameters
> 2 $m' := m \parallel 0^{k_1}$ // Zero pad to $n - k_0$ bits
> 3 $r := \text{rand}(k_0)$ // Generate a random k_0 bit number
> 4 $X := m' \oplus G_{n-k_0}(r)$ // Hash r to length $n - k_0$
> 5 $Y := r \oplus H_{k_0}(X)$ // Hash X to length k_0
> 6 $m'' := X \parallel Y$ // Create message object
> 7 $c := m''^e \bmod N$ // RSA encrypt
> **output**: c

---

4) $\mathcal{S}$ runs $\{m, \perp\} \leftarrow$ Decrypt(sk, c) as seen in Algorithm 3.4 Decrypt. Decrypt inputs the secret key sk $:= (p, q)$ and decrypts ciphertext c using RSA-OEAP encryption and recovers the message m or outputs an error $\perp$. Decrypt also outputs the same RSA-OAEP parameters k_0, k_1, G, H as Encrypt. Next, Decrypt recovers the decryption exponent d on lines 2, 3, 4, where Euclids Extended Algorithm is used. Finally, the RSA-OEAP decrypt algorithm removes the padding and randomness added during the encryption to recover the message m.

Implementation and Performance Analysis. We implement TIDE on a desktop PC and a cluster of raspberry Pis. We show how the timings of Algorithm 3.2 Solve grows linearly with the time parameter t, whilst the other algorithms grow by $O(1)$ in the time parameter. We provide timings with several RSA moduli of practical relevance, and note in particular that with a modulus size of 2048, the average time to run Solve was one second on a desktop PC. The full description of the implementation and our results can be found in Appendix A of our full paper [28].

Algorithm 3.4: Decrypt runs on secret key sk and ciphertext c, to produce message m.

---

input : $\mathsf{sk} := (p', q'), c$

1 $k_0, k_1, G, H \leftarrow \mathsf{params}(1^\kappa)$ // OAEP parameters
2 $N := p'q'$
3 $\phi(N) := (p' - 1)(q' - 1)$
4 $d := e^{-1} \bmod \phi(N)$ // recover d using EEA
5 $m'' := c^d \bmod N$
6 $X := \lfloor c'' \cdot 2^{-k_0} \rfloor$ // Extract X
7 $Y := m'' \bmod 2^{k_0}$ // Extract Y
8 $r := Y \oplus H_{k_0}(X)$ // Recover r
9 $m' := X \oplus G_{n-k_0}(r)$ // Recover padded message
10 $m := m' \cdot 2^{-k_1}$ // Remove padding

output: m

---

4   Security

We provide a security analysis of our construction. To this end, we recall the formal definition of Timed-Release Encryption (TRE), following Chvojka et al. [12][1], along with the definitions of correctness and security for a TRE scheme.

Definition 3. *A timed-release encryption scheme with message space $\mathcal{M}$ is a tuple of algorithms TRE = (Gen, Solve, Encrypt, Decrypt) defined as follows.*

- *(pk,sk, P, t) ← Gen $(1^\kappa, t)$ is a probabilistic algorithm which takes as input a security parameter 1^κ and a time hardness parameter t, and outputs a public encryption parameter pk, a secret key sk, and a puzzle P. We require that Gen runs in time poly $((\log t), \kappa)$.*
- *sk ← Solve(pk, P, t) is a deterministic algorithm which takes as input a public key pk, a puzzle P, and a time parameter t, and outputs a secret key sk. We require that Solve runs in time at most $t \cdot poly(\kappa)$.*
- *c ← Encrypt (pk, m) is a probabilistic algorithm that takes as input public encryption parameter pk and message $m \in \mathcal{M}$, and outputs a ciphertext c.*
- *m/ ⊥← Decrypt (sk, c) is a deterministic algorithm which takes as input a secret key sk and a ciphertext c, and outputs $m \in \mathcal{M}$ or $\perp$.*

Definition 4 (Correctness)

A TRE scheme is correct if for all $\kappa \in \mathbb{N}$ and hardness parameter t, it holds that

$$\Pr\left[m = m' : \begin{array}{l} (\textsf{pk,sk}, P, t) \leftarrow \textsf{Gen}\,(1^\kappa, t)\,, \textsf{sk} \leftarrow \textsf{Solve}\,(\textsf{pk}, P, t) \\ m' \leftarrow \textsf{Decrypt}\,(\textsf{sk}, \textsf{Encrypt}\,(\textsf{pk}, m)) \end{array}\right] = 1$$

---

[1] In [12] they offer a generalised version of this definition, to incorporate what they define *sequential timed-release encryption*. This is beyond the scope of this work, and we instead specify the "non-sequential" case.

Definition 5 (Security). *A timed-release encryption scheme is secure with gap $0 < \epsilon < 1$ if for all polynomials n in κ there exists a polynomial $\tilde{t}(\cdot)$ such that for all polynomials t fulfilling that $t(\cdot) \geq \tilde{t}(\cdot)$, and every polynomial-size adversary $\mathcal{A} = \{(\mathcal{A}_{1,\kappa}, \mathcal{A}_{2,\kappa})\}_{\kappa \in \mathbb{N}}$ there exists a negligible function $\mathsf{negl}(\cdot)$ such that for all $\kappa \in \mathbb{N}$ it holds*

$$\mathbf{Adv}_{\mathcal{A}}^{\mathrm{TRE}} = \left| Pr \left[b = b' : b \xleftarrow{s} \{0,1\}; c \leftarrow \mathsf{Encrypt}(\mathsf{pk}, m_b) \begin{array}{c} \mathsf{pk}, P \leftarrow \mathsf{Gen}(1^{\kappa}, t) \\ (m_0, m_1, \mathsf{st}) \leftarrow \mathcal{A}_{1,\kappa}(\mathsf{pk}, P) \\ \\ b' \leftarrow \mathcal{A}_{2,\kappa}(c, \mathsf{st}) \end{array} \right] - \frac{1}{2} \right| \leq \mathsf{negl}(\kappa)$$

It is required that $|m_0| = |m_1|$ and that the adversary $\mathcal{A}_{\kappa} = (\mathcal{A}_{1,\kappa}, \mathcal{A}_{2,\kappa})$ consists of two circuits with total depth at most $t^{\epsilon}(\kappa)$ (i. e., the total depth is the sum of the depth of $\mathcal{A}_{1,\kappa}$ and $\mathcal{A}_{2,,\kappa}$).

In what follows, we will refer to algorithms 'taking t time to compute', and 'bounding computation time by t'. In both cases, we are referring to evaluating a polynomial sized arithmetic circuit of depth at most t.

In order to prove the security of TIDE, we must first define a new hardness assumption. Informally, this states that the terms x, x_0 and x_{-t} provide a negligible advantage to factoring a Blum integer N, or distinguishing between ciphertexts encrypted to a Blum integer N, when the computational time is bounded by t.

Definition 6 (BBS Shortcut Assumption). *Let the RSA Assumption be that for any $N \leftarrow_R \mathsf{Gen}(1^{\kappa})$ and $e = 65537$, it is hard for any probabilistic polynomial-time algorithm to find the e-th root modulo N of a random $y \leftarrow_R \mathbb{Z}_N^*$ [34].*

The BBS Shortcut Assumption states that given (N', e) and terms (x, x_0, x_{-t}), where $N' \leftarrow_R \mathsf{Gen}(1^{\kappa})$ is a randomly sampled Blum integer, $e = 65537$, x is a randomly sampled integer such that $x \in QNR_N^{-1}$, $x_0 := x^2 \bmod N$, and x_{-t} is the term $t + 1$ steps before x_0 in a BBS_CSPRNG sequence, it is no easier to find the e-th root of a random $y' \leftarrow_R \mathbb{Z}_{N'}^*$ than to find the e-th root modulo N of a random $y \leftarrow_R \mathbb{Z}_N^*$ in a standard RSA instance, without first factoring N'.

We now analyse this security assumption, in order to relate it to the RSA assumption that RSA with OAEP relies on [20].

Recall $P = (x, x_0, x_{-t})$ consists of a randomly sampled integer x, and two terms x_0, x_{-t} which by construction are part of the BBS-CSPRNG sequence, and hence are pseudorandom. As we will see in Lemma 1, the relation between these integers exactly relates to the evaluation of the BBS-CSPRNG sequence, which allows N' to be factored, and cannot be evaluated in time less than t, for some $t \in \mathbb{N}$. The crux of the assumption is that x_{-t} is only related to the terms x and x_0 by the repeated squaring property, which allows the Blum integer N' to be factored. By the RSW time-lock assumption, we know that this will take t time to evaluate, and hence we assume that $P = (x, x_0, x_{-t})$ are only useful when factoring N'.

Theorem 7. *TIDE is correct.*

Proof. First, consider the following statement:

For any message $m \in \{0,1\}^*$, $\mathsf{Decrypt}\big(\mathsf{Encrypt}(\mathsf{N}, m), (p, q)\big)$ outputs m, where $\mathsf{Encrypt}$ and $\mathsf{Decrypt}$ are described in Algorithms 3.3 Encrypt and Algorithm 3.4 Decrypt respectively.

This corresponds to the statement that the RSA cryptosystem with OAEP is correct, which is known to be true [20].

Now suppose Algorithm 3.1 Gen has been run, such that the following parameters have been generated: a public key N, puzzle $P = (x, x_0, x_{-t})$ and time parameter t, and a secret key $\mathsf{sk} = (p, q)$. What remains is to prove that Solve outputs $\mathsf{sk} = (p, q)$. This proof will require a sequence of arguments based on the Theorems outlined in Sect. 2.

First we must prove that Algorithm 3.1 Gen correctly selects the term x such that $x \in \mathcal{QNR}_N^{-1}$.

Corollary 2 *(of Theorem 2). The while loop on lines 8–12 of Algorithm 3.1 Gen selects $x \in \mathcal{QNR}_N^{-1}$ with overwhelming probability.*

Proof. The while loop on lines 8–12 of Algorithm 3.1 Gen selects a quadratic non-residue with Jacobi Symbol equal to -1 by running a series of Bernoulli trials with probability $\mathrm{P}\left(x = \mathcal{QNR}_N^{-1}\right) = \frac{1}{2}$. This forms a geometric distribution $G \sim \mathrm{Geo}(\frac{1}{2})$. Therefore, we can expect to find $x \in \mathcal{QNR}_N^{-1}$ in $\mathbb{E}\{G\} = 2$ trials.

Second we prove that Algorithm 3.1 Gen correctly calculates the term x_{-t}, which is the tth principal square root of x_0. This proof begins by proving Theorem 3, and subsequently uses the Chinese Remainder Theorem for the final proof.

Proof. (Theorem 3). Let $\alpha = r^{\frac{p+1}{4}} \bmod p$. Then $\alpha^2 \equiv (r^{\frac{p+1}{4}})^2 \equiv r^{\frac{2p+2}{4}} \equiv r^{\frac{p+1}{2}} \bmod p$. Next, let $\frac{p+1}{2} = 1 + \frac{p-1}{2}$. Therefore, by Euler's Criterion (Theorem 1) $\alpha^2 \equiv r^1 r^{\frac{p-1}{2}} \equiv r \bmod p$. We refer to α as the principal square root of $r \bmod p$.

Theorem 8. *The Algorithm 3.1 Gen correctly calculates the tth principal square root x_{-t} of the seed x_0.*

Proof. Let $\omega = \frac{p+1}{4}$. If Algorithm 3.1 Gen provides the seed term $x_0 \in \mathcal{QR}_N$, then, by Theorem 3, the tth principal square root of $x_0 \bmod p$ is $\alpha_t := x_0^{\omega^t} \bmod p$ and the tth principal square root of $x_0 \bmod q$ is $\beta_t := x_0^{\omega^t} \bmod q$. Then, the Chinese Remainder Theorem is used to calculate:
$x_{-t} := [\alpha_t q(q^{-1} \bmod p) + \beta_t p(p^{-1} \bmod q)] \bmod N$.

Third we must prove that the Algorithm 3.2 Solve correctly calculates the term $x' \in \mathcal{QR}_N$ using Algorithm 2.1.

Theorem 9. *Algorithm 2.1 Square and Multiply correctly calculates the term x_i, where $x_i \equiv x_0^{2^i} \bmod N$.*

Proof. The input to calculate the term x_i in Algorithm 2.1 Square and Multiply is $(x_0, 2^i, N)$, where $x_0 \in \mathcal{QR}_N$ is the seed term, and $N = pq$, where p and q are distinct odd primes. By Definition 2, selecting $x_0 \in \mathcal{QR}_N$ can be done by uniformly selecting $x \in \mathbb{Z}_N^*$ and setting $x_0 \equiv x^2 \bmod N$. Consider the base case when $i := 1$. The algorithm proceeds as follows: d is set to 1 and the exponent $b := 2^1$ is set to the binary string $B = 10$. Next, the algorithm enters the for loop on the first iteration. On the first iteration j is the first digit of B, which is 1. Next $d := 1$ is squared to output 1. Then the first conditional **if** statement is met as $j = 1$, therefore $d := 1 \cdot x_0 = x_0 \bmod N$, and the first iteration of the loop is done. On the second iteration j is the second digit of B, which is 0. Next, as d was set to x_0 on the first iteration d is now set to $x_0^2 \bmod N$ on the second iteration. The first conditional **if** statement is not met, and the loop terminates as the final digit of B was processed. The algorithm then returns $d := x_1 \equiv x_0^2 \equiv x_0^{2^1} \bmod N$, as required. Therefore, the base case is true.

By the inductive hypothesis we claim that for any $i := k$, the loop invariant of Algorithm 2.1 returns the term $x_0^{2^k} \bmod N$ after k iterations. Therefore after k iterations, where b was set to 2^{k+1}, Algorithm 2.1 will have $d := x_0^{2^k} \bmod N$, and j will be the final digit of $B := 10\ldots 0$. For any k, the variable B will be a binary string starting with the digit 1 followed by a trail of k digits equal to 0. This means after the first iteration of the for loop all remaining $j \in B$ will be 0. Thus, at the $k+1$ iteration of the for loop d will be set to $x_k^2 \bmod N$, and by definition $x_k^2 \equiv x_{k+1} \equiv x_0^{2^{k+1}} \bmod N$. Finally, Algorithm 2.1 will terminate at the $k+1$ iteration as the final digit of B was processed, and the algorithm will return $d := x_0^{2^{k+1}} \bmod N$.

Finally, Theorem 6 is proven to show that Algorithm 3.2 Solve calculates $\gcd(x' - x, N)$ to recover a non-trivial factor of N [33].

Proof (Theorem 6). As x and x' are distinct we have $x^2 \equiv x'^2 \bmod N$. This implies that $pq \mid x^2 - x'^2$. As p and q are both prime this indicates that $p \mid (x - x')(x + x')$ and $q \mid (x - x')(x + x')$. Also, because p is prime it must be the case that $p \mid (x - x')$ or $p \mid (x + x')$. Similarly, it must be the case that $q \mid (x - x')$ or $q \mid (x + x')$. Without loss of generality, assume that $p \mid (x - x')$ is true and that $q \mid (x - x')$ is true. This implies that $pq \mid (x - x')$, which indicates that $x \equiv x' \bmod N$. This is a contradiction because x and x' are distinct. Then it must be the case that $p \mid (x - x')$ and $q \nmid (x - x')$. Therefore, one of the factors of N can be recovered by calculating $p' := \gcd(x - x', N)$ using Euclid's Extended Algorithm, and the other factor of N can be recovered by calculating $q' := \frac{N}{\gcd(x-x',N)} = \frac{N}{p'}$.

We now prove that Solve outputs $\mathsf{sk} = (p, q)$, and hence Theorem 7: the correctness of TIDE.

Proof (Theorem 7). For any pk, sk, and puzzle generated by Gen, we show that sk can be recovered by Solve. More precisely, let $N = pq, P := (x, x_0, x_{-t}), t$ be output by Gen, before being input into Algorithm 3.2 Solve. Algorithm 3.2 Solve will calculate the term x' by entering the following parameters $(x_{-t}, 2^{t-1}, N)$ into

Algorithm 2.1, which will output $x' := x_{-t}^{2^{t-1}} \bmod N$. The term x' is guaranteed to be correct by Theorem 9 and is guaranteed to be in $\mathcal{QR}_N$ by Definition 2, and hence we have that $x \in \mathcal{QNR}_N^{-1}$ and $x' \in \mathcal{QR}_N$. This guarantees that x must be distinct from x'. Therefore, by Theorem 6, calculating $p' = \gcd(x - x', N)$ will recover one factor of N using Euclid's Extended Algorithm, and the other factor can be recovered by calculating $q' = \frac{N}{\gcd(x-x',N)}$.

Theorem 10. *TIDE is a secure TRE scheme under the RSW, RSA and BBS-shortcut assumptions.*

To prove TIDE secure, we show that two messages encrypted using public key (N, e) are indistinguishable under a chosen plaintext attack, where the adversary is bounded by t computation time. We first note that the underlying encryption scheme is RSA with OAEP padding, which is IND-CPA secure [20]. In our proof we provide a reduction from the TRE security of TIDE to IND-CPA security of RSA with OAEP. Explicitly, this requires proving that giving an adversary the additional parameters of P and t, and bounding their computation time by t offers a negligible advantage over the standard RSA-OAEP game.

We first prove the following statement.

Lemma 1. *Given any (N, P, t) output by Algorithm 3.1 Gen, the RSA modulus N cannot be factored in time less than t, with more than negligible probability.*

Proof. Let N be a random Blum integer and P be a puzzle output by Algorithm 3.1 Gen. Note from Algorithm 3.1 that $P = (x, x_0, x_{-t})$, where $x \in \mathcal{QNR}_N^{-1}$, $x_0 \equiv x^2 \bmod N$, and x_{-t} is the tth square root of x_0. To factor N in time less than t, a pair of integers (p^*, q^*) must be computed, such that $p^* \neq 1, q^* \neq 1$, and $p^* q^* = N$, in less than t sequential steps.

We split the proof into two parts: i) Attempts to compute an x', where $x' \equiv \sqrt{x_0} \bmod N$ and $x' \in \mathcal{QR}_N$, in less than t sequential steps, and ii) Attempts to recover the non-trivial factors of N using a method that does not use x'.

We start by proving part (i): that computing x' in time less than t reduces to the RSW time-lock assumption. Specifically, if Solve is honestly run, then $x' := x_0^{2^{t-1}} \bmod N$ is calculated using Algorithm 2.1 with the input $(x_{-t}, 2^{t-1}, N)$. By the RSW time-lock assumption calculating x' using Algorithm 2.1 requires $t - 1$ sequential steps. Once x' is calculated, Algorithm 3.2 Solve recovers the factors of N by calculating $p' := \gcd(x - x', N)$ and $q' = \frac{N}{p'}$.

Next, suppose there exists a PPT algorithm $\mathcal{E}_{<t}$ to evaluate x' in less than $t - 1$ sequential steps. Finding such an x' using $\mathcal{E}_{<t}$ reduces to the RSW time-lock assumption and we obtain a contradiction. Therefore, it is not possible to recover $p^* := \gcd(x - x', N)$ without sequentially evaluating x' with non-negligible probability.

Next, we prove part (ii): that factoring N faster than sequential squaring reduces to an open problem. First note that N is a Blum integer, which is an RSA modulus that is the product of Gaussian primes. Therefore, we assume N cannot be factored by any PPT algorithm with more than negligible probability.

Next, giving $\mathcal{A}$ either (N, x, x_0, t) or (N, x_{-t}, t) also reduces to a standard factoring assumption, as seen in Sect. 4 of Rabin [33]. What remains is to show that giving an adversary all of the puzzle P does not allow them to factorise N. To see this, note that x_0 can be trivially obtained from x, and that by construction x_{-t} and x_0 are terms in a BBS_CSPRNG sequence [5]. Knowledge of these terms does not allow factorisation of N faster than sequential squaring unless $x_{-t}^{2^{\lambda(\lambda(N))}}$ mod N is calculated efficiently. This is an open problem given by Theorem 9 of Blum et al. [5,19,23].

Therefore, the only way a PPT algorithm could factorise N given (pk, P, t) with non-negligible probability is to sequentially evaluate x' and subsequently recover the factors by calculating $p' := \gcd(x - x', N)$ and $q' = \frac{N}{p'}$.

We now use this result to obtain a reduction from the TRE security of TIDE to the standard RSA IND-CPA security.

Proof (sketch) (Theorem 10). We start by assuming that there exists an adversary $\mathcal{A} = (\mathcal{A}_{1,\kappa}, \mathcal{A}_{2,\kappa})$ who can gain a non-negligible advantage in the $\mathbf{Adv}_{\mathcal{A}}^{TRE}$ game defined in Definition 5.

We use Lemma 1 and Definition 6 to show that if the adversary wins the game by factoring N we obtain a contradiction based on the RSW assumption, and if they win the game without factoring N, we obtain a contradiction based on the RSA and BBS-shortcut assumptions.

Recall from Lemma 1 that if the adversary $\mathcal{A}$ factors a Blum integer N output by Algorithm 3.1 in time less than t with more than negligible probability, then the RSW time-lock assumption is broken, and hence we have a contradiction.

Now, recall that RSA with OAEP padding is IND-CPA-secure under the RSA assumption [20]. Suppose $\mathcal{A}$ gained a non-negligible advantage in the TRE security game without factoring. As the underlying encryption scheme is IND-CPA secure, to distinguish between the messages m and m' with any advantage would require decrypting one of the messages, and hence taking an e-th root modulo N. By the BBS shortcut assumption presented in Definition 6, any adversary who gains an advantage in the TRE security game could also gain the same non-negligible advantage in the standard IND-CPA game for RSA-OAEP, and hence break the RSA assumption. This gives us another contradiction. Therefore TIDE is secure under the RSW, RSA and BBS-shortcut assumptions.

5 Conclusion

In this work we introduced TIDE, a new TRE construction which seamlessly integrates the RSA cryptosystem into a time-lock puzzle using powerful number-theoretic concepts. TIDE challenges a solver to factor a special class of RSA modulus, known as a Blum integer. Parties may encrypt to this RSA modulus, and any solver who factors the modulus may easily decrypt all encrypted messages. We demonstrated that this property makes TIDE well-suited to sealed-bid auctions: We compared TIDE to the most recent constructions for sealed-bid auctions, showing that TIDE has advantages both in terms of practicality and efficiency. We proved security of TIDE in the TRE framework introduced by Chvojka et al., and we implemented TIDE on both a Raspberry Pi and on a desktop PC, showing that it is indeed a practical construction.

References

1. Ausubel, L.: A generalized Vickrey auction. Econo0 metrica (1999)
2. Barak, B., et al.: On the (im)possibility of obfuscating programs. In: Kilian, J. (ed.) CRYPTO 2001. LNCS, vol. 2139, pp. 1–18. Springer, Heidelberg (2001). https://doi.org/10.1007/3-540-44647-8_1
3. Bitansky, N., Goldwasser, S., Jain, A., Paneth, O., Vaikuntanathan, V., Waters, B.: Time-lock puzzles from randomized encodings. In: Proceedings of the 2016 ACM Conference on Innovations in Theoretical Computer Science (2016)
4. Blass, E., Kerschbaum, F.: BOREALIS: building block for sealed bid auctions on blockchains. In: Proceedings of the 15th ACM Asia Conference on Computer and Communications Security (2020)
5. Blum, L., Blum, M., Shub, M.: A simple unpredictable pseudo-random number generator. J. Comput. 15(2), 364–383 (1986)
6. Blume, A., Heidhues, P.: All equilibria of the Vickrey auction. J. Econ. Theory 114(1), 170–177 (2004)
7. Bogetoft, P., et al.: Secure multiparty computation goes live. In: Dingledine, R., Golle, P. (eds.) FC 2009. LNCS, vol. 5628, pp. 325–343. Springer, Heidelberg (2009). https://doi.org/10.1007/978-3-642-03549-4_20
8. Boneh, D., Bonneau, J., Bünz, B., Fisch, B.: Verifiable delay functions. In: Shacham, H., Boldyreva, A. (eds.) CRYPTO 2018. LNCS, vol. 10991, pp. 757–788. Springer, Cham (2018). https://doi.org/10.1007/978-3-319-96884-1_25
9. Brandt, F.: Auctions. In: Handbook of Financial Cryptography and Security. Chapman and Hall/CRC (2010)
10. Burdges, J., De Feo, L.: Delay encryption. In: Canteaut, A., Standaert, F.-X. (eds.) EUROCRYPT 2021. LNCS, vol. 12696, pp. 302–326. Springer, Cham (2021). https://doi.org/10.1007/978-3-030-77870-5_11
11. Cathalo, J., Libert, B., Quisquater, J.-J.: Efficient and non-interactive timed-release encryption. In: Qing, S., Mao, W., López, J., Wang, G. (eds.) ICICS 2005. LNCS, vol. 3783, pp. 291–303. Springer, Heidelberg (2005). https://doi.org/10.1007/11602897_25
12. Chvojka, P., Jager, T., Slamanig, D., Striecks, C.: Versatile and sustainable timed-release encryption and sequential time-lock puzzles (extended abstract). In: Bertino, E., Shulman, H., Waidner, M. (eds.) ESORICS 2021. LNCS, vol. 12973, pp. 64–85. Springer, Cham (2021). https://doi.org/10.1007/978-3-030-88428-4_4
13. Cohen, B., Pietrzak, K.: The chia network blockchain (2019)
14. Cormen, T., Leiserson, C., Rivest, R., Stein, C.: Introduction to Algorithms. MIT Press, Cambridge (2009)
15. Crandall, R., Pomerance, C.: Prime Numbers: A Computational Perspective. Springer, New York (2005). https://doi.org/10.1007/0-387-28979-8
16. Ephraim, N., Freitag, C., Komargodski, I., Pass, R.: Continuous verifiable delay functions. In: Canteaut, A., Ishai, Y. (eds.) EUROCRYPT 2020. LNCS, vol. 12107, pp. 125–154. Springer, Cham (2020). https://doi.org/10.1007/978-3-030-45727-3_5

17. De Feo, L., Masson, S., Petit, C., Sanso, A.: Verifiable delay functions from super-singular isogenies and pairings. In: Galbraith, S.D., Moriai, S. (eds.) ASIACRYPT 2019. LNCS, vol. 11921, pp. 248–277. Springer, Cham (2019). https://doi.org/10.1007/978-3-030-34578-5_10
18. Freitag, C., Komargodski, I., Pass, R., Sirkin, N.: Non-malleable time-lock puzzles and applications. In: Nissim, K., Waters, B. (eds.) TCC 2021. LNCS, vol. 13044, pp. 447–479. Springer, Cham (2021). https://doi.org/10.1007/978-3-030-90456-2_15
19. Friedlander, J., Pomerance, C., Shparlinski, I.: Period of the power generator and small values of Carmichael's function. Math. Comput. **70**, 1591–1605 (2000)
20. Fujisaki, E., Okamoto, T., Pointcheval, D., Stern, J.: RSA-OAEP is secure under the RSA assumption. In: Kilian, J. (ed.) CRYPTO 2001. LNCS, vol. 2139, pp. 260–274. Springer, Heidelberg (2001). https://doi.org/10.1007/3-540-44647-8_16
21. Galal, H.S., Youssef, A.M.: Verifiable sealed-bid auction on the ethereum blockchain. In: Zohar, A., et al. (eds.) FC 2018. LNCS, vol. 10958, pp. 265–278. Springer, Heidelberg (2019). https://doi.org/10.1007/978-3-662-58820-8_18
22. Goodstein, R.L.: Boolean Algebra. Dover Publications (2007)
23. Griffin, F., Shparlinski, I.: On the linear complexity profile of the power generator. IEEE Trans. Inf. Theory **46**(6), 2159–2162 (2000)
24. Jain, A., Lin, H., Sahai, A.: Indistinguishability obfuscation from well-founded assumptions. In: Proceedings of the 53rd Annual ACM SIGACT Symposium on Theory of Computing (2021)
25. Juels, A., Szydlo, M.: A two-server, sealed-bid auction protocol. In: Blaze, M. (ed.) FC 2002. LNCS, vol. 2357, pp. 72–86. Springer, Heidelberg (2003). https://doi.org/10.1007/3-540-36504-4_6
26. Katz, J., Lindell, Y.: Introduction to Modern Cryptography, 2nd edn. CRC Press (2014)
27. Liu, J., Garcia, F., Ryan, M.: Time-release protocol from bitcoin and witness encryption for sat. Korean Circ. J. **40**(10), 530–535 (2015)
28. Loe, A.F., Medley, L., O'Connell, C., Quaglia, E.A.: TIDE: a novel approach to constructing timed-release encryption. Cryptology ePrint Archive (2021)
29. Malavolta, G., Thyagarajan, S.A.K.: Homomorphic time-lock puzzles and applications. In: Boldyreva, A., Micciancio, D. (eds.) CRYPTO 2019. LNCS, vol. 11692, pp. 620–649. Springer, Cham (2019). https://doi.org/10.1007/978-3-030-26948-7_22
30. Mao, W.: Timed-release cryptography. In: Vaudenay, S., Youssef, A.M. (eds.) SAC 2001. LNCS, vol. 2259, pp. 342–357. Springer, Heidelberg (2001). https://doi.org/10.1007/3-540-45537-X_27
31. Miller, G.: Riemann's hypothesis and tests for primality. J. Comput. Syst. Sci. **13**(3), 300–317 (1976)
32. Pietrzak, K.: Simple verifiable delay functions. In: 10th Innovations in Theoretical Computer Science Conference, ITCS 2019 (2019)
33. Rabin, M.: Digitalized signatures and public-key functions as intractable as factorization. In: MIT/LCS/TR-212. MIT Laboratory for Computer Science (1979)
34. Rivest, R., Shamir, A., Adleman, L.: A method for obtaining digital signatures and public-key cryptosystems. Commun. ACM **21**(2), 120–126 (1983)
35. Rivest, R., Shamir, A., Wagner, D.: Time-lock puzzles and timed-release crypto. In: MIT/LCS/TR-684. MIT Laboratory for Computer Science (1996)
36. Sako, K.: An auction protocol which hides bids of losers. In: Imai, H., Zheng, Y. (eds.) PKC 2000. LNCS, vol. 1751, pp. 422–432. Springer, Heidelberg (2000). https://doi.org/10.1007/978-3-540-46588-1_28

37. Vickrey, W.: Counterspeculation, auctions, and competitive sealed tenders. J. Finance **16**(1), 8–37 (1961)
38. Zhandry, M.: On ELFs, deterministic encryption, and correlated-input security. In: Ishai, Y., Rijmen, V. (eds.) EUROCRYPT 2019. LNCS, vol. 11478, pp. 3–32. Springer, Cham (2019). https://doi.org/10.1007/978-3-030-17659-4_1

Multi-signatures for ECDSA and Its Applications in Blockchain

Shimin Pan[(✉)], Kwan Yin Chan, Handong Cui, and Tsz Hon Yuen

The University of Hong Kong, Hong Kong, China
{smpan,kychan,hdcui,thyuen}@cs.hku.hk

Abstract. Multi-signatures enable a group of t signers to sign a message jointly and obtain a single signature. Multi-signatures help validating blockchain transactions, such as transactions with *multiple inputs* or transactions from *multisig addresses*. However, multi-signatures schemes are always realised naively in most blockchain systems by directly concatenating t ECDSA signatures.

In this paper, we give the *first* multi-signature scheme for ECDSA. Technically, we design a new ephemeral group public key for the set of signers and introduce an interactive signing protocol to output a single ECDSA signature. The signature can be validated by the ephemeral group public key. Then, we instantiate the ECDSA multi-signature scheme with class group, for which we design a secret exchanging mechanism that ensures the hiding content is well-constructed. Moreover, our scheme is able to identify the malicious party in the signing phase and help to minimize unnecessary resource consumption. This ECDSA multi-signatures can be used in blockchain to reduce the transaction cost and provide accountability for signers and backward compatibility with existing ECDSA addresses.

Keywords: Multi-signatures · ECDSA · Signature

1 Introduction

1.1 Motivation

Multi-signatures [16] have been widely used in different scenarios in the blockchain. This cryptographic primitive allows any group S of parties to jointly sign a message and produce a signature, for which verifiers are convinced that each group member S participated in the signing. It can also be used to divide up responsibility for possession of signing keys among multiple players and avoid a single point of failure. There are two major uses of the functionality of multi-signatures. The first use case is formatting a transaction with *multiple inputs* relative to different addresses. The owner of each input can sign on all of the outputs in this transaction[1] and present a signature for this input. In Bitcoin,

---

[1] This is the default setting in Bitcoin for the signature hash, called SIGHASH_ALL.

K. Nguyen et al. (Eds.): ACISP 2022, LNCS 13494, pp. 265–285, 2022.
https://doi.org/10.1007/978-3-031-22301-3_14

signatures for each input are concatenated. Protocols, such as Taproot, Coin-Join, and PayJoin[2], use multiple inputs and outputs transactions to improve the privacy of Bitcoin transactions. The second use case is the *multisig* address in Bitcoin (and some other blockchain), which contains n public keys. A transaction is valid when there are t valid ECDSA signatures attached relative to public keys among the key list. Each ECDSA signature is verified against one corresponding public key, and these t signers are accountable for generating this multi-signature accordingly.

The efficiency of the naive approach for multi-signatures currently used in Bitcoin is extremely poor. We need k signatures for a transaction with k inputs, or t signatures for a multisig account with a threshold t. Let us consider a transaction with two inputs and two outputs. For the first use case (P2PKH), the transaction size is 374 bytes, and two ECDSA signatures account for 39% (144 bytes) in it. For the second use case (P2SH 2-of-3 multi-signature), the transaction size is 668 bytes, and four ECDSA signatures account for 43% (288 bytes) in it. Therefore, it is important to design a cryptographic solution to reduce the signature size and lower the transaction cost.

1.2   Contribution

We design a new ECDSA multi-signature scheme by introducing the concept of *ephemeral* group public key for a group of signers S. Furthermore, it is integrated with the signing protocol of threshold ECDSA in [15]. The ephemeral group public key is defined *during* the interactive signing and is *different* for each signing instance. Our new scheme is significantly different from existing schemes (e.g., no group public key for [3], or one static group public key for each S [2,4,5,18,19]).

We recall that, in ECDSA, the secret key is x and the public key is $Y = xG$ where G is the group generator. To sign a message m, the signer picks a random k, computes the x-coordinate of $R = k^{-1}G$ as r and calculates $s = k(\mathsf{H}(m)+rx)$ for some hash function H. The signature is (r, s).

A Strawman Protocol. When there are t parties with their keys (x_i, Y_i), a simple multi-signature is setting the group public key as $Y = \sum_i Y_i$. However, this strawman protocol is not secure. For example, an adversary can set $Y_2 = -Y_1 + x_2G$, where Y_1 is the public key of an honest party. Then group key becomes $Y = Y_1 + Y_2 = x_2G$. Hence the adversary can generate a signature using x_2 only. This attack is known as the *rogue public key attack*.

Designing the Group Public Key. In order to deal with the rogue public key attack, the pairing-based multi-signatures [5] and the Schnorr-based multi-signatures [19] defined the group public key as $Y = \sum a_iY_i$ where $a_i = \mathsf{H}_1(S, Y_i)$.[3]

---

[2] Taproot: https://en.bitcoin.it/wiki/BIP_0341.   CoinJoin: https://coinjoin.io. PayJoin: https://en.bitcoin.it/wiki/PayJoin.

[3] The function H_1 is defined in this way for the ease of presentation in the security proof. In practice, we can simply set $a_i = \mathsf{H}_1(i, r, S, m)$ for all i.

Table 1. Comparison of signatures using multiple secret keys.

	# SK	# PK	Size	Accountability	Keygen
Threshold signature	t	1	$O(1)$	No	Involve n parties
Threshold ring signature	t	n	$O(\log n)$	No	No interaction
Bitcoin native multi-signatures	t	t	$O(t)$	Yes	No interaction
Multi-signatures	t	t	$O(1)$	Yes	No interaction

This static group public key is fixed for all signatures signed by the group of signers S. However, this structure cannot be applied to ECDSA multi-signatures because of the security proof. We instead design a new key structure such that the ephemeral group public key is different for each signature (r, s):

$$Y = \sum a_i Y_i, \quad \text{where } (a_1 || \ldots || a_t) = \mathsf{H}(r, \mathsf{S}, m).$$

In the security proof, we show that the unforgeability is reduced to the unforgeability of the standard ECDSA signature with a public key $\hat{Y}$.

1.3   Related Work

Threshold ECDSA and Threshold Ring Signatures. In threshold signatures [11], a signing key is distributed among n parties, and a message can be signed only by a sufficiently large subgroup (Table 1). There are three main differences between threshold signatures and multi-signatures. Firstly, threshold signatures are verified by one public key, while multi-signatures are verified by a set of keys. Secondly, an interactive key generation protocol is needed for threshold signatures, making it hard to cover existing keys and generate new keys. Thirdly, anonymity is a property of threshold signatures while accountability is only offered by multi-signatures. The property of anonymity or accountability may be good for different applications.

Threshold ring signature [6] differs from threshold signature as the group G can be dynamically formed, and there is no interactive setup phase. The drawback of threshold ring signatures is that the verification involves all n public keys in G, and the state-of-the-art signature size is $O(\log n)$.

Multi-signatures. There are two approaches to construct multi-signatures. One is naively implemented by concatenating $|S|$ signatures signed by S signing keys. Alternatively, researchers designed cryptographic algorithms to compress these $|S|$ signatures into a single one, such as Schnorr-based multi-signatures [3,19,20] and pairing-based multi-signatures [4,5,18]. Multi-signatures with a predefined key range G such that $S \subset G$ is also named Accountable-Subgroup Multi-signatures (ASM) [20]. The accountability means that the subgroup S of actual signers is known to the verifiers.

Recent researches on Schnorr follow the paper [19] known as MuSig. MuSig has been proved to be insecure in [13], which states that there is no OMDL reduction to the MuSig. Later in Crypto 2021, other multi-signatures were proposed [1,21]. The recent attractive Schnorr multi-signatures results could not be adapted to ECDSA setting directly due to the complexity of the inversion computation.

An ECDSA-based multi-signature scheme is proposed in [17]. Their scheme relies on a trusted group manager to generate the ECDSA signature from $t - 1$ parties. Moreover, the secret keys of the $t-1$ parties are all derived by the group manager. Apparently, it is not secure in the security model given by [19]. It is also not secure against the rogue public key attack. Konstantinos *et al.* tried to do signature compression in 2021 [10] but their scheme only compresses t signatures into $(t + 1)/2$ and reached a relatively large signature size.

As an ECDSA multi-signature, our scheme requires no trusted party and the signature requires only the same size as the standard ECDSA. Consequently, this scheme shows superiority in functionality and the optimal signature size. Compared to Schnorr multi-signatures, it has better compatibility with current-used ECDSA key pairs in most blockchain systems.

1.4 Paper Organization

This paper is organized as the following. Section 2 shows notations and the multi-signature primitive. Section 3 introduces a modified multiplicative-to-additive scheme. Section 4 presents the generic multi-signature scheme and the security proof. Section 5 shows a scheme instance, which utilizes the Castagnos-Laguillaumie encryption. Section 6 shows the implementation of the previous instance with Rust and the bandwidth analysis. Section 7 shows details of how our scheme interacts with the Bitcoin system. Section 8 draws some conclusions.

2 Preliminaries

We define notations and the multi-signature primitive in this section. Other building components are listed in Appendix A.

Notation $x \leftarrow_\$ S$ is uniformly sampling an element x from the set S and $[n]$ denotes the set $\{1, \ldots, n\}$. PPT stands for probabilistic polynomial time and $\mathsf{negl}(n)$ is a negligible function on n. $\mathcal{G}_{\mathrm{ECC}} = (\mathbb{G}, G, q)$ is the ECC group generated by G with order q.

For the definition of multi-signature, we consider that given in [19], where multi-signature is a tuple of four PPT algorithms (Setup, KeyGen, Sign, Verify):

- Setup(1^λ) → params: it generates system parameters from the security parameter.
- KeyGen(params) → (sk, pk): it is the key generation protocol which, on input parameters, outputs a pair of keys (pk, sk) where pk is the public key and sk is the secret one.

- Sign(params, $\{sk_1, \ldots, sk_t\}, S = \{pk_1, \ldots, pk_t\}, m) \to \sigma/\bot$: it is an interactive protocol. Parties keep their sk_i secret and work with others in S to sign a message m. The protocol outputs either a signature or $\bot$.
- Verify(params, $S = \{pk_1, \ldots, pk_t\}, m, \sigma) \to \{0, 1\}$: it checks whether the signature σ is valid or not.

Correctness. For all messages m, if $\sigma \leftarrow$ Sign(params, $\{sk_1, \ldots, sk_t\}, S = \{pk_1, \ldots, pk_t\}, m)$ where sk_i is the secret key corresponding to the public key pk_i for $i \in [t]$, then $1 \leftarrow$ Verify(params, S, m, σ).

Security model. We use the game-based security definition for multi-signatures [19]. The security game involves one honest party, and all other parties are corrupted by an adversary $\mathcal{A}$. After calling the signing oracle on inputs of the form (m_i, S_i) and getting back valid signatures σ_i, the adversary $\mathcal{A}$ wins the game by outputting a valid signature σ involving the public key of the honest party. A formal definition is given below.

1. The system setups based on the security parameters params $\leftarrow$ Setup(1^λ).
2. The honest party generates a key pair $(sk^*, pk^*) \leftarrow$ KeyGen(params) and the adversary $\mathcal{A}$ receives pk^* as input.
3. For any adversary-specified message m and public-key set $S = \{pk_1, \ldots, pk_t\}$ containing pk^*, the honest party runs Sign(params, sk^*, S, m) interactively with $\mathcal{A}$ and works as the signing oracle for $\mathcal{A}$. It could be abort when wrong messages discovered.
4. Finally, $\mathcal{A}$ returns a message m^*, a public key set S^* and a signature σ^* such that the tuple (m^*, S^*) has not been queried previously. $\mathcal{A}$ wins the game if $pk^* \in S^*$ and the signature is valid, i.e. Verify(params, S^*, m^*, σ^*) = 1.

A multi-signature scheme is said to be unforgeable if no PPT adversary wins the game with non-negligible probability.

3   Multiplicative-to-Additive Share Conversion Protocol

Multiplicative-to-additive (MtA) protocol [14] was introduced as a building block for threshold ECDSA. The MtA protocol involves two parties $\{P_1, P_2\}$ having messages $a \in \mathbb{Z}_p$ and $b \in \mathbb{Z}_p$ as their private input respectively. The protocol turns a multiplicative result $ab \mod q$ to an additive result $\alpha + \beta \mod q$, where P_1 and P_2 outputs α and β respectively.

3.1   Definition

Generic MtA Protocol. The original MtA scheme [14] is constructed with the Paillier encryption, and it requires a range proof. We give a 3 round generic MtA protocol, abstracted from the construction in [7]. This generic protocol relies on any additive homomorphic encryption (Setup, KeyGen, Enc, Dec, EvalSum, EvalScal) with a message space equal to $\mathbb{Z}_q$[4].

---

[4] If the message space of the additive homomorphic encryption is larger than q (e.g., Paillier encryption), then an extra zero-knowledge range proof is needed for all ciphertexts, to ensure that $\alpha = ab - \beta$ in Step 2 is still within the message space.

Setup Phase. For preset system parameters params $\leftarrow$ Setup(1^λ), P_1 generates keys by running (ek, dk) $\leftarrow$ KeyGen(params).

Conversion Phase

1. P_1 encrypts a and generates a zero-knowledge (ZK) proof for it.
   - P_1 computes the encryption $c_A = \mathsf{Enc}_{ek}(a; \rho)$ using a randomness ρ.
   - P_1 creates a zero-knowledge (ZK) proof π_A, relative to the relation R_{Enc}, that c_A is well-formed, where $R_{Enc} = \{(c_A, ek) : (a, \rho) | c_A = \mathsf{Enc}_{ek}(a; \rho)\}$.
   - P_1 sends c_A and π_A to P_2.
2. P_2 manipulates c_A to the ciphertext of $\alpha = ab - \beta \bmod q$, where β is the randomness.
   - P_2 picks a random β in $\mathbb{Z}_q$.
   - P_2 computes $c_B = \mathsf{EvalSum}_{ek}(\mathsf{EvalScal}_{ek}(c_A, b), \mathsf{Enc}_{ek}(-\beta; \rho'))$.
   - P_2 gives the ZK proof π_B, relative to relation R_B, that c_B is calculated from (b, β) and is consistent with $\underline{H = bG}$ where G is the ECC generator.

$$R_B = \left\{ (\underline{H, G}, c_A, c_B, ek) : (b, \beta, \rho') \middle| \frac{\underline{H = bG} \wedge c_B =}{\mathsf{EvalSum}_{ek}(\mathsf{EvalScal}_{ek}(c_A, b), \mathsf{Enc}_{ek}(-\beta, \rho'))} \right\}$$

   - P_2 sends c_B and π_B to P_1.
3. P_1 checks π_B and then computes $\alpha = \mathsf{Dec}_{dk}(c_B)$.

MtAwc Protocol. The standard MtA protocol does not include the underlined steps. If we further want to check b in c_B is consistent with value H, these steps are retained and the protocol is named as MtAwc (Multiplicative-to-additive with check). The MtA(wc) ptotocol could be proved secure even without any ZK proof as shown in [14]. Both MtA and MtAwc are used in our multi-signature.

4   Multi-signatures for ECDSA

In this section, we give a new ECDSA multi-signature scheme. In the naive approach of concatenating t ECDSA signatures, all parties can determine who is not signing correctly. Hence, we choose to build our ECDSA multi-signatures upon the interactive signing protocol with identifiable abort in [15]. Moreover, the new proposed ZK proof technique is detailed in Appendix C.

4.1   Construction

We denote a non-malleable equivocable commitment scheme a tuple of 5 algorithms (KeyGen$_e$, Com$_e$, Decom$_e$, KeyGen$_e'$, Equiv$_e$) and a trapdoor commitment scheme with efficient ZK proof by (KeyGen$_z$, Com$_z$, Decom$_z$, KeyGen$_z'$, TCom$_z$, TDecom$_z$).

   Our protocol contains 4 algorithms (Setup, KeyGen, Sign, Verify).

- Setup$(1^\lambda) \to$ params: On security parameter λ, this algorithm generates an ECC group $\mathcal{G}_{ECC} = (\mathbb{G}, G, q)$. It chooses hash functions $H : \{0,1\}^* \to \mathbb{Z}_q$, and $H_1 : \{0,1\}^* \to \{0,1\}^*$. It runs $\mathsf{pk}_e \leftarrow \mathsf{KeyGen}_e(1^\lambda)$ and $\mathsf{pk}_z \leftarrow \mathsf{KeyGen}_z(1^\lambda)$. It outputs params $= (\mathbb{G}, G, q, H, H_1, \mathsf{pk}_e, \mathsf{pk}_z)$.
- KeyGen(params) $\to$ (sk, pk): Each party picks a random secret key $x_i \leftarrow_\$ \mathbb{Z}_q$ and generates its own public key as $Y = xG$. Each party additionally runs the setup phase of the MtA protocol. This algorithm will finally output the key pair for the current party (x, Y). The key generation is identical to the standard ECDSA.
- Sign(params, $\{\mathsf{sk}_1, \ldots, \mathsf{sk}_t\}$, $S = \{\mathsf{pk}_1, \ldots, \mathsf{pk}_t\}$, $m) \to \sigma/\bot$: On input a group of public keys S of size t and a message m, player P_i with secret key x_i generate and share its MtA public key, then runs the following steps interactively.
  - **Phase 1.** Each player P_i picks $k_i, \gamma_i \leftarrow_\$ \mathbb{Z}_q$. All players broadcast their commitment C_i to $\gamma_i G$, where $(C_i, D_i) \leftarrow \mathsf{Com}_e(\mathsf{pk}_e, \gamma_i G)$.
  - **Phase 2.** For convenience, we define the quantities $k = \sum_{i \in [t]} k_i$, $\gamma = \sum_{i \in [t]} \gamma_i$. As a result $k\gamma = \sum_{i,j \in [t]} k_i \gamma_j \mod q$. Each pair of players P_i and P_j runs MtA together for k_i and γ_j and respectively receives back the result α_{ij} with β_{ij}, such that $k_i \gamma_j = \alpha_{ij} + \beta_{ij} \mod q$. Upon receiving α_{ij} and β_{ji}, P_i constructs $\delta_i = k_i \gamma_i + \sum_{i \neq j} \alpha_{ij} + \sum_{i \neq j} \beta_{ji} \mod q$.
  - **Phase 3.** All parties broadcast their own δ_i and reconstruct $\delta = \sum_{i \in [t]} \delta_i = \sum_{i,j \in [t]} k_i \gamma_j \mod q$.
  - **Phase 4.** Each party P_i broadcasts the decommitment D_i. P_i obtains $\gamma_j G = \mathsf{Decom}_e(\mathsf{pk}_e, C_j, D_j)$ for all $j \neq i$ and constructs $R = \delta^{-1}(\sum_{i \in [t]} \gamma_i G) = (k\gamma)^{-1}(\sum_{i \in [t]} \gamma_i G) = k^{-1}G$ and gets r as the x-coordinate of R.
  - **Phase 5.** Each party broadcasts $\bar{R}_i = k_i R$ and gives a consistency proof π_{k_i} between $\bar{R}_i$ and $\mathsf{Enc}(k_i)$ which is the first message sent in MtA protocol in Phase 2. The protocol aborts if the following check fails

$$G = \sum_{i \in [t]} \bar{R}_i. \tag{1}$$

  - **Phase 6.** All players compute $(a_1 || \ldots || a_t) = H_1(r, S, m)$, in which a_i stands for the masks of all parties' public keys. The group public key is denoted as $Y = \sum_{Y_i \in S} a_i Y_i$. Consequently, the corresponding secret key is $x = \sum_{i \in [t]} a_i x_i$, and it could not be controlled by any single party. As a result, $k \sum_{i \in [t]} a_i x_i = \sum_{i,j \in [t]} k_i(a_j x_j) \mod q$. Each pair of players P_i and P_j runs MtAwc together for k_i and $a_j x_j$, with the public value $B = a_j Y_j$. The return values are respectively marked as μ_{ij} for P_i and ν_{ij} for P_j. Hence $k_i(a_j x_j) = \mu_{ij} + \nu_{ij} \mod q$. Upon receiving μ_{ij} and ν_{ji}, P_i constructs $\sigma_i = k_i a_i x_i + \sum_{i \neq j} \mu_{ij} + \sum_{i \neq j} \nu_{ji} \mod q$
  - **Phase 7.** All parties broadcast T_i, where $(T_i, \cdot) \leftarrow \mathsf{Com}_z(\mathsf{pk}_z, \sigma_i)$, with a zero-knowledge proof π_{T_i} of σ_i.

Table 2. Identify abortion

Phase	Failure	Detecting adversary
2	MtA	Detect directly
4	Decommitment	Detect directly
5	$\bar{R}_i$ consistency	Detect directly
5	Equation (1)	a. P_i publishes k_i, γ_i, α_{ij} and β_{ij} b. All compute δ_i' and check $\delta_i = \delta_i'$
6	MtAwc	Detect directly
7	T_i consistency	Detect directly
8	S_i consistency	Detect directly
8	Equation (2)	a. P_i publishes k_i and μ_{ij} b. P_j computes $\sigma_i G = k_i a_i x_i G + \sum_{i \neq j} \mu_{ij} G + \sum_{i \neq j} \nu_{ji} G$ c. P_i prove $\sigma_i G$ and S_i consistent
9	σ invalid	Detect by checking $s_i R = \mathsf{H}(m)\bar{R}_i + r S_i$

- Phase 8. Each party gives the ZK proof π_{σ_i} on the consistency between T_i in Phase 7 and the newly generated value $S_i = \sigma_i R$. Upon receiving all S_i, parties aborts when

$$Y \neq \sum_{i \in [t]} S_i. \tag{2}$$

- Phase 9. All parties broadcast $s_i = k_i \mathsf{H}(m) + \sigma_i r$ and reconstruct s as $s = \sum_{i \in [t]} s_i$. The protocol aborts if (r, s) is not a valid ECDSA signature for the message m and the public key y.
- Verify(params, $S = \{\mathsf{pk}_1, \ldots, \mathsf{pk}_t\}, m, \sigma) \rightarrow \{0, 1\}$: The algorithm takes as inputs the public keys of signers as $S = \{Y_i\}$, the message m and the signature (r, s). The verification is done in two steps.
  - Generate ephemeral group public key. Compute $(a_1 || \ldots || a_t) = \mathsf{H}_1(r, S, m)$ and $Y = \sum_{i \in [t]} a_i Y_i$.
  - Verify ECDSA signature. Verify $\sigma = (r, s)$ using Y, by computing $R' = \mathsf{H}(m) \cdot s^{-1} G + r s^{-1} Y$ and checking if the x-coordinate of $R' \bmod q$ is r.

Note: Steps with underlining are optional. With these steps, one is able to determine which party did not collaborated properly by referring to Table 2, which uses the technique given by [15]. Otherwise, the protocol will give *anonymous abort*. We could prevent intentionally anonymous aborting by identifying the malicious party.

4.2 Security Proof

Theorem 1. *Our ECDSA multi-signature is unforgeable in the random oracle model if the standard ECDSA is unforgeable.*

Proof. In the bird's eyes, we prove the standard ECDSA is forgeable with non-negligible probability if our multi-signature is threaten by an adversary $\mathcal{A}$ with non-negligible advantage ϵ. The forger $\mathcal{F}$ internally invokes adversary $\mathcal{A}$ for and tries to break the standard ECDSA scheme with the power it.

Without loss of generality, the proof assumes only 1 honest party, named P_1 corresponding to public key pk_1, and other parties $\{P_i\}_{i>1}$ are all corrupted. We assume the adversary to be a *rushing adversary*, which means corrupted parties always send their messages after the honest party in each round.

Simulation of Setup. The simulator $\mathcal{S}$ picks $\mathcal{G}_{\mathrm{ECC}}$ and runs key generation $(\mathsf{pk}_e, \mathsf{tk}_e) \leftarrow \mathsf{KeyGen}'_e(1^\lambda)$ and $(\mathsf{pk}_z, \mathsf{tk}_z) \leftarrow \mathsf{KeyGen}'_z(1^\lambda)$ honestly.

Simulation of KeyGen. The key generation procedure needs to embed the standard ECDSA public key $\hat{\mathsf{pk}} = \hat{Y}$ into the multi-signature scheme. The simulator sets the public key for P_1, i.e. the simulated party, to $Y_1 = \hat{Y}$.

Simulation of H and H_1. $\mathcal{S}$ forwards whatever the standard ECDSA hash function returns for H and simulates H_1 as a normal random oracle query.

Simulation of Sign. For signing on message m, $\mathcal{S}$ firstly queries the ECDSA instance with a random message $\hat{m} \leftarrow_\$ \mathbb{Z}_q$ and gets back the signature $(\hat{r}, \hat{s})$.

They are expected to fulfill the equation $\hat{R} = \mathsf{H}(\hat{m})\hat{s}^{-1}G + \hat{r}\hat{s}^{-1}\hat{Y}$ where $\hat{r}$ is the x-coordinate of $\hat{R}$. Denote $\Delta = \mathsf{H}(\hat{m}) - \mathsf{H}(m)$. $\mathcal{S}$ picks random numbers $d_1, d_2 \in \mathbb{Z}_q$ such that:

$$(\hat{s}/d_2)(d_2\hat{R} + d_1 d_2/\hat{s}G) = \mathsf{H}(\hat{m})G + \hat{r}\hat{Y} + d_1 G = \mathsf{H}(m)G + \hat{r}Y_1 + (d_1 + \Delta)G.$$

Now suppose $R' = d_2\hat{R} + d_1 d_2/\hat{s}G$ and its x-coordinate as r', and denote $s' = \hat{s}/d_2$. Then we have:

$$s'(R') = \mathsf{H}(m)G + r'(\hat{r}/r'Y_1 + (d_1 + \Delta)/r'G).$$

(r', s') is a valid ECDSA signature on a message m and the corresponding group public key is $\hat{r}/r'Y_1 + (d_1 + \Delta)/r'G$. To form such a group public key, we set $a_1 = \hat{r}/r'$ with $\sum_{j>1} a_j x_j = (d_1 + \Delta)/r'$ in Phase 6 by the random oracle model.

The interaction messages will be given on how to simulate the real protocol with the previous $\hat{\mathsf{pk}}$ instance.

- **Phase 1.** P_1 runs the protocol and broadcasts C_1 as required. All other players also broadcast the commitment C_i for $\gamma_i G$.
- **Phase 2.** $\mathcal{S}$ interactively runs MtA with other parties using the MtA encryption keys as the following.
  - **Initiator for MtA with k_1 and γ_j.** $\mathcal{S}$ runs correctly for P_1 using k_1. $\mathcal{S}$ extracts P_j's value γ_j and β_{1j} and computes $\alpha_{1j} = k_1\gamma_j - \beta_{1j} \bmod q$.
  - **Respondent for MtA with k_j and γ_1.** $\mathcal{S}$ runs correctly for P_1 using γ_1. $\mathcal{S}$ extracts P_j's value k_j and computes $\alpha_{j1} = k_j\gamma_1 - \beta_{j1} \bmod q$ using its own share β_{j1}.
- **Phase 3.** $\mathcal{S}$ broadcasts δ_1 according to the scheme and receives back δ_i for $i > 1$. $\mathcal{S}$ reconstructs $\delta = \sum_{i \in [t]} \delta_i$.

- Phase 4a. Party P_i reveals D_i to decommit $\gamma_i G$. $\mathcal{S}$ computes $R = \delta^{-1}(\sum_{i\in[t]} \gamma_i G)$.

$\mathcal{S}$ checks whether the published values are consistent. Using the value k_i extracted in MtA, $\mathcal{S}$ can also validate whether $\sum_{i\in[t]} k_i R = G$. We say that an execution is fail-1 if this checking does not passed. If it is fail-1, $\mathcal{S}$ runs Phase 5 of the protocol as required using k_1 and one of the adversary's ZK proofs will fail and the protocol aborts. If it is not fail-1, then:

- Phase 4b. $\mathcal{S}$ rewinds $\mathcal{A}$ to the decommitment step and computes $\Gamma_1 = \delta R' - \sum_{j>1} \gamma_j G$ using γ_j extracted from Phase 2. Then $\mathcal{S}$ runs $D'_1 \leftarrow \mathsf{Equiv}_e(\mathsf{pk}_e, \mathsf{tk}_e, C_1, \Gamma_1)$. Then $\mathcal{S}$ reveals D'_1 as the decommitment instead.
  All parties can compute $R' = \delta^{-1}(\Gamma_1 + \sum_{j>1} \gamma_j G)$ and get r' as the x-coordinate of R'.
- Phase 5. $\mathcal{S}$ computes $\bar{R}_1 = G - \sum_{j>1} k_j(R')$ using the extracted k_j. $\mathcal{S}$ simulates the consistency proof and outputs $\bar{R}_1$.
- Phase 6. All players compute $(a_1||\ldots||a_t) = \mathsf{H}_1(r', S, m)$.
  $\mathcal{S}$ interactively runs MtAwc with other parties using the MtAwc encryption keys as the following.
    • Initiator for MtAwc with k_1 and $a_j x_j$. $\mathcal{S}$ runs correctly for P_1 using k_1. $\mathcal{S}$ extracts x_j and ν_{1j} from π_B and computes $\mu_{1j} = k_1(a_j x_j) - \nu_{1j} \bmod q$.
    • Respondent for MtAwc with k_j and $a_1 x_1$. $\mathcal{S}$ does not have $\mathsf{sk}_1 = x_1$ of P_1. $\mathcal{S}$ just randomly picks $\tilde{x}_1 \leftarrow_\$ \mathbb{Z}_q$ and interacts with P_i as if it is x_1.

Now $\mathcal{S}$ has already obtained the values $x_2, \ldots, x_t$. $\mathcal{S}$ rewinds $\mathsf{H}_1(r', S, m)$ and sets $a_1 = \hat{r}/r'$ and a_2 such that $\sum_{j>1} a_j x_j = (d_1 + \Delta)/r'$. $\mathcal{S}$ sets new $(a_1||a_2||\ldots)$ as the output of $\mathsf{H}_1(r', \mathsf{S}, m)$. We first consider the distribution of a_2. Since $a_3, \ldots, a_n$ are randomly chosen from $\mathbb{Z}_p$, a_2 itself is uniformly distributed from $\mathbb{Z}_p$. The values of all a_i satisfy the relation $\hat{r}/a_1 = (d_1 + \Delta)/\sum_{j>1} a_j x_j$. The relation is hidden by $\mathcal{S}$'s random choice of d_1 and Δ.

The value a_1 is calculated from $\hat{r}$ (the x-coordinate of $\hat{R}$ generated for a random message $\hat{m}$) and r' (the x-coordinate of R', calculated from the random number d_1, d_2). Assume that the division of the two x-coordinates is uniformly distributed in $\mathbb{Z}_p$, then a_1 is also uniformly distributed from $\mathbb{Z}_p$. Hence rewinding will succeed with non-negligible probability.

We remark that $\mathcal{S}$ cannot get x_1 so it will never get the complete σ_1 by itself. $\mathcal{S}$ can only compute another value: $\sigma_A = \sum_{i,j>1} k_i a_j x_j + \sum_{i>1} \mu_{i1} + \sum_{i>1} \nu_{1i} \bmod q$ using the values extracted from MtAwc.

- Phase 7. $\mathcal{S}$ computes $(T_1, \mathsf{aux}_{T_1}) \leftarrow \mathsf{TCom}_z(\mathsf{pk}_z, \mathsf{tk}_z)$ and uses a simulator of the ZK proof to generate π_{T_1}. $\mathcal{S}$ broadcasts T_1 and π_{T_1}.

$\mathcal{S}$ can detect if the values published by the adversary are consistent. Using the extractor of π_{T_i}, $\mathcal{S}$ can extract σ_i and check if $\sigma_A = \sum_{i>1} \sigma_i$. We say that an execution is fail-2 if this checking is incorrect.

If it is fail-2, then in Phase 8, $\mathcal{S}$ sets $S_1 = (k_1 a_1 \tilde{x}_1 + \sum_{j>1} \mu_{1j} + \sum_{j>1} \nu_{j1})R'$, simulates a consistency proof using the simulator of the ZK proof, and outputs S_1. At least one of the adversary's ZK proofs will fail and the protocol will abort. If it is not fail-2, then:

- Phase 8. $\mathcal{S}$ computes $S_1 = Y - \sum_{j>1} \sigma_i R'$. $\mathcal{S}$ simulates a consistency proof using the simulator of the ZK proof and outputs S_1.
- Phase 9. As the simulator $\mathcal{S}$ already knew k_i, $a_i x_i$ for all $i > 1$, it could compute $s_A = \sum_{i>1} s_i = \mathsf{H}(m)\sum_{i>1} k_i + \sigma_A r$, and outputs $s_1 = s' - s_A$.

Attacking Standard ECDSA. In the final step of the security game, $\mathcal{A}$ is required to present a valid signature (r^*, s^*) on a message m^* such that the honest party's public key Y_1 is inside the public key set $S^* = (y_1^*, \ldots, y_{t^*}^*)$. WLOG, suppose $Y_1^* = Y_1$. Since the signature is valid, we have $(a_1^*||\ldots||a_{t*}^*) = \mathsf{H}_1(r^*, S^*, m^*)$, $Y^* = \sum_{i \in [t^*]} a_i^* Y_i^*$,

$$s^*(R^*) = \mathsf{H}(m^*)G + r^* Y^*, \tag{3}$$

and the x-coordinate of R^* mod q is r^*.

$\mathcal{S}$ rewinds $\mathcal{A}$ to the query of $\mathsf{H}_1(r^*, S^*, m^*)$ and returns another fresh random $(\tilde{a_1}^*||\tilde{a_2}^*||\ldots||\tilde{a_{t*}}^*)$ instead. Now $\mathcal{A}$ returns the signature $(r^*, \tilde{s}^*)$, and

$$\tilde{s}^*(R^*) = \mathsf{H}(m^*)G + r^* \tilde{Y}^*. \tag{4}$$

By dividing Eq. (3) and (4), we have:

$$(s^* - \tilde{s}^*)kG = (s^* - \tilde{s}^*)(R^*) = r^*(a_i^* - \tilde{a_i}^*)\sum Y_i = r^*((a_1^* - \tilde{a_1}^*)Y_1 + \sum_{i>1}(a_i^* - \tilde{a_i}^*)x_i G)$$

Hence $\mathcal{S}$ can extract the discrete logarithm of Y_1 i.e. x_1 from the final equation, which helps itself to generate a valid signature for the underlying standard ECDSA. By the random choice of $\hat{m}$ in the signing oracle query, m^* is different from all existing $\hat{m}$ with an overwhelming probability.

Analysis. The differences between the real and the simulated views can be listed as the following. In Phase 2, the MtA protocol the values $c_i = \mathsf{Enc}_{ek_i}(k_i)$ are published. In the real protocol $R = \sum_i k_i G$ and in the simulated protocol we have R^* instead. The views are indistinguishable as the encryption scheme secure is IND-CPA secure. In Phase 4b of the simulated protocol, the decommitment D_1' is returned. By the non-malleability property of the equivocable commitment, it is indistinguishable from the real decommitment D_1. By the zero-knowledge property of the ZK proofs, the simulation of Phase 5 and 8 are correct. In Phase 6, a_2 is set to $\sum_{j>1} a_j x_j = (d_1 + \Delta)/r'$. It is uniformly distributed in $\mathbb{Z}_q$ by the random choice of $d_1 \in \mathbb{Z}_q$. Also, a_1 is set to $\hat{r}/r'$. Note that $\hat{r}$ is related to $\hat{s} = s'd_2$, which is uniformly distributed in $\mathbb{Z}_p$ by the random choice of $d_2 \in \mathbb{Z}_q$.

5   Instantiating with Class Group

We use the additive homomorphic encryption introduced by Castagnos and Laguillaumie [9] defined on a group with hard subgroup membership (HSM).

5.1 Hard Subgroup Membership Group

HSM Group. It is an abstract group introduced in [5] and named as HSM for the hard subgroup membership assumption [22], which constructs a subgroup where the discrete logarithm (DL) is easy. The generation algorithm takes security parameter 1^λ as input and it outputs the group as $\mathcal{G}_{\mathrm{HSM}} = (\mathbb{G}, \mathbb{G}^q, \mathbb{F}, g, g_q, f, \tilde{s}, q)$. Specifically, the primary group is $(\mathbb{G}, \cdot)$ generated by g, in which the real order $q \cdot \hat{s}$ is unknown but we can determine the prime factor q with $\tilde{s}$ as the upper bound of $\hat{s}$. The subgroup $(\mathbb{F}, \cdot)$ with generator f and order q could be determined. And the subgroup $\mathbb{G}^q$ of order $\hat{s}$ could be generated by g^q. Apparently, we have $\mathbb{G} = \mathbb{G}^q \times \mathbb{F}$. The DL problem in the subgroup $\mathbb{F}$ is easy to solve by a PPT algorithm Solve without any trapdoor. Given the group description $\mathcal{G}_{\mathrm{HSM}} = (\mathbb{G}, \mathbb{G}^q, \mathbb{F}, g, g_q, f, \tilde{s}, q)$ and input $y = f^x$, the algorithm computes discrete logarithm $x \leftarrow \mathsf{Solve}_{\mathcal{G}_{\mathrm{HSM}}}(y)$ in polynomial time.

HSM Group from Class Group. The HSM group could by instantiated by class groups of imaginary quadratic order. The $\mathsf{GGen}_{\mathrm{HSM}}$ first picks a random prime $\tilde{q}$ such that $q\tilde{q} \equiv 1 \pmod 4$ and $(q/\tilde{q}) = -1$. For fundamental discriminant $\Delta_K = -q\tilde{q}$ and non-maximal order of discriminant $\Delta_q = q^2 \Delta_K$, class group $\tilde{\mathbb{G}} = Cl(\Delta_q)$ orders $h(\Delta_q) = q \cdot h(\Delta_K)$ where $h(\Delta_K)$ is the order of $Cl(\Delta_K)$. Let I be the ideal lying above small prime r and ϕ_q^{-1} be the Algorithm 1 in [8]. The generators f and g_q for the subgroup $\mathbb{F} = \langle f \rangle$ and $\mathbb{G}^q = \langle g_q \rangle$ can be computed by $g_q = [\phi_q^{-1}(I^2)]^q$ and $f = [(q^2, q)]$. Accordingly, $g = f \cdot g_q$ generates $\mathbb{G} = \langle g \rangle$. The algorithm outputs $\mathcal{G}_{\mathrm{HSM}} = (\mathbb{G}, \mathbb{G}^q, \mathbb{F}, g, g_q, f, \tilde{s}, q)$.

5.2 CL Encryption for HSM Group

We review the additive homomorphic encryption raised by Castagnos and Laguillaumie [9], in which message space is a cyclic group with prime order q.

- $\mathsf{Setup}(1^\lambda) \to \mathsf{params}$: it calls group generation algorithm $\mathsf{GGen}_{\mathrm{HSM}}$ described previously, then outputs system parameters as $\mathsf{params} = (\mathbb{G}, \mathbb{G}^q, \mathbb{F}, g, g_q, f, \tilde{s}, q)$. Moreover, we define the statistical distance ϵ_d with constant $S = \tilde{s} \cdot 2^{\epsilon_d}$.
- $\mathsf{KeyGen}(\mathsf{params}) \to (\mathsf{ek}, \mathsf{dk})$: it picks $\mathsf{dk} \leftarrow_\$ [0, S]$ and sets public key $\mathsf{ek} = g_q^{\mathsf{dk}}$.
- $\mathsf{Enc}_{\mathsf{ek}}(m) \to C$: it picks random number in $\rho \leftarrow_\$ [0, S]$. It composes the ciphertext $C = (C_1, C_2)$ where $C_1 = f^m \mathsf{ek}^\rho$ and $C_2 = g_q^\rho$.
- $\mathsf{Dec}_{\mathsf{dk}}(C) \to m$: it computes $M = C_1/C_2^{\mathsf{dk}}$ and calls Solve for $m \leftarrow \mathsf{Solve}_{\mathcal{G}_{\mathrm{HSM}}}(M)$.
- $\mathsf{EvalSum}_{\mathsf{ek}}(C, C') \to \hat{C}$: it computes the addition by $\hat{C} = (C_1 C_1', C_2 C_2')$ for $C = (C_1, C_2)$ and $C' = (C_1', C_2')$.
- $\mathsf{EvalScal}_{\mathsf{ek}}(C, s) \to C'$: it scales the message with the scalar s by computing $C' = (C_1^s, C_2^s)$ for inputted ciphertext $C = (C_1, C_2)$.

5.3 ZK Proof with CL Encryption

Instantiating the MtA protocol with CL encryption, the relation R_{Enc} turns to be $\{(m, \rho) | \mathsf{pk} \in \mathbb{G}^q, \rho \in [0, S] : C_1 = f^m \mathsf{pk}^\rho \wedge C_2 = g_q^\rho\}$. And the relation R_B turns to be $\{(\underline{H}, \underline{G}, c_A, c_B, \text{ek}) : (b, \beta, \rho) : \underline{H} = \underline{bG} \wedge C_1 = \hat{C_1}^b \text{pk}^\rho f^{-\beta} \wedge C_2 = \hat{C_2}^b g_q^\rho\}$ where G is the ECC generator. Consequently, the ZK proof for R_{Enc} follows immediately the Algorithm 5 in [22]. And we give the ZK protocol for R_B and its security analysis in Appendix C where the relation is formally named $\mathcal{R}_{\text{Aff}\underline{wc}}$.

Table 3. Bandwidth (bytes) and running time (ms) of each party for a t-party signing

Phase	Sent size	Receive size	Running time
1	32	32 (t − 1)	0.00t + 0.20
2a	4899	4899 (t − 1)	2397.24t + 1832.19
2b	5292 (t − 1)	5292 (t − 1)	588.15t − 2.81
3	32	32 (t − 1)	0.01t + 0.00
4	64	64 (t − 1)	0.03t + 0.37
5	4049	4049 (t − 1)	2749.42t + 1548.67
6	5356 (t − 1)	5356 (t − 1)	584.92t + 5.08
7	128	128 (t − 1)	0.54t + 0.80
8	160	160 (t − 1)	0.92t + 0.70
9	32	32 (t − 1)	0.25t + 0.49
Total	10648t + 9396	20044t − 20044	6321.48t + 3385.70

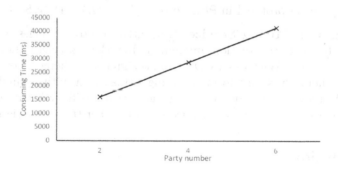

Fig. 1. Total running time of each party for a t-party signing

6   Implementation

We implement the multi-signature with Rust language[5] relying on a modified class group and the related curve library[6] Our implementation targets at 128-bit security and picks the SHA-256 hash function, the Secp256k1 ECC curve and

---

[5] https://github.com/multisig-ecdsa/multisig-ecdsa.
[6] https://github.com/ZenGo-X/class and https://github.com/ZenGo-X/curv.

a class group with $||\Delta_K|| = 3392$ [12] accordingly. The message size and bandwidth requirement analysis are given theoretically, and all broadcast messages are consider as sending it once (Fig. 1 and Table 3). Benchmark is performed on an AMD Ryzen 7 5800H @3.20 GHz computer with 8 GB RAM.

7 Applications in Blockchain

Nowadays, blockchain plays an increasingly essential role among decentralized cryptocurrencies and many of them rely on the ECDSA signatures. In Bitcoin, a flexible way to check the ownership is adopted, which is known as the Bitcoin script. But the Bitcoin script is not Turing-complete and prevents our scheme to work fully native. We discusses how to adapt our scheme to the Bitcoin here.

Advantages for Using ECDSA Multi-signatures. (1) The signature size is minimized in our scheme and could be extremely bandwidth efficient. (2) Compared to the Schnoor-based or pairing-based multi-signatures, our ECDSA multi-signatures could better fit into the current blockchains. (3) Compared to the threshold ECDSA, our scheme does not require interactive key generation.

Construction of t-of-n Multi-signature. In the *multisig* address in Bitcoin, an address can be associated with a set of n public keys G and a threshold value $t \leq n$. Any set of t signers S can authorize a transaction on behalf of G.

From the current method of forming group public key in our ECDSA multi-signature, we could also construct a m-of-n multi-signature. The idea is to replace the key aggregation protocol in Phase 6 to $(a_1||\ldots||a_t) = \mathsf{H}_1(r, \mathsf{S}, G, m)$.

Combining with Mixing Service. Currently, cryptocurrencies utilizes mixing services to make transaction anonymous but these services always takes a high transaction fee. With our ECDSA multi-signature scheme, users could collaborate by themselves and form a mixing transaction with a single ECDSA signature. Moreover, users don't need to generate auxiliary information when signing the message, because we require nothing other than the original keys.

8 Conclusion

In this paper, we give the first multi-signatures for ECDSA by designing a novel *ephemeral group public key* for the set of signers and using a generic MtA protocol for signing. This scheme can identify the malicious party and is adaptable to the class group, which minimizes the communication cost maximally. As it only produces a single signature, this scheme can be used in blockchain to save transaction cost with the accountability for signers and backward-compatibility with existing addresses.

A   Definition for Building Blocks

A.1   ECDSA

ECDSA is a variant of DSA scheme over elliptic curve. It contains a tuple of 4 algorithms (Setup, KeyGen, Sign, Verify). $\mathsf{Setup}(1^\lambda) \to$ params generates parameters and calls $\mathsf{GGen}_{\mathrm{ECC}} = (\mathbb{G}, G, q)$ and picks a hash function $\mathsf{H} : \{0,1\}^* \to \mathbb{Z}_q$. It returns params $= (\mathbb{G}, G, q, \mathsf{H})$. $\mathsf{KeyGen}(\mathrm{params}) \to (\mathsf{sk}, \mathsf{pk})$ takes security parameter params as input and returns a secret key $\mathsf{sk} = x \leftarrow_\$ \mathbb{Z}_q$ with a public key $\mathsf{pk} = xG$. $\mathsf{Sign}(\mathsf{sk}, m) \to \sigma$ computes $R = k^{-1}G$ and takes the x coordinate of $R \bmod q$ as r. It computes $s = k(\mathsf{H}(m) + xr) \bmod q$ and returns signature $\sigma = (r, s)$. $\mathsf{Verify}(\mathsf{pk}, \sigma) \to b$ outputs the verification result $b \in \{0, 1\}$ according to whether $R' = \mathsf{H}(m) \cdot s^{-1}G + rs^{-1}\mathsf{pk}$ and the x coordinate of $R' \bmod q$ is r.

A.2   Additive Homomorphic Encryption

An additive homomorphic encryption allows users to compute the sum of two message in ciphertext. It contains (Setup, KeyGen, Enc, Dec, EvalSum, EvalScal). $\mathsf{Setup}(1^\lambda) \to$ params takes security parameters and outputs the system parameter params. $\mathsf{KeyGen}(\mathrm{params}) \to (\mathsf{ek}, \mathsf{dk})$ computes an encryption key and a decryption key from the system parameters. $\mathsf{Enc}_{\mathsf{ek}}(m) \to C$ gets the encryption of a message m under the encryption key ek as the ciphertext C. $\mathsf{Dec}_{\mathsf{dk}}(C) \to m$ recovers the plaintext m from the decryption key dk. $\mathsf{EvalSum}_{\mathsf{ek}}(C, C') \to \hat{C}$ evaluates the ciphertext $\hat{C} = \mathsf{Enc}_{\mathsf{ek}}(a + b)$ for $C = \mathsf{Enc}_{\mathsf{ek}}(a)$ and $C' = \mathsf{Enc}_{\mathsf{ek}}(b)$. $\mathsf{EvalScal}_{\mathsf{ek}}(C, s) \to C'$ scales $C = \mathsf{Enc}_{\mathsf{ek}}(a)$ to $C' = \mathsf{Enc}_{\mathsf{ek}}(s \cdot a)$.

The security of the additive homomorphic encryption follows the standard definition of indistinguishability against chosen plaintext attack (IND-CPA).

A.3   Trapdoor Commitment

A commitment scheme contains a algorithms tuple as (KeyGen, Com, Decom). $\mathsf{KeyGen}(1^\lambda) \to \mathsf{pk}$ generates a public key pk. $\mathsf{Com}(\mathsf{pk}, M) \to (C, D)$ takes the public key pk with a message M then outputs the commitment string C and decommitment string D. $\mathsf{Decom}(\mathsf{pk}, C, D) \to \{M, \perp\}$ takes the public key pk, the commitment string C, the decommitment string D as input and outputs M if it succeeds and $\perp$ otherwise.

A commitment scheme is considered secure if it fulfills the correctness, hiding and binding properties. For correctness, it requires that for all messages M and $\mathsf{pk} \leftarrow \mathsf{KeyGen}(1^\lambda)$, then $M \leftarrow \mathsf{Decom}(\mathsf{pk}, \mathsf{Com}(\mathsf{pk}, M))$. Hiding means that every message M_1 and M_2 and $\mathsf{pk} \leftarrow \mathsf{KeyGen}(1^\lambda)$, $\mathsf{Com}(\mathsf{pk}, M_1)$ and $\mathsf{Com}(\mathsf{pk}, M_2)$ is statistically indistinguishable. The binding property holds if adversary $\mathcal{A}$ wins the game with probability $\Pr[\mathcal{A} \text{ wins binding game}] \leq \mathsf{negl}(\lambda)$.

Trapdoor Commitment with Efficient ZK Proof. A commitment scheme has the additional algorithms (KeyGen', TCom, TDecom) fulfilling the following. KeyGen'(1^λ) $\rightarrow$ (pk, tk) generates a public key pk and a trapdoor tk. TCom(pk, tk) $\rightarrow$ (C, aux) gives commitment C and auxiliary information aux such that TDecom could open it with any message specified. TDecom(C, aux, M) $\rightarrow D$ give out the decommitment D by using aux.

The additional algorithm is required to be **trapdoorness**. We say a commitment scheme fulfilling the trapdoorness property if for all messages M, the following distributions: $\{(\mathsf{pk}, M, C, D) : \mathsf{pk} \leftarrow \mathsf{KeyGen}(1^\lambda), (C, D) \leftarrow \mathsf{Com}(\mathsf{pk}, M)\}$ and $\{(\mathsf{pk}, M, C, D) : (\mathsf{pk}, \mathsf{tk}) \leftarrow \mathsf{KeyGen}'(1^\lambda), (C, \mathsf{aux}) \leftarrow \mathsf{TCom}(\mathsf{pk}, \mathsf{tk}); D \leftarrow \mathsf{TDecom}(C, \mathsf{aux}, M)\}$ are computationally indistinguishable.

Non-malleable Equivocable Commitment Scheme. The equivocable commitment scheme additionally contains KeyGen' and Equiv. KeyGen'(1^λ) $\rightarrow$ (pk, tk) generates a public key pk and a trapdoor tk. Equiv(pk, tk, C, M') $\rightarrow$ D' generates decommitment string D' using trapdoor tk such that Decom(pk, C, D') = M'.

The additional algorithm is required to be **equivocable** and **non-malleable**. A commitment scheme is called for equivocable if for all messages M, M', (pk, tk) $\leftarrow$ KeyGen'(1^λ), $(C, D) \leftarrow$ Com(pk, M) and $D' \leftarrow$ Equiv(pk, tk, C, M'), then $M' \leftarrow$ Decom(pk, C, D'). Non-malleable means that no adversary $\mathcal{A}$ could generate C' related to C such that the decommitment of C' is computed from M.

B   Trapdoor Commitments and Its ZK Proofs

We instantiate the trapdoor commitment Com_z as the Pedersen commitment $\mathsf{Com}(\mathsf{pk}, m) \rightarrow (C, D)$ for $C = mG + rH$ and $D = (m, r)$. The ZK proof in Phase 5 could be instantiated directly following the Algorithm 6 of [22]. The ZK proofs in Phase 7 and 8 follow the ZK proof in Sect. 3.3 of [15].

C   Zero-Knowledge Proof for MtA(wc)

We give an informal description of assumptions used in HSM group here and refer to [22] for the complete definition. These hard assumptions are defined on prime number $q > 2^\lambda$ and HSM group $\mathcal{G}_{\mathsf{HSM}} = (\mathbb{G}, \mathbb{G}^q, \mathbb{F}, g, g_q, f, \tilde{s}, q)$ for $\mathcal{G}_{\mathsf{HSM}} \leftarrow \mathsf{GGen}_{\mathsf{HSM}}(1^\lambda)$. If we denote H as a generator in the ECC group with prime order q, then

$$\mathcal{R}_{\mathsf{Aff\underline{wc}}} = \left\{ \begin{array}{l|l} (\mathsf{pk}, C_1, C_2, \tilde{C}_1, \tilde{C}_2); & \mathsf{pk}, C_2 \in G^q, C_1 \in G \setminus F, \gamma\beta \in \mathbb{Z}_q, \rho \in [0, S] : \\ (\gamma, \beta, \rho) & \tilde{C}_1 = C_1^\gamma f^\beta \mathsf{pk}^\rho \wedge \tilde{C}_2 = C_2^\gamma g_q^\rho \wedge \underline{H' = \gamma H} \end{array} \right\}.$$

We have 2 important facts in HSM group. The first one if Adaptive root subgroup hardness. Given q and HSM group $\mathcal{G}_{\mathrm{HSM}}$, it's hard to find $u^\ell = w$ and $w^q \neq 1$ for specific $\ell \leftarrow \mathsf{Primes}(\lambda)$. The other one is Non-trivial order hardness, which states that given q and $\mathcal{G}_{\mathrm{HSM}}$, it's hard to find $h \neq 1 \in \mathbb{G}$ such that $h^d = 1$ and $d < q$.

Theorem 2. *The protocol* $\mathsf{ZKPoKAff_{wc}}$ *is an argument of knowledge in the generic group model.*

Proof. We rewind the adversary on fresh challenges ℓ so that each accepting transcript outputs an $(Q_1, Q_2, R_1, R_2, P_1, r_\rho, r_\gamma, \ell)$. Recall that we have $C_2 \in G^q$. By the PoKRepS protocol in [22], with overwhelming probability there exists $\rho^*, \gamma^* \in \mathbb{Z}$ s.t. $\rho^* = r_\rho \bmod \ell$ and $\gamma^* = r_\gamma \bmod \ell$, and $g_q^{\rho^*} C_2^{\gamma^*} = S_2 \tilde{C}_2^c$. Since $S_2 \tilde{C}_2^c = (D_2 E_2)^q g_q^{e_\rho} C_2^{e_\gamma}$, it implies $\rho^* = e_\rho \bmod q$ and $\gamma^* = e_\gamma \bmod q$. Considering 2 cases, $\mathsf{pk}^{\rho^*} C_1^{\gamma^*} f^{u_\beta} = S_1 \tilde{C}_1^c$ is at overwhelming probability.

Next we consider the rewinding of c. The extractor obtains a pair of accepting transcripts with $(\rho^*, \gamma^*, u_\beta, c)$ and $(\rho', \gamma', u'_\beta, c')$. The extractor can compute $\Delta_\rho = \rho^* - \rho'$, $\Delta_\gamma = \gamma^* - \gamma'$ and $\Delta_{u_\beta} = u_\beta - u'_\beta \bmod q$. We denote $\rho = \frac{\Delta_\rho}{\Delta_c}, \gamma = \frac{\Delta_\gamma}{\Delta_c}$ and $\beta = \frac{\Delta_{u_\beta}}{\Delta_c} \bmod q$. Hence we have $\tilde{C}_1^{\Delta_c} = (\mathsf{pk}^\rho C_1^\gamma f^\beta)^{\Delta_c}$. If $\tilde{C}_1 \neq \mathsf{pk}^\rho C_1^\gamma f^\beta$, then $\frac{\mathsf{pk}^\rho f^\beta C_1^\gamma}{\tilde{C}_1}$ is a non-trivial element of order $\Delta_c < q$ which contradicts with the non-trivial element and its order in the generic group model.

As our scheme includes a sub-protocol $\mathsf{ZKPoKRepS}$ on input $\tilde{C}_2$ w.r.t. bases $g_q \in G \setminus F$. Since $\mathsf{ZKPoKRepS}$ is an argument of knowledge, there exists an extractor to extract the same (γ, ρ) such that $\tilde{C}_2 = C_2^\gamma g_q^\rho$. Similar argument applies to H. There exists an extractor to extract the same γ such that $H' = \gamma H$. Hence the extractor can output (β, γ, ρ) such that $\tilde{C}_1 = C_1^\gamma f^\beta \mathsf{pk}^\rho$, $\tilde{C}_2 = C_2^\gamma g_q^\rho$ and $H' = \gamma H$. □

Theorem 3. *The protocol* $\mathsf{ZKPoKAff_{wc}}$ *is an honest-verifier statistically zero-knowledge argument of knowledge for relation* $\mathcal{R}_{\mathsf{Aff_{wc}}}$ *in the generic group model.*

Proof. The simulator Sim randomly picks a challenge $c' \in [0, q-1]$ and a prime $\ell' \in \mathsf{Prime}(\lambda)$. It picks a random $u'_\beta \in \mathbb{Z}_q, q'_\rho, q'_\gamma \in [0, B-1]$ and $r'_\rho, r'_\gamma \in [0, \ell'-1]$. It finds $d'_\rho, d'_\gamma \in \mathbb{Z}$ and $e'_\rho, e'_\gamma \in [0, q-1]$ such that $d'_\rho q + e'_\rho = q'_\rho \ell' + r'_\rho$, $d'_\gamma q + e'_\gamma = q'_\gamma \ell' + r'_\gamma$.

It computes:

$$D'_1 = \mathsf{pk}^{d'_\rho}, \quad D'_2 = g_q^{d'_\rho}, \quad E'_1 = C_1^{d'_\gamma}, \quad E'_2 = C_2^{d'_\gamma},$$

$$Q'_1 = \mathsf{pk}^{q'_\rho}, \quad Q'_2 = g_q^{q'_\rho}, \quad R'_1 = C_1^{q'_\gamma}, \quad R'_2 = C_2^{q'_\gamma}, \quad P'_1 = q'_\gamma H,$$

$$S'_1 = (Q'_1 R'_1)^{\ell'} \mathsf{pk}^{r'_\rho} C_1^{r'_\gamma} f^{u'_\beta} \tilde{C}_1^{-c'}, \quad S'_2 = (Q'_2 R'_2)^{\ell'} g_q^{r'_\rho} C_2^{r'_\gamma} \tilde{C}_2^{-c'},$$

$$S'_3 = \ell' P'_1 + r'_\gamma H + -c' H'.$$

We argue that The simulated transcript is indistinguishable from a real one $(S_1, S_2, \underline{S_3}, c, u_\beta, D_1, D_2, E_1, E_2, e_\rho, \ell, Q_1, Q_2, R_1, R_2, \underline{P_1}, r_\rho, r_\gamma)$ between a prover and a verifier. Sim chooses (ℓ', c') identically to the honest verifier. Both u_β and u'_β are uniformly distributed in $\mathbb{Z}_q$. $(S'_1, S'_2, \underline{S'_3}, D'_1, D'_2, E'_1, E'_2, e'_\rho, e'_\gamma)$ is uniquely defined by the other values such that the verification holds.

We compare the simulated transcript $(Q'_1, Q'_2, R'_1, R'_2, \underline{P'_1}, r'_\rho, r'_\gamma)$ and the real transcript $(Q_1, Q_2, R_1, R_2, \underline{P_1}, r_\rho, r_\gamma)$. We need to prove that, in the real protocol, independent of ℓ and c, the either r_ρ or r_γ has a negligible statistical distance from the uniform distribution over $[0, \ell - 1]$ and each one of $\mathsf{pk}^{q_\rho}, g_q^{q_\rho}, C_1^{q_\gamma}, C_2^{q_\gamma}, q_\gamma H$ has negligible statistical from uniform over $G_k = \langle \mathsf{pk} \rangle, G^q, G_1 = \langle C_1 \rangle, G_2 = \langle C_2 \rangle, \langle h \rangle$ respectively. In addition, each of $Q_1, Q_2, R_1, R_2, \underline{P_1}, r_\rho, r_\gamma$ are independent from others. Then, the simulator produces statistically indistinguishable transcripts. The complete proof is as follows.

Consider fixed values of c, ρ and ℓ. In the real protocol, the prover computes $u_\rho = c\rho + s_\rho$ where s_ρ is uniform in $[-B, B]$ and sets $r_\rho = u_\rho \bmod \ell$. By Fact 1, the value of u_ρ is distributed uniformly over a range of $2B + 1$ consecutive integers, thus r_ρ has a statistical distance at most $\ell/(2B+1)$ from uniform over $[0, \ell - 1]$. This bounds the distance between the real r_ρ and the simulated r'_ρ, which is uniform over $[0, \ell - 1]$. Similarly, $\ell/(2B+1)$ also bounds the distance between r_γ and r'_γ

Next, $g_q^{q_\rho}$ is statistically indistinguishable from uniform in G^q. By the triangle inequality, the statistical distance of $q_\rho \bmod |G^q|$ from uniform is at most $\frac{2^{\lambda+1}}{B} + \frac{2^{\lambda-1}|G^q|}{B+1-2^\lambda}$. We consider the joint distribution of $(\mathsf{pk}^{q_\rho}, g_q^{q_\rho})$ and r_ρ. Consider the conditional distribution of $q_\rho | r_\rho$. Note that $q_\rho = z$ if $(s_\rho - r_\rho)/\ell = z$. We repeat a similar argument as above for bounding the distribution of q_ρ from uniform. For each possible value of z, there always exists a unique value of s_ρ such that $\lfloor \frac{s_\rho}{\ell} \rfloor = z$ and $s_\rho = 0 \bmod \ell$, except possibly at the two endpoints E_1, E_2 of the range of q_ρ. When r_ρ disqualifies the two points E_1 and E_2, then each of the remaining points $z \notin \{E_1, E_2\}$ still have equal probability mass, and thus the probability $\Pr(q_\rho = z | r_\rho)$ increases by at most $\frac{1}{|Y|} - \frac{\ell}{2B+1}$, which also applies to the variable $(\mathsf{pk}^{q_\rho}, g_q^{q_\rho}) | r_\rho$. Similarly, the probability $\Pr(q_\gamma = z | r_\gamma)$ increases by at most $\frac{1}{|Y|} - \frac{\ell}{2B+1}$, which also applies to the variable $(\mathsf{pk}^{q_\gamma}, g_q^{q_\gamma}, h^{q_\gamma}) | r_\gamma$.

We can compare the joint distributions $X'_\rho = (\mathsf{pk}^{q_\rho}, g_q^{q_\rho}, r_\rho)$ to the simulated distribution $Y'_\rho = (\mathsf{pk}^{q'_\rho}, g_q^{q'_\rho}, r'_\rho)$ using Fact 3.

Algorithm 1: Protocol ZKPoKAff<u>wc</u> for the relation $\mathcal{R}_{\mathsf{Aff(wc)}}$

Param: $\mathcal{G}_{\mathrm{HSM}} \leftarrow \mathsf{GGen}_{\mathrm{HSM},q}(1^\lambda)$, $B = 2^{\epsilon_d + \lambda + 3} q\tilde{s}$, where $\epsilon_d = 80$.
Input: $C_1, C_2, \tilde{C}_1, \tilde{C}_2, \mathsf{pk} \in G^q$.
Witness: $\rho \in [0, S], \beta \in \mathbb{Z}_q, \gamma \in \mathbb{Z}_q$, where $S = \tilde{s} \cdot 2^{\epsilon_d}$.

1 Prover chooses $s_\rho, s_\gamma \xleftarrow{\$} [-B, B]$, $s_\beta \xleftarrow{\$} \mathbb{Z}_q$ and computes:

$$S_1 = C_1^{s_\gamma} f^{s_\beta} \mathsf{pk}^{s_\rho}, \quad S_2 = C_2^{s_\gamma} g_q^{s_\rho}, \quad \underline{S_3 = h^{s_\gamma}}.$$

Prover sends $(S_1, S_2, \underline{S_3})$ to the verifier.

2 Verifier sends $c \xleftarrow{\$} [0, q-1]$ and $\ell \xleftarrow{\$} \mathsf{Primes}(\lambda)$ to the prover.
3 Prover computes:

$$u_\beta = s_\beta + c\beta \mod q, \quad u_\rho = s_\rho + c\rho, \quad u_\gamma = s_\gamma + c\gamma.$$

Prover finds $d_\rho \in \mathbb{Z}$ and $e_\rho, e_\gamma \in [0, q-1]$ s.t. $u_\rho = d_\rho q + e_\rho$ and $u_\gamma = d_\gamma q + e_\gamma$.
Prover computes:

$$D_1 = \mathsf{pk}^{d_\rho}, \quad D_2 = g_q^{d_\rho}, \quad E_1 = C_1^{d_\gamma}, \quad E_2 = C_2^{d_\gamma}.$$

Prover sends $(u_\beta, D_1, D_2, E_1, E_2, e_\rho, e_\gamma)$ to the verifier.
4 Verifier check if $e_\rho, e_\gamma \in [0, q-1]$ and:

$$(D_1 E_1)^q \mathsf{pk}^{e_\rho} C_1^{e_\gamma} f^{u_\beta} = S_1 \tilde{C}_1^c, \quad (D_2 E_2)^q g_q^{e_\rho} C_2^{e_\gamma} = S_2 \tilde{C}_2^c,$$
$$\underline{h^{e_\gamma} = S_3 H^c}.$$

If so, the verifier sends $\ell \xleftarrow{\$} \mathsf{Primes}(\lambda)$.
5 Prover finds $q_\rho \in \mathbb{Z}$ and $r_\rho, r_\gamma \in [0, \ell-1]$ s.t. $u_\rho = q_\rho \ell + r_\rho$ and $u_\gamma = q_\gamma \ell + r_\gamma$.
Prover computes:

$$Q_1 = \mathsf{pk}^{q_\rho}, \quad Q_2 = g_q^{q_\rho}, \quad R_1 = C_1^{q_\gamma}, \quad R_2 = C_2^{q_\gamma}, \quad \underline{P_1 = h^{q_\gamma}}.$$

Prover sends $(Q_1, Q_2, R_1, R_2, \underline{P_1}, r_\rho, r_\gamma)$ to the verifier.
6 Verifier accepts if $r_\rho, r_\gamma \in [0, \ell-1]$ and:

$$(Q_1 R_1)^\ell \mathsf{pk}^{r_\rho} C_1^{r_\gamma} f^{u_\beta} = S_1 \tilde{C}_1^c, \quad (Q_2 R_2)^\ell g_q^{r_\rho} C_2^{r_\gamma} = S_2 \tilde{C}_2^c,$$
$$\underline{P_1^\ell h^{r_\gamma} = S_3 H^c}.$$

References

1. Kılınç Alper, H., Burdges, J.: Two-round trip Schnorr multi-signatures via delinearized witnesses. In: Malkin, T., Peikert, C. (eds.) CRYPTO 2021. LNCS, vol. 12825, pp. 157–188. Springer, Cham (2021). https://doi.org/10.1007/978-3-030-84242-0_7
2. Bagherzandi, A., Cheon, J.H., Jarecki, S.: Multisignatures secure under the discrete logarithm assumption and a generalized forking lemma. In: Ning, P., Syverson, P.F., Jha, S. (eds.) CCS 2008, pp. 449–458. ACM (2008)

3. Bellare, M., Neven, G.: Multi-signatures in the plain public-key model and a general forking lemma. In: Juels, A., Wright, R.N., di Vimercati, S.D.C. (eds.) CCS 2006, pp. 390–399. ACM (2006)
4. Boldyreva, A.: Threshold signatures, multisignatures and blind signatures based on the gap-Diffie-Hellman-group signature scheme. In: Desmedt, Y.G. (ed.) PKC 2003. LNCS, vol. 2567, pp. 31–46. Springer, Heidelberg (2003). https://doi.org/10.1007/3-540-36288-6_3
5. Boneh, D., Drijvers, M., Neven, G.: Compact multi-signatures for smaller blockchains. In: Peyrin, T., Galbraith, S. (eds.) ASIACRYPT 2018. LNCS, vol. 11273, pp. 435–464. Springer, Cham (2018). https://doi.org/10.1007/978-3-030-03329-3_15
6. Bresson, E., Stern, J., Szydlo, M.: Threshold ring signatures and applications to ad-hoc groups. In: Yung, M. (ed.) CRYPTO 2002. LNCS, vol. 2442, pp. 465–480. Springer, Heidelberg (2002). https://doi.org/10.1007/3-540-45708-9_30
7. Castagnos, G., Catalano, D., Laguillaumie, F., Savasta, F., Tucker, I.: Two-party ECDSA from hash proof systems and efficient instantiations. In: Boldyreva, A., Micciancio, D. (eds.) CRYPTO 2019. LNCS, vol. 11694, pp. 191–221. Springer, Cham (2019). https://doi.org/10.1007/978-3-030-26954-8_7
8. Castagnos, G., Laguillaumie, F.: On the security of cryptosystems with quadratic decryption: the nicest cryptanalysis. In: Joux, A. (ed.) EUROCRYPT 2009. LNCS, vol. 5479, pp. 260–277. Springer, Heidelberg (2009). https://doi.org/10.1007/978-3-642-01001-9_15
9. Castagnos, G., Laguillaumie, F.: Linearly homomorphic encryption from DDH. In: Nyberg, K. (ed.) CT-RSA 2015. LNCS, vol. 9048, pp. 487–505. Springer, Cham (2015). https://doi.org/10.1007/978-3-319-16715-2_26
10. Chatzigiannis, P., Chalkias, K.: Proof of assets in the diem blockchain. In: Zhou, J., et al. (eds.) ACNS 2021. LNCS, vol. 12809, pp. 27–41. Springer, Cham (2021). https://doi.org/10.1007/978-3-030-81645-2_3
11. Desmedt, Y., Frankel, Y.: Threshold cryptosystems. In: Brassard, G. (ed.) CRYPTO 1989. LNCS, vol. 435, pp. 307–315. Springer, New York (1990). https://doi.org/10.1007/0-387-34805-0_28
12. Dobson, S., Galbraith, S.D.: Trustless groups of unknown order with hyperelliptic curves. IACR Cryptology ePrint Archive, p. 196 (2020). https://eprint.iacr.org/2020/196
13. Drijvers, M., et al.: On the security of two-round multi-signatures. In: 2019 IEEE Symposium on Security and Privacy, SP 2019, San Francisco, CA, USA, 19–23 May 2019, pp. 1084–1101. IEEE (2019). https://doi.org/10.1109/SP.2019.00050
14. Gennaro, R., Goldfeder, S.: Fast multiparty threshold ECDSA with fast trustless setup. In: Lie, D., Mannan, M., Backes, M., Wang, X. (eds.) CCS 2018, pp. 1179–1194. ACM (2018)
15. Gennaro, R., Goldfeder, S.: One round threshold ECDSA with identifiable abort. Cryptology ePrint Archive, Report 2020/540 (2020). https://eprint.iacr.org/2020/540
16. Itakura, K., Nakamura, K.: A public-key cryptosystem suitable for digital multisignatures. NEC Res. Dev. **71**, 1–8 (1983)
17. Khali, H., Farah, A.: DSA and ECDSA-based multi-signature schemes. Int. J. Comput. Sci. Netw. Secur. **7**(7), 11–19 (2007)
18. Lu, S., Ostrovsky, R., Sahai, A., Shacham, H., Waters, B.: Sequential aggregate signatures and multisignatures without random oracles. In: Vaudenay, S. (ed.) EUROCRYPT 2006. LNCS, vol. 4004, pp. 465–485. Springer, Heidelberg (2006). https://doi.org/10.1007/11761679_28

19. Maxwell, G., Poelstra, A., Seurin, Y., Wuille, P.: Simple Schnorr multi-signatures with applications to Bitcoin. Des. Codes Cryptogr. **87**(9), 2139–2164 (2019). https://doi.org/10.1007/s10623-019-00608-x
20. Micali, S., Ohta, K., Reyzin, L.: Accountable-subgroup multisignatures: extended abstract. In: Reiter, M.K., Samarati, P. (eds.) CCS 2001, pp. 245–254. ACM (2001)
21. Nick, J., Ruffing, T., Seurin, Y.: MuSig2: simple two-round Schnorr multi-signatures. In: Malkin, T., Peikert, C. (eds.) CRYPTO 2021. LNCS, vol. 12825, pp. 189–221. Springer, Cham (2021). https://doi.org/10.1007/978-3-030-84242-0_8
22. Yuen, T.H., Cui, H., Xie, X.: Compact zero-knowledge proofs for threshold ECDSA with trustless setup. In: Garay, J.A. (ed.) PKC 2021. LNCS, vol. 12710, pp. 481–511. Springer, Cham (2021). https://doi.org/10.1007/978-3-030-75245-3_18

Post-quantum Cryptography

Fiat-Shamir Signatures Based on Module-NTRU

Shi Bai[✉], Austin Beard[✉], Floyd Johnson[✉], Sulani K. B. Vidhanalage[✉], and Tran Ngo[✉]

Department of Mathematical Sciences, Florida Atlantic University, Boca Raton, USA
{sbai,abeard2019,johnsonf2017,kthakshila2017,ngot2018}@fau.edu

Abstract. Module-NTRU lattices, as a generalization of versatile NTRU lattices, were introduced by Cheon, Kim, Kim and Son (IACR ePrint 2019/1468), and Chuengsatiansup, Prest, Stehlé, Wallet and Xagawa (ASI-ACCS '20). The Module-NTRU lattices possess the benefit of being more flexible on the underlying ring dimension. They also show how to efficiently construct trapdoors based on Module-NTRU lattices and apply them to trapdoor-based signatures and identity-based encryption. In this paper, we construct Fiat-Shamir signatures based on variant Module-NTRU lattices. Further generalizing Module-NTRU, we introduce the inhomogeneous Module-NTRU problem. Under the assumption that a variation of the search and decisional problems associated with Module-NTRU and inhomogeneous Module-NTRU are hard, we construct two signature schemes. The first scheme is obtained from a lossy identification scheme via the Fiat-Shamir transform that admits tight security in the quantum random oracle model (QROM), following the framework of Kiltz, Lyubashevsky and Schaffner (EUROCRYPT '18). The second scheme is a BLISS-like (Ducas et al., CRYPTO '13) signature scheme based on the search Module-NTRU problem using the bimodal Gaussian for the rejection sampling. At last, we analyze known attacks and propose concrete parameters for the lossy signature scheme. In particular, the signature size is about 4400 bytes, which appears to be the smallest provably secure signature scheme in the QROM achieving 128-bit security.

Keywords: Lattice-based signature · Module-NTRU Lattice · Fiat-Shamir

1 Introduction

Lattices have attracted considerable research interest as they can be used to construct efficient cryptographic schemes which are believed to be quantum-resistant. As evidence, many promising candidates submitted to the NIST post-quantum standardization process are based on lattices. Fundamental computational problems in lattice-based cryptography include the Short Integer Solution problem (SIS) [2,35], the Learning With Errors problem (LWE) [11,32,40,41] and the NTRU problem [22,24].

S. Bai—This work was supported in part by NIST award 60NANB18D216 and by the National Science Foundation under Grant No. 2044855 and 2122229.

K. Nguyen et al. (Eds.): ACISP 2022, LNCS 13494, pp. 289–308, 2022.
https://doi.org/10.1007/978-3-031-22301-3_15

Ajtai's seminal work [2] established the worst-to-average connection for the lattice-based primitives based on the SIS problem. It serves as a security foundation for many cryptographic primitives such as hash functions and signatures [2,20,29]. The LWE problem, introduced by Regev [40,41], is extensively used as a security foundation for encryption, signatures and many others [15,20,29,41]. For efficiency, many practical lattice-based cryptosystems are based on assumptions on structured lattices such as the Ring-LWE [32,44], Ring-SIS[31,33,37] and the NTRU problems [23,25]. Introduced by Hoffstein, Pipher and Silverman [23,25], the NTRU assumption is stated informally as follows: given a polynomial h in $R_q := \mathbb{Z}_q[x]/(\phi(x))$, for a cyclotomic polynomial $\phi(x)$ and a positive integer q, where h is the result of dividing one small element by another, find two polynomials $f, g \in R_q$ with small magnitudes such that $h \equiv g/f \pmod{q}$. Following the pioneer work [23,25], the NTRU assumption has been used extensively in various cryptographic constructions such as encryption, signature and many others [15,16,22]. Little is known on the complexity reduction aspects of the NTRU problem (see also [36,38] for progress on this), yet the NTRU assumption with standard parameters remains essentially unbroken after decades of cryptanalysis.

1.1 Previous Work

As an important application, SIS/LWE/NTRU problems have been used extensively to obtain post-quantum digital signatures such as [10,15,18,20,29]. There are two main paradigms for constructing practical lattice-based signature schemes in the literature. The first is to use trapdoor sampling algorithms and the hash-and-sign framework, following the work of Gentry, Peikert, and Vaikuntanathan in [20] (GPV). The second framework, proposed by Lyubashevsky [28,29], utilizes the Fiat-Shamir [17] with aborts for transforming identification schemes into signature schemes using variants of SIS/LWE assumptions. We describe related work for both directions.

Computing a short preimage solution for the SIS and ISIS problems has been proven to be as hard as solving certain lattice problems in the worst case [2]. However, with a trapdoor for the matrix $\mathbf{A}$ one can efficiently derive short solutions. In the pioneer work of GPV [20], they show how to efficiently construct a trapdoor for the ISIS problem; more specifically, they give a provable way to sample short solutions without leaking information about the trapdoor. This leads to a natural way for constructing signatures using the hash-then-sign paradigm in the random oracle model (ROM). More efficient trapdoor constructions based on the SIS and LWE problem have been further proposed in [6,34]. These lattice trapdoors require that the trapdoor dimension to be about $m \approx \Theta(n \log q)$ for achieving the optimal trapdoor quality. In work [16], the authors instantiate the GPV framework using the NTRU lattices, which only requires $m = 2n$. It thus leads to a more efficient Identity-Based Encryption (IBE) (and signature scheme). In practice, a power-of-two is usually used for the underlying ring dimension in NTRU, which leads to inflexibility on the parameter selection for desired security level. To overcome such inflexibility, the Module-NTRU (MNTRU) problem was proposed in [13,14] as a generalization of the NTRU problem. The MNTRU takes the equation $\mathbf{F} \cdot \mathbf{h} = \mathbf{g}$, where $\mathbf{h}, \mathbf{g}$ are vectors of polynomials in R_q^{d-1} and $\mathbf{F}$ is an invertible matrix of dimension $d-1$ with elements in R_q. The elements in $\mathbf{F}, \mathbf{g}$ are small for the MNTRU problem to be well-defined. The work [13,14] constructed trapdoors and proposed instantiations of the hash-then-sign paradigm using the MNTRU assumption. Concrete instantiations of the hash-then-sign signatures include the NIST PQC submissions Falcon [39], pqNTRUSign [45], etc.

The signatures discussed above use the trapdoor functions with the hash-and-sign paradigm. A second paradigm to construct lattice-based signatures is to use the Fiat-Shamir transform [17]. In [28,29], Lyubashevsky utilizes Fiat-Shamir for transforming identification schemes into provably secure signature schemes using variants of SIS/LWE assumptions. In particular, the rejection sampling in Fiat-Shamir is proposed to ensure the distribution of the signatures is independent from the private key and hence preventing the leakage of private keys. An improvement, the so-called BLISS scheme [15], is obtained by using the bimodal Gaussian distribution in the rejection sampling. This leads to a much smaller rejection area for signatures. For practical instantiation, BLISS [15] also devised an efficient signature scheme using the NTRU assumption. Follow-up work such as [5,7,15,21] uses a compression technique to further reduce the signatures size: the common idea is to throw away some bits of the vector to be hashed. The security proofs in these works remain non-tight due to the use of the Forking Lemma [8] with the reprogramming of random oracles. Furthermore, their security is usually studied in the random oracle model.

To construct signature schemes with tight security, Abdalla, Fouque, Lyubashevsky and Tibouchi [1] proposed the lossy identification scheme, and proved that the signatures obtained from Fiat-Shamir admit a tight security in the ROM model. A similar approach has been used in the TESLA signature scheme [4,5]. The general idea is to start with a lossy identification scheme which adopts two security properties, e.g. key indistinguishability and lossiness: it admits a lossy key generation algorithm that produces a lossy public key which is computationally indistinguishable to the genuine public keys, yet it is statistically impossible to win the impersonation game when the public key is lossy. The signature derived from such an identification scheme [1] was known to be secure only in the random oracle model, which does not automatically imply security in the quantum random oracle model (QROM). Kiltz, Lyubashevsky and Schaffner [26] presented a generic Fiat-Shamir framework from lossy identification schemes [1] to obtain tight secure signatures in the QROM. By adaptively re-programming of the random oracle, the same tight security result in the QROM has been obtained for the TESLA signature scheme [4,5]. A concrete instantiation of [26] is to adapt and to modify the Dilithium signature scheme [30], which has tight secure reductions from Module-SIS (MSIS) and Module-LWE (MLWE). A concrete instantiation of the techniques in [4,5] is given in the qTESLA signature [10], whose existential unforgeability under chosen message attack (EUF-CMA) security is reduced from the underlying decisional Ring-LWE problem.

To our knowledge, the minimum signature size that achieves near 128-bit security in the QROM model is from [26] with a pair of parameter sets given. The first set has a signature size of 5690 bytes and public key size 7712 bytes whose public key prevents a BKZ reduction of block size up to 480. The second set admits a larger key security (BKZ block size of 600) has signature size 7098 bytes and public key size 9632 bytes.

1.2 Contributions

In this work we present two Fiat-Shamir signature schemes based on some variant Module-NTRU problems. The first scheme follows the framework of [26], starting from an identification scheme and applying the Fiat-Shamir transform. The second scheme is analogous to the BLISS [15] scheme, but built on the variant Module-NTRU problem, with a fixed q being part of the public key. Thus, they may be viewed as variants of the signatures from [26] and BLISS [15], instantiated with the (inhomogeneous) Module-NTRU assumptions.

We first generalize the Module-NTRU problem proposed in [13,14] to the inhomogeneous MNTRU (iMNTRU) problem and formalize the hardness assumptions used. Briefly, the iMNTRU consists of the equation $\mathbf{F} \cdot \mathbf{h} + \mathbf{g} = \mathbf{t}$, where $\mathbf{t}$ comes from a certain distribution. In our signature, essentially the $\mathbf{F}$ and $\mathbf{g}$ serve as small secrets, while the $\mathbf{h}$ and $\mathbf{t}$ are public keys. The first signature scheme follows the lossy key identification paradigms of [26] using a uniform distribution for nonce generation. We prove the identification scheme achieves completeness of normal keys, simulatability of transcripts, lossy keys, sufficient entropy and computational unique response properties, thus possessing a tight security in the quantum random oracle model to the inhomogeneous Module-NTRU problem. Our second construction is a signature scheme based on the variant MNTRU assumption with a fixed q being part of the public key, and with the bimodal Gaussian distribution. The construction follows a similar framework as the BLISS signature [15], but uses the variant MNTRU assumption, which admits extra flexibility in the choice of parameters for the underlying ring dimension. With these proposed schemes, we analyze known attacks and their efficacy.

We discuss several related works. In [19], Genise et al. described inhomogeneous variants of NTRU problem named MiNTRU. In matrix form, the problem is defined as $\mathbf{A} := \mathbf{S}^{-1}(\mathbf{G} - \mathbf{E}) \pmod{q}$ where $\mathbf{G}$ is a gadget matrix of the form $\mathbf{G} = (\mathbf{0} \mid \mathbf{I} \mid 2\mathbf{I} \mid \cdots \mid 2^{\log q - 1}\mathbf{I})$. The secret matrices $\mathbf{S}$ and $\mathbf{E}$ are sampled from distributions of small magnitudes and the search MiNTRU problem asks an adversary to recover $\mathbf{S}$ and $\mathbf{E}$ from $\mathbf{A}$. In this paper, we introduce a somewhat different assumption by sampling uniformly a vector of polynomials $\mathbf{t} \in R_q^{d-1}$, an invertible matrix of small polynomials $\mathbf{F} \in R_q^{(d-1) \times (d-1)}$ and a vector of small polynomials $\mathbf{g} \in R_q^{d-1}$ so that $\mathbf{h} = \mathbf{F}^{-1}(\mathbf{t} - \mathbf{g})$. In our second BLISS-like signature scheme, we also consider the case where $\mathbf{t}$ is pre-fixed. A work from Chen, Genise and Mukherjee [12] introduced the *approximated* ISIS trapdoor and used it to construct signatures using the hash-and-sign framework, which resulted in reduced sizes on the trapdoor and signature from [34]. For certain distributions, the approximate ISIS problem is shown to be as hard as the standard ISIS problem. The approximate ISIS problem of a given matrix $\mathbf{A} \in \mathbb{Z}_q^{n \times m}$ and a vector $\mathbf{y} \in \mathbb{Z}_q^n$ asks to find a short vector $\mathbf{x}$ from $\mathbb{Z}_q^m$ so that $\mathbf{A}\mathbf{x} = \mathbf{y} + \mathbf{z}$ where $\mathbf{z}$ is a small shift. Note the public matrix $\mathbf{A}$ is drawn uniformly, while in our iMNTRU the public vector $\mathbf{h}$ is computed as $\mathbf{h} = \mathbf{F}^{-1}(\mathbf{t} - \mathbf{g})$. Thus, when $\mathbf{F}$ and $\mathbf{g}$ consist of sufficiently small polynomials, the distribution $(\mathbf{h}, \mathbf{t})$ cannot be uniform, yet depending on the distribution of $\mathbf{t}$, the marginal distribution of $\mathbf{h}$ might be uniform.

Existing signature schemes built on the Fiat-Shamir paradigms such as Dilithium [30] and qTESLA [10] are quite efficient and practical. Our scheme further optimizes the scheme parameters such as the signature size. In particular, we achieve a 128-bit security with a signature size of 4400 bytes and a public key size of 10272 bytes for BKZ block size 490. This appears to be smallest provably secure signature scheme in the QROM achieving 128-bit security. We also have a signature size of 9264 bytes and a public key size of 18464 bytes for BKZ block size 669. In addition to parameter optimization, we think it is also beneficial to investigate a more diverse selection of the underlying hardness assumption. One notes that the schemes [30] and qTESLA [10] are both built on the Module-LWE assumptions.

Finally, compared to the BLISS signature [15], the use of the Module-NTRU enjoys the extra flexibility in the choice of parameters for the underlying ring dimension, since many applications require the NTRU lattice to be defined on the power-of-two cyclotomic rings. Thus, sometimes when a higher security level is needed, the dimension of the NTRU lattice needs to be doubled. Recent progress on the complexity aspects of the NTRU problem [38] may shed light on the hardness of the inhomogeneous Module-NTRU problem used in this work.

2   Preliminaries

We present the notation and definitions used to construct our signatures. Let q be an integer, which is usually a prime in this paper. Let $\mathbb{Z}_q$ be the set of all integers modulo q in the range $(-\frac{q}{2}, \frac{q}{2}]$ when q is even and $[-\lfloor \frac{q}{2} \rfloor, \lfloor \frac{q}{2} \rfloor]$ when q is odd. We will refer to it as the *balanced representation mod q*. We denote R and R_q as the rings $\mathbb{Z}[x]/(x^n + 1)$ and $\mathbb{Z}_q[x]/(x^n + 1)$, respectively. The integer n is usually a power of 2, where $q \equiv 1 \pmod{2n}$. In this case, the polynomial $X^n + 1$ splits completely in $\mathbb{Z}_q$. Throughout, regular font letters such as v denote ring elements in R, R_q and $\mathbb{Z}, \mathbb{Z}_q$. We use bold lower-case letters such as $\mathbf{v}$ to represent vectors of elements from their respective fields. For a vector $\mathbf{v}$, we denote by $\mathbf{v}^t$ its transpose, we also denote $\mathbf{0}$ to be the zero vector. Bold upper case letters denote matrices. A matrix $\mathbf{B} = (\mathbf{b}_1, \cdots, \mathbf{b}_n)$ is also presented in a column-wise way. Abusing notation, we sometimes also use lower-case letters to identify the coefficients of ring elements in R and R_q.

For a polynomial $f = \sum_{i=0}^{n-1} a_i x^i \in R_q$, we identify its *coefficient embedding* as its vector of coefficients $f := (a_0, \ldots, a_{n-1})^T$. For a vector of polynomials $\mathbf{f} = (f_1, \ldots, f_n) \in R_q^n$, we may use $v_{\mathbf{f}}$ as a coefficient vector $(f_1, \ldots, f_n)^T$. A polynomial f in R_q can be associated with an acyclic matrix M_f. Multiplying $f(x)$ by $g(x) = \sum_{i=0}^{n-1} g_i x^i \in R_q$ identifies with the product of $M_f \cdot \mathbf{g}$. For a vector $\mathbf{x}$, we use $\|\mathbf{x}\|$ to denote its ℓ_2-norm and $\|\mathbf{x}\|_\infty = \max_i(|\mathbf{x}_i|)$ to denote its ℓ_∞-norm. The ℓ_2-norm and ℓ_∞-norm of polynomial f are defined as the corresponding norms on the corresponding coefficient vector. Given a vector $\mathbf{f}$ consisting of polynomials f_i, the norm notation extends naturally, i.e., $\|\mathbf{f}\|_\infty = \max_i(\|f_i\|_\infty)$. The inner product of two vectors $\mathbf{x}$ and $\mathbf{y}$ is denoted by $\langle \mathbf{x}, \mathbf{y} \rangle$. For convenience, we define some notations for rounding.

For an integer $c \in \mathbb{Z}$, we denote $[c]_r$ to be the unique integer in the range $(-2^{r-1}, 2^{r-1}]$ such that $[c]_r \equiv c \pmod{2^r}$. We denote $c = \lfloor c \rceil_r \cdot 2^r + [c]_r$, where $\lfloor c \rceil_r$ extracts the higher bits of c. In this paper, the inputs c will be in balanced representation mod q. For a polynomial $f = \sum_{i=0}^{n-1} a_i x^i$ we extend $[.]_r$ and $\lfloor . \rceil_r$ to f on its coefficients coordinate-wise. We define $\mathcal{B}_{n,\kappa}$ to be the set of ternary (or binary) vectors of length n with Hamming weight κ. When the length n is clear in the context, we may write $\mathcal{B}_\kappa$ for short.

We will use the rejection sampling lemma from [29] to ensure the output signature does not leak information about the secret key. We review the definition of various distributions and rejection sampling lemma, and the background on lattices (see full version of this work).

2.1   (Inhomogeneous) Module-NTRU

As a generalization of NTRU, the Module-NTRU (MNTRU) problem was introduced in [13,14], which enables the dimension and parameter flexibility. It was used to construct trapdoors for lattice signatures and identity-based encryption (IBE). Intuitively, given a vector $\mathbf{h}$ such that the inner product of $(1, \mathbf{h})$ and some "small" secret vector $\mathbf{f}$ is zero, the Module-NTRU problem asks to recover the secret $\mathbf{f}$ or close. In this paper, we will use a natural variant of the Module-NTRU, which we denote as the *inhomogeneous* Module-NTRU (iMNTRU) problem. We formalize the problem as follows.

Definition 1 (iMNTRU$_{q,n,d,B}$ instance). *Let $n, d \geq 2$ be integers, and q be a prime. Let B be a positive real number. Denote $R_q = \mathbb{Z}_q[x]/(x^n + 1)$. An iMNTRU$_{q,n,d,B}$ instance consists of a vector $\mathbf{h} \in R_q^{d-1}$ and $\mathbf{t} \in R_q^{d-1}$ such that there exists an invertible matrix $\mathbf{F} \in R_q^{(d-1)\times(d-1)}$ and a vector $\mathbf{g} \in R_q^{d-1}$ with $\mathbf{F} \cdot \mathbf{h} + \mathbf{g} = \mathbf{t} \pmod{q}$ and $\|\mathbf{F}\|, \|\mathbf{g}\| \leq B$. The $(\mathbf{F}, \mathbf{g})$ is called a trapdoor of the MNTRU$_{q,n,d,B}$ instance $\mathbf{h}$. An MNTRU$_{q,n,d,B}$ instance corresponds to an iMNTRU$_{q,n,d,B}$ instance for the case when $\mathbf{t} = \mathbf{0}$.*

Definition 2 (iMNTRU$_{q,n,d,D_1,D_2,T}$ distribution). *Let n, d be positive integers, and q be a prime. Let D_1, D_2, T be distributions defined over $R_q^{(d-1)\times(d-1)}$, R_q^{d-1} and R_q^{d-1} respectively. An iMNTRU$_{q,n,d,D_1,D_2,T}$ sampler is a polynomial-time algorithm that samples matrix $\mathbf{F}$ from D_1, vector $\mathbf{g}$ from D_2, vector $\mathbf{t}$ from T and then computes $\mathbf{h}$ in $\mathbf{F} \cdot \mathbf{h} + \mathbf{g} = \mathbf{t} \pmod{q}$. The sampler outputs a tuple $(\mathbf{h}, \mathbf{F}, \mathbf{g}, \mathbf{t})$. An iMNTRU$_{q,n,d,D_1,D_2,T}$ distribution is the induced marginal distribution of $(\mathbf{h}, \mathbf{t})$*

from an $\mathsf{iMNTRU}_{q,n,d,D_1,D_2,T}$ *sampler. For the distribution to be meaningful, we usually assume* D_1, D_2 *are B-bounded distributions and* D_1 *turns out to be an distribution defined on invertible elements* **F***. An* $\mathsf{MNTRU}_{q,n,d,D_1,D_2}$ *distribution corresponds to the case of an* $\mathsf{iMNTRU}_{q,n,d,D_1,D_2,T}$ *distribution when the support of* T *is always* 0.

In the schemes presented in this work, we will make several different choices for the distribution T, depending on the design and functionality. The decisional variant and search variant of the MNTRU are defined as follows:

Definition 3 (Decisional $\mathsf{iMNTRU}_{q,n,d,D_1,D_2,T,B}$**).** *Let* n, d *be positive integers, and* q *be a prime. Let* D_1, D_2 *be B-bounded distributions defined over* $R_q^{(d-1)\times(d-1)}$ *and* R_q^{d-1} *respectively, and* T *be a distribution over* R_q^{d-1}. *Let* $\mathcal{N}$ *be an* $\mathsf{iMNTRU}_{q,n,d,D_1,D_2,T}$ *distribution. The decisional* $\mathsf{iMNTRU}_{q,n,d,D_1,D_2,T,B}$ *problem asks to distinguish between samples from* $\mathcal{N}$ *and from* $U(R_q^{d-1}) \times T$. *The decisional* $\mathsf{MNTRU}_{q,n,d,D_1,D_2,B}$ *is defined similarly when the support of* T *is always* 0.

Definition 4 (Search $\mathsf{iMNTRU}_{q,n,d,D_1,D_2,T,B}$**).** *Let* n, d *be positive integers, and* q *be a prime. Let* D_1, D_2 *be B-bounded distributions defined over* $R_q^{(d-1)\times(d-1)}$ *and* R_q^{d-1} *respectively, and* T *be a distribution over* R_q^{d-1}. *Let* $\mathcal{N}$ *denote the* $\mathsf{iMNTRU}_{q,n,d,D_1,D_2,T,B}$ *distribution. Given samples* $(\mathbf{h}, \mathbf{t})$ *from* $\mathcal{N}$, *the search* $\mathsf{iMNTRU}_{q,n,d,D_1,D_2,T,B}$ *problem is to recover an invertible* **F** *and* **g** *such that* $\mathbf{F} \cdot \mathbf{h} + \mathbf{g} = \mathbf{t} \pmod{q}$ *and* $\|\mathbf{F}\|, \|\mathbf{g}\| \leq B$. *The search* $\mathsf{MNTRU}_{q,n,d,D_1,D_2,B}$ *is defined similarly when the support of* T *is always* 0. *Given an* $\mathsf{iMNTRU}_{q,n,d,B}$ *instance* $(\mathbf{h}, \mathbf{t})$, *the worst-case search* $\mathsf{iMNTRU}_{q,n,d,B}$ *problem is to recover an invertible* **F** *and* **g** *such that* $\mathbf{F}\cdot\mathbf{h}+\mathbf{g} = \mathbf{t} \pmod{q}$ *and* $\|\mathbf{F}\|, \|\mathbf{g}\| \leq B$. *The worst-case search* $\mathsf{MNTRU}_{q,n,d,B}$ *problem is defined when* **t** *is* 0. *Clearly, the worst-case search* $\mathsf{MNTRU}_{q,n,d,B}$ *problem reduces to worst-case search* $\mathsf{iMNTRU}_{q,n,d,B}$ *problem.*

We are not aware of any reduction between MNTRU and the average cases of inhomogeneous MNTRU assumptions where the **t** is sampled from a distribution. However, one can reduce from MNTRU to inhomogeneous MNTRU by assuming a worst-case oracle on the inhomogeneous MNTRU problem. We will make the assumption that the average-case inhomogeneous MNTRU assumption is as hard as the MNTRU assumption. Our signature scheme relies on an additional assumption that solving a single row of the iMNTRU assumption is as hard as the iMNTRU assumption. Namely, our signature schemes only use a single row **f** of **F** and hence the vectors **g**, **t** are just two polynomials, thus the equation becomes $\langle \mathbf{h}, \mathbf{f} \rangle + g = t \pmod{q}$. The variant search and decisional problems are defined correspondingly and we require that **f** is non-zero.

Our first signature scheme reduces from this variant search and decisional inhomogeneous Module-NTRU assumptions, which we assumed hard to invert and indistinguishable from uniform respectively. Our second signature scheme is based on the variant search Module-NTRU assumption, which is assumed hard to invert as in [13,14].

Remark 1. In the key generation presented in this work, one actually just starts with a single vector $\mathbf{f}$ and pick up an element $\mathbf{h}$ in the left kernel of $t - g$ w.r.t. $\mathbf{f}$. One can pick up $\mathbf{h}$ by choosing h_i for $i \leq d - 2$ first and then computing h_{d-1} in the end. We note here that the distributions of the public keys for our assumption and iMNTRU are not the same. We will make the assumption that this variant assumption is as hard as the iMNTRU assumption. This variant assumption turns out to be analogous to "low-density" inhomogeneous Ring-SIS problem [29]. We leave for future work to study its average-case hardness.

3   Signature Based on iMNTRU in the QROM

In this section, we present a lossy identification scheme based on the variant of inhomogeneous Module-NTRU assumption. Our construction follows the design and paradigm proposed in [1,4,26] via the Fiat-Shamir transformation and thus leads to a tightly-secure signature in the quantum random-oracle model. In this work, the random oracle H takes inputs from $R_q \times \mathcal{M}$, where $\mathcal{M}$ denotes the message space, and outputs a polynomial in R_q. We restrict the output polynomials to be ternary (or binary) and have κ non-zero coefficients, e.g. those can be identified as vectors from $\mathcal{B}_{n,\kappa}$. We refer to [15] for efficient instantiation of random oracles.

3.1   A Lossy Identification Scheme

As in [1,26], we start by constructing a lossy identification scheme ID, given in Fig. 1. The key generation algorithm starts by choosing parameters $d \in \mathbb{N}$ as the rank, n as the ring dimension and a prime q as the modulus. Similar to the key generation of [13,14], one can sample $(\mathbf{h}', \mathbf{F}, \mathbf{g}, \mathbf{t})$ from an iMNTRU$_{q,n,d,D_1,D_2,U(R_q)}$ distribution, where D_1 and D_2 are two distributions for sampling the secret keys. Here we sample each f in $\mathbf{F}$ from U_β^n and each g in $\mathbf{g}$ from U_β^n independently. Note that it is possible to sample them from other "small" distributions such as discrete Gaussian, but we use uniform distribution here. After we sample $\mathbf{g}, \mathbf{t}$ and an invertible $\mathbf{F}$, we compute $\mathbf{h}' = \{h_i\}_{i=1}^{d-1}$ in $\mathbf{F} \cdot \mathbf{h}' + \mathbf{g} = \mathbf{t} \pmod{q}$. Note that for cryptographically sized parameters the probability that a randomly selected matrix of polynomials $\mathbf{F}$ is invertible is close to one.

As previously mentioned, one can only use a single row $(f_1, \ldots, f_{d-1})$ from $\mathbf{F}$ and let g, t be corresponding polynomials in $\mathbf{g}, \mathbf{t}$, respectively. Abusing notation, we denote $f_d := g$ and $\mathbf{f} = (f_1, \ldots, f_{d-1}, f_d)$, which is the secret key for our identification scheme. We also denote $\mathbf{h} = (h_1, \ldots, h_{d-1}, 1)$ and set $(\mathbf{h}, t)$ as the public key. With this rewrite, we see that $\langle \mathbf{h}, \mathbf{f} \rangle = t$. We use balanced representation mod q in the following algorithm.

In the first step of the identification, the prover samples a vector of polynomials $\mathbf{y} := (y_1, \ldots, y_d)$, where each y_i is from the distribution U_γ^n, and computes the commitment $u := \left\lfloor \sum_{i=1}^{d-1} h_i y_i \pmod{q} \right\rceil_r$. The prover then sends u to the verifier. The verifier generates a random challenge c from the distribution $\mathcal{B}_\kappa$ (here we define it to be the set of ternary vectors of length n with weight κ) and sends c to the prover. The number of nonzero coefficients in c is κ, thus the infinity norm of $f_i \cdot c$ is bounded by $\beta \cdot \kappa$. The prover computes $z_i := y_i + c \cdot f_i$ and returns $\mathbf{z}$ if, for all $1 \le i \le d-1$, $\|z_i\|_\infty \le \gamma - \beta \cdot \kappa$, and $|[\sum_{i=1}^{d-1} h_i y_i - c \cdot f_d \pmod{q}]_r| < 2^{r-1} - \beta \cdot \kappa$ together with $\|w\|_\infty < \lfloor q/2 \rfloor - \beta \cdot \kappa$. Otherwise, it

---

Algorithm IGen(q, n, d, β)

1:   Sample $\mathbf{f} = \{f_i\}_{i=1}^d$ and t, where $f_i \hookleftarrow U_\beta^n$ and $t \hookleftarrow U_{R_q}$

2:   Compute $\mathbf{h} = (h_1, \ldots, h_{d-1}, 1)$ such that $\sum_{i=1}^d h_i f_i \equiv t \pmod{q}$

3:   **return** pk $:= (\mathbf{h}, t)$ and sk $:= \mathbf{f}$

Algorithm $P_1(sk)$:

4:   Sample $\mathbf{y} = \{y_i\}_{i=1}^{d-1}$ where $y_i \hookleftarrow U_\gamma^n$

5:   Compute $u = \left\lfloor \sum_{i=1}^{d-1} h_i y_i \pmod{q} \right\rceil_r$

6:   **return** u

Algorithm $P_2(sk, u, c)$:

7:   Compute $\mathbf{z} := (z_1, \ldots, z_{d-1})$ where $z_i = y_i + c \cdot f_i$

8:   Compute $w = \sum_{i=1}^{d-1} h_i y_i - c \cdot f_d \pmod{q}$

9:   **if** any $\|z_i\|_\infty > \gamma - \beta \cdot \kappa$

  or $\|[w]_r\|_\infty \ge 2^{r-1} - \beta \cdot \kappa$

  or $\|w\|_\infty \ge \lfloor q/2 \rfloor - \beta \cdot \kappa$ **then**

10:      **return** $\perp$

11: **return** $\mathbf{z}$

Algorithm $V(pk, u, c, \mathbf{z})$:

12: **if** $\forall 1 \le i \le d-1, \|z_i\|_\infty \le \gamma - \beta \cdot \kappa$ and $\left\lfloor \sum_{i=1}^{d-1} h_i z_i - t \cdot c \pmod{q} \right\rceil_r = u$ **then**

13:      **return** Accept

14: **return** Reject

Fig. 1. A lossy identification scheme based on variant of iMNTRU

returns $\bot$. Verifier accepts $(\mathbf{z}, u)$ if, for all i, we have $\|z_i\|_\infty \leq \gamma - \beta \cdot \kappa$ and $\left\lfloor \sum_{i=1}^{d-1} h_i z_i - t \cdot c \pmod{q} \right\rceil_r$ equals u. Otherwise, it rejects. To optimize slightly, it is possible to record $\sum_{i=1}^{d-1} h_i y_i$ as a state for the prover in Algorithm P_1 and re-use in Algorithm P_2.

In this section, we present the lossy identification scheme in Fig. 1. We show the scheme admits properties including na-HVZK, correctness, lossy, min-entropy and computational unique response (CUR). The proof follows a similar framework as in [26]. For Lemmas 1 to 5, we state them and sketch the proofs in the full version of this work.

We first show that the ID scheme is perfectly na-HVZK. Following the definition of na-HVZK, we set two algorithms $\mathsf{Sim}(.)$ and $\mathsf{Trans}(.)$, shown in Fig. 2. We will show that the distribution of outputs of $\mathsf{Sim}(.)$ and $\mathsf{Trans}(.)$ is identical. For convenience, we denote $B := \beta \cdot \kappa$.

Lemma 1. *The identification scheme of Fig. 1 is perfect* na-HVZK.

We now prove that the identification is correct, up to some rejection rate. We stress that such a bound is not rigorous, as we assumed a specific distribution on the rounded numbers, yet it is sufficient to use in practice. One can get a more accurate rejection rate from a simulation.

Lemma 2. *Under the variant decisional iMNTRU assumption, the identification scheme has correctness error*

$$\delta \approx 1 - \exp\left(-\beta\kappa n \left(\frac{d-1}{\gamma} + \frac{1}{2^{r-1}} + \frac{1}{q}\right)\right).$$

We now show that the identification scheme is lossy. We first define a lossy key generation algorithm $\mathsf{LossyIGen}(q, n, d, \beta)$, shown in Fig. 3, which samples h_i's and t from uniform. First, the public keys generated by $\mathsf{LossyIGen}$ and IGen are indistinguishable due to the variant decisional iMNTRU assumption. It remains to show the scheme admits $\varepsilon_{\mathsf{ls}}$-lossy soundness; that is, for any quantum adversary, the probability of impersonating the prover is bounded by $\varepsilon_{\mathsf{ls}}$.

Lemma 3. *The identification scheme admits* ϵ_{ls}-*lossy soundness for*

$$\epsilon_{\mathsf{ls}} \leq \frac{1}{|\mathcal{B}_\kappa|} + 2 \cdot |\mathcal{B}_\kappa|^2 \cdot \frac{(4(\gamma - B) + 1)^{n(d-1)} \cdot (2^{r+1} + 1)^n}{q^n}.$$

This bound essentially says q should be larger than γ^d asymptotically. This condition is natural, since otherwise, it is intuitive to see there exist many solutions $\mathbf{z}, c$ for $u = \left\lfloor \sum_{i=1}^{d-1} h_i z_i - t \cdot c \right\rceil_r$.

Algorithm Trans(sk)

1 : Sample $\mathbf{y} = \{y_i\}_{i=1}^{d-1}$ where $y_i \hookleftarrow U_\gamma^n$

2 : Compute $u = \left\lfloor \left[\sum_{i=1}^{d-1} h_i y_i \pmod{q} \right] \right\rceil_r$

3 : Sample $c \hookleftarrow \mathcal{B}_\kappa$

4 : Compute $\mathbf{z} = \{z_i\}_{i=1}^{d-1}$ where $z_i = y_i + c \cdot f_i$

5 : Compute $w = \sum_{i=1}^{d-1} h_i y_i - c \cdot f_d \pmod{q}$

6 : **if** any $\|z_i\|_\infty > \gamma - B$ **return** $\perp$

7 : **if** $\left\| [w]_r \right\|_\infty \geq 2^{r-1} - B$

   or $\|w\|_\infty \geq \lfloor q/2 \rfloor - B$ **return** $\perp$

8 : **return** $(\mathbf{z}, c)$

Algorithm Sim(pk)

9 : With probability $1 - \left(\dfrac{|U_{\gamma-B}|}{|U_\gamma|} \right)^{n(d-1)}$

   return $\perp$

10 : Sample $\mathbf{z} = \{z_i\}_{i=1}^{d-1}$ where $z_i \hookleftarrow U_{\gamma-B}^n$

11 : Sample $c \hookleftarrow \mathcal{B}_\kappa$

12 : Compute $w' = \sum_{i=1}^{d-1} h_i z_i - t \cdot c \pmod{q}$

13 : **if** $\left\| [w']_r \right\|_\infty \geq 2^{r-1} - B$

   or $\|w'\|_\infty \geq \lfloor q/2 \rfloor - B$ **return** $\perp$

14 : **return** $(\mathbf{z}, c)$

Fig. 2. Transcript algorithm and simulation algorithm

Algorithm LossyIGen(q, n, d, β)

1 : Sample $\mathbf{h} = (h_1, \ldots, h_{d-1}, 1)$ and t, where $h_i \hookleftarrow U_{R_q}$ and $t \hookleftarrow U_{R_q}$

2 : **return** pk $:= (\mathbf{h}, t)$

Fig. 3. Lossy key generation algorithm LossyIGen

We now prove that the u sent by the prover in Algorithm P_1 is very likely to be distinct across every run of the protocol. We first remark that the public key $\mathbf{h}' \hookleftarrow \mathsf{IGen}$ (i.e. recall that $\mathbf{h} = (\mathbf{h}', 1)$) has a marginal distribution which is uniform in R_q^{d-1}. This is because $\mathbf{h}'$ is computed in equation $\mathbf{F} \cdot \mathbf{h}' + \mathbf{g} = \mathbf{t}$ (mod q) where $\mathbf{t}$ is uniform and $\mathbf{F}$ is invertible. Note that the joint distribution $(\mathbf{h}', \mathbf{t})$ is not uniform for our choice of parameters, but in Algorithm P_1, only $\mathbf{h}'$ is used to produce the commitment.

Lemma 4.   *The identification scheme has $\alpha := n \cdot \log E$ bits of min-entropy, where*

$$E = \min \left\{ (2\gamma + 1)^{d-1}, \ \frac{q}{(4\gamma + 1)^{(d-1)}(2^{r+1} + 1)} \right\}.$$

In the end, we sketch that our scheme satisfies the computational unique response (CUR) property for the strong unforgeability of the signature scheme after the Fiat-Shamir transform.

Lemma 5.   *For any adversary on the identification scheme, the success probability of producing two valid transcripts $(u, c, \mathbf{z})$ and $(u, c, \mathbf{z}')$, such that $\mathbf{z} \neq \mathbf{z}'$, is bounded by $(4(\gamma - B) + 1)^{n(d-1)} \cdot (2^{r+1} + 1)^n \cdot q^{-n}$.*

In the end, we give the signature scheme constructed from the lossy identification scheme (see full version of this work). Theorem 3.1 of [26] concludes that the signature scheme admits a tight security in the QROM. The concrete parameters for the signature scheme will be given in Sect. 5.1.

4   A BLISS-Like Signature Based on MNTRU

In this section, we propose a signature scheme based on the variant MNTRU assumption with a fixed t and the bimodal Gaussian distribution. The construction follows a similar framework as the BLISS signature [15], but uses the variant MNTRU assumption, which admits the extra flexibility in the choice of parameters for the underlying ring dimension.

4.1   Signature Scheme

We give the signature scheme in Fig. 4 and describe the key generation, signing and verification procedure here. In Algorithm Gen, used for key generation, one chooses the following parameters: rank $d \in \mathbb{N}$, a prime modulus q, an integer n as the ring dimension, and a positive odd integer $\beta < q$. We sample $(\mathbf{h}', \mathbf{F}, \mathbf{g})$ from the $\mathsf{MNTRU}_{q,n,d,D_1,D_2}$ distribution, where D_1 is U_β^n and D_2 is $U_{\lfloor \beta/2 \rfloor}^n$ are distributions of secret keys $\mathbf{F}$ and $\mathbf{g}$, respectively. It is sufficient to take a single row $\{f_i\}_{i=1}^{d-1}$ from $\mathbf{F}$ and we denote $\mathbf{s} = (f_1, \ldots, f_{d-1}, f_d)$ where $f_d := 2g + 1$. Note the coefficients of f_d also lie uniformly in $[-\beta, \beta]$. We denote $\mathbf{h} = (h_1, \ldots, h_{d-1}, -1)$ and hence $\langle \mathbf{h}, \mathbf{s} \rangle = 0$ (mod q). In the scheme, we use the vector $\mathbf{a} = (2h_1, \cdots, 2h_{d-1}, q - 2) \in R_{2q}^d$ as the public key and vector $\mathbf{s} \in R_{2q}^d$ as the private key. It can be checked that we have $\langle \mathbf{a}, \mathbf{s} \rangle \equiv q$ (mod $2q$), since

$$\langle \mathbf{a}, \mathbf{s} \rangle \equiv \sum_{i=1}^{d-1} 2h_i f_i - 2f_d \equiv 0 \pmod q,$$

$$\langle \mathbf{a}, \mathbf{s} \rangle \equiv q \cdot (2g+1) \equiv 1 \pmod 2.$$

To sign a message μ, the signer chooses a vector $\mathbf{y} := (y_1, \ldots, y_d)$, where each y_i is sampled from the discrete Gaussian $D_{\mathbb{Z},\sigma}^n$. The signer then computes $c := H(\langle \mathbf{a}, \mathbf{y} \rangle \pmod{2q}, \mu)$ and $\mathbf{z} := \mathbf{y} + (-1)^b c \cdot \mathbf{s}$ for a uniform random bit $b \in \{0, 1\}$. With rejection sampling, the signature $(c, \mathbf{z})$ is outputted with probability $1/M \exp(-\|c \cdot \mathbf{s}\|^2 / (2\sigma^2)) \cosh(\langle \mathbf{z}, c \cdot \mathbf{s} \rangle / \sigma^2)$, where the constant M is the repetition rate for each signing. Upon receiving the signature $(c, \mathbf{z})$, the verification will succeed if $\|\mathbf{z}\|_\infty < q/4$, $\|\mathbf{z}\| \leq \eta \sigma \sqrt{nd}$, and $H(\langle \mathbf{a}, \mathbf{z} \rangle + q \cdot c \pmod{2q}, \mu) = c$. For convenience, we did not use compression in the presented scheme, but mention it should be similar to [15] to compress the signature.

Rejection Sampling. The rejection sampling follows the same as [15]. Consider $\mathbf{z} = (-1)^b \cdot \mathbf{s} \cdot c + \mathbf{y}$. Abusing notation, we denote $\mathbf{s} \cdot c$ as the concatenated coefficient vector as well as a vector of polynomials. The distribution of $\mathbf{z}$ is the bimodal discrete Gaussian distribution $\frac{1}{2} D_{\mathbb{Z}^{nd}, \sigma, \mathbf{s} \cdot c} + \frac{1}{2} D_{\mathbb{Z}^{nd}, \sigma, -\mathbf{s} \cdot c}$. To prevent signatures from leaking the private key, we use rejection sampling that finds a positive integer M such that for all supports except a negligible fraction:

$$D_{\mathbb{Z}^{nd}, \sigma} \leq M \cdot \left(\frac{1}{2} D_{\mathbb{Z}^{nd}, \sigma, \mathbf{s} \cdot c} + \frac{1}{2} D_{\mathbb{Z}^{nd}, \sigma, -\mathbf{s} \cdot c} \right)$$

It is thus sufficient to choose $M \geq \exp(\|\mathbf{s} \cdot c\|^2 / (2\sigma^2))$. Now we bound $\|\mathbf{s} \cdot c\|$. The random oracle H outputs a binary vector c with length n and weight κ (here we define $\mathcal{B}_\kappa$ to be the set of ternary vectors of length n with weight κ), and $\|\mathbf{s}\|_\infty$ is bounded by β, so $\|\mathbf{s} \cdot c\| \leq (\kappa \cdot \beta) \sqrt{nd}$. Hence, the number of repetitions M is approximately $\exp(\kappa^2 \beta^2 nd / (2\sigma^2))$.

Correctness. Let $(\mathbf{z}, c)$ be a valid signature for message μ. The rejection sampling shows that $\mathbf{z}$ follows a discrete Gaussian $D_{\mathbb{Z}^{nd}, \sigma}$. By [29, Lemma 4.4], we have $\|\mathbf{z}\| \leq \eta \cdot \sigma \sqrt{nd}$, except with probability $\approx \eta^{nd} e^{nd/2(1-\eta^2)}$ for some small constant $\eta > 1$. In the security proof, we will also need $\|\mathbf{z}\|_\infty < q/4$. This is usually satisfied whenever $\|\mathbf{z}\| \leq \eta \sigma \sqrt{nd}$. Finally, check that $\langle \mathbf{a}, \mathbf{z} \rangle + q \cdot c = \langle \mathbf{a}, \mathbf{y} \rangle + (-1)^b \cdot c \cdot \langle \mathbf{a}, \mathbf{s} \rangle + q \cdot c \pmod{2q}$.

4.2 Security Proof

We sketch the proof that the signature in Fig. 4 is secure under existential forgery using the Forking Lemma of Bellare-Neven [8] which follows similarly to [15]. We reduce the security of the signature to the variant MNTRU problem.

We construct two games, Hybrid 1 and Hybrid 2, as in Fig. 5, and use them to simulate the genuine signature scheme. The distributions of outputs in Hybrid 1 and outputs in Hybrid 2 are the same due to rejection sampling. Thus, it is sufficient to show the genuine signature is statistically close to Hybrid 1.

Algorithm Gen(q, n, d, β)

1:     Sample $\mathbf{f} = \{f_i\}_{i=1}^{d-1}$ and $f_d := 2g + 1$ where $f_i \hookleftarrow U_\beta^n$ and $g \hookleftarrow U_{\lfloor \beta/2 \rfloor}^n$

2:     Compute $\mathbf{h} = (h_1, \ldots, h_{d-1}, -1)$ such that $\displaystyle\sum_{i=1}^{d-1} h_i f_i \equiv f_d \pmod{q}$

3:     Set $\mathbf{a} = (2h_1, \cdots, 2h_{d-1}, q-2) \in R_{2q}^d$ and $\mathbf{s} = (f_1, \cdots, f_d) \in R_{2q}^d$

4:     **return** $\mathsf{pk} := \mathbf{a}$ and $\mathsf{sk} := \mathbf{s}$

Algorithm Sign$(\mathsf{sk}, \mu, \sigma)$:

5:     Sample $\mathbf{y} := (y_1, \ldots, y_d)$ where $y_i \hookleftarrow D_\sigma^n$

6:     Compute $c = H(\langle \mathbf{a}, \mathbf{y} \rangle \pmod{2q}, \mu)$

7:     Sample a random bit $b \in \{0, 1\}$

8:     Compute $\mathbf{z} = (z_1, \ldots, z_d)$ where

       $z_i = y_i + (-1)^b \cdot c \cdot f_i$

9:     **return** $(\mathbf{z}, c)$ with probability

$$1 / \left(M \exp\left(-\frac{\|c \cdot \mathbf{s}\|^2}{2\sigma^2} \right) \cosh\left(\frac{\langle \mathbf{z}, c \cdot \mathbf{s} \rangle}{\sigma^2} \right) \right)$$

Algorithm Ver$(\mathsf{pk}, \mu, \mathbf{z}, c)$:

10:     **if** $\|\mathbf{z}\|_\infty < q/4$ **and** $\|\mathbf{z}\| < \eta\sigma\sqrt{nd}$ **and**

       $H(\langle \mathbf{a}, \mathbf{z} \rangle + qc \pmod{2q}, \mu) = c$ **then**

11:        **return** Accept

12:     **return** $\bot$

Fig. 4. A BLISS-like signature scheme based on MNTRU

Lemma 6. *Let $\mathcal{D}$ be an algorithm with the goal to distinguish the outputs of the genuine signing algorithm in Fig. 4 and Hybrid 1 in Fig. 5. Let $\mathcal{D}$ have access to two oracles: $\mathcal{O}_H$ and $\mathcal{O}_{\mathsf{Sign}}$. $\mathcal{O}_H$ is the hash oracle which, given an input x, outputs $H(x)$. $\mathcal{O}_{\mathsf{Sign}}$ is the oracle which, given an input, returns either the output of the signing algorithm or the output of Hybrid 1. If $\mathcal{D}$ makes at most q_H calls to $\mathcal{O}_H$ and q_S calls to $\mathcal{O}_{\mathsf{Sign}}$, then $Adv(\mathcal{D}) \leq q_S(q_H + q_S)2^{-n}$.*

We now prove the BLISS-like signature scheme in Fig. 4 admits security against existential forgery under adaptive chosen-message attacks. First, we observe that if there exists an adversary capable of forging Hybrid 2 with advantage δ in polynomial time, then by the previous lemma, the adversary is capable of forging the genuine signature of Fig. 4 with probability $\approx \delta$ in polynomial time. Thus, it is sufficient to reduce the variant MNTRU to the forging problem on Hybrid 2. We sketch it in the following theorem.

Theorem 1. *If there exists a polynomial-time algorithm $\mathcal{A}$ to forge the signature of Hybrid 2 with at most q_S signing queries to Hybrid 2 and q_H hash queries to the random oracle H, and it succeeds with probability δ, then there exists a polynomial-time algorithm that solves the variant $\mathsf{MNTRU}_{q,n,d,D_1,D_2,B}$ search problem with advantage $\approx \delta^2/(q_S + q_H)$, where distributions D_1 and D_2 sample each coordinate-wise polynomial from $D_{\mathbb{Z},\sigma}^n$ and $B := 2\eta\sigma\sqrt{nd}$.*

We sketch the proof of Lemma 6 and Theorem 1 in the full version of this work.

Hybrid 1: $\mathsf{Sign_1(sk, \mu, \sigma)}$

---

1 : Sample $\mathbf{y} := (y_1, \ldots, y_d)$ where $y_i \hookleftarrow D_\sigma^n$

2 : Sample $c \hookleftarrow \mathcal{B}_\kappa$

3 : Sample a random bit b

4 : Compute $\mathbf{z} = \mathbf{y} + (-1)^b \cdot c \cdot \mathbf{s}$

5 : **return** $(\mathbf{z}, c)$ with probability

$$1 / \left(M \exp \left(-\frac{\|c \cdot \mathbf{s}\|^2}{2\sigma^2} \right) \cosh \left(\frac{\langle \mathbf{z}, c \cdot \mathbf{s} \rangle}{\sigma^2} \right) \right)$$

Program $H(\langle \mathbf{a}, \mathbf{z} \rangle + q\,c \pmod{2q}, \mu) = c$

Hybrid 2: $\mathsf{Sign_2(\sigma)}$

---

1 : Sample $c \hookleftarrow \mathcal{B}_\kappa$

2 : Sample $\mathbf{z} = (z_1, \ldots, z_d)$ where $z_i \hookleftarrow D_\sigma^n$

3 : **return** $(\mathbf{z}, c)$ with probability $1/M$

Program $H(\langle \mathbf{a}, \mathbf{z} \rangle + q\,c \pmod{2q}, \mu) = c$

Fig. 5. Hybrid games of Fig. 4

5   Security Analysis and Parameters

In this section, we discuss known attacks for the MNTRU assumptions based on lattice reduction [42,43] for MNTRU lattices. We assume that the variant iMNTRU problem used in our signatures admits a similar security of the same dimension. Let $\mathcal{N}$ be an $\text{MNTRU}_{q,n,d,B}$ distribution, and a vector of polynomials $\mathbf{h} \in R_q^{d-1}$ be a sample from $\mathcal{N}$. The lattice associated to $\mathbf{h}$ is defined as

$$\Lambda_\mathbf{h} := \left\{ (x_1, \ldots, x_d) \in R_q^d : x_1 h_1 + \ldots + x_{d-1} h_{d-1} + x_d = 0 \pmod{q} \right\}.$$

It has a basis generated by the columns of

$$\mathbf{B} := \begin{bmatrix} I_n & 0_n & \cdots & 0_n & 0_n \\ 0_n & I_n & \cdots & 0_n & 0_n \\ \vdots & \vdots & \ddots & \vdots & \vdots \\ 0_n & 0_n & \cdots & I_n & 0_n \\ -M_{h_1} & -M_{h_2} & \cdots & -M_{h_{d-1}} & qI_n \end{bmatrix}$$

The lattice $\mathcal{L}(\mathbf{B})$ has rank $d \times n$ and determinant q^n. Let $(\mathbf{f}, g)$ from $R_q^{d-1} \times R_q$ be a solution of a search $\text{MNTRU}_{q,n,d,B}$ problem. One can verify that $(\mathbf{f}, g)$ is a short vector of $\Lambda_\mathbf{h}$ by the relation $\mathbf{B} \cdot \begin{bmatrix} v_\mathbf{f} \\ 0 \end{bmatrix} = \begin{bmatrix} v_\mathbf{f} \\ g \end{bmatrix}$. Thus if one can solve the SVP problem in $\Lambda_\mathbf{h}$, one can find a solution for the corresponding MNTRU problem.

We review the methodology for estimating the Core-SVP security in the full version of this work and use them to develop the concrete parameters in Table 1.

5.1   Concrete Instantiation

Table 1. Concrete parameters for signature in Sect. 3

	I	II	III	IV	V	VI
Ring dimension n	2048	1024	4096	2048	1283	2003
Module rank d	2	4	2	3	3	2
Ring modulus $\log_2(q)$	39.93	78.68	53.47	71.37	55.89	38.95
κ	32	37	28	32	35	32
r	21	22	34	33	18	20
γ	47668	80205	79918	91335	71583	48041
Acceptance rate	0.237	0.238	0.238	0.238	0.202	0.233
Block-size b	490	500	839	669	494	492
Public key pk (bytes)	10272	10144	27680	18464	9013	9797
Signature size z (bytes)	4400	6963	9262	9264	5824	4305

We propose the concrete parameters for our signature scheme in Sect. 3, with an 128-bit security level achieved by using Theorem 3.1 of [26]. The size of the public key is $n \cdot \lceil \log q \rceil + 256$ bits when using a 256-bit seed to generate the randomness. The signature size is $n \cdot (d-1) \cdot \lceil \log 2(\gamma - \beta \cdot \kappa) \rceil + \kappa(\log(n) + 1)$ bits. For all parameters, the rejection rate is chosen such that the repetition rate is approximately 4.2–4.3, which is comparable to the rejection rate of the 127 bit security scheme in [26] which has the smallest signature size for schemes provable in the QROM. The secret key is taken to be ternary in all cases, that is to say that $\beta = 1$ in all columns in the table. Columns I-IV are arranged with increasing signature size. These four columns are proven secure in Sect. 3 of this work. Columns I and II have BKZ block sizes close to the bound of 128 bit security while columns III and IV have block sizes suitable for higher security considerations. Note that columns II and IV have very large prime moduli, making them potentially weak to subfield attacks [3,27]. To heuristically combat this, one may change β to increase the space of valid secret keys at the cost of signature and public key sizes. Updated choices for β resilient to subfield attacks are left to future works. The optimal provably secure signature size in [26] is 5690 bytes and has public key size 7712 bytes. Comparing this to column I in the table we see that our scheme achieves comparable security and acceptance rates with a signature 77% the size of theirs at the expense of having public key 133% the size. This tradeoff makes their scheme have better overall channel weight if one message is to be signed, but if more than one is to be sent, then our parameter set in column I has a lower overall channel weight.

Columns V and VI use the NTRU-prime [9] like polynomials with irreducible polynomials $x^n - x - 1$ for prime n; thus the underlying rings do not correspond to power-of-two cyclotomics. The flexibility of choosing n leaves room for improvement on provable parameters, as one sees that NTRU-prime constructions give the smallest signature size (VI) and smallest public key size (V). We remark that the security of these two columns is not proven here since our proofs (e.g. Lemma 3) use the underlying ring structure. We leave them to future works.

For the BLISS-like signature scheme in Sect. 4, the public key and the secret key are vectors of polynomials in $U_{R_q}^{d-1}$ and U_β^{nd}, thus amounting to $n \cdot (d-1) \cdot \lceil \log q \rceil$ bits and $n \cdot d \cdot \lceil \log 2\beta \rceil$ bits, respectively. The signature is $(\mathbf{z}, c)$, where $\mathbf{z} \in R_q^d$ with $\|\mathbf{z}\|_\infty < q/4$, and c sampled from the set of binary vectors of length n with Hamming weight κ. Thereby, the size of signature is $(n \cdot d \cdot \lceil \log(q/4) \rceil + n)$ bits. The signature in Sect. 4 utilizes the same framework as the BLISS signature. We expect it yields more flexibility in selecting parameters due to the usage of module lattices. It remains an interesting question to understand whether the BLISS-like signature is secure in the QROM, and thus we leave the parameter selection for future work.

Acknowledgement. The authors thank the reviewers for their helpful discussions and remarks.

References

1. Abdalla, M., Fouque, P.-A., Lyubashevsky, V., Tibouchi, M.: Tightly-secure signatures from lossy identification schemes. In: Pointcheval, D., Johansson, T. (eds.) EUROCRYPT 2012. LNCS, vol. 7237, pp. 572–590. Springer, Heidelberg (2012). https://doi.org/10.1007/978-3-642-29011-4_34
2. Ajtai, M.: Generating hard instances of lattice problems (extended abstract). In: 28th ACM STOC, pp. 99–108. ACM Press (May 1996)
3. Albrecht, M., Bai, S., Ducas, L.: A subfield lattice attack on overstretched NTRU assumptions. In: Robshaw, M., Katz, J. (eds.) CRYPTO 2016. LNCS, vol. 9814, pp. 153–178. Springer, Heidelberg (2016). https://doi.org/10.1007/978-3-662-53018-4_6
4. Alkim, E., Barreto, P.S.L.M., Bindel, N., Krämer, J., Longa, P., Ricardini, J.E.: The lattice-based digital signature scheme qTESLA. In: Conti, M., Zhou, J., Casalicchio, E., Spognardi, A. (eds.) ACNS 2020. LNCS, vol. 12146, pp. 441–460. Springer, Cham (2020). https://doi.org/10.1007/978-3-030-57808-4_22
5. Alkim, E., et al.: Revisiting TESLA in the Quantum Random Oracle Model. In: Lange, T., Takagi, T. (eds.) PQCrypto 2017. LNCS, vol. 10346, pp. 143–162. Springer, Cham (2017). https://doi.org/10.1007/978-3-319-59879-6_9
6. Alwen, J., Peikert, C.: Generating shorter bases for hard random lattices. Theor. Comp. Syst. **48**(3), 535–553 (2011)
7. Bai, S., Galbraith, S.D.: An improved compression technique for signatures based on learning with errors. In: Benaloh, J. (ed.) CT-RSA 2014. LNCS, vol. 8366, pp. 28–47. Springer, Cham (2014). https://doi.org/10.1007/978-3-319-04852-9_2
8. Bellare, M., Neven, G.: Multi-signatures in the plain public-key model and a general forking lemma. In: Juels, A., Wright, R.N., De Capitani di Vimercati, S. (eds.) ACM CCS 2006, October/November 2006, pp. 390–399. ACM Press (2006)

9. Bernstein, D.J., et al.: NTRU Prime. Technical report, National Institute of Standards and Technology (2020). https://csrc.nist.gov/projects/post-quantum-cryptography/round-3-submissions

10. Bindel, N., et al.: qTESLA. Technical report, National Institute of Standards and Technology (2019). https://csrc.nist.gov/projects/post-quantum-cryptography/round-2-submissions

11. Brakerski, Z., Langlois, A., Peikert, C., Regev, O., Stehlé, D.: Classical hardness of learning with errors. In: Boneh, D., Roughgarden, T., Feigenbaum, J. (eds.) 45th ACM STOC, pp. 575–584. ACM Press (June 2013)

12. Chen, Y., Genise, N., Mukherjee, P.: Approximate trapdoors for lattices and smaller hash-and-sign signatures. In: Galbraith, S.D., Moriai, S. (eds.) ASIACRYPT 2019. LNCS, vol. 11923, pp. 3–32. Springer, Cham (2019). https://doi.org/10.1007/978-3-030-34618-8_1

13. Cheon, J.H., Kim, D., Kim, T., Son, Y.: A new trapdoor over module-NTRU lattice and its application to ID-based encryption. Cryptology ePrint Archive, Report 2019/1468 (2019). https://eprint.iacr.org/2019/1468

14. Chuengsatiansup, C., Prest, T., Stehlé, D., Wallet, A., Xagawa, K.: ModFalcon: compact signatures based on module-NTRU lattices. In: Sun, H.-M., Shieh, S.-P., Gu, G., Ateniese, G. (eds.) ASIACCS 2020, pp. 853–866. ACM Press (October 2020)

15. Ducas, L., Durmus, A., Lepoint, T., Lyubashevsky, V.: Lattice signatures and bimodal gaussians. In: Canetti, R., Garay, J.A. (eds.) CRYPTO 2013. LNCS, vol. 8042, pp. 40–56. Springer, Heidelberg (2013). https://doi.org/10.1007/978-3-642-40041-4_3

16. Ducas, L., Lyubashevsky, V., Prest, T.: Efficient identity-based encryption over NTRU lattices. In: Sarkar, P., Iwata, T. (eds.) ASIACRYPT 2014. LNCS, vol. 8874, pp. 22–41. Springer, Heidelberg (2014). https://doi.org/10.1007/978-3-662-45608-8_2

17. Fiat, A., Shamir, A.: How to prove yourself: practical solutions to identification and signature problems. In: Odlyzko, A.M. (ed.) CRYPTO 1986. LNCS, vol. 263, pp. 186–194. Springer, Heidelberg (1987). https://doi.org/10.1007/3-540-47721-7_12

18. Fouque, P.-A., et al.: FALCON: fast-Fourier lattice-based compact signatures over NTRU (2017). https://falcon-sign.info/

19. Genise, N., Gentry, C., Halevi, S., Li, B., Micciancio, D.: Homomorphic encryption for finite automata. In: Galbraith, S.D., Moriai, S. (eds.) ASIACRYPT 2019. LNCS, vol. 11922, pp. 473–502. Springer, Cham (2019). https://doi.org/10.1007/978-3-030-34621-8_17

20. Gentry, C., Peikert, C., Vaikuntanathan, V.: Trapdoors for hard lattices and new cryptographic constructions. In: Ladner, R.E., Dwork, C. (eds.) 40th ACM STOC, pp. 197–206. ACM Press (May 2008)

21. Güneysu, T., Lyubashevsky, V., Pöppelmann, T.: Practical lattice-based cryptography: a signature scheme for embedded systems. In: Prouff, E., Schaumont, P. (eds.) CHES 2012. LNCS, vol. 7428, pp. 530–547. Springer, Heidelberg (2012). https://doi.org/10.1007/978-3-642-33027-8_31

22. Hoffstein, J., Howgrave-Graham, N., Pipher, J., Silverman, J.H., Whyte, W.: NTRUSign: digital signatures using the NTRU lattice. In: Joye, M. (ed.) CT-RSA 2003. LNCS, vol. 2612, pp. 122–140. Springer, Heidelberg (2003). https://doi.org/10.1007/3-540-36563-X_9

23. Hoffstein, J., Pipher, J., Silverman, J.H.: NTRU: a new high speed public key cryptosystem, 1996. Draft Distributed at Crypto'96. http://web.securityinnovation.com/hubfs/files/ntru-orig.pdf

24. Hoffstein, J., Pipher, J., Silverman, J.H.: NTRU: a ring-based public key cryptosystem. In: Buhler, J.P. (ed.) ANTS 1998. LNCS, vol. 1423, pp. 267–288. Springer, Heidelberg (1998). https://doi.org/10.1007/BFb0054868
25. Hoffstein, J., Pipher, J., Silverman, J.H.: NTRU: a ring-based public key cryptosystem. In: ANTS, pp. 267–288 (1998)
26. Kiltz, E., Lyubashevsky, V., Schaffner, C.: A concrete treatment of Fiat-Shamir signatures in the Quantum Random-Oracle model. In: Nielsen, J.B., Rijmen, V. (eds.) EUROCRYPT 2018. LNCS, vol. 10822, pp. 552–586. Springer, Cham (2018). https://doi.org/10.1007/978-3-319-78372-7_18
27. Kirchner, P., Fouque, P.-A.: Revisiting lattice attacks on overstretched NTRU parameters. In: Coron, J.-S., Nielsen, J.B. (eds.) EUROCRYPT 2017. LNCS, vol. 10210, pp. 3–26. Springer, Cham (2017). https://doi.org/10.1007/978-3-319-56620-7_1
28. Lyubashevsky, V.: Fiat-Shamir with aborts: applications to lattice and factoring-based signatures. In: Matsui, M. (ed.) ASIACRYPT 2009. LNCS, vol. 5912, pp. 598–616. Springer, Heidelberg (2009). https://doi.org/10.1007/978-3-642-10366-7_35
29. Lyubashevsky, V.: Lattice signatures without trapdoors. In: Pointcheval, D., Johansson, T. (eds.) EUROCRYPT 2012. LNCS, vol. 7237, pp. 738–755. Springer, Heidelberg (2012). https://doi.org/10.1007/978-3-642-29011-4_43
30. Lyubashevsky, V., et al.: CRYSTALS-DILITHIUM. Technical report, National Institute of Standards and Technology (2020). https://csrc.nist.gov/projects/post-quantum-cryptography/round-3-submissions
31. Lyubashevsky, V., Micciancio, D.: Generalized compact knapsacks are collision resistant. In: Bugliesi, M., Preneel, B., Sassone, V., Wegener, I. (eds.) ICALP 2006. LNCS, vol. 4052, pp. 144–155. Springer, Heidelberg (2006). https://doi.org/10.1007/11787006_13
32. Lyubashevsky, V., Peikert, C., Regev, O.: On ideal lattices and learning with errors over rings. In: Gilbert, H. (ed.) EUROCRYPT 2010. LNCS, vol. 6110, pp. 1–23. Springer, Heidelberg (2010). https://doi.org/10.1007/978-3-642-13190-5_1
33. Micciancio, D.: Generalized compact knapsacks, cyclic lattices, and efficient one-way functions from worst-case complexity assumptions. In: 43rd FOCS, pp. 356–365. IEEE Computer Society Press (November 2002)
34. Micciancio, D., Peikert, C.: Trapdoors for lattices: simpler, tighter, faster, smaller. In: Pointcheval, D., Johansson, T. (eds.) EUROCRYPT 2012. LNCS, vol. 7237, pp. 700–718. Springer, Heidelberg (2012). https://doi.org/10.1007/978-3-642-29011-4_41
35. Micciancio, D., Regev, O.: Worst-case to average-case reductions based on Gaussian measures. In: 45th FOCS, pp. 372–381. IEEE Computer Society Press (October 2004)
36. Peikert, C.: A decade of lattice cryptography. Found. Trends Theor. Comput. Sci. 10(4) (2016). http://eprint.iacr.org/
37. Peikert, C., Rosen, A.: Lattices that admit logarithmic worst-case to average-case connection factors. In: Johnson, D.S., Feige, U. (eds.) 39th ACM STOC, pp. 478–487. ACM Press (June 2007)
38. Pellet-Mary, A., Stehlé, D.: On the hardness of the NTRU problem. Cryptology ePrint Archive, Report 2021/821 (2021). https://ia.cr/2021/821
39. Prest, T., et al.: FALCON. Technical report, National Institute of Standards and Technology (2020). https://csrc.nist.gov/projects/post-quantum-cryptography/round-3-submissions

40. Regev, O.: On lattices, learning with errors, random linear codes, and cryptography. In: Gabow, H.N., Fagin, R. (eds.) 37th ACM STOC, pp. 84–93. ACM Press (May 2005)
41. Regev, O.: Lattice-based cryptography. In: Dwork, C. (ed.) CRYPTO 2006. LNCS, vol. 4117, pp. 131–141. Springer, Heidelberg (2006). https://doi.org/10.1007/11818175_8
42. Schnorr, C.-P.: A hierarchy of polynomial time lattice basis reduction algorithms. Theor. Comput. Sci. **53**, 201–224 (1987)
43. Schnorr, C.-P., Euchner, M.: Lattice basis reduction: improved practical algorithms and solving subset sum problems. Math. Program. **66**, 181–199 (1994)
44. Stehlé, D., Steinfeld, R., Tanaka, K., Xagawa, K.: Efficient public key encryption based on ideal lattices. In: Matsui, M. (ed.) ASIACRYPT 2009. LNCS, vol. 5912, pp. 617–635. Springer, Heidelberg (2009). https://doi.org/10.1007/978-3-642-10366-7_36
45. Zhang, Z., Chen, C., Hoffstein, J., Whyte, W.: pqNTRUSign. Technical report, National Institute of Standards and Technology (2017). https://csrc.nist.gov/projects/post-quantum-cryptography/round-1-submissions

Speeding-Up Parallel Computation of Large Smooth-Degree Isogeny Using Precedence-Constrained Scheduling

Kittiphon Phalakarn[1](✉), Vorapong Suppakitpaisarn[2], and M. Anwar Hasan[1]

[1] University of Waterloo, Ontario, Canada
{kphalakarn,ahasan}@uwaterloo.ca
[2] The University of Tokyo, Tokyo, Japan
vorapong@is.s.u-tokyo.ac.jp

Abstract. Although the supersingular isogeny Diffie-Hellman (SIDH) protocol is one of the most promising post-quantum cryptosystems, it is significantly slower than its main counterparts due to the underlying large smooth-degree isogeny computation. In this work, we address the problem of evaluating and constructing a *strategy* for computing the large smooth-degree isogeny in the *multi-processor setting* by formulating them as scheduling problems with dependencies. The contribution of this work is two-fold. For the strategy evaluation, we transform strategies into task dependency graphs and apply precedence-constrained scheduling algorithms to them in order to find their costs. For the strategy construction, we construct strategies from smaller parts that are optimal solutions of integer programming representing the problem. We show via experiments that the proposed two techniques together offer more than 13% reduction in the strategy costs compared to the best current results by Hutchinson and Karabina presented at Indocrypt 2018.

Keywords: SIDH · Isogeny-based cryptography · Parallel computing · Precedence-constrained scheduling

1 Introduction

The supersingular isogeny Diffie-Hellman (SIDH) protocol is a post-quantum key exchange protocol introduced by De Feo, Jao, and Plût in 2011 [13], where its security is based on the hardness of supersingular isogeny problems. SIDH was parameterized as the supersingular isogeny key encapsulation (SIKE) protocol [5] and was submitted to the NIST post-quantum cryptography standardization project in 2017 [2]. As announced in 2020, SIKE was selected as one of the alternate candidates [1].

SIDH requires relatively smaller public keys but takes more computation time compared to other schemes [4]. This is because SIDH requires both parties to perform large smooth-degree (i.e., all factors of the degree are small primes) isogeny computations, which are the bottleneck of the protocol. To reduce the computation time of SIDH, an abstraction of large smooth-degree isogeny computation called *strategy* was proposed in [13]. In that paper, the authors gave

K. Nguyen et al. (Eds.): ACISP 2022, LNCS 13494, pp. 309–331, 2022.
https://doi.org/10.1007/978-3-031-22301-3_16

a method to compute the *cost* of a strategy, an abstraction for the computation time. Intuitively, a low-cost strategy will lead to a fast implementation of SIDH. The paper also presented how to construct an *optimal strategy*, a strategy giving the lowest cost among all possible strategies. These optimal strategies are then utilized to implement SIDH and SIKE in order to reduce computation time. Apart from this, several other works were proposed towards lowering the computation time of SIDH [12,14,22,25].

The aforementioned techniques, however, do not consider parallelism and are targeted towards the *single-processor setting*. When we can utilize more than one core or processor, which is the case in many situations these days, we have *multi-processor setting*. Since multiple operations can be performed simultaneously in this setting, we can finish the computation faster. For example, under the multi-processor setting, the SIDH hardware architecture in [21] performed up to 42% faster than previous works. Recently, another fast parallel architecture was introduced in [20].

Apart from strategy construction, another important aspects of the isogeny computation in the multi-processor setting is strategy *evaluation*: the cost of a strategy now depends on how it is evaluated. And to achieve the least cost, both strategy construction and evaluation have to be designed specifically for the number of processors provided. In the works of [20] and [21] mentioned earlier, both implementations evaluate strategies designed for the single-processor setting. Hence, those computation times are not necessarily optimal for the multi-processor setting.

To the best of our knowledge, the only works that construct and evaluate strategies specifically for the multi-processor setting are the work of Hutchinson and Karabina [18], and that of Cervantes-Vázquez et al. [9], where the latter is a software implementation of the former. The two evaluation techniques for the multi-processor setting proposed in [18] are *per-curve parallel (PCP)* and *consecutive curve parallel (CCP)* (see Subsect. 2.4). The results of [18] show that, in the multi-processor setting, strategies constructed specifically for the multi-processor setting lead to lower costs than strategies constructed for the single-processor setting. Moreover, under SIKEp751 parameters with eight processors, their multi-processor setting based approach can achieve more than 50% reduction in the strategy cost compared to the single-processor setting. For two, three, and four processors, the reductions in strategy costs are 30%, 40%, and 46%, respectively. And, the maximum cost reduction achieved when we have arbitrary-many processors is 74%. When utilizing strategies and evaluations from [18] in the implementation of SIKEp751 with three processors, together with other optimizations, [9] could achieve more than 30% speedups in the computation time compared to the single-processor setting.

Nonetheless, the strategy costs reported in [18] are not the least we can achieve as their evaluations do not fully utilize available processors. (We will discuss this in Sect. 3.) In this work, we follow a different approach and formulate this problem as precedence-constrained scheduling problems. To our knowledge, our work is the first for this approach to be applied in reducing the strategy cost for the computation of large smooth-degree isogenies. Our contribution is two-fold and consists of a novel strategy evaluation and construction techniques leading to lower strategy costs:

1. For the strategy evaluation (Sect. 3), we transform strategies into task dependency graphs and then apply two precedence-constrained scheduling algorithms, Hu's [17] and Coffman-Graham's [10] algorithms, to them in order to calculate the cost of strategies.
2. For the strategy construction (Sect. 4), we formalize the problem as an integer linear program (ILP) and then construct efficient strategies as a combination of optimal solutions to the ILP by structures of PCP.

We list techniques for strategy evaluation and construction of related works in Table 1. Our experimental results show that the application of our proposed techniques leads to more than 13% reduction in strategy cost compared to those reported by [18] under the same parameter sets.

Table 1. Strategy evaluation and construction techniques used in various works.

Works	Strategy evaluation	Strategy construction
[13]	Single operation at a time	Optimal for single-processor setting
[20, 21]	PCP	Optimal for single-processor setting
[9, 18]	PCP and CCP	Optimal under PCP (multi-processor)
Ours	Precedence-constrained scheduling	Using ILP and PCP

2 Preliminaries

In this section, we review some preliminaries on SIDH, strategies for computing large smooth-degree isogeny, how strategies can be evaluated in the single-processor and multi-processor settings, and precedence-constrained scheduling algorithms.

2.1 SIDH

Let E and E' be elliptic curves over a field F where their identity elements are ∞ and ∞', respectively. An isogeny from E to E' is a morphism $\phi : E \to E'$ satisfying $\phi(\infty) = \infty'$. When specifying an elliptic curve E and a point $R \in E(F)$, one can compute the unique isogeny $\phi : E \to E' = E/\langle R \rangle$ satisfying $\ker \phi = \langle R \rangle$ using Vélu's [27] or √élu's [6] formulas. The degree of ϕ is equal to the order of R. Using these notations, SIDH can be described as follows.

Setup: Alice and Bob agree on the following set of public parameters:

- a prime p of the form $\ell_A^{e_A} \ell_B^{e_B} \cdot f \pm 1$ where ℓ_A, ℓ_B are small primes, e_A, e_B are exponents giving $\ell_A^{e_A} \approx \ell_B^{e_B}$, and f is a positive integer,
- a supersingular elliptic curve E_0 over $\mathbb{F}_{p^2}$ with $\#E_0(\mathbb{F}_{p^2}) = (\ell_A^{e_A} \ell_B^{e_B} \cdot f)^2$,
- bases $\{P_A, Q_A\}$ of $E_0[\ell_A^{e_A}]$ and $\{P_B, Q_B\}$ of $E_0[\ell_B^{e_B}]$.

Key Exchange:

1. Alice randomly chooses $m_A \in \mathbb{Z}_{\ell_A^{e_A}}$. She computes an isogeny $\phi_A : E_0 \to E_A$ with kernel $\langle R_A \rangle$ where $R_A = P_A + [m_A]Q_A$, and then sends E_A, $\phi_A(P_B)$, $\phi_A(Q_B)$ to Bob.
2. Similarly, Bob randomly chooses $m_B \in \mathbb{Z}_{\ell_B^{e_B}}$. He computes $\phi_B : E_0 \to E_B$ with kernel $\langle R_B \rangle$ where $R_B = P_B + [m_B]Q_B$, and sends E_B, $\phi_B(P_A)$, $\phi_B(Q_A)$ to Alice.
3. Upon receiving $E_B, \phi_B(P_A), \phi_B(Q_A)$ from Bob, Alice computes an isogeny $\phi'_A : E_B \to E_{AB}$ with kernel $\langle R'_A \rangle$ where $R'_A = \phi_B(P_A) + [m_A]\phi_B(Q_A)$.
4. Similarly, upon receiving $E_A, \phi_A(P_B), \phi_A(Q_B)$ from Alice, Bob computes $\phi'_B : E_A \to E_{BA}$ with kernel $\langle R'_B \rangle$ where $R'_B = \phi_A(P_B) + [m_B]\phi_A(Q_B)$.
5. The shared secret is the j-invariant of the resulting elliptic curves: $j(E_{AB}) = j(E_{BA})$, where $j(E) = 1728\frac{4a^3}{4a^3+27b^2}$ for $E : y^2 = x^3 + ax + b$.

2.2   Large Smooth-Degree Isogeny Computation and Strategies

SIDH requires several computations of isogenies of the form $\phi : E \to E'$ with kernel $\langle R \rangle$ and degree ℓ^e. Theoretically, the degree of isogenies in SIDH can be any sufficiently large integer, but we have not found an efficient way to compute them using Vélu's or $\sqrt{\text{élu}}$'s formulas. For large smooth-degree (e.g., degree-ℓ^e for small ℓ and large e) isogenies, an efficient way exists, which is to decompose ϕ as a chain of degree-ℓ isogenies [13]:

$$\phi : E = E_0 \xrightarrow{\phi_0} E_1 \xrightarrow{\phi_1} E_2 \xrightarrow{\phi_2} \cdots \xrightarrow{\phi_{e-2}} E_{e-1} \xrightarrow{\phi_{e-1}} E_e = E/\langle R \rangle$$

where, for $0 \leq i < e$, $E_{i+1} = E_i/\langle [\ell^{e-i-1}]R_i \rangle$, $R_{i+1} = \phi_i(R_i)$, and $R_0 = R$. We note that $R'_i = [\ell^{e-i-1}]R_i$ is required in order to compute ϕ_i and E_{i+1}. This suggests the following procedure given in Algorithm 1 for computing $\phi_0, \ldots, \phi_{e-1}$.

We can describe Algorithm 1 using a graph with $\frac{e(e+1)}{2}$ vertices arranged in e columns and e rows as shown in Fig. 1(a). Each vertex represents a point where points in each column are on the same elliptic curve. The vertex at the upper left corner represents the point R_0 and the leftmost column are points on E_0. The top-to-bottom arrows depict point multiplications by $[\ell]$ in Line 4 of the algorithm and the left-to-right arrows depict isogeny evaluations in Line 6. Here, ϕ_{e-1}, E_e, and R_e are omitted as they are not relevant for analysis.

In Fig. 1(a), one might notice that R'_1 can also be computed by $R'_1 = \phi_0([\ell^{e-2}]R_0)$. This gives other possible ways of computing large smooth-degree isogenies. By considering how each point in the graph can be computed from other points, we define the graph T_e following [13] which shows all possible point multiplications by $[\ell]$ and isogeny evaluations among all vertices. For simplicity, vertices are referred to by pairs of their column and row numbers, i.e., vertex (i, j) refers to the point $[\ell^j]R_i$ in column i and row j. Vertices representing R'_i, i.e., vertices $(i, e - i - 1)$ for $0 \leq i < e$, are called *leaves*.

Definition 1. *The graph showing all possible operations for computing degree-ℓ^e isogeny is defined as a directed graph $T_e = (V_e, E_e)$ where*

Algorithm 1: An algorithm for computing degree-ℓ^e isogeny.

Input : A supersingular elliptic curve E and a point R of order ℓ^e
Output: $\phi_0, \ldots, \phi_{e-1}$ and $E/\langle R \rangle$

1 $E_0 \leftarrow E, R_0 \leftarrow R$
2 **for** $i = 0$ **to** $e - 1$ **do**
3      $R_i' \leftarrow R_i$
4   **for** $j = 1$ **to** $e - i - 1$ **do** $R_i' \leftarrow [\ell]R_i'$
5   Use Vélu's or $\sqrt{}$élu's formulas to compute ϕ_i and E_{i+1} from E_i and $\langle R_i' \rangle$
6      $R_{i+1} \leftarrow \phi_i(R_i)$
7 **return** $\phi_0, \ldots, \phi_{e-1}, E_e$

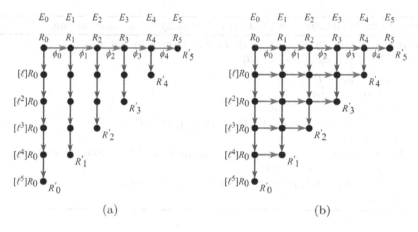

Fig. 1. (a) The graph representing Algorithm 1 and (b) the graph T_e when $e = 6$.

- the set of vertices $V_e - \{(i,j) : 0 \leq i, j < c; \; i + j < c\}$,
- the set of directed edges $E_e = \downarrow_e \cup \rightarrow_e$,
- the set of point multiplication edges $\downarrow_e = \{\langle (i,j),(i,j+1)\rangle : i + j < e - 1\}$,
- the set of isogeny evaluation edges $\rightarrow_e = \{\langle (i,j),(i+1,j)\rangle : i + j < e - 1\}$.

Next, we define a *strategy* for computing degree-ℓ^e isogeny as follows.

Definition 2. *A strategy S for computing degree-ℓ^e isogeny is a subgraph of T_e containing the vertex $(0,0)$ and all leaves where there are paths from the vertex $(0,0)$ to each leaf. A strategy S is* well-formed *if removing any edge from S results in a graph that is not a strategy.*

An example of a strategy is the graph in Fig. 1(a). By the definition, one can use a strategy to compute a degree-ℓ^e isogeny by first performing operations along a path from $(0,0)$ to R_0', then a path from $(0,0)$ to R_1', and so on. Since strategies that are not well-formed have some unnecessary edges, we will consider only well-formed strategies in order to find an efficient strategy.

Now we look at how a strategy can be evaluated which defines the cost of a strategy. We will define the strategy cost using the cost of a single point multiplication by $[\ell]$: $Q \leftarrow [\ell]P$, and the cost of a single degree-ℓ isogeny evaluation: $Q \leftarrow \phi(P)$. We denote their costs as $c_\downarrow$ and $c_\rightarrow$, respectively.

2.3 Single-Processor Setting

When only a single processor is provided, we have to perform all operations sequentially. Formally, given a strategy S, one can compute a degree-ℓ^e isogeny using Algorithm 2.

Algorithm 2: Strategy evaluation in the single-processor setting.

Input : A strategy $S = (V_S, E_S)$, a curve E, and a point R
Output: $\phi_0, \ldots, \phi_{e-1}$ and $E/\langle R \rangle$

1 $E_0 \leftarrow E$, $R_{(0,0)} \leftarrow R$
2 **for** $i = 0$ **to** $e - 1$ **do**
3   **for** $j = 0$ **to** $e - i - 2$ **do**
4   **if** $\langle (i,j), (i,j+1) \rangle \in E_S$ **then** $R_{(i,j+1)} \leftarrow [\ell]R_{(i,j)}$
5     $R' \leftarrow R_{(i,e-i-1)}$
6   Use Vélu's or $\sqrt{}$élu's formulas to compute ϕ_i and E_{i+1} from E_i and $\langle R' \rangle$
7   **for** $j = 0$ **to** $e - i - 2$ **do**
8   **if** $\langle (i,j), (i+1,j) \rangle \in E_S$ **then** $R_{(i+1,j)} \leftarrow \phi_i(R_{(i,j)})$
9 **return** $\phi_0, \ldots, \phi_{e-1}, E_e$

From the above algorithm, we can define the cost of a strategy in the single-processor setting. For a strategy S, let $\#\downarrow_S$ denote the number of point multiplication edges in S and $\#\rightarrow_S$ denote the number of isogeny evaluation edges. Then, the cost of a strategy S in the single-processor setting, denoted by $C_1(S)$, is computed by

$$C_1(S) = \#\downarrow_S \cdot c_\downarrow + \#\rightarrow_S \cdot c_\rightarrow.$$

We emphasize that the strategy cost is only an abstraction for the SIDH computation time since we do not account for the cost of Vélu's or $\sqrt{}$élu's formulas (Line 6 of Algorithm 2) nor other operations required in SIDH (e.g., the cost of Alice computing $R_A \leftarrow P_A + [m_A]Q_A$, etc.). Nevertheless, the strategy cost is a useful measure in order to reduce the computation time of an implementation.

The problem of constructing a least-cost strategy given e, $c_\downarrow$, and $c_\rightarrow$ has been extensively studied in [13]. That work analyzed a particular type of strategies called *canonical* strategies and proved that a least-cost strategy in the single-processor setting must be in this form. A canonical strategy is defined below.

Definition 3. *A* canonical *strategy for computing degree-ℓ^e isogeny is defined recursively as follows:*

– *If $e = 1$, then T_1 is canonical.*

– *Otherwise, let S_n, where $1 \leq n < e$, be a canonical strategy for computing degree-ℓ^n isogeny. If $S = (V_S, E_S)$ is constructed from $S_n = (V_{S_n}, E_{S_n})$ and $S_{e-n} = (V_{S_{e-n}}, E_{S_{e-n}})$ by the following steps, then S is canonical.*
  1. *Rename all vertices (i, j) in S_n to $(i, j + (e - n))$.*
  2. *Rename all vertices (i, j) in S_{e-n} to $(i + n, j)$.*
  3. *Construct $V_S = V_{S_n} \cup V_{S_{e-n}} \cup \{(0, j) : 0 \leq j < e - n\} \cup \{(i, 0) : 0 \leq i < n\}$ and $E_S = E_{S_n} \cup E_{S_{e-n}} \cup \{\langle(0, j), (0, j+1)\rangle : 0 \leq j < e - n\} \cup \{\langle(i, 0), (i + 1, 0)\rangle : 0 \leq i < n\}$.*

In brief, a canonical strategy with e leaves can be split into two canonical strategies with n leaves and $e - n$ leaves. Figure 2 depicts the process explained in Definition 3.

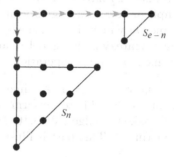

Fig. 2. A canonical strategy.

By exploiting the optimal substructure of the problem, the cost of a least-cost strategy for computing degree-ℓ^e isogeny in the single-processor setting can be calculated by the following recurrence [13]. We abuse the notation C_1 by defining $C_1(e)$ as the cost of a least-cost strategy with e leaves.

$$C_1(e) = \min_{1 \leq n < e} \{C_1(n) + C_1(e - n) + (e - n) \cdot c_{\downarrow} + n \cdot c_{\rightarrow}\}, \quad C_1(1) = 0.$$

2.4   Multi-processor Setting

In this setting, we are provided with $K \geq 2$ processors. At first, a K-time improvement from the single-processor setting might be expected. However, since we need to compute R_i' in order to continue to the next column, the computation is quite restricted and we are not able to fully utilize all processors at all times during the computation. Nevertheless, having multiple processors helps us reduce the cost as discussed next.

Before getting into the strategy cost, we review the implicit restrictions of the degree-ℓ^e isogeny computation. Unlike the single-processor setting, timing plays a crucial role here. Because now we can perform more than one operations at the same time, we have to be careful of which operations are performed first and when they are finished, as they depend closely on each other. This is very important for achieving the least cost in this setting. In this work, we consider two restrictions of how a strategy is evaluated in parallel:

1. To perform a point multiplication by $[\ell]$ corresponding to a directed edge $\langle(i,j),(i,j+1)\rangle$, the vertex (i,j) corresponding to the point $[\ell^j]R_i$ must have been computed.
2. To perform an isogeny evaluation corresponding to a directed edge $\langle(i,j),(i+1,j)\rangle$, two vertices (i,j) and $(i,e-i-1)$ corresponding to the point $[\ell^j]R_i$ and R_i', respectively, must have been computed. Here, the latter vertex R_i' is required to construct ϕ_i.

Even though the computation is restricted, there are still several ways of evaluating a strategy in parallel. To have a clearer picture of the problem, we consider the following example of how a strategy is evaluated. In order to specify which operations are performed at which time, each edge is labeled with its finish time. The cost of evaluating a strategy is then labeled on the edge $\langle(e-2,0),(e-1,0)\rangle$, which must be performed as the last operation.

Example 1. Suppose $K=2$ and $c_\downarrow=c_\rightarrow=1$. At time 0, although we have two processors, the only operation we are able to perform is the edge $\langle(0,0),(0,1)\rangle$. Again, at time 1, we can only take the edge $\langle(0,1),(0,2)\rangle$. We continue until the edge $\langle(0,3),(0,4)\rangle$ is done at time 4. This part is illustrated in Fig. 3(a).

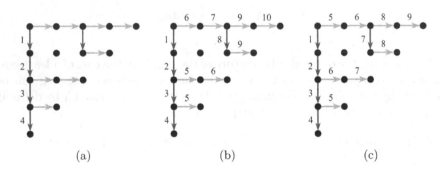

(a)   (b)   (c)

Fig. 3. Examples of parallel evaluations of a strategy with $K=2$.

At time 5, we now have three options: $\langle(0,0),(1,0)\rangle$, $\langle(0,2),(1,2)\rangle$, and $\langle(0,3),(1,3)\rangle$. Because we have two processors, we can choose up to two operations. Figure 3(b) chooses the last two. After performing the remaining operations, the last operation is done at time 10. Thus, the cost of the evaluation in Fig. 3(b) is 10. On the other hand, Fig. 3(c) chooses operations $\langle(0,0),(1,0)\rangle$ and $\langle(0,3),(1,3)\rangle$. By this evaluation, its cost is only 9. We point out that this is the least possible cost from any strategy we can achieve when $e=5$, $K=2$, $c_\downarrow=c_\rightarrow=1$. (Thus, a strategy giving the least cost in the multi-processor setting does not have to be canonical.)

From the above example, the multi-processor setting is much more complicated compared to the single-processor setting. In the rest of this subsection, we present the result of Hutchinson and Karabina [18] on constructing low-cost strategies and evaluations under some constraints called *per-curve parallel (PCP)* and *consecutive-curve parallel (CCP)*.

Per-curve Parallel. Hutchinson and Karabina started with a simple evaluation of a strategy called *per-curve parallel (PCP)*. Under PCP, two rules apply:

1. only operations of the form $\langle(i,j),(i+1,j)\rangle$ and $\langle(i,j'),(i+1,j')\rangle$ (i.e., isogeny evaluations from the same elliptic curve E_i) can be performed in parallel, and
2. point multiplications cannot be done in parallel. In other words, if one processor performs the edge $\langle(i,j),(i,j+1)\rangle$, other processors must be left idle.

The algorithm representing the strategy evaluation under PCP is similar to Algorithm 2, except that we can simultaneously perform up to K isogeny evaluations in Lines 7–8, i.e., when there are n isogeny evaluations from E_i, the cost of performing these isogeny evaluations is $\lceil \frac{n}{K} \rceil \cdot c_\rightarrow$. Let $\#{\rightarrow}_{S,i}$ denote the number of isogeny evaluation edges from E_i in a strategy S, the cost of evaluating S under PCP having K processors is

$$C_K^{\mathrm{PCP}}(S) = \#{\downarrow}_S \cdot c_\downarrow + \sum_{i=0}^{e-2} \left\lceil \frac{\#{\rightarrow}_{S,i}}{K} \right\rceil \cdot c_\rightarrow.$$

Even though the evaluation under PCP does not provide the least cost in the multi-processor setting, it allows an extensive analysis to construct a strategy with smallest $C_K^{\mathrm{PCP}}(S)$. While not stated in [18], the lemma below can be proved.

Lemma 1. *There exists a canonical strategy providing the least cost under PCP.*

Proof (sketch). Suppose we have a least-cost strategy under PCP that is not canonical, we can modify it to have a least-cost canonical strategy. First, we consider the leftmost leaf $(i', e-i'-1)$ connecting to $(0,0)$ via the edge $\langle(0,0),(1,0)\rangle$. If it is not connected to $(0,0)$ via the vertex $(i',0)$, we can remove the existing path and change it to the path $(0,0) \rightarrow (i',0) \rightarrow (i',e-i'-1)$. By this modification, $\#{\downarrow}_S$ and $\#{\rightarrow}_{S,i}$ for $0 \le i < i'$ do not increase. We perform similar actions with the rightmost leaf connecting to $(0,0)$ via the edge $\langle(0,0),(0,1)\rangle$. The modified strategy now has the same structure as a canonical strategy (Fig. 2) except that two smaller strategies might not be canonical. We can apply the same technique recursively to those smaller strategies to convert them into canonical strategies without increasing the cost. Therefore, we have a least-cost canonical strategy under PCP.

By the above lemma, we can construct a least-cost strategy under PCP by finding a least-cost canonical strategy. The optimal substructure of the problem allowed [18] to present a recurrence describing the least cost under PCP. Let $C_K^{\mathrm{PCP}}(e, k)$ denote the least cost of a strategy with e leaves where, in the first iteration of executing Lines 7–8 of Algorithm 2 in parallel for each curve, we can perform isogeny evaluations of only up to k points (instead of K points). Also, let $n' = e - n$. The recurrence for $C_K^{\mathrm{PCP}}(e, k)$ can be described as

$$C_K^{\mathrm{PCP}}(e, k) =
\begin{cases}
0 & \text{if } e = 1, \\
C_K^{\mathrm{PCP}}(e, K) + (e - 1) \cdot c_\rightarrow & \text{if } e > 1 \text{ and } k = 0, \\
\min_{1 \le n < e} \{ C_K^{\mathrm{PCP}}(n, k - 1) + C_K^{\mathrm{PCP}}(n', k) + n' \cdot c_\downarrow + c_\rightarrow \} & \text{otherwise.}
\end{cases}$$

The following theorem describes the least possible cost of a strategy under PCP.

Theorem 1 ([18]). *Let K, $c_\downarrow$, and $c_\rightarrow$ be fixed. The least cost of a strategy under PCP for computing degree-ℓ^e isogeny with K processors is $C_K^{\mathrm{PCP}}(e, K)$ (i.e., evaluating the above recurrence at $k = K$).*

We refer the interested readers to [18] for the detailed proof and explanation of the theorem.

Consecutive-Curve Parallel. Under PCP, we cannot perform any operation in different columns, even though it is allowed to do so and some processors are idle. By this observation, [18] considered another constraint called *consecutive-curve parallel (CCP)*. Let $\downarrow_{S,i}$ denote the set of point multiplication by $[\ell]$ edges for points in E_i in a strategy S and $\rightarrow_{S,i}$ denote that of isogeny evaluation edges. Under CCP, while performing operations in $\rightarrow_{S,i}$, we are allowed to perform operations in $\rightarrow_{S,i+1}$ and $\downarrow_{S,i+1}$ if they are ready to be done.

Because it is more flexible to perform operations in parallel under CCP, it is thus harder to analyze a strategy under this constraint. For this reason, [18] decided to consider only canonical strategies under CCP. As discussed before, operations in $\rightarrow_{S,i+1}$ can be performed after R'_{i+1} is computed. In the case that R'_{i+1} is computed by point multiplication edges in $\downarrow_{S,i+1}$, all operations in $\downarrow_{S,i+1}$ must be done first to obtain R'_{i+1}. By this, CCP uses a greedy heuristic to choose which operations will be performed as described in the following rules:

1. Operations in $\rightarrow_{S,i}$ are performed from bottom to top.
2. If an operation in $\downarrow_{S,i+1}$ is available, then perform one operation in $\downarrow_{S,i+1}$ and $K - 1$ operations in $\rightarrow_{S,i}$.
3. If operations in $\downarrow_{S,i+1}$ are all done or there is no operation in $\downarrow_{S,i+1}$, start performing operations in $\rightarrow_{S,i+1}$ as soon as all in $\rightarrow_{S,i}$ is finished.
4. If operations in $\rightarrow_{S,i}$ are all done before $\downarrow_{S,i+1}$ is exhausted, then perform the remaining operations in $\downarrow_{S,i+1}$ before starting $\rightarrow_{S,i+1}$.

The algorithm for computing the cost under CCP of a canonical strategy S, denoted by $C_K^{\text{CCP}}(S)$, is given in [18, Algorithm 1]. Nonetheless, Hutchinson and Karabina stated that, under CCP, they could find no algorithm for constructing least-cost strategies and no formula for the cost of a least-cost strategy.

We must note that, although performing operations in consecutive columns are allowed, performing operations in other columns are not. Thus, this heuristic could make the cost under CCP larger than the least possible.

2.5   Precedence-Constrained Scheduling Algorithms

The problem of scheduling a set of tasks to processors has been studied for a long time and has many applications in various fields. For a given set of tasks, we need to specify which processor performs which task and the goal is to minimize the time that the last task is finished. In this work, we are interested in the problem of *precedence-constrained* scheduling: we are given, for each task, a list of tasks need to be completed in order to start that task. Thus, we also have to specify the order in which tasks are performed by each processor. The dependency between tasks for this problem is usually specified using a task dependency graph defined as follows.

Definition 4. *Given a set of tasks $T = \{t_1, ..., t_n\}$, the task dependency graph for T is a directed acyclic graph (DAG) $D_T = (V_{D_T}, E_{D_T})$ where $V_{D_T} = T$ and $\langle t_i, t_j \rangle \in E_{D_T}$ if t_i must be performed and finished before t_j can begin.*

There are several variants of this problem, but we restrict ourselves to the case of the graphs D_T with all tasks are of unit-length (i.e., all tasks take the same amount of time to be performed), the number of processors is constant throughout the scheduling, all processors are identical (i.e., no processor performs tasks faster or slower than others) and preemption is not allowed (i.e., tasks cannot be paused and then resumed later). We formally give the definitions of a schedule and the precedence-constrained scheduling problem as follows.

Definition 5. *Let $D_T = (V_{D_T}, E_{D_T})$ be a task dependency graph, and let K be a positive integer. Suppose that all tasks require one unit of time to complete. A scheduling of D_T using K processors is a sequence $\mathcal{S} = \langle s_1, ..., s_n \rangle$ of non-empty sets of tasks where s_i is a set of tasks executed at time i such that (i) $s_1, ..., s_n$ form a partition of V_{D_T}, (ii) $|s_i| \leq K$, and (iii) for all $\langle t, t' \rangle \in E_{D_T}$, if $t \in s_i$ and $t' \in s_j$ then $i < j$. The finished time of $\mathcal{S}$ is n, the size of $\mathcal{S}$, and is denoted by $t(\mathcal{S})$.*

A scheduling $\mathcal{S}$ is optimal if $t(\mathcal{S}) \leq t(\mathcal{S}')$ for any possible scheduling $\mathcal{S}'$ of D_T using K processors. The (precedence-constrained) scheduling problem is to find an optimal scheduling for given D_T and K.

For general DAGs, Ullman [26] proved that the problem is NP-complete, and Garey and Johnson [16] mentioned that complexity remains open when the number of processors $K \geq 3$ is fixed.

In the rest of this subsection, we look at two algorithms. The first algorithm by Hu [17] outputs an optimal scheduling for $K \geq 1$ when the task dependency graph is *tree-like*. The second algorithm by Coffman and Graham [10] produces an optimal scheduling when $K = 2$. When $K \geq 3$, no efficient algorithm has been proposed. Nonetheless, there are many approximation algorithms solving this problem with various approximation ratios [15,24].

Hu's Algorithm. The first algorithm applies with a task dependency graph which is tree-like, i.e., all vertices has out-degrees of at most one. For $u \in V_{D_T}$, let $\ell(u)$ denote the length of a longest path started at u. In a tree-like graph, the longest path started from each vertex is unique since all vertices has at most one out-going edge.

Hu's algorithm can be described as Algorithm 3. In short, the algorithm chooses up to K available tasks with largest $\ell(\cdot)$ in each iteration until all tasks are performed. The chosen tasks and their edges are then removed from the graph in order to show new available tasks.

Algorithm 3: Hu's algorithm [17].

Input : A tree-like task dependency graph $D_T = (V_{D_T}, E_{D_T})$ and the number of provided processors K

Output: An optimal scheduling $\mathcal{S} = \langle s_1, \ldots, s_t \rangle$

1 Compute $\ell(u)$ for all $u \in V_{D_T}$
2 $t \leftarrow 0$
3 **while** $V_{D_T} \neq \emptyset$ **do**
4 $\quad$ $t \leftarrow t + 1$
5 $\quad$ $V' \leftarrow \{u \in V_{D_T} : \text{in-degree of } u = 0\}$
6 $\quad$ Sort V' by $\ell(u)$ in an decreasing order, break ties arbitrarily
7 $\quad$ **if** $|V'| \leq K$ **then** $s_t \leftarrow V'$
8 $\quad$ **else** $s_t \leftarrow \{\text{the first } K \text{ vertices in } V'\}$
9 $\quad$ Remove all vertices in s_t and their associated edges from D_T
10 **return** $\mathcal{S} = \langle s_1, \ldots, s_t \rangle$

Coffman-Graham's Algorithm. Instead of using $\ell(\cdot)$, Coffman and Graham [10] presented another way to label vertices for DAGs of any structure without *transitive edges* defined as follows. After all vertices are labeled, the same technique as in Hu's algorithm is then applied, starting at Line 2.

Definition 6. *Given a directed graph* $G = (V, E)$, *an edge* $e = \langle u, v \rangle \in E$ *is* transitive *if there exists a vertex* $w \notin \{u, v\}$ *in* V *such that* u *reaches* w *and* w *reaches* v.

The labeling process of Coffman and Graham is described as Algorithm 4. We give an example of the function $c(\cdot)$ in Lines 7–8 as follows: Suppose u has three children v_1, v_2, v_3 and all are labeled with $\ell_{CG}(v_1) = 4$, $\ell_{CG}(v_2) = 3$, and $\ell_{CG}(v_3) = 8$. Then, $c(u)$ is the list $[8, 4, 3]$ as it is sorted in decreasing order. In Line 8, lists are compared lexicographically, e.g., $[4, 2, 1] < [4, 3]$, $[5, 4, 2] < [5, 4, 2, 1]$, and $[] < [3, 2]$.

At first, one vertex with no out-going edge is assigned a label of 1. In each iteration, one vertex is labeled. V'' in Line 5 is the set of unlabeled vertices with all children labeled. By the definition of V'', $c(\cdot)$ is well-defined for all vertices in V''. The next vertex to be assigned a label is $u \in V''$ with smallest $c(u)$. The label is assigned from 1 up to $|V_{D_T}|$.

Coffman and Graham proved that, by using $\ell_{CG}(u)$ instead of $\ell(u)$ in Algorithm 3, the output scheduling is optimal when $K = 2$ for a task dependency graph of any structure. Few years later, Lam and Sethi [23] showed that, when applying Coffman-Graham's algorithm with $K \geq 2$, the algorithm is $(2 - \frac{2}{K})$-approximation. When K is small, the approximation ratio is close to 1.

Algorithm 4: Coffman-Graham's labeling algorithm [10].

Input : A task dependency graph $D_T = (V_{D_T}, E_{D_T})$
Output: Coffman-Graham's label $\ell_{CG}(u)$ for all $u \in V_{D_T}$

1 Choose any vertex u with out-degree of 0 and assign $\ell_{CG}(u) \leftarrow 1$
2 $idx \leftarrow 1$
3 **while** there is a vertex without a label **do**
4      $idx \leftarrow idx + 1$
5      $V'' \leftarrow \{u \in V_{D_T} : u$ is not labeled and all its children are labeled$\}$
6   **for** $u \in V''$ **do**
7          $c(u) \leftarrow$ the list of all labels of u's children, sorted in decreasing order
8   Choose $u \in V''$ with smallest $c(u)$ in lexicographical order, break ties arbitrarily
9      $\ell_{CG}(u) \leftarrow idx$

---

3   Proposed Strategy Evaluation Technique

To the best of our knowledge, the evaluation of a canonical strategy under CCP gives the least cost among all existing techniques. In this section, we take a closer look at the problem and propose a new approach to evaluate strategies that gives lower costs. To this end, first we give an example showing that the cost under CCP of a canonical strategy is not the least cost we can achieve.

Example 2. Let $e = 9$, $K = 3$, and $c_\downarrow = c_\rightarrow = 1$. Below shows a canonical strategy which gives the least cost under PCP. When calculating its cost using [18, Algorithm 1], the cost under CCP is 20. The times at which each operation is finished are shown on the corresponding edges as in Fig. 4(a).

Consider another way of evaluating this strategy in Fig. 4(b). Here, the computation is not restricted by CCP. For instance, three isogeny evaluations ϕ_0, ϕ_1,

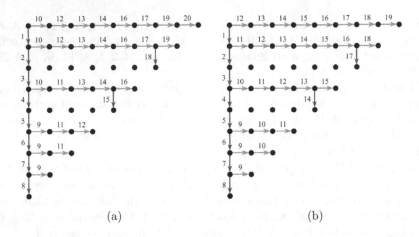

Fig. 4. A strategy giving a cost of 20 under CCP and 19 under another evaluation.

and ϕ_2 are performed in parallel at time 11. As another example, during time 14, two isogeny evaluations ϕ_2, ϕ_3, and a point multiplication on E_4 are done at the same time. These are not permitted under CCP or PCP. As a result, we achieve a lower cost of 19 for this strategy and evaluation.

It is important to note that, unlike the single-processor setting, a strategy in the multi-processor setting does not uniquely correspond to how it is evaluated. This does mean that, in order to obtain the least cost possible, we need to search for a strategy and its evaluation that give the least cost as a pair. Evaluating a good strategy in a wrong way might not give us a low cost. On the other hand, starting with a bad strategy will not give us a low cost under any evaluation. This makes it a challenging problem. Moreover, since it is possible that the least-cost strategy may not be canonical, we might not be able to utilize the recursive structure of canonical strategies to solve the problem.

In this section, we propose a new technique to evaluate strategies. The first part of the technique is to construct the task dependency graph of a strategy, and the second part is to evaluate a strategy by using its task dependency graph and precedence-constrained scheduling algorithms. We tackle the problem of constructing efficient strategies in Sect. 4.

3.1   Task Dependency Graphs of Strategies

Without loss of generality, we assume that for a given strategy $S = (V_S, E_S)$, all vertices in V_S that are unreachable from $(0,0)$ are removed since they are not related to the cost computation. For any well-formed strategy, there is a unique path from $(0,0)$ to any vertices in a strategy. This implies that every vertex in a well-formed strategy that can be reached from $(0,0)$, except for $(0,0)$, must have only one incoming edge. Thus, for a point (i,j) to be available, the operation representing the incoming edge to the point (i,j) must be completed. Therefore, in a strategy, a point and its incoming edge represent the same thing. This concept is important in constructing the task dependency graphs of a strategy.

The task dependency graph of a strategy is defined as follows.

Definition 7. *The task dependency graph of a strategy $S = (V_S, E_S = \downarrow_S \cup \rightarrow_S)$ is a directed acyclic graph $D_S = (V_{D_S}, E_{D_S})$ where $V_{D_S} = V_S \setminus \{(0,0)\}$ and*

$$E_{D_S} = (E_S \cup \{\langle (i, e - i - 1), (i+1, j) \rangle : \langle (i,j), (i+1,j) \rangle \in \rightarrow_S \})$$
$$\setminus \{\langle (0,0), (0,1) \rangle, \langle (0,0), (1,0) \rangle \}.$$

A vertex $(i, j) \in V_{D_S}$ should be thought as a "task" of computing the point (i, j), but it can be thought as the point as well following our discussion earlier. For each isogeny evaluation edge $\langle (i,j), (i+1,j) \rangle$ in S, we add an edge $\langle (i, e - i - 1), (i+1, j) \rangle$ to D_S to explicitly specify the dependency that we need to have R'_i before we can evaluate ϕ_i. We also remove $(0,0)$, since $(0,0)$ is available from the start and we do not have to perform any task to produce it. The next example depicts this process.

Example 3. Consider a strategy from Example 1 as in Fig. 5(a). The first step of constructing the task dependency graph of a strategy is to add a diagonal directed edge for each isogeny evaluation edge to show the dependency described above. The result of the first step is in Fig. 5(b). The second step is to remove the point $(0,0)$ and two edges from it. The task dependency graph D_S is shown in Fig. 5(c).

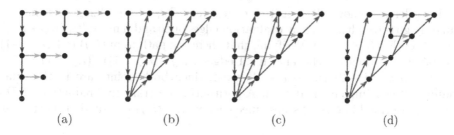

(a)   (b)   (c)   (d)

Fig. 5. Constructing the task dependency graph of a strategy.

3.2 Efficient Algorithm for Removing Transitive Edges

In the second part of the technique, we require that task dependency graphs must not have any transitive edge (Definition 6). We give an example below describing transitive edges in the task dependency graph of a strategy.

Example 4. In Fig. 5(c), the edge $\langle (0,2), (1,2) \rangle$ is transitive as $(0,2)$ reaches $(0,4)$ and $(0,4)$ reaches $(1,2)$. The edge $\langle (0,3), (1,3) \rangle$ is also transitive. These two edges are the only transitive edges in the graph. Figure 5(d) shows the graph with all transitive edges removed.

Aho, Garey, and Ullman [3] presented that, for a general directed graph, the task of removing all transitive edges from a graph, called *transitive reduction*, can be done in $O(|V|^{\log_2 7})$ steps. For D_S, it can be done in a more efficient way using the following lemma.

Lemma 2. *All transitive edges in a graph D_S must be of the form $\langle(i,j),(i+1,j)\rangle$. Also, the edge $\langle(i,j),(i+1,j)\rangle$ is transitive if and only if (i,j) reaches $(i, e - i - 1)$.*

Proof. For an edge $\langle u, v \rangle$ to be transitive in a directed acyclic graph, the out-degree of u and the in-degree of v must be more than 1. Therefore, all point multiplication edges of the form $\langle(i,j),(i,j+1)\rangle$ cannot be transitive.

Next, consider a diagonal edge of the form $\langle(i, e - i - 1),(i+1,j)\rangle$. If there exists another diagonal edge coming out of $(i, e - i - 1)$, its end point must be $(i+1, j')$ with $j' \neq j$. If $j' > j$, it is impossible that $(i+1, j')$ reaches $(i+1, j)$. If $j' < j$, $(i+1, j')$ can reach $(i+1, j)$ by going through a sequence of point multiplication edges. However, $(i+1, j)$ is the end point of the diagonal edge implies that it is the end point of the isogeny evaluation edge $\langle(i,j),(i+1,j)\rangle$. Thus, there is no point multiplication edges coming to $(i+1, j)$. By both cases, all diagonal edges cannot be transitive.

By Definition 7, for an isogeny evaluation edge of the form $\langle(i,j),(i+1,j)\rangle$, there must exist the diagonal edge $\langle(i, e-i-1),(i+1,j)\rangle$. These are only incoming edges to $(i+1, j)$. Therefore, if this isogeny evaluation edge is transitive, (i,j) must reach $(i, e - i - 1)$. This concludes the proof.

In order to remove all transitive edges from D_S, Lemma 2 suggests that we can only go through all isogeny evaluation edges once and remove $\langle(i,j),(i+1,j)\rangle$ if (i,j) reaches $(i, e-i-1)$. Verifying that there is a path from (i,j) to $(i, e-i-1)$ can be simply done by checking if all edges $\langle(i,j),(i,j+1)\rangle, \langle(i,j+1),(i,j+2)\rangle, \ldots, \langle(i, e-i-2),(i, e-i-1)\rangle$ exist, since both points are in the same column. When implemented as in Algorithm 5, the transitive reduction of D_S can be performed in $O(|V|)$ steps since each vertex (i,j) is visited at most once.

Algorithm 5: Transitive reduction algorithm for D_S.

Input : The task dependency graph $D_S = (V_{D_S}, E_{D_S})$ of a strategy S
Output: D_S with all transitive edges removed

1 **for** $i = 0$ **to** $e - 2$ **do**
2   **for** $j = e - i - 2$ **down to** 0 **do**
3   **if** $\langle(i,j),(i,j+1)\rangle \notin E_{D_S}$ **then break**
4   **if** $\langle(i,j),(i+1,j)\rangle \in E_{D_S}$ **then** $E_{D_S} \leftarrow E_{D_S} \setminus \{\langle(i,j),(i+1,j)\rangle\}$
5 **return** D_S

3.3 Proposed Strategy Evaluation Technique

After we construct the task dependency graph from a strategy and remove all transitive edges, precedence-constrained scheduling algorithms (Hu's and Coffman-Graham's algorithms) described in Subsect. 2.5 can be applied to obtain a scheduling. Although both algorithms assume that all tasks are of unit-length when scheduling, which is not the case for SIDH since $c_\downarrow \neq c_\rightarrow$, they can be used as an approximation algorithm in our settings. And even though our task dependency graphs D_S are not tree-like, we get interesting results when evaluating (or scheduling) a strategy using Hu's algorithm, where in our technique $\ell(u)$ is the length of a longest path starting at u. We describe our experiments in Sect. 5.

Because both scheduling algorithms are designed for unit-length tasks, we calculate the cost of a strategy evaluation from a scheduling as shown in Algorithm 6: for each $1 \leq i \leq t(\mathcal{S})$, if all tasks in s_i are point multiplications, the cost of s_i is $c_\downarrow$. If all tasks in s_i are isogeny evaluations, its cost is $c_\rightarrow$. Otherwise, its cost is $\max\{c_\downarrow, c_\rightarrow\}$. The costs of a strategy S when using Hu's and Coffman-Graham's algorithms with K processors are denoted by $C_K^{\mathrm{Hu}}(S)$ and $C_K^{\mathrm{CG}}(S)$, respectively.

Algorithm 6: Computing $C_K^{\mathrm{Hu}}(S)$ and $C_K^{\mathrm{CG}}(S)$ of a strategy S.

Input : A strategy $S = (V_S, E_S)$ for computing degree-ℓ^e isogeny and the number of provided processors K
Output: The cost $C_K^{\mathrm{Hu}}(S)$ or $C_K^{\mathrm{CG}}(S)$

1 Construct D_S from S following Definition 7
2 Remove all transitive edges from D_S following Algorithm 5
3 Label all vertices with $\ell(\cdot)$ or $\ell_{\mathrm{CG}}(\cdot)$ (Algorithm 4)
4 Construct a scheduling $\mathcal{S}$ from (D_S, K) using Algorithm 3
5 $cost \leftarrow 0$
6 **for** $k = 1$ **to** $t(\mathcal{S})$ **do**
7    $cost_k \leftarrow 0$
8   **for** $(i, j) \in s_k$ **do**
9   **if** $\langle(i, j-1), (i, j)\rangle \in E_S$ **then** $cost_k \leftarrow \max\{cost_k, c_\downarrow\}$
10   **else** $cost_k \leftarrow \max\{cost_k, c_\rightarrow\}$
11   $cost \leftarrow cost + cost_k$
12 **return** $cost$

Example 5. We explain how $C_K^{\mathrm{Hu}}(S)$ and $C_K^{\mathrm{CG}}(S)$ are computed for the strategy shown in Fig. 5(a). First, its D_S with all transitive edges removed is as Fig. 5(d). Next, vertices in D_S are labeled. The values of $\ell(\cdot)$ and $\ell_{\mathrm{CG}}(\cdot)$ are provided in Figs. 6(a) and 6(b), respectively. Let $K = 2$, both Hu's and Coffman-Graham's algorithms give the same scheduling $\mathcal{S} = \langle s_1, \dots, s_9 \rangle$ where $s_1 = \{(0, 1)\}$, $\dots$, $s_4 = \{(0, 4)\}$, $s_5 = \{(1, 3), (1, 0)\}$, $s_6 = \{(1, 2), (2, 0)\}$,

$s_7 = \{(2,2),(2,1)\}$, $s_8 = \{(3,1),(3,0)\}$, and $s_9 = \{(4,0)\}$. In s_5, $(1,3)$ and $(1,0)$ are computed by isogeny evaluations, thus $cost_5 = c_\rightarrow$. In s_7, $(2,2)$ is computed by isogeny evaluation and $(2,1)$ is computed by point multiplication, hence $cost_7 = \max\{c_\downarrow, c_\rightarrow\}$. The cost $C_K^{\text{Hu}}(S)$ and $C_K^{\text{CG}}(S)$ is thus $4c_\downarrow + 4c_\rightarrow + \max\{c_\downarrow, c_\rightarrow\}$. The evaluation when $c_\downarrow = c_\rightarrow = 1$ is shown in Fig. 6(c).

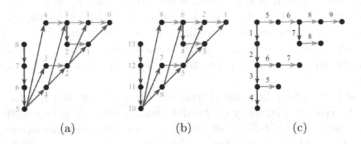

(a)   (b)   (c)

Fig. 6. The process of computing $C_K^{\text{Hu}}(S)$ and $C_K^{\text{CG}}(S)$ of a strategy S: (a) the values of $\ell(\cdot)$, (b) the values of $\ell_{\text{CG}}(\cdot)$, and (c) the evaluation when $K = 2$ and $c_\downarrow = c_\rightarrow = 1$.

4   Proposed Strategy Construction Technique

In addition to an evaluation technique that gives us a low cost from a strategy, we also need efficient strategies that would provide low costs. As discussed earlier, a strategy for the multi-processor setting have to be carefully constructed specifically for the parameter set $(e, c_\downarrow, c_\rightarrow, K)$. To construct those efficient strategies, we first formalize the problem mathematically as an integer linear program (ILP) and then use optimal solutions of the ILP to generate strategies.

4.1   Optimal Strategies and Evaluations

The problem of constructing a strategy and its evaluation is clearly an optimization problem. We call a pair of a strategy and its evaluation that provides the least cost as *optimal*. In this subsection, we will construct an optimal strategy and evaluation in the simplest case of $c_\downarrow = c_\rightarrow = 1$, which can be generalized to the case that $c_\downarrow = c_\rightarrow$.

Let $x_{i,j,t} \in \{0,1\}$ be a decision variable such that $x_{i,j,t} = 1$ if the point represented by the vertex (i,j) is computed and is available no later than time t and 0 otherwise. A discrete optimization problem of finding an optimal strategy and its evaluation can be formalized as an ILP as follows:

$$\underset{x_{i,j,t}}{\text{minimize}} \qquad T + 1 - \sum_{t'=0}^{T} x_{e-1,0,t'}$$

$$\text{subject to} \qquad x_{0,0,0} = 1$$

$$x_{i,j,0} = 0 \qquad (i,j) \neq (0,0)$$

$$x_{i,j,t} \geq x_{i,j,t-1}$$

$$x_{i,j,t} \leq x_{i,j-1,t-c_\downarrow} + \frac{x_{i-1,j,t-c_\rightarrow} + x_{i-1,e-i,t-c_\rightarrow}}{2}$$

$$\sum_{i,j}(x_{i,j,t+1} - x_{i,j,t}) \leq K$$

$$x_{i,j,t} \in \{0,1\}$$

The initial conditions for $x_{i,j,0}$ are $x_{0,0,0} = 1$, since it is available at the start of the isogeny computation, and $x_{i,j,0} = 0$ for $(i,j) \neq (0,0)$. If (i,j) is available no later than time $t - 1$, then it is also available no later than time t. Hence, we have the constraint $x_{i,j,t} \geq x_{i,j,t-1}$. Our objective is thus to minimize t' such that $x_{e-1,0,t'} = 1$, the time that $(e - 1, 0)$ is finished. However, we cannot straightforwardly use this as an objective function because t' is not a decision variable. We instead consider the sum of $x_{e-1,0,t'}$ for $0 \leq t' \leq T$ for some sufficiently large T. The earliest time t' at which $x_{e-1,0,t'} = 1$ can now be expressed by $T + 1 - \sum_{0 \leq t' \leq T} x_{e-1,0,t'}$, which is our objective function.

The fourth constraint comes from two restrictions of the isogeny computation discussed in Subsect. 2.4: $x_{i,j,t}$ can become 1 by one of these two cases: (i) $(i, j-1)$ is ready at time $t - c_\downarrow$ and (i, j) is computed by a point multiplication, or (ii) $(i - 1, j)$ and $(i - 1, e - i)$ are available at time $t - c_\rightarrow$ and (i, j) is computed by an isogeny evaluation. The first case is possible only if $x_{i,j-1,t-c_\downarrow} = 1$. For the second case, both $x_{i-1,j,t-c_\rightarrow}$ and $x_{i-1,e-i,t-c_\rightarrow}$ must be 1. Hence, we can perform the second case only if $\frac{1}{2}(x_{i-1,j,t-c_\rightarrow} + x_{i-1,e-i,t-c_\rightarrow}) = 1$. Because $x_{i,j,t}$ can become 1 by either of the two cases, the value of $x_{i,j,t}$ is restricted to

$$x_{i,j,t} \leq x_{i,j-1,t-c_\downarrow} + \frac{x_{i-1,j,t-c_\rightarrow} + x_{i-1,e-i,t-c_\rightarrow}}{2}.$$

The fifth constraint is the number of processors given. Since we are interested in the case that $c_\downarrow = c_\rightarrow = 1$, there can be up to K decision variables that change from 0 to 1 at each time, those represent points computed at that time. Therefore, we have $\sum_{i,j}(x_{i,j,t+1} - x_{i,j,t}) \leq K$.

Given the integer linear program of the problem, we can use a solver to find an optimal strategy and its evaluation. However, even in the case of small $e < 15$, the solver can take more than 30 min to produce a solution. This is expected due to the nature of integer linear programming which is NP-complete [19]. Although it is not practical to construct optimal strategies and evaluations for large e directly using ILP, we will use solutions for small e to construct a low-cost strategy for large e in the next subsection.

4.2 Proposed Strategy Construction Technique

In Subsect. 2.4, we state Theorem 1 from [18] for computing the cost of a least-cost (canonical) strategy under PCP. The theorem implicitly describes how this least-cost canonical strategy is constructed: a strategy with e leaves is divided into two smaller strategies with n and $e-n$ leaves, and the construction performs recursively until the base case $e = 1$ is reached. With the ILP we obtain in the previous subsection, we propose a new way of constructing a strategy which is by precomputing optimal strategies and evaluations for some e and then using them as base cases. We need to slightly modify the ILP in order to find optimal strategies and evaluations corresponding to $C_K^{\mathrm{PCP}}(e, k)$, but the main idea is the same. Strategies constructed by our proposed technique can then be viewed as a mixture of a canonical part when e is larger than the base case and a possibly non-canonical part when e is one of the base cases.

Similar to the proposed strategy evaluation technique in the previous section, we assume that $c_{\downarrow} = c_{\rightarrow}$ when we formulate the ILP, which is not the case for SIDH. Also, we only solve the ILP for up to some value of e and combine them for large e. Hence, strategies resulted from our construction technique are considered as approximations of a least-cost strategy.

5 Experiments and Results

For each parameter set $(e, c_{\downarrow}, c_{\rightarrow}, K)$, we conduct two experiments using our proposed strategy evaluation (Sect. 3) and construction (Sect. 4) techniques as follows:

- Experiment A: We use Theorem 1 to construct least-cost canonical strategies under PCP. Since there are many such strategies, we randomly sampled 100,000 of them for evaluation. The cost of strategy S is then computed as $\min\{C_K^{\mathrm{Hu}}(S), C_K^{\mathrm{CG}}(S)\}$.
- Experiment B: We randomly constructed 100,000 strategies using our proposed strategy construction technique described in Sect. 4, where we precomputed solutions for ILP for all $e \leq 14$. The cost of strategy S is also computed as $\min\{C_K^{\mathrm{Hu}}(S), C_K^{\mathrm{CG}}(S)\}$.

We conduct experiments under two sets of parameters from [21], which are also used by [18], for the purpose of comparison. Table 2 compares costs obtained by [18] and our experiments under the parameter set $(e, c_{\downarrow}, c_{\rightarrow}) = (186, 25.8, 22.8)$. Rows 3 and 5 show the smallest $\min\{C_K^{\mathrm{Hu}}(S), C_K^{\mathrm{CG}}(S)\}$ among all randomly sampled strategies in Experiment A and B, respectively. Table 3 reports the results under the parameter set $(e, c_{\downarrow}, c_{\rightarrow}) = (239, 27.8, 17)$. The cost reductions in both tables are compared to the costs under CCP.

The experimental results show the reductions of more than 10% in several cases, which is significant due to the fact that CCP has already improved the cost of PCP and the single-processor setting. Our strategy construction technique (Experiment B) works very well when $c_{\downarrow} \approx c_{\rightarrow}$ as seen in Table 2. We expect greater reductions when we precompute solutions of ILP for more values of e.

Table 2. The cost of best strategies under PCP, CCP, and in our experiments under the parameter set $(e, c_\downarrow, c_\rightarrow) = (186, 25.8, 22.8)$. The cost $C_1(e)$ for $K = 1$ is 34256.4.

	K	2	3	4	5	6	7	8
PCP	Cost	25942.2	22521.6	20373.0	19197.0	17941.2	16978.8	16617.0
CCP	Cost	23890.2	20515.2	18252.6	17555.4	16482.0	16021.2	15294.6
Exp. A	Cost	22203.0	18622.8	16337.4	15708.6	15091.2	14949.6	14063.4
	% reduction	7.06	9.22	10.49	10.52	8.44	6.69	8.05
Exp. B	Cost	22081.2	18340.2	16400.4	15269.4	14973.6	14999.4	14184.0
	% reduction	7.57	10.60	10.15	13.02	9.15	6.38	7.26

Table 3. The cost of best strategies under PCP, CCP, and in our experiments under the parameter set $(e, c_\downarrow, c_\rightarrow) = (239, 27.8, 17)$. The cost $C_1(e)$ for $K = 1$ is 41653.8.

	K	2	3	4	7	8
PCP	Cost	31886.0	27858.0	25328.8	21572.6	20851.2
CCP	Cost	29931.0	25835.0	23390.8	20399.6	19814.2
Exp. A	Cost	28265.0	23625.0	21282.8	19073.6	18641.2
	% reduction	5.57	8.55	9.01	6.50	5.92
Exp. B	Cost	28574.6	23731.0	21337.8	19319.0	18900.4
	% reduction	4.53	8.14	8.78	5.30	4.61

In addition, we point out that $C_K^{\mathrm{Hu}}(S)$ and $C_K^{\mathrm{CG}}(S)$ of the same strategy S are equal for all (canonical) strategies sampled in Experiment A, but these costs can be slightly different for some (possibly non-canonical) strategies sampled in Experiment B. When both costs are not equal, $C_K^{\mathrm{Hu}}(S)$ are smaller for some K and strategies, while $C_K^{\mathrm{CG}}(S)$ are smaller for some others. This shows that none of the algorithms provides the least cost for strategy evaluation.

6   Conclusion

We have studied the problem of constructing a strategy for computing degree-ℓ^e isogeny and evaluating it to achieve the least cost possible in the multi-processor setting. The proposed strategy evaluation technique transforms a strategy into a task dependency graph, where we apply precedence-constrained scheduling algorithms to it. Moreover, we have proposed a strategy construction technique which utilizes solutions of ILP for small e. Via experimental results, we have been able to obtain costs that are lower than those under PCP and CCP [18], which already improve the cost of an optimal strategy under the single-processor setting [13]. The improvements can get up to 13.02% under some specific parameter sets.

Although our results outperform those that currently exist in the literature, we note that the proposed strategy evaluation and construction techniques are yet to produce optimal strategy and evaluation. This is because there are several layers of approximation in our techniques: (i) the ILP is formulated only for $c_\downarrow = c_\rightarrow$, (ii) we combine optimal solutions of small e to have strategies for large e, and (iii) the scheduling algorithms also assume $c_\downarrow = c_\rightarrow$. One may need to remove these approximation layers to further reduce the cost.

It is also interesting to apply our techniques to other isogeny-based cryptosystems such as B-SIDH [11], CSIDH [7], and eSIDH [8]. We expect our techniques to be applicable to all schemes but with different degrees of reduction in costs: the techniques may work well with eSIDH as the isogeny degree is quite smooth, but might not work well with B-SIDH and CSIDH as the isogeny degrees are less smooth and they involve several primes with different costs of point multiplications and isogeny evaluations. Moreover, we are yet to implement or benchmark our techniques in hardware or software. These are parts of our future work.

Acknowledgement. The authors would like to thank Jason LeGrow and the reviewers for their constructive comments on improving the manuscript. The first author would like to thank Francisco Rodríguez-Henríquez and Kittiphop Phalakarn for their valuable feedback. The first author is supported by the Ripple Impact Fund through a Ripple Graduate Fellowship. The second author is supported by JSPS Grant-in-Aid for Transformative Research Areas A grant number JP21H05845.

References

1. NIST PQC standardization process: third round candidate announcement. https://csrc.nist.gov/News/2020/pqc-third-round-candidate-announcement. Accessed 2 Feb 2022
2. NIST PQC standardization project. https://csrc.nist.gov/projects/post-quantum-cryptography/post-quantum-cryptography-standardization. Accessed 2 Feb 2022
3. Aho, A.V., Garey, M.R., Ullman, J.D.: The transitive reduction of a directed graph. SIAM J. Comput. **1**(2), 131–137 (1972)
4. Alagic, G., et al.: Status report on the second round of the NIST post-quantum cryptography standardization process. US Department of Commerce, NIST (2020)
5. Azarderakhsh, R., et al.: Supersingular isogeny key encapsulation. Submission to the NIST Post-Quantum Standardization project, vol. 152, pp. 154–155 (2017)
6. Bernstein, D.J., De Feo, L., Leroux, A., Smith, B.: Faster computation of isogenies of large prime degree. Open Book Ser. **4**(1), 39–55 (2020)
7. Castryck, W., Lange, T., Martindale, C., Panny, L., Renes, J.: CSIDH: an efficient post-quantum commutative group action. In: Peyrin, T., Galbraith, S. (eds.) ASIACRYPT 2018. LNCS, vol. 11274, pp. 395–427. Springer, Cham (2018). https://doi.org/10.1007/978-3-030-03332-3_15
8. Cervantes-Vázquez, D., Ochoa-Jiménez, E., Rodríguez-Henríquez, F.: Extended supersingular isogeny Diffie-Hellman key exchange protocol: revenge of the SIDH. IET Inf. Secur. **15**, 364–374 (2021)
9. Cervantes-Vazquez, D., Ochoa-Jimenez, E., Rodriguez-Henriquez, F.: Parallel strategies for SIDH: towards computing SIDH twice as fast. IEEE Trans. Comput. **71**, 1249–1260 (2021)
10. Coffman, E.G., Graham, R.L.: Optimal scheduling for two-processor systems. Acta Informatica **1**(3), 200–213 (1972)

11. Costello, C.: B-SIDH: supersingular isogeny Diffie-Hellman using twisted torsion. In: Moriai, S., Wang, H. (eds.) ASIACRYPT 2020. LNCS, vol. 12492, pp. 440–463. Springer, Cham (2020). https://doi.org/10.1007/978-3-030-64834-3_15

12. Costello, C., Longa, P., Naehrig, M.: Efficient algorithms for supersingular isogeny Diffie-Hellman. In: Robshaw, M., Katz, J. (eds.) CRYPTO 2016. LNCS, vol. 9814, pp. 572–601. Springer, Heidelberg (2016). https://doi.org/10.1007/978-3-662-53018-4_21

13. De Feo, L., Jao, D., Plût, J.: Towards quantum-resistant cryptosystems from supersingular elliptic curve isogenies. J. Math. Cryptol. $8(3)$, 209–247 (2014)

14. Faz-Hernández, A., López, J., Ochoa-Jiménez, E., Rodríguez-Henríquez, F.: A faster software implementation of the supersingular isogeny Diffie-Hellman key exchange protocol. IEEE Trans. Comput. $67(11)$, 1622–1636 (2017)

15. Gangal, D., Ranade, A.: Precedence constrained scheduling in $(2 - \frac{7}{3p+1})$-optimal. J. Comput. Syst. Sci. $74(7)$, 1139–1146 (2008)

16. Garey, M.R., Johnson, D.S.: Computers and Intractability, vol. 174. Freeman San Francisco (1979)

17. Hu, T.C.: Parallel sequencing and assembly line problems. Oper. Res. $9(6)$, 841–848 (1961)

18. Hutchinson, A., Karabina, K.: Constructing canonical strategies for parallel implementation of isogeny based cryptography. In: Chakraborty, D., Iwata, T. (eds.) INDOCRYPT 2018. LNCS, vol. 11356, pp. 169–189. Springer, Cham (2018). https://doi.org/10.1007/978-3-030-05378-9_10

19. Karp, R.M.: Reducibility among combinatorial problems. In: Miller, R.E., Thatcher, J.W., Bohlinger, J.D. (eds.) Complexity of Computer Computations. The IBM Research Symposia Series. Springer, Boston (1972). https://doi.org/10.1007/978-1-4684-2001-2_9

20. Koziel, B., Ackie, A.B., Khatib, R.E., Azarderakhsh, R., Kermani, M.M.: SIKE'd up: fast hardware architectures for supersingular isogeny key encapsulation. IEEE Trans. Circ. Syst. I Regul. Pap. $67(12)$, 4842–4854 (2020). https://doi.org/10.1109/TCSI.2020.2992747

21. Koziel, B., Azarderakhsh, R., Mozaffari-Kermani, M.: Fast hardware architectures for supersingular isogeny Diffie-Hellman key exchange on FPGA. In: Dunkelman, O., Sanadhya, S.K. (eds.) INDOCRYPT 2016. LNCS, vol. 10095, pp. 191–206. Springer, Cham (2016). https://doi.org/10.1007/978-3-319-49890-4_11

22. Koziel, B., Jalali, A., Azarderakhsh, R., Jao, D., Mozaffari-Kermani, M.: NEON-SIDH: efficient implementation of supersingular isogeny Diffie-Hellman key exchange protocol on ARM. In: Foresti, S., Persiano, G. (eds.) CANS 2016. LNCS, vol. 10052, pp. 88–103. Springer, Cham (2016). https://doi.org/10.1007/978-3-319-48965-0_6

23. Lam, S., Sethi, R.: Worst case analysis of two scheduling algorithms. SIAM J. Comput. $6(3)$, 518–536 (1977)

24. Levey, E., Rothvoss, T.: A $(1 + \epsilon)$-approximation for makespan scheduling with precedence constraints using LP hierarchies. SIAM J. Comput. $50(3)$, 201–217 (2019)

25. Seo, H., Liu, Z., Longa, P., Hu, Z.: SIDH on ARM: faster modular multiplications for faster post-quantum supersingular isogeny key exchange. IACR Trans. Crypto. Hardware Embed. Syst. 2018, 1–20 (2018)

26. Ullman, J.D.: NP-complete scheduling problems. J. Comput. Syst. Sci. $10(3)$, 384–393 (1975)

27. Vélu, J.: Isogénies entre courbes elliptiques. CR Acad. Sci. Paris Sér. AB 273, A238–A241 (1971)

An Injectivity Analysis of Crystals-Kyber and Implications on Quantum Security

Xiaohui Ding[1](✉), Muhammed F. Esgin[1,2](✉), Amin Sakzad[1](✉),
and Ron Steinfeld[1](✉)

[1] Faculty of Information Technology, Monash University, Melbourne, Australia
xdin0011@student.monash.edu,
{muhammed.esgin,amin.sakzad,ron.steinfeld}@monash.edu
[2] CSIRO's Data61, Sydney, Australia

Abstract. The One-Way to Hiding (O2H) Lemma proposed by Bindel *et al.* (TCC '19) is a central component of proofs of chosen-ciphertext attack (CCA) security of practical public-key encryption schemes in the Quantum Random Oracle Model (QROM). Recently, Kuchta *et al.* (EUROCRYPT '20) introduced a new technique, called *measure-rewind-measure*, improving upon the O2H lemma. The latter gives a new security reduction that does not suffer from a squared security loss as in Bindel *et al.* (TCC '19) but has the number of queries Q as a multiplicative factor. This result is based on an injectivity assumption that requires the probability of two different messages generating the same ciphertext being negligible. The injectivity analysis of concrete schemes was left as an open problem by Kuchta *et al.* (EUROCRYPT '20).

In this paper, we complement the previous work by investigating the injectivity of a particular scheme in the third round National Institute of Standards and Technology (NIST) Post-Quantum Cryptography (PQC) standardization process. More precisely, we apply the techniques and constructions by Nguyen (ASIACRYPT '19), along with the approach of calculating decryption error by Bos *et al.* (EuroS&P '18), to obtain theoretical and numerical bounds on the injectivity of Crystals-Kyber, which points out a direction of resolving injectivity assumption of concrete scheme in the previous work. Our bounds also give the tightest concrete security guarantees for the QROM CCA security of Crystals-Kyber to date, based on the Module LWE hardness assumption.

Keywords: Post-quantum cryptography · Crystals-Kyber · One-way to hiding · Tight security

1 Introduction

Post-quantum cryptography (PQC) has been considered crucial and been constantly developed for the last two decades since the fast database search algorithm by Grover [10] and the fast integer factorization algorithm by Shor [17] on quantum computers were introduced. When a quantum processor with enough

K. Nguyen et al. (Eds.): ACISP 2022, LNCS 13494, pp. 332–351, 2022.
https://doi.org/10.1007/978-3-031-22301-3_17

qubits is built, it would put many current public-key cryptosystems in danger. That is why in 2016, NIST announced the first round PQC standardization process [13]. Now it is the third and the final round, and several cryptographic schemes have been selected to be the finalists. Crystals-Kyber [7], which utilises module learning with errors (MLWE) as its underlying mathematical problem, is one of the lattice-based cryptographic schemes in the final. There have been many applications of it in real world. For example, it was integrated in the CIRCL cryptography library of Cloudflare [18] and is also supported as one of the post-quantum Transport Layer Security (TLS) protocols in Amazon Web Services (AWS) key management service [20]. Our paper will focus on Kyber and investigate the injectivity of its key encapsulation mechanism.

Crystals-Kyber uses cryptographic hash functions to achieve indistinguishable chosen-ciphertext attack (IND-CCA) security. We model classical (respectively, quantum) attacks on schemes using these hash functions in the Random Oracle Model (respectively, the Quantum Random Oracle Model, QROM). First defined by Bellare and Rogaway in 1993 [4], ROM gives the attacker a mechanism (oracle) $\mathcal{O}$ that takes input query $x \in \{0,1\}^*$ and generates random output $\mathcal{O}(x) \in \{0,1\}^n$. If query x has appeared before, then $\mathcal{O}$ will return the same result as the first output. This is in contrast to a QROM $\mathcal{O}_q$, which was first introduced by Boneh et al. [6]. QROM replaces the query x and the output $\mathcal{O}$ with the qubit query $|\psi\rangle = \sum_i \alpha_i |\psi_i\rangle$ and the qubit output $\mathcal{O}_q |\psi\rangle = \sum_i \alpha_i |\mathcal{O}_q(\psi_i)\rangle$, where $\alpha_i \in \mathbb{C}$ are the complex coefficients of the superposition such that $\sum_i |\alpha_i|^2 = 1$.

One way to measure if a security reduction is tight is to calculate the reduction loss. Assume that the success probability of an adversary $\mathcal{A}$ taking time t to break an algorithm $\mathcal{C}$ is ϵ, and the success probability of a mathematician $\mathcal{B}$ taking time t' to solve the underlying hard mathematical problem of the algorithm $\mathcal{C}$ is ϵ'. The reduction cost and reduction loss are defined by [11] as $T := t - t'$ and $L := \epsilon/\epsilon'$. If L is a constant number or is small, we say the security reduction is tight. The concept is widely used in proving the security reductions from indistinguishable chosen-plaintext attack (IND-CPA) of a Public-Key Encryption (PKE) to indistinguishable chosen-ciphertext attack (IND-CCA) of a Key-Encapsulation Mechanism (KEM). By applying Fujisaki-Okamoto (FO) Transformation [8,9], the IND-CCA security of a KEM can be reduced to the IND-CPA security of its underlying PKE in the ROM. However, when the adversary has quantum access, the QROM should be taken into consideration.

Providing a tight security proof of FO transform under QROM has been the goal of a number of recent studies. In 2015, Unruh [19] introduced an approach called One Way to Hiding (O2H) lemma for (tighter) security proof. Several variants of O2H have been developed to investigate different aspects in the advantage of an adversary with the help of various assumptions. Ambainis et al. [2] put forward a semi-classical O2H to mitigate the problem of measuring in QROM. Adapting this work, Bindel et al. [5] introduced another O2H variant called 'double-sided', which has some additional assumptions than the original O2H [19] but also has a tighter security proof in some particular parameters. Later, Kuchta et al. [12] introduced and applied a novel measure-rewind-measure technique on this double-sided O2H lemma to a deterministic PKE (dPKE) introduced by Saito *et al.* [16] to obtain a result that does not suffer a square-root loss of advantage. In [12], Corollary 4.7, they summarise the advantage inequality as below:

$$\mathsf{Adv}_{\mathsf{FO}^{\not\perp}(\mathsf{P},\mathsf{F},G,H)}^{\mathsf{IND-CCA}}(\mathcal{A}) \leq Q^2 \cdot \mathsf{Adv}_{\mathsf{P}}^{\mathsf{IND-CPA}}(\mathcal{B}_1) + Q^2 \cdot (\delta + \sqrt{\eta}) + Q \cdot \eta + \mathsf{Adv}_{\mathsf{F}}^{\mathsf{PRF}}(\mathcal{B}_2),$$

where $\mathcal{A}$ is the IND-CCA adversary against security under $\mathsf{FO}^{\not\perp}$ transform - an implicit rejection variant of FO transform, $\mathcal{B}_1$ is the IND-CPA adversary against the dPKE P scheme, and $\mathcal{B}_2$ is the Pseudo-Random Function (PRF) adversary against function F. In this equation, Q is the total number of QROM queries, δ is the decryption failure error, and η is the injectivity. This remains an open problem of how to calculate η injectivity of concrete schemes, which is the collision probability of two different messages generating the same ciphertext by the scheme. To achieve the goal of λ-bit security guarantee for small Q, we need the bound on the adversary advantage in the right hand side of the above equation to be in the order of $2^{-\lambda}$ for small Q. Due to the square-root term $\sqrt{\eta}$, this implies that we need an injectivity bound in the order of $\eta \leq 2^{-2\lambda}$.

1.1 Our Contribution

Following the work done by Kuchta *et al.* [12], we initiate the investigation of the injectivity of concrete schemes. We present both theoretical and numerical upper bounds of η-injectivity of Crystals-Kyber giving the tightest concrete QROM security guarantees for the QROM CCA of Crystals-Kyber to date, based on the Module LWE hardness assumption. Our contributions are summarized as follows:

- We divide the injectivity analysis into three parts contributed by centered binomial distribution, module short integer solution (MSIS) problem, and law product and convolution. We then give a theoretical bound on injectivity of Kyber KEM as a combination of probability of these separated parts. A detailed theoretical bound is given in Theorem 2.
- We calculated numerical injectivity bound for Kyber512 to be 2^{-90}, for Kyber768 to be 2^{-433}, and for Kyber1024 to be 2^{-784}. The values of latter two are suitable for our assumption on $\eta \leq 2^{-2\lambda}$, which implies that the effect of injectivity in FO transformed KEM schemes is mild for Kyber768 and Kyber1024. The injectivity bound for Kyber512 is not as small as desired, and we leave it future work to study whether the bound can be further tightened.

2   Preliminaries

Rings, Matrices and Vectors. We use R to represent $\mathbb{Z}[X]/(X^n + 1)$ and R_q to represent $\mathbb{Z}_q[X]/(X^n + 1)$. The degree n of the monic polynomial is fixed to 256 in Kyber. Matrices and vectors are represented as bold upper-case and lower-case letters, respectively. We use $\mathbf{v}^T$ to represent the transpose of $\mathbf{v}$. We also set $[\beta] = \{-\beta, -\beta + 1, \ldots, 0, \ldots, \beta - 1, \beta\} \subseteq \mathbb{Z}_q$, where $\beta \geq 0$, to represent a symmetrical integer set.

Norm and Cardinality. For an element $w \in \mathbb{Z}_q$, we set l_∞-norm of w to be $\|w\|_\infty = |w \bmod^\pm q|$, where $\bmod^\pm q$ is the modulo operation that takes w to the range $\left[\frac{q}{2}\right]$. For a polynomial element $w = w_0 + w_1 X + \cdots + w_{n-1} X^{n-1} \in R$, the l_2 and l_∞ norm can be defined as the followings:

$$\|w\|_\infty = \max_i \|w_i\|_\infty, \quad \|w\| = \sqrt{\|w_0\|_\infty^2 + \cdots + \|w_{n-1}\|_\infty^2}.$$

For vector $\boldsymbol{w} = (w_1, \ldots, w_k) \in R^k$, the norms are defined as:

$$\|\boldsymbol{w}\|_\infty = \max_{1 \le i \le k} \|w_i\|_\infty, \|\boldsymbol{w}\| = \sqrt{\|w_1\|^2 + \cdots + \|w_k\|^2}.$$

As for a finite set $S \subseteq R^k$, we define $|S|$ as the cardinality of S and we have that that:

$$\|S\|_\infty = \max_{\boldsymbol{w} \in S} \|\boldsymbol{w}\|_\infty, \quad \|S\| = \max_{\boldsymbol{w} \in S} \|\boldsymbol{w}\|.$$

Sampling. Let $\mathcal{X}$ be a probability distribution. Then $X \sim \mathcal{X}$ represents random variable X following distribution $\mathcal{X}$, and $x \leftarrow \mathcal{X}$ represents value x being sampled from this distribution. For a polynomial $f \in R_q$ or a vector of such polynomials, this notation is defined coefficient-wise. Particularly, we denote $\beta_{2\eta}$ as the central binomial distribution.

Rounding. Let $x \in \mathbb{R}$ be a real number, then $\lceil x \rfloor$ means rounding to the closet integer with ties rounded up. We also use $\lceil x \rceil$ to represent round up and $\lfloor x \rfloor$ as rounding down.

Compress and Decompress. Let $x \in \mathbb{Z}_q$ and $d \in \mathbb{Z}$ be such that $d < \lceil \log_2(q) \rceil$. Adapted from [7], the Compress and Decompress functions are:

$$\mathsf{Compress}_q(x, d) = \lceil (2^d/q) \cdot x \rfloor \bmod^+ 2^d,$$
$$\mathsf{Decompress}_q(x, d) = \lceil (q/2^d) \cdot x \rfloor.$$

2.1 Injectivity

Adapted from Definition 6 of [5] and Definition 4.3 of [12], the injectivity that we will investigate is defined as below:

Definition 1 (Injectivity of a dPKE [5,12]). *Let $\eta \geqslant 0$. A dPKE scheme* $\mathsf{P} = (\mathsf{KeyGen}, \mathsf{Encr}, \mathsf{Decr})$ *is η-injective if*

$$\Pr\left(\mathsf{Encr(pk, \cdot)} \text{ is not injective: } (\mathsf{pk}, \mathsf{sk}) \leftarrow \mathsf{KeyGen}(1^\lambda), H \xleftarrow{\$} \mathcal{H}\right) \le \eta,$$

where $H \xleftarrow{\$} \mathcal{H}$ is sampling a random element H uniformly from a finite set $\mathcal{H}$ of random function, and a dPKE means PKE that has a deterministic encryption scheme.

2.2   Crystals-Kyber Scheme

The PQC scheme that we are going to investigate is Crystals-Kyber [7]. Let n, k, d_t, d_u, d_v be positive integers and $\mathcal{M}$ denotes the message spaces with 256-bit message. We put the PKE algorithms of Kyber here as a reference.

Sam. Let x be a bit string and S be a distribution taking x as the input, then $y \sim S := \mathsf{Sam}\,(x)$ represents that the output y generated by distribution S and input x can be extended to any desired length.

Algorithm 1. Kyber.CPA.KeyGen(1^λ): key generation [7], pg.5, Algorithm 1

1: $\rho, \sigma \leftarrow \{0,1\}^{256}$
2: $\mathbf{A} \sim R_q^{k \times k} := \mathsf{Sam}(\rho)$
3: $(s, e) \sim \beta_\eta^k \times \beta_\eta^k := \mathsf{Sam}(\sigma)$
4: $t := \mathsf{Compress}_q(\mathbf{A}s + e, d_t)$
5: **return** $(pk := (\mathbf{t}, \rho), sk := s)$

Algorithm 2. Kyber.CPA.Enc $(pk = (\mathbf{t}, \rho), m \in \mathcal{M})$ [7], pg. 5, Algorithm 2

1: $r \leftarrow \{0,1\}^{256}$
2: $\mathbf{t} := \mathsf{Decompress}_q(\mathbf{t}, d_t)$
3: $\mathbf{A} \sim R_q^{k \times k} := \mathsf{Sam}(\rho)$
4: $(\mathbf{r}, e_1, e_2) \sim \beta_\eta^k \times \beta_\eta^k \times \beta_\eta^k := \mathsf{Sam}(r)$
5: $\mathbf{u} := \mathsf{Compress}_q(\mathbf{A}^T \mathbf{r} + e_1, d_u)$
6: $v := \mathsf{Compress}_q(\mathbf{t}^T \mathbf{r} + e_2 + \lceil \frac{q}{2} \rceil \cdot m, d_v)$
7: **return** $c := (\mathbf{u}, v)$

Algorithm 3. Kyber.CPA.Dec($sk = s, c = (\boldsymbol{u}, v)$)[7], pg.5, Algorithm 3

1: $\boldsymbol{u} := \mathsf{Decompress}_q(\boldsymbol{u}, d_u)$
2: $v := \mathsf{Decompress}_q(v, d_v)$
3: **return** $\mathsf{Compress}_q(v - s^T \boldsymbol{u}, 1)$

2.3   Methodologies and Techniques

2.3.1   Operations on Probability

Adapted from [14], we present some techniques of calculating probability as the multiplication of polynomials.

Law Convolution. Suppose A and B are random variables over $[\alpha]$ and $[\beta]$, respectively. Let a_i, b_j be the probability of A, B being equal to i, j for all $i \in [\alpha]$ and $j \in [\beta]$. Then we generate two polynomials

$$A(X) = \sum_{i=-\alpha}^{\alpha} a_i X^i, B(X) = \sum_{j=-\beta}^{\beta} b_j X^j$$

to represent the probability of all possible outcomes of A and B. Now, define

$$C(X) = A(X) \cdot B(X) = \sum_{k=-(\alpha+\beta)}^{\alpha+\beta} c_k X^k$$

to be the product of $A(X)$ and $B(X)$, where $k = i + j$ for each i, j. One can observe that the coefficient c_k is actually the probability of the sum of two independent random variables A and B being equal to k, i.e.,

$$\Pr(A + B = k) = C_k.$$

Thus, $C(X)$ in fact can be used to represent the probability distribution of $A + B$. If we want to investigate the probability of independent multivariate, we can simply repeat the multiplication.

Law Product. Now we want to calculate the probability of the product of two independent random variables A and B. Let $A(X)$, $B(X)$ to be the polynomials as above. Then, define

$$D(X) = \sum_{i=-\alpha}^{\alpha} \sum_{j=-\beta}^{\beta} a_i b_j X^{ij} = \sum_{k=-\alpha\beta}^{\alpha\beta} d_k X^k$$

to be the law product of the two distribution, which represents probability distribution of $A \cdot B$.

Union Bound. Let $\{A_1, A_2, \ldots\}$ be a finite set of events (don't have to be independent), then the probability of at least one happens is less or equal to the the summarized probability of every events as described below:

$$\Pr\left(\cup_{i=1}^{\infty} A_i\right) \leq \sum_{i=1}^{\infty} \Pr(A_i).$$

This is also called Boole's inequality.

2.3.2   Operations on R_q

Adapted from [14], an efficient way to calculate polynomial multiplication over the module quotient ring R_q is converting the coefficients in the polynomials into a matrix and a vector in the original integer commutative ring. Let $a, b \in R_q$, and f denotes the monic polynomial $f(X)$ as the quotient of the ring. For convenience, we set the degree to be d for both a and b. The multiplication of a and b can be written as:

$$a \cdot b \bmod f = a \cdot \left(\sum_{i=0}^{d-1} b_i X^i\right) \bmod f = \sum_{i=0}^{d-1} (aX^i \bmod f) \cdot b_i.$$

We now define $\mathcal{V}_b \in \mathbb{Z}_q^{d \times 1}, \mathcal{M}_a \in \mathbb{Z}_q^{d \times d}$ as below:

$$\mathcal{V}_b = \begin{pmatrix} b_0 \\ b_1 \\ \vdots \\ b_{d-1} \end{pmatrix}, \quad \mathcal{M}_a = \begin{bmatrix} \mathcal{V}_a & \mathcal{V}_{aX \bmod f} & \cdots & \mathcal{V}_{aX^{d-1} \bmod f} \end{bmatrix}.$$

The multiplication $a \cdot b$ then can be represented as $\mathcal{M}_a \mathcal{V}_b \in \mathbb{Z}_q^{d \times 1}$. Similarly, if we expand this technique and apply it on vector $\boldsymbol{a}, \boldsymbol{b} \in R_q^k$, the rotated vector and matrix can also be defined as:

$$
\mathcal{V}_b = \begin{pmatrix} \mathcal{V}_{b_0} \\ \mathcal{V}_{b_1} \\ \vdots \\ \mathcal{V}_{b_{k-1}} \end{pmatrix} = \begin{pmatrix} b_{0,0} \\ \vdots \\ b_{0,d-1} \\ \vdots \\ b_{k-1,d-1} \end{pmatrix} \in \mathbb{Z}_q^{dk \times 1},
$$

and

$$
\begin{aligned}
\mathcal{M}_{\boldsymbol{a}^T} &= \begin{bmatrix} \mathcal{M}_{a_0} \ \mathcal{M}_{a_1} \ \cdots \ \mathcal{M}_{a_{k-1}} \end{bmatrix} \\
&= \begin{bmatrix} \mathcal{V}_{a_0} \ \mathcal{V}_{a_0 X \bmod f} \ \cdots \ \mathcal{V}_{a_0 X^{d-1} \bmod f} \ \cdots \ \mathcal{V}_{a_{k-1} X^{d-1} \bmod f} \end{bmatrix} \in \mathbb{Z}_q^{d \times dk}.
\end{aligned}
$$

Now, if we want to calculate $\boldsymbol{a}^T \cdot \boldsymbol{b} \in R_q$, the representation on the integer ring will be:

$$
\mathcal{M}_{\boldsymbol{a}^T} \cdot \mathcal{V}_b = \mathcal{V}_{\boldsymbol{a}^T \cdot b} \in \mathbb{Z}_q^{d \times 1}.
$$

Special Coefficients. Even with the algebraic representation of a polynomial, the modulo operation on each polynomial is still difficult to calculate. Thus, the monic polynomial f can be set to $X^n \pm 1$ with special property that the integer elements of the matrix and vector are consistent with the original coefficients in the polynomial. For example, the quotient polynomial is set to be $X^n + 1$ in Kyber, where $n = 256$. Let $a, b \in R_q$, the multiplication of a and b can be represented the same way above:

$$
\begin{aligned}
\mathcal{M}_a \cdot \mathcal{V}_b &= \begin{pmatrix} a_0 & -a_{n-1} & \cdots & -a_2 & -a_1 \\ a_1 & a_0 & \cdots & -a_3 & -a_2 \\ \vdots & \vdots & \ddots & \vdots & \vdots \\ a_{n-2} & a_{n-3} & \cdots & a_0 & -a_{n-1} \\ a_{n-1} & a_{n-2} & \cdots & a_1 & a_0 \end{pmatrix} \cdot \begin{pmatrix} b_0 \\ b_1 \\ \vdots \\ b_{n-2} \\ b_{n-1} \end{pmatrix} \\
&= \begin{pmatrix} R_0 \ R_1 \ \cdots \ R_{n-2} \ R_{n-1} \end{pmatrix} \otimes \begin{pmatrix} a_0 \\ a_1 \\ \vdots \\ a_{n-2} \\ a_{n-1} \end{pmatrix} \cdot \begin{pmatrix} b_0 \\ b_1 \\ \vdots \\ b_{n-2} \\ b_{n-1} \end{pmatrix},
\end{aligned}
$$

where $R_0 = I_n$, $R_i = \begin{pmatrix} 0 & -I_i \\ I_{n-i} & 0 \end{pmatrix}$ for $i = 1, ..., n-1$. It can be easily seen that all the columns in $\mathcal{M}_a$ are transformation of the first column with coefficients 1 or -1. This is also why most cryptographic schemes operate on $\mathbb{Z}_q[X]/(X^n \pm 1)$. This property will also be used in our later proof.

2.3.3   Centred Binomial Distribution

The coefficient of x^k in the binomial expansion $(x+1)^{\eta_0}$ is given by $\binom{\eta_0}{k} = \frac{\eta_0!}{k!(\eta_0-k)!}$. When sampled symmetrically around 0, the coefficient becomes: $\binom{2\eta_0}{i} = \frac{(2\eta_0)!}{(\eta_0+i)!(\eta_0-i)!}$, where $i \in [\eta_0]$. Therefore, we give the definition of a centred binomial distribution as below:

Definition 2 (Centred Binomial Distribution). *Let $X \sim \beta_{2\eta_0}$ represent random variable X sampled from integer range $[\eta_0]$ that follows centered binomial distribution (CBD), where $\eta_0 > 0$. The probability of each outcome of X can be defined as:*

$$\Pr(X = i) = \frac{(2\eta_0)!}{(\eta_0+i)!(\eta_0-i)!} \cdot 2^{-2\eta_0}.$$

If we represent the probability of all outcomes of X in one polynomial:

$$\Pr(X) = \sum_{i=-\eta_0}^{\eta_0} \frac{(2\eta_0)!}{(\eta_0+i)!(\eta_0-i)!} \cdot 2^{-2\eta_0} \cdot X^i,$$

the polynomial then can be used to calculate the probability of the difference between 2 independent random variables X_1, X_2 being some value by combining technique in Sect. 2.3.1. Let $X_1, X_2 \sim \beta_{2\eta_0}$, the probability distribution of $X_1 - X_2$ can be written as:

$$\Pr(X_1 - X_2) = \Pr(X_1) \cdot \Pr(X_2) = \sum_{i=-2\eta_0}^{2\eta_0} p_i X^i. \tag{1}$$

2.3.4   Module Short Integer Solution Problem

The short integer solution (SIS) problem can be briefly described as finding a short vector in a random lattice. When the lattice is defined on a module polynomial ring R_q, we call finding a short vector in such a lattice as module short integer solution (MSIS) problem. We adapt Theorem 1.1 and Corollary 3.9 of [15] for calculating the probability of MSIS problem.

Theorem 1. *[Adapted from [15], Theorem 1.1 and Corollary 3.9] Denote $S_\alpha := \{y \in R_q : \|y\|_\infty \le \alpha\}$ and let $l, k, \alpha_1, \alpha_2 \in \mathbb{N}$. q is a prime number with no further assumption. d is the degree of splitting the quotient polynomial $f(X) = X^n + 1$. Also, for $i = 1, ..., d$, define $W_i \subseteq R_q$ to be a set of polynomials st. $\forall u, v \in W_i$,*

$|\mathsf{Zero}(u - v)| < i$. *Then*

$$\Pr_{A \leftarrow R_q^{k \times l}}[\exists (z_1, z_2) \in S_{\alpha_1}^l \setminus \{0\} \times S_{\alpha_2}^k : Az_1 + z_2 = 0]$$

$$\leq \frac{|S_{\alpha_1}|^l \cdot |S_{\alpha_2}|^k}{q^{nk}} + \sum_{i=1}^{e} \frac{\binom{d}{i} \cdot |S_{\alpha_1 + \|W_i\|_\infty}|^l \cdot |S_{\alpha_2 + \|W_i\|_\infty}|^k}{|W_i|^{l+k} \cdot q^{nk(1-i/d)}},$$

where e is the largest number such that $\alpha_1 \sqrt{n} \geq q^{e/d}$, and $|\mathsf{Zero}(y)|$ is a finite set such that:

$$\mathsf{Zero}(y) := \{i : y \equiv 0 \, (\mathrm{mod} \, (f_i(X), q))\}.$$

3   Theoretical Bounds for Crystals-Kyber

Now we give details of calculating the η-injectivity of Kyber.

3.1   Main Result

We first give a theorem for Kyber injectivity as below and later demonstrate some essential lemmas for calculating the final equation.

Theorem 2 (η-injectivity of Kyber). *Let k, η_1, η_2 be positive integer parameters. Let n represent the number of coefficients in a polynomial in the ring R_q, d represent the splitting degree, and $d_u, d_v < \lceil \log_2(q) \rceil$ be compression parameters. The injectivity defined in Definition 1 of Kyber is upper bounded by:*

$$\eta \leq \binom{2n}{2} \cdot \left[r_0 \cdot \sum_{j \in [\gamma_u]} e_j + (1 - r_0) \cdot \left\{ \left(\frac{(4\eta_1 + 1)(4\eta_2 + 2\gamma_u + 1)}{q} \right)^{nk} \right. \right.$$

$$\left. \left. + \sum_{i=1}^{e} \binom{d}{i} \cdot \frac{1}{|W_i|^{2k}} \cdot \left\{ \frac{(4\eta_1 + 2\|W_i\|_\infty + 1)(4\eta_2 + 2\gamma_u + 2\|W_i\|_\infty + 1)}{q^{(1-i/d)}} \right\}^{nk} \right\} \right]$$

$$\cdot n \cdot \sum_{i=\gamma_m - \gamma_v}^{\gamma_m + \gamma_v} p_i, \tag{2}$$

where $e = \lfloor d \cdot \log_q(2\eta_1\sqrt{n}) \rfloor$, r_0, e_j and p_i are from (9), (10), and (14), respectively. The set W_i is constructed from (12). The integers $\gamma_u, \gamma_v, \gamma_m$ are defined as $\gamma_u := \lfloor \frac{q}{2^{d_u}} \rfloor$, $\gamma_v := \lfloor \frac{q}{2^{d_v}} \rfloor$, and $\gamma_m := \pm \lceil \frac{q}{2} \rceil$.

Proof. Let $m, m' \in \mathcal{B}^{32}$ be 32-byte (256-bit) stream messages. According to Algorithm 2, Definition 1, if we want to find η-injectivity for Kyber KEM, we have to calculate the upper bound of the probability of at least one pair of 2 different messages such that the output ciphertexts of them are the same. We first apply union bound on the total message space:

$$\eta = \Pr\left(\cup_{m \neq m'} c(m) = c(m') \right) \leq \sum_{m \neq m'} \Pr(\exists m \neq m' \text{ s.t. } c(m) = c(m'))$$

$$= M \cdot \max_{m \neq m'} [\Pr(c(m) = c(m'))],$$

where M is the total number of pairs $m \neq m'$. Since each message has 256 bits, M takes the value of $\binom{2^n}{2}$, where $n = 256$. Then, we plug in definitions of c_1 and c_2 from line 5 and 6 of Algorithm 2, respectively:

$$\eta \leq M \cdot \max_{m \neq m'} \left[\Pr(c_1 = c_1' \text{ and } c_2(m) = c_2(m')) \right]$$

$$= M \cdot \max_{m \neq m'} \left[\Pr \left(\Delta\mathsf{Compress}_q(\boldsymbol{u}, d_u) = \boldsymbol{0} \text{ and } \Delta\mathsf{Compress}_q(v, d_v) = 0 \right) \right],$$

where

$$\Delta\mathsf{Compress}_q(\boldsymbol{u}, d_u) := \mathsf{Compress}_q(\boldsymbol{u}, d_u) - \mathsf{Compress}_q(\boldsymbol{u}', d_u), \qquad (3)$$

$$\Delta\mathsf{Compress}_q(v, d_v) := \mathsf{Compress}_q(v, d_v) - \mathsf{Compress}_q(v', d_v). \qquad (4)$$

From Algorithm 1 and Algorithm 2, we can clearly see that v and u are dependent. Thus, if we define the compression of $\mathbf{u}$ and $\mathbf{u}'$ being equal as event U and the compression of v and v' being equal as V, we can further write the injectivity as:

$$\eta \leq M \cdot [\Pr(U \cap V)] = M \cdot [\Pr(U) \cdot \Pr(V \mid U)]. \qquad (5)$$

We first look at $\Pr(U)$. By applying Lemma 1, we get the coefficient-wise equation below:

$$\Delta\mathsf{Compress}_q(\boldsymbol{u}, d_u) = \boldsymbol{0} \Rightarrow \|\boldsymbol{u} - \boldsymbol{u}'\|_\infty < \frac{q}{2^{d_u}}$$

for (3). By line 5, Algorithm 2, we substitute $\boldsymbol{u} := \boldsymbol{A}^T \boldsymbol{r} + \boldsymbol{e}_1 \in R_q^k$ into the above equation to obtain:

$$\left\| \left(\boldsymbol{A}^T \boldsymbol{r} + \boldsymbol{e}_1 \right) - \left(\boldsymbol{A}^T \boldsymbol{r}' + \boldsymbol{e}_1' \right) \right\|_\infty = \left\| \boldsymbol{A}^T \Delta \boldsymbol{r} + \Delta \boldsymbol{e}_1 \right\|_\infty < \frac{q}{2^{d_u}}.$$

It is also noticed that the numbers are all integers. Thus, we get:

$$\Pr \left(\left\| \boldsymbol{A}^T \Delta \boldsymbol{r} + \Delta \boldsymbol{e}_1 \right\|_\infty < \frac{q}{2^{d_u}} \right) = \Pr \left(\boldsymbol{A}^T \Delta \boldsymbol{r} + \Delta \boldsymbol{e}_1 \in [\gamma_u] \right),$$

where $\gamma_u := \lfloor \frac{q}{2^{d_u}} \rfloor$, and the equation is also coefficient-wise. We can further split this probability into two parts by letting $\Delta \boldsymbol{r} = \boldsymbol{0}$ or $\Delta \boldsymbol{r} \neq \boldsymbol{0}$. This defines:

$$P_{CBD} := \Pr \left(\boldsymbol{A}^T \Delta \boldsymbol{r} + \Delta \boldsymbol{e}_1 \in [\gamma_u] \cap \Delta \boldsymbol{r} = \boldsymbol{0} \right)$$

and

$$P_{MSIS} := \Pr \left(\boldsymbol{A}^T \Delta \boldsymbol{r} + \Delta \boldsymbol{e}_1 \in [\gamma_u] \cap \Delta \boldsymbol{r} \neq \boldsymbol{0} \right).$$

with this, we have: $\Pr(U) = P_{CBD} + P_{MSIS}$. By adapting Lemma 2, we have:

$$P_{CBD} = r_0 \cdot \sum_{j \in [\gamma_u]} e_j,$$

where r_0 is the probability of $\Delta r = 0$, and e_j is the probability of $\Delta e_1 = j$, for all coefficients of j in range $[\gamma_u]$. Now using Lemma 3 gives:

$$P_{MSIS} \leq (1 - r_0) \cdot \left\{ \left(\frac{(4\eta_1 + 1)(4\eta_2 + 2\gamma_u + 1)}{q} \right)^{nk} + \sum_{i=1}^{e} \binom{d}{i} \cdot \frac{1}{|W_i|^{2k}} \right.$$
$$\left. \cdot \left\{ \frac{(4\eta_1 + 2\|W_i\|_\infty + 1) \cdot (4\eta_2 + 2\gamma_u + 2\|W_i\|_\infty + 1)}{q^{(1-i/d)}} \right\}^{nk} \right\}.$$

We now look at $\Pr(V \mid U)$. Similarly as U part, we have:

$$\Delta \mathsf{Compress}_q(v, d_v) = 0 \Rightarrow \|v - v'\|_\infty < \frac{q}{2^{d_v}}.$$

We substitute Line 4 in Algorithm 1 to obtain:

$$\Delta v = \left(t^T r + e_2 + \left\lceil \frac{q}{2} \right\rceil m \right) - \left(t^T r' + e_2' + \left\lceil \frac{q}{2} \right\rceil m' \right)$$
$$= t^T \Delta r + \Delta e_2 + \left\lceil \frac{q}{2} \right\rceil \Delta m = \left(s^T A^T + e^T \right) \Delta r + \Delta e_2 + \left\lceil \frac{q}{2} \right\rceil \Delta m. \quad (6)$$

It can be calculated on the condition that U part holds $A^T \Delta r = e_u - \Delta e_1$, where e_u is a polynomial vector whose coefficients are all in range $[\gamma_u]$. Therefore, (6) can be written as:

$$\Delta v = s^T e_u - s^T \Delta e_1 + e^T \Delta r + \Delta e_2 + \left\lceil \frac{q}{2} \right\rceil \Delta m.$$

In fact, let $P_V := \Pr(V \mid U)$. Later, we calculate $P_V \leq n \cdot \sum_{i=\gamma_m - \gamma_v}^{\gamma_m + \gamma_v} p_i$, where all parameters and p_i are defined in Lemma 4.

Finally, we summarise the above steps to obtain the theoretical bound of Kyber injectivity:

$$\eta \leq M \cdot [\Pr(U) \cdot \Pr(V \mid U)] \leq M \cdot [P_{CBD} + P_{MSIS}] \cdot P_V,$$

which results in (2). $\square$

3.2   Associated Lemmas and Their Proofs

Now we demonstrate several lemmas to help us compute each component of η-injectivity.

Lemma 1 (Compress$_q$ Equality Condition). *Let $x, x' \in \mathbb{Z}_q$ and $d \in \mathbb{Z}$ be such that $d < \lceil \log_2(q) \rceil$, then we have:*

$$\mathsf{Compress}_q(x, d) - \mathsf{Compress}_q(x', d) = 0 \Rightarrow |x - x'| < \frac{q}{2^d}. \quad (7)$$

Proof. We first look at the rounding of x, x'. If $\lceil x \rfloor - \lceil x' \rfloor = 0$, then we have $|x - x'| < 1$. If x, x' are multiplied by a constant c, this can be further written as:

$$\lceil cx \rfloor - \lceil cx' \rfloor = 0 \Rightarrow |cx - cx'| < 1 \Longleftrightarrow |x - x'| < \frac{1}{|c|}.$$

Now, we look at the equation defined by [3]:

$$\mathsf{Compress}_q(x, d) = \lceil (2^d/q) \cdot x \rfloor \bmod^+ 2^d.$$

Since

$$\lceil (2^d/q) \cdot x \rfloor \in [0, \dots, 2^d) \ \ for \ \forall x \in \mathbb{Z}_q,$$

the mapping is one-to-one. Therefore, the difference between two compressed inputs is calculated by:

$$\begin{aligned} \Delta\mathsf{Compress}_q(x, d) &:= \mathsf{Compress}_q(x, d) - \mathsf{Compress}_q(x', d) \\ &= \lceil (2^d/q) \cdot x \rfloor \bmod^+ 2^d - \lceil (2^d/q) \cdot x' \rfloor \bmod^+ 2^d \\ &= \lceil (2^d/q) \cdot x \rfloor - \lceil (2^d/q) \cdot x' \rfloor. \end{aligned}$$

This is the condition for two compressed inputs being equal as in (7). This results can be generalised to vectors in a component-wise fashion. □

Lemma 2 (CBD Injectivity). *Let $r, r' \in R_q^k$ be samples from $\beta_{2\eta_1}$ and $e_1, e_1' \in R_q^k$ be samples from $\beta_{2\eta_2}$. Let d_u be a positive integer that $d_u < \lceil \log_2(q) \rceil$. The probability P_{CBD} of CBD part injectivity is given by:*

$$P_{CBD} = r_0 \cdot \sum_{j \in [\gamma_u]} e_j, \tag{8}$$

where $\gamma_u := \lfloor \frac{q}{2^{d_u}} \rfloor$, and

$$\sum_{j=-2nk\eta_1}^{2nk\eta_1} r_j X^j = \left(\sum_{i=-\eta_1}^{\eta_1} \frac{(2\eta_1)!}{(\eta_1+i)!(\eta_1-i)!} \cdot 2^{-2\eta_1} \cdot X^i \right)^{2nk}, \tag{9}$$

$$\sum_{j=-2nk\eta_2}^{2nk\eta_2} e_j X^j = \left(\sum_{i=-\eta_2}^{\eta_2} \frac{(2\eta_2)!}{(\eta_2+i)!(\eta_2-i)!} \cdot 2^{-2\eta_2} \cdot X^i \right)^{2nk}. \tag{10}$$

Proof. The probability is an intersection of two independent events, which can be written as:

$$P_{CBD} = \Pr(\Delta r = 0) \cdot \Pr(\Delta e_1 \in [\gamma_u]).$$

Let R, R', E_1, E_1' be random variables which represent single coefficient of r, r', e_1, e_1'. By applying (1), the probability polynomials of Δr and Δe_1 are given by:

$$\Pr(\Delta r) = (\Pr(R) \cdot \Pr(R'))^{nk} = \Pr(R)^{2nk}$$

$$= \left(\sum_{i=-\eta_1}^{\eta_1} \frac{(2\eta_1)!}{(\eta_1+i)!(\eta_1-i)!} \cdot 2^{-2\eta_1} \cdot X^i \right)^{2nk} = \sum_{j=-2nk\eta_1}^{2nk\eta_1} r_j X^j.$$

and $\Pr(\Delta e_1) = \left(\sum\limits_{i=-\eta_2}^{\eta_2} \frac{(2\eta_2)!}{(\eta_2+i)!(\eta_2-i)!} \cdot 2^{-2\eta_2} \cdot X^i \right)^{2nk} = \sum\limits_{j=-2nk\eta_2}^{2nk\eta_2} e_j X^j.$

Thus, we obtain the total probability of CBD injectivity as (8), where r_0 is from (9) by setting $j = 0$ and e_j is from (10). □

Lemma 3 (MSIS Injectivity). *Let* $r, r' \in R_q^k$ *be samples from* $\beta_{2\eta_1}$ *and* $e_1, e'_1 \in R_q^k$ *be samples from* $\beta_{2\eta_2}$. *Let* d_u *be a positive integer such that* $d_u < \lceil \log_2(q) \rceil$. *The probability* P_{MSIS} *of MSIS part injectivity is given by:*

$$P_{MSIS} \leq (1 - r_0) \cdot \left\{ \left(\frac{(4\eta_1 + 1)(4\eta_2 + 2\gamma_u + 1)}{q} \right)^{nk} + \sum_{i=1}^{e} \binom{d}{i} \cdot \frac{1}{|W_i|^{2k}} \right.$$
$$\left. \cdot \left\{ \frac{(4\eta_1 + 2\|W_i\|_\infty + 1) \cdot (4\eta_2 + 2\gamma_u + 2\|W_i\|_\infty + 1)}{q^{(1-i/d)}} \right\}^{nk} \right\}, \tag{11}$$

where $\gamma_u := \lfloor \frac{q}{2^{d_u}} \rfloor$, r_0 *is the probability of* Δr *being* $\mathbf{0}$ *in* (9), e *is the largest number such that* $2\eta_1 \sqrt{n} \geq q^{e/d}$, *and* W_i *is a finite set constructed by* [15].

Proof. The probability of $\Delta r \neq \mathbf{0}$ and $A^T \Delta r + \Delta e_1 \in [\gamma_u]$ can be calculated by using Theorem 1 on concrete Kyber parameters. Assume $A^T \Delta r + \Delta e_1 = e_u$, then e_u is a vector of polynomials whose coefficients are in the finite set $[\gamma_u]$. This equation then can be written as

$$A^T \Delta r + (\Delta e_1 - e_u) = \mathbf{0}.$$

We want to replace z_1, z_2 in Theorem 1 by our $\Delta r, (\Delta e_1 - e_u)$ so that we can have:

$$\Pr_{A \leftarrow R_q^{k \times k}} \left[\exists (\Delta r, \Delta e_1 - e_u) \in S_{\theta_1}^k \setminus \{\mathbf{0}\} \times S_{\theta_2}^k : A^T \Delta r + (\Delta e_1 - e_u) = \mathbf{0} \right]$$

$$\leq \frac{|S_{\theta_1}|^k \cdot |S_{\theta_2}|^k}{q^{nk}} + \sum_{i=1}^{e} \frac{\binom{d}{i} \cdot |S_{\theta_1 + \|W_i\|_\infty}|^k \cdot |S_{\theta_2 + \|W_i\|_\infty}|^k}{|W_i|^{k+k} \cdot q^{nk(1-i/d)}}$$

$$\leq \left(\frac{|S_{\theta_1}| \cdot |S_{\theta_2}|}{q^n} \right)^k + \sum_{i=1}^{e} \binom{d}{i} \cdot \left(\frac{|S_{\theta_1 + \|W_i\|_\infty}| \cdot |S_{\theta_2 + \|W_i\|_\infty}|}{|W_i|^2 \cdot q^{n(1-i/d)}} \right)^k,$$

where $\theta_1, \theta_2 \in \mathbb{N}$ represent the maximum value of coefficients of polynomials in set $S_{\theta_1}, S_{\theta_2}$. We first construct the sets S_{θ_1} and S_{θ_2}, then calculate the cardinality of the finite sets. By definition in Theorem 1, $S_\alpha := \{y \in R_q : \|y\|_\infty \leq \alpha\}$. Thus, we have:

$$S_{2\eta_1} := \left\{ \Delta r \in R_q^k : \|\Delta r\|_\infty \leq 2\eta_1 \right\},$$
$$S_{2\eta_2 + \gamma_u} := \left\{ \Delta e_1 - e_u \in R_q^k : \|\Delta e_1 - e_u\|_\infty \leq 2\eta_2 + \gamma_u \right\}.$$

The cardinality of S_α is:

$$|S_\alpha| = (2\alpha + 1)^n,$$

where n is the number of coefficients. Thus, the first component becomes:

$$\left(\frac{|S_{\theta_1}| \cdot |S_{\theta_2}|}{q^n}\right)^k = \left(\frac{|S_{2\eta_1}| \cdot |S_{2\eta_2+\gamma_u}|}{q^n}\right)^k = \left(\frac{(4\eta_1 + 1)(4\eta_2 + 2\gamma_u + 1)}{q}\right)^{nk}.$$

The second component is dependent on the size of set W_i. We use the construction from Sect. 3.3 of [15]:

$$
\begin{cases}
i = 1, & \begin{cases} |W_1| = 2n, \\ \|W_1\|_\infty = 1 \end{cases} \\[2ex]
i \geq 2, & \begin{cases}
t < \sqrt{n}, & \begin{cases} |W_i| = \sum_{j=0}^{t^2} \binom{n}{j} \cdot 2^j, \\ \|W_i\|_\infty = 1 \end{cases} \\[3ex]
t \geq \sqrt{n} & \begin{cases}
\text{Set 1} & \begin{cases} |W_i| \geq V_n(\frac{1}{2}q^{i/d} - \sqrt{n}), \\ \|W_i\|_\infty = \lfloor \frac{1}{2}q^{i/d} \rfloor \end{cases} \\[3ex]
\text{Set 2} & \begin{cases} |W_i| = (2\lfloor \frac{t}{\sqrt{n}} \rfloor + 1)^n, \\ \|W_i\|_\infty = \lfloor \frac{t}{\sqrt{n}} \rfloor \end{cases}
\end{cases}
\end{cases}
\end{cases}
\tag{12}
$$

where $V_n(R)$ is the volume of n-dim ball with radius r, which can be calculated by $V_n(R) = \frac{(\pi/2)^{\lfloor \frac{n}{2} \rfloor}}{n!!}(2R)^n$. For $t \geq \sqrt{n}$, we choose the one which can produce smaller bound from Set 1 and Set 2.

Therefore, the second component is simplified as:

$$\sum_{i=1}^{e} \binom{d}{i} \cdot \left(\frac{|S_{\theta_1 + \|W_i\|_\infty}| \cdot |S_{\theta_2 + \|W_i\|_\infty}|}{|W_i|^2 \cdot q^{n(1-i/d)}}\right)^k$$

$$= \sum_{i=1}^{e} \binom{d}{i} \cdot \left[\frac{|S_{2\eta_1 + \|W_i\|_\infty}| \cdot |S_{2\eta_2 + \gamma_u + \|W_i\|_\infty}|}{|W_i|^2 \cdot q^{n(1-i/d)}}\right]^k$$

$$= \sum_{i=1}^{e} \binom{d}{i} \cdot \frac{1}{|W_i|^{2k}} \cdot \left\{\frac{(4\eta_1 + 2\|W_i\|_\infty + 1) \cdot (4\eta_2 + 2\gamma_u + 2\|W_i\|_\infty + 1)}{q^{(1-i/d)}}\right\}^{nk}.$$

Now, we summarize the two components to generate our result for MSIS injectivity:

$$\Pr_{A \leftarrow R_q^{k \times k}} \left[\exists (\Delta r, \Delta e_1 - e_u) \in S_{\theta_1}^k \setminus \{0\} \times S_{\theta_2}^k : A^T \Delta r + (\Delta e_1 - e_u) = 0\right]$$

$$= \left(\frac{(4\eta_1 + 1)(4\eta_2 + 2\gamma_u + 1)}{q}\right)^{nk} + \sum_{i=1}^{e} \binom{d}{i} \cdot \frac{1}{|W_i|^{2k}}$$

$$\cdot \left\{\frac{(4\eta_1 + 2\|W_i\|_\infty + 1) \cdot (4\eta_2 + 2\gamma_u + 2\|W_i\|_\infty + 1)}{q^{(1-i/d)}}\right\}^{nk}.$$

Finally, the probability of MSIS part is calculated by probability of $\Delta r \neq 0$ multiplying probability above:

$$P_{MSIS} = [1 - \Pr(\Delta r = 0)] \cdot \Pr_{A \leftarrow R_q^{k \times k}} \left[A^T \Delta r + (\Delta e_1 - e_u) = 0\right],$$

which is (11) in Lemma 3.   □

Lemma 4 (Δv Injectivity). *Let $s, e, r, r' \in R_q^k$ be samples from $\beta_{2\eta_1}$ and $e_1, e_1' \in R_q^k, e_2, e_2' \in R_q$ be samples from $\beta_{2\eta_2}$. Let $e_u \in R_q^k$ and both d_u and d_v be positive integers such that $d_u, d_v < \lceil \log_2(q) \rceil$. All coefficients in e_u are in the range $[\gamma_u]$, where $\gamma_u := \lfloor \frac{q}{2^{d_u}} \rfloor$. And let $\Delta v = s^T e_u - s^T \Delta e_1 + e^T \Delta r + \Delta e_2 + \lceil \frac{q}{2} \rceil \Delta m$. The probability of $\Delta\mathsf{Compress}_q(v, d_v)$ being zero is calculated by:*

$$\Pr(V \mid U) \leq n \cdot \sum_{i=\gamma_m - \gamma_v}^{\gamma_m + \gamma_v} p_i, \tag{13}$$

where n stands for 256 coefficients in one polynomial, $\gamma_v := \lfloor \frac{q}{2^{d_v}} \rfloor$, $\gamma_m := \pm \lceil \frac{q}{2} \rceil$, and p_i is the ith coefficient of $V(X)$ from:

$$V(X) = \sum_i p_i \cdot X^i = \left\{ 4^{-\eta_1} \sum_{i=-\eta_1}^{\eta_1} \binom{2\eta_1}{\eta_1 + i} \cdot X^{i+e_u} \right\}$$

$$\cdot \left\{ 16^{-2\eta_2} \sum_{i=-\eta_2}^{\eta_2} \sum_{j=-\eta_2}^{\eta_2} \binom{2\eta_2}{\eta_2 + i} \binom{2\eta_2}{\eta_2 + j} \cdot X^{i+j} \right\}$$

$$\cdot \left\{ 64^{-(\eta_1+2\eta_2)} \sum_{a=-\eta_1}^{\eta_1} \sum_{b=-\eta_2}^{\eta_2} \sum_{c=-\eta_2}^{\eta_2} \binom{2\eta_1}{\eta_1 + a} \binom{2\eta_2}{\eta_2 + b} \binom{2\eta_2}{\eta_2 + c} \cdot X^{a(b+c)} \right\}^{nk}$$

$$\cdot \left\{ 64^{-3\eta_1} \sum_{i=-\eta_1}^{\eta_1} \sum_{j=-\eta_1}^{\eta_1} \sum_{k=-\eta_1}^{\eta_1} \binom{2\eta_1}{\eta_1 + i} \binom{2\eta_1}{\eta_1 + j} \binom{2\eta_1}{\eta_1 + k} \cdot X^{i(j+k)} \right\}^{nk} \tag{14}$$

Proof. We first move the constant parts to one side:

$$\Delta v - \left\lceil \frac{q}{2} \right\rceil \Delta m = s^T e_u - s^T \Delta e_1 + e^T \Delta r + \Delta e_2.$$

Since we want to calculate different messages, the left-hand side can be further simplified as $\Delta v \mp \lceil \frac{q}{2} \rceil$.

Then we try to find the matrix-vector representation of the polynomial multiplication, then we find the polynomial representation of probability distribution, and finally we calculate the probability of the coefficients locating at the range $[\gamma_v]$. Let us first look at the structure of multiplication of two polynomial vector with same dimension. The matrix representation for $e^T \Delta r$ is:

$$\mathcal{M}_{e^T} \cdot \mathcal{V}_{\Delta r} = \mathcal{V}_{e^T \Delta r} \in \mathbb{Z}_q^{n \times nk} \times \mathbb{Z}_q^{nk \times 1} = \mathbb{Z}_q^{n \times 1},$$

where $n = 256$ is the total number of coefficients of polynomial $e^T \Delta r$. Since the quotient polynomial of R_q is $X^n + 1$, which meets the condition of special case, the nk entries in each row of the matrix will have the same distribution. The dependency of the total matrix vector multiplication is complicated to calculate, but we can adapt a similar technique as in calculating decryption error rate, which is applying union bound on a single coefficient.

Let $A(X), B(X), C(X), D(X)$ represent the distribution of one coefficient of $s^T e_u, s^T \Delta e_1, e^T \Delta r, \Delta e_2$, respectively. We then obtain:

$$A(X) = 4^{-\eta_1} \sum_{i=-\eta_1}^{\eta_1} \binom{2\eta_1}{\eta_1 + i} \cdot X^{i+\gamma_u},$$

$$B(X) = 64^{-(\eta_1+2\eta_2)} \sum_{i=-\eta_1}^{\eta_1} \sum_{j=-\eta_2}^{\eta_2} \sum_{k=-\eta_2}^{\eta_2} \binom{2\eta_1}{\eta_1 + i} \binom{2\eta_2}{\eta_2 + j} \binom{2\eta_2}{\eta_2 + k} \cdot X^{i(j+k)},$$

$$C(X) = 64^{-3\eta_1} \sum_{i=-\eta_1}^{\eta_1} \sum_{j=-\eta_1}^{\eta_1} \sum_{k=-\eta_1}^{\eta_1} \binom{2\eta_1}{\eta_1 + i} \binom{2\eta_1}{\eta_1 + j} \binom{2\eta_1}{\eta_1 + k} \cdot X^{i(j+k)},$$

$$D(X) = 16^{-2\eta_2} \sum_{i=-\eta_2}^{\eta_2} \sum_{j=-\eta_2}^{\eta_2} \binom{2\eta_2}{\eta_2 + i} \binom{2\eta_2}{\eta_2 + j} \cdot X^{i+j}.$$

Here the notation γ_u represents an iteration in range $[\gamma_u]$. Combining nk entries together, let $V(X)$ be the total probability distribution of one particular coefficient, which can be written as:

$$V(X) = A(X) D(X) \{B(X) C(X)\}^{nk} = \sum_i p_i \cdot X^i.$$

We want to sum the probability where the value of the coefficient falls in the range of $\Delta v \mp \lceil \frac{q}{2} \rceil$. Thus, the range of i should be in two intervals $[\lfloor \frac{q}{2^{d_v}} \rfloor] + \lceil \frac{q}{2} \rceil$ and $[\lfloor \frac{q}{2^{d_v}} \rfloor] - \lceil \frac{q}{2} \rceil$. Finally, we apply union bound on the total n coefficients to get an upper bound of v as described in (13) and (14).   □

4   Numerical Result and Analysis

We now calculate the numerical bounds of injectivity of Kyber[1]. As mentioned in Sect. 2, $n = 256$ is the fixed degree of the quotient polynomial, q is the module number of the module ring R_q, and d is the degree of splitting Table 1. The scheme uses k to represent dimension of secrete key vector, η_1 and η_2 to represent the sampling parameters for s, e, r and e_1, e_2 respectively. From security estimation perspective, δ is for δ-correctness, which is the probability of decryption failure attack successfully happening. The security levels λ defined by Call for Proposals [1] of the three parameter sets are consistent with AES128 against 2^{170} MAXDEPTH quantum gates or 2^{143} classical gates as level 1, AES192 against 2^{233} MAXDEPTH quantum gates or 2^{207} classical gates as level 3, and AES256 against 2^{298} MAXDEPTH quantum gates or 2^{272} classical gates as level 5.

We first analyze the total injectivity. Overall, our result in Table 2 indicates the injectivity assumption in [12] holds for Kyber768 and Kyber1024 by showing

---

[1] The code can be accessed at: https://github.com/RdWeirdo981/Injectivity-paper-codes.

Table 1. Third Round Kyber Parameters from specification [3]

	n	d	q	k	η_1	η_2	(d_u, d_v)	δ	Bit security (λ)
Kyber512	256	128	3329	2	3	2	(10, 4)	2^{-139}	128
Kyber768	256	128	3329	3	2	2	(10, 4)	2^{-164}	192
Kyber1024	256	128	3329	4	2	2	(11, 5)	2^{-174}	256

Table 2. Kyber η-Injectivity

	M	P_{CBD}	P_{MSIS}	P_V	η	$\sqrt{\eta}$	$\sqrt{\eta} + \delta$
Kyber512	2^{511}	2^{-1105}	2^{-354}	2^{-338}	2^{-181}	2^{-90}	2^{-90}
Kyber768	2^{511}	2^{-1445}	2^{-937}	2^{-440}	2^{-867}	2^{-433}	2^{-164}
Kyber1024	2^{511}	2^{-2419}	2^{-1687}	2^{-392}	2^{-1569}	2^{-784}	2^{-174}

that $\sqrt{\eta} \leq 2^{-\lambda}$. As for Kyber512, we only obtain a loose upper bound which doesn't meet the requirement but still is good enough for practical uses. Thus, we take a further look at Table 2 to analyze the separated components.

Again, M, P_{CBD}, P_{SIS}, P_V are consistent with previous definitions, and η is calculated from $\eta \leq M \cdot [P_{CBD} + P_{MSIS}] \cdot P_V$. The square-root values of η are also calculated because we want to investigate the injectivity assumption in [12]:

$$\mathsf{Adv}^{\mathsf{IND-CCA}}_{\mathsf{FO}^{\not\perp}(P,F,G,H)}(\mathcal{A}) \leq Q^2 \cdot \mathsf{Adv}^{\mathsf{IND-CPA}}_{\mathsf{P}}(\mathcal{B}_1) + Q^2 \cdot (\delta + \sqrt{\eta}) + Q \cdot \eta + \mathsf{Adv}^{\mathsf{PRF}}_{\mathsf{F}}(\mathcal{B}_2).$$

Since $2^{-90} > 2^{-128}$, the bound on $\sqrt{\eta}$ is not as small as desired. We leave it to future work to determine if the bound can be further improved below 2^{-128}. Some interesting observations are also summarized as below.

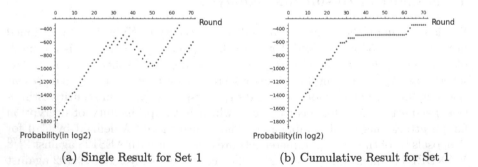

(a) Single Result for Set 1   (b) Cumulative Result for Set 1

Fig. 1. Output of τ Function in MSIS Part

- It was initially considered that only U part is enough for proving the injectivity assumption. The CBD part for these parameters are all small which are not our concern, but the numerical result of MSIS part in Kyber512 with total message space is $M \cdot P_{MSIS} = 2^{511} \cdot 2^{-354}$, which is even larger than 1. The reason why Kyber512 has really large injectivity in MSIS part should be investigated to better understand the huge difference.

- Theorem 1 of [15] constructs 4 sets of W_i as summarized in (12). In the numerical calculation, for $t \geq \sqrt{n}$, Set 2 will always minimize the probability result rather than Set 1. This is because Set 1 uses the volume of n-dimensional ball with radius $\frac{1}{2}q^{i/d} - \sqrt{n}$. If we take a further look at the equation of the volume, it can be calculated that the constant part. $\frac{(\pi/2)^{\lfloor \frac{n}{2} \rfloor}}{n!!}$ is really big, which makes Set 1 to always generate the larger result than Set 2. When the iteration of the sum goes up to about 62, we will obtain the largest single round result as seen in Fig. 1a. And that is why the final cumulative result goes large in Fig. 1b. But Kyber768 and Kyber1024 don't have this issue because they have larger vector dimensions, i.e. larger k. Since k is the exponent in the MSIS part, it will cause exponentially huge influence.

- Therefore, V part is involved for further analysis. It can be seen that the differences between different parameter sets in V part are not as significant as before. This is because the probability distribution of Δv nearly follows normal distribution that is symmetrical around 0, and $\pm \lceil \frac{q}{2} \rceil$ is far away from 0. Thus, there would be no big difference comparing other parts in the total injectivity. The relatively small difference of V part between Kyber512 and Kyber768 mainly comes from the values of η_1, and the injectivity will decrease as η_1 decreases. The result of Kyber1024 is also larger than the one of Kyber768, which is mainly caused by the different choices of k. This indicates that k is positively correlated to the injectivity. The effects of k and η_1 are approximately cancelling out each other as k increases and η_1 decreases. It would be useful to investigate the theoretical correlation between these parameters by improving the estimation technique of V part.

- The result of Table 2 does not indicate the injectivity assumption fails in Kyber512, in general. Looking at the last two columns of Table 2 and the advantage equation given above, for small Q (e.g. highly parallelised attacks with small number of QROM queries) the overall bound differs by at most $\approx 2^{-90}$ from the advantage against MLWE and PRF hardness assumptions, which is nearly optimal. The main reason for the loose bound is the use of union bound over one coefficient of the resulting polynomial being equal. If the total probability of 256 coefficients being zero can be calculated, the bound would be more tight. This dependency refinement might be tackled by using multi-variate distributions.

5   Conclusion

We have followed the work of [12] and taken a step further to investigate and analyze the injectivity of Crystals-Kyber, which uses FO transformation to convert an IND-CPA public key encryption into IND-CCA key encapsulation mechanism. The theoretical bound and corresponding numerical results are provided and have shown that Kyber768 and Kyber1024 are reasonably safe with respect to the injectivity assumption in [5,12], which means that the collision probability of two different messages having the same output ciphertext is negligible in these two parameter sets. The analysis method for Kyber512 still needs to be further improved/refined. The columns of the corresponding matrices over the special quotient polynomial $X^n + 1$ are all rotated version of the original coefficients, which means, to calculate the combined probability for the total 256 coefficients, more advanced mathematical techniques like probability of multivariate and random matrix distribution should be utilised. We leave this as an open problem.

Other schemes using the FO transformation like Saber can be investigated by similar method. The reason why we cannot retake the steps for calculating Kyber injectivity for Saber is that it uses 2^n module number. It makes the approach in [15] not valid to be adapted for Saber. Also, the error of Saber is given by rounding and module switching rather than sampling directly from a centered binomial distribution of noises, which is another difference from Kyber, hence needs further analysis and investigation requiring totally different techniques used in our paper.

References

1. Submission requirements and evaluation criteria for the post-quantum cryptography standardization process. Tech. rep., National Institute of Standards and Technology, Gaithersburg, MD (2017). https://csrc.nist.gov/CSRC/media/Projects/Post-Quantum-Cryptography/documents/call-for-proposals-final-dec-2016.pdf
2. Ambainis, A., Hamburg, M., Unruh, D.: Quantum security proofs using semi-classical oracles. In: Boldyreva, A., Micciancio, D. (eds.) CRYPTO 2019. LNCS, vol. 11693, pp. 269–295. Springer, Cham (2019). https://doi.org/10.1007/978-3-030-26951-7_10
3. Avanzi, R., et al.: Algorithm specifications and supporting documentation (version 3.0). Tech. Rep., Submission to the NIST postquantum project (2020). https://pq-crystals.org/
4. Bellare, M., Rogaway, P.: Random oracles are practical: a paradigm for designing efficient protocols. In: Proceedings of the 1st ACM Conference on Computer and Communications Security, pp. 62–73 (1993)
5. Bindel, N., Hamburg, M., Hövelmanns, K., Hülsing, A., Persichetti, E.: Tighter proofs of CCA security in the quantum random oracle model. In: Hofheinz, D., Rosen, A. (eds.) TCC 2019. LNCS, vol. 11892, pp. 61–90. Springer, Cham (2019). https://doi.org/10.1007/978-3-030-36033-7_3
6. Boneh, D., Dagdelen, Ö., Fischlin, M., Lehmann, A., Schaffner, C., Zhandry, M.: Random oracles in a quantum world. In: Lee, D.H., Wang, X. (eds.) ASIACRYPT 2011. LNCS, vol. 7073, pp. 41–69. Springer, Heidelberg (2011). https://doi.org/10.1007/978-3-642-25385-0_3
7. Bos, J., et al.: CRYSTALS-Kyber: a CCA-secure module-lattice-based KEM. In: 2018 IEEE European Symposium on Security and Privacy (EuroS&P), pp. 353–367. IEEE (2018)

8. Fujisaki, E., Okamoto, T.: How to enhance the security of public-key encryption at minimum cost. In: Imai, H., Zheng, Y. (eds.) PKC 1999. LNCS, vol. 1560, pp. 53–68. Springer, Heidelberg (1999). https://doi.org/10.1007/3-540-49162-7_5

9. Fujisaki, E., Okamoto, T.: Secure integration of asymmetric and symmetric encryption schemes. In: Wiener, M. (ed.) CRYPTO 1999. LNCS, vol. 1666, pp. 537–554. Springer, Heidelberg (1999). https://doi.org/10.1007/3-540-48405-1_34

10. Grover, L.K.: A fast quantum mechanical algorithm for database search. In: Proceedings of the Twenty-Eighth Annual ACM Symposium on Theory of Computing, pp. 212–219. STOC '96, Association for Computing Machinery. https://doi.org/10.1145/237814.237866

11. Guo, F., Susilo, W., Mu, Y.: Introduction to Security Reduction. Springer (2018). https://doi.org/10.1007/978-3-319-93049-7

12. Kuchta, V., Sakzad, A., Stehlé, D., Steinfeld, R., Sun, S.-F.: Measure-Rewind-Measure: tighter quantum random oracle model proofs for one-way to hiding and CCA security. In: Canteaut, A., Ishai, Y. (eds.) EUROCRYPT 2020. LNCS, vol. 12107, pp. 703–728. Springer, Cham (2020). https://doi.org/10.1007/978-3-030-45727-3_24

13. Lily, C.N., et al.: Report on post-quantum cryptography. Tech. Rep., National Institute of Standards and Technology, Gaithersburg, MD (2016). https://doi.org/10.6028/NIST.IR.8105

14. Lyubashevsky, V.: Basic lattice cryptography: encryption and fiat-shamir signatures (2019)

15. Nguyen, N.K.: On the non-existence of short vectors in random module lattices. In: Galbraith, S.D., Moriai, S. (eds.) ASIACRYPT 2019. LNCS, vol. 11922, pp. 121–150. Springer, Cham (2019). https://doi.org/10.1007/978-3-030-34621-8_5

16. Saito, T., Xagawa, K., Yamakawa, T.: Tightly-secure key-encapsulation mechanism in the quantum random oracle model. In: Nielsen, J.B., Rijmen, V. (eds.) EUROCRYPT 2018. LNCS, vol. 10822, pp. 520–551. Springer, Cham (2018). https://doi.org/10.1007/978-3-319-78372-7_17

17. Shor, P.W.: Polynomial-time algorithms for prime factorization and discrete logarithms on a quantum computer. SIAM Rev. **41**(2), 303–332 (1999)

18. Sullivan, N.: Securing the post-quantum world (2021). https://blog.cloudflare.com/securing-the-post-quantum-world/

19. Unruh, D.: Revocable quantum timed-release encryption. J. ACM (JACM) **62**(6), 1–76 (2015)

20. Weibel, A.: Round 2 post-quantum TLS is now supported in AWS KMs (2020). https://aws.amazon.com/blogs/security/round-2-post-quantum-tls-is-now-supported-in-aws-kms/

Cryptographic Protocols

Verifiable Decryption in the Head

Kristian Gjøsteen[1], Thomas Haines[1,2], Johannes Müller[3],
Peter Rønne[3,4], and Tjerand Silde[1(✉)]

[1] Norwegian University of Science and Technology, Trondheim, Norway
{kristian.gjosteen,tjerand.silde}@ntnu.no
[2] Australian National University, Canberra, Australia
thomas.haines@anu.edu.au
[3] University of Luxembourg, Esch-sur-Alzette, Luxembourg
johannes.mueller@uni.lu
[4] Université de Lorraine, CNRS, LORIA, Vanduvre-lés-Nancy, France

Abstract. In this work we present a new approach to verifiable decryption which converts a 2-party passively secure distributed decryption protocol into a 1-party proof of correct decryption. This leads to an efficient and simple verifiable decryption scheme for lattice-based cryptography, especially for large sets of ciphertexts; it has small size and lightweight computations as we reduce the need of zero-knowledge proofs for each ciphertext. We believe the flexibility of the general technique is interesting and provides attractive trade-offs between complexity and security, in particular for the interactive variant with smaller soundness.

Finally, the protocol requires only very simple operations, making it easy to correctly and securely implement in practice. We suggest concrete parameters for our protocol and give a proof of concept implementation, showing that it is highly practical.

Keywords: Verifiable decryption · Distributed decryption ·
Lattice-based crypto · MPC-in-the-head · Zero-knowledge proof ·
Implementation

1 Introduction

There are many applications where we not only need to decrypt a ciphertext, but also prove that we have decrypted the ciphertext correctly without revealing the secret key. This is called *verifiable decryption*. Examples include mix-nets used for anonymous communication [42], decryption of ballots in electronic voting [29], and various uses of verifiable fully homomorphic encryption [35]. In particular, such applications usually require the decryption of a large number of ciphertexts.

It is well-known how to do verifiable decryption for public-key encryption schemes based on discrete logarithms (for ElGamal, proving the equality of two discrete logarithms [19] will do). Except for the recent publication by Lyubashevsky *et al.* [38] (which provides a rather complicated decryption proof by

K. Nguyen et al. (Eds.): ACISP 2022, LNCS 13494, pp. 355–374, 2022.
https://doi.org/10.1007/978-3-031-22301-3_18

combining proofs of linear relations, multiplications and range proofs), no efficient and straight-forward zero-knowledge proofs of correct decryption are known for lattice-based cryptography or other post-quantum encryption schemes. This state-of-affairs is unsatisfying, in particular because many applications that require zero-knowledge proofs of correct decryption should also be secure in the face of quantum computers which are becoming increasingly more powerful. For example, the electronic voting system Helios [1] and the Estonian voting protocol [30] are using classical encryption schemes and decryption proofs with corresponding quantum threats to the long-term privacy of the voters.

On the contrary, there do exist efficient and straightforward passively secure lattice-based encryption schemes with distributed decryption. In such a scheme, the decryption key is shared among several players. Decryption is done in a distributed fashion by each player creating a decryption share, which can be individually verified, and a reconstruction algorithm can recover the message from the decryption shares. *Distributed decryption* allows more general methods to recover the message, such as general multi-party computation. There are many useful and efficient lattice-based threshold cryptosystems and distributed decryption schemes [11,13,16,21,22,24]. In particular, if the security requirements are relaxed, lattice-based distributed decryption can be very straight-forward.

Our main idea is to use MPC-in-the-head [31] in conjunction with a 2-party passively secure distributed decryption scheme to construct a very simple verifiable decryption scheme; however, we shall see that there are various technical challenges. To achieve the desired level of security, we run the 2-party decryption scheme on the ciphertexts many times locally, and then reveal a random subset of keys, one for each run, allowing others to verify that it was done correctly.

1.1   Contribution

Our main contribution is a transformation from a 2-party passively secure distributed decryption scheme to a 1-party verifiable decryption scheme. To achieve this, we use MPC-in-the-head with the 2-party decryption scheme. The idea is that the prover runs the 2-party decryption protocol many times and reveals the resulting decryption shares. The interactive verifier will then, for each run of the decryption scheme, ask to see one of the two decryption keys and any randomness involved in creating the corresponding decryption shares. With this information, it is straight-forward for the verifier to ensure that half of the decryption shares were generated honestly.

As usual, the idea is that if the prover cheats, the verifier will have probability (close to) $1/2$ of detecting this in each round. If a cheating prover is consistently successful, we can use rewinding to extract both secret shares. Furthermore, if the 2-party decryption scheme is passively secure, revealing one share will not reveal anything about the secret key itself.

There are four remaining obstacles, two easy and two somewhat trickier. The first easy obstacle is that in a threshold public key encryption scheme or distributed decryption scheme, the decryption key shares are generated as part of key generation. We already have a decryption key, but we need to create many independent sharings of that key. For discrete logarithm-based schemes like ElGamal, this is usually trivial. For the schemes we consider, it is still not hard, but it follows that we do not have a fully general reduction from 2-party distributed decryption to (1-party) verifiable decryption. The second easy obstacle is that given both secret key shares we want to recover the secret key. We solve this by extending the notation of a distributed decryption function with a function which recovers the key from the shares. This is easy to satisfy in practice.

The third obstacle is that the verifier needs to make sure that the revealed key share is correct. For ordinary threshold decryption schemes, this can often be avoided, either because the dealer is trusted or replaced by some multi-party computation. Therefore, we need to use a non-generic solution here. For batched decryption, the main observation is that we only verify the key once for each run of the 2-party decryption scheme, not once per ciphertext in the batch. The number of runs essentially corresponds to the security parameter, which in many applications will be significantly smaller than the number of ciphertexts.

The final obstacle is related to our security proof. We need to simulate shares of the decryption key, any auxiliary information related to them, and decryption shares. Although similar techniques are common in the construction of threshold public key encryption scheme, the security definitions do not actually require their presence. Since we need them, our approach is again somewhat non-generic.

On the other hand, since we intend to verify correctness of decryption shares by revealing decryption key shares and any randomness involved, we can make do with a passively secure distributed decryption scheme, simplifying our work.

The result is a construction from a somewhat specialized 2-party distributed decryption scheme to a verifiable decryption scheme. Since the security requirements for the distributed decryption scheme are shifted compared to traditional threshold decryption schemes, this will allow us to use very simple threshold decryption. This means that it can be very efficient, both with respect to computational time and size of the decryption shares. Even though the decryption is run many times, the result will still be efficient compared to the alternatives.

Note that in an interactive setting, it may make sense to use a very small security parameter, making the protocol extremely cheap. For instance, in any system where detected cheating will have a significant penalty, rational actors will be deterred by even a small chance of detection. However, when the protocol is made non-interactive, this clearly does not work.

In the full version we prove in the interactive theorem prover Coq [12] a simplified variant of our transform and an ElGamal toy example. Regrettably, we are unable to prove the full transform and the lattice example due to limitations in the interactive theorem prover. Indeed, to our knowledge, no interactive theorem prover exists which provides adequate support. Nevertheless, the proof of the simplified variant increases confidence in the result.

It is worth emphasizing that our protocol is very simple to implement (using Stern-based zero-knowledge proofs [32,34] to ensure that key-shares are well-formed), lowering the bar for deploying our scheme in practice. We note that lattice-based zero-knowledge proofs in general can be very complicated, involving a combination of proofs of linear relations, proofs of shortness and range proofs, in addition to Gaussian sampling, rejection sampling and optimizations exploiting partially splitting rings and automorphisms [6,38]. Correctly and securely implementing voting systems using primitives based on discrete logarithms is hard [28], and lattice-based primitives makes it harder. In our protocol we only need to sample uniformly random or short elements in any ring of our choice, and use standard cut-and-choose techniques to open committed values, making it easy to use in practice. Concretely, this means that we are not vulnerable to side-channel attacks against Gaussian sampling [18] or rejection sampling [25].

Combined with the main contribution, this gives us a verifiable decryption scheme for a lattice-based public key encryption scheme that is very efficient when the number of ciphertexts is much larger than the security parameter. The protocol is fast and simple, and the proof size is small. We give concrete parameters and a proof of concept implementation of our protocol in Sect. 6.

1.2 Related Work

Verifiable decryption for ElGamal can be done by proving the equality of two discrete logarithms [19], and can be batched for significantly improved performance when decrypting many ciphertexts [27,40].

The "dual" Regev system [39] can be used by making the randomness public. However, this is not zero-knowledge and opens for so-called "tagging-attacks" to de-anonymize users in privacy-preserving applications (e.g., e-voting).

Threshold encryption schemes [23] and distributed decryption schemes are now well-understood, and many constructions exist [11], in particular those related to SPDZ [20,22,33]. When only passive security is required, these schemes can be quite efficient. Threshold decryption with active security implies verifiable decryption when the verification of decryption shares is a public operation. The problem is that it is often costly to provide a threshold decryption scheme with active security. Our approach gives away a decryption key share and randomness involved, and it is trivial to verify that the key share has been used correctly.

We compare more in detail with recently developed verifiable decryption protocols [11,15,38,44] in Sect. 7.

2 Passively Secure 2-Party Decryption

A *distributed decryption scheme* enables a set of players to distribute the decryption of ciphertexts, in such a way that only authorized subsets of players can do the decryption. Usually, the decryption key shares are created once during key generation. As discussed in the introduction, we will generate independent decryption key sharings repeatedly, so we need to define the syntax of our variant of distributed decryption schemes precisely.

Consider a public key cryptosystem with key generation algorithm KeyGen, encryption algorithm Enc and decryption algorithm Dec. We extend the notation with a predicate KeyM for key-matching which takes as input a public and secret key. We require for all matching public and secret keys pk, sk and all messages m, that $\mathsf{Dec}(\mathsf{sk}, \mathsf{Enc}(\mathsf{pk}, m)) = m$ (with overwhelming probability).

A *distributed decryption protocol* for this public key cryptosystem consists of four algorithms, a *dealer* algorithm, a *verify* algorithm, a *player* algorithm, and a *reconstruction* algorithm. We consider only two parties where both decrypt.

The dealer algorithm (Deal) takes as input a public key and corresponding secret key and outputs two *secret key shares* and some *auxiliary data* aux.

The verify algorithm (Verify) takes as input a public key, auxiliary data, an index and a secret key share and outputs *yes* (1) or *no* (0).

The player algorithm (Play) takes as input a secret key share and a ciphertext and outputs a *decryption share* ds.

The reconstruction algorithm (Rec) takes as input a ciphertext and two decryption shares and outputs either $\perp$ or a message.

Intuitively, the protocol is *correct* if Play and Rec collectively recover the encrypted message and verification accepts when the dealer is honest.

Definition 1 (Correctness). *A distributed decryption protocol is* correct *if for any key pair* (pk, sk) *s.t.* $\mathsf{KeyM}(\mathsf{pk}, \mathsf{sk}) = 1$, *all* $c = \mathsf{Enc}(\mathsf{pk}, m)$, *any* $(\mathsf{sk}_0, \mathsf{sk}_1, \mathsf{aux})$ *output by* $\mathsf{Deal}(\mathsf{pk}, \mathsf{sk})$, *then, for* $i = 0, 1$, $\mathsf{Verify}(\mathsf{pk}, \mathsf{aux}, i, \mathsf{sk}_i) = 1$, *and*

$$\Pr[\, m \leftarrow \mathsf{Dec}(\mathsf{sk}, c); \mathsf{Rec}(c, \mathsf{Play}(\mathsf{sk}_0, c), \mathsf{Play}(\mathsf{sk}_1, c)) = m \,] \geq 1 - \mathsf{negl}.$$

For a distributed decryption protocol, we must trust the dealer for privacy, but not for integrity. The integrity property below says that if both secret shares given by the dealer are valid (according to the Verify algorithm), then the Play and Rec will collectively recover the encrypted message.

Definition 2 (Integrity). *A distributed decryption protocol has* integrity *if there exists an efficient algorithm (named* FindKey *which takes as input the public key, the two secret key shares and the auxiliary information, and returns a secret key) such that for all public keys* pk, *ciphertexts* $c = \mathsf{Enc}(\mathsf{pk}, m)$, *secret key shares* $(\mathsf{sk}_1, \mathsf{sk}_2)$, *and auxiliary data* aux *and* sk *output by* $\mathsf{FindKey}(\mathsf{pk}, \mathsf{sk}_0, \mathsf{sk}_1, \mathsf{aux})$ *satisfying* $\mathsf{Verify}(\mathsf{pk}, \mathsf{aux}, i, \mathsf{sk}_i) = 1$, *for* $i = 0, 1$, *we have that*

$$\Pr[\, \mathsf{KeyM}(\mathsf{pk}, \mathsf{sk}) \wedge \mathsf{Rec}(c, \mathsf{Play}(\mathsf{sk}_0, c), \mathsf{Play}(\mathsf{sk}_1, c)) = \mathsf{Dec}(\mathsf{sk}, c) \,] \geq 1 - \mathsf{negl}.$$

For threshold cryptosystems and distributed decryption, security is typically defined through the usual security games for public key cryptosystem, allowing the adversary access to the decryption key shares through decryption share oracles. This security notion is not very convenient for us, so we shall instead rely on a variant of simulatability, namely we must be able to simulate both decryption key shares and decryption shares in a consistent fashion.

$Exp_{\mathcal{A}}^{ddp-sim-0}(\mathsf{pk},\mathsf{sk})$
$(i,(c_0,...,c_\tau),(m_0,...,m_\tau)) \leftarrow \mathcal{A}(\mathsf{pk})$
$(\mathsf{sk}_0,\mathsf{sk}_1,\mathsf{aux}) \leftarrow \mathsf{Deal}(\mathsf{pk},\mathsf{sk})$
$\forall j: \mathsf{ds}_j \leftarrow \mathsf{Play}(\mathsf{sk}_{1-i},c_j)$
$b = \mathcal{A}(\mathsf{aux},\mathsf{sk}_i,(\mathsf{ds}_0,...,\mathsf{ds}_\tau))$
return b

$Exp_{\mathcal{A}}^{ddp-sim-1}(\mathsf{pk})$
$(i,(c_0,...,c_\tau),(m_0,...,m_\tau)) \leftarrow \mathcal{A}(\mathsf{pk})$
$(\mathsf{sk}_i,\mathsf{aux}) \leftarrow \mathsf{DealSim}(\mathsf{pk},i)$
$\forall j: \mathsf{ds}_j \leftarrow \mathsf{PlaySim}(\mathsf{pk},\mathsf{sk}_i,c_j,m_j)$
$b = \mathcal{A}(\mathsf{aux},\mathsf{sk}_i,(\mathsf{ds}_0,...,\mathsf{ds}_\tau))$
return b

Fig. 1. The passively secure experiment for distributed decryption protocols.

Definition 3 (Simulatability). *Consider a pair of algorithms* DealSim *and* PlaySim *and an adversary* $\mathcal{A}$ *playing the experiments from Fig. 1, where* $\mathcal{A}$ *always outputs* $\boldsymbol{c} = (c_0,...,c_\tau), \boldsymbol{m} = (m_0,...,m_\tau)$ *such that* $\{m_j = \mathsf{Dec}(\mathsf{sk},c_j)\}_{j=1}^{\tau}$. *The simulatability advantage of* $\mathcal{A}$ *is*

$$Adv^{ddp-sim}(\mathcal{A},\mathsf{pk},\mathsf{sk}) =$$
$$|\Pr[Exp_{\mathcal{A}}^{ddp-sim-0}(\mathsf{pk},\mathsf{sk}) = 1] - \Pr[Exp_{\mathcal{A}}^{ddp-sim-1}(\mathsf{pk}) = 1]|,$$

where the probability is taken over the random tapes and $(\mathsf{pk},\mathsf{sk})$ *output by* KeyGen. *We say that a distributed decryption protocol is* (t,ϵ)-*simulatable (or just* simulatable*) if no t-time algorithm* $\mathcal{A}$ *has advantage greater than* ϵ.

We give an ElGamal toy example in the full version to showcase our technique.

3   Verifiable Decryption from Distributed Decryption

We will now construct a (batch) zero-knowledge proof system of correct decryption from the distributed decryption protocol. The protocol is given in Fig. 2. More precisely, our proof system is a sigma protocol with completeness, special soundness, and honest verifier-zero knowledge.

For any public key cryptosystem, a public key output by the key generation algorithm uniquely defines a decryption function that for all messages agrees with the decryption algorithm for any ciphertext output by the encryption algorithm, except those that lead to decryption failure.

Recall that for a batched verifiable decryption protocol the statement consists of a public key, a vector of ciphertexts and a vector of messages, where the ciphertexts have been output by the encryption algorithm. The statement is in the language if and only if the messages correspond to the decryption function applied to the ciphertexts. The secret key (witness) satisfies the relationship with the statement if it corresponds to the public key and the message vector is the decryption of the ciphertexts with the secret key.

The protocol works as follows: the prover creates λ sharings of the secret key by calling the Deal algorithm λ times. For each sharing and each ciphertext, the prover uses the Play algorithm to construct the decryption share. The prover sends the auxiliary information from Deal and all the shares to the verifier. Then, the verifier returns a challenge which is a binary vector of length λ. The prover finally reveals the corresponding parts of the shares as well as any randomness used in the Play algorithms with this key share. The prover checks that (1) all the revealed shares verify, (2) the decryption shares are consistent with the revealed key shares, and (3) the messages correspond to the decryption shares.

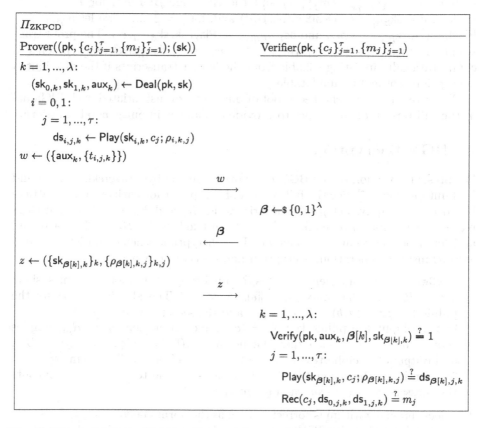

Fig. 2. Proof of correct decryption. $\rho_{i,k,j}$ denotes the random tape used by the Play algorithm to create the ith share of the jth ciphertext in the kth run of the protocol.

Completeness. Up to the possible negligible error introduced by decryption failures, completeness follows immediately by construction and the correctness of the underlying distributed decryption protocol.

Special Soundness. By rewinding, any cheating prover with a significant success probability can be used to create two accepting conversations (w, β, z) and

362 K. Gjøsteen et al.

(w, β', z'), with $\beta \neq \beta'$. From this it follows that $\beta[k] \neq \beta'[k]$ for at least one k, and the verify algorithm has accepted both secret key shares and every decryption share in this round has been correctly created using the Play algorithm. Then, since the ciphertexts are encryptions of the first message vector, integrity implies that FindKey will recover a witness which matches the public key and for which the messages match the output of the decryption function.

Honest-Verifier Zero-Knowledge. Our simulator works as follows, given the statement $(\mathsf{pk}, \{c_j\}_{j=1}^{\tau}, \{m_j\}_{j=1}^{\tau})$ and the challenge β: First, for $i = 1, ..., \lambda$, we let $(\mathsf{aux}_i, \mathsf{sk}_{\beta[i],i}) \leftarrow \mathsf{DealSim}(\mathsf{pk}, \beta[i])$ and, for $j = 1, ..., \tau$, we let $\mathsf{ds}_{\beta[i],j,i} \leftarrow \mathsf{PlaySim}(\mathsf{pk}, \mathsf{sk}_{\beta[i],i}, c_i, m_i)$ and $\mathsf{ds}_{1-\beta[i],j,i} \leftarrow \mathsf{Play}(\mathsf{pk}, \mathsf{sk}_{\beta[i],i}, c_i)$. The proof transcripts is then $((\mathsf{pk}, \{c_j\}_{j=1}^{\tau}, \{m_j\}_{j=1}^{\tau}), (\mathsf{aux}_i, \mathsf{ds}_{0,j,i}, \mathsf{ds}_{1,j,i}), \beta, \mathsf{sk}_{\beta[i],i})$. This is computationally indistinguishable from the honest transcripts if the distributed decryption protocol is simulatable.

We give a machine checked proof of our protocol instantiated with ElGamal in the full version of this paper to provide confidence in our general transform.

4 BGV Encryption

We present a version of the BGV encryption scheme by Brakerski, Gentry and Vaikuntanathan [17]. See the full version of this paper for background on lattice-based cryptography. Let $p \ll q$ be primes, let R_q and R_p be polynomial rings modulo the primes q or p and $X^N + 1$ for a fixed N, let $B_\infty \in \mathbb{N}$ be a bound and let κ be the security parameter. The encryption scheme consists of three algorithms: key generation, encryption and decryption, where

- KeyGen samples an element $a \leftarrow_\$ R_q$ uniformly at random, samples short $s, e \leftarrow_\$ R_q$ such that $\max(\|s\|_\infty, \|e\|_\infty) \leq B_\infty$. The algorithm outputs the public key $\mathsf{pk} = (a, b) = (a, as + pe)$ and the secret key $\mathsf{sk} = (s, e)$.
- Enc, on input the public key $\mathsf{pk} = (a, b)$ and an element m in R_p, samples short $r, e', e'' \leftarrow_\$ R_q$ such that the norm $\max(\|r\|_\infty, \|e'\|_\infty, \|e''\|_\infty) \leq B_\infty$, and outputs the ciphertext $c = (u, v) = (ar + pe', br + pe'' + m)$ in R_q^2.
- Dec, on input the secret key $\mathsf{sk} = (s, e)$ and a ciphertext $c = (u, v)$, outputs the message $m = (v - su \mod q) \mod p$ in R_p.

The decryption algorithm is correct as long as the norm $\max\|v - su\|_\infty = B_{\mathsf{Dec}} < \lfloor q/2 \rfloor$. It follows that the BGV encryption scheme is secure against chosen plaintext attacks if the $\mathsf{DKS}_{N,q,\beta}^\infty$ problem is hard for some $\beta = \beta(N, q, p, B_\infty)$.

Furthermore, we present the passively secure distributed decryption technique by Bendlin and Damgård [11] used in the MPC-protocols by Damgård *et al.* [20,22]. When decrypting, we assume that each decryption server $\mathcal{D}_j$, for $1 \leq j \leq \xi$, has a uniformly random share $\mathsf{sk}_j = s_j$ of the secret key $\mathsf{sk} = (s, e)$ such that $s = s_1 + s_2 + ... + s_\xi$. Then they partially decrypt in the following way:

- DistDec, on input a secret key-share $\mathsf{sk}_j = s_j$ and a ciphertext $c = (u, v)$, computes $m_j = s_j u$, sample some large noise $E_j \leftarrow_\$ \mathbb{E} \subset R_q$ such that $\|E_j\|_\infty \leq 2^{\mathsf{sec}}(B_{\mathsf{Dec}}/p\xi)$ for some statistical security parameter sec and upper error-bound $\max\|v - su\|_\infty \leq B_{\mathsf{Dec}}$, then outputs $\mathsf{ds}_j = t_j = m_j + pE_j$.

We obtain the full decryption of the ciphertext (u, v) as $m \equiv (v - t \mod q)$ mod p, where $t = t_1 + t_2 + \dots + t_\xi$. This will give the correct decryption as long as the noise $\max\|v - t\|_\infty \leq (1 + 2^{\sec})B_{\mathsf{Dec}} < \lfloor q/2 \rfloor$ (see [20, Appendix G]). Here, t will be indistinguishable from random except with probability $2^{-\sec}$.

5 Zero-Knowledge Protocol of Correct Decryption

5.1 Lattice-Based Distributed Decryption

Setup. We will be working over the ring $R_q = \mathbb{Z}_q[X]/\langle X^N + 1 \rangle$ together with a modulus $p \ll q$, both prime. These are the public parameters of the protocol, together with security parameter κ, soundness parameter λ, bound B_∞ and maximal ciphertext error-bound B_{Dec}. We define commitments, their security and give a concrete instantiation based on lattices in the full version of this paper. The commitments are both computationally hiding and computationally binding, in addition to being linearly homomorphic. Finally, let $(\Pi_{\mathsf{ZKPoS}}, \Pi_{\mathsf{ZKPoSV}})$ be a non-interactive zero-knowledge protocol for the following relation:

$$R_{\mathsf{DKS}^\infty_{\tilde{N}, q, 1}} = \{((\boldsymbol{A}, \boldsymbol{y}); \boldsymbol{x}) \colon \boldsymbol{A}\boldsymbol{x} = \boldsymbol{y} \mod q \wedge \|\boldsymbol{x}\|_\infty = 1\}.$$

Scheme. We present a distributed decryption version of the BGV encryption scheme [17], where KeyGen, Enc and Dec are defined in Sect. 4.

The dealer algorithm (Deal) takes as input a public key $\mathsf{pk} = (a, b)$ and corresponding secret key $\mathsf{sk} = (s, e)$, samples uniform s_0 and e_0 from R_q, and computes $s_1 = s - s_0$ and $e_1 = e - e_0$. Then it commits to the values as $c_{s_i} = \mathsf{Com}(s_i)$, $c_{e_i} = \mathsf{Com}(e_i)$, and computes $b_i = as_i + pe_i$ so that $b = b_0 + b_1$. Finally, it computes non-interactive zero-knowledge proofs π_{S_i} proving that the sums $s_0 + s_1$ and $e_0 + e_1$ are short (see details in Sect. 6). It outputs key shares $\mathsf{sk}_0 = (s_0, e_0)$, $\mathsf{sk}_1 = (s_1, c_1)$ and $\mathsf{aux} = (b_0, b_1, c_{s_0}, c_{s_1}, c_{e_0}, c_{e_1}, \pi_{S_0}, \pi_{S_1})$.

The verify algorithm (Verify) takes as input a public key $\mathsf{pk} = (a, b)$, an index i, a secret key share $\mathsf{sk}_i = (s_i, e_i)$, openings d_{s_i} and d_{e_i}, and aux. It outputs 1 if and only if $(b_i \overset{?}{=} as_i + pe_i) \wedge (b \overset{?}{=} b_0 + b_1) \wedge \mathsf{Open}(c_{s_i}, d_{s_i}) \wedge \mathsf{Open}(c_{e_i}, d_{e_i}) \wedge (\Pi_{\mathsf{ZKPoSV}}(\mathsf{sk}_i, \mathsf{aux}, \pi_{S_i}))$, and 0 otherwise.

The player algorithm (Play) takes as input a key share $\mathsf{sk}_i = (s_i, e_i)$, a ciphertext $c = (u, v)$, samples bounded E_i and outputs $\mathsf{ds}_j = t_i = s_i u + p E_i$.

The reconstruction algorithm (Rec) takes as input a ciphertext $c = (u, v)$, decryption shares (t_0, t_1), and outputs $m = (v - t_0 - t_1 \mod q) \mod p$.

5.2 Security

Theorem 1 (Correctness). *The distributed decryption scheme in 5.1 is correct with respect to Definition 1 when* $\max\|v - t\|_\infty \leq (1 + 2^{\sec})B_{\mathsf{Dec}} < \lfloor q/2 \rfloor$.

Theorem 2 (Integrity). *Suppose the protocol* Π_{ZKPoS} *is (computationally) sound and that* Com *is (computationally) binding. Let* $\mathcal{A}_0$ *be an adversary against integrity of the distributed decryption scheme with advantage* ϵ_0, *and let* λ *be* *the number of rounds in the protocol. Then there exists adversaries A_1 and A_2 against soundness of Π_{ZKPoS} and binding of Com, respectively, with advantages ϵ_1 and ϵ_2, such that $\epsilon_0 \leq \epsilon_1 + \epsilon_2 + 2^{-\lambda}$. The runtime of A_1 and A_2 are essentially the same as the runtime of A_0.*

Proof. We sketch the argument. There are essentially three possible ways to attack the integrity of the protocol: an attacker that knows the secret decryption key but correctly guess the challenge in each round is able to decrypt to arbitrary messages, and otherwise, if the attacker does not know the secret key, needs to break the underlying schemes. The guessing attack has success probability $2^{-\lambda}$.

For Verify to accept for both $i = 0$ and $i = 1$, we need that $b = b_0 + b_1$, $b_0 = as_0 + pe_0$, $b_1 = as_1 + pe_1$ and that the zero-knowledge proof of shortness π_S of the sums $s_0 + s_1$ and $e_0 + e_1$ are accepted. If either of the key shares are incorrect then Verify accept with probability 0, and if the key shares are correct, then Rec outputs m except with negligible probability. An attacker can choose s_0, s_1, e_0 and e_1 such that all equations are correct, but the sums are not short. The soundness of Verify then reduces to the soundness of the zero-knowledge protocol, and an attacker A_0 against this part of the protocol with advantage ϵ_0 can be turned into an attacker A_1 against Π_{ZKPoS} with the same advantage.

The last option is for the attacker to produce commitments to a true but unrelated statement with respect to the secret key used in the encryption scheme. This allows the attacker to produce a valid proof of shortness without cheating, but for an unrelated key. However, Verify only accepts if both the opening of the commitments are correct and the zero-knowledge proof of shortness verifies. Hence, and attacker A_0 that is able to produce valid openings and proofs with advantage ϵ_0 can be turned into an attacker A_2 against Com with the same advantage by rewinding the prover for the zero-knowledge proof of knowledge of short openings and then extract two different but valid openings to the commitment.

Theorem 3 (Privacy). *Suppose the protocol Π_{ZKPoS} is (statistically) honest-verifier zero-knowledge, that Com is (computationally) hiding and that Enc is (computationally) CPA secure. Then there exists a simulator for the verifiable decryption protocol such that for any distinguisher A_0 for this simulator with advantage ϵ_0 there exists an adversary A_2 against hiding for the commitment scheme with advantage ϵ_2, an adversary A_3 against CPA security for the encryption scheme with advantage ϵ_3, and a distinguisher A_1 for the simulator of Π_{ZKPoS} with advantage ϵ_1, such that $\epsilon_0 \leq \epsilon_1 + \epsilon_2 + \epsilon_3$. The runtime of A_1, A_2 and A_3 are essentially the same as the runtime of A_0.*

Proof. Let Sim_{Short} be a simulator for Π_{ZKPoS}. We present a simulator DealSim for the Deal-algorithm and a simulator PlaySim for the Play-algorithm in Fig. 3.

DealSim: We create the simulator in three steps. We first replace π_S by the simulated proof π_S^* produced by Sim_{Short}. An attacker A_0 with advantage ϵ_0 against this change can be turned into an attacker A_1 against the simulator Sim_{Short} of protocol Π_{ZKPoS} with the same advantage.

DealSim(pk $= (a, b), i$)	PlaySim(sk$_{1-i} = (s_{1-i}, e_{1-i}), c = (u, v), i, m$)
$i = 0, 1\colon s_i^* \leftarrow\!\$\, R_q, \quad e_i^* \leftarrow\!\$\, R_q$	$E_{1-i} \leftarrow\!\$\, \mathbb{E}$
$b_i^* = a s_i^* + p e_i^*, \quad b_{1-i}^* = b - b_i^*$	$t_{1-i} = s_{1-i} u + p E_{1-i}$
$c_{s_i}^* \leftarrow \mathsf{Com}(s_i^*), c_{s_{1-i}}^* \leftarrow \mathsf{Com}(s_{1-i})$	$t_i^* = v - m - t_{1-i} \mod p$
$c_{e_i}^* \leftarrow \mathsf{Com}(e_i^*), c_{e_{1-i}}^* \leftarrow \mathsf{Com}(s_{1-i})$	**return** $(\mathsf{ds}_i^* = t_i^*)$
$\pi_S^* \leftarrow \mathsf{Sim}_{\mathrm{Short}}(c_{s_i}^*, c_{s_{1-i}}^*, c_{e_i}^*, c_{e_{1-i}}^*)$	
$\mathsf{aux}^* \leftarrow (b_0^*, b_1^*, c_{s_0}^*, c_{s_1}^*, c_{e_0}^*, c_{e_1}^*, \pi_S^*)$	
return $(\mathsf{sk}_i^* = (s_i^*, e_i^*), \mathsf{aux}^*)$	

Fig. 3. Simulators DealSim and PlaySim.

Next, we replace the key shares by uniformly random key-shares s_i^* and e_i^* that give correctness, that is, the public key-shares b_0^* and b_1^* sum to b, but s_0^* and s_1^* does not need to sum to a short key s^* and e_0^* and e_1^* does not need to sum to short noise e^*. This ensures that Verify outputs 1. An attacker $\mathcal{A}_0$ with advantage ϵ_0 against this change can then be turned into an attacker $\mathcal{A}_3$ against CPA security of the encryption scheme with the same advantage.

Finally, we replace the commitments to unopened values by commitments to random values. This way, none of the values in the protocol any longer depends on the secret key in the protocol, and b_i^* are simulated perfectly. An attacker $\mathcal{A}_0$ with advantage ϵ_0 against this change can then be turned into an attacker $\mathcal{A}_2$ against hiding of the commitment scheme with the same advantage.

PlaySim: we start by sampling bounded E_{1-i} from $\mathbb{E}$ and computing $t_{1-i} = s_{1-i}u + pE_{1-i}$. Then we find t_i such that $(v - t_0 - t_1 \mod q) \mod p = m$. This ensures that Rec outputs the message m when reconstructing the shares. Here, the values are sampled according to the exact same distribution as in the real protocol, and the statistical distance is negligible in the security parameter κ.

5.3 Zero-Knowledge Proof of Verifiable Decryption

We present the different phases of our sigma protocol for proving correct decryption. The protocol is given in Fig. 4. The security of the construction follows directly from the results in Sect. 3 in combination with Theorem 1, 2 and 3.

Setup. We are given a honestly generated public key $\mathsf{pk} = (a, b = as + pe)$, where $\max(\|s\|_\infty, \|e\|_\infty) \le B_\infty$. The secret key $\mathsf{sk} = (s, e)$ is given to the prover. We are given a set of honestly generated ciphertexts $\{(u_j, v_j) = (ar_j + pe_j', br_j + pe_j'' + m_j)\}_{j=1}^\tau$, where $\max(\|r\|_\infty, \|e'\|_\infty, \|e''\|_\infty) \le B_\infty$, and set of messages $\{m_j\}_{j=1}^\tau$.

Commit phase. For soundness parameter λ, the prover does the following for $k = 1, ..., \lambda$. First, it runs the Deal algorithm on sk and pk to produce $\mathsf{sk}_{0,k}, \mathsf{sk}_{1,k}$ and aux_k. It uses Π_{ZKPoS} to prove that the shares are correctly computed. Then, for $i = 0, 1$ and each $j = 1, ..., \tau$, it runs the Play algorithm on each key-share $\mathsf{sk}_{i,k}$ and ciphertext c_j to produce $t_{0,j,k}$ and $t_{1,j,k}$. Finally, it sends $w \leftarrow (\{\mathsf{aux}_k, \{t_{i,j,k}\}_{i=0,j=1}^{1,\tau}\}_{k=1}^{\lambda})$ to end the commitment phase.

Challenge phase. The verifier independently samples a random binary challenge vector β of length λ. It sends β to the prover.

Respond phase. The prover sends openings $z = (\{d_{s_{\beta[k],k}}, d_{e_{\beta[k],k}}\})$, for each of the commitments to each index k of β, to the verifier.

Verification phase. For each $k = 1, ..., \lambda$, the verifier runs the Verify algorithm to make sure that the openings of $s_{\beta[k],k}$ and $e_{\beta[k],k}$ are valid, check that all shares of the public key are computed correctly as $b_{\beta[k],k} = as_{\beta[k],k} + pe_{\beta[k],k}$, verify the public key $b = b_{0,k} + b_{1,k}$ and ensure that each $\pi_{S_{i,k}}$ is valid. Further, for each $j = 1, ..., \tau$, the verifier runs the Rec algorithm to make sure that all decryption shares are correct and that all messages are decrypted correctly. It outputs 1 if all checks hold, and 0 otherwise.

Fiat-Shamir. To make the scheme non-interactive we can use the Fiat-Shamir transform [26] by hashing the output of the commit phase and use the hash as challenge, before outputting the response. We note that this can be done similarly to the optimizations described for estimating the size in the next section. We also note that the soundness parameter λ initially can be very small in the interactive case, while it should be (approximately) as large at the security parameter κ in the non-interactive setting, increasing the size of the proof of decryption.

Hybrid proof. We note that the interaction in the protocol opens for a hybrid proof: if we wish for a quick result to get confidence in the decrypted ciphertexts but at the same time can wait longer to be completely certain, we can ask for two proofs. First, we ask the prover for a proof where $\lambda_I = 10$ or $\lambda_I = 20$, and sample a random challenge ourselves. If we accept the proof, we ask the prover to compute a non-interactive proof for the same statement but with $\lambda_N = 100$. This proof can be received, stored and verified later, knowing already that the messages most likely are correctly decrypted. The interactive proof also allows the verifier to arbitrarily increase λ_I by sending more challenges on the fly, where we tell the prover when we are done, and he creates the proofs of shortness in the end. This is particularly useful in real-world applications, e.g., e-voting.

6   Performance

In this section, we shall carefully analyze the performance of our decryption proof. Along the way, we make several easy optimizations with respect to the protocol in Fig. 4. In particular, we use a commitment in the first message, and then send only the values that the verifier cannot recompute himself in the second message. Finally, we compute the zero-knowledge proofs of shortness in the response phase instead of the commit phase, reducing the number of proofs by a factor of two in each round of the protocol.

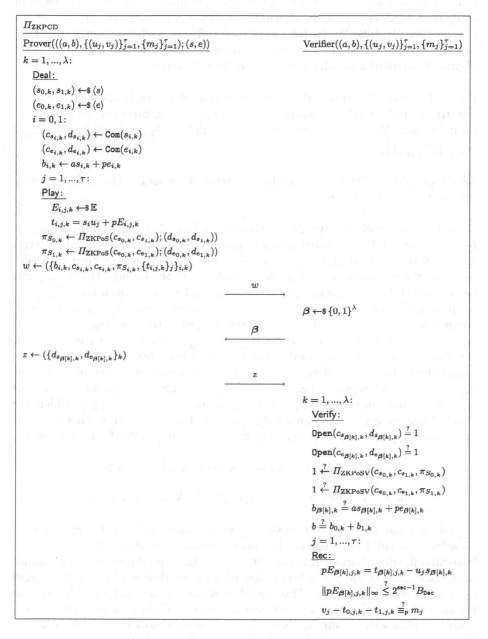

Fig. 4. Zero-knowledge proof of correct decryption.

6.1 Proof Size

Each element in R_q is of size $N \log q$ bits, which might be large, and each element in R_p is of size $N \log p$ bits, which will be small. Short elements bounded by B_∞ is of size $N \log B_\infty$ bits. We let H be a collision resistant hash-function with output of length 2κ. Note that the soundness parameter λ may be chosen independently of, and in particular smaller than, the security parameter κ.

Commit phase. To reduce the number of ring elements being sent, we commit to the output of the commit phase using a hash-function, and send the hash instead. More concretely, we let $w = \mathtt{H}(\{b_{0,k}, b_{1,k}, c_{s_{0,k}}, c_{s_{1,k}}, c_{e_{0,k}}, c_{e_{1,k}}, \{t_{i,j,k}\}_{i=0,j=1}^{1,\tau}\}_{k=1}^{\lambda})$.

Challenge phase. The verifier sends the vector β consisting of λ independently sampled bits to the prover.

Respond phase. Note that we do not need to send the partial decryptions $t_{\beta[k],j,k}$, because they can be computed uniquely from u_j, $s_{\beta[k],k}$ and $E_{\beta[k],j,k}$, and we can let a uniform binary seed $\rho_{\beta[k],k}$ of length 2κ bits can be used to deterministically generate the randomness used in each round. Next, we also note that $b_{\beta[k],k}$ can be computed directly from $s_{\beta[k],k}$ and $e_{\beta[k],k}$, and $b_{1-\beta[k],k}$ from b and $b_{\beta[k],k}$.

It follows that, for each $k = 1, ..., \lambda$, the prover sends $s_{\beta[k],k}$ and $e_{\beta[k],k}$, commitments $c_{s_{1-\beta[k],k}}$ and $c_{e_{1-\beta[k],k}}$ together with the openings $d_{s_{\beta[k],k}}$ and $d_{e_{\beta[k],k}}$, and the partial decryptions $\{t_{1-\beta[k],j,k}\}_{j=1}^{\tau}$. Since the commitments to the sharings of s and e are used in the zero-knowledge proof of shortness, these commitment is computed using lattice-based commitments. We observe that $c_{s_k} = c_{s_{1-\beta[k],k}} + \mathtt{Com}(s_{\beta[k],k})$ and $c_{e_k} = c_{e_{1-\beta[k],k}} + \mathtt{Com}(e_{\beta[k],k})$, with randomness zero, are commitments to $s_{\beta[k],k} + s_{1-\beta[k],k}$ and $e_{\beta[k],k} + e_{1-\beta[k],k}$, which are short. Then we use the zero-knowledge proof of shortness to prove that we know openings of c_{s_k} and c_{e_k} to get π_{S_0} and π_{S_1}. Denote all proofs of shortness by π_S.

Total communication. The total proof size sent by the prover is

$$2\kappa + \lambda N(4 \log q + 2\kappa + 2 \log B_\infty) + \lambda\tau N \log q + |\pi_S| \text{ bits.}$$

Zero-knowledge proof of shortness. There are many options for π_S, proving knowledge of valid openings of the commitments c_{s_k} and c_{e_k}. We can use the Fiat-Shamir with aborts framework [36,37], but this would give us a large soundness slack, that is, we prove knowledge of a vector that might be much larger than what we started with. This would increase the parameters to be used in the overall protocol. Other alternatives are the exact proofs using MPC-in-the-head techniques by Baum and Nof [9] or the range proofs by Attema *et al.* [6]. However, we note that even though these are efficient, both protocols are very complex and are complicated to implement correctly for use in the real world. Another approach is to use generic proof systems like Ligero [4] or Aurora [10], adding more complexity to the overall protocol. We can also use the amortized proof by Bootle *et al.*. [7] to prove that all λ executions are done correctly at the same time. This is the most efficient proof system for these relations today.

However, assuming that the soundness parameter λ is much smaller than the number of ciphertexts τ, the size of the proofs of shortness does not matter much. To keep the protocol as simple as possible, to make it easier to implement the protocol and avoid bugs in practice, we choose to use the Stern-based proofs by Kawachi *et al.* [32] and Ling *et al.* [34] in our implementation and estimates.

Concrete parameters. For a concrete instantiation, we use the example parameters in Table 1, estimated to $\kappa = 128$ bits of long-term security using the LWE-estimator [3] with the *BKZ.qsieve* cost-model. Inserting these parameters into the proof of shortness, then each proof $\pi_{S_{i,k}}$ is of size $\approx 87\mu$ KB. This makes $|\pi_S| \approx 175\mu\lambda$ KB. Furthermore, using the improvements by Beullens [14] we can shrink the proofs down to $18\mu\lambda$ KB. If we replace π_S with the amortized proof by Bootle *et al.*. [7] we get a proof of total size 520 KB[1]. However, if the number of ciphertexts τ is very large, we can ignore all other terms and get a proof of correct decryption π_D of size $\approx 14\lambda\tau$ KB. See Table 1 for details. The given ciphertext modulus q is chosen to be large enough to ensure correct decryption.

Table 1. Notation, explanation, constraints and concrete parameters for the protocol. We also provide size and timings for decryption proof π_D and proofs of shortness π_S.

Parameter	Explanation	Constraints	Value
N	Dimension	Power of two	2048
q	Ciphertext modulus	$B_{\mathsf{Dec}} \ll q \equiv 1 \mod 2N$	$\approx 2^{55}$
p	Plaintext modulus		2
κ	Security parameter	Long-term privacy	128
sec	Statistical security		40
λ	Soundness parameter		10, ..., 128
μ	Repetitions of Π_{ZKPoS}	$\mu \geq \lambda \cdot \ln(2)/\ln(3/2)$	17, ..., 218
B_∞	Bounds on secrets		1
B_{Dec}	Decryption bound	$\|v - su\|_\infty \leq B_{\mathsf{Dec}}$	$\approx 2^{13}$
Size of π_D	Timings for π_D	Size of π_S	Timings for π_S
$14\lambda\tau$ KB	$4\lambda\tau$ ms	$175\lambda\mu$ KB	$30\lambda\mu$ ms

6.2 Implementation

We wrote a proof of concept implementation of our scheme in C++ using the NTL-library [43]. The implementation was benchmarked on an Intel Core i5 running at 2.3 GHz with 16 GB RAM. We ran the protocol with $\lambda = 40, \tau = 1000, \mu = 68$. The timings are given in Table 1. The implementation is very

---

[1] Setting $m = 2048, \log q = 55, r = 90, b = 3, \tau = 50, k = 2398, l = 5000$ and $h = 100$ for soundness 2^{-45} and run the protocol twice, see [7, Section 4.1] for details.

simple, and consists of a total of 400 lines of code. Our source code is available online[2]. We note that our implementation does not use the number theoretic transform for fast multiplication of elements in the ring to reduce complexity. A rough comparison to NFLlib [2], where they show clear improvements compared to NTL, indicates that an optimized implementation should provide a speedup by at least an order of magnitude.

7   Comparison

7.1   Comparison to DistDec (TCC'10)

We sketch an extension of the passively secure distributed decryption protocol Π_{DistDec} given by Bendlin and Damgård [11], which is used in SPDZ [20, 22]. The main difference compared to our protocol is that this protocol requires zero-knowledge proofs to ensure correct computation at each step of the protocol to achieve active security instead of repeating the decryption procedure several times. The protocol works roughly as following:

1. Each party $\mathcal{D}_i$ samples uniform $E_{i,j}$ such that $\|E_{i,j}\|_\infty \leq 2^{40} B_{\text{Dec}}/\xi p$ (for 40 bits statistical security) and computes the partial decryptions $t_{i,j} = s_i u_j + p E_{i,j}$ for each ciphertext $c_j = (u_j, v_j)$.
2. Each party $\mathcal{D}_i$ publish a zero-knowledge proof $\pi_{L_{i,j}}$ of the linear relation for $t_{i,j}$, using the lattice-based commitments together with their zero-knowledge proof of linear relations by Baum et al. [8].
3. Each party $\mathcal{D}_i$ use the amortized ZKP by Baum et al. [7] for batch-size N to prove that each $E_{i,j}$ is bounded by $2^{\text{sec}} B_{\text{Dec}}/\xi p$, given commitments $c_{E_{i,j}}$.
4. The verifier checks the relations $(v_j - t_{0,j} - t_{1,j} \mod q) \equiv m_j \mod p$ and that all the zero-knowledge proofs are valid.

Elements t_j and commitments $c_{E_{i,j}}$ are $N \log q$ and $2N \log q$ bits, respectively. Each proof of linearity $\pi_{L_{i,j}}$ is $6N \log(6\bar{\sigma})$ bits. The amortized proof is $540 \log(6\hat{\sigma})$ bits. The total size, for each $\mathcal{D}_i$, is

$$(3 N \log q + 6 N \log(6\bar{\sigma}) + 540 \log(6\hat{\sigma}))\tau \text{ bits.}$$

Then one party can split the key into $\xi = 2$ shares, run Π_{DistDec} on each key-share locally, and return the outputs from both $\mathcal{D}_1$ and $\mathcal{D}_2$ together with an additional proof that the key-splitting was correct. We based the estimate on the parameters from Table 1, with $\bar{\sigma} \approx 2^{16}$ and $\hat{\sigma} \approx 2^{66}$ (see e.g. Aranha et al. [5] for details about proofs and sizes). However, the amortized proof is not exact, which means that we must increase q to $q \approx 2^{78}$ to ensure correct decryption. For security $\kappa = 128$ we also need to increase N to $N = 4096$. The proof is then of size $\approx 363\tau$ KB. We conclude that Π_{ZKPCD} is of equal size as Π_{DistDec} for $\lambda = 26$ and otherwise larger.

   We do not have access to timings for this protocol. However, as the modulus is much larger, the dimension is twice the size, the zero-knowledge proofs include Gaussian sampling and rounds of aborts, we expect the protocol to be much slower than ours despite the large number of repetitions in our construction.

---

[2] https://github.com/tjesi/verifiable-decryption-in-the-head.

7.2   Comparison to Boschini *et al.* (PQ Crypto'20)

Boschini *et al.* [15] presents a zero-knowledge protocol for Ring-SIS and Ring-LWE. Their protocol can be used to prove knowledge of secrets or plaintexts, or prove correct decryption given a message and a BGV ciphertext. Concrete estimates for the latter are not given in the paper, but the number of constraints is higher for decryption than for the former. For a slightly smaller choice of parameters, a single proof of plaintext knowledge is of size 87 KB and takes roughly 3 minutes to compute. We conclude that the proof system by Boschini *et al.* will provide decryption proofs of equal size as protocol when $\lambda = 6$ and smaller otherwise. The time it takes to produce such a proof are several orders of magnitude slower than ours, making the system impossible to use in practice even for moderate sized sets of ciphertexts.

7.3   Comparison to Lyubashevsky *et al.* (PKC'21)

A recent publication by Lyubashevsky, Nguyen and Seiler [38] gives a verifiable decryption protocol for the Kyber encapsulation scheme [41]. Here, the encryption is over a rank 2 module over a ring of dimension $N = 256$ and modulus $q = 3329$ with secret and noise values bounded by $B_\infty = 2$. The proof of correct decryption of binary messages of dimension 256 is of size 43.6 KB, which of equal size as in our protocol for $\lambda = 3$. We note that the message space is smaller than in our protocol, mostly because we are forced to choose larger parameters to ensure correct decryption, and hence, we can not provide a proof of verifiable decryption for Kyber in particular. They do not provide timings, but we notice that the proof system use Gaussian sampling, rejection sampling, partially splitting rings and automorphisms – making the protocol very difficult to implement correctly and securely in practice.

7.4   Comparison to Silde (VOTING'22)

Silde [44] presents a direct verifiable decryption of BGV ciphertexts. The parameters are similar to our scheme, and the proof is of size 47 KB per ciphertext. This the same as in our scheme for $\lambda = 4$, ignoring the setup cost, while smaller for larger λ. The timing of the decryption protocol is 90 ms per ciphertext, which is equal to our timings for $\lambda = 23$ and otherwise up to 6 times faster for $\lambda = 128$.

Acknowledgment. We thank Carsten Baum and the anonymous reviewers for helpful comments.

References

1. Adida, B.: Helios: web-based open-audit voting. In: van Oorschot, P.C. (ed.) USENIX Security 2008, pp. 335–348. USENIX Association (2008)

2. Aguilar Melchor, C., Barrier, J., Guelton, S., Guinet, A., Killijian, M.O., Lepoint, T.: NFLlib: NTT-based fast lattice library. In: Sako, K. (ed.) CT-RSA 2016. LNCS, vol. 9610, pp. 341–356. Springer, Heidelberg (2016). https://doi.org/10.1007/978-3-319-29485-8_20

3. Albrecht, M.R., Player, R., Scott, S.: On the concrete hardness of learning with errors. J. Math. Cryptol. **9**(3), 169–203 (2015)

4. Ames, S., Hazay, C., Ishai, Y., Venkitasubramaniam, M.: Ligero: Lightweight sublinear arguments without a trusted setup. In: Thuraisingham, B.M., Evans, D., Malkin, T., Xu, D. (eds.) ACM CCS 2017, pp. 2087–2104. ACM Press (2017). https://doi.org/10.1145/3133956.3134104

5. Aranha, D.F., Baum, C., Gjøsteen, K., Silde, T.: Verifiable mix-nets and distributed decryption for voting from lattice-based assumptions. Cryptology ePrint Archive, Report 2022/422 (2022). https://ia.cr/2022/422

6. Attema, T., Lyubashevsky, V., Seiler, G.: Practical product proofs for lattice commitments. In: Micciancio, D., Ristenpart, T. (eds.) CRYPTO 2020. LNCS, vol. 12171, pp. 470–499. Springer, Cham (2020). https://doi.org/10.1007/978-3-030-56880-1_17

7. Baum, C., Bootle, J., Cerulli, A., del Pino, R., Groth, J., Lyubashevsky, V.: Sublinear lattice-based zero-knowledge arguments for arithmetic circuits. In: Shacham, H., Boldyreva, A. (eds.) CRYPTO 2018. LNCS, vol. 10992, pp. 669–699. Springer, Cham (2018). https://doi.org/10.1007/978-3-319-96881-0_23

8. Baum, C., Damgård, I., Lyubashevsky, V., Oechsner, S., Peikert, C.: More efficient commitments from structured lattice assumptions. In: Catalano, D., De Prisco, R. (eds.) SCN 2018. LNCS, vol. 11035, pp. 368–385. Springer, Cham (2018). https://doi.org/10.1007/978-3-319-98113-0_20

9. Baum, C., Nof, A.: Concretely-efficient zero-knowledge arguments for arithmetic circuits and their application to lattice-based cryptography. In: Kiayias, A., Kohlweiss, M., Wallden, P., Zikas, V. (eds.) PKC 2020. LNCS, vol. 12110, pp. 495–526. Springer, Cham (2020). https://doi.org/10.1007/978-3-030-45374-9_17

10. Ben-Sasson, E., Chiesa, A., Riabzev, M., Spooner, N., Virza, M., Ward, N.P.: Aurora: transparent succinct arguments for R1CS. In: Ishai, Y., Rijmen, V. (eds.) EUROCRYPT 2019. LNCS, vol. 11476, pp. 103–128. Springer, Cham (2019). https://doi.org/10.1007/978-3-030-17653-2_4

11. Bendlin, R., Damgård, I.: Threshold decryption and zero-knowledge proofs for lattice-based cryptosystems. In: Micciancio, D. (ed.) TCC 2010. LNCS, vol. 5978, pp. 201–218. Springer, Heidelberg (2010). https://doi.org/10.1007/978-3-642-11799-2_13

12. Bertot, Y., Castéran, P., Huet, G., Paulin-Mohring, C.: Interactive theorem proving and program development : Coq'Art : the calculus of inductive constructions. Texts in theoretical computer science, Springer (2004). https://doi.org/10.1007/978-3-662-07964-5

13. Bettaieb, S., Schrek, J.: Improved lattice-based threshold ring signature scheme. In: Gaborit, P. (ed.) PQCrypto 2013. LNCS, vol. 7932, pp. 34–51. Springer, Heidelberg (2013). https://doi.org/10.1007/978-3-642-38616-9_3

14. Beullens, W.: Sigma protocols for MQ, PKP and SIS, and fishy signature schemes. In: Canteaut, A., Ishai, Y. (eds.) EUROCRYPT 2020. LNCS, vol. 12107, pp. 183–211. Springer, Cham (2020). https://doi.org/10.1007/978-3-030-45727-3_7

15. Boschini, C., Camenisch, J., Ovsiankin, M., Spooner, N.: Efficient Post-quantum SNARKs for RSIS and RLWE and Their Applications to Privacy. In: Ding, J., Tillich, J.-P. (eds.) PQCrypto 2020. LNCS, vol. 12100, pp. 247–267. Springer, Cham (2020). https://doi.org/10.1007/978-3-030-44223-1_14

16. Boyle, E., Kohl, L., Scholl, P.: Homomorphic secret sharing from lattices without FHE. In: Ishai, Y., Rijmen, V. (eds.) EUROCRYPT 2019. LNCS, vol. 11477, pp. 3–33. Springer, Cham (2019). https://doi.org/10.1007/978-3-030-17656-3_1

17. Brakerski, Z., Gentry, C., Vaikuntanathan, V.: (Leveled) fully homomorphic encryption without bootstrapping. In: Goldwasser, S. (ed.) ITCS 2012, pp. 309–325. ACM (2012). https://doi.org/10.1145/2090236.2090262

18. Groot Bruinderink, L., Hülsing, A., Lange, T., Yarom, Y.: Flush, Gauss, and Reload – a cache attack on the bliss lattice-based signature scheme. In: Gierlichs, B., Poschmann, A.Y. (eds.) CHES 2016. LNCS, vol. 9813, pp. 323–345. Springer, Heidelberg (2016). https://doi.org/10.1007/978-3-662-53140-2_16

19. Chaum, D., Pedersen, T.P.: Wallet databases with observers. In: Brickell, E.F. (ed.) CRYPTO 1992. LNCS, vol. 740, pp. 89–105. Springer, Heidelberg (1993). https://doi.org/10.1007/3-540-48071-4_7

20. Damgård, I., Keller, M., Larraia, E., Pastro, V., Scholl, P., Smart, N.P.: Practical covertly secure MPC for dishonest majority - or: Breaking the SPDZ limits. In: Crampton, J., Jajodia, S., Mayes, K. (eds.) ESORICS 2013. LNCS, vol. 8134, pp. 1–18. Springer, Heidelberg (Sep 2013)

21. Damgård, I., Orlandi, C., Takahashi, A., Tibouchi, M.: Two-Round n-out-of-n and multi-signatures and trapdoor commitment from lattices. In: Garay, J.A. (ed.) PKC 2021. LNCS, vol. 12710, pp. 99–130. Springer, Cham (2021). https://doi.org/10.1007/978-3-030-75245-3_5

22. Damgård, I., Pastro, V., Smart, N., Zakarias, S.: Multiparty Computation from Somewhat Homomorphic Encryption. In: Safavi-Naini, R., Canetti, R. (eds.) CRYPTO 2012. LNCS, vol. 7417, pp. 643–662. Springer, Heidelberg (2012). https://doi.org/10.1007/978-3-642-32009-5_38

23. Desmedt, Y., Frankel, Y.: Threshold cryptosystems. In: Brassard, G. (ed.) CRYPTO 1989. LNCS, vol. 435, pp. 307–315. Springer, New York (1990). https://doi.org/10.1007/0-387-34805-0_28

24. Dodis, Y., Halevi, S., Rothblum, R.D., Wichs, D.: Spooky encryption and its applications. In: Robshaw, M., Katz, J. (eds.) CRYPTO 2016. LNCS, vol. 9816, pp. 93–122. Springer, Heidelberg (2016). https://doi.org/10.1007/978-3-662-53015-3_4

25. Espitau, T., Fouque, P.A., Gérard, B., Tibouchi, M.: Side-channel attacks on BLISS lattice-based signatures: Exploiting branch tracing against strongSwan and electromagnetic emanations in microcontrollers. In: Thuraisingham, B.M., Evans, D., Malkin, T., Xu, D. (eds.) ACM CCS 2017, pp. 1857–1874. ACM Press (2017). https://doi.org/10.1145/3133956.3134028

26. Fiat, A., Shamir, A.: How to prove yourself: practical solutions to identification and signature problems. In: Odlyzko, A.M. (ed.) CRYPTO 1986. LNCS, vol. 263, pp. 186–194. Springer, Heidelberg (1987). https://doi.org/10.1007/3-540-47721-7_12

27. Gordon, D.M.: A survey of fast exponentiation methods. J. Algorithms **27**(1), 129–146 (1998). https://doi.org/10.1006/jagm.1997.0913

28. Haines, T., Lewis, S.J., Pereira, O., Teague, V.: How not to prove your election outcome. In: 2020 IEEE Symposium on Security and Privacy, pp. 644–660. IEEE Computer Society Press (2020). https://doi.org/10.1109/SP40000.2020.00048

29. Haines, T., Müller, J.: SoK: techniques for verifiable mix nets. In: Jia, L., Küsters, R. (eds.) CSF 2020 Computer Security Foundations Symposium, pp. 49–64. IEEE Computer Society Press (2020). https://doi.org/10.1109/CSF49147.2020.00012

30. Heiberg, S., Willemson, J.: Verifiable internet voting in Estonia. In: 6th International Conference on Electronic Voting: Verifying the Vote, EVOTE 2014 (2014)

31. Ishai, Y., Kushilevitz, E., Ostrovsky, R., Sahai, A.: Zero-knowledge from secure multiparty computation. In: Johnson, D.S., Feige, U. (eds.) 39th ACM STOC. pp. 21–30. ACM Press (2007). https://doi.org/10.1145/1250790.1250794

32. Kawachi, A., Tanaka, K., Xagawa, K.: Concurrently secure identification schemes based on the worst-case hardness of lattice problems. In: Pieprzyk, J. (ed.) ASIACRYPT 2008. LNCS, vol. 5350, pp. 372–389. Springer, Heidelberg (2008). https://doi.org/10.1007/978-3-540-89255-7_23

33. Keller, M., Pastro, V., Rotaru, D.: Overdrive: making SPDZ great again. In: Nielsen, J.B., Rijmen, V. (eds.) EUROCRYPT 2018. LNCS, vol. 10822, pp. 158–189. Springer, Cham (2018). https://doi.org/10.1007/978-3-319-78372-7_6

34. Ling, S., Nguyen, K., Stehlé, D., Wang, H.: Improved zero-knowledge proofs of knowledge for the ISIS problem, and applications. In: Kurosawa, K., Hanaoka, G. (eds.) PKC 2013. LNCS, vol. 7778, pp. 107–124. Springer, Heidelberg (2013). https://doi.org/10.1007/978-3-642-36362-7_8

35. Luo, F., Wang, K.: Verifiable decryption for fully homomorphic encryption. In: Chen, L., Manulis, M., Schneider, S. (eds.) ISC 2018. LNCS, vol. 11060, pp. 347–365. Springer, Cham (2018). https://doi.org/10.1007/978-3-319-99136-8_19

36. Lyubashevsky, V.: Fiat-shamir with aborts: applications to lattice and factoring-based signatures. In: Matsui, M. (ed.) ASIACRYPT 2009. LNCS, vol. 5912, pp. 598–616. Springer, Heidelberg (2009). https://doi.org/10.1007/978-3-642-10366-7_35

37. Lyubashevsky, V.: Lattice signatures without trapdoors. In: Pointcheval, D., Johansson, T. (eds.) EUROCRYPT 2012. LNCS, vol. 7237, pp. 738–755. Springer, Heidelberg (2012). https://doi.org/10.1007/978-3-642-29011-4_43

38. Lyubashevsky, V., Nguyen, N.K., Seiler, G.: Shorter lattice-based zero-knowledge proofs via one-time commitments. In: Garay, J.A. (ed.) PKC 2021. LNCS, vol. 12710, pp. 215–241. Springer, Cham (2021). https://doi.org/10.1007/978-3-030-75245-3_9

39. Lyubashevsky, V., Peikert, C., Regev, O.: A toolkit for ring-LWE cryptography. In: Johansson, T., Nguyen, P.Q. (eds.) EUROCRYPT 2013. LNCS, vol. 7881, pp. 35–54. Springer, Heidelberg (2013). https://doi.org/10.1007/978-3-642-38348-9_3

40. Peng, K., Boyd, C., Dawson, E.: Batch zero-knowledge proof and verification and its applications. ACM Trans. Inf. Syst. Secur. 10(2), 6 (2007)

41. Schwabe, P., et al.: CRYSTALS-KYBER. Tech. rep., National Institute of Standards and Technology (2020), available at https://csrc.nist.gov/projects/post-quantum-cryptography/round-3-submissions

42. Shirazi, F., Simeonovski, M., Asghar, M.R., Backes, M., Diaz, C.: A survey on routing in anonymous communication protocols. ACM Comput. Surv. 51(3) (2018). https://doi.org/10.1145/3182658

43. Shoup, V.: NTL: a library for doing number theory (2021). https://libntl.org/index.html

44. Silde, T.: Verifiable Decryption for BGV. Workshop on Advances in Secure Electronic Voting (2022). https://ia.cr/2021/1693

Resumable Zero-Knowledge for Circuits from Symmetric Key Primitives

Handong Zhang[1,2], Puwen Wei[1,2(✉)], Haiyang Xue[3], Yi Deng[4,5], Jinsong Li[1,2], Wei Wang[1,2], and Guoxiao Liu[1,2]

[1] Key Laboratory of Cryptologic Technology and Information Security, Ministry of Education, Shandong University, Jinan, China
{hdzhang,jsli,liuguoxiao}@mail.sdu.edu.cn, {pwei,weiwangsdu}@sdu.edu.cn
[2] School of Cyber Science and Technology, Shandong University, Qingdao, China
[3] The University of Hong Kong, Pokfulam, Hong Kong, China
haiyangxc@gmail.com
[4] State Key Laboratory of Information Security, Institute of Information Engineering, Chinese Academy of Sciences, Beijing, China
deng@iie.ac.cn
[5] School of Cyber Security, University of Chinese Academy of Sciences, Beijing, China

Abstract. Consider the scenario that the prover and the verifier perform the zero-knowledge (ZK) proof protocol for the same statement multiple times sequentially, where each proof is modeled as a session. We focus on the problem of how to resume a ZK proof efficiently in such scenario. We introduce a new primitive called *resumable honest verifier zero-knowledge proof of knowledge* (resumable HVZKPoK) and propose a general construction of the resumable HVZKPoK for circuits based on the "MPC-in-the-head" paradigm, where the complexity of the resumed session is less than that of the original ZK proofs. To ensure the knowledge soundness for the resumed session, we identify a property called extractable decomposition. Interestingly, most block ciphers satisfy this property and the cost of resuming session can be reduced dramatically when the underlying circuits are implemented with block ciphers. As a direct application of our resumable HVZKPoK, we construct a post quantum secure stateful signature scheme, which makes Picnic3 suitable for blockchain protocol. Using the same parameter setting of Picnic3, the sign/verify time of our subsequent signatures can be reduced to 3.1%/3.3% of Picnic3 and the corresponding signature size can be reduced to 36%. Moreover, by applying a parallel version of our method to the well known Cramer, Damgård and Schoenmakers (CDS) transformation, we get a compressed one-out-of-N proof for circuits, which can be further used to construct a ring signature from symmetric key primitives only. When the ring size is less than 2^4, the size of our ring signature scheme is only about 1/3 of Katz et al.'s construction.

Keywords: Resumable · Honest verifier zero-knowledge · MPC-in-the-head · Stateful signature · Ring signature · Blockchain

© The Author(s), under exclusive license to Springer Nature Switzerland AG 2022
K. Nguyen et al. (Eds.): ACISP 2022, LNCS 13494, pp. 375–398, 2022.
https://doi.org/10.1007/978-3-031-22301-3_19

1   Introduction

Zero-knowledge (ZK) proofs [29,30] and their non-interactive form (NIZK) [12], which allow a prover to convince a verifier of a certain statement without revealing any additional information, are among the most fundamental and important cryptographic primitives. It is known that there exists ZK proof [29] for any NP language, while the resulting construction is rather inefficient. A lot of works have been done to propose efficient (NI)ZK proofs for arbitrary circuits or specific algebraic computation, e.g., zk-SNARKs [9,25], which have short proof for a statement. Some works focus on the efficient composition of ZK proofs for several statements [1,20,24]. Other works such as [14,34,40] investigate the batch ZK proofs, which enable many instances of the same relation to be proved and verified simultaneously. Amongst most of those constructions, the randomness and the related transcripts are "recycled" or compressed in *one* execution of the resulting ZK protocol in order to reduce the cost of computation or communication.

Notice that one common case of ZK proof, however, is proving the same statement repeatedly multiple times. For example, a user may be required to provide digital signatures on different messages periodically, where each signature can be thought of as one execution of the NIZK proof of knowledge of the signing key [7]. One typical application is validating the authenticity of firmware updates for IoT devices. The manufacturer periodically offers firmware updates and the corresponding signatures, and the IoT devices verify these signatures in order to ensure the authenticity of the updates. Another direct application of ZK is the identification protocol, which could be used by a company to determine the identity of a user each time he tries to access company resources.

Hence, it is worth considering the efficiency of ZK protocols in a scenario where the prover and the verifier need to run the ZK proof of a statement many times (sequentially). In practice, the state information derived from previous sessions could be reused in the following sessions to achieve significant savings in processing load and bandwidth, e.g., session resumption of TLS 1.3 [41]. It is desired that the ZK protocol for the subsequent sessions be much more efficient than that of the original one. Therefore, a natural question is that

How can we resume a session of ZK proofs efficiently?

An intuitive way is to reuse the information of previous ZK sessions (of the same statement). In fact, similar issues have been considered in the research of NIZK. A series of works explored how to reuse the common reference string (CRS) of NIZK for multiple theorems and multiple provers [12,22,33], which implies the case of CRS reuse in multiple sessions (or executions). On the interactive ZK protocols, how to securely reuse previous transcripts among different sessions is, however, more subtle and tends to result in a breach of security. For instance, the witness in many Σ protocols can be extracted when the same commitments are reused in different sessions (with different challenges).

In another recent line of works, researchers have shown how to use secure multiparty computation (MPC) to obtain (NI)ZK proofs, and further quantum-resistant signatures. Ishai et al. [35] showed how to use the so-called "MPC-in-the-head" approach to obtain public-coin ZK proofs. Their scheme was further improved by [18,26] to obtain quantum-resistant signature via Fiat-Shamir transformation [23]. The resulting signature Picnic [16], which was submitted to the NIST post-quantum standardization effort, is very competitive, since its security is based entirely on symmetric-key primitives. But it is still less efficient than lattice-based CRYSTALS-DILITHIUM [4] and multivariate-based Rainbow [21]. So we would like to ask whether we could reduce the overall complexity of Picnic when considering multiple sequential signing requests. In other words, *how can we resume the signing/verifying procedure of* Picnic *efficiently?*

1.1 Our Contributions

We introduce the notion of *resumable honest verifier ZK proof of knowledge* (resumable HVZKPoK) to capture the security and efficiency of HVZKPoK in the scenario of session resumption. In that scenario, the prover and the verifier can perform the ZK proofs multiple times sequentially, where each proof is executed in a session. Informally, we say an HVZKPoK is resumable if it satisfies (1) *resumable zero-knowledge*, i.e., no additional information about the witness is revealed from *all* sessions; (2) *resumable knowledge soundness*, i.e., the witness can be extracted from *every* session; (3) *resumption efficiency*, i.e., the cost of the resumed session in terms of both computation and communication should be much less than that of the initial session (or the original ZK proofs).

The main challenge of constructing resumable HVZKPoK is to achieve resumable knowledge soundness while preserving resumption efficiency, since removing or reusing partial transcripts of the original ZK proofs would undermine or break its soundness property in general. To overcome that problem, we investigate the "MPC-in-the-head" paradigm in the preprocessing model proposed by Katz, Kolesnikov and Wang (KKW) [38], and find that their proofs can be separated according to the decomposition of circuits, where the proofs for the corresponding partial circuits can be further rerandomized without breaking the security. By making use of such separability of the KKW proofs, we provide a general construction of the resumable HVZKPoK. The main idea is that the underlying circuits are decomposed into two parts, where the proofs for the partial circuits with smaller size can be rerandomized. Once the initial session of proofs for the entire circuits is finished, both the prover and the verifier can resume a session by running the rerandomized proofs for the partial circuits only. Since the cost of the KKW proofs is closely related to the number of the AND gates of the circuits, the cost of the resumed session is reduced significantly due to the size of the partial circuits.

Notice that only proofs for the partial circuits usually cannot achieve knowledge soundness implied by the proofs for the entire circuits. To mitigate that problem, we identify a property called extractable decomposition, which guarantees that the witness can be extracted from the inputs of the separated partial circuits. Interestingly, most block ciphers satisfy this property. In addition, the circuits of block ciphers can be decomposed such that the separated partial circuits have no AND gates. Hence, the cost for resuming sessions can be made very small when implemented with block ciphers. By applying the Fiat-Shamir heuristic [23], our resumable HVZKPoK can be transformed into a stateful post-quantum signature scheme. Comparing with the typical chain-based stateful signature [37], the main advantage of our scheme is that, once the initial signature has been generated, the subsequent signatures are much more efficient than the initial one.

We implement our signature and give a comparison with Picnic3 [36]. The sign/verify time of our subsequent signatures can be reduced to 3.1%/3.3%-9.2%/8.8% of Picnic3 and the corresponding signature size can be reduced to 36.0%-38.1%. (For the fixed verifier, the size of the state information needed to be stored is about 2.9 KB-10.9KB.) Although the complexity of our first signature is slightly higher than Picnic3, it is worthy for the reducing cost of subsequent signatures. In particular, our stateful signatures make the symmetric-based signatures, such as Picnic3, suitable for the post-quantum secure blockchain protocol. That is, the previous signatures (or the states) can be stored in the history blocks efficiently and publicly. The verifier only needs to check the validity of the current signature without checking all previous signatures, since the validity of the previous signatures is implied by the consistency of the underlying consensus protocol.

Moreover, applying our method to the Cramer, Damgård and Schoenmakers (CDS) technique [20], we construct a compressed one-out-of N proof, where most of the transcripts for the simulation in CDS technique can be removed. Furthermore, we can construct a ring signature from symmetric key primitives using our compressed one-out-of N proof (without resorting to the Merkle-tree based accumulator). Comparing with the ring signatures from symmetric key primitives proposed by [38], the size of our ring signature is about 1/3 of [38] when the ring size is less than 2^4.

1.2 Related Works

Zero-Knowledge from Symmetric Primitives. Most efficient ZK proofs exist for a restricted set of languages, e.g., languages relying on algebraic structures. To construct efficient ZK proofs for a larger class of languages, many works focus on ZK proofs for arbitrary circuits [8–11,13,15,19,25,31,32,39,43], which have relatively short proofs size and verification time. However, most efficient constructions require a trusted setup or rely on assumptions, which are insecure in the quantum setting.

Ishai et al. [35] introduced a novel way of constructing ZK proofs, called "MPC-in-the-head", which is based on secure multi-party computation (MPC) protocols. Following the idea of [35], Giacomelli et al. [26] proposed ZKBoo which supports efficient non-interactive (NI) ZKPoKs for arbitrary circuits. Chase et al. [18] improved the performance of ZKBoo and proposed ZKB++, which is used to construct the post-quantum secure signature scheme, called Picnic. Compared with other post-quantum secure signature candidates, Picnic relies on the security of the underlying symmetric-key primitives instead of structured hardness assumptions. Although Picnic has good performance on the speed when implemented on hardware, it has a large signature size which is linear in the size of the circuits. Ames et al. [3] proposed Ligero with sublinear proof size, which asymptotically outperforms ZKBoo and ZKB++. Katz et al. [38] instantiated the MPC-in-the-head paradigm in the preprocessing model, which can reduce the number of parallel repetitions, and provided an improved version of Picnic, called Picnic2. Guilhem et al. [42] applied the "MPC-in-the-head with preprocessing" approach to the arithmetic circuit of AES and implemented a signature scheme, called BBQ, whose security is based on AES. Baum et al. [6] proposed a novel way to construct an AES-based signature scheme, called Banquet, which reduces the signature size compared with BBQ and its implementation results show that Banquet can be made almost as efficient as Picnic2 . Baum and Nof [5] incorporated the "sacrificing" paradigm into "MPC-in-the-head" to reduce the proof size for arithmetic circuits. Kales and Zaverucha [36] made further optimizations and presented a new parameter set for Picnic2, called Picnic3. Goel et al. [27] introduced a general framework for constructing Σ-protocols of disjunctive proof which can be used to implement ring signature. Recently, Goel et al. [28] proposed a novel technique for efficiently adding set membership proofs to any MPC-in-the-head based ZK protocol and the resulting ring signatures outperform Katz et al.'s construction by a factor of 5 to 8.

2 Preliminaries

Notations. Let $[n]$ denote $\{1, \ldots, n\}$ and κ denote the security parameters. Let C and C' be the boolean circuit representation of F and f, respectively, where C and C' consists of XOR and AND gates. Let $|C|$ denotes the number of AND gates in the circuit C and $|C_{in/out}|$ denotes the number of input/output wires of C. Let $L_R \subseteq \{0,1\}^*$ be an NP language and R be the related NP-relation for circuit C. $A \approx_c B$ denotes computational indistinguishability between distributions A and B. Let Com denote a commitment scheme. A commitment to a message m is denoted as $\text{com} = \text{Com}(m; r)$ where $r \in \{0,1\}^\kappa$ is chosen uniformly. We say Com is secure if it satisfies the following properties: (1) *Hiding*: $\text{Com}(m; r)$ reveals noting about m; (2) *Binding*: it is hard to find two messages $m \neq m'$ such that $\text{Com}(m; r) = \text{Com}(m'; r')$. Let H denote the hash function. We say H is collision-resistant if the probability that any PPT adversary finds x and x' such that $H(x) = H(x')$ and $x \neq x'$ is negligible.

2.1 MPC-in-the-head with Preprocessing

MPC-in-the-head paradigm [35] is a novel technique to construct ZK proofs from MPC protocols. Suppose the statement to be proven is (C, y), where $C(w) = y$ and w is the witness. Following the MPC-in-the-head paradigm, the prover simulates an MPC protocol which evaluates the circuit C among all the parties *in his head* and the input of each party is a secret sharing of the witness w. The prover then commits to the views of each party in the execution of the MPC protocol. The verifier randomly chooses a subset of these commitments as the challenge. Once receiving the challenge, the prover opens the challenged commitments. The verifier checks the correctness and consistency of these views.

MPC-in-the-head with preprocessing (KKW) [38] improves MPC-in-the-head paradigm and the resulting scheme can achieve the required soundness with much shorter proofs. Loosely speaking, the KKW protocol has two phases, the *preprocessing* phase and the *online* phase. In the *preprocessing* phase, the prover generates random masks for each party, which are used to hide the witness. In the *online* phase, the prover simulates the execution of the MPC protocol using the masked shares of each party and the masked input (or the masked witness) of the circuit. Note that the verifier needs to challenge both phases. The main techniques of MPC-in-the-head with preprocessing are described below.

Let $[x]$ denote an n-out-of-n (XOR-based) secret sharing scheme of a bit x, i.e., $x = [x]_1 \oplus \cdots \oplus [x]_n$, where $[x]_i$ for $1 \leq i \leq n$ is the secret share. Suppose the underlying n-party MPC protocol is Π, which is executed by n parties $P_1, \cdots, P_n$. Let z_α denote the value of wire α of $C(w)$. z_α will be masked by a random bit λ_α, say, $\hat{z}_\alpha = z_\alpha \oplus \lambda_\alpha$. Each party P_i will hold $[\lambda_\alpha]_i$, which is a share of λ_α.

- **Preprocessing phase.** In the preprocessing phase, the prover generates the masks for each party P_i. More precisely, P_i is given the following values.
  - $[\lambda_\alpha]_i$ for each input wire α.
  - $[\lambda_\gamma]_i$ for the output wire γ of each AND gate.
  - $[\lambda_{\alpha,\beta}]_i$ for each AND gate with input wires α and β such that $\lambda_{\alpha,\beta} = \lambda_\alpha \cdot \lambda_\beta$.

  $[\lambda_\alpha]_i$ and $[\lambda_\gamma]_i$ can be generated using a pseudorandom generator (PRG) with a random seed seed_i, for $i = 1, \ldots, n$, where $[\lambda_\alpha]_1 \oplus \cdots \oplus [\lambda_\alpha]_n = \lambda_\alpha$ and $[\lambda_\gamma]_1 \oplus \cdots \oplus [\lambda_\gamma]_n = \lambda_\gamma$. Hence, seed_i instead of $\{[\lambda_\alpha]_i\}$ and $\{[\lambda_\gamma]_i\}$ is given to P_i so that the total proof size can be reduced. Notice that $[\lambda_{\alpha,\beta}]_n$ cannot be generated using seed_n only due to $\lambda_{\alpha,\beta} = \lambda_\alpha \cdot \lambda_\beta$. Actually, $n-1$ shares of $\lambda_{\alpha,\beta}$ are generated using PRG, while the share of P_n is computed by $[\lambda_{\alpha,\beta}]_n := \lambda_\alpha \lambda_\beta \oplus [\lambda_{\alpha,\beta}]_1 \oplus \cdots [\lambda_{\alpha,\beta}]_{n-1}$, which plays the role of "correction bits". Therefore, party P_n needs to be given $\mathsf{aux}_n = \{[\lambda_{\alpha,\beta}]_n\}$ for all AND gates in addition to seed_n.

- **Online phase.** During the online phase, each party P_i runs the underlying n-party MPC protocol Π to evaluate the circuit C gate-by-gate in topological order. For each gate with input wires α and β and output wire γ,
  - For an XOR gate, P_i can locally compute $\hat{z}_\gamma = \hat{z}_\alpha \oplus \hat{z}_\beta$ and $[\lambda_\gamma]_i = [\lambda_\alpha]_i \oplus [\lambda_\beta]_i$, since P_i already holds $\hat{z}_\alpha$, $[\lambda_\alpha]_i$, $\hat{z}_\beta$ and $[\lambda_\beta]_i$.
  - For an AND gate, P_i locally computes $[s]_i = \hat{z}_\alpha[\lambda_\beta]_i \oplus \hat{z}_\beta[\lambda_\alpha]_i \oplus [\lambda_{\alpha,\beta}]_i \oplus [\lambda_\gamma]_i$, publicly reconstructs s, and computes $\hat{z}_\gamma = s \oplus \hat{z}_\alpha \hat{z}_\beta$ which satisfies $\hat{z}_\gamma = z_\gamma \oplus \lambda_\gamma$. Note that party P_i holds $[\lambda_{\alpha,\beta}]_i$ and $[\lambda_\gamma]_i$ in addition to $\hat{z}_\alpha$, $[\lambda_\alpha]_i$, $\hat{z}_\beta$ and $[\lambda_\beta]_i$ for each AND gate.

Finally, each party P_i can compute $\hat{z}_\gamma$ for the output wire γ of the circuit, and the output value z_γ is computed as $z_\gamma = \hat{z}_\gamma \oplus \lambda_\gamma$, where λ_γ is reconstructed publicly.

Security of the underlying MPC protocol. [17, Lemma 6.1] proves that the underlying MPC protocol Π_{mpc} is secure against an all-but-one corruption in the semi-honest model by showing that there exists a simulator for the MPC protocol Π_{mpc} such that the real execution of Π_{mpc} is computational indistinguishable from the simulated execution of Π_{mpc} under the assumption of secure PRG.

3 Resumable HVZK Proof of Knowledge

Let R be an efficiently decidable binary NP-relation which is polynomially bounded, and L_R be the NP-language defined by R. That is, $\exists w$ such that $(x, w) \in R$ iff $x \in L_R$. In our setting, the prover and the verifier can sequentially perform the zero-knowledge proofs for L_R polynomially-many times, say $q(\kappa)$ times, where each proof is modeled as a session and the t-th session is denoted as $\mathsf{session}(t)$, for $t \in \{1, \ldots, q(\kappa)\}$. In each $\mathsf{session}(t)$, the prover aims to convince the verifier that he knows the witness w for statement x by running the HVZKPoK protocol $\Pi = \{(\mathcal{P}^{(t)}, \mathcal{V}^{(t)})\}$. Let $\mathcal{P}^{(t)} = \mathcal{P}(x, w, pr_t, ps_t)$ denote the prover's strategy of $\mathsf{session}(t)$, which takes as input the common-input x, witness w, prover's randomness pr_t and state ps_t. Here, ps_t is the prover's state after $\mathsf{session}(t-1)$. Similarly, let $\mathcal{V}^{(t)} = \mathcal{V}(x, vr_t, vs_t)$ denote the verifier's strategy of $\mathsf{session}(t)$, which takes as inputs the common-input x, verifier's randomness vr_t and state vs_t.

In this paper, we transform an "ordinary" HVZKPoK $\Pi' = (\mathcal{P}', \mathcal{V}')$ to a resumable HVZKPoK $\Pi = \{(\mathcal{P}^{(t)}, \mathcal{V}^{(t)})\}$, the security of which is more subtle. In particular, we have to ensure that the adversary who does not have the knowledge of the witness cannot convince the verifier in any session, even that the adversary can have access to the transcripts of all previous sessions. Consider the following game on soundness. The adversary A can invoke the "honest" prover to run Π for $x \in L_R$ with the verifier for polynomially-many sequential sessions, say, $\mathsf{session}(1), \ldots, \mathsf{session}(q(\kappa) - 1)$, where A can get all the transcripts of these sessions. For the next session, say $\mathsf{session}\ q(\kappa)$, A runs Π with the verifier for $x \in L_R$, trying to convince the verifier without the help of the "honest" prover. The soundness of the resumable HVZK is defined according the above game, which requires that A can win the game only with negligible probability. Formal definition of resumable HVZKPoK is described below.

Definition 1 (Resumable HVZK Proof of Knowledge). $\Pi = \{(\mathcal{P}^{(t)}, \mathcal{V}^{(t)})\}$ *is a resumable honest verifier zero-knowledge proof of knowledge for the relation R with soundness error ξ if the following properties hold:*

- **Completeness:** *If the prover and the verifier follow the protocol $(\mathcal{P}^{(t)}, \mathcal{V}^{(t)})$ on inputs $x \in L_R$ and witness $w \in R_x$, then the verifier always accepts in each $\mathsf{session}(t)$, for $t \in \{1, \ldots, q(\kappa)\}$.*

- **Resumable Honest Verifier Zero-Knowledge:** *Let* $\mathsf{view}_{\mathcal{V}}^{\mathcal{P}}(x, w)$ *be the transcripts of all the sessions run by the prover and the verifier. There exists a PPT simulator* Sim *such that* $\mathsf{Sim}(x) \approx_c \mathsf{view}_{\mathcal{V}}^{\mathcal{P}}(x, w)$ *for all* $x \in L_R$ *and* $w \in R_x$.
- **Resumable Knowledge Soundness:** *For each* $\mathsf{session}(t)$, *there exists a probabilistic knowledge extractor* $\mathcal{E}$, *such that for every* $\hat{\mathcal{P}}^{(t)}$ *and every* $x \in L_R$, *the algorithm* $\mathcal{E}$ *satisfies the following condition:*
  - *Let* $\delta_t(x)$ *denote the probability that the verifier accepts on input* x *for* $(\hat{\mathcal{P}}^{(t)}, \mathcal{V}^{(t)})$ *of* $\mathsf{session}(t)$. *If* $\delta_t(x) > \xi_t(x)$, *then upon input* $x \in L_R$ *and oracle access to* $\hat{\mathcal{P}}^{(t)}$, *the algorithm* $\mathcal{E}$ *outputs a valid witness* $w \in R_x$ *in expected number of steps bounded by* $O(\frac{1}{\delta_t(x) - \xi_t(x)})$.

  Here, ξ_t *denotes the soundness error of* $\mathsf{session}(t)$ *for* $t \in \{1, \ldots, q(\kappa)\}$. *Let* $\xi = \max\{\xi_1, \ldots, \xi_{q(\kappa)}\}$.
- **Resumption efficiency:** *For each* $\mathsf{session}(t)$ *with* $t > 1$, *the computational and communicational complexity of* $(\mathcal{P}^{(t)}, \mathcal{V}^{(t)})$ *should be less than that of the original HVZKPoK* $\Pi' = (\mathcal{P}', \mathcal{V}')$ *for R. That is, resumable HVZK proof of knowledge should be efficient in each resumed session.*

Here, the statement x of R is of the form (F, y), such that $(x, w) \in R$ iff $F(w) = y$, where F denotes a function. Let C be the circuit representation of F. So the statement can be rewritten as (C, y), such that $(x, w) \in R$ iff $C(w) = y$. As mentioned in Sect. 1, the function F needs to satisfy a special property called extractable decomposition, which is defined as follows.

Definition 2 (Extractable Decomposition). *Let* $F : \{0,1\}^{\kappa} \to \{0,1\}^{\kappa'}$ *be a function which has a decomposition as* $F = f \circ g$. *We say the decomposition is extractable if, for all* $x \in \{0,1\}^{\kappa}$, *there exists an efficient extractor* $\mathcal{E}_D$ *such that* $\mathcal{E}_D(g(x)) = x$.

Consider the case that $F(w) = \mathsf{Enc}(w, m)$, where $\mathsf{Enc}(w, m)$ is a block cipher with the private key w and the plaintext m. It is known that a typical block cipher consists of multiple rounds, where each round takes as inputs the output of previous round and the corresponding subkey (or round key) derived from the *master* key w. Note that the subkey schedule of most block ciphers is reversable, which implies most block ciphers naturally satisfy the property of extractable decomposition. Concretely, given a block cipher with n rounds, the first $n - 1$ rounds as well as the key schedule can be taken as g, and the last round is taken as f. Suppose the output of $g(w)$ is w', which consists of the output of the $(n - 1)$-th round and n-th round key k_n. f takes as input w' and outputs the final ciphertext. Obviously, w can be extracted from w', which implies the extractability of the decomposition.

4   General Construction for Resumable HVZKPoK

In this section, we present the general construction of resumable HVZKPoK from the KKW protocol. We first abstract the construction of the original KKW protocol [38] for $F(w) = y$, where F has a decomposition as $F = f \circ g$. Then, we show how to efficiently resume HVZKPoK for w' such that $f(w') = y$ and $w' = g(w)$. Recall that C and C' denote the circuit representation of F and f, respectively. So $F(w) = y$ and $f(w') = y$ can be rewritten as $C(w) = y$ and $C'(w') = y$, respectively.

4.1 KKW Protocol for F

The KKW protocol π^F for $C(w) = y$, i.e., $F(w) = y$, consists of the preprocessing phase π_{pre}^F and the online phase π_{on}^F. π_{pre}^F shows that the n parties' states are generated randomly and correctly by "cut-and-choose", and π_{on}^F ensures that each party's view in the MPC protocol are correct and consistent. Let M denote the number of repetitions for reducing the soundness error.

Preprocessing phase $\pi_{pre}^F(1^\kappa)$.

- Round 1. *Commit* to the masks of M instances.
  The prover prepares the masks λ_j of the MPC protocol for the circuit C as described in Sect. 2.1 for each instance $j \in [M]$. Since λ_j is determined by n parties' states $\{\text{state}_{j,1}, \ldots, \text{state}_{j,n}\}$, which are the random seeds and the n-th party's auxiliary information, the prover only needs to commit to those states. The corresponding commitments are denoted as com_{pre}^F. The prover sends com_{pre}^F to the verifier.
- Round 2. *Challenge* for the preprocessing phase.
  The verifier chooses a random subset $\mathcal{C} \in [M]$ with $|\mathcal{C}| = \tau$, which is used to challenge the prover to open the commitments of instances in $[M] \backslash \mathcal{C}$, so that the verifier can check the randomness and correctness of λ_j for each instance $j \in [M] \backslash \mathcal{C}$. The verifier sends $\mathcal{C}$ to the prover.
- Round 3-a. *Respond* to the challenge for the preprocessing phase.
  The prover computes the openings of the commitments of instances in $[M] \backslash \mathcal{C}$. Denote these openings as resp_{pre}^F. The prover sends resp_{pre}^F to the verifier.

Online phase $\pi_{on}^F(w, \{\text{state}_{j,i}\}_{j \in \mathcal{C}, i \in [n]})$.

- Round 3-b. *Commit* to the views of each party.
  The prover runs the n-party MPC protocol for $C(w) = y$ using the masks λ_j and the witness w for each instance $j \in \mathcal{C}$, and computes the commitments to the views of each party in the MPC protocol execution. Let com_{on}^F denote these commitments. (For simplicity, the masked values of input, e.g., $\hat{w}_j = w \oplus \lambda_{j,w}$, is considered to be part of com_{on}^F.) The prover sends com_{on}^F to the verifier.
- Round 4. *Challenge* for the online phase.
  The verifier chooses a random set $\mathcal{P} = \{p_j\}_{j \in \mathcal{C}}$ with $p_j \in [n]$, which is used to challenge the prover to open the views of all but the p_j-th party for each instance $j \in \mathcal{C}$, so that the verifier can check the consistency of $n - 1$ parties' views for that instance. The verifier sends $\mathcal{P}$ to the prover.

– Round 5. *Respond* to the challenge for the online phase.
  The prover computes the openings of all but the p_j-th party's commitments for each instance $j \in \mathcal{C}$. Let resp_{on}^F denote these openings. The prover sends resp_{on}^F to the verifier.

Verification Strategy.

1. For the opened instances in $[M]\backslash\mathcal{C}$, the verifier uses resp_{pre}^F to recover parts of the openings of com_{pre}^F, which are also used to check the randomness and correctness of the masks.
2. For each unopened instance in $\mathcal{C}$, the verifier uses resp_{on}^F and the masked values of input to simulate the MPC protocol for $C(w) = y$ and recover the openings of com_{on}^F and the remaining openings of com_{pre}^F.
3. The verifier checks the output of the simulation of the MPC protocol and the consistency of com_{pre}^F and com_{on}^F.

4.2   Intuitive Construction for Resumable HVZKPoK

Once the verifier accepts the proof, he is convinced not only that the prover has the witness in the current session, but also the correctness and randomness of the transcripts implied by the proof. We notice that the verifier's trust on some transcripts of KKW protocol can be "reused" to reduce the cost of proofs when resuming sessions. An intuitive construction of resumable HVZKPoK for F is described as follows, where the decomposition $F = f \circ g$ is public. For simplicity, we only consider the case of two sessions.

– **HVZKPoK for the initial session.** It is similar to the original KKW protocol, except that the prover needs to prepare preprocessing values for the next session and proves the consistency of w' and w. Let $\pi^f = (\pi_{pre}^f, \pi_{on}^f)$ denote the KKW proof for $C'(w') = y$, i.e., $f(w') = y$. HVZKPoK for the initial session consists of the following phases.
  1. π^F: The original KKW proof for w such that $C(w) = y$.
  2. π_{pre}^f: Prepare the preprocessing values of $C'(w') = y$ for the next session. In particular, π^F and π_{pre}^f can be merged with the same preprocessing challenge $\mathcal{C}$, which will be explained later.
  3. π_{cert}: Consistency proof for w and w'. That is, we need to guarantee that w' used in the next session is the correct intermediate value of $C(\cdot)$ when evaluating on input w.
– **HVZKPoK for the second session.**
  1. π_{on}^f: Online phase of the KKW proof for $C'(w') = y$.

Note that π_{pre}^f and π_{on}^f constitutes the complete KKW protocol for $C'(w') = y$. Intuitively, if the verifier can be convinced that the preprocessing data in π_{pre}^f is generated correctly, the prover only needs to run π_{on}^f for the second session. Suppose the verifier has accepted the initial session. Combining with the consistency proof π_{cert} for w and w', the verifier can be convinced that the prover has the knowledge of w in the second session. Therefore, the prover needs to provide efficient consistency proof for w and w', while ensuring that the preprocessing data in π^f_{pre} are generated by the "honest" prover, who has the knowledge of w. (Recall the soundness game mentioned in Sect. 3, where we do not consider the malicious prover who has the knowledge of witness.) To do so, we modify the KKW protocol π^f_{pre} for $C'(w') = y$.

4.3   Modified KKW for f and Consistency Proof

Suppose $\lambda_{w'}$ is the random masks for w' in π^F, i.e., the masked intermediate value $\hat{w}' = w' \oplus \lambda_{w'}$. The main modification of π^f is that the generation of the preprocessing data in π^f_{pre} is based on $\lambda_{w'}$. More specifically, the prover rerandomizes $\hat{w}'$ using a random and public value Δ, i.e., $\bar{w}' = w' \oplus \lambda_{w'} \oplus \Delta$. Then, the prover generates the corresponding preprocessing values for the KKW proof for $C'(w') = y$ using $\lambda'_{w'} = \lambda_{w'} \oplus \Delta$ as the mask. Here, the prover generates $n-1$ secret shares of $\lambda'_{w'}$ by running PRG with $n-1$ random seeds, while the n-th secret share $[\lambda'_{w'}]_n$ is determined by $[\lambda'_{w'}]_n = \lambda'_{w'} \oplus [\lambda'_{w'}]_1 \oplus \cdots \oplus [\lambda'_{w'}]_{n-1}$ and is sent to the verifier. (com^f_{pre} commits to the corresponding seeds for each party.) Hence, the verifier only needs to challenge the prover to open $n-2$ parties' views in the online phase.

Based on the above modification, we can provide a simple and efficient construction for the consistency proof π_{cert}. After π^f_{pre}, the prover computes a commitment com_{on}, which commits to $\mathsf{com}^F_{on}||\mathsf{com}^f_{pre}||\Delta||[\lambda'_{w'}]_n$, and sends com_{on} as well as $\mathsf{com}^f_{pre}||\Delta||[\lambda'_{w'}]_n$ to the verifier. Since the verifier accepted the initial session, the consistency of com^F_{on} and the preprocessing data of the initial session, e.g., $\lambda_{w'}$, has been checked. Due to the binding property of com_{on}, the rerandomized mask $\lambda'_{w'} = \lambda_{w'} \oplus \Delta$, which is determined by $\mathsf{com}^f_{pre}||\Delta$, is hard to be modified. In the second session, by checking the openings of com^f_{pre}, it is implicitly guaranteed that $\lambda'_{w'}$ is generated by the same "honest" prover of the initial session. Therefore, the witness w' implied by $\bar{w}'$ is the same as that of the initial session, i.e., $\bar{w}' = w' \oplus \lambda'_{w'}$, and the verifier does not need to check the correctness and randomness of the preprocessing data for the second session by "cut-and-choose". Notice that only the unopened instances in the initial session need the simulated executions of the MPC protocol, which means only in these instances, we need to rerandomize the masked intermediate value $\hat{w}'$. That is why π^F and π^f_{pre} can be merged with the same preprocessing challenge $\mathcal{C}$. To summarize, the modified KKW $\pi^f = (\pi^f_{pre}, \pi^f_{on})$ for the partial circuits C' is described as follows.

Preprocessing phase $\pi^f_{pre}(\{\lambda_{j,w'}\}_{j \in \mathcal{C}}, \mathcal{C})$.

– Round 1-a. *Rerandomize* the masks for the instances in $\mathcal{C}$.
  1. The prover chooses a random seed^Δ to generate Δ_j for each instance $j \in \mathcal{C}$. Then, the prover computes the rerandomized masks $\lambda'_{j,w'} = \lambda_{j,w'} \oplus \Delta_j$, where $\lambda_{j,w'}$ is the mask of $\hat{w}'_j$.
  2. For each instance $j \in \mathcal{C}$, the prover chooses a random $\mathsf{seed}_{j,i}$ for each party P_i to generate the share $[\lambda'_{j,w'}]_i$ for $i \in [n-1]$, while $[\lambda'_{j,w'}]_n$ is computed by $[\lambda'_{j,w'}]_n = \lambda'_{j,w'} \oplus [\lambda'_{j,w'}]_1 \oplus \cdots \oplus [\lambda'_{j,w'}]_{n-1}$. Other preprocessing values

are generated as described in Sect. 2.1. $[\lambda'_{j,w'}]_n$ is included as part of the auxiliary information aux_n. So we have $\mathsf{aux}_n \in \{0,1\}^{|C'|+|C'_{in}|}$. The prover sets $\mathsf{state}'_{j,i} = \mathsf{seed}_{j,i}$ for $i \in [n-1]$, and $\mathsf{state}'_{j,n} = \mathsf{seed}_{j,n}\|\mathsf{aux}_n$. Compute com^f_{pre}, which commits to the n parties' states.

3. The prover sends $\mathsf{state}'_{j,n}$, seed^Δ and com^f_{pre} to the verifier.

Online phase $\pi^f_{on}(w', \{\mathsf{state}'_{j,i}\}_{j\in\mathcal{C}, i\in[n]})$.

- Round 1-b. *Commit* to the views of each party.
  The prover runs the MPC protocol for $C'(w') = y$ using the rerandomized masks $\lambda'_{j,w'}$ (determined by $\{\mathsf{state}'_{j,i}\}_{i\in[n]}$) and the witness w' for each instance $j \in \mathcal{C}$. The prover computes the commitment to the views of each party during the MPC protocol. Denote these commitments as com^f_{on}. Send com^f_{on} to the verifier.
- Round 2. *Challenge* for the online phase.
  The verifier chooses a random set $\mathcal{P} = \{p_j\}_{j\in\mathcal{C}}$ with $p_j \in [n-1]$ in order to challenge the prover to open the views of all but the p_j-th party for each instance $j \in \mathcal{C}$, so that the verifier can check the consistency of $n-2$ views for that instance. The verifier sends $\mathcal{P}$ to the prover.
- Round 3. *Respond* to the challenge for the online phase.
  The prover computes the openings of the commitments of those challenged parties for each instance $j \in \mathcal{C}$. Denote the response by resp^f_{on}. Send resp^f_{on} to the verifier.

Verification Strategy. The verification strategy is similar to that of the original KKW, except that there is no need to check the randomness and correctness of the masks by cut-and-choose.

1. For each instance $j \in \mathcal{C}$, the verifier uses resp^f_{on}, $\hat{w}'_j$, seed^Δ and $\mathsf{state}'_{j,n}$ to simulate the MPC protocol for $C'(w') = y$ and recover the openings of com^f_{on} and com^f_{pre}. (Here, the verifier can get $\hat{w}'_j$ after the initial session.)
2. The verifier checks the output of the simulation of the MPC protocol for C' and the consistency of com^f_{on} and com^f_{pre}.

5   Resumable HVZKPoK from KKW

Using the KKW protocol π^F for $C(w) = y$ and the modified version π^f for $C'(w') = y$ as building blocks, we can construct the resumable HVZKPoK protocol Π_{Res}, which consists of two sub protocols $\Pi_{Res,1}$ and $\Pi_{Res,2}$. $\Pi_{Res,1}$ is for the initial session and $\Pi_{Res,2}$ is for the resumed session. Figure 1 shows the relations of the sub protocols of our general construction.

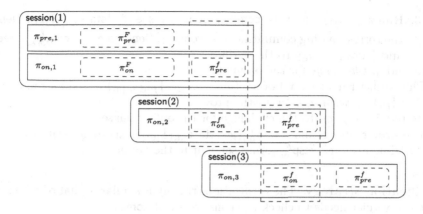

Fig. 1. General construction for resumable HVZKPoK

5.1 Resumable HVZKPoK for Initial Session $\Pi_{Res,1}$

The resumable HVZKPoK $\Pi_{Res,1} = (\pi_{pre,1}, \pi_{on,1})$ for the initial session is described as follows.

Preprocessing phase $\pi_{pre,1} = \pi_{pre}^F(1^\kappa)$. The preprocessing phase is the same as that of $\pi_{pre}^F(1^\kappa)$.

- Round 1. *Commit* to the masks of M instances.
  The prover runs round 1 of $\pi_{pre}^F(1^\kappa)$, which computes the commitments $com_{pre,1}^F$ to $\{state_{j,i,1}\}_{j\in[M],i\in[n]}$ for M instances, and sends $com_{pre,1}^F$ to the verifier.
- Round 2. *Challenge* for the preprocessing phase.
  The verifier runs round 2 of $\pi_{pre}^F(1^\kappa)$ to send a random τ-sized set $\mathcal{C}$ to the prover.
- Round 3-a. *Respond* to the challenge for the preprocessing phase.
  The prover runs round 3 of $\pi_{pre}^F(1^\kappa)$ to generate the corresponding response, denoted by $resp_{pre,1}^F$, and sends it to the verifier.

Online phase $\pi_{on,1} = (\pi_{on}^F(w, \{state_{j,i,1}\}_{j\in\mathcal{C},i\in[n]}) \wedge \pi_{pre}^f(\{\lambda_{j,w'}\}_{j\in\mathcal{C}}, \mathcal{C}) \wedge \pi_{cert})$. The prover's strategy of $\pi_{on,1}$ includes: (1) Run $\pi_{on}^F(w, \{state_{j,i,1}\}_{j\in\mathcal{C},i\in[n]})$ as the original KKW protocol; (2) Prepare the masks for the next session; (3) Certify these masks for the next session to ensure that the witness w' which will be used in the next session is consistent with w.

- Round 3-b.
  1. Run round 3-b of $\pi_{on}^F(w, \{state_{j,i,1}\}_{j\in\mathcal{C},i\in[n]})$ to generate the corresponding commitment $com_{on,1}^F$. Denote the corresponding intermediate mask as $\lambda_{j,w'}$ for each instance $j \in \mathcal{C}$.
  2. Run round 1-a of $\pi_{pre}^f(\{\lambda_{j,w'}\}_{j\in\mathcal{C}}, \mathcal{C})$ to generate a random $seed_2^\Delta$, the state of each party $\{state_{j,i,2}'\}_{j\in\mathcal{C},i\in[n]}$ and $com_{pre,2}^f$ as described above for the next session.

3. Run π_{cert} to commit to $\mathsf{com}_{on,1}^F \| \mathsf{com}_{pre,2}^f \| \mathsf{seed}_2^\triangle \| \{\mathsf{state}_{j,n,2}'\}_{j\in\mathcal{C}}$. Denote the corresponding commitment as $\mathsf{com}_{on,1}$. Send $\mathsf{com}_{on,1}$, $\mathsf{com}_{pre,2}^f$, $\mathsf{seed}_2^\triangle$ and $\{\mathsf{state}_{j,n,2}'\}_{j\in\mathcal{C}}$ to the verifier.

- Round 4. *Challenge* for the online phase.
  The verifier runs round 4 of $\pi_{on}^F(w, \{\mathsf{state}_{j,i,1}\}_{j\in\mathcal{C},i\in[n]})$ to send a random set $\mathcal{P} = \{p_j\}_{j\in\mathcal{C}}$ with $p_j \in [n]$ to the prover.
- Round 5. *Respond* to the challenge for the online phase.
  The prover runs round 5 of $\pi_{on}^F(w, \{\mathsf{state}_{j,i,1}\}_{j\in\mathcal{C},i\in[n]})$ to generate the corresponding response $\mathsf{resp}_{on,1}^F$, and sends it to the verifier.

Verification Strategy. The verification strategy is similar to that of π^F, except that the verifier needs to check the consistency of $\mathsf{com}_{on,1}$.

1. For the opened instances in $[M]\backslash\mathcal{C}$, the verifier uses $\mathsf{resp}_{pre,1}^F$ to recover parts of the openings of $\mathsf{com}_{pre,1}^F$, which are also used to check the randomness and correctness of masks.
2. For each unopened instance in $\mathcal{C}$, the verifier uses $\mathsf{resp}_{on,1}^F$ to simulate the MPC protocol for $C(w) = y$ and recover the openings of $\mathsf{com}_{on,1}^F$ and the remaining openings of $\mathsf{com}_{pre,1}^F$.
3. The verifier checks the output of the simulation of the MPC protocol and the consistency of $\mathsf{com}_{pre,1}^F$.
4. The verifier checks the consistency of $\mathsf{com}_{on,1}^F$ and $\mathsf{com}_{on,1}$.

State Update. The prover and the verifier need to maintain states for session resumption. The prover's initial state is $\mathsf{pstate} = w$, and the verifier's is $\mathsf{vstate} = \perp$. After the initial session, the prover and the verifier update their states as follows.

- Prover's state update: $\mathsf{pstate} = \{\hat{w}_j'\}_{j\in\mathcal{C}} \| \mathsf{seed}_2^\triangle \| \{\mathsf{state}_{j,i,2}'\}_{j\in\mathcal{C},i\in[n]}$, where $\hat{w}_j'$ is the masked intermediate value for each instance $j \in \mathcal{C}$.
- Verifier's state update: $\mathsf{vstate} = \{\hat{w}_j'\}_{j\in\mathcal{C}} \| \mathsf{seed}_2^\triangle \| \{\mathsf{state}_{j,n,2}'\}_{j\in\mathcal{C}} \| \mathsf{com}_{pre,2}^f$.

We emphasize that vstate can be made public.

5.2   Resumable HVZKPoK for Second Session $\Pi_{Res,2}$

For simplicity, we present the resumable HVZKPoK $\Pi_{Res,2}$ for the second session, which can be easily extended to the case of $\mathsf{session}(t)$ for any $t > 1$.

Online phase $\pi_{on,2} = (\pi_{on}^f(w', \{\mathsf{state}_{j,i,2}'\}_{j\in\mathcal{C},i\in[n]}) \wedge \pi_{pre}^f(\{\lambda_{j,w'}\}_{j\in\mathcal{C}}, \mathcal{C}) \wedge \pi_{cert})$.

The prover's strategy $\pi_{on,2}$ is similar to $\pi_{on,1}$, except that he simulates the MPC protocol for $C'(w') = y$ instead of $C(w) = y$. Note that all the inputs of $\pi_{on,2}$ can be extracted from pstate.

- Round 1.
  1. Run round 3-b of $\pi_{on}^f(w', \{\mathsf{state}_{j,i,2}'\}_{j\in\mathcal{C},i\in[n]})$ to generate the corresponding commitment $\mathsf{com}_{on,2}^f$.

2. Run round 1-a of $\pi_{pre}^f(\{\lambda_{j,w'}\}_{j\in\mathcal{C}},\mathcal{C})$ to generate a random $\mathsf{seed}_3^\triangle$, the state of each party $\{\mathsf{state}_{j,i,3}'\}_{j\in\mathcal{C},i\in[n]}$ and $\mathsf{com}_{pre,3}^f$ as described above for the next session.

3. Run π_{cert} to generate $\mathsf{com}_{on,2}$, which is the commitment of $\mathsf{com}_{on,2}^f||\mathsf{com}_{pre,3}^f||\mathsf{seed}_3^\triangle||\{\mathsf{state}_{j,n,3}'\}_{j\in\mathcal{C}}$. Send $\mathsf{com}_{on,2}$, $\mathsf{com}_{pre,3}^f$, $\mathsf{seed}_3^\triangle$ and $\{\mathsf{state}_{j,n,3}'\}_{j\in\mathcal{C}}$ to the verifier.

– Round 2. *Challenge* for the online phase.
  The verifier runs round 2 of $\pi_{on}^f(w',\{\mathsf{state}_{j,i,2}'\}_{j\in\mathcal{C},i\in[n]})$ to send a random set $\mathcal{P}=\{p_j\}_{j\in\mathcal{C}}$ with $p_j\in[n-1]$ to the prover.

– Round 3. *Respond* to the challenge for the online phase.
  The prover runs round 3 of $\pi_{on}^f(w',\{\mathsf{state}_{j,i,2}'\}_{j\in\mathcal{C},i\in[n]})$ to generate the corresponding response $\mathsf{resp}_{on,2}^f$. Send $\mathsf{resp}_{on,2}^f$ to the verifier.

Verification Strategy.

1. For each unopened instance $j\in\mathcal{C}$, the verifier uses $\mathsf{resp}_{on,2}^f$, $\hat{w}_j'$, $\mathsf{seed}_2^\triangle$ and $\mathsf{state}_{j,n,2}'$ to simulate the MPC protocol for $C'(w')=y$ and recover the openings of $\mathsf{com}_{on,2}^f$ and $\mathsf{com}_{pre,2}^f$. Note that $\hat{w}_j'$, $\mathsf{seed}_2^\triangle$ and $\mathsf{state}_{j,n,2}'$ can be extracted from vstate.

2. The verifier checks the output of the simulation of the MPC protocol.

3. The verifier checks the consistency of $\mathsf{com}_{pre,2}^f$, $\mathsf{com}_{on,2}^f$ and $\mathsf{com}_{on,2}$.

State Update. The prover and the verifier update their states as follows.

– Prover's state update: $\mathsf{pstate}=\{\hat{w}_j'\}_{j\in\mathcal{C}}||\mathsf{seed}_3^\triangle||\{\mathsf{state}_{j,i,3}'\}_{j\in\mathcal{C},i\in[n]}$.

– Verifier's state update: $\mathsf{vstate}=\{\hat{w}_j'\}_{j\in\mathcal{C}}||\mathsf{seed}_3^\triangle||\{\mathsf{state}_{j,n,3}'\}_{j\in\mathcal{C}}||\mathsf{com}_{pre,3}^f$.

5.3 Security

Theorem 1. *Assume that π^F, the underlying commitment scheme and pseudo-random generator are secure, and F has an extractable decomposition as $f\circ g$. Then Π_{Res} is a resumable honest verifier zero-knowledge proof of knowledge.*

The proof of zero-knowledge in Theorem 1 is similar to that of [38], while we should consider the zero-knowledge property of all the sessions as a whole. For the proof of resumable knowledge soundness, we show the consistency between w' of $\mathsf{session}(t)$ and w, and use the method of [5,38] to construct a witness extractor $\mathcal{E}$ for each session. Formal proof of Theorem 1 is in Appendix A.

Parallel Repetition. The soundness error ξ_t of $\Pi_{Res,2}$ for $\mathsf{session}(t)$ may be higher than ξ_1. We could reduce ξ_t with parallel executions of $\Pi_{Res,2}$ as follows.

– In round 3 of the online phase $\pi_{on,1}$ (or round 1 of $\pi_{on,2}$) for $\mathsf{session}(t-1)$, the prover repeats round 1 of π_{pre}^f for ℓ times. In other words, the prover rerandomizes intermediate masked values for ℓ times with ℓ random $\{\Delta_i\}_{i\in[\ell]}$.

- For session(t), the prover and the verifier run $\Pi_{Res,2}$ for ℓ times with the corresponding masked values generated in the previous session, where the verifier needs to send ℓ random challenges in round 2 of $\pi_{on,2}$.

Indeed, the above method can be interpreted as compacting ℓ executions of $\Pi_{Res,2}$ for ℓ sessions into one session, which will not break the security of our resumable HVZKPoK due to the honest verifier setting. In this way, we can reduce ξ_t to $\frac{1}{(n-1)^{\tau \cdot \ell}}$. By choosing appropriate ℓ, M, n and τ, we can gain a better soundness error for session(t). (Note that there is a trade-off between the soundness error and the proof size.) The proof of the following theorem are similar to that of Theorem 1 and hence omitted.

Theorem 2. *Assume that π^F, the underlying commitment scheme and pseudorandom generator are secure, and F has an extractable decomposition as $f \circ g$. Then Π_{Res} with parallel executions is a resumable honest verifier zero-knowledge proof of knowledge.*

5.4   3-Round Resumable HVZKPoK

Our 5-round $\Pi_{Res,1}$ can be transformed into a 3-round protocol using the similar method of [38] with the modification that the prover needs to prepare the random masks of the next session for every instance in $[M]$. Such modification has no effect on the security of the initial session, as those random masks could be considered as redundant information if there are no subsequent sessions. A concrete construction of our 3-round resumable HVZKPoK Π_{Res}^3, in which F is instantiated with LowMC [2] as in [38], is shown in our full paper [44]. The security proof of the following theorem is similar to that of Theorem 1 and hence omitted.

Theorem 3. *Assume that the underlying hash function, commitment scheme and pseudorandom generator are secure. Then Π_{Res}^3 is a resumable honest verifier zero-knowledge proof of knowledge.*

6   Resumable-Picnic

As in the previous works [18,38], our 3-round protocol can be transformed into a resumable *non-interactive* ZKPoK (NIZKPoK) using the Fiat-Shamir heuristic in each session, and the resulting NIZKPoK can be used to construct a stateful signature scheme. More precisely, we instantiate F with $\mathsf{Enc}(\cdot, 0^\kappa)$ for some symmetric encryption scheme $\mathsf{Enc}(\cdot, \cdot)$ in which the first input is the key and the second input is the plaintext. The signing key is a uniform $\mathsf{sk} \in \{0,1\}^\kappa$ and the verification key is $\mathsf{pk} = \mathsf{Enc}(\mathsf{sk}, 0^\kappa)$. By applying Fiat-Shamir heuristic to each session of our 3-round protocol for the relation $(\mathsf{pk}, \mathsf{sk}) \in R$, we can obtain a sequence of signatures, where the t-th signature is denoted as σ_t. We denote our stateful signature scheme as Resumable-Picnic.

Theorem 4. *Resumable-Picnic is strongly unforgeable under chosen message attacks in the QROM when* Com *is a collapse-binding commitment scheme and* H *is a collapsing hash function.*

Due to page restrictions, more details of Resumable-Picnic and the proof of Theorem 4 are presented in the full version [44].

Application. One of the possible applications of Resumable-Picnic is in the blockchain setting, where each σ_i can be stored in the corresponding block publicly. The verifier only needs to check the validity of σ_t of the current block, since the validity of $\{\sigma_i\}_{i<t}$ in previous blocks are implied by the consistency of the underlying consensus protocol. More specifically, the signer can sign a transaction tx_1 using Resumable-Picnic with pk and generate the signature σ_1. Then the miner generates a block B_i for a set of transactions with corresponding signatures, which includes $(\mathsf{tx}_1, \sigma_1)$. Afterwards, when the signer wants to sign another transaction tx_2 with pk, he can generate σ_2 efficiently using the state ss_1. Due to the blockchain protocol, $(\mathsf{tx}_2, \sigma_2)$ will be included in some block, say B_j, for $j > i$. If block B_i has been confirmed, which implies the validity of the signatures included in B_i have been confirmed by the majority of miners, the verifier of σ_2 does not need to check the validity of σ_1 any more. Due to the efficiency of session resumption, σ_2 is more efficient than the original Picnic. (Note that there is usually a confirmation delay in most blockchain protocols. For instance, the confirmation delay of Bitcoin is about 6 blocks, which means a block is confirmed if it is followed by at least 6 blocks.)

Table 1. Comparison between Picnic3 and resumable-Picnic. "Size" denotes the signature size. The results are the median time for running 10000 times.

Scheme	M	n	τ	ℓ	Sign (ms)	Verify (ms)	Size (Bytes)
Picnic3-Level 1	252	16	36		71.68	51.37	12595 ± 223
Resumable-Picnic [session(1)]	252	16	36	1	99.99	76.23	14277 ± 243
Resumable-Picnic [session(2)]	252	16	36	1	8.31	4.78	4796
Resumable-Picnic [session($t > 2$)]	252	16	36	1	6.59	4.11	4796
Picnic3-Level 3	419	16	52		170.37	119.45	27104 ± 455
Resumable-Picnic [session(1)]	419	16	52	1	220.45	163.91	31166 ± 466
Resumable-Picnic [session(2)]	419	16	52	1	13.15	7.90	10088
Resumable-Picnic [session($t > 2$)]	419	16	52	1	10.60	6.67	10088
Picnic3-Level 5	601	16	68		487.45	290.22	48716 ± 721
Resumable-Picnic [session(1)]	601	16	68	1	512.56	332.24	55043 ± 673
Resumable-Picnic [session(2)]	601	16	68	1	18.28	11.26	17536
Resumable-Picnic [session($t > 2$)]	601	16	68	1	14.97	9.52	17536

Experimental Results and Comparison. We implement Resumable-Picnic using the same parameters as Picnic3 [36], and give an efficiency comparison with Picnic3. Our benchmarks run on a platform with an Intel Core i7-8700 CPU clocked at 3.2 GHz and 16GB RAM. The parameters are chosen as Picnic3 did which fits security level 1, 3, and 5 recommended by NIST. The comparison between Picnic3 and Resumable-Picnic are shown in Table 1. As shown in Table 1, although the cost of Resumable-Picnic's initial session is slightly higher than that of Picnic3, the efficiency of Resumable-Picnic for the subsequent sessions are improved dramatically. Compared with Picnic3 with security level 1, 3 and 5, the sign/verify time of Resumable-Picnic for session($t > 2$) is reduced to 9.2%/8.0%, 6.2%/5.6%, and 3.1%/3.3%, respectively, and the signature size is reduced to 38.1%, 37.2% and 36.0%, respectively.

7   Compressed 1-out-of-N Proof and Ring Signatures

[20] provides a novel method of the one-out-of-N proof for the relation R_{OR} defined by $(x_1, \ldots, x_N \in L_R; w) \in R_{OR} \iff \exists t \in [N], s.t.(x_t, w) \in R$. By applying the parallel version of $\Pi_{Res,2}$ described in Sect. 5.3 to the CDS method [20], we can get a compressed one-out-of-N proof when the N statements share the same circuit. The main idea is that, for the $N - 1$ statements which the prover does not know the witness, the prover runs the simulator of the resumable HVZKPoK $\Pi_{Res,2}$ for the partial circuit C' in parallel. Hence, most transcripts of the simulation for the $N - 1$ statements can be removed. Furthermore, based on our compressed one-out-of-N proof, we can construct a ring signature from symmetric-key primitives. More details of our compressed one-out-of-N proof and the resulting ring signature are presented in the full version [44].

Using the same parameter set of Picnic2, we make a comparison between the ring signature of [38] and ours in Table 2. It shows that the size of our ring signature is smaller than that of [38] when the ring size is less than 2^6. In particular, it is just about 1/3 of the ring signature size of [38] when the ring size is less than 2^4.

Table 2. Comparison between ring signature [38] and our work.

Ring size	2	2^2	2^3	2^4	2^5	2^6	2^7
$\lvert\sigma\rvert$ ([38])	70KB	106KB	142KB	177KB	213KB	249KB	285KB
$\lvert\sigma\rvert$ (Ours)	21KB	30KB	47KB	82KB	151KB	290KB	567KB

Acknowledgements. We would like to thank the anonymous reviewers for their insightful and helpful comments. Handong Zhang, Puwen Wei, Jinsong Li, Wei Wang and Guoxiao Liu were supported by the National Key Research and Development Program of China (Grant No. 2018YFA0704702), Shandong Provincial Key Research and

Development Program (Major Scientific and Technological Innovation Project) (Grant No.2019JZZY010133) and Shandong Provincial Natural Science Foundation (Grant No. ZR2020MF053). Haiyang Xue was supported by the National Natural Science Foundation of China (Grant No. 62172412). Yi Deng was supported by the National Natural Science Foundation of China (Grant No. 61932019 and No. 61772522), the Key Research Program of Frontier Sciences, CAS (Grant No. QYZDB-SSW-SYS035) and Natural Science Foundation of Beijing (Grant No. M22003).

A   Proof of Theorem 1

Proof. **Completeness.** This property follows from the correctness of the underlying MPC protocol Π used in π^F and π^f.

Resumable Honest Verifier Zero-Knowledge. We need to consider the simulator for all $q(\kappa)$ sessions instead of only one, where the simulation for the transcripts generated by π^F and π^f follows the idea of [38]. Let Sim_Π denotes the simulator of the MPC protocol Π. The simulator Sim of Π_{Res} is described as follows.

- Simulation for initial session $\mathsf{session}(1)$.
  1. Sim chooses random $\mathcal{C}$ and $\mathcal{P}$ as the challenge for the preprocessing phase and the online phase respectively.
  2. For each instance $j \notin \mathcal{C}$, Sim prepares λ_j using $\{\mathsf{state}_{j,i,1}\}_{i\in[n]}$ and generates the corresponding $\mathsf{resp}^F_{pre,1}$ as an honest prover would do in the preprocessing phase.
  3. For each instance $j \in \mathcal{C}$, Sim chooses a random masked input for the MPC protocol and $n-1$ random states for $n-1$ parties determined by $\mathcal{P}$. Then, Sim runs Sim_Π to simulate the views of the n parties during the MPC protocol and computes corresponding $\mathsf{com}^F_{on,1}$. Notice that Sim can get the corresponding intermediate masked value $\hat{w}'_j$ for each instance $j \in \mathcal{C}$ from the simulated views. As mentioned in Sect. 2.1, the indistinguishability between the simulated execution of Sim_Π and the real execution relies on the security of the underlying PRG.
  4. Sim computes $\mathsf{com}^F_{pre,1}$ and $\mathsf{resp}^F_{on,1}$ according to the transcripts generated in step 2 and 3. For the generation of $\mathsf{com}^F_{pre,1}$, the state of the party in $\mathcal{P}$ of each instance can be set by 0-string with appropriate length.
  5. Sim randomly chooses seed^Δ_2 and $\{\mathsf{state}'_{j,i,2}\}_{j\in\mathcal{C},i\in[n]}$, and computes the corresponding commitment $\mathsf{com}^f_{pre,2}$. Generate $\mathsf{com}_{on,1}$ as the commitment to $\mathsf{com}^F_{on,1}\|\mathsf{com}^f_{pre,2}\|\mathsf{seed}^\Delta_2\|\{\mathsf{state}'_{j,n,2}\}_{j\in\mathcal{C}}$.
- Simulation for subsequent session $\mathsf{seesion}(t)$, where $1 < t \le q(\kappa)$.
  1. Sim chooses a random $\mathcal{P}$ as the challenge for the online phase.
  2. For each instance $j \in \mathcal{C}$, Sim computes the rerandomized intermediate masked input $\hat{w}'_j \oplus \Delta_j$, in which $\hat{w}'_j$ is the intermediate masked value of $\mathsf{seesion}(1)$ and Δ_j is generated by seed^Δ_t. Note that Sim has $n-2$ parties' states determined by $\mathcal{P}$. Then, Sim runs Sim_Π to simulate the views of n parties during the MPC protocol, and computes corresponding $\mathsf{com}^f_{on,t}$.

3. Sim randomly chooses $\mathsf{seed}_{t+1}^{\Delta}$ and $\{\mathsf{state}_{j,i,t+1}'\}_{j\in\mathcal{C},i\in[n]}$, and computes the corresponding commitment $\mathsf{com}_{pre,t+1}^{f}$. Generate $\mathsf{com}_{on,t}$ as the commitment to $\mathsf{com}_{on,t}^{f}\|\mathsf{com}_{pre,t+1}^{f}\|\mathsf{seed}_{t+1}^{\Delta}\|\{\mathsf{state}_{j,n,t+1}'\}_{j\in\mathcal{C}}$.

Following a standard hybrid argument, we have that the transcript generated by Sim is computationally indistinguishable from that of a real protocol, where the indistinguishability relies on the indistinguishability of the simulated transcripts generated by Sim_Π and the hiding property of the commitment scheme.

Resumable Knowledge Soundness. The proof of the resumable knowledge soundness is similar to that of [5,38], except that we need to show that there exists a witness extractor $\mathcal{E}$ for each session, especially the resumed session.

We first show the soundness error $\xi(M,n,\tau)$. Since $\Pi_{Res,1}$ is similar to that of the original KKW except additional processing for the masks of the next session. The soundness error ξ_1 of $\Pi_{Res,1}$ is the same as that of [38]. That is,

$$\xi_1(M,n,\tau) = \max_{0\leq c\leq\tau}\left\{\frac{\binom{M-c}{M-\tau}}{\binom{M}{M-\tau}\cdot n^{\tau-c}}\right\},$$

where c denotes the number of preprocessing emulations where the malicious prover cheats.

On the soundness error of $\Pi_{Res,2}$, recall the soundness game mentioned in Sect. 3, where the malicious prover can invoke the "honest" prover to interact with the verifier for polynomially-many sessions, say $\mathsf{session}(1),\ldots,\mathsf{session}(t-1)$ for $1 < t \leq q(\kappa)$, and tries to convince the verifier in $\mathsf{session}(t)$ without the help of the "honest" prover. Note that the masks for $\mathsf{session}(t)$ are generated by the honest prover in $\mathsf{session}(t-1)$. So a malicious prover of session t can cheat only in the online phase, where he must cheat in one of the views of the $n-1$ parties. Thus, the probability that the prover will not be detected in $\Pi_{Res,2}$ is $\xi_t(M,n,\tau) = \frac{1}{(n-1)^\tau}$. Therefore, we have $\xi(M,n,\tau) = \max\{\xi_1(M,n,\tau),\xi_t(M,n,\tau)\}$, for any $1 < t \leq q(\kappa)$. Next, we proceed to prove the resumable knowledge soundness property by showing how to construct $\mathcal{E}$ to extract a valid witness for each session. As explained above, the proof of knowledge soundness in [5] can be applied to $\Pi_{Res,1}$ directly. We focus on $\Pi_{Res,2}$ of $\mathsf{session}(t)$, where $1 < t \leq q(\kappa)$. For simplicity we assume that the commitment scheme is perfectly binding.

We first prove that if the success probability of cheating $\delta_t(x) > \xi_t(M,n,\tau)$, then there exists at least one MPC instance of $\mathcal{C}$, where the prover has committed to a valid intermediate value w'. Considering the deterministic prover with fixed random tape, let $\mathbf{v}$ be a 0/1-vector with length $(n-1)^\tau$, where each entry corresponds to a possible challenge for the online phase of $\mathcal{V}^{(t)}$ and 1 denotes the event of success. Hence, we have that $\delta_t(x)$ is the fraction of '1' entries in $\mathbf{v}$ and the number of '1' entries in $\mathbf{v}$ is higher than 1 due to $\delta_t(x) > \xi_t(M,n,\tau) = \frac{1}{(n-1)^\tau}$. That is, there must exist two accepting transcripts with different challenges $\{p_j\}_{j\in\mathcal{C}}$ and $\{p_j'\}_{j\in\mathcal{C}}$ such that $p_j \neq p_j'$ for an MPC instance j. That means all the views of the parties in instance j are correct and the witness used in this instance must be a valid intermediate value w'.

However, since f is just a part of F, it may be easy for a malicious prover to find a different $w^* \neq w'$ such that $f(w^*) = 1$. It seems that any malicious prover who can find such a w^* can cheat in the next session by computing $\lambda_{w^*} = w' \oplus \lambda_{w'} \oplus w^*$ and generating the corresponding n shares of $\lambda_{w^*} \oplus \Delta$. ($w' \oplus \lambda_{w'}$ can be extracted during the verification of the initial session.) Thanks to the binding property of the commitment $\text{com}_{on,t}$ in π_{cert}, it is hard for the adversary to provide consistency proof using such w^* and λ_{w^*}. For instance, in $\text{session}(t-1)$, $\text{com}_{on,t-1}$ is the commitment of $\text{com}^f_{on,t-1}\|\text{com}^f_{pre,t}\|\text{seed}^\Delta_t$ $\|\{\text{state}'_{j,n,t}\}_{j\in\mathcal{C}}$, where $(\text{com}_{on,t-1}, \text{com}^f_{pre,t}, \text{seed}^\Delta_t, \{\text{state}'_{j,n,t}\}_{j\in\mathcal{C}})$ are public. The rerandomized mask for $\text{session}(t)$, say $\lambda_{w'} \oplus \Delta$, is determined by $(\text{com}^f_{pre,t},$ $\text{seed}^\Delta_t, \{\text{state}'_{j,n,t}\}_{j\in\mathcal{C}})$ and is hard to be modified due to $\text{com}_{on,t-1}$. (The use of mask λ_{w^*} such that $\lambda_{w^*} \neq \lambda_{w'} \oplus \Delta$ will be detected by checking the consistency of $\text{com}_{on,t-1}$ and $\text{com}^f_{pre,t}$.) Therefore, a malicious prover needs to (1) guess the challenge sent by the verifier successfully, which happens with probability $\frac{1}{n-1}$ for each instance, or (2) find $n-1$ random seeds which can be used to generate an $(n-1)$-out-of-$(n-1)$ secret-sharing of $\lambda_{w^*} \oplus \Delta \oplus [\lambda_{w'} \oplus \Delta]_n$, where each share is generated by running PRG with the corresponding random seed. This can be done with negligible probability assuming the underlying PRG is secure. Hence, $\text{com}_{on,t-1}$ and $\text{com}^f_{pre,t}$ guarantee the consistency of w' in $\text{session}(t)$ with w.

Next, we show how to extract the witness using two accepting transcripts with $\{p_j\}_{j\in\mathcal{C}}$ and $\{p'_j\}_{j\in\mathcal{C}}$ when the challenge for j is different. Since $p_j \neq p'_j$, the transcripts with p_j reveals $n-1$ shares of the masks of the intermediate masked input, whereas the transcripts with p'_j reveals the remaining shares (Notice that the shares of the n-th party is public). Hence, we can get all the shares to recover the intermediate value w'. Due to the special property of the decomposition for F, the witness w can be further extracted from w'.

To sum up, the extractor $\mathcal{E}$ is described as follows.

1. Run $\Pi_{Res,2}$ with the prover in session t until the event of success happens, in order to find an '1' entry of the vector $\mathbf{v}$, where the corresponding challenge is $\{p_j\}_{j\in\mathcal{C}}$.
2. Run $\Pi_{Res,2}$ with the prover in session t (using different challenges) until a different '1' entry is found, where the corresponding challenge is $\{p'_j\}_{j\in\mathcal{C}}$ such that $p_j \neq p'_j$.
3. Extract the witness ω in execution j using the related transcripts with $\{p_j\}_{j\in\mathcal{C}}$ and $\{p'_j\}_{j\in\mathcal{C}}$. If $F(w) = y$, output w and halt.

Let $\delta_t(x) = \xi_t(M, n, \tau) + \epsilon_t(x)$ for some $\epsilon_t(x) > 0$. The expected running time of the step 1 and 2 is $\frac{1}{\delta_t(x)} < \frac{1}{\epsilon_t(x)}$ and the running time of step 3 depends on the running time of $F(w)$ with common input x, which is supposed to be more efficient than step 1 and 2. Therefore, a valid witness can be extracted in $O(\frac{1}{\epsilon_t(x)})$ expected number of steps.

Resumption Efficiency. $\Pi_{Res,2}$ consists of π^f and the consistency proof π_{cert}. Since π^f is a simplified KKW proof for the partial circuits of F (without cut-and-choose), the complexity of π^f is much smaller than that of the original KKW proof for F. Recall that π_{cert} mainly consists of $\mathsf{com}_{on,2}$ and $\mathsf{seed}_3^\triangle$. So the complexity of π_{cert} just takes a very small portion of π^f. Hence, although the overall complexity of $\Pi_{Res,2}$ depends on the concrete decomposition of F, $\Pi_{Res,2}$ is much efficient than that of the original KKW proof Π' for F in general.

□

References

1. Abe, M., Ambrona, M., Bogdanov, A., Ohkubo, M., Rosen, A.: Non-interactive composition of sigma-protocols via share-then-hash. In: Moriai, S., Wang, H. (eds.) ASIACRYPT 2020. LNCS, vol. 12493, pp. 749–773. Springer, Cham (2020). https://doi.org/10.1007/978-3-030-64840-4_25
2. Albrecht, M.R., Rechberger, C., Schneider, T., Tiessen, T., Zohner, M.: Ciphers for MPC and FHE. In: Oswald, E., Fischlin, M. (eds.) EUROCRYPT 2015. LNCS, vol. 9056, pp. 430–454. Springer, Heidelberg (2015). https://doi.org/10.1007/978-3-662-46800-5_17
3. Ames, S., Hazay, C., Ishai, Y., Venkitasubramaniam, M.: Ligero: lightweight sublinear arguments without a trusted setup. In: ACM CCS 2017, pp. 2087–2104. ACM Press, New York (2017). https://doi.org/10.1145/3133956.3134104
4. Avanzi, R., et al.: Crystals-kyber. NIST PQC Round **3**, 4 (2020)
5. Baum, C., Nof, A.: Concretely-efficient zero-knowledge arguments for arithmetic circuits and their application to lattice-based cryptography. In: Kiayias, A., Kohlweiss, M., Wallden, P., Zikas, V. (eds.) PKC 2020. LNCS, vol. 12110, pp. 495–526. Springer, Cham (2020). https://doi.org/10.1007/978-3-030-45374-9_17
6. Baum, C., de Saint Guilhem, C.D., Kales, D., Orsini, E., Scholl, P., Zaverucha, G.: Banquet: short and fast signatures from AES. In: Garay, J.A. (ed.) PKC 2021. LNCS, vol. 12710, pp. 266–297. Springer, Cham (2021). https://doi.org/10.1007/978-3-030-75245-3_11
7. Bellare, M., Goldwasser, S.: New paradigms for digital signatures and message authentication based on non-interactive zero knowledge proofs. In: Brassard, G. (ed.) CRYPTO 1989. LNCS, vol. 435, pp. 194–211. Springer, New York (1990). https://doi.org/10.1007/0-387-34805-0_19
8. Ben-Sasson, E., Bentov, I., Horesh, Y., Riabzev, M.: Scalable zero knowledge with no trusted setup. In: Boldyreva, A., Micciancio, D. (eds.) CRYPTO 2019. LNCS, vol. 11694, pp. 701–732. Springer, Cham (2019). https://doi.org/10.1007/978-3-030-26954-8_23
9. Ben-Sasson, E., Chiesa, A., Genkin, D., Tromer, E., Virza, M.: SNARKs for C: verifying program executions succinctly and in zero knowledge. In: Canetti, R., Garay, J.A. (eds.) CRYPTO 2013. LNCS, vol. 8043, pp. 90–108. Springer, Heidelberg (2013). https://doi.org/10.1007/978-3-642-40084-1_6
10. Ben-Sasson, E., Chiesa, A., Riabzev, M., Spooner, N., Virza, M., Ward, N.P.: Aurora: transparent succinct arguments for R1CS. In: Ishai, Y., Rijmen, V. (eds.) EUROCRYPT 2019. LNCS, vol. 11476, pp. 103–128. Springer, Cham (2019). https://doi.org/10.1007/978-3-030-17653-2_4

11. Ben-Sasson, E., Chiesa, A., Tromer, E., Virza, M.: Succinct non-interactive zero knowledge for a von neumann architecture. In: 23rd USENIX Security Symposium, pp. 781–796. USENIX Association, San Diego, CA (2014). https://www.usenix.org/conference/usenixsecurity14/technical-sessions/presentation/ben-sasson
12. Blum, M., De Santis, A., Micali, S., Persiano, G.: Noninteractive zero-knowledge. SIAM J. Comput. **20**(6), 1084–1118 (1991). https://doi.org/10.1137/0220068
13. Bootle, J., Cerulli, A., Chaidos, P., Groth, J., Petit, C.: Efficient zero-knowledge arguments for arithmetic circuits in the discrete log setting. In: Fischlin, M., Coron, J.-S. (eds.) EUROCRYPT 2016. LNCS, vol. 9666, pp. 327–357. Springer, Heidelberg (2016). https://doi.org/10.1007/978-3-662-49896-5_12
14. Bootle, J., Groth, J.: Efficient batch zero-knowledge arguments for low degree polynomials. In: Abdalla, M., Dahab, R. (eds.) PKC 2018. LNCS, vol. 10770, pp. 561–588. Springer, Cham (2018). https://doi.org/10.1007/978-3-319-76581-5_19
15. Bünz, B., Bootle, J., Boneh, D., Poelstra, A., Wuille, P., Maxwell, G.: Bulletproofs: short proofs for confidential transactions and more. In: 2018 IEEE Symposium on Security and Privacy, pp. 315–334 (2018). https://doi.org/10.1109/SP.2018.00020
16. Chase, M., et al.: The picnic signature scheme, design document v2. 1 (2019)
17. Chase, M., et al.: The picnic signature scheme, design document v2. 2. Available at https://microsoft.github.io/Picnic/ (2020)
18. Chase, M., et al.: Post-quantum zero-knowledge and signatures from symmetric-key primitives. In: ACM CCS 2017, pp. 1825–1842. ACM Press, New York (2017). https://doi.org/10.1145/3133956.3133997
19. Costello, C., et al.: Geppetto: versatile verifiable computation. In: 2015 IEEE Symposium on Security and Privacy, pp. 253–270 (2015). https://doi.org/10.1109/SP.2015.23
20. Cramer, R., Damgård, I., Schoenmakers, B.: Proofs of partial knowledge and simplified design of witness hiding protocols. In: Desmedt, Y.G. (ed.) CRYPTO 1994. LNCS, vol. 839, pp. 174–187. Springer, Heidelberg (1994). https://doi.org/10.1007/3-540-48658-5_19
21. Ding, J., Chen, M.S., Petzoldt, A., Schmidt, D., Yang, B.Y.: Rainbow. NIST PQC Round **3**, 4 (2020)
22. Feige, U., Lapidot, D., Shamir, A.: Multiple noninteractive zero knowledge proofs under general assumptions. SIAM J. Comput. **29**(1), 1–28 (1999). https://doi.org/10.1137/S0097539792230010
23. Fiat, A., Shamir, A.: How to prove yourself: practical solutions to identification and signature problems. In: Odlyzko, A.M. (ed.) CRYPTO 1986. LNCS, vol. 263, pp. 186–194. Springer, Heidelberg (1987). https://doi.org/10.1007/3-540-47721-7_12
24. Fischlin, M., Harasser, P., Janson, C.: Signatures from sequential-or proofs. In: Canteaut, A., Ishai, Y. (eds.) EUROCRYPT 2020. LNCS, vol. 12107, pp. 212–244. Springer, Cham (2020). https://doi.org/10.1007/978-3-030-45727-3_8
25. Gennaro, R., Gentry, C., Parno, B., Raykova, M.: Quadratic span programs and succinct NIZKs without PCPs. In: Johansson, T., Nguyen, P.Q. (eds.) EUROCRYPT 2013. LNCS, vol. 7881, pp. 626–645. Springer, Heidelberg (2013). https://doi.org/10.1007/978-3-642-38348-9_37
26. Giacomelli, I., Madsen, J., Orlandi, C.: ZKBoo: faster zero-knowledge for Boolean circuits. In: 25th USENIX Security Symposium, pp. 1069–1083. USENIX Association, Austin, TX (2016). https://www.usenix.org/conference/usenixsecurity16/technical-sessions/presentation/giacomelli
27. Goel, A., Green, M., Hall-Andersen, M., Kaptchuk, G.: Stacking sigmas: a framework to compose σ-protocols for disjunctions. Cryptology ePrint Archive, Report 2021/422 (2021). https://ia.cr/2021/422

28. Goel, A., Green, M., Hall-Andersen, M., Kaptchuk, G.: Efficient set membership proofs using MPC-in-the-head. In: Proceedings on Privacy Enhancing Technologies **2022**(2), 304–324 (2022). https://doi.org/10.2478/popets-2022-0047

29. Goldreich, O., Micali, S., Wigderson, A.: Proofs that yield nothing but their validity and a methodology of cryptographic protocol design. In: SFCS 1986, pp. 174–187. IEEE Computer Society Press (1986). https://doi.org/10.1109/SFCS.1986.47

30. Goldwasser, S., Micali, S., Rackoff, C.: The knowledge complexity of interactive proof systems. SIAM J. Comput. **18**(1), 186–208 (1989). https://doi.org/10.1137/0218012

31. Groth, J.: Short pairing-based non-interactive zero-knowledge arguments. In: Abe, M. (ed.) ASIACRYPT 2010. LNCS, vol. 6477, pp. 321–340. Springer, Heidelberg (2010). https://doi.org/10.1007/978-3-642-17373-8_19

32. Groth, J.: On the size of pairing-based non-interactive arguments. In: Fischlin, M., Coron, J.-S. (eds.) EUROCRYPT 2016. LNCS, vol. 9666, pp. 305–326. Springer, Heidelberg (2016). https://doi.org/10.1007/978-3-662-49896-5_11

33. Groth, J., Ostrovsky, R., Sahai, A.: Perfect non-interactive zero knowledge for NP. In: Vaudenay, S. (ed.) EUROCRYPT 2006. LNCS, vol. 4004, pp. 339–358. Springer, Heidelberg (2006). https://doi.org/10.1007/11761679_21

34. Henry, R., Goldberg, I.: Batch proofs of partial knowledge. In: Jacobson, M., Locasto, M., Mohassel, P., Safavi-Naini, R. (eds.) ACNS 2013. LNCS, vol. 7954, pp. 502–517. Springer, Heidelberg (2013). https://doi.org/10.1007/978-3-642-38980-1_32

35. Ishai, Y., Kushilevitz, E., Ostrovsky, R., Sahai, A.: Zero-knowledge from secure multiparty computation. In: STOC 2007, pp. 21–30. ACM Press, New York (2007). https://doi.org/10.1145/1250790.1250794

36. Kales, D., Zaverucha, G.: Improving the performance of the picnic signature scheme. Cryptology ePrint Archive, Report 2020/427 (2020). https://eprint.iacr.org/2020/427

37. Katz, J.: Digital signatures. Springer Science & Business Media (2010)

38. Katz, J., Kolesnikov, V., Wang, X.: Improved non-interactive zero knowledge with applications to post-quantum signatures. In: ACM CCS 2018, pp. 525–537. ACM Press, New York (2018). https://doi.org/10.1145/3243734.3243805

39. Parno, B., Howell, J., Gentry, C., Raykova, M.: Pinocchio: nearly practical verifiable computation. In: 2013 IEEE Symposium on Security and Privacy, pp. 238–252 (2013). https://doi.org/10.1109/SP.2013.47

40. Peng, K., Bao, F.: Batch ZK proof and verification of OR logic. In: Yung, M., Liu, P., Lin, D. (eds.) Inscrypt 2008. LNCS, vol. 5487, pp. 141–156. Springer, Heidelberg (2009). https://doi.org/10.1007/978-3-642-01440-6_13

41. Rescorla, E., Dierks, T.: The transport layer security (TLS) protocol version 1.3. RFC 8446, https://doi.org/10.17487/RFC8446, August 2018 (2018)

42. de Saint Guilhem, C.D., De Meyer, L., Orsini, E., Smart, N.P.: BBQ: using AES in picnic signatures. In: Paterson, K.G., Stebila, D. (eds.) SAC 2019. LNCS, vol. 11959, pp. 669–692. Springer, Cham (2020). https://doi.org/10.1007/978-3-030-38471-5_27

43. Wahby, R.S., Tzialla, I., Shelat, A., Thaler, J., Walfish, M.: Doubly-efficient zksnarks without trusted setup. In: 2018 IEEE Symposium on Security and Privacy (SP), pp. 926–943 (2018). https://doi.org/10.1109/SP.2018.00060

44. Zhang, H., Wei, P., Xue, H., Deng, Y., Li, J., Wang, W., Liu, G.: Resumable zero-knowledge for circuits from symmetric key primitives. Cryptology ePrint Archive, Report 2022/556 (2022). https://eprint.iacr.org/2022/556

On Security of Fuzzy Commitment Scheme for Biometric Authentication

Donghoon Chang[1,2], Surabhi Garg[1,3]([✉]) [ID], Munawar Hasan[1,2,5],
and Sweta Mishra[4] [ID]

[1] IIIT-Delhi, New Delhi, India
{donghoon,surabhig,munawarh}@iiitd.ac.in
[2] NIST, Gaithersburg, MD, USA
{donghoon.chang,munawar.hasan}@nist.gov
[3] TCS Research, Chennai, India
surabhi.garg@tcs.com
[4] Shiv Nadar University, Kalavakkam, India
sweta.mishra@snu.edu.in
[5] Irisys Co. Ltd., Seoul, Korea
munawar@irisys.co.kr

Abstract. Biometric security is a prominent research area with growing privacy and security concerns related to biometric data, generally known as biometric templates. Among the recently proposed biometric template protection schemes, fuzzy commitment is the most popular and reliable. It uses error correcting codes to deal with the significant number of bit errors present in the biometric templates. The high error correcting capability of the underlying error correcting codes is crucial to achieving the desired recognition performance in the biometric system. In general, it is satisfied by padding the input biometric template with some additional bits. The fixed padding approaches proposed in the literature have security vulnerabilities that could disclose the user's biometric data to the attacker, leading to an impersonation attack. We propose a user-specific, random padding scheme that preserves the recognition performance of the system while it prevents the impersonation attack. The empirical results show that the proposed scheme provides 3 times better recognition performance on the IIT Delhi iris database than the baseline, unprotected systems. Through security analysis, we show that the attack complexity of our proposed work is 2^k, where k is the length of the secret message used to generate codeword, with $k \geq 128$ bits.

Keywords: Fuzzy commitment · Error correcting codes · Bit padding · Biometric security · Authentication · BCH Codes

1 Introduction

Biometric-based authentication systems are being recently deployed on a widespread level in multiple diverse sectors. One of the most significant examples of

K. Nguyen et al. (Eds.): ACISP 2022, LNCS 13494, pp. 399–419, 2022.
https://doi.org/10.1007/978-3-031-22301-3_20

biometric authentication is India's Aadhaar project [8]. Typically, the biometric data, commonly known as a biometric template, is stored during enrolment in its original, unprotected form on public database servers from where it can be stolen or modified by the attackers [18,37]. Unlike passwords, if the biometric data is stolen or lost, it remains compromised forever. Therefore, it is crucial to protect the biometric templates to safeguard users' privacy and security. Hashing could be used to protect biometric templates. However, different biometric samples of a particular instance are never the same, returning an entirely different hash output, which makes authentication infeasible.

Recently, several biometric template protection schemes have been proposed [4,5,10,31,34] that generate the protected templates such that the protected templates reveal no significant information about the original templates. These schemes are broadly categorized as cancelable biometrics, homomorphic encryption schemes and biometric cryptosystems or biocryptosystems. In the cancelable biometric approaches [5,11,14,39], the original biometric template is transformed into a protected template using a key/password dependent transformation function. The comparisons are performed between two protected templates. However, the recognition performance is highly degraded. The homomorphic encryption schemes [13,45] encrypt the biometric templates such that the comparisons during authentication are performed on the encrypted biometric templates, providing high security. They require huge computations. Biocryptosystems [4,6,10,15, 19,20,40] have been prominently used that generate biometric-dependent helper data from the original biometric template. Fuzzy commitment [20] is a popular biocryptosystem which is being used in wide applications including face template protection using deep learning model [31] and key generation from biometric templates [5]. In this paper, we focus on the implementation and security aspects of the fuzzy commitment schemes (refer Sect. 2).

Due to the noisy biometric templates, it is not possible to transform them directly into the protected templates without incorporating any error tolerance mechanisms. It is, therefore, necessary to use error correcting codes (ECC) [30] [10, 44]. Several error correcting codes [30] are proposed in the literature such as Reed Solomon (RS) Codes [12], Hadamard Codes [32], Binary Bose-Chaudhuri-Hocquenghem (BCH) Codes [3], Turbo Codes [2] and the various combinations of these codes. Our work focuses on BCH codes as they have been extensively used in the literature [4,5,31] in the domain of biometric security. Also, it has been observed from [35] that these are simple to perform and are more advantageous over other codes such as RS codes for correcting random and burst errors in the biometric data. The details of the BCH code are given in Sect. 2.

Motivation. Fuzzy commitment schemes have been widely used as an underlying architecture in multiple schemes, some are summarized in Table 1. As inferred from the limitations of these schemes discussed in Sect. 4, the efficient implementation and the security of fuzzy commitment schemes majorly rely on implementing underlying error correcting code. The efficiency is measured in terms of the recognition performance accuracy and the time taken to perform the user authentication. Further, the security of the fuzzy commitment scheme depends on the length of the secret message, K used to generate the underlying error correcting

Table 1. The existing prominent biometric template protection schemes that use fuzzy commitment scheme. Here, K represents the secret key used to generate the error correcting code C, t denotes the maximum number of errors C can correct.

Approach	Underlying ECC	Limitation (s)
Baseline A [10, 16]	BCH or RS code	small t, low recognition performance
Baseline B [6, 15]	RS and Hadamard code or BCH code	$|K| \leq 128$
Zero padding [22, 24, 25, 38]	RS and Hadamard code	impersonation attack [42, 44]
Fixed padding [22, 23, 25, 38]	RS and Hadamard code	require additional key/password
Bit-wise encryption [5]	BCH code	small t, low recognition performance
BIOFUSE [4]	BCH code	small t, low recognition performance
Secure Face [31] (based on DL model [9, 26, 43])	RS or BCH code	$|K| \leq 128$

code. In a fuzzy commitment scheme, the length of the biometric template B should be exactly equal to the length of error correcting codeword C. It is due to the XOR operation between these parameters to generate the secure sketch value S given as $B \oplus C \longrightarrow S$. Here, if C is revealed to the attacker, the original biometric template B could be obtained. Furthermore, in real-life scenarios, the biometric templates contain multiple bit errors, which could be higher than the error correcting capability t of the underlying error correcting codeword. In such cases, it is challenging to implement the error correcting code with a sufficiently large secret message K, preferably with $k \geq 128$ bits and $k = |K|$, where $|.|$ denotes the length. In general, to mitigate the mentioned challenges, the following techniques are introduced in the literature.

1. The significant bits are extracted from the biometric templates [9, 17] with the error correcting code applied on the significant bits, providing a good recognition performance. To equalize the length of B and C, a few extra bits from the input biometric template are discarded from the beginning or the end [21]. It may lead to loss of discrimination [44] between the biometric templates of different users as the discarded bits may be relevant.
2. A larger size codeword is taken so that it could correct more number of bit errors. It can be done by padding the biometric template with some extra bits such that the corresponding codeword's size would increase [22, 22, 24, 25, 38]. The details are given in Sect. 4. The padding technique results in higher accuracy; however, it leads to impersonation attack [42] (refer Sect. 5).
3. Considering a small-sized secret key used to generate the random error correcting codeword [6, 9, 15, 26, 31, 43]. The smaller is the key size, the more errors an error correcting codeword can correct, the higher is the recognition performance. Such an approach is vulnerable to the brute force attack.

The implementation challenges with the fuzzy commitment schemes prompt the need for an efficient implementation of error correcting codewords. We propose a user-specific, random padding scheme to prevent the impersonation attack on error correcting codewords while providing high recognition performance. The application of our contribution exists in all such scenarios where fuzzy commitment schemes are applied to generate a secure biometric template or to derive the secure key from biometrics.

The Paper Makes the Following Contributions.

- We introduce a user-specific, random bit-padding approach for implementing the error correcting codes in the fuzzy commitment scheme that improves the recognition performance of the system.
- The existing fixed, zero padding schemes lead to an impersonation attack discussed in Sect. 5. We propose to the best of the authors' knowledge, first and a novel padding approach that prevents such an attack.
- We exclude the use of any additional password or key as a secret parameter.
- We evaluate the recognition performance of our proposed system that shows a tremendous improvement in performance accuracy measured in terms of true match rate (TMR) as compared to the existing schemes, which are discussed in Sect. 4 (in our proposed scheme, TMR = 0.63).
- Further, the empirical experiments performed to evaluate the performance in terms of time taken for enrolment and authentication show that our proposed approach can be implemented for a wide-scale deployment of biometric authentication systems. As an instance, our proposed scheme takes around 0.3 seconds to authenticate a user.
- We provide a thorough security analysis that shows that our proposed scheme's attack complexity is equivalent to the brute force attack complexity.

2   Preliminaries

2.1   Notations

B denotes the original biometric template represented in the form of a binary string, C denotes the error correcting codeword generated from a secret message K of length k. n denotes the length of the codeword C. H denotes the hash function. The error correcting capability of an error correcting codeword is denoted by t. S denotes the secure sketch value. $\|$ denotes the concatenation operation and $\oplus$ denotes the XOR operation. HD denotes the public helper data which is stored on the database server during the enrolment phase.

2.2   Definitions

We use several concepts in our construction discussed below.

- **Fuzzy Commitment Scheme:** The fuzzy commitment (FC) scheme is a combination of two functions, a commitment and a de-commitment function.
  1. A commitment function on input $B \in \{0,1\}^n$, selects a random error correcting code $C \in \{0,1\}^n$ and returns a random secure sketch value $S \in \{0,1\}^n$ where $S = B \oplus C$. S and $H(C)$ are stored on server as a part of helper data HD during enrolment.
  2. The de-commitment function takes a n-bit query template B' and the secure sketch value S. It computes $(S \oplus B')$ to generate C'. With an efficient error correcting code decoding function, if the Hamming distance

between two strings B and B', denoted as $\|B \oplus B'\| \leq t$, where t is the maximum number of errors that can be corrected in the bit string, C' is decoded to the nearest codeword C''. If $(H(C'') = H(C))$, the user is authenticated and B is recovered.

- **BCH Codes:** Given the mapping as an injective function, the error correcting codes map k-symbols to n-symbols such that $\{0,1\}^k \longrightarrow \{0,1\}^n$. Each error correcting code is a set of unique, random codewords denoted by C. One of the prominent examples of error correcting codes used in biometrics is Bose-Chaudhuri-Hocquenghem codes. BCH codes are random error-correcting cyclic codes constructed using polynomials over a finite field (Galois field). For any positive integers $(q \geq 3)$ and $(t < 2^{(q-1)})$, there exists a t-error-correcting BCH code generated with the random, secret message K of length k with the following parameters [3,30]:
  Size of error correcting codeword: $n = 2^q - 1$
  Number of parity-check bits: $n - k \leq qt$
  Minimum distance: $d_{min} \geq 2t + 1$
  The codeword C is denoted as $(n, k, t)-$ BCH codeword. The parity-check bits are used to recover the original, transmitted codeword from a received codeword with some error(s). Minimum distance gives the minimum distance between any two codewords, such that each codeword corrects a maximum of t error bits. In our paper, the security attack is explained in Sect. 5 with BCH codes into consideration.

3 Models and Settings

We discuss the system participants, assets and the possible attack scenarios. We consider the biometric system with a fuzzy commitment scheme as the underlying architecture.

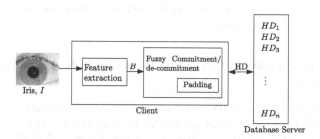

Fig. 1. System model for our proposed scheme. Here, HD denotes the helper data stored on the database server.

3.1 System Model and Participants

The system consists of users (genuine or impostors) and a server. Figure 1 shows the system model for our proposed scheme. The user provides input as the biometric characteristics, such as iris, from which features are extracted to get the template. The client device consists of a feature extraction module, a fuzzy commitment and a de-commitment module. Further, the padding module is present within the fuzzy commitment/de-commitment modules. The padding is assumed to be done on the original biometric templates. We consider the generation of helper data to be done on the client device. The database server stores the helper data generated using the iris template for each user. The helper data constitutes the secure sketch value and the hash of the error correcting codeword used in the underlying fuzzy commitment scheme as discussed in Sect. 2.

3.2 Attack Model

- In the real world, an attack is possible where the attacker can access the server database to get the helper data corresponding to each enroled user.
- When the padding approach is used (whether fixed, zero padding [22,38] or random, secret padding (proposed approach)), the attacker may know the positions in the biometric template where the fixed (such as all $0's$) or random padding has been done.
- In the case if padding bits are also known to the attacker (such as in the case of all $0's$), it would lead to the security attack as discussed in Sect. 5 which reveals the original biometric template of a particular enroled/genuine user to the attacker. The disclosed biometric template could be used for any malicious activities. For example, the attacker may impersonate the genuine user by providing the disclosed biometric template to authenticate successfully. It results in an impersonation attack.

4   Related Work

This section describes the literature work related to existing biometric template protection schemes including the padding schemes that use fuzzy commitment as an underlying architecture.

4.1   Existing Biometric Cryptosystems (Including Padding-Based Schemes)

Hao et al. [15] are the first to introduce the fuzzy commitment scheme for iris template protection by integrating two error correcting codes, Hadamard and Reed-Solomon, in the fuzzy commitment scheme. Kanade et al. [21,25] introduce a secret shuffling of iriscode using a password or a key [22,24,38]. It is followed by zero insertion in iriscode to improve the error correcting capability of Hadamard codes (increased beyond 25%). Two zeros are inserted after every three bits of iriscode. However, padding with all $0's$ results in an impersonation attack, discussed in Sect. 5. Also, using an additional key or a password is not a reliable solution since keys or passwords need to be memorized or require secret storage, which is an overhead.

Most of the recent work on biometric cryptosystems [4,6,16] that incorporate fuzzy commitment schemes implement BCH codes as the error correcting codes. In [28], a biometric cryptosystem is constructed by combining fingerprint templates with various error correcting codes, including BCH code which gives promising results. Hoang et al. [16] propose an authentication system on mobile devices for gait characteristics in which BCH code is employed. Deploying the same scheme for iriscodes with no padding results in an unsatisfactory recognition performance if $k \leq 128$ bits. Similarly, an improved scheme is proposed in [6], where additional security parameters are included in the generation of error correcting codeword. However, implementing BCH or RS code with no padding and $k \geq 128$ bits results in low recognition performance accuracy on the real databases. In [4], the fuzzy commitment scheme is combined with the fuzzy vault scheme using the format preserving encryption. The scheme is highly secure. However, high recognition performance is achieved on the assumption that the error correcting codes can correct all or most of the bit errors in the input biometric templates.

4.2 Existing Cancelable and Deep Learning Based Schemes

A cancelable biometric scheme is proposed in [5] that uses a fuzzy commitment scheme to generate a secret key from the input biometric template while preserving the recognition performance with the assumption that the error correcting code can correct all the bit-errors in the biometric template. In the area of deep learning [31], the fuzzy commitment scheme is used to extract the secret key, which is used to activate or deactivate the layers of the neural network to get a protected template as an output. The security of the underlying fuzzy commitment scheme is limited to around 56 bits. In [9,43], a face template protection scheme is proposed while using error correcting codes to correct bit-errors; however, the security of the fuzzy commitment scheme is not taken into consideration. A reconstruction of the protected biometric template to get the original biometric template is shown in [26]. The attack is possible due to the use of a fuzzy commitment scheme. However, the attack considers all the bit-errors to be corrected by the error correcting codes, which is not always feasible.

5 Impersonation Attack on Error Correcting Codewords

In this section, we describe an attack on error correcting codes mentioned in [42,44]. The security of the codeword (considering BCH codes) depends on k message bits from which it is generated. Therefore, the brute force attack to get the correct codeword will take 2^k number of trials. However, the following attack allows an attacker to reveal the entire biometric template by solving a set of linear equations with a complexity less than that of a brute force attack. Considering the case when a zero-padding or fixed padding (can be used interchangeably) is performed on the biometric template, we assume that the attacker knows the relative positions where the $0's$ or fixed padding bits are inserted [21]. If the input biometric template is zero-padded with k or more than k bits, after padding, the fuzzy commitment scheme is given as

$$B\|\{0\}^{k^+} \oplus C = S \qquad (1)$$

where $\{0\}^{k^+}$ denotes that k or more than k zeros are inserted. Because of the zero insertions and public value S, the attacker would know the corresponding k or more than k bits of the codeword C by inverting the XOR operation.

The Step-by-Step Procedure of the Attack is Described as Follows

The encoding of BCH codeword aims as finding a polynomial that has generator polynomial $g(x)$ as a factor. The secret message $K = K_{k-1}K_{k-2}\cdots K_0$ of length k bits is represented in the form of a polynomial given as $K(x)$. Considering the Euclidean division of polynomials, we take dividend as secret message bits $K(x)$ multiplied with x^{n-k} and subtract the remainder given as $P(x)$ from the dividend to get the output as a multiple of divisor (which denotes the generator polynomial $g(x)$). The division is denoted as

$$x^{n-k}K(x) - P(x) = g(x) \times q(x) \qquad (2)$$

where $q(x)$ represents the multiplicative factor.

The systematic error correcting codeword includes the secret message bits verbatim within the codeword itself. Such a codeword in polynomial form is denoted as $C(x)$ and is given as $C(x) = K(x) * P(x)$. Here, $P(x)$ is denoted as the parity-check bits (in the polynomial form) of the error correcting codeword $C(x)$. It is of size $(n - k)$. Parity check bits is derived from Eq. (2) as

$$P(x) = x^{n-k}K(x) \bmod(g(x)) \qquad (3)$$

The Eq. (3) is linear under modulus operation, therefore,

$$P(x) = x^{n-k}K_{k-1}x^{k-1}mod(g(x)) \oplus x^{n-k}K_{k-2}x^{k-2}mod(g(x)) \oplus \cdots$$
$$\oplus x^{n-k}K_0 mod(g(x))$$
$$= K_{k-1}x^{n-1}mod(g(x)) \oplus K_{k-2}x^{n-2}mod(g(x)) \oplus \ldots \oplus K_0 x^{n-k}mod(g(x)).$$

Representing $x^{n-i}mod(g(x))$ as vector V_{n-i}, where $1 \leq i \leq k$, $P(x)$ is given as

$$P(x) = K_{k-1}V_{n-1} \oplus K_{k-2}V_{n-2} \oplus \ldots \oplus K_0 V_{n-k}. \qquad (4)$$

The generator polynomial $g(x)$ is public and is known for a particular pair (n, k) of the codeword, implying vector V_{n-i} would be known.

Given: k or more than k bits of the codeword C, where these known k bits are considered as a part of parity-check bits.

Goal: Find the secret message $K(x)$ with k bits from which the original error correcting codeword is generated.

Constructing $(n - k)$ linear equations from Eq. (4) with K_j as unknowns, where $0 \leq j \leq (k - 1)$, we get

$$
\begin{bmatrix}
V_{n-1}^{1} & V_{n-2}^{1} & \cdots & V_{(n-k)}^{1} \\
V_{n-1}^{2} & V_{n-2}^{2} & \cdots & V_{(n-k)}^{2} \\
V_{n-1}^{3} & V_{n-2}^{3} & \cdots & V_{(n-k)}^{3} \\
\vdots & \vdots & \cdots & \vdots \\
\vdots & \vdots & \cdots & \vdots \\
V_{n-1}^{(n-k)-1} & V_{n-2}^{(n-k)-1} & \cdots & V_{(n-k)}^{(n-k)-1} \\
V_{n-1}^{(n-k)} & V_{n-2}^{(n-k)} & \cdots & V_{(n-k)}^{(n-k)}
\end{bmatrix}_{(n-k)\times k}
\begin{bmatrix}
K_{k-1} \\
K_{k-2} \\
K_{k-3} \\
\vdots \\
\vdots \\
K_1 \\
K_0
\end{bmatrix}_{k\times 1}
=
\begin{bmatrix}
P_{(n-k)-1} \\
P_{(n-k)-2} \\
P_{(n-k)-3} \\
\vdots \\
\vdots \\
P_1 \\
P_0
\end{bmatrix}_{(n-k)\times 1}
\tag{5}
$$

Since the input biometric template is padded with k or more than k zeros, the attacker get the corresponding k or more than k bits in error correcting codeword. We consider that the revealed codeword bits are a part of parity-check bits P_u, where $0 \leq u \leq ((n-k)-1)$. Using Eq. (5) with k or more than k known parity-check bits on the right-hand side of the matrix, it generates k independent linear equations with k unknown secret message bits (given by K), forming a system of linear equations $EX = F$ with a unique solution $X = E^{-1}F$ [7].

Taking X as the unknown secret message K, E as the known vector V and F as the parity check matrix P with $\geq k$ known values, the attacker solves the linear equations to get k unknown secret message bits to get the codeword C. B can be obtained by simply XORing C with secure sketch value S using Eq. (1), leading to an impersonation attack. In the case of brute force, the attack complexity would be 2^k bits, whereas, in our case, the attack complexity becomes equal to the complexity of solving a system of linear equations. The attack mentioned above is mainly documented on BCH codes. However, it is also possible to perform the attack on the family of BCH codes, including the Reed Solomon codes and other members of the same family [42, 44].

6 Proposed Work

We propose a user-specific, random padding approach for the efficient implementation of a fuzzy commitment scheme that enhances the overall system's security while preserving high recognition performance. The proposed scheme works on the principle that unique but random padding bits must be used during enrolment and authentication for a particular individual. The padding bits are derived from the underlying error correcting codeword. At the same time, the padding bits are random and are not stored anywhere during the enrolment to avoid being guessed by the attacker.

6.1 User-Specific, Random Padding Using Codeword Bits

The user provides its biometric template in the form of a binary string $B \in \{0,1\}^n$. A random, error correcting codeword $C \in \{0,1\}^m$ is used to correct the bit-errors present in the biometric template. Taking inspiration from the existing approaches [25,38], we introduce random padding on the input biometric template. Insertion of a few random padding bits increases the size of B while keeping the bit errors the same as that of the original B (before padding). Since the length of the biometric template and error correcting codeword is kept the same, a corresponding larger-sized codeword is required for the modified biometric template (with padding). Generally, larger the codeword size, the more errors it will correct [44] (observed in Fig. 2). Thus, it is possible to correct more bit-errors in the biometric template by using a larger-size codeword.

Algorithm 1: Enrolment Phase

Input: Iriscode B

Output: Secure sketch values S_j for $1 \leq j \leq i$ and $i \geq 2$, hash value

1. $B = B_1 \| B_2 \| \ldots \| B_{i-1} \| B_i$
2. **For** $1 \leq j \leq i-1$
3. $C_j \xleftarrow{k_j} K_j,$ $\triangleright K_j$ denotes j-th random secret message
4. $S_j = B_j \oplus C_j,$ $\triangleright |C_j| = |B_j|$
5. $j = j+1$
6. **For** $j = i$
7. $C_i \xleftarrow{k_i} K_i,$ $\triangleright |C_i| = |B_i\|\{C_{i-1}\}^{pad}|$
8. $H(C_i) \xleftarrow{H} C_i$
9. $B_i\|\{C_{i-1}\}^{pad} \oplus C_i = S_i$
10.   **Return** $S_1, S_2, \ldots, S_i, H(C_1\|C_2\|\ldots\|C_i)$

During enrolment phase, on providing B as input, we split it into i different blocks such that $B = B_1\|B_2\|\ldots\|B_{i-1}\|B_i$.

Each block B_j with $1 \leq j \leq i$ is of length $n_1, n_2, \ldots, n_{i-1}, n_i$ respectively, where the length could vary for each block. For each block B_j, a codeword C_j of length m_j is generated. We can split the biometric template into any number of blocks of biometric templates with 2 minimum blocks, i.e. $i \geq 2$. In Sect. 7, we perform our experiments with biometric templates splitted into 2 blocks. For the purpose of generality and simplicity, we consider applying padding to only the last block B_i of the biometric template.

For $1 \leq j \leq i-1$, a secure sketch value S_j is derived using fuzzy commitment scheme with B_j and corresponding C_j as inputs. It is given as

$$B_1 \oplus C_1 = S_1$$
$$B_2 \oplus C_2 = S_2$$
$$\vdots$$
$$B_{i-1} \oplus C_{i-1} = S_{i-1}$$

To introduce padding in the last block B_i, we propose to use a few codeword bits from the codeword C_{i-1} belonging to a previous block. The number of padding bits required is denoted by *pad*. These padding bits are replicated from the codeword C_{i-1} and are appended to block B_i.

Algorithm 2: Authentication Phase

Input: Iriscode B', Secure sketch values S_j, where $1 \leq j \leq i$ and
$\qquad i \geq 2$, hash value $H(C_1 \| C_2 \| \ldots \| C_i)$

Output: a bit 1/0

1. $B' = B'_1 \| B'_2 \| \ldots \| B'_{i-1} \| B'_i$
2. **For** $1 \leq j \leq i - 1$
3. $\qquad C'_j = B'_j \oplus S_j$, $\quad \triangleright |C_j| = |B'_j|$ and error correcting
    capability of C_j is t_j
4. $\qquad C'_j$ is decoded to C''_j if $HD(B_j, B'_j) < t_j$
5. $\qquad j = j + 1$
6. **For** $j = i$
7. $\qquad B'_i \| \{C_{i-1}\}^{pad} \oplus S_i = C'_i$
8. $\qquad C'_i$ is decoded to C''_i if $HD(B_i, B'_i) < t_i$
9. **if** $H(C''_1 \| C''_2 \| \ldots \| C''_i) = H(C_1 \| C_2 \| \ldots \| C_i)$
10. $\qquad$ **Return** 1, $\quad \triangleright$ User is successfully authenticated
11. **else**
12. $\qquad$ **Return** 0

The enrolment phase for the last block of the biometric template is given as,

$$B_i \| \{C_{i-1}\}^{pad} \oplus C_i = S_i$$

$\{C_{i-1}\}^{pad}$ denotes that the *pad* number of bits from C_{i-1} are taken for concatenation. Here, the codeword C_i is chosen such that its length is exactly equal to the length of the padded biometric template, denoted as

$$|C_i| = |B_i \| \{C_{i-1}\}^{pad}|$$

The secure sketch values $S_1, S_2, \ldots, S_{i-1}, S_i$ are stored on the database server as public values along with the hash of all the codewords concatenated together denoted as $H(C_1 \| C_2 \| \ldots \| C_i)$. The values S_1 to S_i and $H(C_1 \| C_2 \| \ldots \| C_i)$ constitute the helper data. The enrolment phase is described in Algorithm 1.

During the authentication phase, the user provides $B' \in \{0,1\}^l$ which is splitted into i blocks of the respective lengths as in the enrolment phase such that $B' = B'_1 \| B'_2 \| \ldots \| B'_{i-1} \| B'_i$. From the secure sketch values S_j for $1 \leq j \leq i - 1$ and $i \geq 2$ stored as a part of helper data on the database server, the original codeword C_j is decoded as

$$B'_1 \oplus S_1 = C'_1$$
$$B'_2 \oplus S_2 = C'_2$$
$$\vdots$$
$$B'_{i-1} \oplus S_{i-1} = C'_{i-1}$$

If B'_j, B_j (for $1 \leq j \leq i-1$) satisfy the condition that $HD(B'_j, B_j) \leq t$, where HD calculates the hamming distance between two binary strings, C'_j is decoded using t-error correcting codeword to get the codeword $C''_j = C_j$.

For $j = i$, i.e. for the last block, $|B_i'| \neq |S_i|$, thus, we need padding. The *pad* number of bits are replicated from the decoded codeword $C_{i-1}'' = C_{i-1}$ and appended to the B_i'. We then perform, $B_i' \| \{C_{i-1}\}^{pad} \oplus S_i = C_i'$ If B_i', B_i satisfy the condition: $HD(B_i', B_i) \leq t$, C_i' would be decoded to the codeword C_i''. If $H(C_1'' \| C_2'' \| \dots \| C_i'') = H(C_1 \| C_2 \| \dots \| C_i)$, the user is authenticated successfully. The authentication phase is described in Algorithm 2.

We can design multiple constructions by taking the blocks in any order while maintaining their order during the enrolment and authentication phase. According to the statistical distribution of bit errors among multiple datasets, the design flexibility helps to achieve high-performance accuracy while preserving security.

7   Experiments and Performance Analysis

We analyze the performance of our proposed scheme in terms of recognition accuracy and the time taken to perform biometric authentication. We perform the experiments on the publicly available IIT-Delhi iris database [27] consisting of 420 instances, 5 samples per instance. To obtain the iriscodes, we use several open-source libraries such as OSIRIS [36] and University of Salzburg Iris Toolkit v1.0 [41] and the Daugman-like 1D-Log Gabor (LG) algorithm proposed by Masek [33] for feature extraction in the iris. An iriscode of length 10240 bits is generated. We perform a statistical test on the database to find the general distribution of errors in the iriscodes. On about 4200 genuine samples with a threshold of 0.21 (considering a suitable BCH codeword with $k \geq 128$ bits, we partition each iriscode into 3 parts and observed that the last partition contains more number of bit errors (greater than 21%) as compared to the other two partitions for most of the iriscodes. Hence we prefer padding on the second block of the iriscode when the iriscode is split into 2 blocks. We use BCH codes for implementation[1] of various configurations (shown in Table 2).

7.1   Recognition Performance Evaluation

We evaluate the recognition performance in terms of the true match rate and false match rate generated by the system for various values of the length k of secret message K. The higher the length of K, the more is the security. The recognition performance of our proposed scheme is shown in Fig. 2. The true match rate decreases by increasing the length of secret message K and increases with the decreasing length of K. It is implicit that the higher the length of secret message K, the fewer errors t would be corrected by a particular error correcting codeword [29]. Therefore, a performance-security trade-off always exists in the implementation of error correcting codes. Figure 3 shows the comparison of recognition performance of our proposed approach with the existing approaches. We select the value of K such that $k \geq 128$ for our proposed approach and compare our proposed approach in Table 2 with the existing constructions given as follows.

---

[1] http://www.eccpage.com/bch3.c.

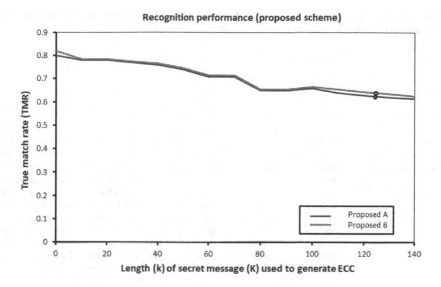

Fig. 2. The recognition performance (true match rate (TMR)) of Proposed A and Proposed B schemes with respect to the length k of secret message K. The markers show the TMR at $k = 128$.

- **Baseline A** [10,16]: It denotes the original fuzzy commitment scheme proposed by Dodis et al. [10] (without padding). The extra bits from the biometric template are discarded.
- **Baseline B** [6,15]: It denotes the scheme proposed by Hao et al. [15] with BCH code with $k = 19$ bits so that the maximum number of errors would be corrected by the underlying error correcting codeword.
- **Zero Padding** [22,24,25,38]: We append several zeros in the biometric template B of length 10240 to get the modified length of 16383 bits.
- **Fixed Padding** [22,23,25,38]: We append some fixed padding bits derived using an additional key or a password.
- **Bit-wise encryption** [5]: In [5], we ignore the cancelable template generation module and focus on the fuzzy extractor. BCH code is used to correct the bit errors in the input biometric template.
- **BIOFUSE** [4]: For BIOFUSE, we consider the performance of the fuzzy commitment scheme while ignoring the fuzzy vault scheme's performance since a Boolean AND operation is performed.
- **Secure Face** [31]: We consider the fuzzy extractor module for generating the secure key from iriscode using BCH code.
- **Proposed:** We split the iriscode into $i = 2$ blocks as described in Sect. 6. We consider the two best cases given as:
  - **Proposed A:** B_1=8191 with C_1=8191 bits and B_2=2049 padded with 6142 bits of C_1. The length of codeword C_2=8191 bits.
  - **Proposed B:** B_1=8191 with C_1=8191 bits and B_2=2049 padded with 2046 bits of C_1. The length of codeword C_2=4095 bits.

Table 2. True match rate (TMR) along with security comparison for various fuzzy commitment schemes designed for iris biometric templates.

Approaches	Biometric template B		Codeword C, (n,k,t)		TMR	Security (in k bits)
	B_1	B_2	C_1	C_2		
Baseline A [10,16]	8191	2047	(8191,131,1759)	(2047,133,365)	0.19	$k_1, k_2 \geq 128$
	2047	8191	(2047,133,365)	(8191,131,1759)	0.17	$k_1, k_2 \geq 128$
Baseline B [6,15]	8191	2047	(8191, 14, 2047)	(2047, 12, 511)	0.49	$k_1, k_2 \leq 128$
	2047	8191	(2047,12,511)	(8191, 14,2047)	0.61	$k_1, k_2 \leq 128$
Zero padding [22,24,25,38]	$10240\|\{0\}^{6143}$		(16383,134,3575)		0.93	$k_1, k_2 \geq 128^a$
Fixed padding [22,23,25,38]	$10240\|\{0\}^{6143}$		(16383,134,3575)		0.93	$k_1, k_2 \geq 128^a$
Bit-wise encryption [5]	8191	2047	(8191,131,1759)	(2047,133,365)	0.19	$k_1, k_2 \geq 128$
	2047	8191	(2047,133,365)	(8191,131,1759)	0.17	$k_1, k_2 \geq 128$
BIOFUSE [4]	8191	2047	(8191,131,1759)	(2047,133,365)	0.19	$k_1, k_2 \geq 128$
	2047	8191	(2047,133,365)	(8191,131,1759)	0.17	$k_1, k_2 \geq 128$
Secure Face [31]	8191	2047	(8191,131,1759)	(2047,133,365)	0.19	$k_1, k_2 \geq 128$
	2047	8191	(2047,133,365)	(8191,131,1759)	0.17	$k_1, k_2 \geq 128$
Proposed	**8191**	$2049\|\{C_1\}^{6142}$	**(8191,131,1759)**	**(8191,131,1759)**	**0.63**	$k_1, k_2 \geq 128$
	8191	$2049\|\{C_1\}^{2046}$	**(8191,131,1759)**	**(4095,134,763)**	**0.64**	
	$2049\|\{C_2\}^{2046}$	8191	(4095,134,763)	(8191,131,1759)	0.59	
	$2049\|\{C_2\}^{6142}$	8191	(8191,131,1759)	(8191,131,1759)	0.59	

Following are the observations

- The proposed scheme gives the best recognition performance accuracy among all the secure schemes (no impersonation attack and $k \geq 128$ bits). We achieve a true match rate of approximately 64% as the best case.
- The zero and fixed padding schemes [21–25,38] show highest accuracy (93%); however, they lead to the impersonation attack (refer Sect. 5).
- The Baseline B has recognition performance equivalent to the performance of proposed approach, it is not secure due to the small length of the secret message ($k = 19$), resulting in a brute force attack (refer Sect. 8).
- We also calculate the false match rate (FMR) of our proposed approach as well as the existing approaches. It is almost negligible for all the causes contributing to high security in critical systems when the priority is to reject an intruder or an impostor rather than to keep the true match rate high.
- In Table 2 and Fig. 3, we observe that the recognition performance of some existing schemes [4,5,31] is low (TMR = 0.19), given $k = 128$ bits. By implementing our proposed padding approach, the recognition performance of such schemes could be improved to 3 times (with TMR = 0.63).
- In Table 2, we also consider padding on the first block of iriscode. In comparison to the Baseline A (TMR= 0.17) where B_1=2047 and B_2=8191 bits, a significant improvement (TMR = 0.59) is shown in the proposed case with padding where B_1=$2049\|\{C_2\}^{6142}$ and B_2=8191. Thus, in the scenarios, where the distribution of error is more in the first block, the padding on the first block could help to improve the overall performance rates of the system.
- We further evaluate the results on different number of block partitions, considering 3 blocks as B_1=2047 bits with codeword C_1=2047 bits, B_2=6144 bits padded with 2047 bits of codeword C_1 and B_3=2047 bits padded with 6144

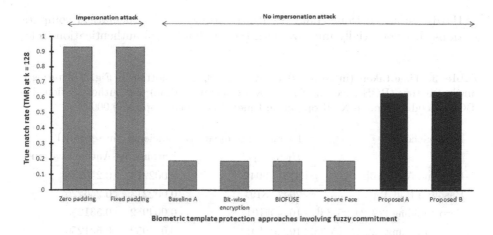

Fig. 3. Recognition performance of various approaches (best cases from Table 2).

bits of codeword C_2. The length of codeword C_2 and C_3=8191 bits. Similar to the above-mentioned case, we observe the degradation of accuracy (TMR= 0.48) as compared to the Proposed A and Proposed B cases.

- While the overall accuracy of our proposed scheme is quite low for implementation in real-life scenarios; it still surpasses the accuracy achieved with baseline approaches by a significant number. For real-life implementations, the configurations can be manipulated according to the database and the error distribution in the particular database to get the desired accuracy.

7.2   Efficiency in Terms of Authentication Time

We evaluate the efficiency of our proposed scheme in terms of the time taken during the enrolment and authentication phase (measured in terms of seconds on an average of over 200 runs each). The experiments are performed on a server-grade processor; Intel i7 2.6 GHz quad core processor (with hyper-threading) with 16 GB RAM architecture for profiling BCH encoding and decoding subroutines. Further, we have used several compiler flags that allow fast compilation of the code. Following are the inferences from Table 3:

- We obtain the authentication time as approximately 0.3 seconds for one of the best cases- Proposed B. Shorter authentication time helps to achieve the deployability of our proposed approach on wider scale biometric systems where real-time processing is a major requirement.
- For the configuration with 3 block partition (B_1=2047, B_2=6144 and B_3=2047 bits), we obtain the enrolment time as 0.0039 seconds and authentication time as 0.46 seconds approximately which shows that as the length of codewords and the number of codewords used increase, the time also increases.
- Small authentication time proves the fact that the entire authentication process is not resource-intensive. Hence, our proposed scheme could also be scaled to low powered or IoT devices.

- Hardware instructions could be utilized for several mathematical computations that potentially improve both the enrolment and authentication time.

Table 3. Time taken (in seconds) by various schemes plotted in Fig. 2 in terms of enrolment time (BCH encoding time + XOR operation time) and authentication time (BCH decoding time + XOR operation time). XOR takes approx. 0.00002 s.

Approaches	Biometric template B		Efficiency (in seconds)	
	B_1	B_2	Enrolment	Authentication
Baseline A [10, 16]	8191	2047	0.002213	0.256226
Baseline B [6, 15]	2047	8191	0.002213	0.256226
Zero Padding [22, 24, 25, 38]	$10240\|\|\{0\}^{6143}$		0.004952	0.531250
Fixed Padding [22, 23, 25, 38]	$10240\|\|\{0\}^{6143}$		0.004952	0.531250
Bit-wise encryption [5]	8191	2047	0.002213	0.256226
BIOFUSE [4]	8191	2047	0.002213	0.256226
Secure Face [31]	8191	2047	0.002213	0.256226
Proposed A	8191	$2049\|\|\{C_1\}^{6142}$	0.003536	0.409550
Proposed B	8191	$2049\|\|\{C_1\}^{2046}$	0.002694	0.308337

8   Security Analysis

The security of our proposed work majorly depends on two parameters: the input biometric template B and the secret message K of length k used to generate C.

8.1   Brute Force Attack Complexity

We discuss the brute force attack complexity for an attacker to reveal B or C.

1. **Brute force complexity for getting the biometric template B:** While the attacker tries to perform an exhaustive search over B, the number of trials to get B is given in terms of the entropy of B. Hao et al. [15] introduce the concept of security based on the sphere-packing bound [1] to calculate the entropy estimation on iriscode as a biometric template which gives the probability of how difficult or easy it is to guess a correct iriscode by an attacker. It computes a degree of freedom that requires the correlation information [15] in a large real-time database, which is not a practical approach.
2. **Brute force complexity for getting the error correcting codeword C:** In the fuzzy commitment scheme, we store the hash of the codeword C on the server as a part of the helper data. The authentication is successful when $(H(C'') = H(C))$.

To compromise C, there could be 2 different approaches:

- In the first approach, the target would be to obtain C. Given $H(C)$, the attacker could perform pre-image attack on C to satisfy the authentication condition that $(H(C'') = H(C))$. The attack complexity is given by the number of trials required to guess C which limits to $|H(C)|$ since $|C| >> |H(C)|$. It is equal to $2^{|H(C)|}$.
- In the second approach, the attacker could perform a brute force attack on the secret message K with the number of trials as 2^k, where k is the length of K. Therefore, the security bound is given in terms of the number of trials as $2^{min(|H(C)|,k)}$. Usually, $k \leq |H(C)|$, therefore, attacker chooses to perform brute force on secret message K.

To prevent the attacks given in the two approaches mentioned above, first, the size of the hash output should be considerably large. For example, we use SHA-256 as the hash function, which gives 256 bits hash value. Second, the secret message bits K used to generate codewords must be preferably equal to or greater than 128 bits. We further suggest that for every block of the biometric template B_j, with $1 \leq j \leq i$ obtained after splitting the biometric template B into i blocks, the secret message bits used for generating the respective codewords must have lengths $k_j \geq 128$ bits.

8.2   Attack Complexity of the Proposed Scheme

Our proposed random-padding scheme prevents the impersonation attack discussed in Sect. 5. The following result justifies the security of our scheme.

Statement: The security of the overall scheme lies on the security of the k bits of the secret message K, which is used to generate C.

Proof. To compromise the system, an attacker could follow two approaches:

- **Case 1: Guessing K:** K is assumed to be a uniformly distributed random value. The number of trials required to obtain K is equal to the brute force complexity and is given as 2^k, where k is the length of K.
- **Case 2: Guessing padding bits** *pad* **in our proposed random padding scheme:** The fuzzy commitment scheme for the $i - th$ block of biometric template following our proposal is shown as

$$B_i \| \{C_{i-1}\}^{pad} \oplus C_i = S_i$$

The padding bits are random, secret bits and are not stored on the server during enrolment. It is ensured that the number of padding bits, *pad* $\geq k$, where k is the length of secret message K used to generate the underlying codeword C and $k \geq 128$ bits. In case if *pad* $< k$ bits, an attacker can perform a brute force approach and can be successful with attack complexity less than 2^{128}, leading to the impersonation attack, described in Sect. 5.

Since the padding bits are unknown, the attacker aims at guessing at least k padding bits out of pad number of bits which requires 2^k number of trials to guess the k bits. To prevent the impersonation attack, we consider the number of padding bits $pad \geq k \geq 128$. Besides, it is always easy to avoid the case when $pad < 128$. For an example, let we have i blocks of biometric template, out of which the padding is required for the block B_j such that $1 \leq j \leq i$ and $i \geq 2$. Then, the error correcting codeword of a specific length m_j could be chosen by the system for block B_j in a way that, we get $m_j - n_j \geq 128$ where n_j is the length of block B_j and $m_j - n_j$ gives the number of padding bits required for the particular block.

Therefore, the whole system's security depends on the security of k bits of the secret message, equivalent to the brute force attack complexity as 2^k.

9 Conclusions

We propose, first in our knowledge, a novel, user-specific, random padding scheme for an efficient implementation of error correcting codes to enhance the security of existing fuzzy commitment schemes. Our proposed padding scheme prevents the impersonation attack that could reveal the whole biometric template to the attackers. While the existing approaches often use an additional key or a password to enhance security or recognition performance, we did not use any of these. The experimental results show that our proposed padding scheme tremendously improves the recognition performance of the baseline, unprotected schemes by approximately 3 times by providing a true match rate of 0.64. The time taken for authentication is around 0.30 seconds on an average of over 200 trials. We provide a thorough security analysis for our proposed work. It shows that our proposed random padding scheme provides the attack complexity of k bits equivalent to the brute force attack complexity, where k denotes the length of the secret message used to generate the codeword and $k \geq 128$ bits.

We conclude that our proposed scheme is simple and efficient to implement. It significantly improves recognition performance and efficiency in terms of authentication time while preserving the overall system's security. Other than for user authentication, our scheme could be applied in the areas where the fuzzy commitment scheme is prominently used to generate a secret key from the biometric templates [4, 5, 31]. Since the secret, the cryptographic key generated from a particular instance is unique, it is very important to preserve maximum bit errors in different samples of the same instance. In such scenarios, our proposed padding scheme would enhance the error preservation, hence the system's performance. Further, the performance accuracy can be significantly increased by considering multiple configurations of the blocks of biometric templates according to the distribution of bit errors in a particular database.

References

1. Al-Assam, H., Jassim, S.: Security evaluation of biometric keys. Cmput. Secur. **31**(2), 151–163 (2012)
2. Berrou, C., Glavieux, A., Thitimajshima, P.: Near shannon limit error-correcting coding and decoding: Turbo-codes. 1. In: Proceedings of ICC'93-IEEE International Conference on Communications, vol. 2, pp. 1064–1070. IEEE (1993)
3. Bose, R.C., Ray-Chaudhuri, D.K.: On a class of error correcting binary group codes. Inf. Control **3**(1), 68–79 (1960)
4. Chang, D., Garg, S., Ghosh, M., Hasan, M.: Biofuse: a framework for multi-biometric fusion on biocryptosystem level. Inf. Sci. **546**, 481–511 (2021)
5. Chang, D., Garg, S., Hasan, M., Mishra, S.: Cancelable multi-biometric approach using fuzzy extractor and novel bit-wise encryption. IEEE Trans. Inf. Forensics Secur. **15**, 3152–3167 (2020)
6. Chauhan, S., Sharma, A.: Improved fuzzy commitment scheme. Int. J. Inf. Technol. **14**, 1321–1331(2019)
7. Cullen, C.G.: Matrices and Linear Transformations. Courier Corporation (2012)
8. Daugman, J.: 600 million citizens of India are now enrolled with biometric id. SPIE Newsroom **7** (2014)
9. Dayal Mohan, D., Sankaran, N., Tulyakov, S., Setlur, S., Govindaraju, V.: Significant feature based representation for template protection. In: Proceedings of the IEEE/CVF Conference on Computer Vision and Pattern Recognition Workshops (2019)
10. Dodis, Y., Reyzin, L., Smith, A.: Fuzzy extractors: how to generate strong keys from biometrics and other noisy data. In: Cachin, C., Camenisch, J.L. (eds.) EUROCRYPT 2004. LNCS, vol. 3027, pp. 523–540. Springer, Heidelberg (2004). https://doi.org/10.1007/978-3-540-24676-3_31
11. Drozdowski, P., Garg, S., Rathgeb, C., Gomez-Barrero, M., Chang, D., Busch, C.: Privacy-preserving indexing of iris-codes with cancelable bloom filter-based search structures. In: 2018 26th European Signal Processing Conference (EUSIPCO), pp. 2360–2364. IEEE (2018)
12. Gao, S.: A new algorithm for decoding reed-solomon codes. In: In: Bhargava, V.K., Poor, H.V., Tarokh, V., Yoon, S. (eds.) Communications, Information and Network Security, pp. 55–68. Springer, Boston (2003). https://doi.org/10.1007/978-1-4757-3789-9_5
13. Gomez-Barrero, M., Maiorana, E., Galbally, J., Campisi, P., Fierrez, J.: Multi-biometric template protection based on homomorphic encryption. Pattern Recogn. **67**, 149–163 (2017)
14. Gomez-Barrero, M., Rathgeb, C., Galbally, J., Busch, C., Fierrez, J.: Unlinkable and irreversible biometric template protection based on bloom filters. Inf. Sci. **370**, 18–32 (2016)
15. Hao, F., Anderson, R., Daugman, J.: Combining crypto with biometrics effectively. IEEE Trans. Comput. **55**(9), 1081–1088 (2006)
16. Hoang, T., Choi, D., Nguyen, T.: Gait authentication on mobile phone using biometric cryptosystem and fuzzy commitment scheme. Int. J. Inf. Secur. **14**(6), 549–560 (2015). https://doi.org/10.1007/s10207-015-0273-1
17. Hollingsworth, K.P., Bowyer, K.W., Flynn, P.J.: The best bits in an iris code. IEEE Trans. Pattern Anal. Mach. Intell. **31**(6), 964–973 (2008)
18. Jain, A.K., Nandakumar, K., Nagar, A.: Biometric template security. EURASIP J. Adv. Signal Process. **2008**, 113 (2008)

19. Juels, A., Sudan, M.: A fuzzy vault scheme. In: Proceedings of IEEE International Symposium on Information Theory, 2002, p. 408. IEEE (2002)
20. Juels, A., Wattenberg, M.: A fuzzy commitment scheme. In: Proceedings of the 6th ACM conference on Computer and Cmmunications Security, pp. 28–36. ACM (1999)
21. Kanade, S., Camara, D., Krichen, E., Petrovska-Delacrétaz, D., Dorizzi, B.: Three factor scheme for biometric-based cryptographic key regeneration using iris. In: Biometrics Symposium, 2008. BSYM 2008, pp. 59–64. IEEE (2008)
22. Kanade, S., Camara, D., Petrovska-Delacrtaz, D., Dorizzi, B.: Application of biometrics to obtain high entropy cryptographic keys. World Acad. Sci. Eng. Tech **52**, 330 (2009)
23. Kanade, S., Petrovska-Delacrétaz, D., Dorizzi, B.: Cancelable iris biometrics and using error correcting codes to reduce variability in biometric data. In: 2009 IEEE Conference on Computer Vision and Pattern Recognition, pp. 120–127. IEEE (2009)
24. Kanade, S., Petrovska-Delacrétaz, D., Dorizzi, B.: Multi-biometrics based cryptographic key regeneration scheme. In: 2009 IEEE 3rd International Conference on Biometrics: Theory, Applications, and Systems, pp. 1–7. IEEE (2009)
25. Kanade, S.G., Petrovska-Delacrétaz, D., Dorizzi, B.: Enhancing information security and privacy by combining biometrics with cryptography. Synth. Lect. Inf. Sec. Privacy Trust **3**(1), 1–140 (2012)
26. Keller, D., Osadchy, M., Dunkelman, O.: Fuzzy commitments offer insufficient protection to biometric templates produced by deep learning. arXiv preprint arXiv:2012.13293 (2020)
27. Kumar, A., Passi, A.: Comparison and combination of iris matchers for reliable personal authentication. Pattern Recogn. **43**(3), 1016–1026 (2010)
28. Li, P., Yang, X., Qiao, H., Cao, K., Liu, E., Tian, J.: An effective biometric cryptosystem combining fingerprints with error correction codes. Expert Syst. Appl. **39**(7), 6562–6574 (2012)
29. Lin, S., Costello, D.J.: Error Control Coding. Prentice Hall, Englewood Cliffs (2001)
30. MacWilliams, F.J., Sloane, N.J.A.: The Theory of Error-Correcting Codes, vol. 16. Elsevier, New York (1977)
31. Mai, G., Cao, K., Lan, X., Yuen, P.C.: Secureface: face template protection. IEEE Trans. Inf. Forensics Secur. **16**, 262–277 (2020)
32. Malek, M.: Hadamard Codes. California State University, p. 112 (2018)
33. Masek, L., et al.: Recognition of human iris patterns for biometric identification. Ph.D. thesis, Citeseer (2003)
34. Nandakumar, K., Jain, A.K.: Biometric template protection: Bridging the performance gap between theory and practice. IEEE Signal Process. Mag. **32**(5), 88–100 (2015)
35. NL, F.: Uk," comparison bose-chaudhuri-hocquenghem bch and reed solomon. CCITT SGXV, Doc.# 476, Working Party XV/4, Specialists Group on Coding for Visual Telephony (2004)
36. Othman, N., Dorizzi, B., Garcia-Salicetti, S.: OSIRIS: an open source iris recognition software. Pattern Recogn. Lett. **82**, 124–131 (2016)
37. Ratha, N.K., Connell, J.H., Bolle, R.M.: Enhancing security and privacy in biometrics-based authentication systems. IBM Syst. J. **40**(3), 614–634 (2001)
38. Rathge, C., Uhl, A., Wild, P.: Reliability-balanced feature level fusion for fuzzy commitment scheme. In: 2011 International Joint Conference on Biometrics (IJCB), pp. 1–7. IEEE (2011)

39. Rathgeb, C., Breitinger, F., Busch, C.: Alignment-free cancelable iris biometric templates based on adaptive bloom filters. In: 2013 International Conference on Biometrics (ICB), pp. 1–8. IEEE (2013)
40. Rathgeb, C., Uhl, A.: The state-of-the-art in iris biometric cryptosystems. In: State of the Art in Biometrics, pp. 179–202 (2011)
41. Rathgeb, C., Uhl, A., Wild, P., Hofbauer, H.: Design decisions for an iris recognition SDK. In: Bowyer, K.W., Burge, M.J. (eds.) Handbook of Iris Recognition. ACVPR, pp. 359–396. Springer, London (2016). https://doi.org/10.1007/978-1-4471-6784-6_16
42. Stoianov, A.: Security of error correcting code for biometric encryption. In: 2010 Eighth Annual International Conference on Privacy Security and Trust (PST), pp. 231–235. IEEE (2010)
43. Talreja, V., Valenti, M.C., Nasrabadi, N.M.: Zero-shot deep hashing and neural network based error correction for face template protection. In: 2019 IEEE 10th International Conference on Biometrics Theory, Applications and Systems (BTAS), pp. 1–10. IEEE (2019)
44. Teoh, A.B.J., Kim, J.: Error correction codes for biometric cryptosystem: an overview. Inf. Commun. Mag. **32**(6), 39–49 (2015)
45. Zhou, K., Ren, J.: PassBio: privacy-preserving user-centric biometric authentication. IEEE Trans. Inf. Forensics Secur. **13**(12), 3050–3063 (2018)

SoK: Decentralized Randomness Beacon Protocols

Mayank Raikwar$^{(\boxtimes)}$ and Danilo Gligoroski

Norwegian University of Science and Technology (NTNU), Trondheim, Norway
{mayank.raikwar,danilog}@ntnu.no

Abstract. The scientific interest in the area of Decentralized Randomness Beacon (DRB) protocols has been thriving recently. Partially that interest is due to the success of the disruptive technologies introduced by modern cryptography, such as cryptocurrencies, blockchain technologies, and decentralized finances, where there is an enormous need for a public, reliable, trusted, verifiable, and distributed source of randomness. On the other hand, recent advancements in the development of new cryptographic primitives brought a huge interest in constructing a plethora of DRB protocols differing in design and underlying primitives.

To the best of our knowledge, no systematic and comprehensive work systematizes and analyzes the existing DRB protocols. Therefore, we present a Systematization of Knowledge (SoK) intending to structure the multi-faced body of research on DRB protocols. In this SoK, we delineate the DRB protocols along the following axes: their underlying primitive, properties, and security. This SoK tries to fill that gap by providing basic standard definitions and requirements for DRB protocols, such as Unpredictability, Bias-resistance, Availability (or Liveness), and Public Verifiability. We classify DRB protocols according to the nature of interactivity among protocol participants. We also highlight the most significant features of DRB protocols such as scalability, complexity, and performance along with a brief discussion on its improvement. We present future research directions along with a few interesting research problems.

Keywords: Random beacon · Bias-resistance · Unpredictability ·
Secret sharing · Verifiable delay function

1 Introduction

Public digital randomness is an essential building component for a large spectrum of applications and protocols. For example, a reliable source of continuous randomness providing high entropy, also known as *random beacon*, is crucial for many security applications. A notion of *coin tossing protocol* [9] was proposed by Blum in 1983 that addressed the question of generating the trustworthy random value in a network of mutually distrustful participants. Further, Rabin [58] formalized the notion of the random beacon. Since then, randomness generation has been advanced significantly due to the underlying modern cryptography.

K. Nguyen et al. (Eds.): ACISP 2022, LNCS 13494, pp. 420–446, 2022.
https://doi.org/10.1007/978-3-031-22301-3_21

Lately, coin tossing protocols became more appealing in Proof-of-Work (PoW) or Proof-of-Stake (PoS) [39] consensus. Random beacon has a range of applications that includes cryptographic parameter generation [49], design of byzantine fault tolerant (BFT) protocols [16,39], privacy-preserving message services [40], e-voting protocols [1], online gaming [13], publicly auditable selections [13], anonymous browsing [41], sharded blockchains [23] and smart contracts [48].

Due to the applicability of shared randomness in a variety of applications, a rich body of literature has emerged that proposes many DRB protocols differing in their designs and underlying cryptography. Nevertheless, the system models and design challenges in these DRB protocols are highly disparate. Therefore, to address these challenges and to provide a general definition of a DRB protocol, we present a Systematization of Knowledge (SoK). The purpose of this SoK is to provide a systematic overview of existing DRB protocols that can help researchers and practitioners to find suitable solutions for randomness generation.

Background. An easy approach to achieve continuous randomness is through a single node or a trusted third party such as NIST [46], Random.org [43] or Oraclize.it [56]. The NIST beacon continuously outputs hardware-generated random values from a quantum-mechanical effect. Since these beacon services are centralized, they can be unreliable. Moreover, in the past, they suffered a significant public trust deterioration after the revealed backdoor in the NSA-designed Dual elliptic curve pseudorandom number generator [68]. Due to these problems, these centralized beacon services are undesirable for secure applications.

As a consequence, *Decentralized Randomness Beacon* (DRB) protocols were proposed and constructed where trust is distributed across multiple nodes that jointly generate random values at a regular interval. More concretely, a consortium of organizations launched a distributed publicly verifiable randomness beacon that periodically provides unbiasable and unpredictable random outputs. The deployment is known as League of Entropy (LoE)) [51] that aims to provide collaborative governance for protection of its random beacon. The consortium believes that their beacon can become a fundamental service on the internet.

DRB protocols can be constructed by employing different cryptographic primitives e.g. Publicly Verifiable Secret Sharing schemes (PVSS) [8,17,18,25,47,66,69], Threshold Crypto-Systems [16,20,31,45,55], Verifiable Random Functions (VRF) [22,24,27,36,39,71], Verifiable Delay Functions (VDF) [30,34,44,49,65]. Randomness can also be extracted from external data sources such as [7,13,21] or from the blockchain schemes having their own random beacon [36,45,47]. These DRB protocols are not equally-suited in all applications or use-cases due to the diversity in their designs, characteristics, and underlying assumptions.

DRB protocols differ significantly due to their underlying techniques. A DRB protocol should have a list of desirable beacon properties along with low communication complexity, low computational cost, and low trust requirement (e.g., setup assumptions). Additionally, the DRB protocol should be efficient in practical settings. Therefore, despite having many constructions of DRB protocols, a few problems such as scalability, trust, and network assumptions need to be addressed to construct a desirable DRB protocol for practical applications.

Motivated by the above, the contributions of this SoK are as follows:

1. We provide a formal definition of a Decentralized Randomness Beacon (DRB) with a brief description of its security properties (Sect. 2).
2. We present a classification of DRB protocols in Interactive and Non-interactive DRB protocols and we describe these protocols in detail (Sect. 3).
3. We give a brief discussion on several crucial issues related to DRB protocols, including complexity, scalability, and assumptions. We also identify a few efficient building components to construct efficient DRB protocols (Sect. 4).

2   Decentralized Randomness Beacon (DRB)

A DRB allows a group of participants to collaboratively produce random values without the need of a central party. A DRB consists of n participants[1] $\mathcal{P} = (P_1, P_2, \ldots, P_n)$. These participants are connected in a distributed manner. Without loss of generality, we assume that a DRB protocol works in rounds and maintains a beacon state st for each round. For every round $e \in \{1, 2, \ldots\}$, given the current state st_{e-1}, the DRB protocol collectively produces a random output v_e; the state st_0 is jointly computed and agreed from the protocol participants during the bootstrapping of the DRB protocol. Following, we present a formalization of DRB and we formally define the required security properties of a DRB. Additionally, we define a secure DRB protocol in Appendix A.

Definition 1. *(Decentralized Randomness Beacon (DRB)) A DRB on a set of participants $\mathcal{P} = (P_1, \ldots, P_n)$ is defined as a tuple $\mathcal{B}$ of polynomial algorithms:*
$$\mathcal{B} = (\mathsf{Setup}, \mathsf{LocalRand}, \mathsf{GlobalRand}, \mathsf{VerifyRand}, \mathsf{UpdateSt})$$

- $\mathsf{Setup}(1^\lambda, n)$: *Given input security parameter λ, and n participants, it generates public parameter pp and keypair for each participant (pk_i, sk_i). All participants agree on public parameter pp and $\{pk_i\}$.*
- $\mathsf{LocalRand}(st_{e-1}, pp, sk_i, s_{e,i})$: *Given input state st_{e-1} from round $e-1$, public parameter pp, and input seed $s_{e,i}$, a participant P_i computes a local output value $v_{e,i}$ with a proof $\pi_{e,i}$ using sk_i and $s_{e,i}$ for round e. Output $(i, v_{e,i}, \pi_{e,i})$.*
- $\mathsf{GlobalRand}(st_{e-1}, pp, \mathcal{S} = \{(i, v_{e,i}, \pi_{e,i})\}, m)$: *Given input state st_{e-1}, public parameter pp, a set $\mathcal{S}$ of local output values from $|\mathcal{S}|$ participants, if $|\mathcal{S}| \geq m$, where m is the minimum number of required local output values, the algorithm computes the beacon output v_e for round e by executing a function f on $\{v_{e,i}\}$ from set $\mathcal{S}$. It also computes proof of correctness π_e using $\{\pi_{e,i}\}$ from set $\mathcal{S}$. Output (v_e, π_e) or $\perp$.*
- $\mathsf{VerifyRand}(st_{e-1}, pp, v_e, \pi_e)$: *Given input state st_{e-1}, public parameter pp, a beacon output v_e, and a proof π_e, the algorithm verifies the beacon value v_e and the corresponding proof π_e. Output 0 or 1.*
- $\mathsf{UpdateSt}(st_{e-1}, pp, v_e, \pi_e)$: *Given input state st_{e-1}, public parameter pp, a beacon output v_e, and a proof π_e generated at the round e, the algorithm updates the state from st_{e-1} to st_e for round e. Output st_e or $\perp$.*

---

[1] We use node and participant interchangeably in protocols throughout the paper.

The security properties of a DRB corresponds to: *Unpredictability*: An adversary should not be able to predict (precompute) future beacon outcomes; *Bias-Resistance*: A single participant or a colluding adversary cannot bias the future beacon values; *Availability (or Liveness)*: A single participant or a colluding adversary can not prevent the generation of the new beacon value; *Public Verifiability*: Any third party can verify the correctness of the new beacon value. **Note:** *We use DRB protocols and DRBs interchangeably throughout the paper.*

These formal security guarantees of a DRB protocol are evolved during the time. Initial proposals lack the formal definitions and mathematical proofs of their DRB protocols. Nevertheless, the recent proposals put an emphasis on the security of their protocols. These protocols define and prove the security properties of their DRB using the mathematical properties of the underlying cryptographic primitives. Due to different designs, setting up a formal provability framework for DRBs should define the least common security requirements, therefore, we formulate the desiderata of a DRB protocol as follows where λ is a security parameter and $\mathsf{negl}(\lambda)$ is a negligible function of λ.

Definition 2. *(Unpredictability) Let $\mathcal{A}(v_1, \ldots, v_e, st_e)$ be a probabilistic polynomial time algorithm that receives the values $v_1, \ldots, v_e$ and the current state st_e as the input values. Let $\mathcal{A}$ outputs a value v_{e+f} for any value (future rounds) $f \geq 2$, and for all rounds $e \geq 1$. Then*

$$\Pr[\mathcal{A}(v_1, \ldots, v_e, st_e) = v_{e+f}] \leq \mathsf{negl}(\lambda) \tag{1}$$

Definition 3. *(Bias-Resistance) Let $\mathsf{bit}_i(v_e)$ denotes the i-th bit in the binary representation of v_e, let $b = |v_e|$ is the number of bits of v_e, and let $\mathcal{A}_i(v_1, \ldots, v_{e-1}, st_{e-1})$ for $i = 1, \ldots, b$, be b probabilistic polynomial-time algorithms that receive the values $v_1, \ldots, v_{e-1}$ and the current state st_{e-1} as input and output one bit: 0 or 1. Then for every round $e \geq 1$, every $\mathcal{A}_i(\ )$ and for all $i = 1, \ldots, b$*

$$\Pr[\mathsf{bit}_i(v_e) = \mathcal{A}_i(v_1, \ldots, v_{e-1}, st_{e-1})] \leq \frac{1}{2} + \mathsf{negl}(\lambda) \tag{2}$$

$$\Pr[\mathsf{bit}_i(v_e) = 0] \leq \frac{1}{2} + \mathsf{negl}(\lambda) \tag{3}$$

More concretely, we say that a DRB protocol is Bias-resistant if predicting any single bit of the random beacon output v_e has only a non-negligible advantage over the trivial guessing strategy that has a probability of $1/2$.

Definition 4. *(Availability) Let $\mathcal{A}$ be an adversary controlling a fraction of participants and $\mathcal{P}^h \subseteq \mathcal{P}$ be a set of honest participants in the DRB protocol. Given v_e, π_e, pp and st_{e-1}, for every round $e \geq 1$ and for every participant $P_i \in \mathcal{P}^h$*

$$\Pr[\mathsf{UpdateSt}(st_{e-1}, pp, v_e, \pi_e) \neq st_e] \leq \mathsf{negl}(\lambda) \tag{4}$$

Definition 5. *(Public Verifiability) Given $\mathsf{VerifyRand}(\ )$ as a public probabilistic polynomial-time algorithm run by an external verifier $P_x \notin \mathcal{P}$ that receives v_e, π_e*

and the state st_{e-1} at the end of round e as input values and outputs a bit 0 or 1 based on the verification of v_e using π_e. Then for every round $e \geq 1$

$$\Pr[\mathsf{VerifyRand}(v_e, \pi_e, st_{e-1}) \neq 1] \leq \mathsf{negl}(\lambda) \tag{5}$$

3   DRB Classification

We classify DRB protocols in two ways: *Interactive* and *Non-Interactive*. *Interactive* DRB protocols generate a beacon output in an interactive manner which involves multiple rounds of communication among participants. However, *Non-Interactive* DRB protocols do not involve interactions among participants to produce a random beacon value for each round. Therefore, non-interactive DRBs are preferable for decentralized applications. Nevertheless, the setup for the public parameter generation can be interactive for both types of DRBs.

3.1   Interactive Decentralized Randomness Beacon Protocols

Interactive DRB protocols employ multiple rounds of interaction among participants in order to produce one beacon output. These protocols are constructed using interactive cryptographic primitives such as Publicly Verifiable Secret Sharing (PVSS) or Interactive Threshold Signature Scheme. The existing interactive DRB protocols are based on PVSS involving two logical rounds of coin-tossing wherein the first round, the participants broadcast commitments to their shares, and further, these commitments are revealed in another round. Constructions of DRBs with other interactive cryptographic primitives, we left as open problems.

Research Problem 1. *Construct a DRB protocol based on interactive threshold signature scheme with better complexity compared to existing interactive DRBs.*

The main advantage of PVSS-based DRBs is that the generated randomness is indistinguishable from uniform. Nevertheless, due to the interaction and broadcast, interactive DRBs incur high communication cost. Some of the PVSS-based DRBs improve upon the general PVSS scheme to reduce the communication complexity by utilizing a threshold version of PVSS or electing a committee to perform PVSS or introducing a leader to relay the messages. Hence, these optimized versions of DRB protocols can be used to obtain periodic fresh randomness in real-world applications. A PVSS scheme consists of a tuple of algorithms (PVSS.Setup, PVSS.Share, PVSS.Verify, PVSS.Recon) described in Appendix B.

PVSS-based DRB protocols are mainly of two types: with leader [8,25,66] and without leader [17,18,47]. In a leader-based protocol, a leader L_e is elected in each round e which is responsible for performing the distribution of the secret shares of the PVSS scheme. A further illustration can be found in Appendix B. Following we present a description of PVSS-based interactive DRB protocols.

- Ouroboros [47]: Ouroboros is a PoS-based blockchain where a set of elected participants run the DRB protocol to fetch the randomness for the leader election. It operates in two phases *commit* and *reveal*. In *commit* phase, participants encrypt the shares for all other participants by running PVSS.Share and submit the shares on the blockchain. In *reveal* phase, each participant decrypts all the encrypted shares that are encrypted using his public key. Then, each participant computes a local random value using all the decrypted shares and posts it in the blockchain. Finally, a beacon output is computed by performing an XOR operation on all the published local random values.

- RandHound, RandHerd [69]: Syta et al. constructed scalable randomness generation protocols by following client-server architecture and threshold cryptography. RandHound is a one-shot on-demand protocol to generate single randomness. However, RandHerd is a beacon protocol that emits continuous random values. RandHound divides the servers into groups, and each group is responsible for running PVSS among the group members. RandHound employs the commit-reveal technique as defined in Ouroboros for each group. Finally, to produce global randomness in RandHound, a client operates on all the received valid local randomness from each server group. RandHerd improves upon the complexity of RandHound by leveraging communication trees among the server groups and collective signing to produce beacon outputs.

- SCRAPE [17]: Cascudo et al. constructed an honest majority coin-tossing protocol SCRAPE with guaranteed output delivery. It constructs a threshold PVSS scheme where sharing, verification, and reconstruction take only a linear number of exponentiations compared to quadratic in basic PVSS scheme [67]. In SCRAPE, all participants have access to a ledger where messages are posted similar to Ouroboros. Cascudo et al. constructed an efficient share verification procedure with linear complexity by observing the fact that sharing a secret using PVSS is equivalent to encoding the secret with a Reed Solomon error correcting code [61]. The dealer in the PVSS scheme [67] not only encrypts the shares but also commits to the shares. Therefore, to prove that shares in encrypted shares are the same as shares in commitments, the efficient share verification procedure involving error-correcting code is applied. SCRAPE improves the computation and verification cost compared to Ouroboros.

- HydRand [66]: HydRand improves upon the complexity of SCRAPE's PVSS protocol. HydRand works in rounds consisting of three phases: *propose*, *acknowledge* and *vote*. In each round, a leader is selected deterministically from the set of potential leaders and by using the last round randomness. In *propose* phase, the leader reveals his previously committed value which is acknowledged, signed and further broadcast by the other participants in *acknowledge* phase. In *vote* phase, each participant performs some checks, including the checks on the number of received acknowledgments. If the leader does not reveal his secret, the secret is reconstructed using PVSS.Recon. The beacon value is computed using the revealed secret and the last round randomness.

- ALBATROSS [18]: ALBATROSS significantly improves, amortizes the computation complexity of SCRAPE and provides a universal composability (UC)-secure model. It shows efficiency gain through the packed Shamir secret sharing scheme in PVSS or by using a linear t-resilient function to extract randomness as a vector of random group elements. It utilizes Cooley-Tukey fast Fourier transformation to amortize the complexity and for further improvement, it uses $\sum$-protocol to prove that the published sharing is correct. ALBATROSS provides two variants of UC security: 1) First variant uses UC-Non-Interactive Zero-Knowledge (NIZK) proofs for discrete logarithm, 2) Second variant introduces and uses a new primitive named "designated verifier" homomorphic commitments where a sender can open a commitment for one specific receiver. Later, the receiver can prove the same opening to a third party.
- RandPiper [8]: Bhat et al. constructed a reconfiguration-friendly DRB protocol RandPiper with strong security guarantees and quadratic communication complexity. It combines PVSS with State-Machine Replication protocol and presents two protocols: GRandPiper and BRandPiper. GRandPiper is a communication optimal DRB with strong unpredictability in the presence of a static adversary. However, BRandPiper shows the best communication complexity and the best possible unpredictability in case of a dynamic adversary.
- SPURT [25]: SPURT protocol constructs a new PVSS scheme using pairing to produce beacon output and involves a leader. The new PVSS scheme relies on Decisional Bilinear Diffie-Hellman (DBDH) assumption [12]. In addition, SPURT uses State Machine Replication to lower the communication complexity compared to the broadcast channel used by other DRBs e.g., HydRand. SPURT operates in a semi-synchronous network and has no trusted setup.

3.2 Non-Interactive Decentralized Randomness Beacon Protocols

We categorize Non-Interactive DRB (NI-DRB) protocols based on the main constituent cryptographic primitive, further, we illustrate these protocols in Table 1.

VDF-Based. These DRBs are based on stand-alone Verifiable Delay Function $\mathsf{VDF} = (\mathsf{VDF.Setup}, \mathsf{VDF.Eval}, \mathsf{VDF.Verify})$ described in Appendix C. A VDF is a function $f : \mathcal{X} \to \mathcal{Y}$ that takes a prescribed number of sequential steps to compute the output and provides exponentially easy verification of the output. In a VDF-based DRB, the participants evaluate an Iteratively Sequential Function (ISF) to generate their local random values. The verification of these values can be efficiently done using VDF.Verify. Due to the non-parallelizable property of VDF, an adversary cannot bias the output of the random beacon.

Lenstra and Wesolowski [49] constructed a DRB protocol, Unicorn, using a slow-time hash function named *sloth*. This function takes inputs from a set of distrusting participants and outputs a random value. Keeping Unicorn protocol as a successor to VDF, the following VDF-based DRB protocols are constructed.

- Minimal VDF Randomness Beacon [30]: Justin Drake constructed a minimal randomness beacon using RANDAO [59] and VDF. RANDAO is a smart contract based DRB where participants submit their local entropy to the smart contract, and further, the smart contract produces a single global entropy. RANDAO biasable entropy is used as input to the VDF to produce unbiasable randomness. Nevertheless, there is no formal security analysis of this protocol.
- Continuous VDF [34]: Ephraim et al. presented a new notion of Continuous Verifiable Delay Function (cVDF) by adapting Pietrzak scheme [57]. A cVDF f provides the output computation of each intermediate steps (i.e. $f(t)$ for $t < T$) with an efficient proof π^t (used for public verification of the output). A cVDF can be used to construct a DRB protocol where beacon outputs are generated by applying a suitable hash to the intermediate outputs of each step. The drawback with this protocol is that the nodes having the most efficient (fastest) processors can always learn the beacon outputs before the other participating nodes. A similar argument goes for the Unicorn protocol.
- RandRunner [65]: RandRunner leverages trapdoor VDF with strong uniqueness to construct a DRB protocol. Each participant P_i of RandRunner initializes its public parameter pp_i with a corresponding trapdoor sk_i. The participants exchange their public parameters and verify the received ones. RandRunner executes in consecutive rounds where in each round, a leader is elected. Further, the leader tries to solve the VDF using its trapdoor, and other participants attempt to solve the VDF using the common VDF.Eval algorithm. The drawback with the RandRunner protocol is that once a powerful adversary becomes a leader, it can keep corrupting the round leaders (e.g., via DoS), withhold its output computed via trapdoor, and keep working on for the next outputs for many subsequent rounds hence breaking unpredictability.
- RANDCHAIN [44]: RANDCHAIN is a competitive DRB where in each round, nodes compete to be a leader which solely produces the beacon output. RANDCHAIN constructs a non-parallelizable Sequential Proof-of-Work (SeqPoW) puzzle by employing VDF or Sloth. A node solves the SeqPoW puzzle by incrementing an ISF for a randomized time. RANDCHAIN works as a Nakamoto-based blockchain where nodes synchronize their local blockchains and keep solving the puzzle to mine new blocks to the main blockchain. RANDCHAIN mimics a blockchain structure, so it can suffer from frontrunning (block withholding) attacks and can also have forks due to problems with blocks' finality.

VRF-Based. These DRBs compute randomness using Verifiable Random Function VRF = (VRF.KeyGen, VRF.Eval, VRF.Verify) described in Appendix D. A VRF is a pseudorandom function that produces pseudorandom output along with proof about the correctness of the output. Participants in these DRBs apply VRF on an input seed to generate their local entropy which is used to compute the beacon output. VRF-based DRBs are explained as follows:

- Blockchain Protocol Designs: Ouroboros Praos [27], Algorand [39] and Erlond [33] blockchains have their DRB as a byproduct. In these DRBs, each participant P_i runs VDF.Eval on a seed (e.g., previous output or state) using its secret key sk_i and the DRB output is computed from the participants' VRF outputs. These DRBs do not guarantee generation of uniformly random values and do not have strong bias-resistance as an adversary can include/exclude the corrupted participants' VRF outputs used for DRB output computation.
- Distributed VRF-based DRBs: A distributed VRF (DVRF) [29] based DRB was first introduced by DFINITY [45]. Later DRBs [22,24] employed DFINITY-DVRF along with BLS cryptography. Nevertheless, these DRBs do not provide formal security analysis. A recent paper [36] provides two new constructions of DVRF: 1) DDH-DVRF based on elliptic curve cryptography; 2) GLOW-DVRF based on cryptographic pairings. These constructions also formalize a security model with proper security analysis. DRBs based on DDH-DVRF, and GLOW-DVRF show strong bias resistance and strong pseudorandomness.
- RandChain [71]: RandChain follows *commit-and-reveal* strategy by building a sub-routine *RandGene* using VRF. RandChain has a two-layer hierarchical blockchain structure where nodes form distinct committees. Each committee has a local blockchain and generates local entropy through the RandGene protocol, further, global randomness is computed from these local entropy by forming a RandChain block. RandChain security depends on a secure sharding process, followed by a leader election for each shard (committee). However, both processes can be influenced by an adversary to obstruct DRB properties.

HE-Based. These DRBs utilize homomorphic encryption scheme HE = (HE. Setup, HE.KeyGen, HE.Enc, HE.Dec, HE.Eval). Homomorphic encryption allows performing arithmetic operations on ciphertext directly without decryption (details in Appendix E). Following DRBs employ ElGamal encryption [32] as partial HE.

- Nguyen-Van et al. [55]: Their DRB has three components: a Requester, a Public Distributed Ledger (PDL), and a Core Layer. The protocol works in rounds where, first, the Requester sends a nonce to the PDL that computes a ticket T and publishes it. Further, participants of the core layer run a VRF using the ticket T to check if they are selected as a contributor. Each contributor publishes a ciphertext computed on a random value using the Requester's public key. Later, the Requester performs a homomorphic operation on the published ciphertexts and computes a single ciphertext. Finally, the Requester publishes the decrypted value as DRB output with a proof of correct decryption. There are two drawbacks: 1) A malleable ElGamal encryption, 2) The Requester can collude with contributors or refuse to decrypt the resulting ciphertext.
- HERB [20]: Homomorphic Encryption Random Beacon (HERB) DRB uses threshold ElGamal encryption scheme with a distributed key generation

(DKG) protocol. DKG is used to generate a common public key and secret key shares for participants. Each participant publishes a ciphertext share with proof of correct encryption (NIZK Proof) on a public bulletin board. These shares generate an aggregated ciphertext through ElGamal aggregation which is subsequently decrypted by a threshold of participants to produce the DRB output.

External Source-Based. In these DRBs, participants extract the randomness from an external entropy source, i.e., real-world entropy. These entropy sources can be public blockchains [7,14], real-time financial data [21] or national lottery results [3]. PoW-based blockchains are promising sources but an adversarial miner can manipulate the generated randomness. Therefore, to achieve most of the beacon properties, the following DRBs apply different defense mechanisms.

- Rand Extractor [21]: Clark et al. [21] created a model to generate randomness by combining the information theory with computational finance. They used the closing prices of the stock market to compute a random output. During the market's closing in the day, one entity publishes this random output in the protocol. This entity can also induce its own local entropy to transparently construct a publicly verifiable final randomness, but liveness is hard to achieve.
- Proofs of Delay [14]: In this DRB, a beacon smart contract (BC) publishes the random beacon values on a public blockchain. The DRB is built on *Proof-of-Delay* which uses an ISF such as sloth [49]. In this DRB, a beacon maintainer executes this ISF and publishes the result to BC with queryable access to the beacon output using a *refereed delegation of computation* protocol. To show the honest behavior, the maintainer is incentivized; otherwise punished.
- Bitcoin Beacon [13] [7]: These DRBs extract randomness from the bitcoin blockchain [53] and follows the security of the bitcoin. In [13], an extractor fetches the randomness from the block headers. As each block contains several transactions involving ECDSA signatures [37] that rely on strong randomness for security hence, the extractor gives good public randomness as a beacon output. Bentov et al. [7] constructed a bitcoin beacon protocol that fetches m consecutive blocks $B_1, B_2, \ldots, B_m$ such that the block B_m already have l subsequent blocks. Further, the protocol acquires a bit b_i from each block and runs a majority function on all these bits as input to get the DRB output.

Threshold Signature-Based. These DRBs are based on a non-interactive threshold signature scheme that requires a single round of communication among participants to produce the unique group signatures from a threshold number of participants' signature shares. Most of the existing threshold signature-based DRBs employ threshold BLS signature. These DRBs require a setup to generate the secret shares for the participants. Additionally, the complexity of unique signature construction comply with DRB protocol for practical use.

Table 1. Advantages and disadvantages of different non-interactive DRB protocols

Scheme	Advantages	Disadvantages
VDF-based	1. These DRBs achieve liveness under the period of full asynchrony 2. These DRBs avoid byzantine agreement consensus hence have less communication complexity 3. It shows strong bias-resistance as long as there is an honest node	1. Front-running attack can hinder some DRB properties 2. In most of these DRBs, the significant powerful adversary can learn the output of DRB earlier than other nodes 3. These protocols rely on the new assumptions of VDF
VRF-based	1. Most of these DRBs do not have any trusted setup and achieve strong notion of pseudo-randomness and bias-resistance [36] 2. These DRBs incur less computation and communication cost	1. In some of these DRBs, leader uniqueness is not guaranteed that introduces additional consensus protocol to agree on the beacon output
HE-based	1. The output of these DRBs for a round e does not depend on the output of the previous round $e - 1$ 2. Partial homomorphic encryption schemes used in these DRBs can be replaced by a lattice-based fully homomorphic scheme to ensure the post-quantum security	1. Scalability issue due to the homomorphic evaluation of multiple ciphertexts 2. The existing DRBs use public ledger to publish the local and global entropy. But distributing the local entropy in DRBs using a consensus incur a high communication cost
External Source -based	1. These DRBs do not incur communication cost as the DRB output is published in a public bulletin board 2. These DRBs work perfectly even in the asynchronous network	1. Most of these DRBs do not provide public verifiability 2. Proof-of-Work based beacons are not energy efficient and nodes with better hardware can outperform other nodes in producing the beacon output
Threshold Signature -based	1. These DRBs provide strong bias resistance and unpredictability 2. Consortium of organizations can participate to construct such beacon due to threshold property (e.g. Drand [31])	1. These DRBs require either a trusted setup or DKG, hence do not offer a reconfiguration-friendly setup 2. Security of the DRBs depend on the security assumptions of elliptic curve pairings due to the use of BLS-signature

- Cachin et al. [16], Drand [31]: Cachin et al. presented a common coin protocol using threshold signature along with a random-access coin-tossing scheme. In this DRB, a trusted dealer distributes the secret key shares to the participants. The DRB output is a unique signature on the hash of a counter (epoch number). Drand [31] follows a similar idea, but it replaces the threshold secret to the threshold BLS key. Drand can be considered as an implementation of the Cachin et al. scheme. Drand utilizes the DKG protocol of Gennaro et al. [38] during the setup phase that yields a high communication complexity.
- DFINITY [45]: It also employs a threshold BLS signatures scheme but the selection of the best initialization vector in the scheme creates a challenge. The protocol works well even in the partial synchronous network model. It employs a non-interactive DKG setup and achieves better communication complexity than Drand. The DRB acts as a VRF that produces unbiasable output.

Note: We present Hybrid DRB protocols in Appendix F.

4 Discussion

4.1 Security Assumptions

The security of all these DRBs depends on well-defined security assumptions. These assumptions can be assumptions about the underlying network, adversary, setup, or cryptographic primitives. If these assumptions are failed in some cases, then the DRB using these assumptions will break its security properties.

- *Cryptographic Assumptions (Primitive):* As the above described DRBs are based on cryptographic primitives such as PVSS, VDF, VRF, these DRBs inherit the security assumptions from the primitives. These assumptions are well-known hard problems of cryptography such as standard decisional or computational Diffie-Hellman assumptions [10] (or their variants) depending on the underlying cryptographic scheme (e.g., PVSS, DVRF). VDF-based DRBs depend on the new security assumptions on sequential computation (e.g., iterated squaring over groups of unknown order [62]) that are not well studied and understood in the current literature. Modeling of the hash function as a random oracle [6] is also considered in security assumptions in some DRBs.
- *Network Assumptions (Model):* Most of the PVSS-based and VRF-based DRBs assume a strong *synchronous* network which can be an unrealistic setting in the real world. Hence, these DRBs require a lock-step synchronous network where the messages are delivered before the end of each round. In case of no lock-step synchrony, participants might employ round synchronization protocols [54,74]. Some of the DRBs work well in *semi-synchronous* network where the messages are delivered within a known finite time-bound. VDF-based and external-source-based DRBs work well in an *asynchronous* network where messages are delivered without a known time-bound. However, the trust of these models depends on the underlying setup assumptions

or on the public blockchain, where the local entropy of the participants are posted.

- *Setup Assumptions*: Many DRB protocols [8,20,31,45,69] require an initial trusted setup assumption where private keys for the participants and uniformly random public parameters are generated by a trusted third party (dealer) or by a distributed key generation (DKG) protocol. The Security of DRBs with a trusted third party crucially depends on the action and ability of the trusted party. Nevertheless, DKG incurs a considerable setup cost (high communication complexity) with its limitation of adding or replacing the participants. Therefore, DKG-based DRBs are preferred when the participants are fixed. Hence, many recent DRB protocols [2,17,27,39,66] have a transparent setup where the public parameters are trapdoor free.

Following the above security assumption, most of the DRB protocols perform well in permissioned systems. However, permissionless systems have a highly dynamic set of nodes that maintain the system state. Due to the dynamically changing participants, integrating an existing DRB with the system is challenging. Moreover, setting the assumption on a number of adversarial nodes is hard.

Research Problem 2. *Study the hardness of embedding the existing DRB protocols in permissionless systems, based on Proof-of-Work (PoW) or-Stake (PoS).*

4.2   Complexity

DRB protocols following different approaches exhibit different complexity. Finding a good balance between computation and communication complexity in a DRB protocol is a challenging task. Therefore, an extensive amount of work has been devoted to reduce the complexity of DRB protocols.

- *Communication Complexity*: Most of the interactive DRB protocols assume a broadcast channel. Therefore, Ouroboros [47], RandShare [69], and SCRAPE [17] have a communication complexity of $\mathcal{O}(n^3)$ due to the broadcasting of $\mathcal{O}(n)$ size message. HydRand [66] improves upon the communication complexity to $\mathcal{O}(n^2)$ by having a leader-based approach where a leader node performs the PVSS share distribution. Relaying the messages through a single node to reduce the communication complexity is also embraced by ALBATROSS [18], GLOW [36]. RandHound, RandHerd [69], DFINITY [45] employ sharding to sample a committee for output generation that results in lower communication complexity. But such a procedure can be immediately subject to attacks by an adaptive adversary who can corrupt the committee once it is determined.
  Most of the non-interactive DRBs [14,27,39,55] have less communication complexity as a successful participant (e.g., leader) usually need to perform one broadcast. Therefore, it incurs the communication complexity in $\mathcal{O}(n)$. Moreover, most of the NI-DRBs involving blockchain [44,59] to publish shared local and global randomness also have lower communication complexity.

DKG setup based DRBs [16,20,31,45] suffer from additional communication cost. Complexity of DRBs can be improved using asynchronous data dissemination (ADD) [26] or using hbACSS [75](for PVSS-based DRBs).

Research Problem 3. *Design a DRB protocol with sub-quadratic communication complexity together with optimal fault-tolerance.*

- *Computation Complexity*: It is defined as the number of operations needed to be performed by a participant during one round of DRB protocol. PVSS-based protocols such as RandShare [69] and Ouroboros [47] requires a computation complexity of $\mathcal{O}(n^3)$. An improved version of PVSS further reduces this cost in SCRAPE [17]. Puzzle-based DRBs [13,14] have a high computational cost due to the involved puzzle. VDF-based DRBs also have the drawback of high computational complexity due to the repeated squaring. On the contrary, VRF-based DRBs incur a minimum computation cost.

Research Problem 4. *Design a puzzle-based DRB protocol incurring low computation complexity.*

- *Verification Complexity* Verification cost refers to the number of operations performed by an external participant to verify the output of a beacon protocol. Although VDF-based DRBs have high computational costs, they do provide efficient verification hence incur less verification cost. The most efficient DRB protocols with regard to computation and verification complexity are based on VRF [27,39,71] or threshold crypto-systems [16,31,45,55].

Research Problem 5. *Design a PVSS-based DRB protocol with a constant verification complexity, linear communication cost and no trusted setup.*

4.3 Scalability

Despite a decade of research on DRB protocols, only quite a few recent DRBs emphasize the scalability of their DRB. Scalability in a DRB protocol refers to the number of participants it can support. Many of the described DRB protocols do not offer good scalability. Especially, DRBs involving DKG setup provide poor scalability as DKG does not support frequent modification in the set of key holders. In addition, the high complexity along with the underlying network model in many of these DRBs significantly affect the scalability of the DRBs.

A general approach for achieving good scalability is *"sharding"* which is considered in recent DRBs, including RandHerd [69], DFINITY [45] and Algorand [39] with the cost of slightly degrading the fault-tolerance. RandHerd shows a direct consequence of the sharding where nodes are split into smaller groups. Each group produces local entropy and each group's entropy is combined to produce the DRB output. Algorand and DFINITY show selection of a committee to generate the DRB output. Therefore, this orthogonal technique of randomly sampling a committee for protocol execution can improve scalability.

Another way for improving scalability is using a *leader-based approach* where a leader relays the messages to the participants. Moreover, having a *public ledger* where participants post their local entropy messages also improves scalability.

Reconfiguration Friendliness directly impact scalability. A protocol is reconfiguration friendly when the parameters and list of participants can be changed dynamically without affecting the current execution. When there is no binding between the setup and the system, the reconfiguration becomes easier. DRBs involving DKG setup are not reconfiguration-friendly, hence poor scalability. On the contrary, non-interactive DRBs (with no DKG) show better scalability.

Research Problem 6. *Study the (im)possibility of designing a reconfiguration-friendly sub-quadratic DRB protocol that do not employ committee sampling.*

4.4   Adversarial Model

Most of these DRBs consider a fixed set of n nodes; out of these nodes, f nodes may exhibit byzantine behavior. An adversary in these DRBs can be defined as:

Active vs. Passive An active adversary actively modifies the messages (e.g., public shares, DRB output) in DRB; a passive adversary observes the transcript (i.e. messages) of an honest run of the DRB and predicts the DRB's next output.

Adaptive vs. Static An adaptive adversary corrupts the nodes during the protocol execution, while a static adversary does corruption before the execution.

An adversary can affect the security guarantees of a DRB in many ways, such as by trying to bias the produced random output, withholding the output, predicting the future output, or tricking an outsider (third party) into accepting invalid beacon output. Leader-based DRBs suffer from targeted attacks, however, blockchain-based DRBs suffer from blockchain-specific attacks. Moreover, unpredictability can be affected by network model.

Research Problem 7. *Choose a static secure DRB protocol and transform it to an adaptively secure DRB that retains the efficiency standard of the static one.*

4.5   Throughput Evaluation

We report throughput of state-of-the-art public implementations of various DRBs in Fig. 1. DFINITY and SPURT operate on a semi-synchronous network but BRandPiper, Drand, GLOW, and HydRand assume synchronous networks. The network delay parameter in these DRBs directly affects the throughput of DRBs.

Drand is a practically deployed DRB protocol. However, when the number of nodes increases to more than 64, nodes in the DRand abort the DKG step of the protocol, and yet it suffers from significant network delay. For HydRand, we chose the public implementation [64] available on Github. For BRandPiper, we depict throughput for the Merkle-tree-based implementation, which is quantitatively

Table 2. Comparison of existing decentralized randomness beacon protocol

Protocol	Network Model	Adaptive Adversary	Liveness	Unpredictability	Bias-Resistance	Fault-tolerance	Communication Complexity	Computation Complexity	Verification Complexity	Cryptographic Primitive	No Trusted Dealer or DKG required
ALBATROSS [18]	syn.	✗	✓	✓	✓	1/2	$O(n)$	$O(\log n)$	$O(n)$	PVSS	✓
Algorand [39]	semi-syn.	✗	✓	✓‡	✗	1/3◇	$O(cn)$	$O(c)$	$O(1)$	VRF	✓
BRandPiper [8]	syn.	✓	✓	✓	✓	1/2	$O(n^3)$	$O(n^2)$	$O(n^2)$	PVSS	✓
Cachin et.al [16]	asyn.	✗	✓	✓‡	✓	1/3	$O(n^2)$	$O(n)$	$O(1)$	Uniq. thr-sig	✗
Caucus [2]	syn.	✗	✓‡	✓	✗	1/2	$O(1)$	$O(1)$	$O(1)$	Hash func	✓
Continuous VDF [34]	asyn.	✗	✓‡	✓	✓	1/2	$O(1)$	VDF	$O(1)$	VDF	✓
DFINITY [45]	semi-syn.	✗	✓	✓	✓	1/3	$O(n^2)$	$O(n)$	$O(1)$	BLS thr-sig	✗
Drand [31]	syn.	✗	✓	✓	✓	1/2	$O(n^2)$	$O(n)$	$O(1)$	Uniq. thr-sig	✗
GLOW [36]	syn	✗	✓	✓‡	✓	1/3	$O(n^2)$	$O(n)$	$O(1)$	DVRF	✗
GRandPiper [8]	syn	✗	✓	✓‡	✓	1/2	$O(n^2)$	$O(n^2)$	$O(n^2)$	PVSS	✓
HERB [20]	syn.	✗	✓	✓	✓	1/3	$O(n^2)*$	$O(n)$	$O(n)$	PHE	✗
HydRand [66]	syn.	✗	✓	✓‡	✓	1/3	$O(n^2)$	$O(n)$	$O(n)$	PVSS	✓
Nguyen-Van et.al [55]	syn.	✗	✗	✓	✗	1/2	$O(n)$	$O(1)$	$O(n)$	PHE, VRF	✓
Ouroboros [47]	syn.	✗	✓	✓	✓	1/2	$O(n^3)$	$O(n^3)$	$O(n^3)$	PVSS	✓
Ouroboros Praos [27]	semi-syn.	✓	✓	✓	✗	1/2	$O(n)*$	$O(1)*$	$O(1)*$	VRF	✓
Proof-of-Delay [14]	syn.	✗	✓	✓	✓	1/2	$O(n)$	very high	$O(\log \Delta)^\circ$	Hash func	✓
Proof-of-Work [53]	syn.	✗	✓	✓‡	✗	1/2	$O(n)$	very high	$O(1)$	Hash func	✓
RandChain [71]	syn.	✓	✓	✓	✓	1/3	$O(cn)$	$O(cn)$	$O(n)$	VRF	✓
RANDCHAIN [44]	syn.	✓	✓	✓	✓	1/3	$O(n)$	VDF	$O(1)$	VDF	✓
RANDAO [59]	asyn.	✗	✓	✗	✗	1/2	$O(n)$	VDF	$O(1)$	VDF	✓
RandHerd [69]	syn	✗	✓	✓	✓	1/3	$O(c^2 \log n)$	$O(c^2 \log n)$	$O(1)$	PVSS, CoSi	✗
RandHound [69]	syn.	✗	✓	✓	✓	1/3	$O(c^2 n)$	$O(c^2 n)$	$O(c^2 n)$	PVSS	✓
RandRunner [65]	syn.	✓	✓	✓‡	✓	1/2	$O(n^2)$	VDF	$O(1)$	VDF	✓
RandShare [69]	asyn.	✗	✓◎	✓	✓	1/3	$O(n^3)$	$O(n^3)$	$O(n^3)$	VSS	✓
Rand Extractor [13,21]	asyn.±	✗	✓∥	✓	✓	1/2	$O(1)$	$O(1)$	$O(1)$	Hash func	✓
SCRAPE [17]	syn.	✗	✓	✓	✓	1/2	$O(n^3)$	$O(n^2)$	$O(n^2)$	PVSS	✓
SPURT [25]	semi-syn.	✗	✓	✓	✓	1/3	$O(n^2)$	$O(n)$	$O(n)$	PVSS, Pairing	✓
Unicorn [49]	asyn.	✗	✓‡	✓	✓	1/2	$O(1)$	high	$O(1)$	Sloth	✓

Fault-tolerance refers to number of byzantine faults a DRB can tolerate and c is average committee size.

‡ refers to probabilistic guarantees for unpredictability, and has a bound on the number of future rounds an adaptive rushing adversary can predict the beacon output.

◇ Due to the randomly sampling a committee of size c in Algorand, the fault-tolerance reduces slightly.

† The node with more computational power learns the beacon output earlier than others.

* HERB achieves communication complexity of $O(n^2)$ when nodes use Avalanche algorithm or public blockchain to share their ciphertexts.

* Ouroboros Praos is not a stand-alone DRB and does not describe randomness generation approach, so the presented complexity does not account the additional complexity for communication or verification.

◎ The verification in beacon smart contract has complexity $O\log \Delta)$ in the security parameter Δ.

⊙ An additional synchrony assumption is needed to provide liveness in RandShare.

± DRB protocols built on public blockchain also follow the network structure of the respective blockchain. Therefore, [13] uses a synchronous network as it relies on the bitcoin blockchain.

∥ Liveness can be hindered due to the limited availability of financial data caused by closed exchanges in [21] or due to the fork situation in the blockchain in [13].

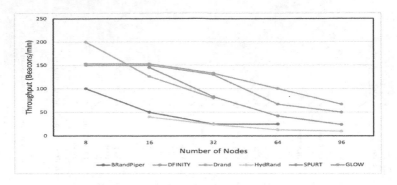

Fig. 1. Overview of throughput for various DRB protocols

practical for real-world scenarios. For SPURT, we used the throughput values directly from their paper. For DFINITY and GLOW, we followed the public implementation [35] of DVRFs to get the throughput while assuming no failure.

4.6 Others

- *Incentive* Some DRBs [14,59] involve incentivizing or punishing the partic- ipants to enforce fairness against rational adversaries. In particular, these (dis)incentivizing approaches (e.g., [4]) are considered mostly in smart contract-based DRBs. Putting an economic incentivization scheme to reward the participants of beacon enforces the honest behavior from the participants. An incentivization scheme can also reward the right computation or verifi- cation. Interesting research would be to create an *incentive structure* for a DRB.
- *Output Uniqueness* It states that the DRB produces a unique output even in the presence of an adversary having the trapdoor information of honest participants. It implies strong bias-resistance in DRBs. Therefore, DRBs such as RandRunner [65], DFINITY [45] and GLOW [36] provide strong bias- resistance due to their output uniqueness. Having this property also prevents an adversary from manipulating the beacon output for any financial gain.
- *Universal Composability* (UC) It is arguably one of the strongest security guarantees. A UC-secure protocol ensures that the protocol can be employed as a building block in more complex systems while preserving its security. The earlier UC-secure DRBs [47] do not provide bias-resistance. The first UC- secure DRB ALBATROSS [18] leverages UC-secure NIZK proofs. UC-secure time-lock puzzles (TLP) [5] can be scrutinized to construct a UC-secure DRB.

5   New Components for Construction of DRB Protocols

There have been many new efficient constructions of cryptographic primitives in recent years. These primitives can be embedded as new building blocks or replace old ones in the DRB protocols to improve the performance of DRBs.

– *Using New Verifiable Functions*: Gurkan et al. [42] constructed a new aggregatable DKG scheme that leverages gossip instead of broadcast communication to reduce the communication complexity. Further, they introduced an efficient Verifiable Unpredictable Function (VUF) and combined it with DKG. This threshold VUF can be utilized to construct a DRB protocol.

VDF-based DRBs can benefit from the recent work [63] about batch verification of VDF in which the verification of beacon outputs during the last several rounds can be batched and verified efficiently. Work [52] on VDF can be investigated and applied to construct a practical VDF-based DRB protocol.

Current DRBs are not Post-Quantum (PQ) secure (except DRB [50] that does not depend on any third party to construct a quantum-safe beacon). Recent constructions of Post-Quantum VRF [15] and Post-Quantum VDF [19] can be carefully studied and applied to construct practical PQ-secure DRB protocols.

– *Using New Threshold Signatures*: Tomescu et al. [70] designed a fast BLS-based threshold signature scheme (BLS-TSS). Their scheme has fast signature aggregation and verification. There are some DRBs that use the BLS signature scheme. The new BLS-TSS scheme can be directly applied to these DRBs to improve their performance. Otherwise, a new large-scale, simple DRB protocol can be designed and implemented using this new BLS-TSS scheme.

– *Using New Erasure Codes*: All known Verifiable Secret Sharing (VSS) schemes published so far in the open literature (without exception) use the well-known Reed-Solomon codes [61]. Reed-Solomon codes are Maximum Distance Separable (MDS) erasure codes of type (t, n), where the original message is equally split in t parts and is encoded to n (where $n > t$) parts. In the recent decade, the coding theory community constructed new MDS erasure codes. The most significant line of work was done by Dimakis et al., in [28] where they constructed Minimum Bandwidth Regenerating (MBR) codes (optimal in terms of the repair bandwidth) and Minimum Storage Regenerating (MSR) codes (optimal in terms of the storage). Soon after that, those MDS codes were practically employed in Facebook data centers [60], and new variants of MDS codes e.g. [73] were proposed. Therefore, it would be interesting to research the potential replacement of the Reed-Solomon code in VSS schemes with another MDS (MSR) code to improve the performance of VSS-based DRBs.

6 Conclusion

Within recent years, there has been a dramatic surge in the construction of new Decentralized Randomness Beacon (DRB) protocols due to its emergence in cryptographic protocols. We present the first systematization of knowledge (SoK) for the existing efforts on DRB protocols. This SoK provides a comprehensive review of the design paradigms and approaches of DRB protocols. This SoK can serve as a starting point to explore DRB protocols and can help researchers or practitioners to pick a DRB protocol well-suited for their application.

In this SoK, we presented basic standard definitions of a DRB protocol and its required properties. We discussed the key components and the most significant features of DRB protocols and summarized the existing DRB protocols in Table 2. We identified several research challenges related to the complexity, scalability, and security of DRB protocols. We highlighted respective solutions to encounter some of the challenges. Finally, we proposed promising research directions for the future design of DRB protocols by employing the new cryptographic components that can help to advance the state-of-the-art of DRB protocols.

A   Secure DRB Protocol

A DRB protocol is said to be secure if for any probabilistic polynomial-time adversary $\mathcal{A}$ corrupting at most t parties in a round e, in a security game $\mathcal{G}$ played between the adversary $\mathcal{A}$ and a challenger $\mathcal{C}$, $\mathcal{A}$ has negligible advantage.

1. $\mathcal{C}$ executes the setup and sends the public parameters of the system to $\mathcal{A}$.
2. $\mathcal{A}$ corrupts up to t participants and informs about t corrupted nodes to $\mathcal{C}$.
3. $\mathcal{C}$ creates the secret and public keys of honest nodes and sends the public keys of honest nodes to $\mathcal{A}$.
4. $\mathcal{A}$ sends the remaining public parameters (e.g. public keys) of t nodes to $\mathcal{C}$.
5. $\mathcal{C}$ and $\mathcal{A}$ runs the protocol execution interactively per round where:
   (a) $\mathcal{C}$ sends all the honest participants' messages to $\mathcal{A}$.
   (b) $\mathcal{A}$ decides on the delivery (sends / does not send) of the messages.
   (c) At the end of a round e, an honest node outputs the protocol transcript.
6. $\mathcal{C}$ samples a bit $b \in \{0, 1\}$ and sends either the DRB output based on transcript or a random element.
7. $\mathcal{A}$ makes a guess b' and the advantage of $\mathcal{A}$ is defined as $|\Pr[b = b'] - \frac{1}{2}|$.

B   Publicly Verifiable Secret Sharing (PVSS)

In a PVSS scheme, a dealer shares a randomly selected secret s among a set of n nodes using an $(n, t + 1)$ threshold access-structure. That means, secret s can be recovered from a set of $t + 1$ valid shares.

Definition 6. *(PVSS): It is defined as a collection of following algorithms:*

- Setup(λ): *Given a security parameter λ, generates the public parameters pp and the public-private key-pair for each node, output the public parameter and public keys (pp, pk). pp is an implicit input to all the other algorithms.*
- Share(s): *For a randomly chosen secret s, a dealer creates the secret shares for each node $\vec{S} = (s_1, s_2, \ldots, s_n)$ along with the encryption of the shares $\vec{E} = (c_1, c_2, \ldots, c_n)$ where $c_i = Enc(s_i)$ and proof of correct encryption $\vec{\pi} = (\pi_1, \pi_2, \ldots, \pi_n)$. It outputs $(\vec{S}, \vec{E}, \vec{\pi})$.*
- Verify($\vec{E}, \vec{\pi}$): *Given the encrypted shares and the proofs, any external $\mathcal{V}$ can non-interactively verifies if the sharing is correct. It outputs 0 or 1.*

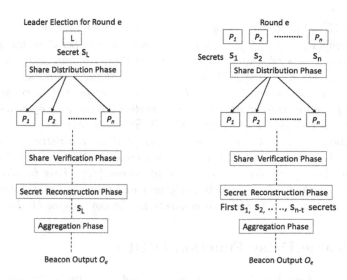

Fig. 2. PVSS-based DRB protocols with and without leader

- Recon($\vec{S}$): *Given valid set $\vec{S} \subseteq \{s_1, s_2, \ldots, s_n\}^{t+1}$ of $t+1$ decrypted shares, it reconstructs the secret and outputs s.*

In a DRB protocol involving a leader, once the setup phase is completed, for the round e, first a leader election algorithm LeaderElec($e, O_{e-1}, P_1, P_2, \ldots, P_n$) is executed and a leader L_e is selected. The election algorithm can be *round-robin selection* or *sampling uniformly at random*. The leader L_e chooses a secret value s_{L_e} (either a new value or previously committed value in the previous round) and executes the PVSS scheme for secret s_{L_e}. At the end of round e, DRB output O_e is generated using the reconstructed secret and the previous round (or rounds') output value. Figure 2 depicts leader and non-leader-based DRB protocols. In the first sub-figure, a leader is elected, followed by leader's secret is shared and beacon output is produced. In the second sub-figure, all participants randomly choose secrets at the start of the round and further share the encrypted shares of the secret to all the other participants. In the final stage, the first n-t reconstructed (or decrypted) shares are used to obtain beacon output.

Definition 7. *(PVSS-based Interactive Decentralized Randomness Beacon (I-DRB)) Given a set of participants $\mathcal{P} = (P_1, P_2, \ldots, P_n)$, a PVSS-based I-DRB without leader can be defined as a tuple $\mathcal{B}$ of polynomial-time algorithms:*
$$\mathcal{B} = (\mathsf{Setup}, \mathsf{Share}, \mathsf{Verify}, \mathsf{Recon}, \mathsf{Aggregation})$$

- Setup(e, λ): *Set the round $e = 1$. Run PVSS.Setup(λ) and generate public parameter pp and key-pairs (sk_i, pk_i) for each participant.*
- Share(e): *For a round e, each participant P_i runs PVSS.Share(s_i) for a randomly chosen value s_i from the input space and gets $(\vec{S}_i, \vec{E}_i, \vec{\pi}_i)$. P_i shares the encrypted shares and corresponding proofs $(\vec{E}_i, \vec{\pi}_i)$ with other participants.*

- Verify$(e, \{\vec{E}, \vec{\pi}\})$: *Each party P_j runs the share verification algorithm* PVSS.Verify$(\vec{E}_i, \vec{\pi}_i); \forall i, i \neq j$ *on every shared secret. Let $\mathcal{C}$ be the set of first $n - t$ participants who have correctly shared their random secret values.*
- Recon$(e, \{\vec{S}_i\})$: *Each party P_i in* C *opens the Shamir secret s_i and the randomness used, other participants $P_j; \forall j, j \neq i$ verify if it is consistent with sharing posted during* Share *phase. If a party P_i refuses to open its secret s_i, the secret is reconstructed by executing* PVSS.Recon$(\vec{S}_i)$.
- Aggregation$(e, \{s_i\})$: *Once the valid decrypted or reconstructed shares are available for the parties $P_i \in \mathcal{C}$. The beacon output is generated by executing a function f on input a set of valid shares $\{s_i\}$. This function f takes all the valid shares $\{s_i\}$ (additionally previous beacon outputs) as input and aggregates these input values to generate the beacon output O_e for round e.*

C   Verifiable Delay Function (VDF)

Verifiable delay function $f : \mathcal{X} \to \mathcal{Y}$ was defined formally by Boneh et al. [11]. After the introduction of VDF, two new proposals [57,72] were presented. A VDF has properties of *Sequentiality, Uniqueness* and *ϵ-Evaluation time.*

Definition 8. *(VDF): A VDF is defined as a tuple of following algorithms:*

- Setup(λ, T): *It is a randomized algorithm that takes security parameter λ, time parameter T and outputs public parameter pp $:= (\mathbb{G}, N, H, T)$, where $\mathbb{G}$ is a finite abelian group of unknown order, N is an RSA modulus, and $H : \mathcal{X} \to \mathbb{G}$ is a hash function.*
- Eval(pp, x, T): *The evaluation algorithm applies T squarings in $\mathbb{G}$ starting with $H(x)$ and outputs the value $y \leftarrow H(x)^{(2^T)} \bmod N$, along with a proof π.*
- Verify(pp, x, y, π, T): *The verification algorithm outputs a bit $\in \{0, 1\}$, given the input as public parameter* pp, *input value x, output value y, proof π, and time parameter T.*

D   Verifiable Random Function (VRF)

VRF has properties of Uniqueness, Collision resistance and Pseudorandomness.

Definition 9. *(VRF): A VRF is defined as a tuple of following algorithms:*

- KeyGen(r): *On input value r, the algorithm generates a secret key sk and a verification key vk.*
- Eval(sk, M): *Evaluation algorithm produces pseudorandom output O and the corresponding proof π on input sk and a message M.*
- Verify(vk, M, O, π): *Verify algorithm outputs 1 if and only if the output produced by evaluation algorithm is O and it is verified by the proof π given the verification key vk and the message M.*

E Homomorphic Encryption (HE)

Definition 10. *(HE): An HE scheme is defined as a set of following alogorithms:*

- Setup(1^λ): *Given security parameter λ, Output global parameters params.*
- KeyGen(*params*): *Given global parameters param, output a public-private key-pair (pk, sk).*
- Enc(*params*, *pk*, μ): *Given a message $\mu \in R_\mathcal{M}$, output a ciphertext c.*
- Dec(*params*, *sk*, *c*): *Given a ciphertext c, output a message $\mu^* \in R_\mathcal{M}$.*
- Eval($pk, f, c_1, ..., c_l$): *Given the inputs as public key pk, a function $f : R_\mathcal{M}^l \rightarrow R_\mathcal{M}$ which is an arithmetic circuit over $R_\mathcal{M}$, and a set of l ciphertexts $c_1, ..., c_l$, output a ciphertext c_f.*

In the above scheme, the message space $\mathcal{M}$ of the encryption schemes is a ring $R_\mathcal{M}$, and the functions to be evaluated are represented as arithmetic circuits over this ring, composed of addition and multiplication gates. HE can be categorized into: *Partially HE* that supports only addition or multiplication; *Somewhat HE* that allows both operations but with limited times; *Fully HE* that supports arbitrary computation by allowing both operations with unlimited times.

F Hybrid DRB Protocols

There are many more DRB protocols. Some of these protocols use more than one crypto primitive to achieve all DRB properties with better efficiency/optimization.

- Mt. Random (PVSS + T(VRF))(eprint 2021/1096): It is a multi-tiered DRB protocol that combines PVSS, VRF, and Threshold VRF (TVRF) to construct a DRB with optimal efficiency and without compromising security guarantees of DRB. It is a flexible architecture for DRB where each tier runs a separate beacon based on PVSS, VRF, and TVRF, and output of one tier works as a seed for the next tier. Being constructed using different crypto-primitives, each tier differs in the provided randomness and complexity. Due to that, a high-level application can decide on which tier to use to obtain randomness.
- Harmony (VRF + VDF)(https://harmony.one/whitepaper.pdf): Harmony is a sharding-based, provably secure, and scalable blockchain. In Harmony, nodes compute local entropy by executing VRF using their secret keys. DRB output is computed using VDF where the input for the VDF is constructed from a threshold number of VRF evaluations from pairwise different nodes. DRB output is made pseudorandom by applying a random oracle on VDF output.
- CRAFT (TLP + VDF)(eprint 2020/784): Baum et. al first construct UC-secure publicly verifiable TLP and UC-secure VDF. To construct DRB, they replace the commitments with the UC-secure TLP in the standard commit-reveal coin-tossing protocol. Their construction achieves $O(n)$ communication

to generate DRB output. DRB output can be obtained as fast as the communication channel delay allows when nodes communicate their TLPs faster.

- VeeDo (STARK+VDF)(https://github.com/starkware-libs/veedo): It is based on STARK-based VDF. STARK is a post-quantum secure zero-knowledge proof protocol. VeeDo is a smart-contract-based DRB where a beacon smart contract and a verifier smart contract is placed on-chain. However, heavy computational parts involving VDF and STARK prover are kept off-chain. A VDF is run on a seed s from a block hash to compute the DRB output and a proof is computed using the STARK prover. The VDF output and the proof are sent to the on-chain contracts for verification and subsequently publishing.

- STROBE (RSA-based)(eprint 2021/1643): It is a history-generating DRB (HGDRB). It allows efficient generation of previous beacon outputs given only the current beacon value and public key. It is based on origin squaring based RSA approach of Beaver. It is well-suited for practical applications especially in streaming designs where it allows client software to generate game states by computing every missing beacon value and state. It is NIZK-free, concisely self-verifying and can be efficiently used in blockchain and voting systems.

- OptRand (Bilinear paring-based PVSS + NIZK)(eprint 2022/193): It is an optimally responsive DRB protocol. It employs a pairing-based PVSS scheme together with a NIZK proof system to produce DRB outputs. Despite the synchrony of the network, it can provide an optimal response and can progress. Therefore, OptRand can provide availability at actual network speed during optimistic conditions. It is reconfiguration-friendly and has low communication complexity and low latency while generating beacon outputs.

References

1. Adida, B.: Helios: Web-based open-audit voting. In: USENIX Security Symposium. vol. 17, pp. 335–348 (2008)
2. Azouvi, S., McCorry, P., Meiklejohn, S.: Winning the caucus race: continuous leader election via public randomness. arXiv preprint arXiv:1801.07965 (2018)
3. Baigneres, T., Delerablée, C., Finiasz, M., Goubin, L., Lepoint, T., Rivain, M.: Trap me if you can-million dollar curve. IACR Cryptol. ePrint Arch. p. 1249 (2015)
4. Baum, C., David, B., Dowsley, R.: Insured MPC: efficient secure computation with financial penalties. In: Bonneau, J., Heninger, N. (eds.) FC 2020. LNCS, vol. 12059, pp. 404–420. Springer, Cham (2020). https://doi.org/10.1007/978-3-030-51280-4_22
5. Baum, C., David, B., Dowsley, R., Nielsen, J.B., Oechsner, S.: TARDIS: a foundation of time-lock puzzles in UC. In: Canteaut, A., Standaert, F.-X. (eds.) EUROCRYPT 2021. LNCS, vol. 12698, pp. 429–459. Springer, Cham (2021). https://doi.org/10.1007/978-3-030-77883-5_15
6. Bellare, M., Rogaway, P.: Random oracles are practical: a paradigm for designing efficient protocols. In: Proceedings of the 1st ACM Conference on Computer and Communications Security, pp. 62–73 (1993)
7. Bentov, I., Gabizon, A., Zuckerman, D.: Bitcoin beacon. arXiv preprint arXiv:1605.04559 (2016)

8. Bhat, A., Shrestha, N., Kate, A., Nayak, K.: Randpiper-reconfiguration-friendly random beacons with quadratic communication. IACR Cryptol. ePrint Arch. **2020**, 1590 (2020)
9. Blum, M.: Coin flipping by telephone a protocol for solving impossible problems. ACM SIGACT News **15**(1), 23–27 (1983)
10. Boneh, D.: The decision diffie-hellman problem. In: International Algorithmic Number Theory Symposium, pp. 48–63. Springer, Boston (1998). https://doi.org/10.1007/978-1-4419-5906-5_443
11. Boneh, D., Bonneau, J., Bünz, B., Fisch, B.: Verifiable delay functions. In: Shacham, H., Boldyreva, A. (eds.) CRYPTO 2018. LNCS, vol. 10991, pp. 757–788. Springer, Cham (2018). https://doi.org/10.1007/978-3-319-96884-1_25
12. Boneh, D., Lynn, B., Shacham, H.: Short signatures from the weil pairing. In: Boyd, C. (ed.) ASIACRYPT 2001. LNCS, vol. 2248, pp. 514–532. Springer, Heidelberg (2001). https://doi.org/10.1007/3-540-45682-1_30
13. Bonneau, J., Clark, J., Goldfeder, S.: On bitcoin as a public randomness source. IACR Cryptol. ePrint Arch. **2015**, 1015 (2015)
14. Bünz, B., Goldfeder, S., Bonneau, J.: Proofs-of-delay and randomness beacons in ethereum. In: IEEE Security and Privacy on the blockchain (IEEE S&B) (2017)
15. Buser, M., et al.: Post-quantum verifiable random function from symmetric primitives in POS blockchain. IACR Cryptol. ePrint Arch. **2021**, 302 (2021)
16. Cachin, C., Kursawe, K., Shoup, V.: Random oracles in constantinople: practical asynchronous byzantine agreement using cryptography. J. Cryptol. **18**(3), 219–246 (2005)
17. Cascudo, I., David, B.: SCRAPE: scalable randomness attested by public entities. In: Gollmann, D., Miyaji, A., Kikuchi, H. (eds.) ACNS 2017. LNCS, vol. 10355, pp. 537–556. Springer, Cham (2017). https://doi.org/10.1007/978-3-319-61204-1_27
18. Cascudo, I., David, B.: ALBATROSS: publicly attestable batched randomness based on secret sharing. In: Moriai, S., Wang, H. (eds.) ASIACRYPT 2020. LNCS, vol. 12493, pp. 311–341. Springer, Cham (2020). https://doi.org/10.1007/978-3-030-64840-4_11
19. Chavez-Saab, J., Henríquez, F.R., Tibouchi, M.: Verifiable isogeny walks: towards an isogeny-based postquantum VDF. Cryptology ePrint Archive, Report 2021/1289
20. Cherniaeva, A., Shirobokov, I., Shlomovits, O.: Homomorphic encryption random beacon. IACR Cryptol. ePrint Arch. **2019**, 1320 (2019)
21. Clark, J., Hengartner, U.: On the use of financial data as a random beacon. In: EVT/WOTE. vol. 89 (2010)
22. Corestar: Corestar arcade: Tendermint-based byzantine fault tolerant (BFT) middleware with an embedded BLS-based random beacon (2019)
23. Croman, K., et al.: On scaling decentralized blockchains. In: Clark, J., Meiklejohn, S., Ryan, P.Y.A., Wallach, D., Brenner, M., Rohloff, K. (eds.) FC 2016. LNCS, vol. 9604, pp. 106–125. Springer, Heidelberg (2016). https://doi.org/10.1007/978-3-662-53357-4_8
24. DAOBet: Daobet to deliver on-chain random beacon based on BLS cryptography (2019). https://daobet.org/blog/on-chain-random-generator/
25. Das, S., Krishnan, V., Isaac, I.M., Ren, L.: Spurt: scalable distributed randomness beacon with transparent setup. IACR Cryptol. ePrint Arch. **2021**, 100 (2021)
26. Das, S., Xiang, Z., Ren, L.: Asynchronous data dissemination and its applications. IACR Cryptol. ePrint Arch. (2021)

27. David, B., Gaži, P., Kiayias, A., Russell, A.: Ouroboros Praos: an adaptively-secure, semi-synchronous proof-of-stake blockchain. In: Nielsen, J.B., Rijmen, V. (eds.) EUROCRYPT 2018. LNCS, vol. 10821, pp. 66–98. Springer, Cham (2018). https://doi.org/10.1007/978-3-319-78375-8_3

28. Dimakis, A.G., Godfrey, P.B., Wu, Y., Wainwright, M.J., Ramchandran, K.: Network coding for distributed storage systems. IEEE Trans. Inf. Theory 56(9), 4539–4551 (2010). https://doi.org/10.1109/TIT.2010.2054295

29. Dodis, Y.: Efficient construction of (distributed) verifiable random functions. In: Desmedt, Y.G. (ed.) PKC 2003. LNCS, vol. 2567, pp. 1–17. Springer, Heidelberg (2003). https://doi.org/10.1007/3-540-36288-6_1

30. Drake, J.: Minimal VDF randomness beacon. Ethereum Research (2018)

31. drand: Drand - a distributed randomness beacon daemon (2020). https://github.com/drand/drand

32. ElGamal, T.: A public key cryptosystem and a signature scheme based on discrete logarithms. IEEE Trans. Inf. Theory 31(4), 469–472 (1985)

33. Elrond, A.: Highly scalable public blockchain via adaptive state sharding and secure proof of stake (2019)

34. Ephraim, N., Freitag, C., Komargodski, I., Pass, R.: Continuous verifiable delay functions. In: Canteaut, A., Ishai, Y. (eds.) EUROCRYPT 2020. LNCS, vol. 12107, pp. 125–154. Springer, Cham (2020). https://doi.org/10.1007/978-3-030-45727-3_5

35. Fetch.ai.: Distributed verifiable random functions: an enabler of decentralized random beacons (2020). https://github.com/fetchai/research-dvrf

36. Galindo, D., Liu, J., Ordean, M., Wong, J.M.: Fully distributed verifiable random functions and their application to decentralised random beacons. IACR Cryptol. ePrint Arch. 2020, 96 (2020)

37. Gennaro, R., Goldfeder, S., Narayanan, A.: Threshold-optimal DSA/ECDSA signatures and an application to bitcoin wallet security. In: Manulis, M., Sadeghi, A.-R., Schneider, S. (eds.) ACNS 2016. LNCS, vol. 9696, pp. 156–174. Springer, Cham (2016). https://doi.org/10.1007/978-3-319-39555-5_9

38. Gennaro, R., Jarecki, S., Krawczyk, H., Rabin, T.: Secure distributed key generation for discrete-log based cryptosystems. In: International Conference on the Theory and Applications of Cryptographic Techniques, pp. 295–310 (1999)

39. Gilad, Y., Hemo, R., Micali, S., Vlachos, G., Zeldovich, N.: Algorand: Scaling byzantine agreements for cryptocurrencies. In: Proceedings of the 26th Symposium on Operating Systems Principles, pp. 51–68 (2017)

40. Goel, S., Robson, M., Polte, M., Sirer, E.: Herbivore: a scalable and efficient protocol for anonymous communication. Cornell University, Tech. rep. (2003)

41. Goulet, D., Kadianakis, G.: Random number generation during tor voting. In: Tor's protocol specifications-Proposal, p. 250 (2015)

42. Gurkan, K., Jovanovic, P., Maller, M., Meiklejohn, S., Stern, G., Tomescu, A.: Aggregatable distributed key generation. In: Canteaut, A., Standaert, F.-X. (eds.) EUROCRYPT 2021. LNCS, vol. 12696, pp. 147–176. Springer, Cham (2021). https://doi.org/10.1007/978-3-030-77870-5_6

43. Haahr, M.: Random.org: True Random Number Service. School of Computer Science and Statistics, Trinity College, Dublin, Ireland, p. 10 (2010)

44. Han, R., Yu, J., Lin, H.: RandChain: decentralised randomness beacon from sequential proof-of-work. IACR Cryptol. ePrint Arch. 2020, 1033 (2020)

45. Hanke, T., Movahedi, M., Williams, D.: Dfinity technology overview series, consensus system. arXiv preprint arXiv:1805.04548 (2018)

46. Kelsey, J., Brandão, L.T., Peralta, R., Booth, H.: A reference for randomness beacons: Format and protocol version 2. Tech. rep, National Institute of Standards and Technology (2019)
47. Kiayias, A., Russell, A., David, B., Oliynykov, R.: Ouroboros: a provably secure proof-of-stake blockchain protocol. In: Katz, J., Shacham, H. (eds.) CRYPTO 2017. LNCS, vol. 10401, pp. 357–388. Springer, Cham (2017). https://doi.org/10.1007/978-3-319-63688-7_12
48. Kosba, A., Miller, A., Shi, E., Wen, Z., Papamanthou, C.: Hawk: The blockchain model of cryptography and privacy-preserving smart contracts. In: 2016 IEEE Symposium on Security and Privacy (SP), pp. 839–858 (2016)
49. Lenstra, A.K., Wesolowski, B.: A random zoo: sloth, unicorn, and TRX. IACR Cryptol. ePrint Arch. **2015**, 366 (2015)
50. Li, Z., Tan, T.G., Szalachowski, P., Sharma, V., Zhou, J.: Post-quantum VRF and its applications in future-proof blockchain system (2021)
51. LoE: League of entropy : Decentralized randomness beacon (2019). https://www.cloudflare.com/it-it/leagueofentropy/
52. Loe, A.F., Medley, L., O'Connell, C., Quaglia, E.A.: A practical verifiable delay function and delay encryption scheme. Cryptology ePrint Archive (2021)
53. Nakamoto, S.: Bitcoin: a peer-to-peer electronic cash system. http://bitcoin.org/bitcoin.pdf (2009)
54. Naor, O., Baudet, M., Malkhi, D., Spiegelman, A.: Cogsworth: Byzantine view synchronization. arXiv preprint arXiv:1909.05204 (2019)
55. Nguyen-Van, T., et al.: Scalable distributed random number generation based on homomorphic encryption. In: 2019 IEEE International Conference on Blockchain (Blockchain), pp. 572–579. IEEE (2019)
56. Oraclize.it: Provable random number generator. https://provable.xyz
57. Pietrzak, K.: Simple verifiable delay functions. In: 10th Innovations in Theoretical Computer Science Conference (ITCS 2019) (2018)
58. Rabin, M.O.: Transaction protection by beacons. J. Comput. Syst. Sci. **27**(2), 256–267 (1983)
59. Randao: Randao: A dao working as rng of ethereum, https://github.com/randao/randao. Accessed 1 Nov 2021
60. Rashmi, K.V., Shah, N.B., Gu, D., Kuang, H., Borthakur, D., Ramchandran, K.: A solution to the network challenges of data recovery in erasure-coded distributed storage systems: a study on the facebook warehouse cluster. In: 5th USENIX Workshop on Hot Topics in Storage and File Systems, USENIX (2013)
61. Reed, I.S., Solomon, G.: Polynomial codes over certain finite fields. J. Soc. Ind. Appl. Math. **8**(2), 300–304 (1960)
62. Mahmoody, M., Moran, T., Vadhan, S.: Time-lock puzzles in the random oracle model. In: Rogaway, P. (ed.) CRYPTO 2011. LNCS, vol. 6841, pp. 39–50. Springer, Heidelberg (2011). https://doi.org/10.1007/978-3-642-22792-9_3
63. Rotem, L.: Simple and efficient batch verification techniques for verifiable delay functions. Cryptology ePrint Archive (2021)
64. Schindler, P.: Hydrand. https://github.com/PhilippSchindler/hydrand
65. Schindler, P., Judmayer, A., Hittmeir, M., Stifter, N., Weippl, E.: Randrunner: distributed randomness from trapdoor VDFs with strong uniqueness. IACR Cryptol. ePrint Arch. **2020**, 942 (2020)
66. Schindler, P., Judmayer, A., Stifter, N., Weippl, E.: Hydrand: efficient continuous distributed randomness. In: 2020 IEEE Symposium on Security and Privacy (SP), pp. 73–89. IEEE (2020)

67. Schoenmakers, B.: A simple publicly verifiable secret sharing scheme and its application to electronic voting. In: Wiener, M. (ed.) CRYPTO 1999. LNCS, vol. 1666, pp. 148–164. Springer, Heidelberg (1999). https://doi.org/10.1007/3-540-48405-1_10

68. Shumow, D., Ferguson, N.: On the possibility of a back door in the NIST sp800-90 dual EC PRNG. In: Proceedings of the Cryptology, vol. 7 (2007)

69. Syta, E., et al.: Scalable bias-resistant distributed randomness. In: 2017 IEEE Symposium on Security and Privacy (SP), pp. 444–460. IEEE (2017)

70. Tomescu, A., et al.: Towards scalable threshold cryptosystems. In: 2020 IEEE Symposium on Security and Privacy (SP), pp. 877–893 (2020)

71. Wang, G., Nixon, M.: Randchain: practical scalable decentralized randomness attested by blockchain. In: 2020 IEEE International Conference on Blockchain (Blockchain), pp. 442–449. IEEE (2020)

72. Wesolowski, B.: Efficient verifiable delay functions. In: Ishai, Y., Rijmen, V. (eds.) EUROCRYPT 2019. LNCS, vol. 11478, pp. 379–407. Springer, Cham (2019). https://doi.org/10.1007/978-3-030-17659-4_13

73. Ye, M., Barg, A.: Explicit constructions of high-rate MDS array codes with optimal repair bandwidth. IEEE Trans. Inf. Theory **63**(4), 2001–2014 (2017)

74. Yin, M., Malkhi, D., Reiter, M.K., Gueta, G.G., Abraham, I.: HotStuff: BFT consensus with linearity and responsiveness. In: Proceedings of the 2019 ACM Symposium on Principles of Distributed Computing, pp. 347–356 (2019)

75. Yurek, T., Luo, L., Fairoze, J., Kate, A., Miller, A.K.: hbACSS: how to robustly share many secrets. IACR Cryptol. ePrint Arch. **2021**, 159 (2021)

Blockchain

CCOM: Cost-Efficient and Collusion-Resistant Oracle Mechanism for Smart Contracts

Xiaofei Wu[1], Hao Wang[1], Chunpeng Ge[1(✉)], Lu Zhou[1], Qiong Huang[2], Lanju Kong[3], Lizhen Cui[3], and Zhe Liu[1]

[1] Nanjing University of Aeronautics and Astronautics, Nanjing, China
{wuxiaofei,wangh24,gecp,lu.zhou,zhe.liu}@nuaa.edu.cn
[2] South China Agricultural University, Guangzhou, China
qhuang@scau.edu.cn
[3] Shandong University, Jinan, China
{klj,clz}@sdu.edu.cn

Abstract. Smart contracts, that allow parties to establish agreements based on predefined rules without a trusted third-party, have been explored in various applications. However, the main drawback of smart contracts is that they cannot access the external data required to trigger the execution of inner logic. The Oracle technology is an interactive bridge between on-chain smart contracts and off-chain data, which is designed to introduce external data into the blockchain system. A superior oracle mechanism should achieve reliable data acquisition with easy data parsing, deployable services, high system efficiency, and cost-effectiveness. The current smart contracts oracle mechanisms either rely on a trusted third-party or introduce high computation overhead and difficulty in deployment. This paper, for the first time, proposes a decentralized and efficient on-chain oracle mechanism *CCOM*. In our scheme, a prisoner's contract is introduced for users who want to obtain specific information. The user introduces two oracles to complete the same task of obtaining data, and the contract can prevent oracles from collusion. Rational oracles will not collude but honestly submit the correct result to increase self-interest. We also demonstrate that the proposed scheme can resist a single potentially malicious oracle service and prevent collusion from occurring. Finally, we perform experiments on Ethereum test network Rinkeby and show that our scheme is time-efficient and cost-effective.

Keywords: Oracle · Smart contract · Collusion-resistant · Game theory

1 Introduction

A blockchain system is a separate "information island" where data is transmitted between blockchain participants. It can only access data within the blockchain and lacks a reliable mechanism to query information outside (i.e., off-chain data) [2]. However, the execution of blockchain smart contracts relies on reliable external data [8]. Consider a smart contract that allows betting on the score of a football match. Designing a smart contract that defrays the reward based on the game's result is simple. While getting a reliable game score from the real world to trigger the smart contract is challenging. Therefore, it is essential to efficiently obtain reliable data to trigger the correct execution of smart contracts.

Oracles (also known as data feeds) [5,10,13,18,29] that get data from off-chain and feed it into the smart contract is a promising technique to bridge the smart contracts and the real world data. A straightforward approach is involving a trusted third-party oracle service to obtain the outside data. However, a malicious oracle service may provide manipulated data according to its own profit. Data reliability entirely relies on the trusted third-party oracle service. Another possible approach is leveraging decentralized oracle service where multiple oracles collaborate to obtain data. Decentralized oracles also are considered as consensus oracles, in which the oracle nodes reach an agreement through the consensus mechanism. Nevertheless, this approach is inefficient and increases resource consumption and overhead. Moreover, the decentralized oracle services cannot achieve high economic security [18], which means that if the financial benefits do not outweigh the costs, compromising a network would not be beneficial. Additionally, decentralized oracle schemes are difficult to deploy.

To overcome the above issues, we propose an efficient and low-overhead on-chain oracle mechanism that is resistant to a single potentially malicious oracle service, called $CCOM$. Our scheme constructs a prisoner's contract between the client and two oracles, which adopts cryptographic commitment and game theory. The key idea is to leverage smart contracts to implement a collusion-resistant payment protocol. (1) By requiring the oracle to pay the deposit in advance as a security guarantee for delivering the correct result. If the oracle delivers the incorrect result, it will be punished and lose the deposit. Such a mean weakens the oracle's incentive to collude. (2) Incentivize oracles to act honestly by redistributing confiscated deposits, which rewards honest oracles that submit correct results. (3) By requiring the oracle to submit the commitment to bid for the task, which once again weakens the oracle's motivation for collusion after successful bidding. Because in the next stage of delivering the original data, changing the result will cause the hash verification to fail.

Contributions. To summarize, we make the following contributions in this paper.

1. We propose a cost-efficient and collusion-resistant blockchain oracle mechanism, $CCOM$, which uses hash commitment and game theory-based methods to resist collusion. Detailed game theory analysis proves that two oracles submitting correct results are the only sequential equilibrium of the game (see Sect. 2.2).
2. The proposed $CCOM$ can resist to a single potentially malicious oracle service while taking into account the efficiency and overhead on the basis of ensuring the degree of decentralization.

3. We implement a lightweight smart contract scheme based on Ethereum and conduct detailed tests on Rinkeby. The results show that our scheme is time-efficient and cost-effective.

2   Preliminaries

2.1   Games and Strategies

Strategic Game [17] is a model of interaction between decision-makers (also known as players). Each player has a set of possible actions. This model captures the interaction between players by allowing each player to be affected by all player actions, not just his own actions.

Definition 1. *A **strategic game (with ordinal preferences)** consists of the following three elements.*

- *Players: a set of players.*
- *Actions: for each player, a set of actions.*
- *Preferences: for each player, preferences over the set of action profiles.*

The preferences defined as the payoff function, which associates a number with each action in such a way that actions with higher numbers are preferred. More precisely, the payoff function u represents a decision-maker's preferences if, for any actions a and b in A, $u(a) > u(b)$ if and only if the decision-maker prefers a to b.

The Prisoner's Dilemma [16] is one of the well-known situations of strategic games. The players of the game are two prisoners suspected of major crimes rather than two Internet users. The two prisoners were locked up in different interrogation rooms. However, there was enough evidence to convict each of them of minor crimes, but there was not enough evidence to convict any of them of major crimes unless one of them informed the public. Everyone can admit or deny their crime while being silent or betraying each other. If they both remain silent, everyone will be sentenced to a misdemeanor and go to prison for one year. If only one of them informs, the informant will be released and the other will spend four years in prison. If they betray each other, each of them will spend three years in prison.

This situation may be modeled as a strategic game:

- Players: The two suspects.
- Actions: Each player's set of actions is Silent, Betray.
- Preferences: Suspect A's action profiles, from best to worst, are (Betray, Silent) (A is freed), (Silent, Silent) (A gets one year in prison), (Betray, Betray) (A gets three years in prison), (Silent, Betray) (A gets four years in prison). Suspect B's action profiles are also similar.

We choose payoff functions that represent the suspects' preference orderings. For suspect A we let function u_1(Betray, Silent)=3 > u_1(Silent, Silent) = 2 >

u_1(Betray, Betray) $= 1 > u_1$(Silent, Betray) $= 0$. For suspect B we similarly choose the function u_2 for which u_2(Silent, Betray) $= 3 > u_2$(Silent, Silent) $= 2 > u_2$(Betray, Betray) $= 1 > u_2$(Betray, Silent) $= 0$. Using such payout functions, the game can be presented in the form of Table 1, where the rows correspond to player A's actions, the columns correspond to player B's actions, and the content of the box is the payoff function for the selected action configuration.

Table 1. The example of prisoner's dilemma.

Suspect A	Suspect B	
	Silent	Betray
Silent	$(2, 2)$	$(0, 3)$
Betray	$(3, 0)$	$(1, 1)$

The Prisoner's Dilemma simulates a situation in which cooperation will bring benefits (that is, each player remains silent instead of choosing to betray), but no matter what the other party does, each player has the incentive to choose to betray to gain higher returns.

Perfect Information Game: [15] The player specifies the action they will take at each choice node of the game, and the player knows the node where they are in and all previous choices, including the choices of other agents. However, in more realistic situations, such assumptions are too strong, and many scenarios need to simulate agents that partially or completely do not know the actions taken by others, or even agents with limited knowledge of their own past actions.

The Imperfect-Information Game [15] is an extended form of a game that solves this limitation.

In the extensive form, a game is captured as a game tree. Each node represents a player's choice, each edge represents a possible action, the leaves represent the final result, and each player has a utility function. Formally, we define it as follows.

Definition 2. *An **imperfect-information game** in extensive form is a tuple* $(N, A, H, Z, \chi, \rho, \sigma, u)$ *where:*

1. *N is a set of n players;*
2. *A is a (single) set of actions;*
3. *H is a set of non-terminal choice nodes;*
4. *Z is a set of terminal nodes, disjoint from H;*
5. *$\chi: H \mapsto 2^A$ is the action function, which assigns to each choice node a set of possible actions;*
6. *$\rho: H \mapsto N$ is the player function, which assigns to each non-terminal node a player $i \in N$ who chooses an action at that node;*
7. *$\sigma: H \times A \mapsto H \cup Z$ is the successor function, which maps a choice node and an action to a new choice node or terminal node such that for all $h_1, h_2 \in H$ and $a_1, a_2 \in A$, if $\sigma(h_1, a_1) = \sigma(h_2, a_2)$ then $h_1 = h_2$ and $a_1 = a_2$;*

8. $u = (u_1, ..., u_n)$, *where $u_i : Z \mapsto R$ is a real-valued utility function for player i on the terminal nodes Z.*

9. $I = (I_1, ..., I_n)$, *where is an equivalence relation that partitions player i's choice nodes $\{h \in H : \rho(h) = i\}$ into k_i information sets $I_{i,1}, ..., I_{i,k_i}$ with the property that $\chi(h) = \chi(h')$ and $\rho(h) = \rho(h')$ whenever there exists a j for which $h \in I_{i,j}$ and $h' \in I_{i,j}$.*

In the definition, the tuple $(N, A, H, Z, \chi, \rho, \sigma, u)$ captures the setting and rules of the game, which same as the perfect-information game, and I captures the imperfection of information. The strategy set A captures the actions that players will take at any stage of the game. This paper considers mixed behavior strategies that are more common than pure strategies.

Definition 3 (Behavior strategies). *Let $G = (N, A, H, Z, \chi, \rho, \sigma, u)$ be an imperfect-information extensive-form game. Then the behavior strategies s_i of player i is a function that assigns each information set $I_{i,j} \in I_i$ a probability distribution over the actions in $\chi(I_{i,j})$, with the property that each probability distribution is independent of the others. A **completely mixed behavior strategy** is a behavior strategy in which every action is assigned a positive probability. A **strategy profile** is a list of all players' strategies $s = (s_i)_{i \in N}$. A strategy profile without player i's strategy is defined as $s_{-i} = (s_1, ..., s_{i-1}, s_{i+1}, ..., s_n)$. We can also write $s = (s_i, s_{-i})$.*

2.2 Sequential Equilibrium

The state of the stable optimal solution in game theory is called a **Nash equilibrium** [17]. Informally, in a Nash equilibrium, each player's strategy is the best given the other players' strategies, and no one can do better by changing their strategies if the other players do not change their strategies. However, the player's strategy may include irrational behavior that leads to his own lower payoff, thus forming a weaker Nash equilibrium.

We employ an improvement scheme that excludes unreasonable equilibrium-**sequential equilibrium** [17] -consisting of a behavior strategy profile and a belief system. The equilibrium should not only specify the players' strategies, and the belief system should also specify their beliefs about each set of information about the history that occurred. They must move according to the set of information about the history that happened. We refer to such a pair (s, β) as an **assessment**, in which s is a **behavior strategy profile** and β is a **belief system**.

Definition 4. *In a game G, a (**belief system**) $\beta = (\beta_i)_{i \in N}$ is as follows: for each player i, β_i assigns each information set $I_{i,j} \in I_i$ a probability distribution over the nodes in $I_{i,j}$. For each node $h \in I_{i,j}$, the belief $\beta_i(h) = Pr[h|I_{i,j}]$, i.e. the probability that player i is at h given that he is at $I_{i,j}$.*

Definition 5. *In a game G, the player i's **expected payoff** at h, given the play of the game is at node h when the players implement the strategy profile s, is the* *sum of the utility of each terminal nodes, weighted by the probability of reaching the node:*

$$u_i(s;h) = \sum_{z \in Z} Pr[z|(s,h)] \cdot u_i(z) \tag{1}$$

The player i's expected payoff at $I_{i,j}$ is the sum of expected payoff at each $h \in I_{i,j}$, weighted by the belief $\beta_i(h)$:

$$u_i(s;I_{i,j},\beta) = \sum_{h \in I_{i,j}} \beta_i(h) \cdot u_i(s;h) \tag{2}$$

Definition 6. *In a game G, (s,β) be an assessment, the strategy profile $s = (s_i, s_{-i})$ is called **rational** at information set $I_{i,j}$, relative to β, if for each behavior strategy $s_i' \neq s_i$ of player i:*

$$u_i(s;I_{i,j},\beta) \geq u_i((s_i',s_{-i});I_{i,j},\beta) \tag{3}$$

*The assessment is called **sequentially rational** if for each player i and each information set $I_{i,j} \in I$, the strategy profile s is rational at $I_{i,j}$ relative to β.*

Definition 7. *An assessment (s,β) is said to be **consistent** if there exists a sequence of fully mixed behavior strategy profiles $(s^k)_{k \in N}$ satisfying the following conditions:*

(1) The profile $(s^k)_{k \in N}$ converges to s, which is $\lim_{k \to \infty}(s^k) \to s$;
(2) The sequence of beliefs $(\beta^k)_{k \in N}$ induced $(s^k)_{k \in N}$ (by Bayes' rule) converges to the belief system β, which is $\lim_{k \to \infty}(\beta^k) \to \beta$.

Definition 8. *An assessment (s,β) is called a **sequential equilibrium** if it is sequentially rational and consistent.*

Due to imperfect information, players must make decisions under uncertainty. When a player is asked to make a decision, the belief system allows the player to construct the strategy that is optimal at every point in the tree.

2.3   Smart Contract and Oracle

Blockchain is a new type of distributed ledger paradigm that integrates multiple existing technologies. It uses distributed consensus algorithms to generate and update data and peer-to-peer networks for data transmission between nodes. The distributed ledger that combines cryptography principles and time stamping technologies ensures that the stored data cannot be tampered with and uses automated script codes or smart contracts to implement upper-level application logic. **Smart contracts** are programs with specific addresses that are executed on the blockchain, which are event-driven, self-executing, and tamper-resistant. They consume transaction fees based on the complexity of the code (for example, **Gas** consumed by deployment in the Ethereum blockchain) and use the resources available on the blockchain network. The introduction of smart contracts to the blockchain has increased the programmability of the blockchain and revolutionized the software ecosystem.

Although the prospects are promising, smart contracts that perform specific functions need to access data about real-world state and events from outside the blockchain system [30,31]. However, since the blockchain system is isolated from the external world [25], the blockchain and smart contracts cannot access off-chain data (outside the p2p network). The availability of smart contracts in terms of performance and programmability will be limited to data on the chain. To overcome this limitation of smart contracts, the **Oracle** (also known as **Data Feed**) [4,14,28] represented by smart contracts on the blockchain came into being. Oracles act as agents, servicing data requests from other smart contracts, discovering and validating real-world events, and feeding the data to smart contracts. Lack of reliable data feeding mechanism limits the applicability of smart contracts.

3   The Architechture of *CCOM*

3.1   Adversary Model and Assumption

In our system model, the client who publishes a data request task and introduces two oracles to get the required data is thought to be honest. The client's goal is to get the correct data it wants while minimizing the cost. A single oracle may behave in-honestly and return incorrect data so as to get extra profit. Each oracle is thought to be a separate rational adversary, which means that the oracle always considers all possible outcomes and rationally chooses the strategy that will maximize its profits. The parties involved are risk-neutral. For other risk profiles (i.e., risk-seeking or risk-averse), the utility function can be adjusted to the risk profile, and equilibrium is maintained by choosing deposits based on the risk profile. Beyond that, we have the following assumptions:

- We assume that oracles can provide incorrect but reasonable results with no cost.
- For simplicity, we also assume that different oracles consume the same cost to complete the task, and the cost is public.
- Combined with real-world scenarios, we assume that the data required by the smart contract is not complicated. Considering the high cost and low demand of uploading large amounts of data to the blockchain, complex data acquisition tasks are beyond the scope of this paper for the time being.

3.2   The System Architecture of *CCOM*

The *CCOM* involves two types of participants as shown in Fig 1.

- *Users (Clients):* A user wants to access the specific data which service provided by oracles, then he creates and distributes the prisoner's contract on blockchain to publish a task.

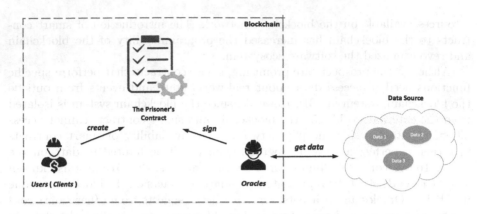

Fig. 1. System architecture of $CCOM$.

- *Oracles:* An oracle who wants to accept the task needs to bid and sign the prisoner's contract with the client.

When on-chain users need to access off-chain data sources to complete some interactions, the client instantiates a prisoner's contract according to the specific requirements and distributes the smart contract on the blockchain. Two oracles which are selected randomly, sign the contract with the client. Then oracles fetch data from data sources and deliver it to the contract. If there is any dispute, the trusted third oracle(TTO) will be introduced, which is served by a reputable oracle service provider. This oracle can provide results and resolve disputes. However, if the oracle is rational, TTO will never be called.

To incentivize honest behavior, oracles are required to prepay deposit, which is stated in the contract in advance. If the oracle acts honestly, the deposit will be refunded; if the oracle is detected cheating, the client will confiscate the deposit. In addition, in the case where one oracle is honest and the other cheats, the honest oracle will get extra profits from the cheating oracle's deposit. Although, collusion may bring higher profits than both parties acting honestly. However, there will be a higher profit if one person can induce the other party to cheat while being honest with himself. Once both oracles understand that collusion is unstable, the other oracle always tries to deviate from it. Any attempt to persuade the other party to collude without a credible and enforceable promise will be considered a trap, therefore, will not succeed.

3.3 Monetary Variables

We use some non-negative currency variables in the contract — see Table 2.

Obviously, there are some relationships between these currency variables.

- $w \geq c$: Oracle will not accept low-paying jobs at a loss.

Table 2. Summary of monetary notations.

Notation	Description
c	The essential cost of an oracle completes the task of obtaining specific data
th	The cost of calling TTO to re-complete the task of obtaining specific data and resolving disputes
d	The deposit an oracle needs to pay to the client for a job
w	The amount the client agrees to pay to an oracle to complete the task of obtaining specific data

- $th > 2 * w$: Otherwise, the oracle service will not be needed. The client can directly select the TTO, which is slightly more expensive, to complete the task of obtaining specific data.
- $d > c + th$: In order to establish an ideal Nash equilibrium, d is set by the client in the prisoner's contract.

In addition, th will be paid by the oracle that submitted the wrong result. Honest customers pay no more than the cost of requesting two oracle services plus the gas cost of initiating the transaction.

3.4   The Prisoner's Contract

The prisoner's contract is established between a user (client) and two oracles (o_1 and o_2), the contract is summarized in Algorithm 1, and the specific protocol is as follows:

Init: The client instantiates the prisoner's contract according to the specific data service request (including content and format, etc.) and sets the deadline $T_1 < T_2 < T_3$. Then he publishes it on the blockchain.

Create: The client creates a task through the contract, declares the data he wants to access, and sets the d that oracle needs to pay. Agree to pay the w to each oracle who completes the task honestly and select o_1 and o_2 that provide corresponding services randomly to prevent oracle collusion in advance to a certain extent. Determine TTO and the th, if any disputes will be resolved by TTO. In addition, the client pays $(2 * w) + th$ to the contract when publishing the task.

Bid: The o_1 and o_2 assigned the task need to bid within T_1. Oracle accepts the task to pay the d to the contract and upload the HASH of the data required by the client, namely $hash(data)$. If any oracle fails to do so, the contract will be terminated, and any deposit paid will be refunded.

Deliver: The o_1 and o_2 must submit the original data before T_2. The contract verifies whether the result submitted by oracle is consistent with those submitted during the Bid period. If they are the same, the submission is successful.

Pay: If the time exceeds T_2, o_1 and o_2 have not delivered the results, the d will be forfeited in full. If both o_1 and o_2 deliver the results and the results are equal, the w will be paid and the d will be refunded. Otherwise, a dispute will be raised with TTO.

Only when there is an obvious problem, that is, no oracle delivers the result, or the client is satisfied with the result, can the contract be directly terminated.

Dispute: After TTO receives the dispute, it completes the task of obtaining specific data and submits the $result_0$ to the contract, and the contract determines it.

(1) If both oracles fail to submit the results correctly within the deadline, their deposits will be forfeited in total, and th will be paid to TTO.
(2) If the result submitted by one oracle is correct and the other oracle is wrong, the dishonest oracle will be charged for the deposit in total, and the contract will pay the honest oracle the w, additional $bonus$ ($bonus = d-th$) and the d.

When only one result is received successfully, or the results do not match, the contract will determine the cheating behavior and settle the amount based on the result of TTO. If the client is honest, disputes will only be raised when there is a problem, and the th will be paid by the cheating oracle's d.

Liquidate: If after T_3, the client neither pays nor raises a dispute, for the oracle that delivers the result before T_2, the client must pay the w and refund the d to the oracle, and all the remaining balance of the contract will be transferred to the client.

The client is honest in theory, but if the client maliciously manipulates-neither pays nor raises a dispute, the oracle can call the Timer function in the contract to ensure that its funds are not locked.

Reset: After a task ends, the client can call the reset function to reset the contract parameters before releasing a new task. There is no need to redeploy contracts frequently, saving gas consumption.

The contract has three deadlines to enforce timeliness and avoid locking up funds when some parties refuse to advance the contract. The contract may permanently lock the balances if the code does not specify what to do after the deadline. So the deadline is crucial for smart contracts.

Algorithm 1. The Prisoner's Contract pseudocode.

Init:
  Set state := Init, T_1, T_2, T_3, Do := false;
Create:
  Upon receiving ("create", w, d, th, o_1, o_2 , TTO) from *client*:
  if state := Init and $T < T_1 < T_2 < T_3$ and $bal[client] \geq \$(2 * w + th)$ **then**
    state := Created;
    $bal[ledger] := \$(2 * w + th)$;
    worker = $\{o_1, o_2\}$;
Bid:
  Upon receiving ("bid", $hash(data)_i$) from o_i:
  if state := Created and $T < T_1$ and
    $o_i \in$ worker and $bal[o_i] \geq \$d$ **then**
    $bal[ledger] := bal[ledger]+\$d$;
    $hash_i := hash(data)_i$;
    $hasBid[o_i] := true$;
  else
    $hasBid[o_i] := false$;
  if $hasBid[o_1]$ and $hasBid[o_2]$ **then**
    state := GetData;
Deliver:
  Upon receiving ("deliver", $data_i$) from o_i:
  if state := GetData and $T < T_2$ and
    $o_i \in$ worker **then**
    $result_i := data_i$;
    if $hash(data_i) := hash_i$ **then**
      $hasDeliver[o_i] := true$;
    else
      $hasDeliver[o_i] := false$;
    state := Pay;
Pay:
  Upon receiving ("pay") from *client*:
  while state := Pay and $T > T_2$ **do**
    if $hasDeliver[o_1]$ and $hasDeliver[o_2]$ **then**
      $bal[client] := bal[client] + \$(2 * w + th + 2 * d)$;
      state := Done;
      Do := false;
    else if $hasDeliver[o_1]$ and $hasDeliver[o_2]$
    and $result_1 := result_2$ **then**
      $bal[o_1] := bal[o_1] + \$(w + d)$;
      $bal[o_2] := bal[o_2] + \$(w + d)$;
      $bal[client] := bal[client] + \$(th)$;
      state := Done;
      Do := true;
    else

      state := Error;
      Do := false;
    return Do;
Dispute:
  Upon receiving ("Dispute", *result*) from TTO:
  while state := Error **do**
    for i =1 to 2 **do**
      if $hasDeliver[o_i]$ and $result = result_i$
  then
        $hasCheat[o_i] := false$;
      else
        $hasCheat[o_i] := true$;
    if $hasCheat[o_1]$ and $hasCheat[o_2]$ **then**
      $bal[o_2] := bal[o_2] + \$(w + 2 * d - th)$;
      $bal[client] := bal[client] + \$(w + th)$;
    else if $hasCheat[o_1]$ and $hasCheat[o_2]$
  then
      $bal[o_1] := bal[o_1] + \$(w + 2 * d - th)$;
      $bal[client] := bal[client] + \$(w + th)$;
    else if $hasCheat[o_1]$ and $hasCheat[o_2]$
  then
      $bal[client] := bal[client] + \$(2 * (w + d))$;
    $bal[TTO] := bal[TTO] + \$(th)$;
    state := Done;
Liquidate:
  Upon receiving ("Timer"):
  while state := Created and $T > T_1$ **do**
    $bal[client] := bal[client] + \$(2 * w + th)$;
    for i =1 to 2 **do**
      if $hasBid[o_i]$ **then**
        $bal[o_i] := bal[o_i] + \$(d)$;
    state := Aborted;
  while state := GetData and $T > T_2$ **do**
    state := Pay;
  while state := Pay and $T > T_3$ **do**
    for i =1 to 2 **do**
      if $hasDeliver[o_i]$ **then**
        $bal[o_i] := bal[o_i] + \$(w + d)$;
    $bal[client] := bal[client] + bal[ledger]$;
    state := Done;
Reset:
  Upon receiving ("reset"):
  if state := Done or state := Aborted **then**
    clear cache of all parameters;
    state := Init;

4   Discussion and Analysis

An imperfect information game created by the above prisoner's contract is shown in Fig. 2. In the game, the players are two oracles. Although the contract also involves the client and TTO, who are honest and have only one deterministic strategy, we exclude them from the players. We formalize the game. The player set is $N = \{o_1, o_2\}$. The action set $A = \{T - result, F - result, other\}$, where

$T-result$ means that the participant sent the correct result before the deadline, and $F-result$ means that the participant sent the wrong result before the deadline. Other refers to other behaviors that submit incorrect data or fail to submit data within the specified time. The game has two information sets: $I_1 = \{v_0\}$ belongs to o_1, and $I_2 = \{v_1, v_2, v_3\}$ belongs to o_2. $(H, Z, \chi, \rho, \sigma)$ are captured by the tree structure. We use u_1 and u_2 to denote the utility functions of o_1 and o_2, respectively. Both parties' payoff (utilities) are listed below the terminal nodes.

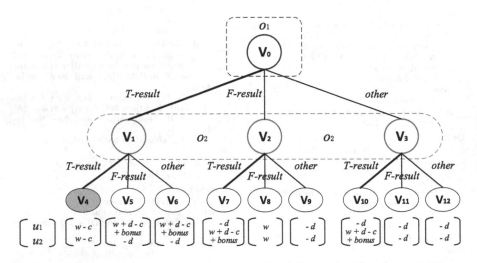

Fig. 2. The game created by the prisoner's contract. Bold edges indicate the actions that parties will play in the unique sequential equilibrium.

Next, we prove that the game has a unique sequential equilibrium. To be precise, if $d > c + th$, the probability of both parties of the game submitting the correct data $T - result$ is 1, and the only achievable node of the game is v_4. The significance of balance is that for each oracle node, submitting the correct data will always bring itself the highest payoff. In detail, we see the decision point v1 of o_2: if o_2 chooses $T - result$, it will go to the terminal node v_4, the game is over, and the payoff of o_2 is $w - c$; while choosing $F - result$ or other will go to v_5 and v_6 respectively, o_2's payoff is all $-d$. Since $w - c$ is positive, it's a better choice than $-d$ anyway. Similarly, for the decision point v_2 of o_2, if o_2 chooses $T - result$, it will go to the terminal node v_7, and the payoff is $w + d - c + bonus$, that is $w + 2 * d - c - th$. If o_2 chooses $F - result$ or other, it will go to v_8 and v_9, and the payoff is w and $-d$, respectively. Obviously, if $d > c + th$, the payoff in v_7 is higher than that in v_8 and v_9. Correspondingly, at decision point v_3, if o_2 chooses $T - result$, it will go to terminal node v_{10}, and the payoff is $w - c + bonus$, which is better than the payoff of choosing $F - result$ or other which is $-d$. Regardless of how o_1 chooses his actions, o_2 will prefer to submit the correct result, and terminal nodes will only be spawned in v_4, v_7, and v_{10}. From the payoff of o_1 in these three nodes, it is obvious that the oracle will choose to execute $T - result$ to get the best payoff, so if the oracles are all rational, v_4 is the only outcome of the game.

From the definition in Sect. 2.2, we can draw the following conclusions.

Lemma 1. *If* $d > c+th$, *then Game in Fig. 2 has a unique sequential equilibrium* $((s_1, s_2), (\beta_1, \beta_2))$ *where*

$$
\begin{cases}
s_1 = ([1(T - result), 0(F - result), 0(other)]); \\
s_2 = ([1(T - result), 0(F - result), 0(other)]); \\
\beta_1 = ([1(v_0)]); \\
\beta_2 = ([1(v_1), 0(v_2), 0(v_3)]);
\end{cases}
\tag{4}
$$

Theorem 1. *If* $d > c + th$ *and* o_1, o_2 *are rational, Game in Fig. 2 will always terminate at* v_4.

Lemma 1 states that for o_1 and o_2, the best strategy is to always submit correct results $T - result$ in time (with a probability 1). Informally, beliefs can be reasoned like this: for o_1, since I_1 has only one node, o_1 knows that it is always at v_0 when it reaches I_1 (that is $\beta_1 = ([1(v_0)])$); for o_2, knowing that o_1's strategy is always select to send $T - result$ and it always reaches v_1 and not the other two nodes in I_2 (that is $\beta_2 = ([1(v_1), 0(v_2), 0(v_3)])$).

Given Lemma 1, Theorem 1 can be easily proved: if both parties always send $T - result$ with a probability 1, the game always ends at v_4.

In the above analysis, when both parties submit the same incorrect result at the deadline, the contract cannot distinguish the authenticity. It will still offer the incorrect result to the client. At this time, we assume that both oracles have intentionally reached collusion. The probability of such a situation occurring in the absence of collusion is extremely low and can be ignored.

Next, we consider the case of collusion. From a rational point of view, in the game created by our prisoner's contract, the oracles participating in the collusion earn less than the payoff for submitting the correct result. However, there is also the possibility that colluding oracles may obtain extra benefits from other channels. For example, after the oracle reaches collusion, the result is manipulated so that the client suffers a loss when using the incorrect data to execute other smart contracts, and the loss makes the collusion oracle obtain a higher profit.

Considering that oracles are rational and selfish adversaries, collusion is unreliable unless credible and enforceable commitments are made in the form of smart contracts that explicitly regulate the rewards of collusion and the penalties for the betrayal of collusion. In addition, if collusion is reached, the oracle also can betray the collusion and report to the client to obtain higher profits. Therefore, collusion is unstable.

Moreover, the above collusion is difficult to achieve in CCOM. First of all, our scheme adopts the principle of randomness to select two oracles. The oracle node that receives the task cannot determine who also received the task because anyone can serve as an oracle node on the $p2p$ network to provide data. Then, our prisoner's contract has a clear deadline for the oracle to submit the result. The deadline is within a few minutes, and it is almost difficult for a potentially malicious oracle to quickly find another oracle and sign a collusion contract to do evil together. It is tantamount to finding a needle in a haystack in a short period. When the oracle accepting the task pays the deposit for bidding, the identity of the oracle that issued the transaction is disclosed. However, the hash of the result has been submitted simultaneously in bidding and cannot be changed in delivering, so collusion cannot be realized.

To summarise, in the scenario where oracles obtain off-chain data for smart contracts, $CCOM$ can resist collusion in the face of rational and selfish oracles.

5   Implementation

The experiments is conducted on a ThinkBook 13X with a CPU of 11th Gen Intel(R)Core(TM) i5-1130G7@ 2.90 GHz and 16 GB RAM. The contract was implemented in Solidity 0.4.10 [23] and tested on the Ethereum testnet Rinkeby. Simultaneously, we use the built-in hash function—$Keccak256$ of solidity to upload encrypted information to the smart contract. Contracts are loosely coupled with external services provided by oracles. The task of fetching the data can be viewed as a black box, and the contract does not need to know their internal details. The contract is only called before/during/after executing the task. The source code of our scheme's contracts can be found at https://github. com/job00001/CCOM.

5.1   Cryptographic Primitives - HASH Function

Hash function is a one-way irreversible and input-sensitive algorithm that is cryptographically secure. It is precisely that input a random v yields a unique $c = H(v)$ which is uniformly distributed and unpredictable. The hash algorithm has the following two characteristics: (1) One-Way: it is difficult to deduce the sensitive data v through the hash value $H(v)$; (2) Collision-Resistant: it is difficult to find different sensitive data v' produces the same hash value $H(v)$.

Cryptographic commitments allow one to commit to a chosen value (or chosen statement) while keeping it hidden to others, with the ability to reveal the committed value later. The receiver cannot know the chosen value at that time (which provides hiding property). The chosen value in the commit phase must be the only one that the sender can compute and validate during the reveal phase (which provides binding property). Hash function is simple in construction and easy to use, satisfying the essential characteristics of cryptographic commitments – hiding and binding. In our experiments, we use solidity's built-in $keccak256$ function, which is briefly described below for what it does for our contracts.

Select Oracles Randomly: In the create phase of the prisoner's contract, the client uses the $keccak256$ algorithm to select two oracles randomly. It is too expensive for solidity to generate random numbers through complex algorithms.

We use one of the most commonly used algorithms–"Linear Congruence Generator (LCG)". Enter the current timestamp and the client's address as parameters to obtain a hash value of type *uint*256, and then modulo the total number of oracles n to obtain a random number. Although this method is not secure enough on Ethereum, in practice, nodes generally do not have enough resources to launch an attack. Attacks are unprofitable unless we have a ton of money on our random function, so we decided to accept this shortcoming.

Encrypt Information: The oracle converts the result into a *keccak* value and then feeds it to the contract so that other nodes cannot replicate or initiate acollusion. When two oracles have delivered their original data, the contract can verify whether the results are consistent with the previous bidding to judge whether they act honestly. Hashing is a commitment scheme that is strongly collision-resistant while providing verifiability of results. We replace the actual input/output values that should be placed on the blockchain with hash values, temporarily hiding the information of the input/output and avoiding collusion well (see Sect. 5).

We implement contracts on the blockchain (such as Ethereum) to assist in realizing a cost-efficient and collusion-resistant oracle mechanism by using a collision-resistant hash function. Blockchain has limited space for storing data, and nodes in the network need to verify all transactions. The size and complexity of transactions are limited, so such an approach is efficient and has very little overhead (see Sect. 5.2 for details).

5.2   Overhead and Cost

Cryptography Overhead and Gas Cost: We use the built-in hash function of solidity. Each oracle only needs to generate one *keccak* value, each client needs to generate two *keccak* values, and each prisoner's contract requires to verify at most two *keccak* values. So the additional overhead caused by cryptography primitives is small. In Table 3, we show the cost of setting up and executing our contracts on the Ethereum testnet Rinkeby. The cost is in the amount of gas consumed by each function. In all transactions, the gas price was $1\ gas = 0.0000000025\ ether$.

The cost is roughly related to the computational and storage complexity of the function. For example, In our prisoner's contract, Init (deploying the contract on the blockchain), Create (publishing specific tasks), and Dispute (calling the third oracle to resolve disputes) cost more than other functions. Deploying our contract costs 2.96×10^6 gas, but if the reset function is called to reset the parameters, the contract can be reused without deploying again. Then each task can save about 2.87×10^6 gas, and the cost can be further reduced. If there is no dispute for a task, the total cost (client and two oracles) is about 0.57×10^6 gas, and if there is a dispute to be resolved, the total cost is about 0.76×10^6 gas. It can be seen that the cost of using our constructed prisoner's contract on Ethereum is very cheap, *CCOM* is cost-effective.

Table 3. The cost of using the smart contracts on Rinkeby.

(a) The example with dispute treatment

Function	Gas	Txn Fee(Ether)	Time-consuming(s)	Txn Hash
Init	2962477	0.007406192	14.89	0x59e14baab5d2269f32760f12bbae0dd52a7ec33695c3b0fe2a69ec13f87b231
Creat	271108	0.000677770	18.13	0xf932bf63f59db63b4b996b2e96536dac2a404f1682c883a0065ec1ea02dc458b
Bid	80222	0.000200555	8.53	0xc5479e5d376a50caf6fbccca236d1033f0e994c534b657310af01ac60150657d
Deliver	83506	0.000208765	5.93	0x1f2e8876c64e309d1a5d1e24e9adfaf5068e845e96649a553b78326a3872e04a
Pay	42420	0.000106050	14.13	0x6fe639334f773f74ab8471c239a9cd70370f909d95f21720d8ab440df7ffd85
Dispute	126749	0.000316872	16.25	0xe7eb3f360def52c2ca63dc034727aed646759ae385cc66bf3ef872c6bab88e7e
Timer	27780	0.000069450	15.64	0xb1cb2eb577b78a3dc6b6cf296e2c7abe42b49083e00b44c783a9880c295791eb
Reset	86995	0.000217487	5.46	0x5f54e2e506e1210c3b88a14c53e3f6d031363faac7907589a0e8732a25557eac

(b) The example without dispute treatment

Function	Gas	Txn Fee(Ether)	Time-consuming(s)	Txn Hash
Creat	253465	0.000633662	17.28	0x50202f0bd5139d84c4b8a4d69704b8b03c818a4a19f28ada4ce7bbd00483386a
Bid	60322	0.000150805	6.33	0xa609bcf20450f44859332099d24221de56fb95857f84fc7bc1d374a0319a2a973
Deliver	60519	0.000151297	16.02	0xc1999702843336d154ddf2847b066e106c6f89c8480caf96113d958f55561022f1
Pay	77071	0.000192677	17.01	0x975c2d591ftdb51ecbebb4cc53a67b93c2f4ab29db4b562b269de0bb2b8ce0
Reset	84755	0.000211887	11.82	0x9e2e40960494f2a967d21e624cedbf9e2c73807b8885ea593be3c3b187c8ec01

Time Cost: We also consider the time-consuming of *CCOM*. Since our oracle mechanism is wholly based on the modeling of Ethereum smart contracts, the time-consuming cost does not involve the setting of initial parameters, writing solidity contracts, and other preprocesses. We only consider the time consumed by the *CCOM* mechanism to execute transactions on Ethereum.

We recorded the time consumption of each transaction made on Rinkeby, as shown in Table 3. For an example of interaction without dispute treatment, the total time consumption for six transactions is about 79 s. For an example of interaction with dispute treatment, the total time consumption for seven transactions is 77.5 s. If the time exceeds T3 and the client has not settled, the contract may involve another liquidating transaction. The current network situation of Ethereum has affected our results to a certain extent, so the transaction time is irregular, but a single transaction basically does not exceed 20 s. To sum up, the time cost of *CCOM* is also very small.

6 Related Work

Scholars around the world have conducted extensive research on blockchain oracles. The earliest smart contracts use the secure HTTP connection supported by the Transport Layer Security protocol (TLS) to obtain information. Still, the TLS protocol cannot fully guarantee that the content of the HTTP session has not been tampered with. TLS-N [21] is a more general approach to provide non-repudiation to the TLS protocol. However, to achieve this, significant changes were made to the TLS protocol, and the scheme was poorly deployable. These schemes are dedicated to achieving safe and reliable data transmission.

Provable [3] (previously known as Oraclize) is a pioneering centralized oracle service (operating since 2015) that fetches external data from a Web API and uses TLSNotary/SafetyNet to build proofs of authenticity to provide security. Provable is based on a Trusted Execution Environment (TEE) and an auditable virtual machine. Although the supply of audit data is guaranteed, the performance of Provable is not good enough. In 2016, Zhang F et al. [31] proposed Town Crier (TC), a framework based on Intel Software Extensions Protection (SGX), and the Enclave instance of SGX acts as a link between HTTPS-enabled data source websites and Ethereum blockchain smart contracts. TC's security relies on the SGX framework's security and authentication infrastructure. However, Intel CPU and SGX have been severely attacked and damaged [24,27], which link security is weak. Furthermore, TC only supports limited APIs and data feeds dedicated to the Ethereum mainnet. PriceGeth [7] is implemented as a smart contract for trusted entities to publish real-time price pairs to the Ethereum blockchain and keep all historical prices on-chain so that prices can be accessed without gas. The solution is centralized, there is no incentive mechanism for oracles that publish and store price pairs, and the application scenarios are relatively limited. The above three solutions are typical of centralized oracles, providing off-chain solutions connected to on-chain smart contracts to transmit data.

Augur [20] utilizes the trust decentralization of blockchain to provide a low-cost oracle platform for prediction markets of online transactions. Witnet [19] is a reputation-based decentralized oracle network (DON) protocol that connects smart contracts with external data providers. Witnet's reputation system maintains the credibility and honesty of participants by rewarding successful majority-consistent provers and punishing contradictory provers. ChainLink [22] is the first decentralized oracle solution proposed on Ethereum, which pushes data between smart contracts and Web-API, maintaining the integrity, confidentiality, and authenticity of smart contract data and both providing on-chain and off-chain components. All three schemes select oracle nodes based on reputation, which can easily lead to Matthew Effect and are prone to collusion and targeted attacks. Aeternity [11] is an open-source, decentralized application platform utilizing public blockchain technology, using Bitcoin-NG as the consensus mechanism to agree on the state of the outside world.

Bitcoin-NG enables high transaction throughput, making Aeternity a viable platform for data-intensive oracles. Nevertheless, adopting the consensus mechanism as the authentication mechanism wastes many resources. ASTRAEA [6] is a decentralized blockchain oracle that runs on the public chain and relies on the voting-based game strategy. ASTREA assumes that all rational players act honestly, analyzes the game-theoretic incentive structure, and proves that an ideal Nash equilibrium exists. However, external data feeds can still break the Nash equilibrium by generating off-chain collusion attacks, and there is still a risk of Sybil attacks. Dos Network [1] is a decentralized oracle service network that supports multiple mainstream public chains, such as Ethereum, EOS, TRON, and Zilliqa. The scheme adopts Verifiable Random Function (VRF) and zero-knowledge proof (zkSNARK) to select working groups safely and randomly. The chosen node obtains the data and uses the threshold signature algorithm to synergistically generate the proof of data integrity.

The above solutions [1,6,11,19,20,22] are decentralized oracle platforms, in which Chainlink and Dos Network provide both on-chain and off-chain components, while others only provide on-chain components. Our scheme, $CCOM$, mainly provides on-chain components and is implemented as lightweight smart contracts. It can resist a single potentially malicious oracle, is more secure than the centralized oracle service, and has no single point of failure. At the same time, compared with the decentralized oracle service, it can save resources and have a lower cost. In short, $CCOM$ balances efficiency and decentralization.

After that, many oracle research schemes realize specific properties, but they are not comprehensive. The PDFS [9] scheme focuses on achieving non-repudiation, the zk-AuthFeed [26] scheme uses zero-knowledge proof to achieve good privacy protection, and GRUB [12] considers the problem of saving gas overhead.

7   Conclusion

Smart contracts are programs that can be executed autonomously on the blockchain. In recent years, research on smart contracts has played an indispensable role in the prosperity and development of the blockchain field. The oracle technology is crucial for solving the need for blockchain and smart contracts to access data about real-world state and events from the outside. This paper proposed a cost-effective and collusion-resistant oracle mechanism $CCOM$, which constructs a prisoner's contract between the clients and oracles, and adopts cryptographic commitment and game theory to resist collusion deception. For rational oracles, always being honest can maximize their benefits. Under the umbrella of our scheme, the malicious behavior of a single oracle service in the case of centralization can be resolved while considering both efficiency and overhead.

Acknowledgements. This work was supported by the National Key R&D Program of China (Grant No. 2020YFB1005900, 2020B0101090002), the National Key R&D Program of Guangdong Province (Grant No. 2020B0101090002), the National Natural Science Foundation of China (Grant No. 62032025, 62071222, U21A201710, U20A201092), and the Natural Science Foundation of Jiangsu Province (Grant No.BK20200418).

References

1. Dos network: a decentralized oracle service boosting blockchain usability with off-chain data & verifiable computing power. https://s3.amazonaws.com/whitepaper.dos/DOS (2019)
2. Ethereum blockchain. https://ethereum.org/en/whitepaper/ (2020)
3. Provable documentation. https://docs.provable.xyz/. January 2020
4. Al Breiki, H., Al Qassem, L., Salah, K., Rehman, M.H.U., Sevtinovic, D.: Decentralized access control for IoT data using blockchain and trusted oracles. In: 2019 IEEE International Conference on Industrial Internet (ICII), pp. 248–257. IEEE (2019)
5. Al-Breiki, H., Rehman, M.H.U., Salah, K., Svetinovic, D.: Trustworthy blockchain oracles: review, comparison, and open research challenges. IEEE Access **8**, 85675–85685 (2020)
6. Berryhill, R., Veneris, A.: Astraea: A decentralized blockchain oracle. IEEE Blockchain Tech. Briefs **2**(2) (2019)
7. Eskandari, S., Clark, J., Sundaresan, V., Adham, M.: On the feasibility of decentralized derivatives markets. In: Brenner, M., et al. (eds.) FC 2017. LNCS, vol. 10323, pp. 553–567. Springer, Cham (2017). https://doi.org/10.1007/978-3-319-70278-0_35
8. Greenspan, G.: Why many smart contract use cases are simply impossible. https://www.coindesk.com/three-smart-contract-misconceptions (2016)
9. Guarnizo, J., Szalachowski, P.: Pdfs: practical data feed service for smart contracts (2018)
10. Heiss, J., Eberhardt, J., Tai, S.: From oracles to trustworthy data on-chaining systems. In: 2019 IEEE International Conference on Blockchain (Blockchain), pp. 496–503. IEEE (2019)
11. Hess, Z., Malahov, Y., Pettersson, J.: Æternity blockchain. https://aeternity.com/aeternity-blockchainwhitepaper.pdf (2017)
12. Li, K., Tang, Y., Chen, J., Yuan, Z., Xu, C., Xu, J.: Cost-effective data feeds to blockchains via workload-adaptive data replication (2019)

13. Mammadzada, K., Iqbal, M., Milani, F., García-Bañuelos, L., Matulevičius, R.: Blockchain oracles: a framework for blockchain-based applications. In: Asatiani, A., et al. (eds.) BPM 2020. LNBIP, vol. 393, pp. 19–34. Springer, Cham (2020). https://doi.org/10.1007/978-3-030-58779-6_2

14. Moudoud, H., Cherkaoui, S., Khoukhi, L.: An IoT blockchain architecture using oracles and smart contracts: the use-case of a food supply chain. In: 2019 IEEE 30th Annual International Symposium on Personal, Indoor and Mobile Radio Communications (PIMRC), pp. 1–6. IEEE (2019)

15. Myerson, R.: Game Theory: Analysis of Conflict. Harvard University Press, Cambridge (1991)

16. Osborne, M.J.: An Introduction to Game Theory. New York vol. 3 (2004)

17. Osborne, M.J., Rubinstein, A.: A Course in Game Theory. MIT Press, Cambridge (1994)

18. Pasdar, A., Dong, Z., Lee, Y.C.: Blockchain oracle design patterns. arXiv preprint arXiv:2106.09349 (2021)

19. de Pedro, A.S., Levi, D., Cuende, L.I.: Witnet: a decentralized oracle network protocol. arXiv preprint arXiv:1711.09756 (2017)

20. Peterson, J., Krug, J., Zoltu, M., Williams, A.K., Alexander, S.: Augur: a decentralized oracle and prediction market platform. arXiv preprint arXiv:1501.01042 (2015)

21. Ritzdorf, H., Wüst, K., Gervais, A., Felley, G., Capkun, S.: Tls-n: non-repudiation over tls enabling-ubiquitous content signing for disintermediation. Cryptology ePrint Archive (2017)

22. Ellis, S., Juels, A., Nazarov, S.: Chainlink: a decentralized oracle network, March 2017

23. Solidity, E.: Solidity documentation (2017)

24. Van Bulck, J., et al.: Foreshadow: extracting the keys to the intel {SGX} kingdom with transient out-of-order execution. In: 27th {USENIX} Security Symposium ({USENIX} Security 18), pp. 991–1008 (2018)

25. Van Mölken, R.: Blockchain across Oracle: Understand the details and Implications of the Blockchain for Oracle Developers and Customers. Packt Publishing Ltd, Birmingham (2018)

26. Wan, Z., Guan, Z., Zhou, Y., Ren, K.: zk-authfeed: how to feed authenticated data into smart contract with zero knowledge. In: 2019 IEEE International Conference on Blockchain (Blockchain) (2019)

27. Weisse, O., et al.: Foreshadow-ng: breaking the virtual memory abstraction with transient out-of-order execution (2018)

28. Xu, X., et al.: The blockchain as a software connector. In: 2016 13th Working IEEE/IFIP Conference on Software Architecture (WICSA), pp. 182–191. IEEE (2016)

29. Xu, X., Weber, I., Staples, M.: Blockchain Patterns. In: Architecture for Blockchain Applications, pp. 113–148. Springer, Cham (2019). https://doi.org/10.1007/978-3-030-03035-3_7

30. Yamashita, K., Nomura, Y., Zhou, E., Pi, B., Jun, S.: Potential risks of hyperledger fabric smart contracts. In: 2019 IEEE International Workshop on Blockchain Oriented Software Engineering (IWBOSE), pp. 1–10. IEEE (2019)

31. Zhang, F., Cecchetti, E., Croman, K., Juels, A., Shi, E.: Town crier: an authenticated data feed for smart contracts. In: Proceedings of the 2016 aCM sIGSAC Conference on Computer and Communications Security, pp. 270–282 (2016)

DeChain: A Blockchain Framework Enhancing Decentralization via Sharding

Shenwei Chen, Zhen Liu$^{(\boxtimes)}$, Yu Long, and Dawu Gu

Shanghai Jiao Tong University, Shanghai, China
{sjtucmcsw1998,liuzhen,dwgu}@sjtu.edu.cn, longyu@cs.sjtu.edu.cn,

Abstract. In a blockchain system, full nodes store all the history data generated by the whole network. As time goes by, the increasing data will place a heavy burden on the full nodes. Rational nodes may discard history data, which results in the decrease of the number of full nodes. Moreover, huge storage requirement prevents storage-constrained users from participating in the network. These factors weaken decentralization and are harmful to the whole blockchain network. In this paper, we propose a new shard-based blockchain framework called DeChain which distributes the blockchain database into different nodes in protocol level. Specifically, we design a new mechanism to shard the UTXOs into specific nodes and set special rules for transaction generation. Each node in DeChain is in charge of the verification of some specified transactions. We propose an RSA accumulator-based method to support inter-shards verification of transactions. With this framework, users can participate in the consensus of the whole network by only maintaining a small portion of blockchain database. This greatly reduces the storage burden and enhances the decentralization of blockchain network.

Keywords: Blockchain · Sharding · Decentralization · Data management

1 Introduction

Since Bitcoin [25] was introduced in 2008, blockchain technology has become a promising tool to build trust in digital world. Its success depends on the feature of decentralization, which means no centralized entity is in charge of the authenticity of the data but each participant works together to build consensus. Blockchain technology has shown its success in building digital currency in the past decade. Combining with other technology, it also enables smart contract (Ethereum [27]), anonymous transactions (Monero [22]) and other applications.

However, a great challenge faced by blockchain systems in real world is the storage problem. Without a centralized entity, the data generated by the blockchain network should be stored in each node. This design intends to enhance decentralization originally, but shows its drawback in long run. For a full node in a blockchain system, the storage it needs to store the whole history data becomes

© The Author(s), under exclusive license to Springer Nature Switzerland AG 2022
K. Nguyen et al. (Eds.): ACISP 2022, LNCS 13494, pp. 469–488, 2022.
https://doi.org/10.1007/978-3-031-22301-3_23

larger and larger as time goes by. Currently (January, 2022), it takes over 380 gigabytes [3] to run a Bitcoin full node. Things are even worse for Ethereum, which takes over 500 gigabytes [27] to run an already pruned full node, let alone archive node which records all the history data.

Some solutions have been proposed to conquer the storage problem, including light client, block pruning, stateless blockchain and so on. However, these solutions do not consider the importance of decentralization and may do harm to overall health of the whole network. Specifically, light clients [7,16,25] only validate the workload of main chain and store block headers in their database. They should rely on full nodes to verify transactions and cannot provide concrete data for other nodes. Lacking the ability to verify transactions independently, light clients cannot participate in the consensus since they cannot include transactions into blocks. Hence, light client is only a tool for accessing blockchain network but do not contribute to the whole network. Data pruning approach [10,15,20] aims at getting rid of a part of the history data. This can be achieved by techniques like checkpoint, snapshot or cryptographic aggregation function. However, this may cause permanent loss of some history data. Recently, the concept of stateless blockchain [6,9,11] is proposed. In a stateless blockchain, the state of the current network, for example, unspent transaction outputs (UTXOs) are compressed into a short commitment. The validator or the miner only needs to store the block header (including the commitment) and there is no need to store concrete transaction data. When issuing a transaction, the transaction proposer should send the transaction along with its witness to prove its validity. The witness is usually very large because it should contain the original transactions referenced by the inputs and proof of existence in the commitment. This greatly inflates the size of transaction and puts a heavy burden on transaction proposer. Although these three approaches indeed reduce the storage requirements for participating in the blockchain network while guaranteeing safety, they ignore the fact that the existence of full nodes is still necessary. With these approaches, rational nodes tend not to store all the data because it does not affect their ability to verify the transactions and generate the block. Hence, the number of full nodes will decrease, which leads to difficulty in obtaining history data and weakens the decentralization.

In this paper, we aim at achieving the balance between storage usage and decentralization, which means reducing the storage usage of a participating node as well as maintaining enough copies of full blockchain data. The basic idea is natural: since history data is valuable but full blockchain data is too large for a node, we can split these data and distribute it to different nodes. To achieve this goal, we need to handle two challenges: how to split the data reasonably and how to ensure the nodes' ability to verify transactions and propose blocks. To address these challenges, we propose a new shard-based blockchain framework called DeChain which can reduce storage of a single node as well as maintain the ability of transaction verification and block proposing. We achieve this goal in protocol level. Specifically, our contributions are summarized as follows:

1. We propose a blockchain framework called DeChain which classifies participating nodes into different shards and distributes the whole blockchain database to them. We design a reasonable data splitting method based on UTXO hash. Each shard is only in charge of a small portion of data and maintaining a part of UTXO pool.
2. According to the shard-based structure, we design a special rule for transactions in DeChain. We add restrictions to the inputs of a transaction. Therefore, a transaction will belong to a specific shard and can be correctly verified by shard members.
3. We propose an RSA accumulator-based method to handle the inter-shards transaction verification. Inter-shards transaction verification is crucial since a node should verify the blocks proposed in other shards.

The rest of the paper is organized as follows. We review some related work and introduce some background knowledge in Sect. 2. In Sect. 3, we present the overview of the whole framework and crucial concepts in DeChain. The detailed operations of DeChain is shown in Sect. 4. In Sect. 5, we make some theoretical analysis and simulation experiments. Finally, some discussions and conclusion are given in Sect. 6 and Sect. 7.

2   Background and Related Work

2.1   Sharding

Sharding in blockchain is originally proposed to overcome the scalability and performance problem. By dividing all the nodes in the network into different shards, each shard can verify transactions and propose blocks in parallel, thus elevating the throughput of the whole network. In blockchain sharding, how to split the nodes and how to deal with intra-shard and inter-shards verification are big challenges.

Some blockchain sharding protocols [17,19,29] adopt Byzantine agreement-based designs. In these sharding approaches, nodes are pre-assigned to specific shards and a leader shard or an atomic commit scheme should be used to deal with inter-shards verification. In comparison, our work is simpler and does not involve pre-assignment and complex inter-shards verification. Nodes are free to join any shards and can still verify transactions and blocks relatively independently. Yu et al. [28] propose a protocol called OHIE, which composes parallel instances of Nakamoto consensus securely. However, it only focuses on scalability issue and the node still needs to store all the blockchain data. Our work also adopt the design of parallel chains but the node only needs to store a part of blockchain data. We borrow the concept of sharding and design a reasonable method to distribute data to different nodes, which alleviates the storage burden of a single node and enhances decentralization of blockchain network.

2.2   Aggregating TXOs

Aggregating TXOs (transaction outputs), which was first mentioned in Bitcoin Forum [1], is a good idea to implement light nodes in a blockchain system. By compressing TXO state into a short field called TXO root and adding it into block header, a node can quickly acquire the latest state of the blockchain. This is also the core technique of stateless blockchain [26]. To aggregate TXOs, how to effectively organize the TXOs is a big challenge.

Different data structures have been proposed to aggregate TXOs. Chepurnoy et al. [11] propose a stateless blockchain using sparse Merkle tree [12] to aggregating UTXOs. However, it requires complex pruning technique to correctly store the sparse Merkle tree, which is hard to implement in real world. Dryja [13] proposes a Merkle tree forest to organize UTXOs (unspent TXOs) and aggregates the roots of forest to compress state. However, adding and deleting UTXOs need recomputing of the tree and are very inefficient. Zhang et al. [30] adopt balanced binary tree to aggregate UTXOs, which is also inefficient and impractical because of expensive cost in adding and deleting UTXOs from tree. In comparison, we use RSA accumulator to aggregate TXOs and do not involve inefficient deleting operation in our design. Chen and Wang [9] propose miniChain, which also utilizes RSA accumulator to store spent transaction outputs. This work does alleviate the storage burden of a single node but places great burden on transaction proposers because they should store and update their transaction proof frequently. Our work does not put heavy burden on transaction proposers. Moreover, we introduce RSA accumulator into sharding to handle the inter-shards verification.

2.3   Cryptographic Accumulator

Cryptographic accumulator [2] is a technique that can combine a group of elements into a short commitment. A prover can generate a membership or nonmembership proof for an element. Then the validator can validate whether the element is included in the commitment or not with the proof.

Cryptographic accumulator can be divided into static accumulator and dynamic accumulator. In a static accumulator, if the element in the set changes, the commitment and membership proof should be computed again and cannot be updated efficiently. Merkle tree [21] is a kind of static accumulator, which can accumulate all the elements into a constant-sized Merkle root. The membership proof is the Merkle path. However, the Merkle root and the membership proof cannot be updated efficiently since adding or removing an element will result in recalculation of the whole tree. This is unsatisfactory when the number of elements is very large. Hence, few systems aggregate the UTXO set into a single commitment using Merkle Tree.

In contrast, the update efficiency of dynamic accumulator will not be affected by the number of elements in the set. In this paper, we use a dynamic accumulator called RSA accumulator, which is constructed based on strong RSA assumption. It supports both membership proof and nonmembership proof. Specifically, the elements in RSA accumulator should be prime numbers to avoid collision.

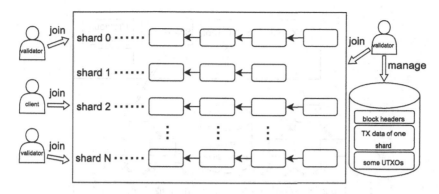

Fig. 1. DeChain architecture

However, a universal RSA accumulator [8,18] does not meet the requirement in public blockchain since it needs trusted setup. Hence, we use RSA accumulator described in Boneh's work [5]. Boneh's RSA accumulator supports batch membership and nonmembership proof and does not need trusted setup. Boneh's work also discusses the application of RSA accumulator in blockchain, namely aggregating UTXOs by RSA accumulator. However, deleting UTXOs from the accumulator is still inefficient. In contrast, our work avoids this expensive delete operation and only uses the efficient update operation of RSA accumulator.

3   Framework of DeChain

In this section, we present the overview of DeChain and introduce some important concepts used in DeChain. The terms "node" or "validator" mean a normal node which participates in the consensus of the blockchain network. We assume each "node" is equal in status. We adopt PoW (Proof of Work) as our consensus mechanism. Hence, a "node" will invest in computing power to propose blocks and earn reward in the network. The term "client" means a node which issues transactions. It does not participate in the consensus of the network. Of course, a user usually acts as "node" and "client" at the same time. However, a client does not need to store large amounts of data to issue transactions. It only needs to know its UTXOs to issue transactions using a light client or relying on other nodes, which is out of scope of this paper.

3.1   Design Principles

The design of DeChain needs to meet the following principles.

- Reasonable work division: We observe the fact that to ensure the overall health of the whole blockchain network, nodes should be responsible for the work of storing the blockchain database since they participate in the consensus and earn reward. Clients do not need to undertake this work and can send transactions without concrete data on the chain.

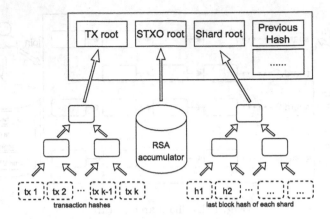

Fig. 2. Block header of DeChain

- Relatively low storage: The storage usage of a single node should be relatively low and the network should operate normally even if there is no full node in the network. This requires us to design a feasible data distribution scheme.
- Complete verification ability: Nodes should still be able to verify transactions and blocks even if they only maintain a small part of blockchain data.

3.2   Architecture

Figure 1 shows the architecture of DeChain. The whole network is split into N shards and there exists an independent blockchain in each shard. The node and the client participate in the network by joining one (or more) shard. Which shard to join is up to node itself. The node collects transactions and proposes blocks independently on its chain and takes the responsibility of managing a part of data, including the block headers of all shards, concrete block data of its shard and a part of UTXOs. If a node or a client join shard n, we say it belongs to shard n.

3.3   Block

A block in DeChain is composed of the block header and concrete transaction data included in the block. The structure of DeChain block header is shown in Fig. 2. It needs to contain the following fields,

- **TX root** is the Merkle tree root of transaction hashes in this shard. We denote this field as $txRoot$.
- **STXO root** is the RSA accumulate value of all spent transaction outputs (STXOs) of this shard. We denote this field as $stxoRoot$.
- **Shard root** is the Merkle tree root of the last block hash of each shard. We denote this field as $shardRoot$.

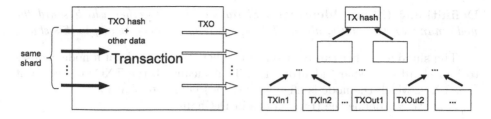

Fig. 3. DeChain transaction

- **Previous hash** is the hash of the previous block of this shard. We denote this field as *previousHash*.

These are the most important fields in DeChain. Other fields such as timestamp, difficulty are omitted here.

3.4 Transaction

The structure of a transaction in DeChain is shown in Fig. 3. Each transaction in DeChain can be represented as several inputs and outputs. The input is a TXO hash and other data (e.g. witness, signature).

Definition 1 (TXO hash). *TXO hash is the hash value of the content of a transaction output. It is a unique identifier of a TXO.*

Generally, the information in a TXO contains output information like receiver, amount, locking script and so on. We add a new field **salt** in TXO. This is used to generate specific TXO hash later. To simplify the model, we suppose **salt** is a 32-bit value. Hence, TXO hash can be calculated by

$$TXOhash = H(outputInformation\|salt) \tag{1}$$

where $H(x)$ is a secure cryptography hash function. In addition, we stipulate that all the TXO hashes in DeChain should be prime numbers in order to support RSA accumulator. We will explain it in detail in the following section.

Since our design requires nodes to manage different shard of UTXOs, we utilize a simple method to classify them, namely by taking the remainder of TXO hash. Suppose there are N shards in total and h is the TXO hash. Remember that all the TXO hash should be prime numbers (also odd numbers).

Definition 2 (TXO Classification). *To which shard the TXO belongs can be calculated by*

$$CalculateShard(h, N) = \frac{h-1}{2} \bmod N. \tag{2}$$

Based on the TXO classification, we define the shard identifier.

Definition 3 (Shard Identifier). *Shard identifier specifies which shard the node manages. Generally, all the TXOs owned by the node belong to this shard.*

The shard identifier can be a single number. For example, if a node chooses to join shard i, its shard identifier is i. That means all the TXOs owned by it (i.e. TXOs which the node is eligible to spend) belong to shard i.

Now we can define the transactions in DeChain.

Definition 4 (Transaction). *A valid transaction in DeChain consumes several UTXOs generated before as inputs and generate some new UTXOs as outputs. Moreover, the consumed UTXOs should belong to the same shard. The transaction hash in DeChain is the root hash of Merkle tree whose leaves are hashes of inputs and hashes of outputs of the transaction.*

We require the consumed UTXOs of a transaction in DeChain should belong to the same shard. That means only TXOs belong to the same shard can be used as inputs together to form a transaction, which is the reason why we say all the TXOs owned by a node should belong to the same shard. In addition, if all input TXOs of a transaction belong to shard i, we say this transaction belongs to shard i. That means this transaction will be verified and included in the blocks by nodes in shard i.

Moreover, the transaction hash in DeChain is not computed simply by hashing the transaction data. Instead, the transaction hash is the root hash of Merkle tree whose leaves are TXO hashes consumed in inputs and TXO hashes of outputs of the transaction, which is shown in Fig. 3. The advantage is that we can simply prove some specific inputs or outputs belong to a transaction by providing Merkle path.

4   System Details

In this section we introduce detailed operations of DeChain, including the transaction generation and propagation, inter-shards proof generation and verification. To simplify the notation, block m means the mth block of one shard. We omit the shard number here.

4.1   Setup

Once a node connects with a new node, the first thing it should do is to exchange the shard identifier with new node. This process allows nodes to have a knowledge of what shard their peers belong to, which will affect the following behavior.

4.2   Transaction Generation

In the above section, we mention that each TXO hash should be a prime number. This is because we will add it into RSA accumulator later and the elements in RSA accumulator should be prime. While the output of hash function is almost

---

Algorithm 1: Transaction Generation

Input: Consumed UTXO hash set $U = \{u_1, u_2, ...\}$, transaction output
    information set $O = \{o_i, o_2, ..., o_n\}$, payee shard identifier set
    $S = \{s_1, s_2, ..., s_n\}$, number of shard N
Output: Generated transaction tx
    `// setup inputs (e.g. add signature to consumed UTXOs)`
1 $Inputs = SetupInputs(U)$
    `// setup outputs`
2 $Outputs = \{\}$
3 **for** *each o in O* **do**
4     $salt = 0$
5   **while** *true* **do**
6         $h = Hash(o\|salt)$
7   **if** $CalculateShard(h, N) = s$ *and* $IsPrime(h)$ **then**
            `// find TXO that satisfies the requirement`
8   break
9         $salt = salt + 1$
10    $txo = [o, salt]$
11    $Outputs = Outputs \cup \{txo\}$
12 $tx = (Inputs, Outputs)$

---

uniform, we can iterate over the input until we find an output that satisfies our requirement (namely prime number).

Of course we can remove this restriction of TXO hash and transfer this procedure to validators (e.g. the validator first converts the TXO hash to prime number using a deterministic hash to prime function [14] and then adds it to the RSA accumulator). However, generating a prime number takes too much time and all the validators need to repeat this procedure. This is unsatisfactory since long validation time will damage the synchronization of the whole network. Hence, we let transaction proposer finish this time-consuming procedure when generating the transaction since transaction generation is not a frequent thing. Then the validator only needs to test if the TXO hash is a prime or not without wasting time generating a prime number. To judge if a large number is a prime number or not, we can use probabilistic algorithms such as Miller-Rabin primality test [24].

The transaction generation algorithm is shown in Algorithm 1. Suppose Alice wants to send some coins to Bob. She should first know which shard Bob belongs to and iterate over salt to find one that make the corresponding TXO hash belong to this shard.

It should be noticed that this iteration process may cause the collision of TXO hash (i.e. two TXOs have the same hash value, mostly due to same input). This can be avoided by adding more randomness into the TXO (e.g. add current timestamp into TXO). Then because of the collision resistance property of secure hash function, the probability of collision is negligible with different inputs. Even if it does happen, we can still avoid it in the consensus layer of blockchain. That means if transaction proposer finds a hash value which collides with a previous one, he should generate the TXO again. Otherwise, this transaction will be rejected by the network.

The Number of Iterations Needed to Generate a TXO that Satisfies the Requirement: Randomly pick a positive integer that is not larger than M, the probability that it is a prime number is about $\frac{1}{\ln M}$ (Prime number theorem [23]). Suppose there are N shards in total. Since the outputs of hash function are distributed uniformly, the probability that finding a TXO that satisfies the requirement with x times of iterations is about

$$1 - \left(1 - \frac{1}{N \ln M}\right)^x. \tag{3}$$

For SHA-256 and 64 shards, the probability of finding a TXO that satisfies the requirement with 100000 iterations is larger than 99.98%, which is acceptable. We should notice that the distribution of prime numbers is not uniform. However, this distribution is hard to describe, so we only calculate the average probability above. With enough iterations, a TXO that satisfies the requirement will be found eventually.

4.3   Transaction Propagation

Each node is in charge of storing UTXOs belong to its shard. To be specific, a node in shard k will maintain a UTXO pool of UTXOs belong to shard k. Then it can simply decide if a TXO belongs to shard k exists or not and verify the transaction inputs. Hence, the node can verify transactions belong to shard k independently without the help of other nodes from other shards.

The transaction proposer creates transaction and propagates it to the network. When other nodes receive the transaction, they should first check its basic integrity, namely

– whether all the consumed UTXO hashes belong to the same shard,
– whether all the consumed UTXO hashes are prime numbers,
– whether all the TXO hashes of transaction outputs are prime numbers.

If the transaction does not meet the above requirements, it will be discarded. Then the nodes' behaviors vary depending on the shard which they manage. If the transaction does not belong to the shard managed by the node, which means that the node cannot further check the validity of the transaction since it does not have the concrete data, the node just propagates it to peer nodes.

If the transaction belongs to the shard managed by the node, the node will check

– whether the consumed UTXOs exist in UTXO pool,
– authentication and authorization of the transaction.

If the transaction passes all the checks, it will be put into transaction candidate pool and may be included in the block later. Finally, the node will propagate this transaction to its peer nodes.

4.4   Update and Verification of STXO Root

When generating blocks, a node needs to correctly update the STXO root, this is achieved by adding all STXO hashes into the STXO root of the previous block. Then the verifier, namely other node, needs to check if the STXO root has been updated correctly or not. Verifying the TXO root is a time-consuming task because the value added to accumulator is very large, which can be accelerated by NI-PoE (Non-Interactive Proof of Exponentiation) [4]. Suppose a prover wants to convince a verifier $w = u^x$ where $w, u \in \mathbb{G}$, $x \in \mathbb{Z}$. The algorithms of NI-PoE prove and verify are shown in Algorithm 2. The algorithms hold because $Q^l u^r = ((u^q)^l u^r) = u^{ql+r} = u^x$.

Algorithm 2: NI-PoE (Non-Interactive Proof of Exponentiation)

    // $w, u \in \mathbb{G}$, $x \in \mathbb{Z}$, Claim $w = u^x$
    // $H_{prime}()$ is a hash-to-prime function
1 **Function** NI-PoE-Prove(x, u, w):
2      $l = H_{prime}(x, u, w)$
3      $q = \lfloor x/l \rfloor$
4      $Q = u^q$
5   **return** Q

6
7 **Function** NI-PoE-Verify(x, u, w, Q):
8      $l = H_{prime}(x, u, w)$
9      $r = x \bmod l$
10   **return** $Q^l u^r \overset{?}{=} w$

The algorithms of update and verification of STXO root are shown in Algorithm 3 and 4. The prover adds all the consumed UTXO hashes of this block into the STXO root of previous block and generates a proof using NI-PoE. This proof is also broadcast with the new block. Then the verifier can check the correctness of new STXO root in a short time.

Algorithm 3: STXO Root Update

    Input: Consumed UTXO hash set H, old STXO root A_m
    Output: New STXO root A_{m+1}, Proof Q
1 $x = 1$
2 **for** *each h in H* **do**
3      $x* = h$
4 $A_{m+1} = A_m^x$
5 $Q =$NI-PoE-Prove(x, A_m, A_{m+1})

Algorithm 4: STXO Root Verification

Input: Consumed UTXO hash set H, old STXO root A_m, new STXO root
A_{m+1}, Proof Q
Output: true/false

1 $x = 1$
2 **for** *each h in H* **do**
3 $\quad \lfloor\ x* = h$
4 return NI-PoE-Verify(x, A_m, A_{m+1}, Q)

4.5   Proof of Transaction Validity

For a new block belongs to shard i, if the node also manages this shard, it can quickly verify the transactions included in it. This is because it has the concrete data of this shard and can check the existence of TXOs, authorization and authentication of the transactions and so on.

However, for a node that does not belong to this shard, the validity of the transactions cannot be checked directly since the node only has block header of other shards. To make other nodes believe the transactions are valid, the block proposer needs to provide proof of transaction validity. This means the inputs of transactions exist and have not been spent before.

We mentioned in Sect. 3.4 that the transaction hash is computed by building a Merkle tree with all inputs and outputs. Hence, the existence of a transaction input is easy to prove by providing the Merkle path from the transaction input to the transaction hash and the Merkle path from the transaction hash to TX root of block header.

In comparison, proving a specific TXO has not been spent before is not that easy. Remember there is a field called STXO root in block header, which is the accumulate value of all STXOs before. The block proposer can generate a batch nonmembership proof for all consumed TXOs with the help of RSA accumulator. The algorithms of batch nonmembership proof generation and verification in DeChain are shown in Algorithm 5 and 6. Bezout(x, y) means calculating a, b which satisfy $ax + by = 1$ using extended Euclidean algorithm.

Algorithm 5: Batch Nonmembership Proof Generation

Input: STXO root A_m, A_n, STXO hash set $H_{m:n}$ spent between block m and
block n, the hash set X of TXOs which need to be proved
Output: Nonmembership proof u_x for all elements in X

1 $x^* = \prod_{x \in X} x$
2 $h^* = \prod_{h \in H_{m:n}} h$
3 $(a, b) =$ Bezout(h^*, x^*)
4 $B = A_m^b$
5 $u_x = (a, B)$

Algorithm 6: Batch Nonmembership Proof Verification

Input: STXO root A_m,A_n, nonmembership proof $u_x = (a, B)$, the hash set X
of TXOs which need to be proved

Output: true/false

1 $x^* = \prod_{x \in X} x$

2 return $A_n^a B^{x^*} \stackrel{?}{=} A_m$

The block proposer generates the nonmembership proof for consumed TXOs included in his block. A_m is the STXO root of the block that generated the earliest TXO included in the transaction inputs of new block and A_n is the TXO root of previous block. With this proof, other nodes can ensure the inputs of transactions have not been spent before. The algorithms hold because $A_n^a B^{x^*} = (A_m^{h^*})^a (A_m^b)^{x^*} = A_m^{ah^* + bx^*} = A_m$.

The proof size $|a| \approx |x^*|$ and B is a group element, which is acceptable. However, the time complexity of nonmembership proof generation is about $O(N)$, where N is the number of STXOs between block m and block n, which is not satisfactory when N is very large. If a TXO that is consumed in a transaction was generated a long time ago, it may take too much time to generate the nonmembership proof. Suppose each block consumes 50 TXOs and a transaction included in the new block consumes a TXO that was generated 2000 blocks prior to the latest block, it is estimated that the generate time will exceed 10 minutes. One solution is to maintain the nonmembership proof of those old TXOs and update them periodically. The update algorithm is shown in Algorithm 7. This means generating separate nonmembership proof for it and batch nonmembership proof for others. The time to update nonmembership proof is acceptable compared to the time interval between blocks. Once the nonmembership proof of a transaction is ready, the transaction can be included in new block. The node can also cache the product of previous STXO hashes periodically to accelerate computing. Another solution is to resort to a service provider to provide nonmemebership proof for those TXOs.

Algorithm 7: Nonmembership Proof Update

Input: STXO root A_n of last update, old proof $u_x = (a, B)$, latest STXO root A_k, STXO hash set $H_{n:k}$ spent between block n and block k, TXO hash x which needs to be proved

Output: New nonmembership proof u'_x for x

1 $h^* = \prod_{h \in H_{m:n}} h$

2 $(a', b') = \text{Bezout}(h^*, x)$

3 $r = b'a$

4 return $u'_x = (a'a, BA_n^r)$

4.6   Block Generation and Validation

The process of block generation includes collecting transactions and constructing block that meets the requirement of becoming a leader. Since we adopt PoW as the consensus protocol, block generation can also be referred to as mining, which means that each node invests computing power to "mine" a solution of a puzzle (e.g. Hash function).

To generate a block, a block proposer should first correctly fill in the fields of block header, which we have introduced in Sect. 3.3. The TX root and shard root are easy to construct by building Merkle trees with all transaction hashes and all the last block hashes of shards. For STXO root, algorithms introduced in Sect. 4.4 are used. Moreover, the existence of UTXOs should also be proved. This is done by providing the Merkle path of each UTXO and a batch nonmembership witness computed by algorithm introduced in Sect. 4.5. These proofs will be broadcast with the block later.

Once a node mines a new block, it will broadcast it to the whole network. Other nodes need to validate the block before they insert it into their database. Nodes which manage different shards will behave differently when validating a new block.

To validate a block, these components should be checked:

- Whether each transactions included in the block belong to the same shard.
- Whether each TXO of the transactions included in the block has not been spent before.
- Whether the transactions included in the block are valid. This includes checking the authentication and authorization of each transaction.
- Whether the STXO root is correctly updated.
- Other checks (e.g. whether the Merkle root of transactions matches the TX root, whether the difficulty meets the requirement).

Verifying whether a TXO has been spent or not is easy for a node which belongs to the same shard as the block since the node maintains an UTXO pool of this shard. It only needs to check if the TXO is in the pool or not. However, it does not work for nodes belong to other shards since these TXOs are not in their UTXO pool. Remember that existence proof (Merkle path from TXO to TX root) and unspent proof (nonmembership witness) are also broadcast with the new block. Hence, for a node belongs to other shard, it can ensure TXOs consumed in a block exist and have not been spent before using these proof.

After validating a block, the node will search for TXOs that belong to its shard in each transaction and then add them into its UTXO pool. Then it will insert the whole block into its database if this block belongs to its shard. Otherwise, it only needs to store block header and can discard all the concrete transaction data.

5 Analysis and Simulation

5.1 Experiment Setup

The block and transaction data used in our simulation experiments is from Bitcoin. We extract the meta data of Bitcoin from block 0 (genesis block) to block 720000 (2022/1), including block size, transaction count, the number of inputs and outputs of each transaction. We run our experiments on Ubuntu 20.02 with Intel i5-11600KF and 16 GB RAM.

5.2 Storage Usage

The storage usage of a DeChain node is composed of two parts: block headers and transaction data (transaction data of a shard and UTXOs belong to this shard). Compared with Bitcoin, the block header of DeChain has two additional fields, STXO root and Shard root, which are 32 bytes for each. Then the block header is 144 bytes. In addition, the transaction output contains a new field called salt. Suppose salt is a 32-bit value.

We simulate the operation of DeChain and evaluate its storage usage using the real data from Bitcoin. Suppose there are 64 shards in DeChain and the transactions are randomly distributed to each shard. The block generation speed of each shard is the same as that of Bitcoin. That means the throughput is also the same as that of Bitcoin. The storage usage growth of a DeChain node and a Bitcoin node is shown in Fig. 4.

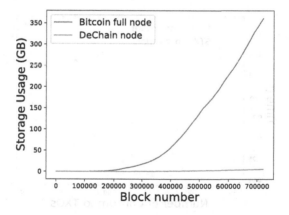

Fig. 4. Storage usage

The results show that with the same number of blocks generated (and the same throughput), a DeChain node consumes much lower storage space (about 7 GB) comparing to a Bitcoin full node (about 360 GB). The reason is that the whole database of DeChain is distributed in different nodes and a single node only needs to store concrete data of one shard. We can also find that the storage consumed is a little larger than 360/64, which is because besides concrete transaction data of one shard, some additional data is also needed (salt, block headers of other shards, concrete TXO data that belongs to this shard but is generated by transactions of other shards).

5.3 Efficiency

The efficiency of proof generation and verification will affect the network performance. Hence, we test the efficiency of the algorithms used in DeChain to show the feasibility. Suppose the RSA accumulator has 2048 bit-modulus and the length of TXO hash is 256-bit (SHA-256 function). We run each test for 100 times and take the average for each data point.

Update and Verification of STXO Root. We first test the performance of updating and verifying the STXO root. The result is shown in Fig. 5. We can find that as the number of consumed TXO grows, the time of update and verification grow linearly. Verification is much faster than update, which is because NI-PoE greatly reduces the number of group operations. From the real transaction data of Bitcoin, we can obtain that the average number of transactions in each block is about 980 and the average number of inputs (consumed TXOs) is about 3. Hence, to achieve the same throughput with Bitcoin, for a block in DeChain with 64 shards, the average number of consumed UTXOs in a block is about $980 * 3/64 \approx 46$. That is about 0.25s to update the STXO root and 0.02s to verify the proof, which is acceptable.

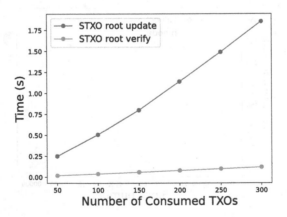

Fig. 5. Update and verification of STXO root

Update and Verification of Nonmembership Proof. The performance of updating and verifying nonmembership proof is also important. The time to generate the batch nonmembership proof is hard to test because it depends on the earliest TXO consumed in the block. Hence, we assume that nonmembership proof will be updated periodically and only test the efficiency of update and verification. Suppose 50 TXOs are consumed in new block. The result is shown in Fig. 6. We can find that the time of update grows linearly with the number of STXOs accumulated (i.e. the number of STXOs since last update). If each block consumes 50 TXOs, it takes about 6s to update the proof every 20 blocks. The time of verification is stable because it only depends on the number of TXOs consumed in new block.

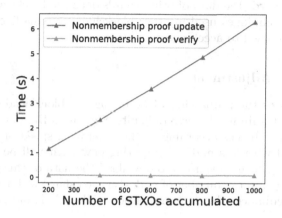

Fig. 6. Update and verification of nonmembership proof

6   Discussion

6.1   Bridge Transaction

Usually, all the UTXOs owned by a user belong to the same shard, which are easy to form a valid transaction. However, in some special cases (e.g. two wallets merge into one wallet and these wallets are from different shards A and B), we can not use these UTXOs in a single transaction. The solution is simple. We can create a special transaction called bridge transaction that consumes all the UTXOs from shard A and generates a new UTXO which belongs to shard B.

6.2   Shard Choice

We have mentioned above that which shard to join is up to node itself. Usually a node will join one shard in default. Of course it can join two or more shards in order to collect more transactions and mine on a shard that has the most transaction fee. It can even choose to become a full node (i.e. store the data of all shards) if it is willing to. In fact, full node is not necessarily needed in DeChain. All nodes can still verify the validity of the blocks by only maintaining a small portion of the whole database. This lowers the threshold for a new node to participate in the network.

6.3   Synchronization

When a new node joins the network, it needs to keep in sync with other nodes. This requires the node to download and verify the data starting from the genesis block from other nodes and obtain the current UTXO pool. Since the whole database is distributed in different nodes, we can download the data of each shard in parallel from multiple nodes. A node only needs to store the data of its shard and discards the data of other shards once the blocks are validated. In addition, some techniques used in other blockchain systems like checkpoints or snapshots can be used to accelerate this process.

6.4   Difficulty Adjustment

Difficulty indicates the probability of becoming the block leader. Each shard's blockchain in DeChain has its own difficulty. Similar to Bitcoin, the difficulty is adjusted every few blocks according to the generation speed of last few blocks. Hence, for shard with less nodes (computing power), it will be easier to find a valid block. This encourages users to download the data of this shard and mine on it. In the long run, the number of nodes on each shard will maintain dynamic balance, which enhances the decentralization of the whole blockchain network.

6.5   Bandwidth Management

According to our framework, we propose two optimization methods to reduce bandwidth usage.

Transaction Cache. When a node receives a transaction from others, it can store this transaction temporarily (and set an expire time). Later when a new block is mined, the block proposer only needs to propagate the block headers as well as all transactions hashes included in the block. If the network is well-connected, these transactions must have already been propagated to all nodes. Thus there is no need to transmit the transactions again. If some transactions are missing, the node can ask peer nodes for them.

Transmission on Demand. According to DeChain framework, a node will store three parts of data: (1) all the block headers, (2) transactions belong to its shard and (3) UTXOs belong to its shard (UTXO pool). Remember that a transaction input only contains a TXO hash which refers to previous UTXO. Some nodes may not store the concrete data of this UTXO. Hence, apart from block headers and transaction hashes, the details of this UTXO should also be transmitted. However, there is no need to transmit this data to two kinds of nodes: (1) the nodes which belong to the same shard as the block and (2) the nodes which belong to the same shard as the transaction that generates this UTXO. Thus we can transmit the UTXO data on demand according to the shard identifier of the peer nodes. This method can also save the bandwidth.

7   Conclusion

In this paper, we propose DeChain, a shard-based blockchain framework to reduce the storage usage for a participating node. We introduce a reasonable data splitting method, accompanied by a special transaction generation rule. An RSA accumulator-based method is used to prove the existence of inter-shards UTXOs. With these techniques, each node in DeChain only needs to keep a small portion of blockchain data while still having the ability to verify transactions and blocks and also propose blocks. This lowers the storage requirement for participating in the consensus and encourages more users to join the network, thus enhancing the decentralization. The analysis and simulation experiments show the feasibility of our framework.

Acknowledgements. We would like to thank all the anonymous reviewers for their constructive and detailed comments. This work was supported by the National Natural Science Foundation of China (No. 62072305), the Key (Keygrant) Project of Chinese Ministry of Education (No. 2020KJ010201), and the Key Research and Development Plan of Shandong Province (No. 2021CXGC010105).

References

1. Ultimate blockchain compression. https://bitcointalk.org/index.php?topic=88208
2. Benaloh, J., de Mare, M.: One-way accumulators: a decentralized alternative to digital signatures. In: Helleseth, T. (ed.) EUROCRYPT 1993. LNCS, vol. 765, pp. 274–285. Springer, Heidelberg (1994). https://doi.org/10.1007/3-540-48285-7_24
3. Blockchain charts: Bitcoin block size. https://blockchain.info/charts/blocks-size/
4. Boneh, D., Bonneau, J., Bünz, B., Fisch, B.: Verifiable delay functions. In: Shacham, H., Boldyreva, A. (eds.) CRYPTO 2018. LNCS, vol. 10991, pp. 757–788. Springer, Cham (2018). https://doi.org/10.1007/978-3-319-96884-1_25
5. Boneh, D., Bünz, B., Fisch, B.: Batching techniques for accumulators with applications to IOPs and stateless blockchains. In: Boldyreva, A., Micciancio, D. (eds.) CRYPTO 2019. LNCS, vol. 11692, pp. 561–586. Springer, Cham (2019). https://doi.org/10.1007/978-3-030-26948-7_20
6. Bonneau, J., Meckler, I., Rao, V., Shapiro, E.: Coda: decentralized cryptocurrency at scale. IACR Cryptol. ePrint Arch. p. 352 (2020)
7. Bünz, B., Kiffer, L., Luu, L., Zamani, M.: Flyclient: super-light clients for cryptocurrencies. In: IEEE Symposium on Security and Privacy, SP. pp. 928–946. IEEE (2020)
8. Camenisch, J., Lysyanskaya, A.: Dynamic accumulators and application to efficient revocation of anonymous credentials. In: Yung, M. (ed.) CRYPTO 2002. LNCS, vol. 2442, pp. 61–76. Springer, Heidelberg (2002). https://doi.org/10.1007/3-540-45708-9_5
9. Chen, H., Wang, Y.: Minichain: a lightweight protocol to combat the UTXO growth in public blockchain. J. Parall. Distrib. Comput. **143**, 67–76 (2020)
10. Chepurnoy, A., Larangeira, M., Ojiganov, A.: Rollerchain, a blockchain with safely pruneable full blocks (2016)
11. Chepurnoy, A., Papamanthou, C., Zhang, Y.: Edrax: a cryptocurrency with stateless transaction validation. IACR Cryptol. ePrint Arch, p. 968 (2018)

12. Dahlberg, R., Pulls, T., Peeters, R.: Efficient sparse merkle trees - caching strategies and secure (non-)membership proofs. In: Secure IT Systems - 21st Nordic Conference, vol. 10014, pp. 199–215 (2016)

13. Dryja, T.: Utreexo: a dynamic hash-based accumulator optimized for the bitcoin UTXO set. IACR Cryptol. ePrint Arch, p. 611 (2019)

14. Fouque, P., Tibouchi, M.: Close to uniform prime number generation with fewer random bits. IEEE Trans. Inf. Theory **65**(2), 1307–1317 (2019)

15. Bruce, J.D.: The mini-blockchain scheme (2014). http://cryptonite.info/files/mbc-scheme-rev3.pdf

16. Kiayias, A., Miller, A., Zindros, D.: Non-interactive proofs of proof-of-work. In: Bonneau, J., Heninger, N. (eds.) FC 2020. LNCS, vol. 12059, pp. 505–522. Springer, Cham (2020). https://doi.org/10.1007/978-3-030-51280-4_27

17. Kokoris-Kogias, E., Jovanovic, P., Gasser, L., Gailly, N., Syta, E., Ford, B.: Omniledger: a secure, scale-out, decentralized ledger via sharding. In: IEEE Symposium on Security and Privacy, SP. pp. 583–598 (2018)

18. Li, J., Li, N., Xue, R.: Universal accumulators with efficient nonmembership proofs. In: Katz, J., Yung, M. (eds.) ACNS 2007. LNCS, vol. 4521, pp. 253–269. Springer, Heidelberg (2007). https://doi.org/10.1007/978-3-540-72738-5_17

19. Luu, L., Narayanan, V., Zheng, C., Baweja, K., Gilbert, S., Saxena, P.: A secure sharding protocol for open blockchains. In: Proceedings of the 2016 ACM SIGSAC Conference on Computer and Communications Security, pp. 17–30. ACM (2016)

20. Matzutt, R., Kalde, B., Pennekamp, J., Drichel, A., Henze, M., Wehrle, K.: Coinprune: Shrinking bitcoin's blockchain retrospectively. IEEE Trans. Netw. Serv. Manag. **18**(3), 3064–3078 (2021)

21. Merkle, R.C.: A digital signature based on a conventional encryption function. In: Pomerance, C. (ed.) CRYPTO 1987. LNCS, vol. 293, pp. 369–378. Springer, Heidelberg (1988). https://doi.org/10.1007/3-540-48184-2_32

22. Monero Foundation: Monero whitepaper (2014). https://cryptoverze.com/monero-whitepaper/

23. Newman, D.J.: Simple analytic proof of the prime number theorem. Am. Math. Monthly **87**, 693–696 (1980)

24. Rabin, M.O.: Probabilistic algorithm for testing primality. J. Number Theor. **12**(1), 128–138 (1980)

25. Nakamoto, S.: Bitcoin: a peer-to-peer electronic cash system (2008). http://bitcoin.org/bitcoin.pdf

26. Vbuterin: the stateless client concept. https://ethresear.ch/t/the-stateless-client-concept/172.2017

27. Wood, G.: Ethereum: a secure decentralised generalised transaction ledger (2014). http://gavwood.com/Paper.pdf

28. Yu, H., Nikolic, I., Hou, R., Saxena, P.: OHIE: blockchain scaling made simple. In: IEEE Symposium on Security and Privacy, SP. pp. 90–105 (2020)

29. Zamani, M., Movahedi, M., Raykova, M.: Rapidchain: Scaling blockchain via full sharding. In: Proceedings of the 2018 ACM SIGSAC Conference on Computer and Communications Security, CCS. pp. 931–948. ACM (2018)

30. Zhang, W., Yu, J., He, Q., Guan, N.: TICK: tiny client for blockchains. IACR Cryptol. ePrint Arch, p. 792 (2019)

Garrison: A Novel Watchtower Scheme for Bitcoin

Arash Mirzaei[(✉)], Amin Sakzad, Jiangshan Yu, and Ron Steinfeld

Faculty of Information Technology, Monash University, Melbourne, Australia
{arash.mirzaei,amin.sakzad,jiangshan.yu,ron.steinfeld}@monash.edu

Abstract. In this paper, we propose Garrison, which is a payment channel with watchtower for Bitcoin. For this scheme, the storage requirements of both channel parties and their watchtower would be $\mathcal{O}(\log(N))$ with N being the number of channel updates. Furthermore, using properties of the adaptor signature, Garrison avoids state duplication. It means both parties store the same version of transactions for each state and hence the number of off-chain transactions does not exponentially increase with the number of applications built on top of each other in the channel. Moreover, the new proposal avoids punish-per-output pattern, meaning that all outputs of a revoked state can be claimed using a single revocation transaction. Garrison can be implemented without any update in Bitcoin script.

Keywords: Bitcoin · Payment channel · Watchtower

1 Introduction

Payment channel is a promising technique to mitigate the scalability issue of blockchains. To establish a payment channel, two parties lock their funds in a 2-of-2 multisignature address on the blockchain. Then, parties privately carry out multiple payments by exchanging off-chain transactions. Finally, parties close the channel by publishing the last channel state on-chain.

Since the channel parties are generally untrusted and blockchain miners are unaware of the off-chain transactions, a mechanism must be adopted to prevent parties from publishing an old state. In Lightning Network [15], as the most widely used Bitcoin payment channel network, with 31,483 nodes, 82,776 channels and total capacity of 159 Million US dollars[1], when a channel party publishes an old channel state on the blockchain, a period called *dispute period* starts. In this period, the other party can publish a *revocation* transaction and penalize the cheating party by claiming all the channel funds.

However, the dispute process works based on the assumption that parties are always online to detect malicious behaviours. This requirement can be practically violated due to crash failures or DoS attacks against the channel party [13,15]. To relax this assumption, [15] suggests that channel parties delegate the monitoring task to a third party called the *watchtower*. The watchtower is an always-online

---

[1] https://1ml.com/statistics,datafetchedon06/12/2021.

K. Nguyen et al. (Eds.): ACISP 2022, LNCS 13494, pp. 489–508, 2022.
https://doi.org/10.1007/978-3-031-22301-3_24

service provider that monitors the blockchain and acts on behalf of its customers to secure their funds. In other words, once channel parties update their channel, each party gives the revocation transaction to the watchtower. Then, once an old state appears on the ledger, the watchtower broadcasts its corresponding revocation transaction.

Monitor [15] and DCWC [4] are two watchtower schemes for the Lightning Network where the storage size of the watchtower in both schemes linearly increases with each channel update and hence the watchtower's storage costs would be $\mathcal{O}(N)$ with N being the number of channel updates. Generalized channel [1], Cerberus [5] and FPPW [14] are also other payment channels that work based on the dispute period idea. However, for all these schemes, the storage size of the watchtower linearly increases with the number of channel updates.

Outpost [11] is a novel payment channel with watchtower scheme that reduces the watchtower's storage requirements per channel from $\mathcal{O}(N)$ to $\mathcal{O}(\log(N))$. This consequently reduces the operational costs of maintaining watchtowers. Although elegantly designed, Outpost suffers from following shortcomings,

- The storage cost of each channel party is still $\mathcal{O}(N)$.
- Each party has his own version of the channel state where this state duplication causes the number of transactions to exponentially increase with the number of applications on top of each other [1]. In other words, to add an application (e.g. *Virtual channel* [2]) on top of the channel, parties must split their channel into sub-channels. If parties recursively split their channel k times, then to update their last layer sub-channel, they must create $\mathcal{O}(2^k)$ different versions of the channel state.
- Outpost works based on "punish-per-output" pattern, meaning that if there are M outputs in the published old state, the cheated party must claim each output separately [1]. Then, the required on-chain transactions upon dispute would be $\mathcal{O}(M)$ with M being the number of outputs in the published old state.

Therefore, the main motivation of this paper is designing a Bitcoin payment channel with watchtower scheme which is storage-efficient for channel parties and the watchtower and also avoids state duplication and punish-per-output pattern.

1.1 Our Contributions

The contribution of this paper is to present a new payment channel with watchtower for Bitcoin, called Garrison, for which the storage cost of channel parties and the watchtower would be logarithmic in the maximum number of channel updates. Furthermore, both channel parties store the same version of transactions. Additionally, regardless of the number of outputs in each channel state, there exists a single revocation transaction per state. Table 1 presents a comparison between Garrison and other Bitcoin payment channels that work based on dispute period. We also prove security of the Garrison channel under security of its underlying cryptographic primitives.

Table 1. Comparison of different dispute period-based payment channels with N channel updates, M outputs on average per state and k channel splits on top of each other.

Scheme	Party's St. Cost	Watch. St. Cost	on-chain TX.[a]	off-chain TX.[b]
Lightning [8]	$\mathcal{O}(\log(N))$	$\mathcal{O}(N)$	$\mathcal{O}(M)$	$\mathcal{O}(2^k)$
Generalized [4]	$\mathcal{O}(\log(N))$	$\mathcal{O}(N)$	$\mathcal{O}(1)$	$\mathcal{O}(1)$
Outpost [11]	$\mathcal{O}(N)$	$\mathcal{O}(\log(N))$	$\mathcal{O}(M)$	$\mathcal{O}(2^k)$
FPPW [14]	$\mathcal{O}(N)$	$\mathcal{O}(N)$	$\mathcal{O}(1)$	$\mathcal{O}(1)$
Cerberus [5]	$\mathcal{O}(N)$	$\mathcal{O}(N)$	$\mathcal{O}(M)$	$\mathcal{O}(2^k)$
Garrison	$\mathcal{O}(\log(N))$	$\mathcal{O}(\log(N))$	$\mathcal{O}(1)$	$\mathcal{O}(1)$

[a]Number of on-chain transactions upon dispute.
[b]Number of off-chain transactions per state.

1.2 Related Works

The first payment channels were introduced in [18] but they suffered from being unidirectional. DMC [6] and Lightning [15] were the first bidirectional payment channels where the former uses decrementing timelocks to replace the current channel state with a newer one and the latter revokes the current state upon authorizing a new state. Generalized channels [1] use adaptor signatures to avoid state duplication. Then, both parties would store the same copy of the channel transactions.

Lightning and generalized channels require parties to be always online to prevent their counter-parties from finalizing the channel with an old state. Since this requirement could be difficult to achieve, parties might delegate it to watchtowers. Monitor [15] is a privacy preserving watchtower scheme for Lightning Network. DCWC [4] proposes using a network of watchtowers to minimize the chance of malicious channel closure. In the above mentioned watchtower schemes, the watchtower is unaccountable, i.e. watchtowers do not guarantee their clients' funds. Cerberus [5] and FPPW [14] are two payment channel with watchtower schemes that focus on fairness with respect to the watchtowers' clients. Outpost [11] presents a payment channel with watchtower that reduces the storage costs of the watchtower from $\mathcal{O}(N)$ to $\mathcal{O}(\log(N))$ where N denotes the number of channel updates. Sleepy channel [3] is a payment channel without watchtower where parties are allowed to go offline for a long time period.

2 Preliminaries and Notations

In this section, we closely follow [1,14] to introduce the underlying cryptographic primitives of Garrison and notations.

2.1 Preliminaries

Digital Signature. A digital signature scheme Π includes three algorithms as following:

- **Key Generation.** $(pk, sk) \leftarrow \mathsf{Gen}(1^\kappa)$ on input 1^κ (κ is the security parameter), outputs the public/private key pair (pk, sk).
- **Signing.** $\sigma \leftarrow \mathsf{Sign}_{sk}(m)$ on inputs the private key sk and a message $m \in \{0,1\}^*$ outputs the signature σ.
- **Verification.** $b \leftarrow \mathsf{Vrfy}_{pk}(m; \sigma)$ takes the public key pk, a message m and a signature σ and outputs a bit b.

In this work, we assume that the utilized signature schemes are existentially unforgeable under an chosen-message attack ($\mathsf{EUF} - \mathsf{CMA}$). It guarantees that it is of negligible probability that an adversary, who has access to a signing oracle, outputs a valid signature on any new message. In this paper, we call such signature schemes secure. ECDSA [10] is a secure signature scheme that is currently being used in Bitcoin. Schnorr [17] is another important secure signature scheme that has been proposed to be introduced in Bitcoin due to its key aggregation and signature aggregation properties.

Hard Relation. A relation $\mathcal{R}$ with statement/witness pairs $(Y; y)$ is called a hard relation if (i) There exists a polynomial time generating algorithm $(Y; y) \leftarrow \mathsf{GenR}(1^\kappa)$ that on input 1^κ outputs a statement/witness pair $(Y; y) \in \mathcal{R}$; (ii) The relation between Y and y can be verified in polynomial time, and (iii) For any polynomial-time adversary $\mathcal{A}$, the probability that $\mathcal{A}$ on input Y outputs y is negligible. We also let $L_\mathcal{R} := \{Y \mid \exists Y \ s.t. \ (Y, y) \in \mathcal{R}\}$. Statement/witness pairs of $\mathcal{R}$ can be public/private key of a signature scheme generated by Gen algorithm.

Adaptor Signature. Given a hard relation $\mathcal{R}$ and a signature scheme Π, an adaptor signature protocol $\varXi$ includes four algorithms as follows:

- **Pre-Signing.** $\tilde{\sigma} \leftarrow \mathsf{pSign}_{sk}(m, Y)$ is a probabilistic polynomial time (PPT) algorithm that on input a private key sk, message $m \in \{0,1\}^*$ and statement $Y \in L_\mathcal{R}$, outputs a pre-signature $\tilde{\sigma}$.
- **Pre-Verification.** $b \leftarrow \mathsf{pVrfy}_{pk}(m, Y; \tilde{\sigma})$ is a deterministic polynomial time (DPT) algorithm that on input a public key pk, message $m \in \{0,1\}^*$, statement $Y \in L_\mathcal{R}$ and pre-signature $\tilde{\sigma}$, outputs a bit b.
- **Adaptation.** $\sigma \leftarrow \mathsf{Adapt}(\tilde{\sigma}, y)$ is a DPT algorithm that on input a pre-signature $\tilde{\sigma}$ and witness y, outputs a signature σ.
- **Extraction,** $\mathsf{Ext}(\sigma, \tilde{\sigma}, Y)$ is a DPT algorithm that on input a signature σ, pre-signature $\tilde{\sigma}$, and statement $Y \in L_\mathcal{R}$, outputs $\perp$ or a witness y such that $(Y, y) \in \mathcal{R}$.

An adaptor signature scheme is "secure" if it is existentially unforgeable under chosen message attack ($\mathsf{aEUF} - \mathsf{CMA}$ security), pre-signature adaptable and witness extractable. The $\mathsf{aEUF} - \mathsf{CMA}$ security guarantees that it is of negligible probability that any PPT adversary with access to signing and pre-signing oracles outputs a valid signature for any arbitrary new message m even given a valid pre-signature and its corresponding Y on m. Pre-signature adaptablity guarantees that every pre-signature (possibly generated maliciously) w.r.t. Y can adapt to a valid signature using the witness y with $(Y, y) \in \mathcal{R}$. Witness extractablity guarantees that it is of negligible probability that any PPT adversary with access to signing and pre-signing oracles outputs a valid signature and a statement Y for any new message m s.t. the valid signature does not reveal a witness for Y even given a valid pre-signature on m w.r.t. Y. The ECDSA-based and Schnorr-based adaptor signature schemes were constructed and analyzed in [1].

2.2 Notations

Throughout this work, we define different attribute tuples. Let U be a tuple of multiple attributes and one of its attributes is denoted by attr. To refer to this attribute, we use U.attr.

Our focus in this work is on Bitcoin or any other blockchains with UTXO model. In this model, units of value which we call coins are held in *outputs*. Formally, an output θ is a tuple of two attributes, $\theta = (\mathsf{cash}, \varphi)$, where θ.cash denotes the amount of coins held in this output and $\theta.\varphi$ denotes the condition that needs to be fulfilled to spend the output θ. The condition $\theta.\varphi$ is encoded using any script supported by the underlying blockchain. If the condition $\theta.\varphi$ contains a user P's public key, we say that P controls or owns the output θ because satisfying the condition requires a valid signature corresponding with that public key. Satisfying a condition might require authorizations by multiple parties. Such conditions contain public keys of all the involved parties separated by $\wedge$ operation(s). The relative timelock of T rounds in an output condition is denoted by Δ_T. It means the output cannot be spent within T rounds of the blockchain.

A condition might also have several subconditions, one of which must be satisfied to spend the output. Different subconditions of an output are separated by $\vee$ operation(s). The OP_RETURN output is a special output which does not hold any coins and is used to add some arbitrary data to the blockchain. Such an output is denoted by $\theta = (0, data)$ where $data$ is its arbitrary data.

A transaction changes ownership of coins, meaning that it takes a list of existing outputs and transfers their coins to a list of new outputs. To distinct between these two lists, we refer to the list of existing outputs as *inputs*. A transaction TX is formally defined as the tuple (txid, Input, Output, Witness). The identifier TX.txid $\in \{0, 1\}^*$ is computed as TX.txid $:= H([\mathsf{TX}])$, where $[\mathsf{TX}]$ is called the *body* of the transaction defined as $[\mathsf{TX}] := (\mathsf{TX.Input}, \mathsf{TX.Output})$ and H is a hash function which is modeled as a random oracle. The attribute TX.Input is a list of identifiers for all inputs of TX. The attribute TX.Output $= (\theta_1, \ldots, \theta_n)$ is a list of new outputs. The attribute TX.Witness $= (\mathsf{W}_1, \ldots, \mathsf{W}_m)$ is a list of tuples where its ith tuple authorizes spending the output that is taken as the ith input of TX. The tuple $\mathsf{W}_i = (\eta, \zeta)$ of the witness TX.Witness contains two attributes where $\mathsf{W}_i.\zeta$ denotes the data, e.g. the signature(s), that is (are) required to meet the $\mathsf{W}_i.\eta^{\text{th}}$ subcondition of the output that is taken as the ith input of TX. The signature (pre-signature) of P for TX.Witness.$\mathsf{W}_i.\zeta$ is denoted by $\sigma_{\mathsf{TX}}^{P,i}$ $(\tilde{\sigma}_{\mathsf{TX}}^{P,i})$, where i can be removed for single-input transactions. The ith entry of a list L is denoted by $L[i]$ with $i > 0$. Table 2 summarizes the notations.

Table 2. Notations

Notation	Description
U.attr	Attribute attr of the tuple U
$\theta = (\mathsf{cash}, \varphi)$	Output with value cash and script condition φ
$\theta = (0, data)$	OP_RETURN output with $data$ as its data
TX	Transaction TX = (txid, Input, Output, Witness)
[TX]	Tuple (TX.Input, TX.Output)
TX.txid	Identifier of the transaction TX
TX.Input	List of identifiers for all inputs of TX
TX.Output	List of new outputs $(\theta_1, \ldots, \theta_n)$ for TX
TX.Witness	List of witnesses $(W_1, \ldots, W_m)$ for TX where W_i corresponds with i^{th} input of TX
$W = (\eta, \zeta)$	Witness that fulfills η^{th} subcondition of an output using data ζ
$\sigma_{\mathsf{TX}}^{P,i}$	Signature of party P on TX for TX.Witness.$W_i.\zeta$
$\tilde{\sigma}_{\mathsf{TX}}^{P,i}$	Pre-signature of P on TX for TX.Witness.$W_i.\zeta$
Δ_T	Relative timelock of T rounds
$L[i]$	i^{th} entry of a list L

We additionally use charts to illustrate the connections between different transactions. Doubled edge and single edge rectangles respectively illustrate transactions that are already published on-chain or are ready to be published. Dotted edge rectangles show transactions that still lack the required witness for at least one input and hence are unprepared to be propagated in the blockchain network. Directional arrows from i^{th} output of transaction TX to j^{th} input of transaction TX′ shows that the transaction TX′ takes i^{th} output of the transaction TX as its jth input. If an output has multiple subconditions, it is shown by a diamond shape with multiple arrows where each arrow corresponds with one subcondition. OP_RETURN outputs are illustrated by blocked lines (instead of directional arrows). As an example, Fig. 1 shows that TX_i and TX_j are published and unpublished, respectively. The transaction TX_k is still unprepared to be published on the ledger. The transaction TX_i has two subconditions, where one of the subconditions is owned by both A and B and is relatively timelocked by T rounds and another subcondition is owned by C. The second output of TX_k is an OP_RETURN output.

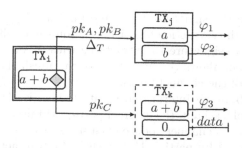

Fig. 1. A sample transaction flow.

3 Garrison Overview

3.1 System Model

Channel parties exchange data using an authenticated and secure communication channel. Channel participants might deviate from the protocol if it increases their profit. Furthermore, the underlying blockchain contains a distributed ledger that achieves security [9]. If a valid transaction is propagated in the blockchain network, it is included in the blockchain ledger within τ rounds (i.e. the confirmation delay is τ).

3.2 Garrison Overview

This section overviews the Garrison channel between A (Alice) and B (Bob). We start with a simple payment channel and then modify it step by step to mitigate its limitations.

A Simple Payment Channel. Figure 2 depicts the simple payment channel, introduced in [14]. This channel is created once channel parties publish a funding transaction on the blockchain and hence fund a 2-of-2 multisignature output on the ledger. The ith channel state includes a commit transaction $\text{TX}_{\text{CM},i}$ as well as a split transaction $\text{TX}_{\text{SP},i}$. The commit transaction sends the channel funds to a new joint account which is shared between the channel parties. Output of the commit transaction has two subconditions. The first subcondition which is not timelocked, as we will explain later, is used for revocation purposes. The second subcondition is relatively timelocked by T rounds with $T > \tau$ and is met by the corresponding split transaction. Split transaction distributes the channel funds among the channel parties and hence represents the channel state.

The transaction $\text{TX}_{\text{CM},i}$ requires signatures of both parties A and B to be published. To generate $\sigma^B_{\text{TX}_{\text{CM},i}}$, party A generates a statement/witness pair $(Y_{A,i}, y_{A,i})$ and sends the statement $Y_{A,i}$ to B. Then, party B uses the pre-signing algorithm pSign of the adaptor signature and A's statement $Y_{A,i}$ to generate a pre-signature $\tilde{\sigma}^B_{\text{TX}_{\text{CM},i}}$ on $[\text{TX}_{\text{CM},i}]$ and sends the result to A. Thus, whenever it is necessary, A is able to use the adaptation algorithm adapt of the adaptor signature to transform

the pre-signature to the signature $\sigma^B_{\text{TX}_{\text{CM},i}}$ and publish $\text{TX}_{\text{CM},i}$ on-chain. This also
enables B to apply the extraction algorithm Ext on the published signature and
its corresponding pre-signature to extract the witness value $y_{A,i}$. The witness
value, as will be seen, allows the honest party to punish the dishonest channel
party by claiming all the channel funds.

As one may submit an intermediate state (which is already replaced by a
later state) to the blockchain, the channel parties will need to punish such mis-
behaviours. Thus, upon channel update from state i to $i+1$, a revocation transaction $\text{TX}_{\text{RV},i}$ is created by parties. Unlike the split transaction, the revocation
transaction can immediately spend output of the corresponding commit transaction $\text{TX}_{\text{CM},i}$ using its first subcondition which does not contain any timelock.
Thus, if the revoked commit transaction $\text{TX}_{\text{CM},i}$ is published by a channel party,
let's say A, party B can immediately publish the revocation transaction $\text{TX}_{\text{RV},i}$.
Moreover, since commit transactions are signed using the adaptor signature,
once $\text{TX}_{\text{CM},i}$ is published by A, the witness $y_{A,i}$ is revealed to B. Thus, only B
who knows both $y_{A,i}$ and $y_{B,i}$ can meet the condition $Y_{A,i} \wedge Y_{B,i}$ in the output
of the revocation transaction and hence B will actually be the owner of all the
channel funds. Broadcast of the latest commit transaction does not pose any risk
to its broadcaster because parties have not signed its corresponding revocation
transaction yet.

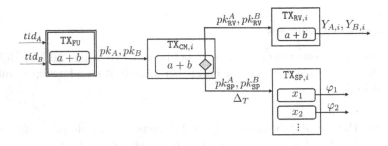

Fig. 2. A simple payment channel

Reducing the Storage Requirements of the Watchtower. All revocation
transactions in the introduced scheme must be stored by channel parties or their
watchtowers to be published upon fraud. To reduce the storage requirements of
the watchtower, similar to Outpost [11], our main idea is storing the revoca-
tion transaction $\text{TX}_{\text{RV},i}$ inside the commit transaction $\text{TX}_{\text{CM},i}$. Then, once $\text{TX}_{\text{CM},i}$ is
published, the watchtower extracts $\text{TX}_{\text{RV},i}$ and records it on the blockchain. How-
ever, we have $\text{TX}_{\text{RV},i}.\text{Input} = \text{TX}_{\text{CM},i}.\text{txid}\|1$. Thus, if $\text{TX}_{\text{RV},i}$ is created, signed and
finally stored inside $\text{TX}_{\text{CM},i}$, then $[\text{TX}_{\text{CM},i}]$ and hence $\text{TX}_{\text{CM},i}.\text{txid}$ and $\text{TX}_{\text{RV},i}$ change.
Thus, there is a self-loop situation [11]. To solve this issue, we add an auxil-
iary output with the value of ϵ to commit transactions where ϵ is the minimum

value supported by the Bitcoin blockchain. We also add an auxiliary transaction between each commit transaction and its corresponding split transaction. This new transaction $TX_{AU,i}$ spends the auxiliary output of the commit transaction. The signatures of party A and party B on $[TX_{RV,i}]$ are stored in an OP_RETURN output of the auxiliary transaction $TX_{AU,i}$. The split transaction $TX_{SP,i}$ spends the main output of $TX_{CM,i}$ as well as the main output of the auxiliary transaction $TX_{AU,i}$. Based on this design, parties can be sure that once the revoked commit transaction $TX_{CM,i}$ is published on the blockchain, its split transaction $TX_{SP,i}$ cannot be published unless $TX_{AU,i}$ is also on the blockchain. Furthermore, due to the timelock in the main output of $TX_{AU,i}$, once this transaction is published on-chain, $TX_{SP,i}$ cannot be published within $T - 1$ rounds. However, the honest party or the watchtower can extract the signatures on $[TX_{RV,i}]$ from $TX_{AU,i}$ and publish $TX_{RV,i}$ immediately. Figure 3 depicts the transactions flows.

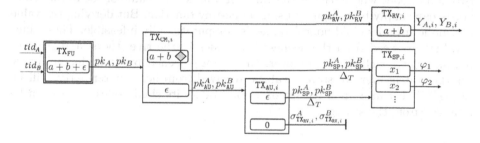

Fig. 3. Reducing the storage requirements of the watchtower

However, this scheme has the following issues:

- To create and publish the revocation transaction, the watchtower must also know the value of $Y_{A,i}$ and $Y_{B,i}$.
- Typically, revocation transaction of state i must be created once parties update the channel state from state i to $i + 1$. However, in the proposed scheme signatures for $TX_{RV,i}$ is stored in $TX_{AU,i}$ and hence $TX_{RV,i}$ must actually be created once parties update the channel state from state $i-1$ to i. It means if an honest party records the latest commit and auxiliary transactions on the blockchain, the counter-party might publish the revocation transaction and take all the channel funds.

To solve the first mentioned issue, $Y_{A,i}$ and $Y_{B,i}$ are stored in an OP_RETURN output that is added to the commit transaction $TX_{CM,i}$. To solve the second mentioned issue, we add two statements from the hard relation $\mathcal{R}$, $R_{A,i}$ and $R_{B,i}$, to the first subcondition of the main output of $TX_{CM,i}$, where $R_{A,i}$ ($R_{B,i}$) is generated by A (B) for the state i. Then, once the latest commit and auxiliary transactions are published by A, party B cannot record the revocation transaction as he does not know his counter-party's witness $r_{A,i}$. The witnesses $r_{A,i}$ and $r_{B,i}$ are exchanged between the parties and are given to the watchtower once parties have created $\text{TX}_{\text{CM},i+1}$, $\text{TX}_{\text{AU},i+1}$ and $\text{TX}_{\text{SP},i+1}$. Thus, $\text{TX}_{\text{FU}}.\text{txid}$, public keys pk_{RV}^A, pk_{RV}^B, pk_{SP}^A and pk_{SP}^B as well as r values of both parties are all data needed by the watchtower to watch the channel for both parties. Figure 4 depicts the mentioned modifications.

The security requirement for r values is that B (or the watchtower) must not be able to compute $r_{A,j}$ given that he knows $r_{A,i}$ with $i < j$. Otherwise, when A submits the latest commit transaction $\text{TX}_{\text{CM},j}$, party B uses $r_{A,i}$ to compute $r_{A,j}$. Then, B publishes the revocation transaction $\text{TX}_{\text{RV},j}$ and claims its output. If r values are randomly generated, the mentioned security requirement is met but storage cost of channel parties and the watchtower would be $\mathcal{O}(N)$. To reduce the storage and meeting the stated security requirement, parties generate their r values in a binary Merkle tree and use them from the deepest leaf nodes in the tree to the root [7]. In more details, in a binary Merkle tree, each node has two child nodes where having the value of a node, the value of each of its child nodes can simply be computed using a one-way function. But deriving the value of a node from its child nodes' values is computationally infeasible. Thus, since r values are used from the deepest leaf nodes in the tree, the stated security requirement is achieved. Moreover, the storage needed by each channel party (or the watchtower) to store r values, received from her counter-party, will be $\mathcal{O}(\log(N))$ because upon receipt of a node value, its child nodes' values can be removed from the storage.

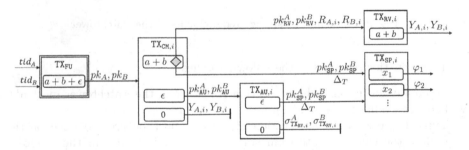

Fig. 4. Adding Y and R values to commit transactions

Reducing the Storage Requirements of Channel Parties. Although the storage of the watchtower is $\mathcal{O}(log(N))$, channel parties still have to store all the signatures of their counter-parties on the revocation transactions. Otherwise, the dishonest channel party publishes a revoked commit transaction $\text{TX}_{\text{CM},i}$ without publishing its auxiliary transaction $\text{TX}_{\text{AU},i}$. Then, the channel funds could be locked forever. This raises a hostage situation. The scheme Outpost suffers from this problem which is why storage requirement of channel parties is $\mathcal{O}(N)$. To solve this problem, we add one subcondition, $Y_{A,i} \wedge Y_{B,i} \wedge \Delta_{3T}$, to the main output of the commit transaction $\text{TX}_{\text{CM},i}$. This subcondition allows the honest channel party to claim all the channel funds in such hostage situations. In other words, if party A publishes the revoked commit transaction $\text{TX}_{\text{CM},i}$, she has $3T$ rounds time to publish $\text{TX}_{\text{AU},i}$ and $\text{TX}_{\text{SP},i}$ before B can claim the channel funds by meeting the subcondition $Y_{A,i} \wedge Y_{B,i} \wedge \Delta_{3T}$. If during this interval, $\text{TX}_{\text{AU},i}$ is published, party B instantly establishes and publishes $\text{TX}_{\text{RV},i}$ and claims its output. To do so, each party must have r values of both parties stored. Since these keys are generated in a Merkle tree, the storage requirements of each channel party for storing these values would be $\mathcal{O}(log(N))$ (See Fig. 5).

Once party A publishes $\text{TX}_{\text{CM},i}$, party B must be able to use Ext algorithm to extract the value of $y_{A,i}$. To do so, he must know the corresponding pre-signature $\tilde{\sigma}^{B}_{\text{TX}_{\text{CM},i}}$. If parties store all their own pre-signatures, their storage cost would be $\mathcal{O}(N)$. To acquire lower storage costs, parties must be able to regenerate the required pre-signature, once a commit transaction is published. To achieve this goal, random values which are required to generate pre-signatures must be generated in a Merkle tree and be used from the root to the deepest leaf node in the tree. In this way, once the commit transaction $\text{TX}_{\text{CM},i}$ is published by A, party B can regenerate the required random value, recompute the corresponding pre-signature $\tilde{\sigma}^{B}_{\text{TX}_{\text{CM},i}}$ and finally extract the value of $y_{A,i}$. Thus, the storage requirements would be still $\mathcal{O}(log(N))$.

Additionally, party B must know the value of $y_{B,i}$ to meet $Y_{A,i} \wedge Y_{B,i}$. The security requirement for y values is that A must not be able to compute $y_{B,i}$ given that he knows $y_{B,j}$ with $j > i$. Otherwise, once B submits the latest commit transaction $\text{TX}_{\text{CM},j}$, A computes $y_{B,j}$ and hence derives $y_{B,i}$ with $i < j$ and then try to publish $\text{TX}_{\text{CM},i}$ before $\text{TX}_{\text{CM},j}$ being published on the ledger. Then, A might be able to claim all the channel funds by meeting the third sub-condition of the main output of $\text{TX}_{\text{CM},i}$ or by publishing the revocation transaction $\text{TX}_{\text{RV},i}$ and claiming its output. If y values are randomly generated, the mentioned security requirement is met but parties' storage cost would be $\mathcal{O}(N)$. To reduce the storage and simultaneously meet the stated security requirement, parties generate their y values in a Merkle tree and give the corresponding Y values to their counter-parties from the root to the deepest leaf nodes in the tree.

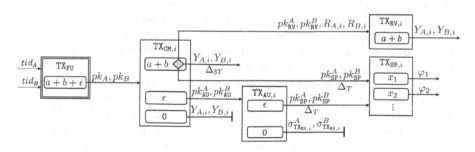

Fig. 5. Reducing storage requirements of channel parties

4   Garrison Channel

We introduce different transactions of a Garrison channel in Sect. 4.1. Then, in Sect. 4.2, we explain its protocol.

4.1   Garrison Transactions

Transactions of a Garrison channel are as following:

Funding Transaction. Parties A and B fund the channel by recording the funding transaction TX_{FU} on the blockchain. The output of the funding transaction is a 2-of-2 multisignature address shared between A and B. If A (B, respectively) uses the xth (y^{th}, respectively) output of a transaction with transaction identifier of $txid_A$ ($txid_B$, respectively) to fund the channel with a (b, respectively) coins, the funding transaction is as follows[2]:

$$\text{TX}_{\text{FU}}.\text{Input} := (txid_A \| x, txid_B \| y),$$
$$\text{TX}_{\text{FU}}.\text{Output} := \{(a + b, pk_A \wedge pk_B)\},$$
$$\text{TX}_{\text{FU}}.\text{Witness} := ((1, \sigma_{\text{TX}_{\text{FU}}}^{A,1}), (1, \sigma_{\text{TX}_{\text{FU}}}^{B,2})).$$

Commit Transaction. The commit transaction for state i is denoted by $\text{TX}_{\text{CM},i}$ and is as follows:

$$\text{TX}_{\text{CM},i}.\text{Input} := \text{TX}_{\text{FU}}.txid \| 1,$$
$$\text{TX}_{\text{CM},i}.\text{Output} := ((a + b, \varphi_1 \vee \varphi_2 \vee \varphi_3),$$
$$(\epsilon, pk_{\text{AU}}^A \wedge pk_{\text{AU}}^B),$$
$$(0, (Y_{A,i}, Y_{B,i})))$$
$$\text{TX}_{\text{CM},i}.\text{Witness} := \{(1, \{\sigma_{\text{TX}_{\text{CM},i}}^A, \sigma_{\text{TX}_{\text{CM},i}}^B\})\}$$

with $\varphi_1 := (pk_{\text{RV}}^A \wedge pk_{\text{RV}}^B \wedge R_{A,i} \wedge R_{B,i})$, $\varphi_2 := (Y_{A,i} \wedge Y_{B,i} \wedge \Delta_{3T})$, and $\varphi_3 := (pk_{\text{SP}}^A \wedge pk_{\text{SP}}^B \wedge \Delta_T)$ where $Y_{A,i}$ and $R_{A,i}$ ($Y_{B,i}$ and $R_{B,i}$) are statements of a hard relation $\mathcal{R}$ generated by A (B) for the ith state and T is any number such that $T > \tau$. The first and second output of the transaction are the main and auxiliary outputs. Normally, if $\text{TX}_{\text{CM},i}$ is the last commit transaction and is published on-chain, first its auxiliary output and then its main output are spent by the auxiliary and split transactions, respectively. The third output of $\text{TX}_{\text{CM},i}$ is an OP_RETURN output containing values of $Y_{A,i}$ and $Y_{B,i}$. Parties A and B use their counter-parties' statements $Y_{B,i}$ and $Y_{A,i}$ and the underlying adaptor signature to generate a pre-signature on the commit transaction for their counter-parties. Thus, once A publishes the commit transaction $\text{TX}_{\text{CM},i}$, she also reveals her witness $y_{B,i}$.

---

[2] We assume that funding sources of TX_{FU} are two typical UTXOs owned by A and B.

Remark 1. Each Bitcoin transaction can have at most one OP_RETURN output with the size constraint of 80 bytes. To store $Y_{A,i}$ and $Y_{B,i}$ inside an OP_RETURN output, their compressed version, each with 33-byte length, are stored.

Revocation Transaction. The revocation transaction for state i is denoted by $\text{TX}_{\text{RV},i}$ and is as follows:

$$\text{TX}_{\text{RV},i}.\text{Input} := \text{TX}_{\text{CM},i}.\text{txid}\|1,$$
$$\text{TX}_{\text{RV},i}.\text{Output} := \{(a + b, Y_{A,i} \wedge Y_{B,i})\},$$
$$\text{TX}_{\text{RV},i}.\text{Witness} := \{(1, \{\sigma^A_{\text{TX}_{\text{RV},i}}, \sigma^B_{\text{TX}_{\text{RV},i}}, r_{A,i}, r_{B,i}\})\}$$

The $\text{TX}_{\text{RV},i}$ spends the main output of $\text{TX}_{\text{CM},i}$ using its non-timelocked subcondition $pk^A_{\text{RV}} \wedge pk^B_{\text{RV}} \wedge R_{A,i} \wedge R_{B,i}$ and sends all the channel funds to an output with the condition $Y_{A,i} \wedge Y_{B,i}$. When a dishonest party, let's say A, publishes the revoked $\text{TX}_{\text{CM},i}$, she must publish $\text{TX}_{\text{AU},i}$ and then wait for T rounds before being able to publish $\text{TX}_{\text{SP},i}$. However, given that the state i is revoked, B knows the value of $r_{A,i}$ and hence creates the revocation transaction $\text{TX}_{\text{RV},i}$ and instantly publishes it on the blockchain. The output of $\text{TX}_{\text{RV},i}$ can only be claimed by B because no one else knows the witness $y_{B,i}$.

Auxiliary Transaction. Auxiliary transaction for state i is as follows:

$$\text{TX}_{\text{AU},i}.\text{Input} := \text{TX}_{\text{CM}}.\text{txid}\|2,$$
$$\text{TX}_{\text{AU},i}.\text{Output} := ((\epsilon, pk^A_{\text{SP}} \wedge pk^B_{\text{SP}} \wedge \Delta_T),$$
$$(0, (\sigma^A_{\text{TX}_{\text{RV},i}}, \sigma^B_{\text{TX}_{\text{RV},i}})))$$
$$\text{TX}_{\text{AU},i}.\text{Witness} := \{(1, \{\sigma^A_{\text{TX}_{\text{AU},i}}, \sigma^B_{\text{TX}_{\text{AU},i}}\})\}$$

This transaction spends the auxiliary output of the commit transaction and its output is spent by the split transaction. In other words, split transaction cannot be published unless auxiliary transaction is on the blockchain. The second output of $\text{TX}_{\text{AU},i}$ is an OP_RETURN output containing signatures of both parties on the corresponding revocation transaction.

Remark 2. Each encoded Bitcoin signature can be up to 73 bytes long. Thus, due to the size constraint of the OP_RETURN output, two separate signatures do not fit into the auxiliary transaction. To solve this issue, A and B can aggregate their public keys pk^A_{RV} and pk^B_{RV} to form an aggregated public key pk_{RV} [12] and change φ_1 in $\text{TX}_{\text{CM},i}$ to $(pk_{\text{RV}} \wedge R_{A,i} \wedge R_{B,i})$. Then, rather than two separate signatures on the revocation transaction, they generate a multisignature (with up to 73 byte size) and store it inside the OP_RETURN output of $\text{TX}_{\text{AU},i}$.

Split Transaction. $TX_{SP,i}$ actually represents the ith channel state and is as follows:

$$TX_{SP,i}.\text{Input} := (TX_{CM,i}.\text{txid}\|1, TX_{AU,i}.\text{txid}\|1),$$
$$TX_{SP,i}.\text{Output} := (\theta_1, \theta_2, \cdots),$$
$$TX_{SP,i}.\text{Witness} := ((3, \{\sigma^A_{TX_{SP,i}}, \sigma^B_{TX_{SP,i}}\}), (1, \{\sigma^A_{TX_{SP,i}}, \sigma^B_{TX_{SP,i}}\}))$$

The split transaction spends the main output of the commit transaction and the first output of the auxiliary transaction.

4.2   Garrison Protocol

The lifetime of a Garrison channel can be divided into 4 phases including *create*, *update*, *close*, and *punish*. These phases are explained, hereinafter.

Create. The channel creation phase completes once the funding transaction TX_{FU}, the commit transactions $TX_{CM,0}$, the split transaction $TX_{SP,0}$, the auxiliary transaction $TX_{AU,0}$ and body of the revocation transaction $[TX_{RV,0}]$ are created, and TX_{FU} is published on the blockchain. In this phase, parties do not have access to $TX_{RV,0}$ as they have not exchanged $r_{A,i}$ and $r_{B,i}$ yet. At the end of the channel creation phase, the channel would be at state 0. Since output of the funding transaction can only be spent if both parties agree, one party might become unresponsive to raise a hostage situation. To avoid this, parties must sign the commit, revocation, auxiliary and split transactions before signing and publishing the funding transaction. Figure 6 summarizes the channel creation phase.

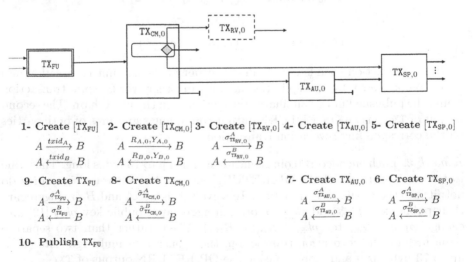

1- Create $[TX_{FU}]$ **2- Create** $[TX_{CM,0}]$ **3- Create** $[TX_{RV,0}]$ **4- Create** $[TX_{AU,0}]$ **5- Create** $[TX_{SP,0}]$

$A \xrightarrow{txid_A} B$ $A \xrightarrow{R_{A,0},Y_{A,0}} B$ $A \xrightarrow{\sigma^A_{TX_{RV,0}}} B$
$A \xleftarrow{txid_B} B$ $A \xleftarrow{R_{B,0},Y_{B,0}} B$ $A \xleftarrow{\sigma^B_{TX_{RV,0}}} B$

9- Create TX_{FU} **8- Create** $TX_{CM,0}$ **7- Create** $TX_{AU,0}$ **6- Create** $TX_{SP,0}$

$A \xrightarrow{\sigma^A_{TX_{FU}}} B$ $A \xrightarrow{\tilde{\sigma}^A_{TX_{CM,0}}} B$ $A \xrightarrow{\sigma^A_{TX_{AU,0}}} B$ $A \xrightarrow{\sigma^A_{TX_{SP,0}}} B$
$A \xleftarrow{\sigma^B_{TX_{FU}}} B$ $A \xleftarrow{\tilde{\sigma}^B_{TX_{CM,0}}} B$ $A \xleftarrow{\sigma^B_{TX_{AU,0}}} B$ $A \xleftarrow{\sigma^B_{TX_{SP,0}}} B$

10- Publish TX_{FU}

Fig. 6. Summary of garrison channel creation phase.

Update. Let the channel be in state $i \geq 0$ and channel parties decide to update it to state $i+1$. The update process is performed in two sub-phases. In the first sub-phase, channel parties create $TX_{CM,i+1}$, $TX_{SP,i+1}$, $TX_{AU,i+1}$, and $[TX_{RV,i+1}]$ for the new state. In the second sub-phase, channel parties revoke the state i by exchanging $r_{A,i}$ and $r_{B,i}$ and giving these values to the watchtower. We assume that the watchtower is also paid after each channel update. Figure 7 summarizes the channel update phase.

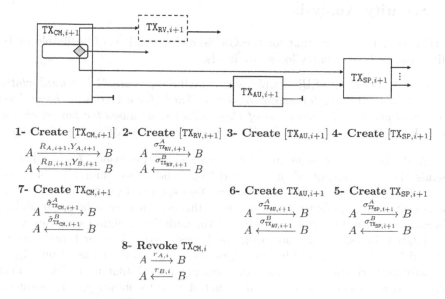

1- Create $[TX_{CM,i+1}]$ **2- Create** $[TX_{RV,i+1}]$ **3- Create** $[TX_{AU,i+1}]$ **4- Create** $[TX_{SP,i+1}]$

$$A \xrightarrow{R_{A,i+1},Y_{A,i+1}} B \qquad A \xrightarrow{\sigma^A_{TX_{RV,i+1}}} B$$
$$A \xleftarrow{R_{B,i+1},Y_{B,i+1}} B \qquad A \xleftarrow{\sigma^B_{TX_{RV,i+1}}} B$$

7- Create $TX_{CM,i+1}$ **6- Create** $TX_{AU,i+1}$ **5- Create** $TX_{SP,i+1}$

$$A \xrightarrow{\tilde{\sigma}^A_{TX_{CM,i+1}}} B \qquad\qquad A \xrightarrow{\sigma^A_{TX_{AU,i+1}}} B \quad A \xrightarrow{\sigma^A_{TX_{SP,i+1}}} B$$
$$A \xleftarrow{\tilde{\sigma}^B_{TX_{CM,i+1}}} B \qquad\qquad A \xleftarrow{\sigma^B_{TX_{AU,i+1}}} B \quad A \xleftarrow{\sigma^B_{TX_{SP,i+1}}} B$$

8- Revoke $TX_{CM,i}$

$$A \xrightarrow{r_{A,i}} B$$
$$A \xleftarrow{r_{B,i}} B$$

Fig. 7. Summary of garrison channel update phase from state i to $i+1$.

Close. Assume that the channel parties A and B have updated their channel n times and then A and/or B decide to close it. They can close the channel cooperatively. To do so, A and B create the below transaction, called modified split transaction $TX_{\overline{SP}}$, and publish it on the blockchain:

$$TX_{\overline{SP}}.\mathsf{Input} := TX_{FU}.txid \| 1,$$
$$TX_{\overline{SP}}.\mathsf{Output} := TX_{SP,n}.\mathsf{Output},$$
$$TX_{\overline{SP}}.\mathsf{Witness} := \{(1, \{\sigma^A_{TX_{\overline{SP}}}, \sigma^B_{TX_{\overline{SP}}}\})\}.$$

If one of the channel parties, e.g. party B, becomes unresponsive, A can still non-collaboratively close the channel. To do so, she publishes $TX_{CM,n}$ and $TX_{AU,n}$ on the ledger. Then, she waits for T rounds, and finally publishes $TX_{SP,n}$.

Punish. Let the channel be at state n. If a channel party, e.g. party A, publishes $TX_{CM,i}$ and then $TX_{AU,i}$ with $i < n$ on the blockchain, party B or his watchtower can create the transaction $TX_{RV,i}$ and publish it within T rounds. If only $TX_{CM,i}$

is published, party B claims its first output by meeting its second subcondition $Y_{A,i} \wedge Y_{A,i} \wedge \Delta_{3T}$.

Remark 3. If the watchtower is non-responsive, the channel might be closed with an old state. The paper [16] proposes a reputation system, called HashCashed, which forces watchtowers to be responsive without requiring them to lock any funds as collateral. We assume that Garrison is used with HashCashed system.

5   Security Analysis

In this section we prove that for the Garrison channel, it is of negligible probability that an honest party loses any funds.

Lemma 1. *Let Π be a $\mathsf{EUF-CMA}$ secure digital signature, $\mathcal{R}$ be a hard relation and Ξ be a secure adaptor digital signature. Then, for a Garrison channel with n channel updates, the broadcast of $\mathrm{TX}_{\mathrm{RV},i}$ with $i < n$ causes the honest channel party $P \in \{A, B\}$ to lose any funds in the channel with negligible probability.*

Proof. Without loss of generality let $P = A$. The transaction $\mathrm{TX}_{\mathrm{RV},i}$ with $i < n$ spends the main output of the revoked $\mathrm{TX}_{\mathrm{CM},i}$ and hence cannot be published unless $\mathrm{TX}_{\mathrm{CM},i}$ is on-chain. The transaction $\mathrm{TX}_{\mathrm{CM},i}$ spends the output of $\mathrm{TX}_{\mathrm{FU}}$. Since the condition in $\mathrm{TX}_{\mathrm{FU}}$.Output contains pk_A, this output cannot be spent without A's authorization. Otherwise, security of the underlying digital signature would be violated. Based on the protocol, the honest party A never broadcasts the revoked $\mathrm{TX}_{\mathrm{CM},i}$ on-chain and her pre-signature $\tilde{\sigma}_{\mathrm{TX}_{\mathrm{CM},i}}$ on the transaction $\mathrm{TX}_{\mathrm{CM},i}$ is the only authorization he grants for spending $\mathrm{TX}_{\mathrm{FU}}$.Output using $\mathrm{TX}_{\mathrm{CM},i}$. Thus, if $\mathrm{TX}_{\mathrm{CM},i}$ is published, the probability that A fails to obtain $y_{B,i}$ is negligible. Otherwise, $\mathsf{aEUF-CMA}$ security or witness extractability of the used adaptor signature is violated. Furthermore, $\mathrm{TX}_{\mathrm{RV},i}$ has only one output with the condition of $Y_{A,i} \wedge Y_{B,i}$ and the value of $a+b$. Since A privately preserves its witness value $y_{A,i}$, the probability that any PPT adversary claims $\mathrm{TX}_{\mathrm{RV},i}$.Output is negligible. Otherwise, the utilized hard relation would break. Therefore, it is of negligible probability that A (who knows both $y_{A,i}$ and $y_{B,i}$) fails to claim $\mathrm{TX}_{\mathrm{RV},i}$.Output and obtain all the channel funds.

Lemma 2. *Let Π be a $\mathsf{EUF-CMA}$ secure digital signature, $\mathcal{R}$ be a hard relation and Ξ be a secure adaptor digital signature. Then, for a Garrison channel between A and B with $P \in \{A, B\}$ being the honest party, if P's counter-party publishes $\mathrm{TX}_{\mathrm{CM},i}$, it is with negligible probability that*

- *P fails to obtain the data required to meet the second subcondition of $\mathrm{TX}_{\mathrm{CM},i}$.Output[1].$\varphi$.*
- *any PPT adversary can meet the second subcondition of $\mathrm{TX}_{\mathrm{CM},i}$.Output[1].$\varphi$.*

Proof. Without loss of generality let $P = A$. Similar to the proof of Lemma 1, if B publishes $\mathrm{TX}_{\mathrm{CM},i}$, the probability that A fails to obtain $y_{B,i}$ is negligible. Otherwise, $\mathsf{aEUF-CMA}$ security or witness extractability of the used adaptor signature is violated. The witness $y_{A,i}$ has also been created by A and hence he has the whole data required to meet $Y_{A,i} \wedge Y_{B,i} \wedge \Delta_{3T}$. Furthermore, given that A privately preserves its witness value $y_{A,i}$, the probability that any PPT adversary meets this subcondition is negligible. Otherwise, the utilized hard relation would break.

Lemma 3. *Let Π be a* EUF $-$ CMA *secure digital signature, $\mathcal{R}$ be a hard relation and Ξ be a secure adaptor digital signature. Then, for a Garrison channel with n channel updates, if the honest party $P \in \{A, B\}$ publishes* $TX_{CM,n}$, *P loses funds in the channel with negligible probability.*

Proof. Without loss of generality let $P = A$. We assume that A publishes $TX_{CM,n}$ in the block $\mathcal{B}_j$ of the blockchain and prove that it is of negligible probability that A fails to publish $TX_{SP,n}$. Then, since $TX_{SP,n}$ corresponds with the latest channel state, its broadcast cannot cause A to lose any funds.

The condition $TX_{CM,n}.\mathsf{Output}[2].\varphi$ contains pk_{AU}^A and hence it is of negligible probability that this output is spent without A's authorization. Otherwise, the security of the underlying digital signature is violated. The honest party A grants such an authorization only on the transaction $TX_{AU,n}$ which is held by both A and B. Based on the protocol, once $TX_{CM,n}$ is published on the blockchain by A, he also instantly submits $TX_{AU,n}$ to the blockchain. According to our assumptions regarding the blockchain, $TX_{AU,n}$ is published on the blockchain in the block $\mathcal{B}_{j+k}$ with $0 < k \leq \tau < T$. Similarly, the first output of $TX_{AU,n}$ can only be spent by $TX_{SP,n}$. According to the protocol, A holds $TX_{SP,n}$ and submits it to the blockchain T rounds after $TX_{AU,n}$ is published on-chain. Thus, given that the first input of $TX_{SP,n}$ (or equivalently the first output of $TX_{CM,n}$) is still unspent, based on our assumptions regarding the blockchain, $TX_{SP,n}$ is published on the blockchain in the block $\mathcal{B}_{j+k+l+T}$ with $0 < l \leq \tau < T$. Now, we prove that, when $\mathcal{B}_{j+k+l+T}$ with $0 < l, k < T$ is added to the blockchain, the first output of $TX_{CM,n}$, $TX_{CM,n}.\mathsf{Output}[1]$, is still unspent.

The first and third subconditions of $TX_{CM,n}.\mathsf{Output}[1]$ contains $R_{A,n}$ and pk_{SP}^A, respectively and hence it is of negligible probability that these two subconditions are met without A's authorization. Otherwise, the underlying hard relation or digital signature would break. Party A grants such an authorization only on $TX_{SP,n}$. Moreover, the second subcondition $Y_{A,i} \wedge Y_{B,i} \wedge \Delta_{3T}$ cannot be met in block $\mathcal{B}_{j+k+l+T}$ with $0 < l, k < T$ because $j + k + l + T < j + 3T$.

Lemma 4. *Let Π be a* EUF $-$ CMA *secure digital signature, $\mathcal{R}$ be a hard relation and Ξ be a secure adaptor digital signature. Then, for a Garrison channel with n channel updates and with $P \in \{A, B\}$ being the honest party, if P's counterparty publishes* $TX_{CM,n}$, *it is of negligible probability that P loses any funds in the channel.*

Proof. Without loss of generality let $P = A$. The proof is similar to the proof of Lemma 3. The only difference is that following Lemma 2, it is of negligible probability that A fails to meet the second subcondition of $TX_{CM,n}.\mathsf{Output}[1]$. Therefore, A can either publishes both $TX_{AU,n}$ and $TX_{SP,n}$ or claim $TX_{CM,n}.\mathsf{Output}[1]$

by meeting its second subcondition. None of these two cases can cause the honest party A to lose any funds in the channel.

Lemma 5. *Let Π be a* EUF − CMA *secure digital signature, $\mathcal{R}$ be a hard relation and Ξ be a secure adaptor digital signature. Then, for a Garrison channel with n channel updates and with $P \in \{A, B\}$ being the honest party, if any adversary publishes* $\mathrm{TX}_{\mathrm{CM},i}$ *with $i < n$, it is of negligible probability that P loses any funds in the channel.*

Proof. Without loss of generality let $P = A$. The output $\mathrm{TX}_{\mathrm{CM},i}.\mathrm{Output}[1]$ includes 3 subconditions, one of which must be met to cheat A out of its funds. The first subcondition contains pk_{RV}^A and hence it is of negligible probability that this output is spent without A's authorization. Otherwise, the security of the used digital signature is violated. The honest party A grants such an authorization only on the transaction $\mathrm{TX}_{\mathrm{RV},i}$. However, according to Lemma 1, it is of negligible probability that broadcast of $\mathrm{TX}_{\mathrm{RV},i}$ causes A to lose any funds. Moreover, according Lemma 2, it is of negligible probability that any PPT adversary can meet the second subcondition. Now, we prove that if the third subcondition is used to cheat A out of her funds, it leads to a contradiction.

Assume that the third subcondition of $\mathrm{TX}_{\mathrm{CM},i}.\mathrm{Output}[1]$ is used to cheat A out of her funds. This subcondition contains pk_{SP}^A and hence it is of negligible probability that this condition is met without A's authorization. Otherwise, the security of the underlying digital signature is violated. The honest party A grants such an authorization only on the transaction $\mathrm{TX}_{\mathrm{SP},i}$. Assume that $\mathrm{TX}_{\mathrm{SP},i}$ is included in the block $\mathcal{B}_k$ of the blockchain. The transaction $\mathrm{TX}_{\mathrm{SP},i}$ cannot be added to the blockchain unless its inputs are some unspent outputs on the blockchain. It means that $\mathrm{TX}_{\mathrm{AU},i}$ is also on the blockchain and following the condition in $\mathrm{TX}_{\mathrm{AU},i}.\mathrm{Output}[1]$, the transaction $\mathrm{TX}_{\mathrm{AU},i}$ must have been published in the block $\mathcal{B}_j$ with $j \le k - T$. However, based on the protocol, once A or her watchtower observes $\mathrm{TX}_{\mathrm{AU},i}$ on the blockchain, they create the corresponding revocation transaction $\mathrm{TX}_{\mathrm{RV},i}$ and submit it to the blockchain. According to our blockchain assumptions, this transaction is published on the blockchain in block $\mathcal{B}_l$ with $j < l \le j + \tau < j + T \le k$. However, once $\mathrm{TX}_{\mathrm{RV},i}$ is published in the block $\mathcal{B}_l$ of the blockchain, the transaction $\mathrm{TX}_{\mathrm{SP},i}$ becomes invalid and cannot be published in block $\mathcal{B}_k$ of the blockchain which leads to a contradiction.

Theorem 1. *Let Π be a* EUF − CMA *secure digital signature, $\mathcal{R}$ be a hard relation and Ξ be a secure adaptor digital signature. Then, for a Garrison channel, an honest party $P \in \{A, B\}$ loses any funds in the channel with negligible probability.*

Proof. Without loss of generality let $P = A$. Funds of A are locked in $\mathrm{TX}_{\mathrm{FU}}.\mathrm{Output}$. It is of negligible probability that any PPT adversary $\mathcal{A}$ spends the output of $\mathrm{TX}_{\mathrm{FU}}$ without the honest party A's authorization. Otherwise, the underlying digital signature would be forgeable. Furthermore, $\mathrm{TX}_{\overline{\mathrm{SP}}}$, $\mathrm{TX}_{\mathrm{CM},i}$ with $i = [0, n-1]$, $\mathrm{TX}_{\mathrm{CM},n}$ are the only transactions in the protocol that spend the output of $\mathrm{TX}_{\mathrm{FU}}$ and A grants authorization for. Thus, these transactions will be discussed further. Since $TX_{\overline{SP}}$ represents the final agreed state of the channel, its broadcast cannot cause A to lose any funds. Moreover, according to Lemmas 3 and 4, it is of negligible probability that broadcast of $TX_{CM,n}$ causes A to be cheated out of her funds. Also, based on the protocol, A never publishes $TX_{CM,i}$ with $i = [0, n-1]$ and according to Lemma 5, if one of these transactions is published by the adversary, it causes A to lose any funds with negligible probability. This concludes the proof.

References

1. Aumayr, L., et al.: Generalized bitcoin-compatible channels. IACR Cryptol. ePrint Arch. **2020**, 476 (2020)
2. Aumayr, L., et al.: Bitcoin-compatible virtual channels. In: 2021 IEEE Symposium on Security and Privacy (SP), pp. 901–918. IEEE (2021)
3. Aumayr, L., Thyagarajan, S.A., Malavolta, G., Moreno-Sanchez, P., Maffei, M.: Sleepy channels: bitcoin-compatible bi-directional payment channels without watchtowers. Cryptology ePrint Archive (2021)
4. Avarikioti, G., Laufenberg, F., Sliwinski, J., Wang, Y., Wattenhofer, R.: Towards secure and efficient payment channels. arXiv preprint arXiv:1811.12740 (2018)
5. Avarikioti, Z., Thyfronitis Litos, O.S., Wattenhofer, R.: CERBERUS channels: incentivizing watchtowers for bitcoin. In: Bonneau, J., Heninger, N. (eds.) FC 2020. LNCS, vol. 12059, pp. 346–366. Springer, Cham (2020). https://doi.org/10.1007/978-3-030-51280-4_19
6. Decker, C., Wattenhofer, R.: A fast and scalable payment network with bitcoin duplex micropayment channels. In: Pelc, A., Schwarzmann, A.A. (eds.) SSS 2015. LNCS, vol. 9212, pp. 3–18. Springer, Cham (2015). https://doi.org/10.1007/978-3-319-21741-3_1
7. Developers, L.: Bolt# 3: Bitcoin transaction and script formats (2017)
8. Dryja, T., Milano, S.B.: Unlinkable outsourced channel monitoring. Talk transcript) https://diyhpl.us/wiki/transcripts/scalingbitcoin/milan/unlinkable-outsourced-channel-monitoring (2016)
9. Garay, J., Kiayias, A., Leonardos, N.: The bitcoin backbone protocol with chains of variable difficulty. In: Katz, J., Shacham, H. (eds.) CRYPTO 2017. LNCS, vol. 10401, pp. 291–323. Springer, Cham (2017). https://doi.org/10.1007/978-3-319-63688-7_10
10. Johnson, D., Menezes, A., Vanstone, S.: The elliptic curve digital signature algorithm (ECDSA). Int. J. Inf. Secur. **1**(1), 36–63 (2001)
11. Khabbazian, M., Nadahalli, T., Wattenhofer, R.: Outpost: a responsive lightweight watchtower. In: Proceedings of the 1st ACM Conference on Advances in Financial Technologies, pp. 31–40 (2019)
12. Lindell, Y.: Fast secure two-party ECDSA signing. In: Katz, J., Shacham, H. (eds.) CRYPTO 2017. LNCS, vol. 10402, pp. 613–644. Springer, Cham (2017). https://doi.org/10.1007/978-3-319-63715-0_21
13. McCorry, P., Bakshi, S., Bentov, I., Meiklejohn, S., Miller, A.: Pisa: Arbitration outsourcing for state channels. In: Proceedings of the 1st ACM Conference on Advances in Financial Technologies, pp. 16–30 (2019)
14. Mirzaei, A., Sakzad, A., Yu, J., Steinfeld, R.: Fppw: a fair and privacy preserving watchtower for bitcoin. Cryptology ePrint Archive, Report 2021/117 (2021). https://eprint.iacr.org/2021/117

15. Poon, J., Dryja, T.: The bitcoin lightning network: Scalable off-chain instant payments (2016)
16. Rahimpour, S., Khabbazian, M.: Hashcashed reputation with application in designing watchtowers. In: 2021 IEEE International Conference on Blockchain and Cryptocurrency (ICBC), pp. 1–9. IEEE (2021)
17. Schnorr, C.P.: Efficient signature generation by smart cards. J. Cryptology 4(3), 161–174 (1991). https://doi.org/10.1007/BF00196725
18. Spilman, J.: [bitcoin-development] anti dos for tx replacement. https://lists.linuxfoundation.org/pipermail/bitcoin-dev/2013-April/002433.html (2013)

Shoot Before You Escape: Dynamic Behavior Monitor of Bitcoin Users via Bi-Temporal Network Analytics

Chen Zhao[1,2], Jianing Ding[1,2], Zhenzhen Li[1,2], Zhen Li[1,2], Gang Xiong[1,2], and Gaopeng Gou[1,2(✉)]

[1] Institute of Information Engineering, Chinese Academy of Sciences, Beijing, China
{zhaochen4264,dingjianing,lizhenzhen,lizhen,
xionggang,gougaopeng}@iie.ac.cn
[2] School of Cyber Security, University of Chinese Academy of Sciences, Beijing, China

Abstract. As the first successful decentralized cryptocurrency system, Bitcoin has gradually become a breeding ground for hiding illegal or malicious activities without a central governing authority, in recent years. It remains a challenging task to mine Bitcoin blockchain for better financial forensics and security regulation, due to the hugeness and dynamism of transaction data. In this paper, we propose BitMonitor, which enables dynamic classification of Bitcoin users in real-time. The key module of BitMonitor is the construction of Bi-Temporal transaction network. Through it, on the one hand, we can perform temporal slicing of transactions associated with wallet nodes and sequentially tag the intent of user activity at different stages. On the other hand, it enables deep backtracking and tracing of the relevant financial flows dynamically over time. We demonstrate the effectiveness of the resulting multi-order neighborhood information in a static experimental scenario. Besides, the specificity of the Bi-Temporal transaction network also allows for incremental updating of neighborhood characteristics. Finally, through a weighted voting mechanism by incorporating tags on historical slices, we evaluate the dynamic classification performance from two different aspects. Unlike the static post-mortem analysis among existing work, we are the first to conduct a dynamic behavior monitor for the purpose of identifying Bitcoin accounts as soon as possible.

Keywords: Bitcoin · Address classification · Dynamic behavior analysis · Financial forensics

1 Introduction

Bitcoin, as the most widely used virtual cryptocurrency system, has attracted extensive attention since firstly proposed in [25]. Behind the boom, anomalous behaviors are now proliferating as well. According to [10], nearly one-quarter of

Bitcoin users and one-half of Bitcoin transactions are involved in illegal activities. [18] demonstrated that Bitcoin is still the dominant cryptocurrency used in criminal activities compared to others. Hence, studying and understanding Bitcoin-related activities is an urgent need of critical societal importance.

The prosperity of illegal activities can be greatly attributed to these reasons. a) Based on the decentralized peer-to-peer network, transactions can be carried out more conveniently and autonomously than usual without third-party governing authority. b) Due to the pseudonymous nature, just with a base-58 encoded identifier of 26–35 alphanumeric characters that we call Bitcoin address [25], along with a related private key, everyone can send or receive Bitcoin. There is no need to provide any extra information related to real-world identities in this process, which protects the privacy of participants to a certain extent.

Yet till now, keeping a comprehensive and detailed understanding of the activities in Bitcoin is still an extremely tricky task due to the hugeness and dynamism of transaction data. As of 16th Jan 2021, there are more than one million daily active addresses and 300 thousand daily transactions in Bitcoin (https://studio.glassnode.com/).

However, most existing work dissects the Bitcoin transaction network just from a static perspective (i.e., studying a snapshot of the transaction network at time t). Few schemes considering dynamism either try to analyze behavioral changes of Bitcoin users by dividing the transaction ledger into small temporal batches of different granularities [1,38,39], or introduce various temporal attributes(e.g., temporal features generated by LSTM, node embedded representation capturing the dynamism of the graph sequence and attributed temporal heterogeneous motifs) to improve classification rates of Bitcoin users at a static point in time [20,28,36]. Nevertheless, these efforts simply reveal the fact that the behavior of Bitcoin entities may constantly change over time and the effectiveness of temporal properties proposed in classification tasks, without giving corresponding solutions of real-time classification in dynamic scenarios.

We are the first to conduct a dynamic behavior monitor for the purpose of identifying Bitcoin accounts as soon as possible. The main motivation behind this research is that, with more detailed and targeted regulatory matters deployed actively in advance, we will meet fewer regulatory difficulties, especially those caused by the gradual proliferation of suspicious funds in the vast transaction network. In addition, note that the feature extraction is time-dependent. Regular features like 'total number of transactions' extracted by a wallet node in 2016 may all have been changed in 2019. A natural question arises: whether the features selected at the old-time point can also perform well in the event of data changes at a new point.

Obviously, existing classification methods cannot be applied directly to dynamic scenarios. Unlike our task of trying to identify targets quickly when anomalous behavior occurs, what they do is always a static post-mortem analysis where the target wallet nodes have been inactive for a long time. Thus, it is highly desirable to explore a new classification model for dynamic scenarios.

Certainly, this model should also take into account the subsequent, unbearable space-time overhead.

In this paper, we propose BitMonitor, a powerful scheme for monitoring the dynamic behavior of Bitcoin users. Specifically, the model is built on a Bi-Temporal network where not only the timeline of transactions related to a user is dissected but more detailed temporal information about tracking and tracing money flows associated with these transactions is given. We give a deep insight into these flows based on a natural assumption that malicious accounts often carry out multi-level transactions like money laundering to conceal the true flow of funds and then escape scrutiny. Of course, some existing studies have also demonstrated that multi-order neighbor information may be helpful to the classification of Bitcoin users [15, 30]. To reduce spatial and temporal complexity, we introduce flows extraction and flow sampling in the process of data processing. Finally, we perform sequence tagging and weighted voting to integrate historical information and then realize real-time classification.

Our contributions can be briefly summarized as follows:

- We design BitMonitor for real-time dynamic classification. To achieve this, we first study the Bitcoin blockchain in the form of a bipartite address-transaction graph. The combination of two heterogeneous information adds temporal attributes to the transaction graph.
- The key step in BitMonitor is the construction of Bi-Temporal transaction network, which dissects the trading information in two dimensions. On the one hand, transactions directly related to the target wallet node can be arranged in time series according to the additional timestamp. On the other hand, it is possible to perform deeper backtracking and tracing of the money flows associated with these transactions.
- To facilitate the training and evaluation of the dynamic classification model (BitMonitor), time slicing is performed, together with subsequent dynamic sequence tagging and weighted voting incorporating historical information, we can classify wallet nodes at different time points.
- We evaluate the dynamic classification performance based on two requirements, one is to identify the correct category of nodes as early as possible and the other is to reduce misclassification during the intermediate process. We balance the two requirements by a weighting coefficient w. Additional experiments in static scenarios validate the effectiveness of the feature extraction framework and present some useful findings.

To the best of our knowledge, this is the first to study real-time classification tasks in dynamic scenarios. The remainder of this paper is structured as follows. After this introduction, Sect. 2 summarizes the related work. Section 3 provides the preliminaries needed for the paper. A detailed description of the proposed methodology BitMonitor can be found in Sect. 4. Section 5 presents the experimental results and analysis. After a brief discussion of BitMonitor in Sect. 6, we conclude this paper in Sect. 7.

2   Related Work

Since the birth of Bitcoin, its anonymity has been controversial. On the one hand, transactions related to malicious or illegal activities are heavily deployed due to the unregulated nature and pseudo-anonymity. On the other hand, the transparency of the transaction ledger and the traceability of pseudonyms in Bitcoin have made it possible to attack anonymity [31]. From the perspective of conducting better financial forensics and security regulation, we focus on the latter here. Relevant research can be roughly divided into the following three categories.

Address Deanonymization. Initial methods of de-anonymization (i.e. associating wallet addresses belonging to the same user), mainly used heuristic rules such as 'multi-input' and 'change address' [5,23,31]. The effectiveness of the heuristic was further investigated in [12]. More recently, some new methods of address clustering and community detection have been proposed. In addition, in order to deal with some privacy enhancement technologies that have emerged on Bitcoin [7,34], there have been some corresponding analysis and mitigation measures [14,24,36]. However, the methods proposed above do not achieve true de-anonymization. A laborious but direct approach that correlates the wallet address on the chain with the real-world personal information of the user off-chain is to gather information from social networks. There have been a few attempts to help analyze some particular activities such as hacking subnetworks [11], tor hidden service users [3] and human traffickers [29].

Illegal Activities Detection. Typical illegal activities include darknet market [17,19], ransomware [2,27], money laundering [24,35] and scam [6]. In [2], ransomware-related transactions can be automatically detected by using local topological information available on the Bitcoin transaction graph. [17] proposed a voting-based method to identify newly emerged darknet markets' transactions and addresses. Based on a novel analysis of transactions history, [32] can efficiently collect a large number of the HYIP (High Yield Investment Programs) operators' Bitcoin addresses and achieve a 93.75% detection accuracy on a recent public dataset. In particular, some work has built a Bitcoin transaction network visualization system to help identify illegal abnormal transaction patterns including money laundering and denial of service attacks [8,9,22].

Relevant Services Identification. Analytical research related to the classification of various service types is likewise of considerable significance in financial regulation. For instance, Bitcoin exchange functions as a medium for the exchange of digital and fiat currencies, providing a breakthrough in anti-money laundering tasks [30]. Mechanisms like deep auto-encoder [26] and hybrid motifs [36] have been introduced to identify addresses associated with the mixed currency service. Besides, [37] provided a detailed analysis of mixing services in a generic abstraction manner, and summarized two important mixing mechanisms. More recently, with the popularity of graph learning technology, a series of related algorithms have been introduced to explore more possibilities in node identification tasks [4,28,35].

In short, whether for the task of classifying illegal/legal activities or different types of services, no study exists on dynamic behavior monitoring of Bitcoin users for timely detection. Our work is the first to do such analysis, and the goal is to propose a general framework for Bitcoin user behavior analysis, not specifically for a particular classification task.

3 Preliminaries

In this section, we give a rough overview of Bitcoin's transaction structure. Unlike traditional credit card transactions, the transaction structure of Bitcoin is based on an unspent transaction output (UTXO) model.

A Bitcoin transaction, as shown in the left half of Fig. 1, comprises a list of inputs and outputs. Each input is linked to an existing unspent transaction output (i.e. UTXO) and each output denotes a new generated UTXO associated with the recipient. An UTXO is related to only one specific address whereas an address can be connected to many UTXOs, either by receiving UTXOs generated from transactions or by spending those as inputs of new transactions, as shown in the right half of Fig. 1. Additionally, note that UTXO is indivisible so it can only be spent as a whole.

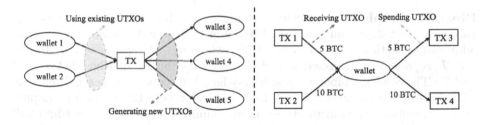

Fig. 1. Transaction structure of Bitcoin (Left: transaction perspective; Right: wallet address perspective)

With such a transaction structure, any Bitcoin can be tracked or traced back easily between transaction nodes and wallet nodes in the form of UTXO. This unique design provides an opportunity to monitor the flow of suspicious funds.

4 Methodology

This section provides a detailed description of our methodology towards identifying Bitcoin users over time. The overview of the proposed scheme BitMonitor is presented in Fig. 2. After the heterogeneous graph information processing module, a Bi-Temporal network based on the perspective of target nodes is established. With the help of Bi-Temporal network dissection, deeper information mining and incremental feature updating can be implemented in the following dynamic behavior classifier.

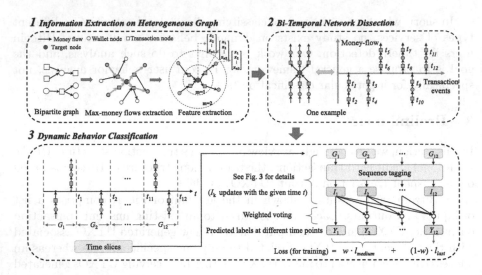

Fig. 2. The overview of the proposed scheme BitMonitor

4.1   Information Extraction on Heterogeneous Graph

Bipartite Graph Construction. Based on the background introduction of Bitcoin in Sect. 3, we can study the Bitcoin blockchain in the form of a bipartite address-transaction graph $\mathcal{G} = (\mathcal{A}, \mathcal{T}, \mathcal{E})$, where $a \in \mathcal{A}$ represents an address, $t \in \mathcal{T}$ represents a transaction and $\mathcal{E}$ represents the set of edges between $\mathcal{A}$ and $\mathcal{T}$. The resulting bipartite graph may have bidirectional edges and multiple edges when the same wallet address node appears in both the inputs and outputs of a transaction, or multiple times in the inputs (outputs). These edges will be unfolded or merged later for the local topological analysis of the nodes to be classified. The combination of two heterogeneous information adds temporal attributes to the transaction graph as well as facilitates the tracking and tracing of money flows. For example, when a Bitcoin user receives a transfer, the source of the funds can be traced back, and similarly, when a Bitcoin user initiates a transfer, we can track where the funds go later.

Max-money Flows Extraction. A Bitcoin user is usually associated with many transactions, and then these transactions are related to a larger number of users. Reasonable simplification is necessary here for that once more in-depth money flow information is taken into account, the number of relevant nodes involved is numerous. Specifically, we perform a max-money flows extraction. Starting one by one from the transactions directly related to a wallet node to be classified (i.e. the user's first-order neighbors), if it is an incoming transaction to receive funds (we note it as *received transaction*), we only select the wallet node sending the largest amount. Accordingly, if it is an outgoing transaction to transfer funds (we note it as *spent transaction*), we only select the wallet node receiving the largest amount. These selected nodes act as second-order neighbors. Third-order neighbors are obtained by selecting the relevant previous or next transaction along with the just max-money flow (if linked to a *received transaction*, then here is the previous one). Extracting deep neighbor information in this way, until there is a Coinbase transaction (a transaction initiated by the system that rewards miners and cannot be tracked back) or an unspent transaction output is encountered (cannot be traced further) or the required maximum number of layers is met.

Feature Extraction. Overall, there are three types of nodes requiring feature extraction: main wallet node, transaction node, and neighbor wallet node. The main wallet node, i.e. the node to be classified, is characterized to grasp global information of the transaction records, then the feature of transaction nodes and neighbor wallet nodes is extracted to incorporate relevant neighborhood characters. Note that, the same wallet address may appear multiple times in the input (output) list of a transaction, possibly to split big funds, so we merge such multi-inputs or multi-outputs during feature extraction.

The main wallet node includes 22 features, which are listed in Table 1. As in most of the existing work, these features are basic first-order statistical features related to the number of transactions, transaction amounts, and transaction time of the target node.

The transaction node includes 12 features, which are listed in Table 2. Here, we extract the basic first-order statistical features from the transaction amount and the list of transaction inputs/outputs.

To simplify the problem of feature updating in dynamic scenarios, feature extraction of the neighbor wallet node is only based on static information at the moment of association with the main wallet node, which is completely different from that of the main wallet node. The neighbor wallet node includes 4 features, which are listed as follows: whether it is related to the Coinbase transaction, whether the output has been spent, the relevant transaction amount, and the interval between the receipt of funds and the outflow of funds.

4.2   Bi-Temporal Network Dissection

After a series of transaction data processing steps in the previous subsection, we can dissect the transaction information related to a wallet address node from the perspective of a Bi-Temporal transaction network. That is, on the one hand, the wallet address node is involved in a large number of transactions and these transactions can be arranged in time series according to the additional timestamp. On the other hand, money flows associated with these transactions can be traced back or tracked over time. As illustrated by the example in Fig. 2, for the already extracted disorderly money flows related to the target node, we can perform temporal profiling from two perspectives: transaction timeline and money-flowing. Then, among the listed time points of transactions: $t_1 < t_3 < t_6 < t_8 < t_9 < t_{12}$, $t_2 < t_1$, $t_4 < t_3$, $t_6 < t_5$, $t_8 < t_7$, $t_{10} < t_9$, $t_{12} < t_{11}$. In a word, the idea of

Table 1. Basic statistical features of main wallet node

Feature	Description
N_{total}	The total number of transactions
$N_{coinbase}$	The number of Coinbase transactions
N_{spent}	The number of *spent transactions*
$N_{received}$	The number of *received transactions*
$V_{total,spent}$	Total spent BTC
$V_{total,received}$	Total received BTC
$V_{max,spent}$	The maximum value of spent BTC
$V_{max,received}$	The maximum value of received BTC,
$V_{min,spent}$	The minimum value of spent BTC
$V_{min,received}$	The minimum value of received BTC
$V_{mean,spent}$	The mean value of spent BTC
$V_{mean,received}$	The mean value of received BTC
$I_{lifetime}$	Total active time (interval between the first transaction and the last transaction, calculated by blocks)
$I_{max,spent}$	The maximum interval of *spent transactions*
$I_{max,received}$	The maximum interval of *received transactions*
$I_{min,spent}$	The minimum interval of *spent transactions*
$I_{min,received}$	The minimum interval of *received transactions*
$I_{mean,spent}$	The mean interval of *spent transactions*
$I_{mean,received}$	The mean interval of *received transactions*
$I_{max,all}$	The maximum interval of transactions
$I_{min,all}$	The minimum interval of transactions
$I_{mean,all}$	The mean interval of transactions

Table 2. Basic statistical features of transaction node

Feature	Description
$Is_{coinbase}$	Whether it is a Coinbase transaction
N_{total}	The total number of wallet nodes involved
$N_{outputs}$	The number of wallet nodes in outputs
N_{inputs}	The number of wallet nodes in inputs
V_{total}	The total BTC amount of the transaction
$V_{max,outputs}$	The maximum value of BTC amount in outputs
$V_{max,inputs}$	The maximum value of BTC amount in inputs
$V_{min,outputs}$	The minimum value of BTC amount in outputs
$V_{min,inputs}$	The minimum value of the amount in inputs
$V_{mean,outputs}$	The mean value of BTC amount in outputs
$V_{mean,inputs}$	The mean value of BTC amount in inputs
V_{fee}	The transaction fee (Satoshi)

Bi-Temporal network dissection lays the foundation for the subsequent dynamic behavioral analysis.

4.3 Dynamic Behavior Classification

In this subsection, we will introduce the main body of the proposed BitMonitor, i.e. the design of a dynamic behavior classifier. First, we slice the Bi-Temporal network of the main wallet node. Then sequence tagging of each time slice is performed. Finally, the historical sequence tagging information is fused to realize the task of classifying wallet nodes at different time points.

Time Slicing. Many wallet nodes are rich in transaction information, with up to ten million transaction records for a single node under extreme conditions. To facilitate training and classification, we focus on the transaction information within the last year of each node and slice it into 12 time slices, with each month as a time slice (about 4320 blocks). Here, the time interval used for slicing is just a hyper-parameter that can be adjusted according to the actual processing capacity and task requirements.

Another reason for slicing is based on such speculation: A wallet node carries out ransomware transaction activity within a certain period, and then is marked as a ransomware malicious node. However, this does not mean that every transaction associated with this wallet node is involved in ransomware activity. Before the ransomware transactions occur, it may only engage in normal transactions such as shopping and investment, and similarly, in the period after the ransomware transactions, it may conduct activities like asset transfer or money laundering. Of course, papers mentioned in Sect. 1 have shown that the behavioral activities of wallet nodes vary over time. So slicing in time, rather than fusing all the information together, is more helpful to analyze this periodic and changing trading activity.

Sequence Tagging. Then, we conduct sequential tagging of each time slice, details of this process can be seen in Fig. 3.

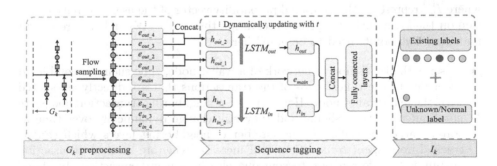

Fig. 3. The details of sequence tagging in BitMonitor

First, for the transaction flows in month k, we sample two flows with the maximum value of received BTC and spent BTC. Set the maximum neighbor order in each direction to N. Following the feature extraction method in Sect. 4.1, we can obtain the embedded representations of the main wallet node denoted as e_{main} and its neighbors denoted as $e_{in\_1}, e_{in\_2}, ..., e_{in\_N}$; $e_{out\_1}, e_{out\_2}, ..., e_{out\_N}$ (here, e_{in_i} corresponds to the i_{th} order neighbor in the direction of money-inflow, while e_{out_i} corresponds the i_{th} order neighbor in the direction of money-outflow).

Second, to ensure homogeneity of the data for subsequent dynamic analysis, we concatenate the neighboring transaction node and wallet node two by two. This results in new neighborhood representations denoted as $h_{in\_1}, h_{in\_2}, ..., h_{in\_n}$; $h_{out\_1}, h_{out\_2}, ..., h_{out\_n}$ $(n = N/2)$.

Then, LSTM algorithm is used to fuse the neighbor information with increasing number of neighbor layers. Details are as follows:

$$h_{in} = LSTM_{in}(h_{in\_1}, h_{in\_2}, ..., h_{in\_n}) \tag{1}$$
$$h_{out} = LSTM_{out}(h_{out\_1}, h_{out\_2}, ..., h_{out\_l}) \tag{2}$$

Here, we use two *Long Short Term Memory* [13] networks $LSTM_{in}$ and $LSTM_{out}$ to aggregate neighboring features in different directions. They have the same operating mechanism with two hidden layers. In parentheses is a series of input values. $LSTM_{in}$ can aggregate n layers neighbor information (using zero padding in case of Coinbase transaction blocking backtracking), for that once a *received transaction* is generated, all information related to the source of funds is immediately exposed; while the number of neighbor layers l that $LSTM_{out}$ can aggregate needs to be determined based on the actual time t for node class determination.

Finally, after concatenating the neighborhood features of incoming and outgoing directions as well as the features of the main wallet node, we can classify the activity intention of the wallet nodes in month k by three fully connected layers as described in Eq. 3,

$$I_k^{(t)} = Softmax(W_3 \cdot Relu(W_2 \cdot Relu(W_1 \cdot CONCAT(e_{main}^{(k)}, h_{in}^{(k)}, h_{out}^{(k,t)})))) \tag{3}$$

where $I_k^{(t)}$ represents the predicted probability vector of the user's activity intention on the k_{th} month at a given observation time t. W_1, W_2 and W_3 are weight matrices. Two points need to be noted here.

- Observe the Bi-Temporal network of a wallet node, time slicing is conducted according to the timestamps of the transactions that are directly associated with the main wallet node. However, other neighboring transaction nodes are not limited by time slicing and they still change dynamically over time as stated earlier. Specifically, the number of neighboring layers which can be tracked from *spent transactions* will increase, when an unspent transaction output is transferred out to someone else in a new transaction. In short, transaction information of a historical time slice is still dynamically changing at different time points. Another advantage of the LSTM algorithm is that it can keep incremental updating. According to the principle of LSTM algorithm [13], if the n_{th} order neighborhood X_n appears, feature representation of the first n orders can be simply computed based on X_n and information passed down from the previous state. So we don't need to keep all the historical source data all the time, which can greatly reduce the spatio-temporal overhead.

- The category labels already revealed in the currently labeled datasets do not encompass all categories of wallet nodes, but only contain a few key categories that need to be paid attention to. However, when the activity intent of a wallet node in a certain period is analyzed, it is likely that the wallet node is only engaged in ordinary transactions or other types of transactions not mentioned. Thus, such category information (unknown/normal) needs to be taken into consideration when tagging the time-slice information.

Weighted Voting. For a given time point t, after sequentially tagging all historical time slices, we need to fuse these results to determine the most likely label of the wallet node at time t. We first summarize these results in a summation fashion (this process is equivalent to voting). The weighting operation is specific to different trading activities, and its purpose is to highlight occasional but noteworthy activities, such as illegal activities. The entire weighted voting mechanism is described in Eq. 4:

$$Y_t = Softmax(W_4 \cdot (\sum_{k=1}^{t} I_k^{(t)})) \qquad (4)$$

where W_4 is a weight matrix, Y_t represents the probability vector indicating the likelihood that the wallet node belongs to each category at time t. Our predicted label is the largest one of Y_t.

Loss Function. Next, we design the loss function used for model training. Note that, due to the dynamic nature of user activity, any other type of transaction activity is possible before or after representative transaction activities (directly related to the real label of wallet nodes) occur. Thus, one necessary assumption should be given that the wallet nodes in our adopted labeled dataset did not perform, or only rarely performed other special activities that may influence the judgment of their categories. What's more, we cannot know the true labeling time of the dataset, the only thing that can be guaranteed is the ground truth label at the last time point (all transactions have been revealed). We balance the need to improve the correctness of classification at the last time point and the need to reduce misclassification during the intermediate process by a weighting coefficient w in the following loss function $\mathcal{L}$. Misclassification during the intermediate process here means being incorrectly classified into other categories other than the true label and normal/unknown label(representative events haven't happened yet).

$$\mathcal{L} = \frac{1}{|X|} \cdot \sum_{i=1}^{|X|} (w \cdot l_{medium}^{(i)} + (1-w) \cdot l_{last}^{(i)})$$

$$= \frac{1}{|X|} \cdot \sum_{i=1}^{|X|} (w \cdot \frac{1}{11} \sum_{t=1}^{11} l_t^{(i)} + (1-w) \cdot l_{12}^{(i)}) \tag{5}$$

$$l_t^{(i)} = \begin{cases} -\sum_{c=1}^{C} \hat{y}_c^{(i)} \cdot log(Y_{t,c}^{(i)} + Y_{t,normal/unknown}^{(i)}) & , t = 1, 2, ..., 11 \\ -\sum_{c=1}^{C} \hat{y}_c^{(i)} \cdot log(Y_{t,c}^{(i)}) & , t = 12 \end{cases} \tag{6}$$

As presented in Eq. 5 and Eq. 6, $|X|$ is the size of the training set, $l_{medium}^{(i)}$ denotes the loss of sample x_i during the intermediate process, $l_{last}^{(i)}$ denotes the loss of sample x_i at the last time point, $l_t^{(i)}$ denotes the loss of sample x_i at time t, $Y_{t,c}^{(i)}$ is the predicted probability of label c for the sample x_i (at time t). $\hat{y}_c^{(i)} = 1$ if the ground truth label of sample x_i is c, else $\hat{y}_c^{(i)} = 0$. C denotes the number of label categories in the dataset. It can be seen that the loss function $\mathcal{L}$ is changed from the cross-entropy function, just distinguishing between the last time point and the intermediate process in the way loss is calculated as well as adding the weighting coefficient w.

5   Experiments

In this section, we are devoted to evaluating the effectiveness of the proposed scheme BitMonitor. After a brief description of the dataset collection module, we illustrate the effectiveness of the Bi-Temporal network construction in static scenarios and present an experimental analysis of some key parameter settings. Finally, we evaluate the classification performance of BitMonitor in dynamic scenarios.

5.1   Dataset Description

It is well known that Bitcoin transaction data is recorded in an open and transparent block ledger, which can be obtained and analyzed by anyone who joins the Bitcoin network. In this paper, we synchronize the first 672,627 transaction blocks (as of 1st Jan 2021) and use BlockSci v0.7 [16] tool to perform block parsing. We use a seven-categories Bitcoin addresses dataset which contains 26,313 addresses [33]. Details of this dataset can be seen in Table 3.

Table 3. Dataset details

Category	Description	Number
Exchange/Wallet	A medium for the exchange of digital and fiat currencies	10,469
Faucet	Offering small amount of Bitcoin to those completing the assigned task	340
Gambling	Various types of gambling activities	6,734
HYIP	High Yield Investment Programs	2,026
Market	Online market place	1,900
Mixer	Helping with money laundering to avoid Bitcoin flow tracking	3,199
Mining pool	An entity that gathers miners for mining	1,645

5.2 Experimental Analysis in Static Scenarios

In this subsection, we first present a simplified model configuration modified from BitMonitor. A series of experimental analyses based on it not only fully illustrate the effectiveness of the feature extraction frame incorporating multi-order neighbors, but also give some interesting conclusions. The feature extraction framework here includes bipartite graph construction, max-money flows extraction and multi-order heterogeneous neighbor information extraction.

A Simplified Model Configuration. The proposed scheme BitMonitor can be modified for static scenarios with a simplified model configuration named BitMonitor_static. It is essentially a feature extraction framework taken from BitMonitor. We show its details in Fig. 4. Here, instead of expanding transactions related to the target wallet node on a timeline, all relevant transactions are roughly placed together. Unlike the Sequence Tagging module in Sect. 4.3, where flows with the largest amount of received BTC and spent BTC are sampled on each time slice to reduce spatio-temporal complexity, we sample the top 5 largest flows in both directions separately here. In general, merging multiple flows is more robust than merging one single flow, so we perform several experiments and choose '5' from the perspective of performance and computational complexity. These flows are then merged by averaging. Finally, after concatenating the neighborhood features of incoming and outgoing directions as well as the

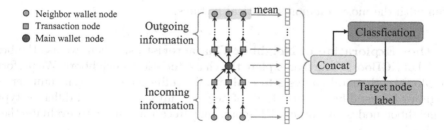

Fig. 4. The feature extraction framework BitMonitor_static used in static scenarios

features of the main wallet node, we can obtain the final node label by using a common machine learning classifier.

Benefit of Bi-Temporal Transaction Network. In addition to facilitating dynamic profiling, another advantage of the Bi-Temporal network is the ability to fuse multi-order neighbor information. Based on the simplified model configuration above, we illustrate the effectiveness of the feature extraction framework by comparing it with the prior best feature processing scheme [21] on this labeled dataset. That work was proposed by Lin et al. mainly to enrich the feature expression by introducing higher-order moments. We cite the results given in that paper directly, keeping the same experimental configuration including Micro-F1 score, Macro-F1 score, and 10-fold cross-validation strategy.

In addition, to facilitate the evaluation, we choose the same six common machine learning classifiers as the original paper. We consider the first 10 orders of neighbor information here. Table 4 shows the detailed results.

Table 4. Performance in static scenarios

Method	High-order moment scheme		BitMonitor_static(ours)	
	Micro-F1	Macro-F1	Micro-F1	Macro-F1
Logistic regression	0.48	0.45	0.77	0.74
SVM	0.47	0.46	0.83	0.79
AdaBoost	0.36	0.36	0.63	0.56
Random Forest	0.83	0.81	0.82	0.79
XGBoost	0.83	0.82	**0.91**	**0.90**
LightGBM	**0.87**	**0.86**	0.90	0.89

Although Lin et al. add high-order moment features to improve performance, the best result of these six classifiers is only 0.87 Micro-F1/0.86 Macro-F1. Our scheme performs better on most classifiers and achieves the best result of 0.91 Micro-F1/0.90 Macro-F1 by XGBoost. Obviously, these results illustrate the effectiveness of the neighborhood information used in performance improvement, even with the most common statistical features.

Further Exploration of Neighbor Characteristics. Then, we use the best model of XGBoost to further explore the characteristics of neighbors. We perform specific experimental analyses to evaluate the influence of different numbers of neighbor layers, different directions of neighbor information, and different types of neighbor nodes. Accuracy, F1 score, and Recall are used to evaluate these results.

Table 5 shows the details of the experimental results. The first column of it presents different experimental configurations in such a form (choice of direction,

Table 5. Results of different experimental parameters in BitMonitor_static

Experimental parameters	Accuracy	Macro-F1	Macro-Recall
BitMonitor_static(main, 0, none)	0.773	0.701	0.676
BitMonitor_static(all, 2, two)	0.898	0.883	0.856
BitMonitor_static(all, 4, two)	0.904	0.899	0.872
BitMonitor_static(all, 6, two)	**0.906**	**0.900**	**0.873**
BitMonitor_static(all, 8, two)	0.905	**0.900**	0.872
BitMonitor_static(all, 10, two)	**0.906**	0.898	0.871
BitMonitor_static(main+in, 10, two)	0.824	0.756	0.722
BitMonitor_static(main+out, 10 , two)	0.901	0.897	0.872
BitMonitor_static(all, 10, wallet)	0.848	0.813	0.779
BitMonitor_static(all, 10, transaction)	0.905	0.899	**0.873**

number of neighbor layers, choice of node type). Specifically, the first parameter term includes four choices: considering only the feature of main wallet node, considering main wallet node and incoming direction neighbors (associated with *received transaction*), considering main wallet node and outgoing direction neighbors (associated with *spent transaction*), and considering all these information. The second parameter term examines different numbers of neighbor layers. The third parameter term includes three options: considering only neighbor wallet nodes, considering only neighbor transaction nodes, and considering both types.

The best result is 0.906 Accuracy/0.900 Macro-F1/0.873 Macro-Recall with BitMonitor_static (all, 6, two), which shows that neighbor information of both directions and both types are all helpful for classification. Further, the result using only the neighbor features in the outgoing direction is significantly better than that in the incoming direction. It can be concluded that the *spent transaction*_related trading pattern of wallet nodes reveals more information for classification. This is not difficult to understand, for example, malicious nodes may intentionally launder money and share the spoils after conducting illegal trading activities. In addition, to some extent, fusing more layers of neighbors will obtain better classification results. We have achieved the best results when fusing 6 layers of neighbors in this experiment.

Experimental Analysis of Flows Extraction and Flow Sampling. In Sect. 4.1 and Sect. 4.3, we propose to reduce the complexity of the data analysis by max-money flows extraction mode (tracking and tracing the maximum funds) as well as sampling flows corresponding to the maximum *spent transaction* and *received transaction*. Other methods that can be used include focusing on the minimum money flow similarly or doing these in a random way (flows extraction: in the process of tracking and tracing the funds, if a transaction has multiple inputs or outputs, randomly select one; flow sampling: for the previously generated transaction flows, randomly select one). We compare these three methods and present the results in Table 6.

Table 6. Results of different options in flows extraction and flow sampling

Option	Accuracy	Macro-F1	Macro-Recall
Max	0.906	0.898	0.871
Min	0.909	0.898	0.869
Rand	0.897	0.888	0.856

From Table 6, we can see that the first two options are slightly better compared with the random option. Although the min option has higher accuracy than the max option, the max option has higher recall. There is only a very slight difference between them. A reasonable explanation is as follows: The generation of small amounts of money may be caused by change wallets (wallets that appear in the transaction output list to make change). These change wallet addresses have the same owner as the main wallet node, so mining the characteristics of these neighboring addresses will deepen our understanding of the main wallet node's behavior pattern. Besides, large amounts of money have a strong user-subject purpose. In all, both options are helpful for classification.

5.3   Performance Evaluation in Dynamic Scenarios

In this subsection, we evaluate the classification performance of BitMonitor in dynamic scenarios. Relevant experimental hyperparameters of BitMonitor are set with the learning rate of 0.1, the batch size of 1000, the epochs of 800, and a SGD optimizer. The num_layers and the hidden_size of $LSTM_{in}/LSTM_{out}$ we used are 2 and 60 respectively. The output dimension of the first fully connected layer is 400 and the output dimension of the second is 200. The ratio of the training set, validation set, and test set is 6:2:2. Besides, we use dropout and BatchNorm function to prevent over-fitting (the rate of dropout we set is 0.2).

As stated in Sect. 4.3, due to the lack of real labels at intermediate time points, it is not possible to evaluate the discriminant results for each time point. In order to demonstrate the effectiveness of BitMonitor, we put forward two requirements. One is to identify the correct category of nodes as early as possible and the other is to reduce misclassification during the intermediate process. Note that early transactions may not have been involved in illegal activities. Instead, they may be just ordinary transfer activities. Thus, 'as early as possible' means that we are able to classify correctly as soon as some representative transaction activities occur, rather than rudely classifying them quickly.

Table 7 shows the details of performance evaluation. It includes the average classification performance during the intermediate process, the classification performance at the last time point, and the average earliest time point t_{early} at which the node's category is consistently and correctly identified (i.e. the target wallet node is correctly classified at all time points after this point). The hyperparameter w is the weighting factor used in Eq. 5 to balance the need to improve the correctness of classification at the last time point and the need to reduce misclassification during the intermediate process. From this table, we can see that when the w increases, misclassification in the intermediate process decreases, but the classification performance is worse at the last time point. Besides, our proposed method can consistently and correctly identify the wallet nodes at a relatively early time (the total number of time points is 12 in this paper).

Table 7. Performance in dynamic scenarios

w	Intermediate process			The last time point			t_{early}
	Accuracy	Macro-F1	Macro-Recall	Accuracy	Macro-F1	Macro-Recall	
0.0	0.470	0.469	0.534	0.854	0.814	0.792	6.25
0.1	0.898	0.880	0.855	0.850	0.813	0.778	6.12
0.2	0.907	0.884	0.860	0.845	0.710	0.680	5.94

Finally, we look at the identification results of a HYIP wallet node(address: "1KoeBcBM5MzqwAJh8E6bsubbq9LtixygqE") at different time points ($w = 0.1$). This node is classified as 'Unknown/Normal' at the first time point, but can be consistently classified as 'HYIP' from the second (i.e. July 24th, 2015). By manual inspection, this node does receive/send small Bitcoins with similar amounts frequently after June 24th, which is consistent with its characteristics: attracting investments and offering daily interest rates to investors.

6   Discussion

In this section, we give a short discussion of the proposed BitMonitor. Firstly, in terms of the model itself, there are three limitations or improvements as follows. a) The focus of our paper is on the implementation of BitMonitor, a model capable of dynamic detection of Bitcoin user behavior. Nevertheless, additional experiments have been carried out on a simplified static scene to illustrate the rationality and effectiveness of the feature extraction framework incorporating multi-order neighbors. Making deeper model improvements to outperform other work in static scenes (not just those for feature optimization) is our next step. b) Although our model has taken spatio-temporal complexity into account, some other aspects of data processing such as the speed of transaction parsing and feature extraction will have a great impact on the model size and update latency. We will specifically analyze these changes as the Bitcoin data grows dynamically in future work. c) Due to the lack of labels at different time points, we can only make a general assessment of dynamic classification performance.

Secondly, in terms of the applicability of the model, the proposed BitMonitor is only applicable to blockchains with an UTXO-based transaction mode like Bitcoin, and cannot be applied to Ethereum (an account-based transaction mode). Nevertheless, the idea of dynamic sequence tagging of time slices as well as weighted voting incorporating historical information can be borrowed. Furthermore, if we shift the main object of model analysis from the wallet address nodes to the transaction hash nodes, we can analyze transaction-related tasks in a similar way, such as conducting a more scientific and comprehensive analysis of mixing behavior to identify the mixing transactions rather than only locating to some possible wallet addresses.

7   Conclusion

In this paper, we propose BitMonitor, which enables dynamic behavioral monitoring of Bitcoin wallet address nodes. Based on the constructed Bi-Temporal transaction network, we are able to dissect the trading information in two dimensions. On the one hand, transactions directly related to the target wallet node can be time-sliced. Together with subsequent dynamic sequence tagging and weighted voting incorporating historical information, we can classify nodes at different time points. On the other hand, it is possible to perform deeper backtracking and tracing of the money flows associated with these transactions. We demonstrate the effectiveness of the resulting multi-order neighborhood information in a static experimental scenario. Finally, we evaluate the dynamic classification performance from two aspects.

Acknowledgement. This work is supported by The National Key Research and Development Program of China No. 2021YFB3101400 and the Strategic Priority Research Program of Chinese Academy of Sciences, Grant No. XDC02040400.

References

1. Agarwal, R., Barve, S., Shukla, S.K.: Detecting malicious accounts in permissionless blockchains using temporal graph properties. Appl. Netw. Sci. **6**(1), 1–30 (2021)
2. Akcora, C.G., Li, Y., Gel, Y.R., Kantarcioglu, M.: Bitcoinheist: topological data analysis for ransomware prediction on the bitcoin blockchain. In: Bessiere, C. (ed.) Proceedings of the Twenty-Ninth International Joint Conference on Artificial Intelligence, IJCAI 2020. pp. 4439–4445. ijcai.org (2020)
3. Al Jawaheri, H., Al Sabah, M., Boshmaf, Y., Erbad, A.: Deanonymizing tor hidden service users through bitcoin transactions analysis. Comput. Secur. **89**, 101684 (2020)
4. Alarab, I., Prakoonwit, S., Nacer, M.I.: Competence of graph convolutional networks for anti-money laundering in bitcoin blockchain. In: Proceedings of the 2020 5th International Conference on Machine Learning Technologies, pp. 23–27 (2020)
5. Androulaki, E., Karame, G.O., Roeschlin, M., Scherer, T., Capkun, S.: Evaluating user privacy in bitcoin. In: Sadeghi, A.-R. (ed.) FC 2013. LNCS, vol. 7859, pp. 34–51. Springer, Heidelberg (2013). https://doi.org/10.1007/978-3-642-39884-1_4
6. Bartoletti, M., Pes, B., Serusi, S.: Data mining for detecting bitcoin ponzi schemes. In: 2018 Crypto Valley Conference on Blockchain Technology (CVCBT), pp. 75–84. IEEE (2018). https://doi.org/10.1109/CVCBT.2018.00014
7. Bonneau, J., Narayanan, A., Miller, A., Clark, J., Kroll, J.A., Felten, E.W.: Mixcoin: anonymity for bitcoin with accountable mixes. In: Christin, N., Safavi-Naini, R. (eds.) FC 2014. LNCS, vol. 8437, pp. 486–504. Springer, Heidelberg (2014). https://doi.org/10.1007/978-3-662-45472-5_31

8. Chen, W., Wu, J., Zheng, Z., Chen, C., Zhou, Y.: Market manipulation of bitcoin: evidence from mining the MT. GOX transaction network. In: IEEE INFOCOM 2019-IEEE Conference on Computer Communications, pp. 964–972. IEEE (2019)

9. Di Battista, G., Di Donato, V., Patrignani, M., Pizzonia, M., Roselli, V., Tamassia, R.: Bitconeview: visualization of flows in the bitcoin transaction graph. In: 2015 IEEE Symposium on Visualization for Cyber Security (VizSec), pp. 1–8. IEEE (2015). https://doi.org/10.1109/VIZSEC.2015.7312773

10. Foley, S., Karlsen, J.R., Putniņš, T.J.: Sex, drugs, and bitcoin: how much illegal activity is financed through cryptocurrencies? Rev. Finan. Stud. 32(5), 1798–1853 (2019). https://doi.org/10.1093/rfs/hhz015

11. Goldsmith, D., Grauer, K., Shmalo, Y.: Analyzing hack subnetworks in the bitcoin transaction graph. Appl. Netw. Sci. 5(1), 1–20 (2020). https://doi.org/10.1007/s41109-020-00261-7

12. Harrigan, M., Fretter, C.: The unreasonable effectiveness of address clustering. In: 2016 Intl IEEE Conferences on Ubiquitous Intelligence & Computing, Advanced and Trusted Computing, Scalable Computing and Communications, Cloud and Big Data Computing, Internet of People, and Smart World Congress (UIC/ATC/ScalCom/CBDCom/IoP/SmartWorld), pp. 368–373. IEEE (2016)

13. Hochreiter, S., Schmidhuber, J.: Long short-term memory. Neural Comput. 9(8), 1735–1780 (1997)

14. Hu, Y., Seneviratne, S., Thilakarathna, K., Fukuda, K., Seneviratne, A.: Characterizing and detecting money laundering activities on the bitcoin network. arXiv preprint arXiv:1912.12060 (2019)

15. Jourdan, M., Blandin, S., Wynter, L., Deshpande, P.: Characterizing entities in the bitcoin blockchain. In: 2018 IEEE International Conference on Data Mining Workshops (ICDMW), pp. 55–62 (2018)

16. Kalodner, H., et al.: {BlockSci}: design and applications of a blockchain analysis platform. In: 29th USENIX Security Symposium (USENIX Security 20), pp. 2721–2738 (2020)

17. Kanemura, K., Toyoda, K., Ohtsuki, T.: Identification of darknet markets' bitcoin addresses by voting per-address classification results. In: 2019 IEEE International Conference on Blockchain and Cryptocurrency (ICBC), pp. 154–158. IEEE (2019)

18. Kethineni, S., Cao, Y.: The rise in popularity of cryptocurrency and associated criminal activity. Int. Crim. Justice Rev. 30(3), 325–344 (2020)

19. Lee, S., et al.: Cybercriminal minds: an investigative study of cryptocurrency abuses in the dark web. In: 26TH Annual Network and Distributed System Security Symposium (NDSS 2019), pp. 1–15. Internet Society (2019)

20. Li, Y., Cai, Y., Tian, H., Xue, G., Zheng, Z.: Identifying illicit addresses in bitcoin network. In: Zheng, Z., Dai, H.-N., Fu, X., Chen, B. (eds.) BlockSys 2020. CCIS, vol. 1267, pp. 99–111. Springer, Singapore (2020). https://doi.org/10.1007/978-981-15-9213-3_8

21. Lin, Y.J., Wu, P.W., Hsu, C.H., Tu, I.P., Liao, S.W.: An evaluation of bitcoin address classification based on transaction history summarization. In: 2019 IEEE International Conference on Blockchain and Cryptocurrency (ICBC), pp. 302–310. IEEE (2019)

22. McGinn, D., Birch, D., Akroyd, D., Molina-Solana, M., Guo, Y., Knottenbelt, W.J.: Visualizing dynamic bitcoin transaction patterns. Big Data 4(2), 109–119 (2016). https://doi.org/10.1089/big.2015.0056

23. Meiklejohn, S., et al.: A fistful of bitcoins: characterizing payments among men with no names. In: Proceedings of the 2013 Conference on Internet Measurement Conference, pp. 127–140 (2013). https://doi.org/10.1145/2504730.2504747

24. Möser, M., Böhme, R., Breuker, D.: An inquiry into money laundering tools in the bitcoin ecosystem. In: 2013 APWG eCrime researchers summit. pp. 1–14. IEEE (2013). https://doi.org/10.1109/eCRS.2013.6805780

25. Nakamoto, S.: Bitcoin: a peer-to-peer electronic cash system. Decentralized Bus. Rev. 21260 (2008)

26. Nan, L., Tao, D.: Bitcoin mixing detection using deep autoencoder. In: 2018 IEEE Third international conference on data science in cyberspace (DSC), pp. 280–287. IEEE (2018). https://doi.org/10.1109/DSC.2018.00047

27. Paquet-Clouston, M., Haslhofer, B., Dupont, B.: Ransomware payments in the bitcoin ecosystem. J. Cybersecur. 5(1), tyz003 (2019)

28. Pareja, A., et al.: Evolvegcn: evolving graph convolutional networks for dynamic graphs. In: Proceedings of the AAAI Conference on Artificial Intelligence, vol. 34, pp. 5363–5370 (2020)

29. Portnoff, R.S., Huang, D.Y., Doerfler, P., Afroz, S., McCoy, D.: Backpage and bitcoin: uncovering human traffickers. In: Proceedings of the 23rd ACM SIGKDD International Conference on Knowledge Discovery and Data Mining, pp. 1595–1604 (2017). https://doi.org/10.1145/3097983.3098082

30. Ranshous, S., et al.: Exchange pattern mining in the bitcoin transaction directed hypergraph. In: Brenner, M., et al. (eds.) FC 2017. LNCS, vol. 10323, pp. 248–263. Springer, Cham (2017). https://doi.org/10.1007/978-3-319-70278-0_16

31. Reid, F., Harrigan, M.: An analysis of anonymity in the bitcoin system. In: Altshuler, Y., Elovici, Y., Cremers, A., Aharony, N., Pentland, A. (eds.) Security and Privacy in Social Networks, pp. 197–223. Springer, New York (2013). https://doi.org/10.1007/978-1-4614-4139-7_10

32. Toyoda, K., Mathiopoulos, P.T., Ohtsuki, T.: A novel methodology for HYIP operators' bitcoin addresses identification. IEEE Access 7, 74835–74848 (2019)

33. Toyoda, K., Ohtsuki, T., Mathiopoulos, P.T.: Multi-class bitcoin-enabled service identification based on transaction history summarization. In: 2018 IEEE International Conference on Internet of Things (iThings) and IEEE Green Computing and Communications (GreenCom) and IEEE Cyber, Physical and Social Computing (CPSCom) and IEEE Smart Data (SmartData), pp. 1153–1160. IEEE (2018)

34. Valenta, L., Rowan, B.: Blindcoin: blinded, accountable mixes for bitcoin. In: Brenner, M., Christin, N., Johnson, B., Rohloff, K. (eds.) FC 2015. LNCS, vol. 8976, pp. 112–126. Springer, Heidelberg (2015). https://doi.org/10.1007/978-3-662-48051-9_9

35. Weber, M., Domeniconi, G., Chen, J., Weidele, D.K.I., Bellei, C., Robinson, T., Leiserson, C.E.: Anti-money laundering in bitcoin: Experimenting with graph convolutional networks for financial forensics. arXiv preprint arXiv:1908.02591 (2019)

36. Wu, J., Liu, J., Chen, W., Huang, H., Zheng, Z., Zhang, Y.: Detecting mixing services via mining bitcoin transaction network with hybrid motifs. IEEE Trans. Syst. Man Cybern. Syst. 52, 1–13 (2021)

37. Wu, L., et al.: Towards understanding and demystifying bitcoin mixing services. In: Proceedings of the Web Conference 2021, pp. 33–44 (2021)

38. Zhang, R., Zhang, G., Liu, L., Wang, C., Wan, S.: Anomaly detection in bitcoin information networks with multi-constrained meta path. J. Syst. Architect. 110, 101829 (2020)

39. Zola, F., Bruse, J.L., Eguimendia, M., Galar, M., Orduna Urrutia, R.: Bitcoin and cybersecurity: temporal dissection of blockchain data to unveil changes in entity behavioral patterns. Appl. Sci. 9(23), 5003 (2019)

Author Index